D0606308

A HISTORY OF PSYCHOLOGY

To OMT—for reminding us what psychology is all about.

A HISTORY OF PSYCHOLOGY

A GLOBAL PERSPECTIVE

ERIC SHIRAEV
George Mason University

Los Angeles | London | New Delhi
Singapore | Washington DC

For information:

SAGE Publications, Inc.
2455 Teller Road
Thousand Oaks, California 91320
E-mail: order@sagepub.com

SAGE Publications Ltd.
1 Oliver's Yard
55 City Road
London EC1Y 1SP
United Kingdom

SAGE Publications India Pvt. Ltd.
B 1/I 1 Mohan Cooperative Industrial Area
Mathura Road, New Delhi 110 044
India

SAGE Publications Asia-Pacific Pte. Ltd.
33 Pekin Street #02-01
Far East Square
Singapore 048763

Printed in the United States of America

Library of Congress Cataloging-in-Publication Data

Shiraev, Eric, 1960-
A history of psychology : a global perspective / Eric Shiraev.
p. cm.
Includes bibliographical references and index.
ISBN 978-1-4129-7383-0 (cloth)
1. Psychology—History. I. Title.

BF81.S55 2011
150.9—dc22 2010021117

This book is printed on acid-free paper.

10 11 12 13 14 10 9 8 7 6 5 4 3 2 1

Acquisitions Editor:	Christine Cardone
Associate Editor:	Eve Oettinger
Editorial Assistant:	Sarita Sarak
Production Editor:	Astrid Virding
Copy Editors:	Pam Suwinsky, Mary Tederstrom, Gillian Dickens
Permissions Editor:	Karen Ehrmann
Typesetter:	C&M Digitals (P) Ltd.
Proofreader:	Dennis W. Webb
Indexer:	Kathy Paparchontis
Cover Designer:	Gail Buschman
Marketing Manager:	Stephanie Adams

Brief Contents

Detailed Contents

Preface

In human years, psychology as a discipline is just about 18 years old. The discipline is in an early period of maturity, a dawn of adulthood when a few accomplishments look very promising and numerous plans remain daringly ambitious. Like every 18-year-old, psychology once was an infant. Many great thinkers of the past—philosophers and doctors in particular—anticipated psychology's future and helped it to take a few cautious steps forward. Mathematicians, physiologists, and natural scientists guarded psychology during its childhood. Psychology learned the meaning of experiments and measurements. Scientific peers began to acknowledge it. It gained its own voice. First shy and insecure, the discipline of psychology grew stronger with every decade. It began to offer advice and practical solutions to human problems. Accomplishments were noticeable. Setbacks were common. The ambition of many beautiful psychological theories was tamed by the ugliness of stubborn facts. Yet, as in life, these victories as well as mistakes have helped psychology to build its self-confidence. Using the allegory of human years, psychology's long history is a short but exciting period of growing and maturing. This book is an account of psychology's maturation over centuries.

The ideas and materials for *A History of Psychology*, like pieces of a jigsaw puzzle, have been assembled over several years and frequent-flyer plans. The ageless streets of Vienna and Zurich, the confident beauty of Cornell University buildings, the old academic glory of Paris and Berlin, the scholarly tradition of Leipzig and Heidelberg, the poise of Harvard and Columbia lecture halls, the rebellious spirit of Berkeley, the casual simplicity of Pavlov's laboratories near St. Petersburg in Russia—all of them and many other travel, research, and teaching experiences have had a lasting impact on this book. Psychology's history is about remarkable individuals. It is also about the amazing times when our ancestors and predecessors lived, created, and laid the foundations of today's psychology.

Main Features

How does the book present its materials? It contains 13 chapters that examine psychology's development through ancient times, mid-millennium transitions, the age of modernity, and through the 20th century. The main emphasis of the book is psychology's formative experiences during the past 150 years. What are the book's main features?

First, psychological science is presented here as increasingly *interdisciplinary*. The book's core is a balanced blend of science and social science, with additions from the fields of humanities, liberal arts, and other relevant disciplines. It emphasizes a complex scientific foundation of psychology that stretches over centuries.

Second, as does no other book on psychology's history, this book emphasizes *diversity.* It has a serious cross-cultural and cross-national focus that emphasizes the global nature of psychology as a research discipline and applied field. Philosophical, cultural, and social traditions of Western and non-Western origins are commonly acknowledged.

Third, *critical thinking* becomes a main method of analysis of the book. Emphasis on critical thinking allows students to retrieve more information from apparently "plain" research data. They also learn to deduce facts from opinions and to be informed skeptics.

Next, the book focuses on the interaction between scientific *psychology* and *society* in different periods of history. Each chapter contains a brief discussion of the impact of psychology on society and, in reverse, societal influences on psychology.

Next, the book pays attention to the *relevance* of yesterday's knowledge to students' diverse experiences today. The role of psychology in fields such as medicine, education, work and professional training, criminal justice, business, advertising, and entertainment is emphasized.

Finally, the book traces psychology's *progressive mission.* From its earliest days, psychology has had a mission to be actively engaged in social progress and in the development of a new society where science, reason, and care are learned and enthusiastically promoted.

Knowledge in Psychology's History

Psychology during its history used four sources of knowledge. The first type is *scientific knowledge.* This type of knowledge is a product of systematic empirical observations, measurement, and evaluation of a wide range of psychological phenomena. The second source is *popular beliefs*—often called *folk theories*—assumptions about human behavior, emotion, cognition, and thought. Some popular beliefs tend to be volatile and change without serious opposition. The third type of ideas concerning psychology is determined by *value-based knowledge.* In contrast to folk beliefs, this type of knowledge stems from a cohesive and stable set of attitudes about the world, the nature of good and evil, and the purpose of human life. Finally, the fourth source is *legal knowledge.* This source includes the rules and principles that exist in the form of law and can be used by authorities to make judgments about human behavior. Although additional facts about the sources of psychological knowledge should make the coverage not only comprehensive but also engaging, the main focus of the book is *scientific knowledge.*

Pedagogy

The following pedagogical tools are used:

- Each chapter contains a *timeline* placing main events, names, and theories in a visual, chronological perspective.

- Each chapter begins with a *vignette* or opening *case*, which serves as an informal introduction.

- Several *Check Your Knowledge* boxes are placed within chapters to help with immediate review of key points and facts.

- *Case in Point* boxes review and illustrate an issue or problem related to an individual, study, or theme; display cases and research findings; and introduce various opinions about the findings.

- *In Their Own Words* boxes display quotes made by famous psychologists and other scholars about psychological research and its applications.

- In *On the Web*, additional support for the text can be found on the book website at www.sagepub.com/shiraev, where you can find biographies, practice and discussion questions, research updates, facts, and links.

- *Chapter Summaries* and lists of *Key Terms* at the end of each chapter will help students to better prepare for exams and may serve as a reference as well.

Intended Audiences and Purposes

This book was designed with the following readers and purposes in mind:

- As a primary or supplementary text for undergraduate college students from a diverse array of majors (including but not limited to psychology, sociology, anthropology, education, history, philosophy, journalism, communication, political science, etc.)

- As a supplementary text for graduate students in areas such as psychology, social work, education, law, journalism, nursing, business, and public administration

- Professional psychologists, counselors, and social workers

- Educators and other practitioners working with people

Teaching Philosophy

The book's teaching philosophy is based on an assumption that over the course of its history psychology played a significantly bigger and more progressive role in a changing world. Psychology as a science was not a passive observer or a wise guru giving answers to those who asked questions. Throughout its history, psychology—rooted in science and people's wisdom—discussed, offered, and demanded concrete actions. Confident about its past, psychology today should play a primary and unique role in helping all of us become more effective global citizens.

Acknowledgments

This book received invaluable contributions, help, and support from scores of individuals. I have benefited from the insightful feedback and advice of colleagues and reviewers, the thorough efforts of research assistants, and the patience and understanding of family members and friends. In particular I acknowledge Laura Pople, Erik Gilg, Erik Evans, and Kirk Bomont for supporting this project from the start. I appreciate support of David Sears and Barry Collins from UCLA, James Sidanius from Harvard University, David Levy from Pepperdine University, Sergei V. Tsytsarev from Hofstra University, Denis Sukhodolsky from Yale University, Cheryl Koopman from Stanford University, Phil Tetlock from the University of California-Berkeley, Denis Snook from Oregon State University, Anton Galitsky from St. Petersburg State University, and Olga Makhovskaya from the Russian Academy of Sciences. Special thanks to York University's Christopher Green, who has created the best online resource for the study of psychology's history. A word of appreciation to John and Judy Ehle, Gerald Boyd, Vlad Zubok, Dmitry Shiraev, Dennis Shiraev, Nicole Shiraev, and Oh Em Tee. I can never thank them enough.

I also want to thank reviewers Michael T. Scoles, Department of Psychology and Counseling, University of Central Arkansas; Cooper B. Holmes, PhD, Emporia State University; Wendy J. Quinton, University at Buffalo, SUNY; Brian J. Cowley, PhD, BCBA, Park University; Michael A. Riley, University of Cincinnati; Madhu Singh, Tougaloo College; Terese A. Hall, Oral Roberts University; Carryl L. Baldwin, George Mason University; Darrell Rudmann, Shawnee State University; Jared A. Montoya, The University of Texas at Brownsville; Christina S. Sinisi, Charleston Southern University; Angela D. Mitchell, Texas Woman's University; Billy L. Smith, University of Central Arkansas; and Janice E. Weaver; Ferris State University, for their insightful comments.

I also take this opportunity to acknowledge the tremendous support I received at virtually every stage of this project's development from the team at Sage: Christine Cardone, Deya Saud, Sarita Sarak, Astrid Virding, copyeditors Pam Suwinsky, Mary Tederstrom, and Gillian Dickens.

A special word of appreciation is due to the administration, faculty, staff, and students at my academic institutions, where I have consistently been provided with an abundance of encouragement, assistance, and validation.

The journey continues.

About the Author

Eric Shiraev is a Russian-born American professor, researcher, and author. He took his academic degrees at St. Petersburg University in Russia and completed a postdoctoral program in the United States at UCLA. He served in various positions at St. Petersburg University, Northern Virginia Community College, Oregon State University, George Washington University, and George Mason University. He is an author, coauthor, and coeditor of 12 books and numerous publications in the fields of cross-cultural psychology, social psychology, political psychology, and comparative studies. In his publications, he develops a multidisciplinary approach to human behavior and experience. He believes in a universally progressive role of psychology to promote awareness, incremental improvements, and social initiative. He resides near Washington, D.C.

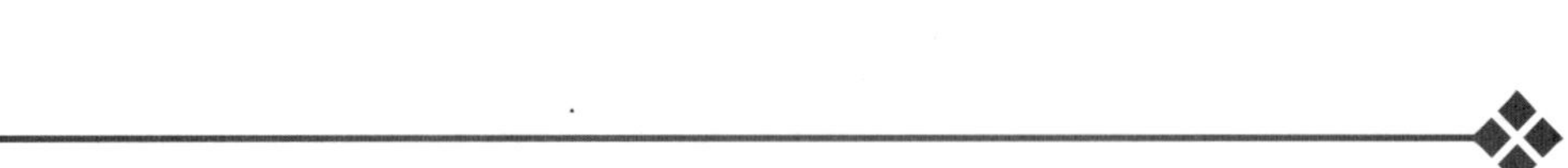

Understanding Psychology's History

What you are, they once were.
What they are, you will be.

An inscription in the crypt of Capuchin monks spotted by John Boyd and Phil Zimbardo

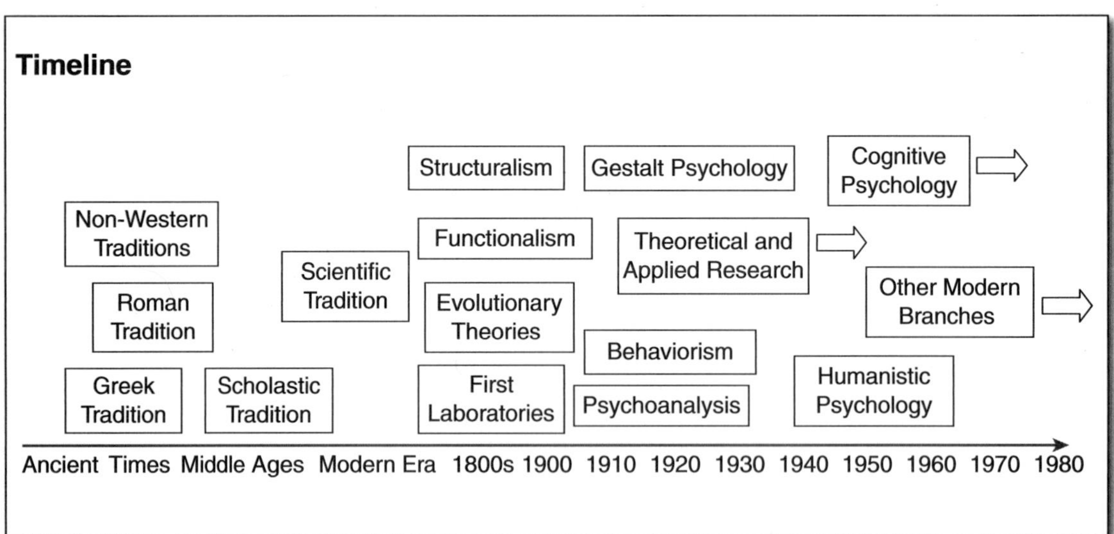

CHAPTER OUTLINE

"Professor, I have figured it out!" With a triumphant smile on his face, Daniel stormed into the professor's office. "In the beginning, you told us to investigate the source of every problem, right?" He pulled out of his pocket a piece of paper. Hastily unfolded and placed on the top of the desk, the paper resembled an exotic white lily with the petals wrinkled in unpredictable directions. "Here it is." Daniel pointed at his handwritten lines that resembled antlers. "Yesterday we discussed why psychologists have trouble identifying the subject of psychology, right? I know the reason why. Psychology was developed by people who had little to do with psychology. Remember you showed us how historians ranked the 10 most important psychologists of all time? Guess how many of them obtained their graduate degrees in psychology?"

"Skinner had a psychology degree for sure," the professor replied.

"Yes, Skinner had, but that's it! Everyone else had not. Wundt, James, and Freud, ranked first, second, and third on the list—they all had medical degrees. John Watson received his master's in theology and a PhD in philosophy. Ivan Pavlov was a physiologist who, by the way, did not believe in psychology as a scientific discipline. Ebbinghaus had a PhD in philosophy. Jean Piaget took a doctorate in zoology. Alfred Binet had an equivalent of a PhD in natural science for studying insects. Gustav Fechner's doctoral degree was in biology. . . ."

Daniel has made an interesting observation. Most top-ranked psychologists on the list, published some time ago in the *American Psychologist,* the top journal of the American Psychological Association (Korn, Davis, & Davis, 1991), did not receive their academic degrees in psychology. They, as did many other prominent psychologists of the past, began their educational careers pursuing degrees in biology, philosophy, or political science.

However, these historic examples must be taken cautiously for several reasons. First, the fact that psychology's prominent founders represented different fields of science is likely to be a sign of psychology's strength, not weakness. Second, it is inaccurate to form an opinion about psychology as a discipline by looking at a "top 10" list as if we are ranking football teams. Psychology's contributions, both theoretical and practical, are measured in many other ways. Third, psychology as a discipline developed in specific social and cultural contexts. Thousands of scholars dedicated their work and lives to the ideas that we study today. Returning to the "top psychologists" list, do you think that three Americans, three Germans, two Frenchmen, one Austrian, and one Russian could fully represent the entire world of psychology? Let's start a more rigorous investigation of psychology's history together!

Prologue

What Do We Study?

History is the study of the past. Historians gather facts, interpret them, dress these interpretations in the clothes of theories, and then present them to the reading, listening, and watching world. Historians focus on civilizations, cultures, countries, and great individuals. The history of psychology is the study of psychology's past. But how can we study it?

Focusing on Knowledge. In this book, we undertake a scientific investigation of psychological knowledge from a historic perspective. We examine major psychological ideas and their development. We will learn how people developed their understanding of behavior and experience. Take depressive symptoms as an example. Early theories attributed depression to a misbalance of vital liquids in the body. Later theories referred to weakness of the nervous system as the cause of depressive symptoms. Yet more recent studies focused on genetic and environmental factors contributing to the symptoms.

Studying psychological knowledge, we examine major psychological schools including structuralism, functionalism, behaviorism, Gestalt psychology, psychoanalysis, cognitive psychology, and humanistic psychology—these and other labels should be familiar to you from an introductory psychology course. We also look at a wide range of ideas and remarkable theories created by psychologists around the world whose work did not necessarily fit into these convenient categories.

Understanding Historical Contexts. Knowledge is inseparable from the social, economic, and cultural contexts in which it develops. Early studies of intelligence at the beginning of the 20th century took place because compulsory education of children was established in many countries and their governments needed a scientific system of assessment of children's learning abilities. Attention to "psychological energy" increased significantly during the period when scientists were making discoveries in the fields of nuclear physics. Cultural taboos prevented psychologists from studying sexuality for a long time. Some psychologists in Nazi Germany worked on theories justifying the supremacy of the Aryan race. To understand psychology fully is to recognize its social and cultural environment. We pay special attention to at least three important features of the social context within which psychological knowledge developed: society's resources, social climate, and academic tradition of the time.

Examining the Roots. Which historic period will we examine? Most attention is paid to psychology's last 150 years. Although psychology as an academic discipline received its initial recognition by the end of the 19th century, its development had begun much earlier. Scholarly papers, books, letters, and diaries written hundreds of years ago reveal the amazing breadth of knowledge that people acquired in different historic periods about their experiences, dreams, decisions, insecurities, and the whole range of normal and abnormal psychological symptoms.

To understand psychology's development, we look at a wide variety of influences on psychology: philosophical, biological, medical, religious, political, and others. Although we study history, our attention is also on today's psychology as an academic discipline, applied field, and profession.

Remembering Great Individuals. Many individual scholars—psychologists, philosophers, doctors, theologians, neurophysiologists, mathematicians, and others—contributed to psychological knowledge and psychology as a discipline. Individual discoveries enhanced global knowledge. In the 19th century, most researchers believed that the main cause of dementia (which is a significant cognitive and behavioral impairment) was a "wrong" set of neuromagnetic processes in the brain. In 1901, the German doctor Alois Alzheimer dismissed these views after he found that certain structural abnormalities in the brain were likely to be major contributors to the symptoms of dementia. Alzheimer's discovery in medicine produced new psychological knowledge explaining the connection between brain pathology on the one hand and the human mind on the other. Most probably, if Alzheimer didn't make his discovery, someone else would have. However, he was the first, and his name remains in history.

Well-known and obscure theories, ambitious hypotheses, remarkable observations, and spectacular experimentations—all of them were the creations of individual scholars and their resourceful minds. Books and articles they published, letters they wrote, and lectures they delivered are like a mirror to their thought processes, concerns, aspirations, and hopes, all of which matter in our understanding of psychology's past and present.

Understanding psychology's past is about comprehending several of its most recurrent topics and themes. What specific and recurrent themes do we pay attention to?

Recurrent Themes

The diversity and complexity of the problems that psychology has tried to address is remarkable. Three most important themes or problems, however, can be identified. Among them:

1. The mind-body problem
2. The interaction of biological and social factors in human behavior and experience, and
3. The balance between theoretical knowledge and its practical applications

We describe these problems only briefly now. We will return to them later in the book.

The Mind-Body Problem. Research shows that people who are ill but believe that they will get healthy again tend to recover somewhat better compared to sour pessimists (Bryan, Aiken, & West, 2004). Is this an example of how our mind affects our body, or is it just that healthy people tend to be more optimistic? And what is optimism anyway? Is it a kind of mental power or simply a set of physiological reactions of the brain? The mechanism of the mind-body interaction is one of the most common themes in intellectual debates in the history of science and one of the most intriguing problems in the history of psychology (Gergen, 2001).

For centuries, many scholars believed that experimental science was incapable of studying the "higher" mental processes, including what we call today optimism, imagination, or beliefs. How could one, they argued, measure compassion or free will? The scientific opposition believed in the possibility of the scientific study of the mind through research on the nervous system and the brain. These opposing views represented a global scientific and even cultural divide. One group, as you can imagine, was accused by the other of making vulgar attempts to reduce the complexity of mental life to the movements of molecules through fibers. This group, in response, accused their critics of scientific ignorance. Today, the debate continues. Even using the advanced research from physiology and computer science, psychologists still have a challenge ahead of them: how to measure the subjective elements of experience.

The Nature-Nurture Debates. Are we born with certain qualities such as shyness or propensity for violence, or do we form them primarily through experience? The debates about complex interactions of natural (biological) factors and social (cultural) influences have always been in the focus of psychology's attention. The essence of the nature-nature debates was not necessarily about the dilemma, is it exclusively nature or is it solely nurture? Scholars of the distant past as well as psychologists of more recent times tended to view human beings as products of both the natural world and social environment (Münsterberg, 1915). The assumption about the dual impact of natural and social factors is generally accepted today. Most debates focus on the extent or degree of the impact of natural (biological) or social (environmental) factors. The outcomes of these debates have significant applications for psychology practitioners.

The Theorist-Practitioner Debates. Should scientists be concerned with practical applications of their research? Two traditions in science influenced psychology in every stage of its history. The first tradition maintained that science should be, above all, a rational pursuit of a true understanding of nature. Whether or not there are practical results of this pursuit is not science's concern. The other tradition claimed that science should, above all, serve to improve humanity (Morawski, 2002). Psychologists of the past tended to support the view that both practical and theoretical goals were important. Yet many of them differed in their personal choices: some were more committed to theory, while others were more actively involved in practical pursuits. The American Psychological Association for many years after its inception in 1891 witnessed heated debates about the degree of psychology's practical involvement outside the university laboratory (Benjamin, 2002; Griffith, 1921). We will see how some psychologists believed that the true value of their research should be found only in its applications. Others were skeptical about their practice-oriented colleagues and criticized them for their alleged misuse of science to satisfy the demands of their sponsors. As we will see in Chapter 5, 100 years ago, psychologists who did a paid research for Coca-Cola were frequently criticized for "selling out" science to help a big corporation to win a legal case.

A history of psychology is a scholarly investigation of development of psychological knowledge, whether it was theoretical, experimental, or practical. If we study knowledge, how can we describe and explain it?

Four Types of Knowledge in Psychology

Knowledge is information that has a purpose or use. People use knowledge for different purposes. Imagine a shaman tells his fellow villagers that their dreams reveal their future. At the same time, in a different place, a licensed therapist tells a client that her dreams reflect little more than the client's past insecurities. Question: Which of these two individuals conveys knowledge? If we accept the definition, the answer should be, both. Throughout centuries, psychological knowledge was developed and used with a particular purpose. Different people and groups used knowledge to pursue specific purposes. As a result, several types of psychological knowledge have emerged (see Table 1.1). Let's examine them from both historic and contemporary perspectives.

Table 1.1 Four Types of Psychological Knowledge

Type of Knowledge	*Sources of Knowledge*
Scientific	Knowledge accumulated through research, systematic empirical observation, and evaluation of a wide range of psychological phenomena. Facts are obtained with the help of scientific research methodologies and rigorous verification by multiple sources.
Popular (or folk)	Everyday assumptions about psychological phenomena; such assumptions are often expressed in the form of beliefs, evaluations, or prescriptions.
Ideological (value-based)	A consistent set of beliefs about the world, the nature of good and evil, right and wrong, and the purpose of human life are all based on a certain organizing principal or central idea.
Legal	Knowledge encapsulated in the law and detailed in rules and principles related to psychological functioning of individuals. These rules are commonly established by legal authorities.

Scientific Knowledge

The first type is **scientific knowledge**. Its major source is science, or systematic empirical observation, measurement, and evaluation of facts. It is rooted in the scientific method, which is based on the use of cautious research procedures designed to provide reliable and verifiable evidence (Gergen, 2001). Supporters of the scientific method saw it as the exclusive arbiter of truth in psychology as a discipline. However, what was accepted as scientific varied greatly throughout history.

Take emotions as an example. Twenty-five hundred years ago, the ancient Greek philosopher Democritus believed that the movement of atoms of different shape and speed cause various emotional states. Four hundred years ago, René Descartes, the French-born thinker, associated emotions with the activities of animal spirits passing through the vascular system. According to the James-Lange theory of the late 19th century, there were bodily reactions that evoked experiences that a person then labeled as emotions. According to the Cannon-Bard theory of the 20th century, emotions occur first as signals, thus causing bodily reactions. A century ago, German psychologist Wilhelm Wundt identified emotions and measured them as elementary foundations of human subjective experience. In the 1920s, physiologist Ivan Pavlov in Russia and psychologist John Watson in the United States described emotions simply as learned reactions. Can you tell which of these views represented scientific knowledge and which of them did not?

In fact, all of them represented science. However, it was a developing science relevant to its times. All these theories attempted different but incomplete descriptions of emotions. We will see that most scientific theories of the past gained initial recognition but were later replaced by other theories. This does not make the earlier theories unscientific. They were probably less accurate. Scientific knowledge can be inaccurate for at least three reasons: incorrect assumptions, imprecise descriptions, and poor applications. Look at three historic cases presented next.

Mesmerism: The Science of Incorrect Assumptions. The French physician and innovator Franz Anton Mesmer claimed in his dissertation in 1766 that human illnesses might be caused by the disruption or blocking of the normal flow of an invisible body fluid, which he called *animal magnetism.* A trained physician, Mesmer insisted that he should be able to find these disruptions and blocks and then remove them by touch (Mesmer, 1766/1980). Mesmer also claimed that he had the ability to magnetize objects and patients. He thought that a trained specialist could learn this skill too. Many apparently successful demonstrations of his method were well documented and led to Mesmer's immense popularity in the late 18th century (Wampold & Bhati, 2004).

However, the skeptics were undaunted. The Royal Commission decided to check the validity of Mesmer's claims. All the attempts to test the existence of animal magnetism irrefutably provided no evidence in support of it. Mesmer had no intent to deceive people. His theories of bodily action were, in some way, extensions of the emerging theories of physics. Sir Isaac Newton postulated gravity as a force between objects and showed how the gravity of the moon and sun formed the tides. Similarly, Mesmer thought that gravity affected the fluids in the body. It was an incorrect assumption, however. Another wrong assumption was related to his patients. In the demonstrations, many of them reported disappearance of pain and other signs of improvement. From today's standpoint, the patients reported improvements probably because they believed in own recovery or wanted to show progress. This effect of a change caused by an anticipation of a change was later called the **placebo effect**. (We examine Mesmer's and similar views in some detail in Chapter 4.)

Neurasthenia: Imprecise Descriptions in Psychology. In the past, doctors and psychologists used the diagnosis **neurasthenia** to identify a mixed cluster of symptoms involving anxiety and depression. Clinicians attributed these symptoms to the weakness of the nervous system, assuming that science in the future would identify the specific neurological causes of neurasthenia. Overall, neurasthenia has been a popular and convenient diagnosis worldwide. Yet despite the widespread use of this diagnosis, there was no agreement on what the "core" characteristics of neurasthenia were (Starcevic, 1999). Overall, neurasthenia was a very imprecise label that allowed professionals to include practically any psychological symptom they saw fit under the umbrella of this name. Today, neurasthenia as a diagnostic category has been excluded from the *Diagnostic and Statistical Manual of Mental Disorders:* what was considered scientific yesterday is no longer viewed the same way today. (We return to neurasthenia in Chapter 6.)

Pavlov's Laws: The Science of Poor Applications. With the aid of multiple quantitative experiments conducted on animals placed in isolated chambers, Ivan Pavlov, the Nobel Prize-winner from Russia, described the laws of the formation, preservation, and extinction of reflexes. Using his findings, he developed a theory of the higher nervous activity associated primarily with the cerebral cortex of the brain. Pavlov believed in the existence of three basic characteristics of nervous processes: strength, balance, and agility. He also suggested that an individual's entire behavior could be described in terms of strength, balance, and agility of the nervous processes. His theory appeared to many to be scientifically sound and simple and seemed unfaultable. Pavlov believed in the experimental method to understand behavior, and he made a significant contribution to psychology (we examine it in detail in Chapter 7). However, later studies showed that his theory did not apply well to explain human behavior. A "strong and balanced" individual in one set of circumstances may be "weak and imbalanced" in another. Besides, physiologists using Pavlov's theory have not been able to show specific physiological mechanisms in the brain that would represent the strength, the balance, and the agility of the nervous system.

At certain points in history, these three apparently scientific theories were substantially revised or, as in case of mesmerism, discarded (see Table 1.2).

Scientific knowledge is supposed to be accumulated through research, systematic empirical observation, and evaluation of a wide range of psychological phenomena. Facts gathered by scientific psychology are obtained with the help of scientific research methodologies, which require rigorous verification by multiple sources. However, relevance of these facts, as well as relevance of scientific knowledge, was continually changing with time (Kendler, 1999).

Table 1.2 Anton Mesmer, Neurasthenia, and Ivan Pavlov: How Scientific Ideas Are Dismantled

Theory, Views	*Critical Points*
 Anton Mesmer formulated a theory about people's ability to magnetize objects and bodies and thus affect bodily processes. Supporters considered his views scientific. Many people today people continue to believe in different forms of bodily magnetism.	Careful investigation showed that the improvement in symptoms was not caused by magnetism as claimed by Mesmer. In addition, there was no verifiable evidence about the existence of the effects of magnetism.
The term **neurasthenia** was widely used by clinicians to explain the etiology of several dysfunctions, including various forms of anxiety and depression.	The concept of *weakness of nervous system* is vague. The symptoms included in neurasthenia are extremely diverse, and clinicians interpret them according to their cultural or educational backgrounds.
Ivan Pavlov's theory suggested the existence of several processes including the strength, the balance, and the speed of processes within the nervous system. 	The assumptions about the strength, balance, and speed of nervous processes did not find many practical applications and turned out to be rather simplistic.

Popular Beliefs

Another type of psychological knowledge manifests in **popular beliefs**, often called *folk theories* because they represent a form of "everyday psychology" created by the people and for the people. Main sources of popular beliefs related to psychology are shared assumptions about certain aspects of behavior and experience. Some of these assumptions, such as the belief in the ability of dreams to predict the future, are very broad. Others, such as a friend's recommendation about how to ask a professor for a deadline extension, are very specific. Popular beliefs are, to some degree, working hypotheses that people use to make sense of themselves and other people.

Contents of Popular Beliefs. Quite often, popular beliefs describe various aspects of human life properly and receive support from science (Lock, 1981). For instance, from our own experience we may learn about the harmful impact of continuous stress, the inspirational value of hope, and the importance of trust in our relationships. In many other cases, popular beliefs are inconsistent, inaccurate, or contradict scientific knowledge. For example, many people today believe in the existence of extrasensory perception. Scientific psychology has little evidence in support of this belief. Some people think that parental mistakes can cause schizophrenia in children when they become adults. Science disagrees and points at a combination of biomedical factors as likely causes of this illness. Scores of parents would tell you that if you startle a child, it may cause the child's permanent stutter. Science again suggests that this is for the most part an incorrect assumption. Some beliefs go away easily, others change slowly. Take, for example, popular assumptions of the past about "irreparable harms" of teenage masturbation—in particular, the beliefs that masturbation causes mental retardation. These beliefs continue to have a significant impact on behavior and self-knowledge of millions of people around the globe. Contemporary science, however, finds little evidence that masturbation causes psychological abnormality (Laqueur, 2004).

Historically, before the birth of mass media, scientific knowledge related to psychology was mostly elitist. In traditional communities, a few self-appointed experts shared their knowledge about psychology and gave advice. They advised on marital problems, child rearing, emotional problems, sleep disturbances, matchmaking, and other issues. Such experts were called different names in different times and cultures. They were astrologists and shamans, psychics and spiritualists, mediums and witch doctors. Today, like many years ago, they claim they can heal depression or anxiety with magic words or magnetism. They advise not to take trips or get married because of a certain lineup of planets. Some of them claim that they can communicate with spirits of the dead.

Pop Psychology. Psychological knowledge designed specifically for mass consumption is often labeled *popular psychology*, or simply **pop psychology**. In the history of psychology, a clear demarcation line between scientific knowledge and popular beliefs began to appear by the end of the 19th century, which was the era of mass literacy in most developed countries (Coon, 1992). Today, most information about psychology reaches people through the media—newspapers, television, radio, popular books, and the Internet. This information tends to be simplified and even sensationalized. An emphasis on simplicity and sensationalism is the essence of pop psychology.

Bookstore shelves display hundreds of pop psychology books. Magazine columns advise on a wide variety of psychological issues, ranging from how to please a husband to how to cure anxiety symptoms. Beginning in the 1990s, television or radio talk shows featuring psychology experts attract multimillions of fans. Countless websites and blogs provide information on a variety of psychological issues. Many contributors to such websites or television shows have degrees in psychology or medicine, and it seems that a lot of information on the Web comes from reliable sources and contains accurate information. Nevertheless, most of the shows featuring psychologists seek sensationalism to increase their ratings. Reliable, scientific knowledge is frequently brushed aside by today's pseudo-psychologists for the sake of ratings increased by a boiling controversy.

Today, as many years ago, popular beliefs continue to influence people's lives, their daily practices, and decisions. Folk theories about child rearing, marriage, mental illness, sexuality, dreams, causes of success, or cures for "bad" behavior continue to influence billions of people. Therefore, in this book, while focusing on scientific knowledge, we continually return to its interaction with popular beliefs.

Ideology and Values

The third type of knowledge is found in human **values**. In contrast to folk beliefs, this type of knowledge stems from established, stable perceptions about the world, the nature of good and evil, right and wrong behavior, purpose of human life, and so forth. **Ideological (value-based)** knowledge is different from popular beliefs because it is grounded on a set of unwavering principles often supported by tradition or powerful authorities. There is another particularly important difference between values and scientific knowledge: value-based ideas often do not require factual scrutiny. Every ideology tends to adhere to some principles and values that are not questioned. For example, the deep-seated belief in the existence of the soul as a nonmaterial and immortal substance is a value. A belief in the necessity of moral behavior to avoid misfortune is a value too. A belief that homosexuality as a sin that has no place in human life may also be a value.

The power of ideology to affect scientific knowledge and people's behavior is significant. History shows that people could ignore or reject science in favor of ideology. Some may turn ideology against science. In Nazi Germany of the 1930s, ideology hijacked science to justify racism and discrimination against ethnic minorities and the mentally ill. In the Soviet Union, psychologists writing papers or dissertations had an obligation to quote Karl Marx or other Communist leaders. In Communist China, in the 1960s, a rare translation of a Western psychology textbook was accompanied by the specially written concluding chapter titled, "The Backwardness of Present Capitalistic Psychology." Chinese psychologists were instructed to view Western psychology critically, within the context of Communism (Whittaker, 1970, p. 758). Evolution still cannot be taught in some U.S. public schools because it conflicts with some people's fundamental values (Tryon, 2002).

Religion is probably the most powerful source of values. People use religion to explain their experience and justify their own behavior (Harrington, 1996). Behavioral prescriptions, such as moderation in needs, respect for strong family ties, frugality, discipline, and thrift are common in the doctrines and practices of Christianity, Judaism, Confucianism, Hinduism, Sikhism, Islam, and other religions. Views of psychological illness are also affected by religious beliefs. Within the Christian tradition, as an illustration, the core beliefs related to sin, confession, and repentance motivated many individuals to believe that some severe forms of mental illness are God's punishment for inappropriate behavior (Shiraev & Levy, 2009). While many people today turn to licensed therapists for help, others reject professionals and turn to religion for behavioral prescriptions.

Values often play a positive role in people's lives. However, in the past, some of these values justified harassment and abuse of individuals whose behavior was different from the prescribed patterns. In the following chapters, you will find examples of authorities in the past who discriminated against individuals who showed symptoms of mental illness.

☞ CASE IN POINT

Social Values and Psychological Knowledge. Consider two cases about how values affected scientific knowledge. The first case is *trappidomania,* or so-called Pathological Craving for Freedom. In the 19th century, this diagnosis was often given to black slaves in the United States who had made repeated attempts to escape from their owners. Medical professionals viewed this behavior of the slave not only as deviant but also pathological. Why? The predominant view was that a person who doesn't understand his "place" in society must have serious psychological problems.

The second case refers to the former Soviet Union. In the 1970s and 1980s, the Communist Party assigned a number of Soviet psychiatrists to treat political dissidents (the opponents of the Communist régime). Many civil rights activists, who did not support Communist ideology, were forcefully hospitalized to mental institutions with the following official diagnosis: Schizophrenia, Slowly Progressing (Sluggish) Type, Delusion of Reformation. These patients received strong medications to suppress their "delusional thoughts" about democracy and political reforms (Bloch & Reddaway, 1977). This was a method by which the government used psychology to create a new category of mental illness.

We should understand that back in their time, the majority of medical professionals in the mentioned countries accepted trappidomania and delusion of reformation as valid scientific categories.

Legal Knowledge

Finally, **legal knowledge** represents the fourth type of judgment related to psychology. This knowledge appears in the form of legal prescriptions established by authorities (ranging from tribal leaders to state governments). Legal knowledge provides legitimate reasons for important decisions about life and death, marriage, people's rationality, sanity, ability to raise children, and so forth. For example, in the United States as well as in many other countries, it is legal to marry for a person who is 18 years old. People in most circumstances don't plan their marriages at 16 and consider the very idea of an early marriage inappropriate. In some other countries parents insist that their children, especially daughters, get married early, at 14 and even earlier. Physical punishment of children is accepted in many countries as an effective method of upbringing. In most Western countries, however, physical abuse of a child is likely to be illegal. The legal definition of death in most Western societies has little to do with people's religious beliefs. No matter what we think of the soul and immortality, the legal indicator of physical death is the extinction of activity in the brain (Truog & Miller, 2008). Furthermore, legal definitions of insanity, which we examine in Chapter 6, are different from science-based definitions of mental illness.

Legal rules are not likely to explain what life and death are. Court documents do not provide scientific information about why individuals in the United States are prohibited from consuming alcohol before they reach 21 years of age. Yet legal rules establish boundaries of acceptable human behavior and affect customs and practices in millions of families. They may directly affect our judgments, emotions, and thought. From the legal standpoint, homosexuality was considered an illness in the United States for most of the 20th century. In the Soviet Union before 1990, a person could end up in prison for being openly gay. In many countries today, governments define homosexuality as an "illegal" lifestyle, which is a punishable crime.

In the next section, we compare the four types of knowledge in psychology and apply them to contemporary contexts.

✓ CHECK YOUR KNOWLEDGE

What are the three recurrent themes in psychology's history?

Why is mesmerism viewed as unscientific today?

Give an example of a scientific fact and popular belief related to human behavior.

Define pop psychology.

The Interaction of the Four Types of Knowledge

Ask a few people a simple question: "What is a dream?" You should expect to receive different answers. Probably you will receive quick and simple replies, such as,

"A dream is when you sleep" or might hear something mysterious such as, "Dreams are your spiritual life." These answers probably reflect some people's popular knowledge. You will also hear refined responses, including, "A dream is a special form of brain activity," and even more sophisticated ones like, "It is a series of images occurring involuntarily in the person during certain stages of sleep." These answers are rooted in scientific knowledge. You can imagine how many different answers we can find when we look back in history and collect views of dreams from a historical perspective.

As another example, in a contemporary American city many individuals who seek treatment for their alcohol-related addiction are likely to turn to professional help. Professionals use scientific knowledge to diagnose addictions and treat them. In other situations, some people turn to popular beliefs. In a traditional Native American therapeutic procedure, individuals who try to stop abusing alcohol take their seats around hot rocks and then pour water on them. Steam from the rocks is believed to purify the people who sit nearby. They believe they can rid themselves of addiction through sweating (Jilek, 1994). Science does not support this belief, however. Studies in Nigeria, in another example, showed that in the recent past a vast majority of health care workers believed that witchcraft and evil spirits were important factors causing people's abnormal psychological symptoms (Turner, 1997). Science and popular beliefs often coexist in the same individual.

Take as another example the main principles of scientology, which is a contemporary religion. One of the goals of healing prescribed by this religion is *dianetics*—a systemic method of identifying the causes of and relieving many of an individual's mental, emotional, or psychosomatic problems. Fundamental to the system is the concept of the *engram,* defined as a permanent trace left by a stimulus on the protoplasm of a tissue. It is believed that such engrams appear during periods of psychological distress or trauma and lie at the root of all mental disorders (Hubbard, 1955). Many educated people trained in science regard dianetics as a kind of ideology or folk belief because dianetics fails to meet the requirements of the scientific method, which is the investigation and acquisition of new knowledge based upon physical evidence. Yet people who follow scientology, many of them highly educated, accept dianetics as science. As you can see, individuals may consider their religious values as scientific knowledge and believe in its accuracy and validity.

In the history of psychology, the four types of knowledge are deeply interconnected. Commonsense assumptions, such as how to deal with deep sadness or how to interpret dreams, have always been part of people's knowledge about mental phenomena. These assumptions have been influenced by a continually changing flow of new facts and opinions. At certain times in history, as we will see later in the book, values-based doctrines, often embedded in organized religion, have had a tremendous impact on popular, scientific, and legal knowledge. Value-based, deeply seated cultural knowledge tends to resist rapid changes, but it transforms too. Legal psychological knowledge changes together with continuous transitions taking place in society.

All four types of knowledge were inseparable parts of the social environment within the developing human civilization.

Society and Psychology's History

Historians agree that the social, political, and academic atmosphere unique to particular historic times and locations was crucial for psychology as a discipline (Danziger, 1990; Leahey, 2002). In the past, specific societal conditions created either favorable or unfavorable circumstances for psychological knowledge and psychology as science. At the end of the 19th century in Germany, for example, experimental, laboratory-based psychology won support in most universities. In France, it was clinical psychology that received support from state-sponsored universities. At least three factors should help us understand the complex interaction among society and psychological knowledge: resources, social climate, and academic tradition. (See Table 1.3.)

Table 1.3 Factors Contributing to the Development of Psychology as Science

Resources and infrastructure	Availability of resources creates conditions for the development of science and inclusion of psychology as a scientific discipline.
Social climate	Favorable social climate creates an opportunity for psychology to be viewed and treated as a legitimate discipline and profession.
Academic tradition	Presence of educated professionals sharing the same principles of understanding of psychology constitutes an academic tradition; this creates a great opportunity for others to join in and develop this tradition further.

Resources

Somebody has to pay for research. The availability of resources such as money, laboratories, equipment, and educational and training facilities is important for the development of any academic discipline. History shows that science-based psychological knowledge developed rapidly in countries and regions with substantial resources invested in education and science. The advancement of knowledge in ancient Greece was inseparable from the financial wealth of Athens and other major Greek cities. The Italian Renaissance in arts and sciences occurred at the time when the bankers of Florence had accumulated enormous wealth (Simonton, 1994). Sultans of the Ottoman Empire and Chinese emperors invested in science and sponsored court scholars. The wealth accumulated in America at the beginning of the 20th century stimulated the rapid development of its universities.

Some researchers, of course, did not need generous help from big universities or resourceful authorities to run their experiments or create theories. Among the most recognized scholars who did not associate themselves directly with a university were, for example, Herbert Spencer in England and Benedict Spinoza in the Netherlands. Hermann Ebbinghaus of Germany conducted his famous memory experiments before he became a university professor. Yet the vast majority of scientists were recipients of financial and organizational support from either government or private sources.

Consider a simple illustration related to early experimental psychology. To study visual or auditory thresholds in the 19th century, a psychologist had to have a specially designed dark and quiet room and relatively expensive research equipment. After Wilhelm Wundt created the famous psychological laboratory in Leipzig (Germany), by 1879 international scholars visiting his lab wanted to repeat his success in their home countries. They pursued two major goals. The first one was academic: to learn more about Wundt's experimental method. The second was practical: to raise funds and build experimental research facilities in their home countries. Many of these scholars were successful in their financial pursuits (Griffith, 1921).

Money and big lecture halls alone will not necessarily move science forward. Science always needs a favorable social climate.

Social Climate

Psychology's history is difficult to separate from specific social conditions within which it developed. **Zeitgeist** is a term standing for the prevalent social climate, or, translated literally, the "spirit" of a particular time or generation. Both favorable and unfavorable social climates accompanied the development of psychological knowledge (Ludy, 1986).

Social opposition could put brakes on any research. Take, for example, human sexuality as a subject of psychological investigation. In the Soviet Union of the 1970s, psychology as a scientific discipline was booming. The government sponsored psychological research, opened new university departments, and created many faculty positions. National conferences and research seminars became frequent. However, government authorities rejected almost any research in the fields of human sexuality, which was considered an ideologically inappropriate field. The public, at least a substantial portion of it, also considered any public discussion of sexuality obscene. Many ordinary people supported strong restrictions on sex education in Soviet schools (Shlapentokh, 2004). The government reinforced the existing social climate of cultural conservatism in the Soviet Union.

Have things been much different in the United States? The publication of Alfred Kinsey's (1894–1956) *Sexual Behavior in the Human Male* (1948/1998), a book based on empirical studies of sexuality, received an angry response from many people, including scientists. The social climate in America was quite ambivalent at that time. Some people thought that researchers should enjoy academic freedom and study anything they chose. Others maintained that research should be separated from what they believed was perversion. The difference between the situations in the United States in the 1940s and the Soviet Union in the 1970s was that in America, despite some strong public opposition, the government was unlikely to interfere in psychological research, while in the Soviet Union it was the government that determined what scientists should and should not have studied.

ON THE WEB

Kinsey is a 2004 semibiographical film written and directed by Bill Condon. It describes the life of Alfred Kinsey, whose 1948 publication *Sexual Behavior in the Human Male* was one of the first recorded works that scientifically addressed and investigated sexual behavior in humans. The book website contains a link to a site related to the film.

Scientific theories, in turn, can affect social climate. How? Scientific knowledge commonly affects values and popular beliefs. One hundred years ago, for instance, many educated people believed that the intellectual development of the people from remote tribes in Africa, Indonesia, or South America was primitive, their behavior immature, and their cultures backward. Most scholars did little to discourage these attitudes. Non-European ethnic and racial groups were commonly presented in simplistic and condescending terms. Literary magazines like *The Cosmopolitan,* for example, in an October 1894 article described Tunis as a place "where the sky is clear, the earth fertile, and man obsequious." The Turks were "proud and unmanageable." The Moors were "honest, mild, polite, and courageous." Similar simplistic descriptions of other groups were common.

However, a growing number of studies began to challenge these simplistic popular perceptions of other cultures. One of the groundbreaking studies was *The Mind of Primitive Man,* written by Franz Boas (1911), one of the founders of modern anthropology. The central premise of his approach, immediately supported by scores of scientists, was the equality of human beings and their cultures and appreciation of human behavior in its diverse forms. This publication gave a boost to a new wave of research in developmental and cultural psychology, social psychology, and anthropology, which certainly affected a gradual shift of social attitudes about history, culture, and social equality. This shift, however, did not take place overnight.

Academic Tradition

Psychology's history is a history of academic traditions. They bring together scholars who share similar views on a particular approach, subject, or method. There are real associations involving interacting individuals, and there are traditions that are used mostly as convenient symbols to indicate a similarity in the views. Certain academic traditions come to stay, while others go. Psychoanalysis was a dominant field in the clinical field of psychology until the 1960s. A shift in priorities took place in the second half of the 20th century. The traditional talk therapy tradition was gradually replaced by a new tradition embracing faster and more efficient methods of behavioral and cognitive treatment. (We discuss this in Chapters 8 and 11.)

Academic traditions serve several functions. The first is communication. Scientists have a chance to discuss their ideas and research. There are passing traditions, such as discussion clubs, in which scholars sharing common views stayed in touch with one another for some time. In the 18th century, the famous French intellectual, Paul-Henri Thiry (known also as Baron d'Holbach) established the *salon:* a regular get-together of progressive thinkers, authors, and educators. Liberal-minded philosophers discussed materialism and atheism and criticized the oppressive rule of the king. In the 19th century, shortly after Wilhelm Wundt had established his laboratory in Germany (1879), in the United States Professor James McCosh organized an informal "Wundt club" among the faculty at Princeton University to discuss the latest psychological research conducted in Europe (Baldwin, 1926). Expectedly, scientific ideas receiving scholarly attention and informal support had a greater chance to develop and win more supporters in the future. Similarly, some well-accepted ideas are likely to fade away under the pressure of their critical evaluations. This is exactly what happened to the theoretical ideas of Wundt, as we will learn in Chapter 4.

The second function is consolidation of knowledge. Several scholars working on the same problem or using the same theoretical approach can work more efficiently than can individual scholars. There are long-term informal associations, the purpose of which is to let their participants collaborate and share research findings and theoretical assumptions. Such associations may gain recognition among scholars of two or more generations. Prominent psychologists of the 20th century such as Sigmund Freud, William James, Kurt Lewin, B. F. Skinner, Jean Piaget, and many others cared about their students and followers—those who could and would continue research traditions of their mentors. Many psychologists actively and deliberately recruited their followers (Krantz & Wiggins, 1973).

The third function of academic traditions is protection and control. In history, quite a few academic traditions—especially those related to philosophy, social and life sciences—were closely associated with government and authority. Sometimes blended with government institutions, formal academic associations frequently played the role of academic sponsors and censors. Some research was enthusiastically promoted while other studies were hastily suppressed. For instance, psychology in Europe and North America in the 19th century could not turn to experimental studies of mental activities until after university authorities and supporting academic associations began to enjoy academic freedom.

In summary, certain academic traditions create favorable conditions for particular types of psychological research and development of psychological knowledge. A strong academic support of a theory, or its rejection, very frequently played a vital role in the history of psychology. (See Figure 1.1.)

Figure 1.1 Societal Impact on Psychological Knowledge

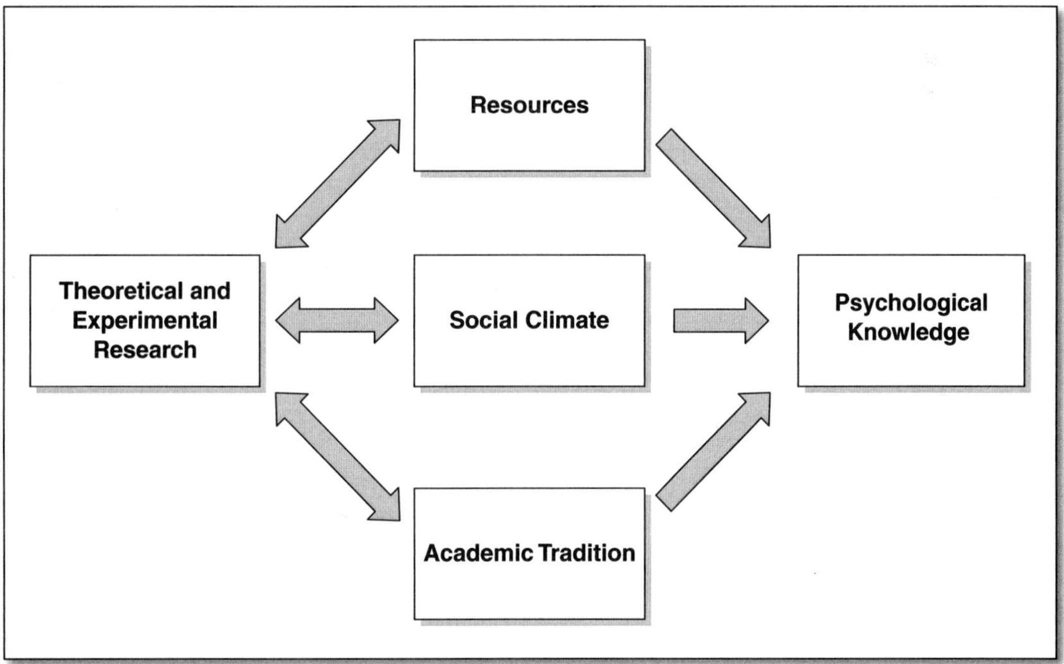

An accurate picture of psychology would be incomplete without introducing the lives and deeds of individual psychologists. Individual scientists wrote the history of psychology. They called themselves philosophers, educators, physicists, doctors, theologians, physiologists, and psychologists; they have created their ideas, exposed them to followers, defended them against critics, and conveyed them to other generations. Years pass by and volumes of published research are forgotten. Colorless book covers on the crowded library shelves are sad reminders of some books' apparent irrelevance for today's students of psychology (Simonton, 1994). But what makes some ideas historically significant? To address this question, we turn to historiography.

✓ CHECK YOUR KNOWLEDGE

Define social climate or Zeitgeist.

Recall three main functions of academic tradition.

Historiography of Psychology

In a broad sense, **historiography** studies the ways by which people obtain and disseminate historical knowledge. Referring to psychology, historiography focuses on the methods used in the study and depiction of psychology's history (Pickren & Dewsbury, 2002). In history books, the accomplishments of entire generations are commonly condensed in several pages or even paragraphs. The history of any academic discipline is a summary. Moreover, it is frequently a creative narrative because historians' accounts of the past are unkindly selective.

Not every psychologist's name will remain in psychology textbooks. Most psychology majors, for example, have heard about the work of John Watson, "Psychology as the Behaviorist Views It," published in 1913. But how many majors are aware of the article "Immortality from a Scientific Point of View" written by Vladimir Bekhterev in 1916? History books have preserved Watson's "Psychology" but have not been so generous to the Bekhterev's article on immortality. Many people know who Sigmund Freud was. But who was Wilhelm Stekel? Most definitely, Katharine Banham (a Canadian psychologist) is less known than Jean Piaget from Switzerland! How many of us have read a 1970 article about the reaction time of 100 male subjects in Finland responding to visual signals? However, there are other studies, like the 1971 Stanford prison experiment by Philip Zimbardo and his colleagues, that became familiar to practically every student majoring in psychology (Zimbardo, 2008).

How do psychologists gather and select the information from years past? Why do some psychological studies remain relatively obscure while others gain prominence? An easy answer might be that significance of psychological knowledge of yesterday is based on its contribution to future knowledge. However, what is called significant is subject to a wide range of interpretations (Kendler, 2002; Lakatos,

1970). Let's address the question of significance by discussing several assumptions related to historiography.

Peer Review and Significance of Knowledge

Who is a good judge of knowledge's relevance? Probably those of us who can make informed evaluations of that knowledge's relevance and impact. Psychological knowledge is likely to remain in history textbooks today if it has been broadly recognized by qualified peers. Peer acceptance is an important factor in determining the value of psychological knowledge. Psychologists today show some consistency in the way they recognize the most important theories of the past. For example, in 10 randomly selected best-selling introductory psychology textbooks published in the United States in 2008, William James is referred to 67 times (ranked number one), the name of John Watson is mentioned 47 times, the name of Ivan Pavlov appears 56 times. Typically, names such as Erik Erikson, B. F. Skinner, Abraham Maslow, and Albert Bandura are mentioned several times in every psychology textbook. Sigmund Freud receives significant attention, mostly for his personality theory. There are always a few references to the works of Wilhelm Wundt, Carl Jung, Alfred Adler, Jean Piaget, and Carl Rogers, among others. Disagreeing about some details, psychologists, as surveys show, generally agree about the top 10 most influential psychologists from the past (Korn et al., 1991).

Nevertheless, peer evaluation is a very complicated and at times controversial process. Very frequently, personal disputes, jealousy, friendship, personal affiliations, favoritism, and many other subjective factors play a role in science. Scientists sometimes use unfair strategies in attempt to secure funding for their research and deny support to others (Fara, 2009). There are also institutional traditions that may or may not be supportive of certain scientific fields. Consider the Nobel Prize, an undeniable indicator of prominence. How many scientists-contributors to psychological knowledge won this most prestigious scientific award? Sigmund Freud was nominated 11 times, and 11 times he lost (optimists say, "He did not win"). Wilhelm Wundt was nominated three times with the same disappointing result. Ivan Pavlov was nominated five times: four times his name was suggested for his research on the nervous system and reflexes; one time he was nominated for his research in physiology of digestion. Pavlov won the Nobel Prize for physiology or medicine in 1904. Physicist Georg von Békésy, who worked on the mechanisms of sensation and psychoacoustics in particular, won the Nobel Prize, also, for physiology or medicine in 1961. Another prize in the same field was awarded in 1973 to three ethologists: Karl von Frisch, Konrad Lorenz, and Nikolaas Tinbergen (*ethology* is the study of animal behavior primarily in a natural environment). Behavioral science was recognized again in 1978 when Herbert A. Simon won the prize in 1978 in economics for his work on organizational decision making. In 1981, Roger Sperry was awarded the prize in medicine for discoveries concerning the functional specialization of the cerebral hemispheres (Dewsbury, 2003). Daniel Kahneman was the first psychologist to win the Nobel Prize, in 2002. However, he won this prize in economics (although Kahneman claimed that he had never taken a single economics course in college) by introducing fundamental research on people's mistakes of judgment in investments and trade.

As you can see, scores of psychologists and other scientists who have contributed to psychology are not on the list. They have been overlooked by the Nobel Prize selection committee. But does this fact make researchers who haven't won the prize less important than those who have? In historiography, peer recognition is an important factor, yet there are other factors affecting the selection and preservation of knowledge in psychology (Pickren, 2003).

Support or rejection by peers does not guarantee that a researcher's name and his or her works will remain in history. Mesmerism, as you recall, was increasingly rejected in academic circles across Europe in the 19th century, yet this theory was popular and remains well known today. Wundt received recognition for his impact on psychology; however, most attention today is given to his organizational talent. His theoretical views lost their perceived significance very rapidly. In addition to receiving positive peer review, psychologists and their studies are often remembered for the impact they make on the discipline. Such impact could be positive or, frequently, controversial.

Impact and Controversy

In the 1930s, a group of psychologists conducted a long-term experimental study in Iowa. The researchers studied children in orphanages and adoptive homes and documented remarkable upward movement in the IQs of young children who were exposed to stimulating environments in well-educated, economically secure families. Filled with methodological errors, this study did not produce reliable data. However, this research became noticeable for its scope, daring goals, and a variety of methods used. It appeared for some time as a research landmark, or as a reminder to psychologists to pay extremely careful attention to methodology (Herman, 2001). This study also illustrated that psychological knowledge can stand out if it affects the work and the views of other scholars. An event in history may be overlooked by a few peers, yet this same event can shape the experience of many others.

Look, for example, at the life and work of Stanley Milgram. He designed, as you might remember from introductory psychology classes, a series of experiments to study obedience to authority. He conducted his experiments at a small laboratory at Yale University in 1961–1962. The research procedure obliged the researcher to place a number of volunteer participants under tremendous psychological pressure. During the experiment, participants had to make difficult moral choices, such as whether to deliver painful electric shocks to other participants. Most peers-critics believed that the subjects in this experiment had been abused and traumatized emotionally. Milgram was heavily criticized for this. Although he later conducted other original experiments, his name is forever associated in psychology books with that original Yale University study, which psychologists call today the *Milgram experiment.* This landmark study showed that obedience to authority is common in ordinary people and that many of us could act unethically if someone else takes responsibility for our behavior. But most important, the study highlighted the vital importance of ethical guidelines in psychology experiments (Blass, 1992; Milgram, 1963).

Research conducted by Harry Harlow also belongs to the category of original landmark projects that sparked attention and encouraged new research. Harlow and his colleagues showed that infant monkeys prefer a soft terrycloth mother surrogate to a wire one, even when only the wire one dispenses milk. The research showed the importance of attachment and its impact on an individual's development (Novak & Harlow, 1975). Attachment became a central topic of psychological studies for many years to come.

Historical significance of a psychologist's work may be overshadowed by his or her controversial behavior or the circumstances surrounding it. Wundt, a founder of experimental psychology, for example, thought of Germany's entrance into World War I as morally justifiable. Wundt expressed a nationalistic belief in Germany's right to defend itself and accused the United States and Great Britain of excessive individualism and materialism (Harrington, 1996; Kendler, 1999). It is doubtful, however, that Wundt's nationalist attitudes have affected his peers' assessment of his laboratory experiments. Yet when scientists make bold decisions or take controversial actions, their views and work receive sudden publicity and attract attention. Social and political activism is one of such actions. William James, a prominent American psychologist of the beginning of the 20th century, had become one of the earliest social activists arguing against wars on moral grounds. Do these pacifist beliefs add points to the score of James's psychological legacy? Probably, yes, although the impact could be indirect. For example, theoretical political science literature today contains references to William James's critical work on the nature of war and attracts attention of students and scholars from other disciplines (Betts, 2005).

In the age of the media, controversy brings public attention. An originator of behaviorism, John Watson, was forced to resign from his key academic positions because of a personal scandal involving him and a female student with whom Watson had intimate relationship. Newspapers were extremely unkind to Watson during the scandal, which quickly became public. As we will see in this book, a controversy surrounding a psychologist's life can fuel significant public attention to researchers and their work.

Most psychologists do not seek controversy or scandal to grab attention. In the history of psychology, however, selective attention has sometimes been given to research associated with social prestige and power.

Social Prestige and Power

Historians admit that in the history of science, individuals of higher social status had a better opportunity to have their scientific ideas initially accepted than anyone else (Fara, 2009). In theory, talent should always win against mediocrity. However, talented scientists and educators serving kings and sultans have always had a greater access to information, superior conditions for research, and better opportunities to publicize their teachings than any talented scholar working in obscurity. We will read in Chapters 2 and 3 that probably the most celebrated philosophers in Europe, the Middle East, India, and China who lived and worked in ancient times and the Middle Ages had their names associated with the most powerful rulers. Similarly, most prominent philosophers of the modern era who made important contributions to psychological knowledge were de facto on kings' and queens' payroll or supported by wealthiest families. Several exceptions, of course, existed. But the association with the powerful was common for most prominent thinkers before the 18th century.

Today's psychologists (with rare exceptions) do not directly serve presidents and prime ministers. For nearly 200 years most scientists contributing to psychology have worked for colleges and universities. Yet in a similar way, the prominence and power of academic institutions may become an important factor empowering psychologists and their creations. Prominent "founding parents" of American psychology studied in and worked for top schools. Edward Thorndike did his studies at Columbia University. John Watson worked at the University of Chicago and Johns Hopkins University. Hugo Münsterberg was at Harvard University. William James and B. F. Skinner also served at Harvard. Edward Titchener worked at Cornell University. It is not a rule that a psychological theory created at Harvard, Cornell, Columbia, or some other "top" school should receive more attention and a better reception from scholars. However, very few will deny that the resources available to researchers in the best schools play a serious role in how knowledge develops. Universities with better funding opportunities often have a greater potential to hire prominent psychologists or accept gifted students. Again, talented researchers supported by generous funding tend to have more opportunities than their equally talented colleagues who are working in less favorable conditions.

There is no reason to become cynical and see the history of psychology only through the prism of money and resources. Funds and prestige do not always buy the best talent in psychology. For example, one of the most quoted early studies of memory was conducted in the 19th century by Hermann Ebbinghaus, who at that time was not a university professor. Wilhelm Wundt's laboratory was in Leipzig, not in Berlin, which was the most prestigious German university with a reputable psychology department. Probably the most quoted early specialist on intelligence, Alfred Binet, couldn't secure employment at the premier French university of his choice. The only psychology professional who won the Nobel Prize had worked at the University of Oregon, which is not an Ivy League school. One of the founders of social psychology, Kurt Lewin, settled down at the University of Iowa. World-renowned Abraham Maslow taught at Brooklyn College. One of the most quoted contributors to psychology, Sigmund Freud, as well as Herbert Spencer, did not hold a full-time professorship.

Wilhelm Stekel, one of Freud's earliest followers, was expelled from the psychoanalytic movement in 1912 because of his alleged personal mistakes (we discuss them in Chapter 8). Although he remained active as a psychoanalyst, most psychologists are unaware of his post-1912 work, which was considerable. Wilhelm Stekel was a productive writer. In the 28 years after his break with Freud until his suicide in 1940, Stekel published at least a book a year as well as numerous papers. Altogether, he wrote 36 books, 179 articles, and 153 abstracts and reviews (Bos, 2003). Should we assume that Freud's poor relations with his former supporter have influenced our perception of Stekel? Most likely this is not the case. Freud had several followers beside Stekel. Two of them were Carl Jung and Alfred Adler, who continued their work after breaking with Freud. Today they remain among the most prominent psychologists of the 20th century. Of course, friendship plays an important role in the history of psychology, but its impact is highly circumstantial and depends on many other factors.

The history of psychology is a product created by academic superstars as well as by scores of individuals who remain virtually unknown today (Leahey, 2002). In our study of psychology's past, we shouldn't overlook the importance of contributions made by lesser-known individuals who took their part in shaping the body of contemporary psychological knowledge.

Paying Selective Attention: Gender and Ethnicity

For years, men dominated the discipline of psychology. Even in the 20th century, restrictions existed in many industrially developed nations regarding enrollment of female students to major universities. Even in cases when equality was protected by law, hiring of female faculty and researchers was limited by custom and prejudice. Glass-ceiling barriers also existed in terms of promotion of women to more advanced positions in university's male-dominated hierarchies. You will observe continuously in many chapters of this book that gender has been a very important factor affecting the development of psychology as a discipline and psychological knowledge as well (Riger, 2002). Consider just one example.

In the very beginning of the 20th century, many experimental psychologists shared a view that only a specially selected and trained group of highly skilled observers could perform the collection and compilation of scientific data in psychological labs. Only trained professionals could conduct scientific observations in strictly controlled conditions of an experiment. These trained professionals should be men. Why? The researcher, as it was widely assumed, should be a watchful and meticulous person. He should be lacking any emotion or passion, like excitement, disappointment, or jealousy. Women at that time were commonly regarded as too subjective, unstable, and sentimental (Keller, 1985). If we follow this logic, the psychology researcher must have been wearing a pair of pants and a mandatory beard. It was further assumed that women—because of their involvement in busy relationships, families, children, and so forth—should play only subsidiary roles in psychological research. In other words, a better role for a woman was research assistant, not principal investigator (Noon, 2004.) As a result of these beliefs and practices, until recent times accomplishments and aspirations of women were too frequently underestimated, overlooked, or simply ignored.

Another factor affecting psychology was **ethnocentrism**, or the tendency—sometimes deliberate but often unintentional—to view psychological knowledge from own national or ethnic positions. We will hardly find psychologists who deliberately ignore research conducted in other countries or by people of different ethnic or cultural background. Yet ethnocentrism, often unintended, existed in history. Why?

One of several factors contributing to ethnocentrism was the language barrier. Historically, due to a rapid development of psychology in the United States in the 20th century, much written communication was conducted in English. Scores of prominent journals and other publications also appear in English. For many years now, most international conferences overseas recommend English as an official language.

Researchers who have limited knowledge of English or no access to international journals, unfortunately, have a diminished opportunity to be recognized.

Another factor feeding ethnocentrism in psychology is the belief that only scholars working within Western cultural tradition deserve attention of most of today's psychologists. In a similar way, there is a tendency in psychology books to portray North American and western European psychological schools as having made the most substantial contribution to the history of psychology compared to other national schools. As a result, most textbooks available today describe various schools of thought and specific theories originated and developed in a relatively small selection of countries. These are, mainly, the United States, France, Germany, and a very short list of other European nations. Without a doubt, scientists from these countries have made the most remarkable and significant contributors to contemporary psychology. However, there are no less noteworthy and outstanding contributions coming from many other parts of the world, including Japan, Russia, South Africa, Turkey, India, Pakistan, Iran, Mexico, China, Congo, and Brazil, to name a few. These names and theories, for a number of reasons, remain unknown to a majority of psychology students. A psychologist paying careful attention to the negative impact of ethnocentrism should pay attention to a history of psychology that is more comprehensive and accurate than many other versions that existed in the past.

ON THE WEB

You can easily access links to the APA article on women in psychology on the book website.

In summary, selective attention to psychological knowledge developed in the past due to gender or ethnic bias is a subtle but substantial factor influencing the researchers'

CASE IN POINT

Women Psychologists in North America. Psychology for centuries has been a male-dominated field. In 1950, only 15 percent and in 1960 only 18 percent of all doctoral degrees in psychology were awarded to women. Yet in the 1970s, the number of women earning doctorates in psychology began to increase steadily, and by the early 1980s, this number had increased dramatically. For the first time in history, the proportion of women doctoral recipients became equal to men. By 2113, if the trend continues, women would receive 70 percent of the doctoral degrees earned in North America. Men and women tend to pursue many similar career choices in psychology. Some careers are different. For example, a vast majority of doctoral degrees in developmental psychology goes to women. Yet most degrees in experimental psychology are awarded to men.

Source: American Psychological Association (2009)

choices in selecting, presenting, and promoting materials related to the history of psychology. In the following chapters, we address these and other cultural biases.

✓ **CHECK YOUR KNOWLEDGE**

What does historiography study?

Who was the first psychologist to win the Nobel Prize? In which field?

What is ethnocentrism in psychology?

Understanding the History of Psychology

The history of psychology as the history of science is not necessarily a straight line of growth and improvement (Kuhn, 1962). There were distinct psychological schools. Each school had a time and place of birth, followed by a period of development, and concluded by a phase of decline. Then a new school was born and developed through similar stages. Studying the history of psychology, we often tend to assemble the known facts into convenient groups with suitable labels attached. For example, it is convenient to understand the development of psychology as a movement from one historical generation of psychologists to another. It is easy to divide psychologists who lived in a certain period into two categories: those who belonged to a scientific school (behaviorists, for instance) and those who didn't.

No Straight Pass

However, by using this straight-line approach, we run the risk of presenting psychology in a very simplistic way. Look at the following deliberately simple presentation of psychology's history over the past 150 years. In the following example, a line in history appears as a sequence of identifiable labels (we will study all these categories and labels mentioned in the case later, in practically every chapter of the book):

> Philosophers and physicians, who studied psychology prior to the 19th century, gave way to phenomenologists. Then it was a battle between structuralists and functionalists. Then behaviorists came in the 20th century and replaced phenomenologists. Psychoanalysts struggled against behaviorists. Both psychoanalysts and behaviorists fell under criticism of Gestalt psychologists, cognitivists, and, most recently, humanistic psychologists.

But wait! Could it be that psychologists—especially those who had lived in the same historic period—wanted to accept these labels standing for distinct psychological traditions? We know today that in the past, psychoanalysts preferred to meet with fellow analysts but not with other types of psychologists. Leading behaviorists attended behaviorist conventions and sought students who would share similar academic views (Rogler, 2002). In fact, there were several distinct psychological schools associated with universities such as the University of Chicago. Many psychologists identified themselves as members of such schools.

Nevertheless, many other psychologists did not want to associate their names with categories, schools, or associations. We will learn that the convenient division of psychology of the early 20th century into structural and functional types was not commonly recognized 100 years ago. Placing every researcher in a specific category frequently simplifies our knowledge about psychology. As a remedy, we will accept an artist's wisdom: between the extremes of black and white there exists a middle ground comprised of innumerable shades of gray (Levy, 2009). In many cases, a "No labels attached" understanding of a psychologist's work helps us to understand that work better.

Categorizing is, to some degree, an American cultural trend: we label and rank everything from college teams, songs, movies, the most attractive male and female dancers and singers, to the silliest acts caught on video and the most beautiful or ugliest outfits of the year. In a similar fashion, it is sometimes tempting to see the history of psychology as a straight line of distinct schools and systems with labels and ranks attached.

What is an alternative to these apparent simplifications? Studying the history of discrete psychological schools, their birth, development, and decline, we will look at many turns, gray areas, theories, and concepts that did not always fit into the convenient boundaries of psychological schools. And you will find that there are plenty of such theories and names!

Fragmentation and Standardization

Since the dawn of psychological research, scientists consistently expressed dissimilar opinions on almost every topic. One hundred years ago they could not even agree on the main subject of psychology. Wundt, Ebbinghaus, and Titchener urged psychologists to study consciousness. Freud and Jung focused on the mechanisms of unconscious processes. Spencer, Galton, and James paid attention to human adoptive activities. Thorndike and Watson put behavior in focus. Some, like Pavlov, preferred to study the reflex as the foundation of all psychological activities. Others, like Titchener, focused on mental elements or mental operations. Some of them supported experimental research, while others believed in free will and self-analysis.

With years passing by, the situation within the field of psychology was becoming more confusing. By the end of the first quarter of the 20th century, scholars belonging to various academic traditions began to design and use their own professional language closely related to the subject and methods of their study. Increasingly, scientific schools grew apart. Psychoanalysts would not read behaviorist publications. Behaviorists would ignore altogether the structuralists and their work. Both behaviorists and psychoanalysis would skip publications of Gestalt psychologists. The fragmentation of knowledge in psychology was evident since the inception of the discipline. The history of psychology appeared for some critics as a narrative of a series of disjointed concepts and theories (Bower, 1993; Yanchar & Slife, 1997).

Despite an apparent fragmentation and specialization of psychologists preoccupied with their own models and methods, psychologists received a great opportunity to look at these branches and theories, compare them, and make comparative evaluations. Some theories revealed their own weaknesses. Reliable scientific data from other theories became universally available. In this process, psychological knowledge was becoming more standard, consistent, and interrelated. We can call his process the standardization of knowledge. Three factors stimulated the process of psychology's standardization.

First, the development of market-oriented principles of governing established in many societies through the 20th century gave psychologists great opportunities to seek practical applications of their research in education, business, assessment, training, and health care fields. Practical needs led many psychologists to acknowledge the existence of some general psychological theories and facts and develop a sort of a universal professional language of psychology.

Second, because of the growing sophistication of psychological research, many psychologists no longer could afford to conduct big and comprehensive studies. It was the time of specialization, which, in effect, led to the recognition that the same phenomenon (parent-child interaction, as an example) could be studied simultaneously from different psychological perspectives and by different methods. Every method would advance knowledge.

Third, rapid developments in education and communication, including the birth and expansion of mass media, have broadened the general audience's knowledge about psychology and diversified the public's attitudes about psychology. More people were aware of psychology as a discipline, more individuals sought and appreciated scientific knowledge, and more people would choose psychology as their educational field and future profession.

The competing process of fragmentation and differentiation in psychology continued for many decades. It continues today.

✓ CHECK YOUR KNOWLEDGE

Explain standardization of knowledge in psychology.

Why couldn't scientists create a single, universal psychological theory?

Conclusion

Pessimists who emphasize fragmentation are likely to look at the history of psychology as a sequence of failed theories. This is how the pessimists see it. First, a theory initially attracts enthusiastic supporters. Then critics find weaknesses in this theory. Criticism grows, thus diminishing the significance of the theory. Finally, it loses support. New theories appear to repeat the sequence. Pessimists argue that psychology has never had a common language and has never been unified. It remained largely fragmented throughout its short history.

But let's look at the history of psychology from a different angle. What if we see these fragmented theories as if they were beams of light coming from different projectors and illuminating one object? Each beam brightens only one side of the object, but together they show a much clearer picture. Using this analogy, we could see psychology's history as a relentless attempt to enlighten our knowledge. Let's call this approach *integrative* as some psychologists suggest (Sternberg & Grigorenko, 2001). From this point of view, in the history of psychology, each psychological theory or assumption was somewhat accurate. Each has illuminated, brightly or not, only a small part of psychological reality. If we take into consideration, for example, anger, we can realize that several theories of the past had different and incomplete interpretations of this emotion. Yet, we can also realize that anger, as well as any other emotion, was studied from an evolutionary, cognitive, behavioral, or other approaches. Each presents a different way of understanding anger.

Why couldn't psychologists put their heads together to create a single theory? Would it be beneficial to have a unified theory instead of many relatively separated from one another approaches? There are serious arguments against an advanced consolidation of psychological knowledge. Any attempt at consolidation would eventually create a monopoly on knowledge. This monopoly would likely mean intellectual domination of one group of researchers over others. It would also mean that only one understanding would be deemed scientific or correct and other eliminated. Competition of ideas no longer will be tolerated. Only a few esteemed psychology leaders would be granted the lifelong right to disseminate their psychological wisdom to forthcoming generations of young psychologists. Would you like to witness this scenario?

Psychological knowledge is strong because of its diversity.

Summary

- The book undertakes a scientific investigation of psychological knowledge from a historic perspective. Psychological knowledge is inseparable from the social, economic, and cultural contexts in which it develops.

- Although psychology as an academic discipline had received its initial recognition by the end of the 19th century, its development began much earlier. Many individual scholars—psychologists, philosophers, doctors, theologians, neurophysiologists, mathematicians, and others—contributed to psychological knowledge and psychology as a discipline.

- Among important themes in psychology, three stand out: the mind-body problem, the interaction of biological and social factors in human behavior and experience, and the balance between theoretical knowledge and its practical applications.

- Different people and groups used psychological knowledge to pursue specific goals. As a result, several types of psychological knowledge have emerged. Among them are scientific, folk, ideological, and legal.

- The social, political, and academic atmospheres that were unique to particular historic times and locations were crucial for psychology as a discipline. At least three factors are used to understand the complex interaction among society and psychological knowledge: resources, social climate, and academic tradition.

• In history books, the accomplishments of entire generations are commonly condensed in several pages or even paragraphs. The history of any academic discipline is a summary based on opinions of peers, social impact of research, controversies involved, and social prestige. Gender bias and ethnocentrism also affected psychology's history.

• The history of psychology as the history of science is not necessarily a straight line of growth and improvement. Psychologists consistently expressed dissimilar opinions on almost every topic. Fragmentation, standardization, and integration of psychological knowledge continued throughout its history.

Key Terms

Ethnocentrism

Historiography

Ideological (value-based) knowledge

Knowledge

Legal knowledge

Neurasthenia

Placebo effect

Pop psychology

Popular (or folk) beliefs

Scientific knowledge

Values

Zeitgeist

2

Early Psychological Knowledge

God provides the wind, but man must raise the sails.

Attributed to Augustine (354–430)

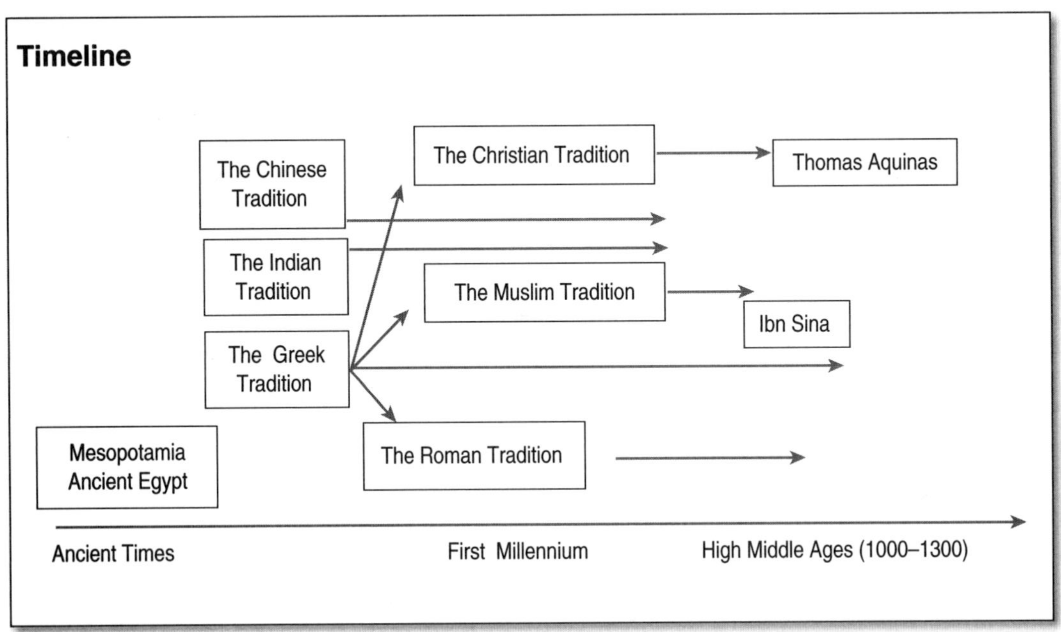

CHAPTER OUTLINE

From a distance, the white piles of the *American Psychologist* on a bookshelf look like a wall of thin horizontal and motionless paper wrinkles. The miniscule characters on the journal covers indicate the chronology of the issues: the older ones are on the bottom; the newest editions are closer to the top. Pull out just a few issues published in recent years. Browse through articles, reports, critiques, and reviews written by contemporary authors about modern day psychology. What you will find is that despite the precious uniqueness of the problems that psychology deals with today, many of the issues at point are not new. It is amazing how many current topics have been discussed in the works of the scientists who lived hundreds or even thousands of years ago! Take a few randomly chosen articles and see that some of today's main topics had already been addressed by thinkers in Greece, Iran, China, or India!

What is psychological truth? A 2002 article argues that although the methods of the natural sciences are appropriate for determining psychological truth, psychology is not a natural science but rather a form of a human science. Therefore, it should use different criteria for interpreting facts related to human activities. It is remarkable that hundreds of years ago, Aristotle, Seneca, and Avicenna also discussed the same subject. Scores of Greek, Indian, or Arab scholar debated the origins of human perception and the nature of scholarly methods in psychology for centuries.

The ideas of individualism in collectivism are better understood if we recognize the religious contexts in which they were formed, suggests an article published in 2000. Is this a brand-new point of view of the 21st century? No. The idea that psychological knowledge, both theoretical and empirical, develops within particular religious conditions, has been already acknowledged by thinkers in ancient Greece and Rome, in Iran and Egypt.

The language is the product not of the mind but of cultural process. A 2001 paper defends the importance of cultural factors in understanding of language. In fact, this point was raised much earlier, by Epicurus and the Roman Stoics.

How can we understand intuitions and thoughts, accessibility of knowledge, and the nature of the deliberate thought process? asked a 2003 article. The same question about intuition was put forward by Plato, Aristotle, and Socrates in Greece, Ibn Sina in Persia, Thomas Aquinas in Paris, and Lao-Tse in China. The miracle of human intuitive thinking continued to occupy the minds of dozens of scholars throughout history.

Prevention programs for children and youth is a sound investment in society's future, insists another contemporary article. The great Chinese thinker Confucius understood this and believed in the importance of prevention in the process of socialization of the child. How long ago? Check his birth date later in this chapter.

Do these all references and quotes mean that contemporary psychology attempts to reexamine knowledge? Probably, yes. Today's psychology tries to give new answers to the never-ending questions related to the miracle of human experience. As we can see in this chapter, many important questions about psychology had been already asked in the past. We examine some of these inquiries and trace the development of psychological knowledge to the earlier stages of human civilization. We begin our studies with an examination of some ideas of the ancient past. But in many ways, this chapter is also about today's psychology.

The following articles from the *American Psychologists* were used for this introductory vignette: Gergen (2001); Kahneman (2003); Kendler (2002); Sampson (2000); Weissberg, Kumpfer, and Seligman (2003).

Psychological Knowledge at the Beginning of Human Civilization

The first human civilizations emerged 5,000 to 6,000 years ago, when people began to live in organized communities under governing social rules. Systematic agriculture brought a substantial change in the lives of large groups who could acquire food on a regular basis, build permanent settlements, and exchange products through trade. People began to develop a new type of connection between themselves and environment. This type of connection, called **subjective culture**, manifested itself in various forms, including early religion, arts, education, and science. People learned about the physical world around them, their bodies, and, certainly, psychological experiences. Systematic knowledge was transforming small human communities and larger civilizations; the developing civilizations stimulated the development of systematic knowledge. The wheel of science began to turn.

What kind of psychological knowledge was accumulated? Early psychological observations began to emerge in written folklore, religious scriptures, and paintings. Although these observations seem grossly incomplete today, they allow us to study people's knowledge related to sensations, emotions, desires, dreams, will, and other experiences. Throughout history, psychological knowledge was never singular or unified (Robinson, 1986).

Who were the people who made early contributions to psychological knowledge? They were physicians, religious scholars, teachers, philosophers, and poets. Most of them occupied special and often privileged positions in society. Most information today is available from sources traced back to the ancient Near East, ancient Greece and Rome, the Middle East, and North Africa; these are commonly referred to today as the roots of Western civilization. Non-Western written sources came primarily from Central Asia, India, and China (see Table 2.1).

Table 2.1 Psychological Knowledge in the Beginning of Human Civilization: An Overview

Observations	*Sources of Knowledge*	*Major Findings*
Behavior and its causes	Observation and generalizations	External forces, primarily supernatural, control human behavior; people could pursue and achieve goals through will.
Cognition	Observation and generalizations	The soul was recognized as an entity associated with cognition.
Emotion	Observation and generalizations	Various emotional states were recognized.
Specific knowledge	Observation and generalizations	Prescriptions were given about appropriate and inappropriate behavior.

Mesopotamia

Located between the Tigris and Euphrates rivers in the area of contemporary Iraq, Mesopotamia was one of the oldest civilizations. Few written sources on social and legal issues have given us even approximate information about the type of psychological knowledge that people of this civilization developed. From Hammurabi's Code, a legal document reflecting the social developments during Hammurabi's rule (c. 1700 BCE), we learn that gods in Mesopotamia were viewed as actual beings and people cared about their good relationships with them to bring health, victory in war, happiness in marriage, or profit in trade deals. People were convinced that forces beyond their control guided their lives. The importance of symbols, signs, and superstitions in people's lives was remarkable. However, by observing religious traditions and following rituals people could feel somewhat confident. Significant wealth was contributed to the construction of temples as places of worship. Mesopotamian civilization was among the first to develop written language. Texts were written on clay tablets, and some of them contain descriptions of dreams, especially of noble individuals. Dreams were used to make predictions about daily events, health, and destiny. The first professional dream interpreters seemed to emerge at that time (Hoffman, 2004).

Ancient Egypt

As in Mesopotamia, religion was also an inseparable element of life in ancient Egypt. Psychological observations come from various sources, including fragments of written prescriptions about how to behave in social situations; how to respect people of a higher status; how not to offend women; or how to avoid embarrassment (Spielvogel, 2005). Educational principles were summarized in a number of ancient Egyptian treatises now commonly called the *Books of Instruction.* From papyrus manuscripts, prepared sometimes between 2900 and 2000 BCE, we infer that the human heart was viewed as the center of the organism. It was the location of the soul, reasoning abilities, emotions, and personality traits. The gods could send people knowledge and imperatives through their hearts.

In summary, Mesopotamia and Egypt are examples of two early civilizations that produced documented but very fragmented histories of peoples' searches for answers about the nature of the world, the role of human beings in it, and supernatural forces. The separation of the material and spiritual—the body and soul—was an important step down the road of a relentless inquiry into human psychology. Similar division of the spiritual and material also appeared in written accounts of the early civilizations of the Assyrians, the Jews, the Persians, and the Babylonians.

Psychological Knowledge in the Civilization of the Greeks

The civilization of the Greeks laid the foundations for Western culture. The history of Greek civilization—and the period to which we direct our attention now is approximately 750 BCE to 100 BCE—was a remarkable account of war and territorial expansion, slavery, discrimination, and violence. At the same time, it was a time of great progress in science, philosophy, engineering, trade, medicine, education, and the arts.

A contemporary psychologist examining that period is likely to establish at least three major sources of systematic knowledge related to psychology. One source is derived from Greek philosophy and its several branches, including ethics (studies of moral values and behavior), metaphysics (philosophy), and epistemology (studies of cognition). Another relates to natural science and includes medicine. The third source is found in mythology. (See Table 2.2.)

Table 2.2 Psychological Knowledge in the Civilization of the Greeks: An Overview

Observations	*Sources of Knowledge*	*Major Findings*
Behavior and its causes	Observation and generalizations, mythology, medical research	Two sources of causation are natural and divine.
Cognition	Observation and generalizations, mythology, research of the sensory organs	Materialism: cognition is a reflection of the outside world. Idealism: cognition is a result of "higher" processes caused by divine sources.
Emotion	Observation and generalizations, mythology	Emotions regulate behavior but can be destructive and interfere with cognition.
Specific knowledge	Observation and generalizations, mythology, medical research	Assumptions were made about the role of the heart, the brain, the nervous system, and other organs in human behavior and experience.

What did the Greeks know about psychology? The following section of the chapter contains a description of the major findings of the ancient Greeks—philosophers, physicians, and natural scientists—in their investigations of psychology. Please notice that most of these findings were rooted in typical Greek beliefs in harmony, proportion, order, and beauty.

Early Concepts of the Soul

In ancient Greece, the separation of the body and soul was generally accepted, with two different schools of thought developing. The first was associated with the view that the human soul originated from the same matter as any other material object. **Materialism** was the fundamental view suggesting that the facts of mental life can be sufficiently explained in physical terms by the existence and nature of matter. The materialist view rejected the existence of anything psychological or mental and teaches that anything referred to as "psychological" is nothing but physical or physiological processes. The second school of thought, **idealism,** claimed the relative independence of the nonmaterial soul from the material body.

Materialism. Many early Greek materialists were atomists. **Atomism** stands for the notion that matter is made up of small, indivisible particles. Although atomism may appear to some of us today as naïve and simplistic, gradually, through centuries, this "simplistic" outlook was developed into a remarkably sophisticated worldview. First written accounts discussing the atomist approach refer to Leucippus (fifth century BCE) and particularly of Thales (640–546 BCE). He was one of the first thinkers who gave materialistic explanations of all natural phenomena, including mental activities (Brumbaugh, 1981).

> **ON THE WEB**
>
> On the book website, read Thales's biographical sketch and brief biographies of other Greek thinkers.

Thales's followers included Anaximander (611–547 BCE) and Anaximenes (550–500 BCE). These three thinkers, who lived in the town of Miletus, are known today as representatives of the Milesian school. Their views are considered as seminal to the tradition called **material monism**, which holds that all things and developments, including psychological processes, no matter how complicated they are, have one similar material origin. Anaximenes considered air as the founding source of everything, including the soul, which was compared with the breath of life. While Thales viewed water as the origin, Anaximander believed in the existence of a special organizing principle or source called *boundless* (Greek: *apeiron*) and taught that life was originated from moisture and people gradually developed from fish. These were early evolutionary views.

These ideas were developed by Heraclitus (530–470 BCE). He introduced a very sophisticated concept of the soul—called *psyche*—that consisted of specific particles of ever-living fire, a founding substance. In this system, the strength and quality of the soul are based on the quality of the fire. Drunkenness, for instance, is associated with a wetness of the soul, which is an unhealthy state. Physical death of the body also means death of the psyche. Heraclitus described different states of awareness or, as we call it today, consciousness. He attributed the difference between sleep and awakening to a weak or strong connection between the body and the soul. Heraclitus also theorized that people gain their intellectual strength through breathing and lessen psychological capacities in sleep because their sensory organs are shut down temporarily (Kirk, Raven, & Schofield, 1995).

Empedocles (c. 490–430 BCE) continued the tradition of materialism. He was a remarkable contributor to rhetoric (the art of using language) and medicine. He maintained that the human soul is more complex than Heraclitus had stated and is comprised of not only one, but several components, including fire, water, and air. Empedocles believed that not only humans but also animals and plants have souls. In humans, the soul is associated with blood and, therefore, with the heart. A different view was developed by Alcmaeon of Croton (c. 500–450 BCE). He believed that sensation and thought are connected with the brain and nervous system. Although animals have brains and, therefore, should have souls, animals use only sensations, while humans have the distinctive ability of intelligence. Alcmaeon assumed that different states of mental awareness are caused by various states of activation and balance of blood in the body: when the blood is active and fills the joints, the person is awake. In Alcmaeon's teachings we find the earliest traces of future theories of various bodily "balances" and their impact on individual functioning. Similar theories were developed in other parts of the ancient world.

Democritus (460–370 BCE) was probably the most influential Greek philosopher of the materialist school. Two of his assumptions are important for today's psychologists. First, like other materialists, Democritus explained human experience as activities of the soul, which is part of the natural world. The soul consists of round atoms of fire, which provide movement to the body, which is life. The soul does not survive the destruction of the body because the atoms disperse as well. Second, Democritus created a three-centric theory of the localization of the soul. He believed that the atoms of the soul are active on three different levels in the human body: around the brain, close to the chest and heart, and in the region of the liver. The atoms located close to the brain are responsible for thinking. The atoms that concentrate around the heart are related to emotional processes. And, finally, those atoms that rotate around the liver are in charge of needs and desires.

The views of Democritus were developed by Epicurus (341–271 BCE). Like Democritus, he taught that the basic constituents of the world are atoms: indivisible particles of matter. Human souls consist of atoms of fire and air. The more atoms of fire are in the soul, the more active the soul is. All psychological processes, states of consciousness, can be explained in materialistic, atomic terms as different states of concentration of atoms. We return to Epicurus's views several times in this chapter.

To find another example of the materialist understanding of the soul in ancient Greece, we now turn to Stoicism (the name derives from the Greek word referring to the porch in Athens around which, supposedly, the members of the school met), the philosophical movement that was developed by Zeno of Citium (344–262 BCE), Cleanthes (331–232 BCE), and Chrysippus (280–206 BCE). The world, according to the Stoics, consists of a passive matter and an active force called *pneuma.* As a result of the interaction between pneuma and matter, the existing world appears in four categories or levels. The more pneuma is involved, the more active the matter becomes. For example, the first level is nature, and the impact of pneuma on it is relatively insignificant. On the second level, pneuma is more active and is responsible for the growth and procreation of matter. This is the level of plants. The third level is the animal kingdom. Here pneuma is more dynamic and enables matter not only to grow and procreate but also to feel and perceive. The fourth and highest level of interaction is achieved on the human level. Pneuma, in the most complete form, represents human soul, which is, in fact, part of nature.

Idealism. The idealist view challenges most assumptions of materialists. Idealism is a fundamental view suggesting that the facts of mental life can be sufficiently explained in mental terms. The soul is nonmaterial, immortal, and can exist alone, separated from the body. The idealist view is well represented in the teachings of Plato (427–347 BCE), one of the most quoted of the Greek philosophers. He is the originator of an influential philosophical view that has been studied and advanced through many generations of thinkers. Plato theorized that the world can be described in three dimensions. The first dimension is the world of the ideal forms (which is the primary reality). The second is the material world created by God. The third is psychological, which is a reflection of the ideal through material. How does the reflection take place? In Plato's famous allegory, human beings are located inside of an imaginary cave, and they observe reflections of forms (the reality) on the cave's walls. The reflections are merely replicas of reality, but humans believe that these reflections are the "real" world. The human body offers only a temporary harbor for the soul that is part of the world of ideas. Souls travel there free of earthly concerns and desires. When back in the human body, the soul is capable of recalling the knowledge gained while it was traveling in the world of ideas.

Plato believed that people differ socially due to the inborn variations in the quality of their souls.

Although the soul is an immortal, undivided, and nonmaterial entity, it can be understood as existing on three levels. This triarchic understanding of the soul as well as triarchic classification of mental activities will appear again many times in various psychological theories including most contemporary (*triarchic* in psychological language stands for anything that is comprised of three elements or governed by three principles). The highest level belongs to the rational soul that is responsible for abstract thinking and wisdom. The brain is a temporary harbor associated with the rational soul. The next level down is affective and is associated with the area of the heart. The affective soul is emotional, courageous, and fearless. The lowest part of the soul is responsible for desires and needs and can be associated with the level of the abdomen.

Plato believed that people differ due to the variations in the quality of their souls. Philosophers and rulers are likely to possess the highest-quality rational souls.

Warriors and fighters have strong affective souls. Slaves should have dominant desirous souls. According to Plato, large groups of people also form categories according to the quality of their souls. Greeks, for example, were likely to have the most advanced rational souls. Tribes that lived in northern Europe had affective souls, and Egyptians possessed lower kinds of souls. Society is built according to the same principles. Because the highest levels of the soul are supposed to dominate the lowest ones, the ideal state is supposed to be organized in a certain way: wise aristocrats rule, brave warriors defend, and other people produce, build, cook, clean, buy, and sell (see Table 2.3). Somewhat similar views differentiating people according to their skills or even size of their brains appeared again in the 19th century to justify policies of social and racial segregation.

Table 2.3 Plato's Views of the Soul

Aspect of Soul	*Associated Social Class*	*Dominant Features*
Highest, rational	Philosophers, rulers, educators	Reason, wisdom, freedom from immediate concerns and desires
Affective	Warriors	Courage, responsibility, and strength
Desirous	Commoners, including merchants, craftsmen, peasants, and slaves	Needs and desires

Plato's theory of different realities is remarkable. In effect, the teachings of Plato about perception may turn an average person's assumptions about psychology upside down. As you remember, Plato believed that the reality of objects, which we detect by our senses, is not real but exists as a reflection of immaterial ideas that comprise the true reality. These and similar fundamental assumptions about human perception occupied the minds of many prominent philosophers. (Some of these ideas are discussed in Chapters 3, 4, and 12.) Various applications of Plato's views are still significant today, for example, in literature and cinematography (see the following Case in Point).

☞ CASE IN POINT

Plato and *The Matrix*. Have you seen the Hollywood blockbuster, *The Matrix*? The movie portrays the mystery and horror of an artificial, virtual world. Appearing real for its inhabitants, it is, in fact, built of sheer perceptions. Based on the idea that what is perceived by us as reality is only an illusion controlled by malevolent forces,

The Matrix is arguably one of the most clearly philosophical movies of the 1990s. The film inadvertently addresses Plato's theory of cognition: the reality of the world is "given" to us through our senses, and our ability to know what is beyond our sensations is limited. Many students with little background in philosophy or psychology were quite surprised to learn that the basic ideas presented in this film were not contemporary but had been created thousands of years ago by philosophers like Plato. Those who are interested in learning more about the linkages between the ideas presented in this movie and other theoretical concepts related to mind and consciousness can check the book by William Irwin called *The Matrix and Philosophy.*

✓ CHECK YOUR KNOWLEDGE

Compare and contrast materialism and idealism in the Greeks' understanding of the soul.

Explain the meaning of Plato's cave allegory.

Hylomorphism of Aristotle. Plato's most prominent student, Aristotle (384–322 BCE), developed an original theory of the soul and its relationship with the body. This theory is frequently called **hylomorphism**, a term composed of the Greek words for matter (*hulê*) and form (*morphê*). He introduced the soul in his manuscript called *De Anima* (The Soul) as the *form* of the body, which is the *matter* of the soul. Before Aristotle, you will keep in mind, philosophers who maintained the materialist view considered the soul as a special kind of matter. Plato, on the other hand, considered the soul as a bodiless substance. Aristotle combined these points of view together. He viewed the soul as an active, creative influence in the body: the body's form but not the body itself. He connected the body and the soul by claiming their coexistence and maintained that the existence of the living organism is impossible without the soul, and conversely the soul cannot exist without the living body.

He further theorized that the soul possesses individual capacities or faculties: nutrition (growth and reproduction), perception (reflection of reality), and reason (highest function associated with thinking). Of all living organisms, only human souls possess all three capacities. Aristotle considered the individual faculties of the soul not as separate entities but as interconnected functions. He advanced the common among Greeks concept of psychological functions divided into three categories: (1) skills associated with growth and strength; (2) skills associated with courage, will, and emotions; and, finally, (3) skills associated with logic and reason. Aristotle also considered the heart as the center of vital activities and believed that blood should be a source of activities of the soul. He referred to the brain as a "coolant" of blood. Cross-culturally, human language today contains references to the brain as a center of reason that cools down or restrains the affective impulses of the heart.

The Greeks' early views of the matter and soul should help us understand better their views of human cognition including sensation, perception, and thinking. Many contemporary debates about the fundamental principles of human cognition and its applications originate in the works of ancient Greeks.

Understanding Cognition

Greek philosophers expressed a wide range of ideas about the mechanisms of cognition. These ideas became a base for **epistemology**—the branch of philosophy that studies the nature of knowledge, its foundations, extent, and validity. Early epistemology grew almost entirely out of observations and their critical discussion. There were no laboratory experiments conducted or quantitative studies performed. Nevertheless, clever assumptions about how people see, hear, remember, and think remain valuable indicators about the sophistication of the knowledge possessed by the ancient Greeks. The most fundamental differences among the scholars were based on their interpretations of the major source of cognition and its mechanisms. At least three schools of thought are discussed here.

Three Views of Cognition. Materialists shared several important assumptions. First, they generally believed that the soul serves as the detector of the processes that take place in reality. Individual experience has the capacity to portray the outside world accurately. Sensation is a foundation of thinking, and without sensation thought is impossible. Thinking helps people to understand what is behind their sensations. Mistakes may occur when people try to make generalizations about their senses using imagination, fantasy, and abstract judgments.

Second, despite some differences, Greek materialists generally supported the view according to which sensation is possible because of a kind of emanation or "discharge" coming from objects. These are particles of matter or atoms of different shape and form. They make an impression on our senses and thus evoke sensation and then thought. This view was later called the **emanation theory** of sensation. How does sensation work? Alcmaeon, for example, was among the first to introduce the principle of similarity to explain the functioning of perception. The human eye, in Alcmaeon's theory, contains substances such as fire and water, and therefore, the eye is set to receive substances that also contain fire and water. The human ear contains air, thus enabling us to perceive sound going through air. These were the earliest views about the specialization of human senses. Science later developed these views in many sophisticated ways, but the core explanatory principle remained the same.

Third, most materialists, including Democritus, believed that characteristics of matter such as color, taste, sound, and smell do not belong to atoms. Properties such as sweetness or white color do not exist at the atomic level because atoms are not sweet or white. All these sensations are products of an interaction between the atoms of the soul and atoms of the external world. These suggestions laid the foundation for the 17th-century discussions about primary and secondary characteristics of human perception, which we describe in Chapter 3.

Fourth, Greek materialists attempted to explain the basic mechanisms of thinking. Epicurus, for example, theorized that people combine impressions to form simple concepts. As a next step, specific concepts are compared to one another, and common features are found. Finally, abstract concepts are formed. Human souls do not have any inborn images; concepts are formed as a result of experience. Consider dreaming. A dreaming person deals with concerns that were simply avoided during the day. Language also has natural origins. It is acquired during life as a result of numerous attempts to identify objects and attach meanings to them. People try to associate objects with sounds, and different languages are formed when, in different places on Earth, people learn to identify objects by dissimilar sounds. These views of language are echoed in the 20th century in the works of behaviorists.

For Plato, who challenged materialist views, human beings possess two kinds of knowledge. One is derived from their sensations, and this knowledge exists in the form of opinion: you may see one thing or one side in a developing story, while other people may see something completely different. Opinions, therefore, cannot represent true knowledge. Individuals can discover truth coming from immortal ideas, which as you keep in mind, existed before these individuals' conception. The soul acquires universal and true knowledge by recollection: they recall the experience they have gained while traveling in the immortal world of ideas. Plato's views about the existence of knowledge prior to experience made a great impact on many psychologists, including our contemporaries.

Another distinct view of cognition belongs to Aristotle. As you remember, Aristotle, like Democritus and Empedocles, believed that the main source of sensation is the external world of objects. Aristotle, however, developed a quite different view of specific mechanisms of sensation. Unlike his many materialist predecessors, he did not use the emanation theory to explain sensation. The process of sensation is the acquisition of a form of an object by the body organs capable of receptive function such as the eye, the ear, the tongue, and so on. Any object is capable of initiating sensation, but there must be a specific environment in which this process takes place. For example, hearing requires air, vision is impossible without light, and so on. Sensory organs cannot produce any images without being affected by objects in the specific environment. Aristotle named five main types of sensation; all of them are recognized today as the basic senses: vision, hearing, taste, smell, and touch. How do people handle so many sensations? An individual's soul uses the mechanism of association including consolidation, comparison, and distinction among sensations.

✓ CHECK YOUR KNOWLEDGE

What is epistemology?

Explain three main views of cognition in ancient Greece.

What is the emanation theory of sensation?

Understanding Basic Emotions and Needs

In many Greek manuscripts, emotions came into view largely as "intruders" in the process of a logical reflection of reality. They were acknowledged as necessary processes, though frequently excessive and inappropriate. Stoic thinkers, for example, insisted that humans should learn how to control their emotions to prevent them from disturbing reason.

Most atomists connected emotions with specific activities of the soul's atoms. Both Democritus and Epicurus believed atomic movements cause emotions. For example, positive emotions are associated with the movement of round and smooth atoms. Negative emotions are associated with the movement of atoms with small hooks and the atoms that do not have to travel in smooth trajectories. Aristotle wrote in *De Anima* that human emotions should link to the biological activities of the body. Similar views of emotions as processes requiring a physiological response appeared in the 19th and 20th centuries (Cannon, 1927; Lange, 1912/1885).

Views of motivation appear primarily in the teachings about ethics, or principles of moral behavior. Heraclitus reflected on the relative character of needs: animals often desire things that no humans would. People learn about pleasure and displeasure through the opposing experiences. A healthy person does not pay attention to his health. Illness makes health pleasant. Similar arguments apply to hunger and fatigue (Kirk, Raven, & Schofield, 1995). Democritus drew a distinction between primary motivation and its secondary effects, that is, an internal impulse versus a reaction to an external event.

The Greeks believed that excessive desires are destructive. For example, Epicurus distinguished between three types of needs. The first type involved natural and necessary for survival desires: those such as hunger or thirst that have a physical limit. The second type contained natural, but nonnecessary, desires, such as the desire to eat only exotic or expensive food. The third type consisted of "vain" or "empty" desires. They included desires for power, wealth, and fame. These desires are difficult to satisfy, mostly because they have no natural limit. Several 20th-century psychologists, such as Carl Rogers and Abraham Maslow, build some of their arguments around a similar point: people can discover happiness if they dedicate themselves to nonmaterial issues, including love, creativity, self-understanding, and compassion.

Self-control was an important virtue. The sign of a reasonable man, according to Democritus, was the ability to fight desire. Epicurus, despite popular misinterpretations of his views and claims that he encouraged people to enjoy life carelessly and satisfy their own unlimited needs, in fact taught people to limit the pursuit of the vain needs and free themselves of unnecessary fears (including fear of God and fear of death). If a person can banish fear about the future and face it with confidence, then the state of joy and tranquility (called *ataraxia*) will be achieved (Annas, 1994). Moral discipline is imperative in dealing with needs. For Epicurus, the avoidance of pain was more important than the pursuit of pleasure. He also favored intellectual pleasures over physical enjoyments (Long & Sedley, 1987).

If self-control is so important, how can a person achieve it? In the teaching of the Greeks, the function of the soul associated with human needs or affects was one level "below" the rational soul associated with thinking and logic. Democritus called the heart "the queen, the nurse of anger" and believed that atoms of the soul near the liver had a lot do with desire. Stoics offered two practical ways in dealing with disturbing desires or affects. The first is to suppress one emotion by initiating another. For example, anger can be suppressed by joy. The second way is based on a better understanding of emotions and better knowledge of the person's future and the past. Emotions, especially negative ones, occur because people have wrong impressions about the past and incorrect expectations about the future. If people learn how to reflect their past and future in the right way, they will be able to rid themselves of unpleasant emotions. There is some resemblance between these assumptions and recommendations—used in contemporary cognitive therapies—about the necessity to develop a different, healthier view of life (Butler, 2008).

Similarly, suggestions by the Stoics many centuries ago resemble core principles of a few distinguished psychological theories developed in recent times. Stoic philosophers maintained that an ideal person is free of harmful emotions and lives according to the law of necessity. A wise person should not surrender to emotions or desires. The main task of human beings is not to change the world but to find ways to adjust to it. Such recommendations are fairly close to some contemporary understanding of the concept of *coping* used in some contemporary multi-cultural forms of psychological counseling with trauma survivors (Bemak, Chung, & Pedersen, 2003).

Understanding the Biological Foundations of Human Psychology

Ancient Greeks emphasized the role of the brain and physiological processes in mental functioning. Alcmaeon of Croton (described earlier in this chapter) attributed mental activities to the brain and nervous system. Herophilus (335–280 BCE), who worked in Alexandria (contemporary Egypt), released the manuscript *On Dissections.* Working in a community where human autopsies were permitted (in many places at that time it was prohibited), he prepared a detailed description of the nervous system that recognized the brain as the base of thought and intelligence. He also recorded his views on the functioning of the retina and distinguished nerves as motor and sensory.

Erasistratus (3rd century BCE) was the leader of a Greek school of medicine in Alexandria. He made insightful comments about the functioning of the nervous system and suggested that air carried from the lungs to the heart is converted into a vital spirit distributed by the arteries. Like Herophilus, he distinguished between motor and sensory nerves. Erasistratus dissected and examined the human brain, noting the convolutions, cerebrum, and cerebellum (although these names had not been given to these parts of the brain yet). He compared the brains of animals and humans to explain more advanced intellectual capacities of humans. Table 2.4 summarizes major assumptions of Greek physicians about the functions of the body and their related mental activities.

Table 2.4 Body and Human Psychology: A Glance Into Greek Medicine and Science

Bodily Functions	*Psychological Functions*
The brain	The brain was associated with the functioning of the soul and primarily with intellectual functions. In some theories (Aristotle) the heart was viewed as a center of mental activities.
The nervous system	The nervous system is a conductor of impulses coming either from the heart or from the brain; such impulses are responsible for bodily movements and the psychological processes including sensation, emotion, and thinking.
Sensory organs	Five basic sensations and the responding sensory organs were recognized. The division in the understanding of their functioning occurred primarily between materialists and idealists.

Understanding Abnormal Symptoms

References to abnormal psychological symptoms usually referred to severe psychological disturbances involving unusual emotional states or outrageous behavioral acts. In translations, a common label for these symptoms was madness. The references to madness, however, are fragmentary, and the observations are very imprecise.

Yet observations about mood and melancholy are particularly interesting. **Melancholy** (often **melancholia**) was the most common label for symptoms that we call today depressive. The term originates from the Greek *melas* (black) and *khole* (bile, the liver-generated bitter liquid stored in the gallbladder). Despite differences in specific details, the Greeks shared several common views of emotions and mood (Simon, 1978; Tellenbach, 1980). Among these views were the following:

- There should be physical (or somatic) causes of mood.
- Either an excessive surplus or deficiency in bodily substances is associated with a certain mood problems.
- Some people have predispositions to develop abnormal mood symptoms.

Initial references to the word *melancholia* are found in the *Corpus Hippocraticum,* a collection of writings that are believed to have been written or compiled by the Greek physician and scientist Hippocrates (460–377 BCE). He wrote that all types of human illness have natural causes. Melancholia results from particular misbalances of blood and other humors. When the blood is contaminated with black bile, it causes misbalance and the mental state of the person is disturbed. This is manifested in a variety of melancholy symptoms, such as feelings of sadness and fear, despondency, sleeplessness, and irritability. Hippocrates also recognized personality types that develop a predisposition to melancholic illnesses. These early observations describe normal and abnormal states of mood and illustrate individual liabilities to certain psychological dysfunctions, which is a topic of serious interest in today's clinical psychology (Krueger & Markon, 2006).

Plato adopted the prevalent Hippocratic doctrine of the balance and proportion and applied it to his concept of human mortal and finite body and immortal and indivisible soul. Illness, in his view, is always disproportion, or *ametria.* Excessive pleasure and pain are sources of soul illness. The soul can be contaminated by bitter and bilious bodily humors, which can generate excessive sadness on one hand or excessive irritability and rage on the other. There was also a special kind of mania—*divine mania*—that did not fall into the illness category but was recognized as a form of inspiration in poets and philosophers.

Aristotle in *Problemata* paid attention to different states of human gall and the temperature of black bile. If it is colder than the norm, it can cause a depressive emotional state. If it is warmer, it can produce an elevated emotional state. To illustrate: a sad, fearful, or numb person has colder bile, while a cheerful person has warmer one. Wine, if it gets in the blood, can also produce effects resembling emotional disturbance. This influence, however, is short term. The bile's influence is long term, which can cause *athymia* and *extaisis,* two opposite forms of melancholia (depressive and manic states, in contemporary terms). Melancholia, in other words, is an enduring emotional imbalance, which has higher incidence in the spring and in the fall because bile was believed to have a seasonal pattern. There are people, according to Aristotle, who tend to be more tempered than others because of the quicker change in the black bile's temperature.

☞ CASE IN POINT

Greek Mythology and an Early Insanity Defense. Greek mythology provides an interesting example of what could be the first case of "insanity defense," a legal procedure that uses the concept of severe psychological dysfunction and inability to understand the nature of the committed crime in order to explain (and often excuse) the actions of the accused. In the myth called "The Madness of Hercules the Strongman and Adventurer," Hercules, one of several illegitimate offspring of Zeus, the most powerful of the Greek gods, was seriously disturbed by Zeus's wife Hera. She was jealous of Hercules because he thought people look at him as a living reminder of Zeus's unfaithfulness to her. She cast a spell of madness upon Hercules, who, as the result of the spell, lost the ability to think rationally. Driven by an emotional outburst, he kills his wife and three children. Yet Hercules was so distressed that he remained unaware of his terrible actions. At long last, he regained rational thought and could understand the terrible crime he had committed. The townspeople, however, forgave him, because they believed that he was temporarily insane and had no control over his actions.

Early Views of Health and Social Psychology

The Greeks made interesting observations about other aspects of human experiences and behavior. Thales commented on the importance of having a healthy body, which provides a person with a healthier soul and good skills. Democritus maintained that happiness, like unhappiness, is a property of the soul. People find happiness neither by means of the body nor through material possessions, but through uprightness and wisdom. People should value the soul first and the body second because perfection of the soul corrects the inferiority of the body, but physical strength without intelligence does very little to improve the mind. Reciprocity in relationships is critical: the person who loves nobody is not loved by anyone; similarities of outlook create good friendship. Psychological sources of moral actions interested many philosophers and particularly Socrates (469–399 BCE). He believed that if people knew the good, they would always do the good. A person goes astray because he or she does not really know how to act rightly. This position of Socrates influenced centuries-long discussions among philosophers, social scientists, and psychologists about the sources of moral behavior and the role of emotions and knowledge in them. This debate continues today (Prinz, 2008).

Epicurus taught that life is made up of three different kinds of events. One kind involves inevitability: there is nothing that we can do about certain things that happen to us. Another kind involves chance. Here, again, people have little control over such events. The third kind of events is manageable. People should know about such circumstances and learn how to deal with them. Contemporary studies in social psychology and social sciences continue to address the issue of rational and irrational choices in our daily decision making (Caplan, 2008).

✓ CHECK YOUR KNOWLEDGE

Compared to logic and reasoning, how did the Greeks generally view emotions?

What was the anatomical center of mental activities according to Aristotle?

How did the Greeks understand melancholy?

Evaluating the Impact of the Greeks

Greek thinkers made a remarkable contribution to philosophy and science by developing original and diverse views of the universe, nature, and the principles of human behavior. Their views laid a strong foundation for the further development of global psychological knowledge. There are at least five major areas of influence: the study of the soul, the teachings about the mechanisms of human cognition, the suggestions about the biological foundations of mental activities, the initial inquiry in the fields of clinical psychology, and the rich observations of social behavior.

In the teachings about the soul, the Greeks set the stage for a continuous debate in the history of psychology about the origins of knowledge, the existence of free will, the place of human beings in the hierarchy of species, and the ability of humans to exercise control over their lives. Today an increasing number of psychologists explore the body-mind relationship and its many applications to health psychology (Epel, 2009). The Greeks developed early theories associating the brain with intellectual functions. They provided valuable assumptions about the role of the nerves in bodily and psychological processes. These assumptions were verified much later in history.

Theories about cognition and its mechanisms set the tone for the debate about the accuracy of knowledge and the possibility of knowledge without prior experience. Atomists such as Democritus and Epicurus provided a powerful set of ideas equating perception with reception, the view that became dominant for some time in science-oriented psychology. Many of Plato's ideas, transformed over the course of centuries, provide an important theoretical basis for the contemporary scientific argument maintaining that the processes in the brain contribute to perception and may create a perceived reality of its own (Gregory, 1997). In terms of practical applications, Greeks introduced memorization techniques and used them to improve their public-speaking skills (Yates, 1966).

Greek thinkers conducted remarkable observations about appropriate and inappropriate behavior, healthy choices, recipes for success, and warnings against failures. Despite the differences in their positions about how much control people could have over their lives, the philosophers emphasized the importance of education, honesty, moderation, friendship, cooperation, hard work, and the ability to persevere in difficult circumstances.

The Greeks also made valuable observations of abnormal behavior understanding it as a deviation from a norm. They provided descriptions of what is identified today as anxiety and mood disorders. The Greeks explained abnormal psychological symptoms as reflections of bodily imbalances, behavioral excesses, or a person's inability to cope with difficult circumstances. These and similar views are common in today's clinical psychology.

Psychological Knowledge in India and China: An Introduction to Non-Western Traditions in Psychology

Great thinkers of Greece, India, and China lived around the same historic period but in different parts of the vast Eurasian continent. Historians maintain that there was very little or no scientific interaction among their respective cultures (Cooper, 2003). You may be surprised, however, to read how similar their psychological observations frequently were.

Early Psychological Views in India

Experts associate the origins of Indian history with the birth of the Indus Valley civilization and its original settlements in the Punjab region, along the Ganga and Yamuna plains, and the migration of the Aryan tribes. With agriculture and trade increased by 500 BCE, many settlements along the Ganga became centers of social life.

As was the case in ancient Greece, in India, philosophers made the earliest observations about human psychology. What we call today psychological knowledge can be picked up in bits and pieces from their writings on religion, metaphysics, and epistemology. One of many remarkable features of the early Indian schools of philosophy is the extraordinary attention they paid to the search for the meaning of the individual psychological experience. The emphasis was on educated human beings who found a way to free the self of the unpleasant constraints of their educations and experiences. Indian philosophies traditionally include six different schools, in addition to Buddhism and Jainism. A comprehensive analysis of these schools is not our goal. We focus instead on the contributions of Indian philosophers to the development of psychological knowledge.

Life Circle. Indian philosophers shared the belief that all living creatures undergo a cycle of rebirth and their souls transmigrate from one body to another. Human actions have consequences, either immediate or delayed. Everything happens for a reason, and all thoughts and behaviors have a special place in an intelligible whole. Another significant unifying assumption of different branches of early Indian thought was that reflections of reality, such as perceptions, feelings, and desires, are largely distorted. People tend to misunderstand their own place in the scheme of things. Reality is substantially different from how it usually appears to us. False beliefs lead to insecurity. Only the right state of mind can bring an individual back to state of security at peace with the self. Similar assumptions about human cognition and how incomplete it is, as you remember, were also made by the philosophers of the Greek civilization. However, cognitive aspects of human psychology attracted only some attention from Greek philosophers, with the exception of Epicurus and a few others. For most Indian philosophers, conversely, cognition was the fundamental case of their teachings.

Cognition. Like the Greeks, Indian philosophers proposed atomic theories. Gautama and Kanada (both about 400 BCE), originators of the Nyaya tradition, expressed an atomist and materialist view according to which the natural world consists of various substances, including objects, space, and time, and that nature is independent of thought and perception. They also expressed a belief that there is the immaterial soul responsible for consciousness and feelings. The biggest challenge for the philosophers of this tradition was the formulation of the criteria for valid, true knowledge. Why do people need true knowledge? Because it brings supreme happiness to individuals.

According to the *Sankhya* tradition, the roots of which are found in texts and ritual hymns called *Vedas* (dated 1500 BCE and earlier and further developed in the oral teachings or *Upanishads,* fundamental and sacred texts of Hinduism), the world is composed of a number of elementary particles. All these elements belong to a single dynamic substance, which has two forms. The first form is the elements composing the external world including material objects. The other form develops into the three entities: (1) senses responsible for perception such as vision and hearing; (2) senses responsible for motivation such as desire and will; and (3) senses responsible for thinking, which puts in order the data received by the senses. Perception, memory, and motivation are material and different from each other only because of different states of matter involved in them. This view echoes not only basic and similar assumptions of the Greeks but also many contemporary interpretations of mental processes as special forms of physiological processes in the brain.

This philosophical tradition, however, contained elements of idealism because it recognized the existence of separate, nonmaterial consciousness. Animals can have perception and desires. However, although animals respond to stimuli because the creatures have sensory systems, they do not possess consciousness, an entity that is outside of nature. Overall, because mental processes are not conscious, they require supervision and direction from consciousness.

Rooted in ancient oral teaching, the *Advaita* tradition appears the most controversial to the contemporary observer. According to this view, what we ordinarily perceive as "real" objects are, in fact, only appearances or illusions. Belief in the existence of the real, material world is caused by ignorance. Liberation from the state of ignorance is possible if a person understands the existence of pure consciousness. This idealist kind of Indian philosophy suggested that there is only one substance—the ideal—and the material world is just a reflection of the ideal (Isaeva, 1995). The Advaita tradition, with its analysis of the material and the ideal, shares similar ideas of Plato.

According to the Hindu tradition, illness is likely to originate from a misbalance within the body. The symptoms of illness manifest in bodily sicknesses and in psychological complaints. The human mind can control and direct activities of the body and other sense organs. This religious concept, in fact, is a fertile ground for modern scientific theories underlying the importance of the patient's own positive attitudes in the course of therapeutic treatment (Rao, 2000).

These and other philosophical traditions represent the teachings of classic *Hinduism*, a fundamental religious system with more than 700 million followers today. Another religious system, *Buddhism*, also was originated in India and has roots in Hinduism as well. Buddhism is a system of knowledge and values based on the belief that liberation from the world of suffering is possible. Liberation of human beings occurs when they are able to accept the right point of view of the world—a view that is often distorted. The founder of Buddhism was Siddarata Gautama (480–400 BCE), who by his life and deeds influenced the minds of millions of followers. He is regarded as the Supreme Buddha, the enlightened one. A branch called *Theravada* Buddhism contains the earliest surviving record of the Buddha's teachings. Most thinkers within this tradition adopted an atomist viewpoint: the external world is real and consists of elementary particles. Complex and visible things are constructed out of these elements. However, the *Mahayana* school of Buddhism accepts a different position, which is anti-atomist. According to Mahayana teachings, the external world is the reflection of the mind itself. Long before the appearance of teachings of George Berkeley in England (discussed in Chapter 3), it was already postulated that no other forms of evidence exist besides the one that exists in our perceptions.

In addition to studies of cognition, Indian philosophers also created a comprehensive set of views about basic mechanisms of thinking, moral and immoral behavior, choice, and duty. They provided detailed descriptions of different types of people (which we call personality types today), the complexity of emotions, and the impact of emotions on behavior. They also described symptoms called today hallucinations, anxiety, and various depressive manifestations. Significant attention was paid to cognition and inner psychological processes, including meditation, concentration, deep self-consciousness, and ability to understand the inner self.

✓ CHECK YOUR KNOWLEDGE

What is the life circle in teachings of Indian philosophers?

Describe psychological views found in the Advaita tradition.

Early Psychological Views in China

The first Chinese emperor (ascending the throne in 246 BCE), pursuing efficiency and order, designed a radiating system of roads, unified different measures of weight, made standard coins and a uniform writing system, and even suggested the typical width of wagons. Historians provide evidence that more than 2,000 years ago, Chinese emperors used a system of written examinations to evaluate potential government employees (Bowman, 1989). Politics and science in China seemed to pursue similar goals: the search for the ultimate effectiveness of society and efficiency of individual actions (Smith, 1991).

Like the ideas of the Greek philosophers that spread around the geographic vicinity of the Mediterranean Sea, the ideas of Chinese philosophers spread across eastern Asia. For nearly two millennia, the minds of people of the world's most populous country were shaped by the teachings of Confucius (c. 551–479 BCE). Confucius did not write books. His teachings were preserved through his students, then students of his students, and scores of followers and commentators. Remember that in Greece, for instance, the teachings of several philosophers were preserved in a similar way.

ON THE WEB

Confucius. A brief biography and related information is posted on the book website.

Confucius believed that people could improve themselves, be happy without fear of God, respect traditions and authority. His views had a great impact on Chinese culture.

Confucianism. Confucian teachings appear as moral prescriptions and can be compared to the views of Epicurus, Socrates, or the Stoics of ancient Greece. Confucius and his followers based their views on the concept of *ren*, which is a lifelong determination of a human being to become a truthful and caring person (Tu, 1979). Virtuous and efficient behavior was the center of attention. Confucius believed that anyone could become a virtuous person. The key to success was a person's commitment to improve. No matter how successful one becomes, there must be motivation to be better. There are no limits to self-perfection. A person is good as long as a genuine effort is made even though the actual achievement may be small.

For Confucius, the ideal person is a balanced one, someone who does not stop doing right things because of the fear of unpleasant consequences. There is no reason to worship God. People can improve themselves and be happy without fear of God. People have to love their neighbors and especially members of their families. They have to respect authority and obey the law. People must avoid disruptions of the social order and learn how to accept it. Learning should advance social purpose (Lee, 1996).

The difficult question about whether or not humans possess moral goodness becomes an important topic of discussions. A great Chinese philosopher and follower of Confucius, Mencius (c. 372–289 BCE), taught that being a good person is natural. People act in moral ways because they are unselfish. For Mencius, the difference between people and animals lay in people's capacity to reason and ability for moral actions. However, not all Chinese philosophers shared the idea about the "good nature" of people. For instance, another prominent follower of Confucius, Hsun Tzu (298–238 BCE), proclaimed that human nature is evil. Without education, people are likely to pursue their selfish interests and turn to animal-like behavior. People learn to act morally because of their fear of punishment. Confucius also advocated that all people should be educated, irrespective of their abilities (Higgins & Zheng, 2002).

Many original ideas introduced by Confucius and his followers were gradually incorporated into Chinese customs and law. The ideas of Confucianism were also gradually recognized as the official philosophy of the government. Leading scholars were even summoned by government officials (for example in 79 CE) to clarify the true meaning of certain Confucian ideas. In China, as in many other places, scientists were frequently summoned to aid the government (Fairbank & Reischauer, 1989).

Holism. One of the prominent features cultivated by many Chinese philosophers is **holism** (often described as *Zheng He Lu*). This is the concept holding that everything is interconnected in the world and body. The holistic mode of thought rests on the assumption that everything exists in the integration of two famous historic Chinese concepts—*yin* and *yang*—the entities that are opposed to one another and yet also are connected as a whole in time and space (Peng & Nisbett, 1999). The ideas of interconnected yin and yang are found in other early Chinese systems of thought. Tung Chung-Shu (179–104 BCE), for example, connected the human body with nature and used comparisons that linked human joints with days in the year, and human organs with basic substances of nature, such as fire, water, and so on. According to his teachings, human nature is associated with yang, which is goodness, and yin, which is a form of natural emotions. Yin is dark, feminine, soft, and hidden. Yang is bright, masculine, firm, and open. The capacity for goodness is planted in human nature but could be retrieved through training and education. People have to restrain their emotions and desires and turn instead to reason.

Taoism. China did not have a powerful institutionalized religion like Christianity, Islam, or Judaism. However, there was an influential system of views called Taoism, a system of philosophical-religious views challenging the Confucian tradition but coexisting alongside it for centuries. The founder of Taoism is believed to be Lao-Tse (604–531 BCE), a contemporary of Confucius. Taoism promotes the development of virtue in the individual and personality traits such as empathy, kindness, self-restraint, and modesty. Human beings should live in accordance with nature and promote simplicity and a healthy approach to life (Mote, 1971).

Like Indian philosophies, Taoism paid significant attention to the harmony of interconnected things. Such emphasis on harmony was associated with Taoist interest in healthy lifestyles, healing, and the prevention of illness. Most valuable for psychologists today are Taoist ideas about coping with the effects of aging, fatigue, and stress. Taoists were interested in health and vitality; they experimented with herbal medicine and pharmacology; they developed systems of gymnastics and massage to keep the body strong and youthful (Bokenkamp, 1997). Many early Taoists despised wealth, prestige, and social status. Taoism was, as it frequently noted, "the other way" (as an opposing way to Confucianism), but it did not threaten the social structure of Chinese society (Welch, 1957).

✓ CHECK YOUR KNOWLEDGE

What is the ideal person in Confucius teachings?

Explain holism.

Like the Greek tradition, both Indian and Chinese ancient traditions developed an extremely sophisticated view of behavior, emotions, thought, and other mental activities. In contrast to Indian thinkers, who were focusing primarily on the complexities of cognition and its distortions, Chinese philosophers were interested, above all, in ethical and social problems. Yet it would be incorrect to state that these were their exclusive interests. Both Indian and Chinese schools, as well as the Greeks, developed a remarkable worldview of the individual, social roles, cognition, and the ability of people to control the outcomes of their behavior. Most important, all these traditions emphasized the interconnectedness of physical and spiritual processes and underlined the meaning of harmony and balance in human behavior and thought. See Figure 2.1 to compare the traditions.

Figure 2.1 Overlapping Interests of the Greek, Indian, and Chinese Traditions

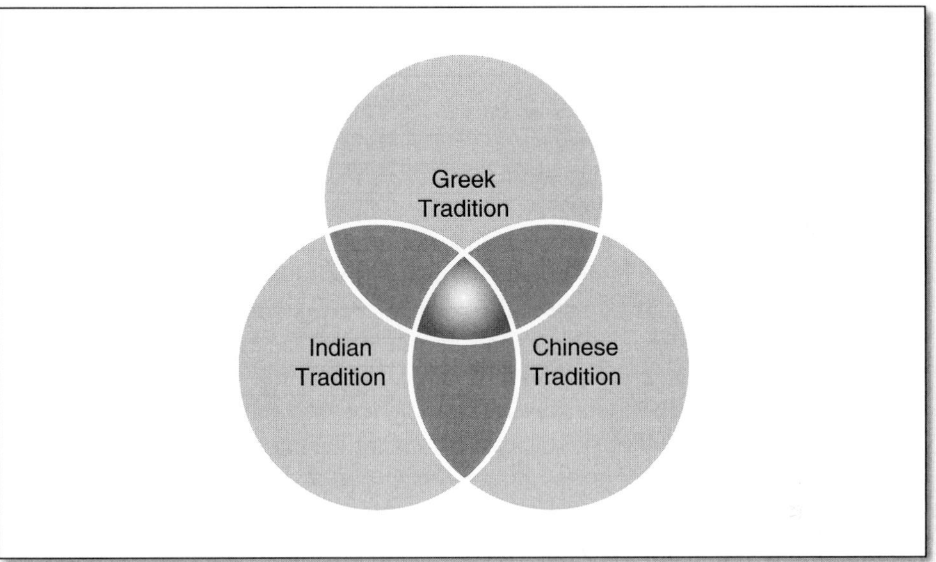

Psychological Knowledge at the Turn of the First Millennium

The impact of Greek science and culture on other regions and civilizations was significant. Many of their works appeared in translations. Prominent thinkers of Rome, North Africa, the Middle East, Persia, and other parts of the world learned from the Greeks. However, other cultures developed their own original psychological views and theories.

The Romans: Psychological Knowledge in Philosophy and Science

The Roman Empire lasted for nearly 500 years before its disintegration in 476 CE. The Romans saw themselves as carriers of the divine mission to rule and enlighten. This sense of exceptionality and mission gave the Roman elites intellectual ammunition to justify slavery, violence, and oppression against other people. On the other hand, the Romans preserved and developed the intellectual heritage of Western civilization. They were impressed with scientific accomplishments of Greece. The Greek language remained popular in the Roman Empire, and most educated Romans spoke it fluently. Most important for the history of psychology remains the Romans' teachings in the fields of medicine and their sophisticated theories of human behavior, moral choices, and an individual's ability to control the outcomes of his own decisions.

Medical Foundations. One of the most notable figures of science and medicine in Rome was Galen (c. 129–200), physician and writer of Greek origin. Born at Pergamon, Asia Minor, into an educated, well-to-do family, he settled in Rome, where he produced most of his works. In the history of psychology, Galen stands out for his views about the soul, structure and functioning of the nervous system, and bodily balances.

The fundamental principle and force of life, according to Galen, was *pneuma,* which exists in three forms. The first kind is located in the brain and is responsible for imagination, reason, and memory. The second, vital pneuma, with its center in the heart, regulates the flow of blood. The third kind of pneuma resides in the liver and is responsible for nutrition and metabolism. The rational faculties of imagination, reason, and memory are located in the ventricles of the brain. The brain receives vital pneuma from the heart, which is mixed into the sanguine humor (blood). The brain then extracts the pneuma and stores it in the ventricles, from where it is distributed throughout the body via the nerves. This mechanism of circulating pneuma controls muscles, organs, and all of the body's activities. The liver is responsible for the desires; the heart is responsible for the emotions, and the brain controls reason.

Galen described the nervous system like a tree. Nervous paths, like branches, are filled with the substance similar to one in the brain, which is pneuma. Two kinds of nerves exist. One is soft, and it connects the sensory organs with the brain. The other kind is harder; it connects brain with the muscles. Each sensory organ has its own pneuma; that is, the eye has a kind of visionary pneuma and the ear contains a kind of auditory pneuma. People do not recognize what is happening in the sensory organs. Only pneuma that is in the brain allows individuals to perceive (Scarborough, 1988). Galen also distinguished two kinds of activities of the body. Automatic activities were typical for organs such as the stomach, the heart, the lungs, and others. Other movements are voluntary and controlled by the soul. This was an early observation of the functions that were later called reflexes.

The Roman philosophical and medical tradition was primarily rooted in earlier Greek studies, which contained the principal ideas about bodily fluids, their misbalances, and the impact they make on mood and behavior. According to Galen, for instance, bodily substances in the brain directly affect manic and depressive symptoms in an individual. The quality of blood affects emotions. For example, hot blood causes unrestricted anger. Intense emotions are not good for the person. Therefore, individuals have to balance emotions by balancing the fluids in their own bodies. Situational and contextual factors could cause acute emotional problems too. For instance, Cicero (106–43 BCE) and Arateus (30–90 CE) suggested that individuals who develop melancholia have predisposing conditions of their bodies or in their lives that lead to emotional problems. According to Cicero, among these contextual factors were fear, grief, and neglect of reason.

Moral Behavior. A remarkable school of philosophy in Rome grew out of the tradition established by the Stoic philosophers in Greece. The only complete works by Stoic philosophers of the Roman period available today are those by Seneca (4 BCE–65 CE), Epictetus (c. 55–135 CE), and Marcus Aurelius (121–180 CE). Most of these works focused on ethical behavior and discussed duty, moral choices, rationality, and free will. Marcus Aurelius stressed the importance of virtues such as wisdom, justice, fortitude, and moderation, believing that the moral life leads to happiness. He also believed that a divine providence had placed reason in people. Marcus Aurelius, who was also a Roman emperor, denounced violence on moral grounds and hoped to rule according to ethical standards rather than political calculations (he knew how difficult it was in reality).

For the Roman Stoics, the ultimate goal of a person's existence was to obtain a state of mind free from immediate desires for pleasure. Unfortunately, most people are "slaves" of their own passions. Nevertheless, people have rational minds that allow them to free themselves from disturbing emotions, such as fear of death. Even when people learn to exercise reason, they shouldn't try to change the world. Instead, they have to adjust to everything that happens in it. Those individuals who understand this wisdom can be happy. The ideas of the central role of moral duty and acceptance of one's own fate were embraced later by many scholars within the religious tradition of European philosophy in high Middle Ages (Yakunin, 2001).

What role did Roman thinkers play in psychology's history? First, they preserved and strengthened the traditional Greek views of the soul, its structure, and functions. Roman philosophers, especially in the beginning of the first millennium, turned their attention to moral behavior, self-restraint, and moderation. They emphasized the importance of reason and patience, goodwill, and hope. The Romans strengthened the view of the distracting role of human emotion and emphasized the importance of self-control. They gave significant attention to reason as a superior form of cognition as compared to sensations and emotions. Scientists of ancient Rome made a significant contribution to anatomy and physiology. Like the Greeks and Chinese did in their traditions of thought, the Romans emphasized the importance of balancing of natural processes within the human body.

Scholars in ancient Greece and Rome used religious teachings sometimes to justify their views of morality or fate, or to explain the fundamentals of the universe. With advancing Christianity, religion began to play an increasingly important role in science and philosophy. Over centuries, organized religion established its virtual monopoly on the developing psychological knowledge. To understand the initial impact of religion on psychology, we turn to the Scholastic tradition.

The Early Christian Tradition

At the beginning of the first millennium, Christianity was spreading beyond its original birthplace near Jerusalem. Christian communities were founded in most big cities in the eastern part of the Roman Empire. Written Gospels about the life of Jesus Christ and his teachings, known as the New Testament, started to circulate widely around the Mediterranean. Early in the third century, the New Testament was translated from Greek to Latin, thus allowing Christianity to find millions of new followers. In the fourth century, Christianity became Rome's official religion and later an integral part of the European culture. The influence of the religion grew in social institutions including education and science. Philosophy was gradually becoming part of **theology**, the study of the nature of God and religious truth. Theology gradually expanded its monopoly on psychological knowledge. **Scholasticism**, the dominant

Western Christian school of thought of the Middle Ages, was based on religious doctrines. Scholastics often referred to Aristotle and his later reviewers.

Immortality of the Soul. An early founder of the Christian tradition, Plotinus (204–270), was also the founder of neo-Platonism. He based his teachings on Plato's main ideas; historians often view Plotinus as a representative of a late movement in Greek philosophy. His views are presented in six books, each containing nine essays or chapters. Therefore, the title of his works is *The Enneads,* from the Greek *ennea,* which means nine. Plotinus developed a complex cognitive theory suggesting that the mind plays an active role in shaping or ordering the objects of perception rather than passively receiving data from experience.

The central concept of his teaching related to psychology is *the soul.* Plotinus believed that the soul is a divine, nonmaterial, and eternal entity possessing three functions. The first one allows the soul to be connected with eternity—with absolute, divine, and perfect soul. The second function connects the soul with the body and individual feelings. The third function gives the soul self-reflection to learn about its own past and present. Through the "lower" functions, the soul undergoes the drama of existence; it suffers, forgets, falls into vice, and so on, while through the "higher" functions the soul remains unaffected and persists in the divine state.

Plotinus also commented on perception of beautiful things. The beauty of physical objects, he wrote, is based on the unity that they exhibit—the statement that resembles some fundamental assumptions of the Gestalt psychology of the 20th century. He explains beauty as the product of the human mind but also as a concept that has divine nature. Beauty is close to God, while ugliness is due to a departure from unity toward evil, from spiritual to material. For example, a person appears ugly when she is dirty. As the soul is purified from material substance, it becomes close to reason and beauty. Being courageous, for instance, means to release the self from fear of physical death, and this is beautiful.

Plotinus's theoretical views of cognition are quite sophisticated. His assumptions about an active function of the soul that is building its own experience may resemble some of today's most intriguing theories of cognition (Scholl, 2005). Yet there was another area that also relates to contemporary psychology: the study of psychological foundations of guilt.

Psychological Foundations of Guilt and Sin. A long-lasting contribution to philosophy and psychology was made by Augustine (354–430). He was born and resided in the Roman Empire, in North Africa, which is present-day Algeria. A creative thinker and prolific writer, he lived at a time when the empire began to collapse, devastated by numerous invaders and its own social and political problems. New separate and smaller states began to develop in place of the empire. To many contemporaries, these rapid changes signified the end of the world: authority, order, and the way of life—as people knew them for centuries—were breaking down. Violence and destruction appeared as unchangeable attributes of human existence. Yet Augustine, a professor in Milan (contemporary Italy) who later became a religious official, used religion to build his optimism. He proposed a psychological solution to people's problems. It was Augustine from whom Christianity will later inherit its position on guilt, sin, and sex—the view embedded in many cultural traditions and values.

Like most of us today, people who lived hundreds of years ago tried to address their own insecurities. In early adulthood, Augustine was confused about his personal ambitions, sexuality, and choices of the right worldview. He studied Plato. To be closer to God, he tried various forms of religious mysticism. He converted to Christianity as an adult. He was preoccupied with the search for explanations about human sin. Augustine became convinced that a single motivational force could explain all the sins that people commit. This force was will. Roman Christians had commonly applied this term to human deeds. It was a common view that human beings have free will—that is, people are responsible for their own decisions. If this is true, why do people commit sinful acts knowingly? Augustine looked for his own answers.

The Dual Nature of the Will. Augustine formulated the principle of two wills. There is a carnal will that is responsible for sinful behavior. But there is also a spiritual will responsible for ethical actions, self-restraint, and virtue. The carnal will, which he called **cupiditas**, stands for excessive desire, violence, and greed. The spiritual will, called **caritas,** stands for good intentions. Cupiditas and caritas are in continual battle against each other. They divide the self into struggling entities: lust versus chastity, greed versus self-control, and cravings versus moderation. Wealth, power, or material possessions could not bring spiritual salvation to a person. Only spiritual will could. To accept the spiritual will is to be on the way to God. Unfortunately, the power of the carnal will continuously distracts human beings from doing the right things. In *Confessions,* Augustine gave the following example. One day, while sitting at his writing table, he spotted a spider weaving a web. Rather than doing the work he was supposed to do, Augustine idly watched the spider. That was negligence: rather than participating in work he should do, he was distracted by the lazy desires of the carnal self (Hooker, 1982).

A dual nature of human will is one of the most fundamental legacies of Augustine found in the European thought: first in theology, then in philosophy and literature, and finally in psychology in the works of Sigmund Freud, Carl Jung, and their followers in the 20th century. Augustine described human sexuality as a feature of carnal will. To guarantee the right path in their lives, human beings should suppress sexuality, leave sex only for procreation purposes, and pursue unconditional chastity. This was a fundamental element in his theory, which was accepted and promoted by the institutions of European Christianity for many centuries to come. This view not only determined many prohibitive views of sexuality; it also set the views on public morality, self-expression, the nature of guilt and shame, good education, and even psychological disorders, which we examine in Chapters 6 and 8.

Why did Augustine's views receive such enduring acceptance in European theology and culture? Why did guilt become an attribute of so many people's beliefs? Let's think critically. For instance, many of us have a tendency to accept blame for misfortunes beyond our control—a seeming paradox in light of many people's tendency to deny personal wrongdoing. However, there is logic in such assumption about self-blame. What would you prefer, to feel guilty or to feel helpless in the face of an illness, an accident, a failure, or other serious difficulties? If we blame others or feel helpless, we are not solving the problem that we face. Guilt, on the other hand, could help us mobilize our own psychological resources to tackle the problem. Furthermore, by accepting the biblical belief about the original sin by Adam and Eve, Christians also accept in theory the idea that all human beings are innately predisposed to sin. This may help some people to explain why bad things sometimes happen to good people (Pagels, 1989).

Do Augustine's views, expressed more than 1,500 years ago, make sense to you today? Some psychological studies provide support for Augustine's assumptions. Research by June Tangney and Ronda Dearing (2003) showed that a person's awareness of his or her own guilt in cases of perceived wrongdoing can be used as a therapeutic tool to help avoid serious anxiety-related and other difficult emotional problems. Guilt according to contemporary research appears as a powerful resource to explain and regulate behavior.

For Augustine, plants and animals also have souls. This was a common view rooted in earlier Greek teachings, and those of Aristotle in particular. The senses are coordinated by the soul's inner capacity, which is another similarity with Aristotle's teachings. The human soul is both immaterial and immortal. The inner capacity combines the information of the senses and passes judgment on the results of this synthesis. People can learn through self-understanding and observation of our own thoughts, emotions, and states. This idea has reappeared later in studies involving introspection, a popular psychological method of the 19th century (see Table 2.5).

Table 2.5 Psychological Knowledge in the Scholastic Period: An Overview

Psychological Phenomena	*Sources of Knowledge*	*Major Findings*
Behavior and its causes	Religious scholarship, observation and generalizations, mythology, medical research	Humans can exercise rational behavior; moderation is the most desirable behavior.
Cognition	Religious scholarship, observation and generalizations, mythology, research of the sensory organs	The existence of the soul is acknowledged as nonmaterial entity.
Emotion	Religious scholarship, observation, and generalizations	Emotions regulate behavior but often become disturbing.
Specific knowledge	Religious scholarship, observation and generalizations, mythology, medical research	Specific facts about human behavior and experience are accumulated.

✓ CHECK YOUR KNOWLEDGE

How did Galen explain the nervous system?

What were the Roman Stoics' views of human emotions?

Describe Augustine's views of sin and guilt.

Further Development of Knowledge in the High Middle Ages (1000–1300s)

The Middle Ages as an epoch begins with the collapse of the Western Roman Empire, although historians debate the precise dates. The High Middle Ages in Europe was a period of economic growth and recovery from an earlier period of violence and political disarray. The development of new agricultural practices, a warming of the Earth's climate, and fewer wars allowed peasants to produce more food. These factors contributed to population growth, the further development of the cities, and a relative social stability. The Catholic Church was the religion of the majority in Europe. It was an extremely influential institution, affecting all aspects of life. After a period of decline, the church restored its influence, and monasteries continued to be centers of education, science, and philosophy. Although life in the monasteries was difficult and the majority of monks were engaged in hard physical labor, these institutions produced many talented thinkers who left a rich written account in the areas of philosophy and theology. One of these individuals was Thomas Aquinas.

Restoring Aristotle's Prestige

Thomas Aquinas (c. 1225–1274) was born to a wealthy influential family in the Neapolitan territory of Italy and was educated in a monastery in which his uncle was abbot. Thomas (as he is commonly addressed by historians) continued the tradition started by Aristotle: he believed that the soul is the form of the body that gives it life and energy. Thomas added that the soul without the body would have no individuality, because such uniqueness comes from matter. For this reason, resurrection of the body, an important Christian belief, is crucial to the idea of personal immortality. Thomas Aquinas followed many of Aristotle's assumptions and distinguished five faculties of the soul. The first is the vegetative faculty involved in nutrition, procreation, and growth. The second is the sensitive faculty engaged in sensations, including higher cognitive functions. The third is the motor faculty responsible for movement. The fourth is appetitive faculty, which is involved in motivation and will. Finally, the fifth faculty is the intellectual faculty, the highest form of reason.

For Thomas, human cognition was not a merely passive process during which atoms irradiate from objects and reach the body and thus cause sensations. The soul should play an active role in sensation and particularly in the complex processes of thinking. Intellect, the fifth faculty, is the greatest treasure of humans, placing them above the animals. Although sensations can portray reality correctly, their accuracy reaches only a certain degree. Only the fifth faculty can lead a person to an understanding of the physical world and human life. Moreover, the soul can understand the self and realize its unique, nonmaterial origin.

The views of Thomas Aquinas, as you can notice, resemble the positions held by Aristotle, especially about the structure and functioning of the soul. Unlike Aristotle, however, Thomas believed in the nonmaterial essence of the soul and a possibility of its independent existence. Aristotle did not use God to explain the major points of his theory of cognition. Thomas believed in exactly the opposite and suggested that the concept of God is vital in the understanding of cognitive activities. Aristotle also assigned a greater role of environment in the formation of thinking, while Thomas believed that the higher mental processes should be understood as the process that belonged to the soul itself.

In summary, what was the impact of the scholastic and early Christian tradition of thought on psychology's history? Psychological knowledge developed, to some degree, as a symbolic alliance of Christian theology and the Greek philosophy. The works of many Greek philosophers, Plato and Aristotle in particular, were thoroughly analyzed and critically evaluated. In fact, the method of critical thinking in analyzing scholarly texts has one of its roots in the early Scholastic tradition. A centuries-long search for moral foundations of an individual's behavior continued in the High Middle Ages. The discussions of free will, guilt, emotion, rationality, belief, and doubt—all of these and many other features of our complex psychological experience—received their early critical evaluation in Scholasticism.

Christian theology had a major impact on the development of psychological knowledge in Europe in the early millennium and during the High Middle Ages. In similar ways, Muslim theology affected philosophy and science in the Middle East, parts of North Africa, and Central Asia in the first millennium after the birth of Islam in the seventh century.

Psychological Views in the Early Arab and Muslim Civilization

Several original and independent schools of thought appeared in different parts of the developing Islamic world, spreading its spiritual and political influence through the Arabic Peninsula through the Middle East. Creative ideas continued to flourish outside the religious tradition. An important factor helping scientific ideas to spread around the broad geographic region was the common language. As in the ancient Greek civilization, when the Greek language dominated the Mediterranean region, Arabic became the language of communication for most educated circles in the Middle East and North Africa. For example, Arabic translations of teachings of Galen and Hippocrates became very influential among scholars in the Middle East. Following Galen's descriptions, many doctors in the Middle East would identify the liver as a location for anger; courage and passion were associated with the heart; fear was linked to the lungs; laughter to the spleen; and greed was associated with the kidneys (Browne, 1962).

As was common in Europe, scholars in the Middle East were proficient in several fields. A scholar could be a philosopher, an astronomer, a natural scientist, a doctor, and a poet—all at the same time. Many philosophers practiced medicine, and physicians wrote brilliant philosophical tractates. A prominent Arab philosopher, Basran al-Kindi (c. 865 CE), was a private teacher of the son of a caliph. He studied the teachings of Aristotle and Plato and promoted the necessity of critical questioning of knowledge. Al-Farabi (870–950 CE), a man of Persian descent born in Turkistan in Central Asia, attempted to blend the ideas of Aristotle and Plato with Sufism—the Islamic tradition of mystical thought. Al-Farabi reportedly wrote 117 books and was employed by many people of power.

Al-Farabi studied knowledge, its extent and validity. He identified three types of social groups—an early contribution to the discipline we now call social psychology. He used allegories to describe these groups. For example, the ideal social group is compared to a *virtuous* city. People are good and happy in this city, like the limbs of a healthy body, with all the functions working properly. There are also other groups in which people are engaged in different types of behavior. Al-Farabi called them inhabitants of the *ignorant* city, the *dissolute* city, the *turncoat* city, and the *straying* city. The souls of the people who inhabit these cities are contaminated and face possible extinction. Yet in the *virtuous* city, people cooperate to earn happiness. Collaboration is what could bring happiness to all people (Fakhry, 1983).

The Greek Influence. There were many Hellenists—supporters of the Greek tradition of thought—in the Middle East who attempted to describe people as guided by reason. In their views of nature, the function of God was diminished to the role of universal creator or universal intelligence. This view, as you may expect, did not match with the most fundamental positions of Islamic scholars, who often did not welcome theories brought from afar.

Despite resistance, there were many attempts to combine Greek teachings with those of Islamic scholars. As an example, in the formative period of Muslim theology, the school called Mutazilites (approximately ninth century and later) promoted the doctrine of free will, rationalism, and Aristotle's logic in attempt to blend them with religious teachings. Abul-Walid Ibn Rushd, better known as Averroes to Europeans (1126–1198) played a decisive role in the defense of Greek philosophy against the criticisms of religious scholars. His views helped him to gain popularity in Europe, especially his commentaries about Aristotle, which sparked discussions among medieval scholars and renewed their interest in Greek philosophy.

Ibn al-Haitham, known to Western scholars as Alhazen (965–1040), was born in Basra, in contemporary Iraq, but taught in Egypt, where he lived throughout his life. Psychologists should acknowledge his valuable observations based on experiments on visual sensations. He contradicted Ptolemy's and Euclid's theory of vision that objects are seen by rays of light emanating from the eyes; according to him the rays originate in the object of vision and not in the eye. He described accurately various parts of the eye and gave a scientific explanation of the process of vision. He also attempted to explain binocular vision and gave a correct explanation of the apparent increase in size of the sun and the moon when near the horizon—a prologue to the concept of constancy of perception developed much later in the 20th century.

The Medical Tradition. An important contribution to psychological knowledge belongs to Ibn Sina (980–1037), best known to Europeans by the Latin version of his name, Avicenna. His two most important works are *The Book of Healing* and *The Canon of Medicine.* Although Avicenna adopted many ideas of Aristotle, there is substantial difference between the two scholars. For example, Avicenna, like Aristotle, described three functions of the soul. However, Avicenna believed that the center of psychological functioning is the brain, not the heart as Aristotle had suggested. Avicenna also maintained that the soul contains abstract concepts, a higher level of reflection independent from direct perception. Abstract concepts cannot be formed as a result of experience. They must exist prior to experience. An idea can exist in our mind without being attached to an existing object. When we think about a chair before building it, the idea about this chair existed before the chair was created. That means that material objects can come out of ideal concepts.

ON THE WEB

Ibn Sina. A brief biography and related information is posted on the book website.

Avicenna followed Galen's teachings in physiology and psychology and offered a remarkable biological model of the psychological processes. He postulated that the nerves contain special endings. A steamlike substance moves back and forth through the nerves from the body's surface back to the soul. Ibn Sina was among the earliest scientists to experiment with perception. He established that if a colored disk is rotated with a certain speed, a person stops seeing different colors on the disk and perceives only one color instead. Memory, according to him, is a summary of perceptions. Emotions accompany perception. Furthermore, emotions could affect the body and its functions. Anger can make the body hotter, grief dries it out, and sadness weakens the strength of the body. Avicenna believed that black bile mixed with phlegm causes depressive symptoms, such as inactivity, passivity, and silence. On the contrary, a mixture of black and yellow bile can cause manic symptoms, including agitation and euphoric excitement.

Views of Social Behavior. Early Islamic scholars expressed various views about personality traits and the connections between behavioral choices and actual behavior. For example, an important question was, Is it good enough to consider yourself a moral individual, or is it imperative to help people? These views are relevant to us today because they emphasize the debate about the sources of moral behavior. For example, we can condemn violence in theory. But what if violence is necessary to help another person to become free from oppression?

Similar to the teachings of European and Asian philosophers, most Middle Eastern thinkers recommended behavioral asceticism, or abstinence from material pleasures. This meant that a person should exercise moderation; pray systematically; display humility, tolerance, repentance, and patience; and keep a simple life. Muslims were taught to use the life of Mohammed as the touchstone for proper thought, decision, and action. His life was the model to follow for millions, as were the lives of Christ and Buddha to their followers in other parts of the world.

There are also many literary sources from the Middle East about the individual's personality and social behavior. One of the most popular forms of art in the Middle East, Iran, and Central Asia was poetry. Creations of Firdawsi, Umar Hayyam, and Nizami are translated and known today in many countries. We learn from these works about passion and romantic love, anger, jealousy, pride, and generosity of people living many hundreds years ago.

Overall, Arabic, Middle Eastern, and Central Asian scholars played a crucial role in preserving knowledge originated in the ancient Greece. Many detailed translations of the Greeks appeared in Arabic. Then, many Arabic texts containing these translations and critical evaluations were brought back to Europe centuries later. This stimulated the development of European sciences and philosophy. Moreover, scholars working within the Islamic tradition produced a complex knowledge about psychological activities; they also studied anatomy and acknowledged the connection between the brain and mental processes; they explained the basic mechanisms of memory, perception, imagination, and thinking. Like Greek, Roman, Indian, and Chinese scholars, they emphasized the importance of moderation, rational choice, and strong moral values as guides of human behavior.

ON THE WEB

An exercise. "Who said this?" You may agree that ancient thinkers could say very contemporary things! Check the book website.

Table 2.6 Psychological Knowledge in Early Middle Eastern Civilizations: An Overview

Psychological Phenomena	*Sources of Knowledge*	*Major Findings*
Behavior and its causes	Islamic scholarship, Greek teachings, observation, generalizations, and medical research	People make rational choices; behavior is motivated by external and internal forces.
Cognition	Islamic scholarship, Greek teachings, observation and generalizations, research of the sensory organs	Existence of the soul is acknowledged. Sensory organs give accurate impressions of reality. Higher cognitive functions have divine origins.
Emotion	Islamic scholarship, Greek teachings, observations and generalizations	Emotions regulate behavior but can be disturbing.
Specific knowledge	Islamic scholarship, observations and generalizations, mythology, medical research	Various facts were accumulated about behavior, decision making, and moral choices.

✓ CHECK YOUR KNOWLEDGE

How did Thomas Aquinas view the soul?

What was the major impact of Greek thought on Middle Eastern science?

What was the "color experiment" by Ibn Sina?

What is behavioral asceticism?

Assessments

Throughout centuries, psychological knowledge emerged within many scientific and cultural traditions. Scholars of those epochs underlined a distinction between material and ideal worlds, the body and mind, but offered different views about the interaction between them. How different were these views?

Today we should acknowledge but not misjudge the differences between so-called Eastern and Western views of the body-mind interactions. The differences exist, but they must not be exaggerated. In short, scholars in ancient Greece and Rome did not separate the material and spiritual; similarly, scholars in India and China did not put the body and mind "back" together. Idealism and materialism are neither Eastern nor Western intellectual accomplishments exclusively.

The Greeks and later the Romans recognized sensation, perception, emotion, thinking, and motivation as distinct processes. Yet they were not isolated from one another. The earliest ideas of interconnectedness and complexity of psychological processes are found in the statements of Heraclitus and the comprehensive logic of Aristotle. A similar view was shared by scholars in India and the Middle East. The holistic view of the individual was, in fact, a major accomplishment of those scholars. This view allowed them to understand the balance, harmony, and interdependence of psychological processes (Peng & Nisbett, 1999).

Scholars in Europe, Africa, and Asia made remarkable assumptions about the biological foundations of psychology. Although their views were inaccurate from today's perspective, most ancient scholars made right assumptions about the role of the brain and the nervous system in regulating behavior and mental functions. They made fascinating observations about emotions and their regulatory role in behavior. Almost in a similar fashion, scholars in Greece and India believed in the importance of rational choice over immediate emotional impulses. In Rome and Medina, scholars emphasized the importance of a healthy lifestyle, rationality, and moderation—the key foundations of today's health psychology.

It is also inaccurate to perceive all knowledge developed within religious traditions as dogmatic, noncreative. It is true that organized religion, be it Islam or Christianity, sets limits on what can be research. We will later see how religious institutions opposed experimental research in psychology. Religion often requires putting faith before experience. Nevertheless, religious prescription gave inspiration and guidance to a great number of scholars in the Islamic, Christian, Buddhist, Hindu, Jewish, Taoist, and other religious systems. Semantic analysis of religions across the world shows that they underlined similar basic human strengths—including justice, humanity, wisdom, and temperance—and provided people with knowledge about their self-improvement (Dahlsgaar, Peterson, Christopher, & Seligman, 2005). The religious understanding of the soul as a nonmaterial, independent, eternal, and active substance, as well as one capable of being separated from the body, generally corresponds with many contemporary views on the nature of the psychological processes that emphasizes its active character, the role of the will, and the importance of individual responsibility, perseverance, and self-regulation. Psychological idealism, the position supported in many religious schools of thought was also a cornerstone of many scientific theories of the 19th and 20th centuries.

An interesting question remains about specialization of thought among the Greek and Roman academics, Chinese and Indian philosophers, and, to a certain extent, Middle Eastern scholars. Some critics suggest that the Greeks had developed a generally universal system of knowledge that involved the understanding of psychological phenomena by observing the natural (physics) and philosophical (metaphysics) perspectives. In China, to the contrary, the fundamental knowledge was mainly concerned with the theoretical justification of the principles of efficient human behavior in society within human networks, such as local community, family, and so on (Kleinman & Kleinman, 1991). In India, as critics continue, the systematic knowledge was primarily preoccupied with the cognitive aspects of human psychology: the understanding of the self, the nature of perception and thinking, and the accuracy of human knowledge. Middle Eastern science and philosophy held a unique position between the East and West because it was partially rooted in the findings of Greek philosophers and partly in its own scientific discoveries in natural sciences and medicine. It also developed its unique perspective of psychology within the framework of the Islamic theology.

These arguments are interesting but incomplete. Knowledge developed within major scholarly traditions was very much comprehensive. Cognition was studied in India and by Greek philosophers. Studies of happiness appear in many teachings, not only in the works of Indian philosophers, but in many others including Aristotle, Seneca, and Epicurus. We can find remarkable similarities in specific psychological observations. For example, scholars of the past emphasized almost unanimously that honesty and hard work were desirable behaviors, while drunkenness and carefree lifestyles were not good choices.

There were many differences, of course. On the one hand, most philosophers in Rome and Greece accepted homosexual feelings and behavior as normal. In Islamic and Christian traditions, on the other hand, homosexuality was rejected outright. According to some philosophers, such as Epicurus, human beings are supposed to be independent thinkers, critical and skeptical about the words they hear. According to other traditions (Stoics and followers of Confucianism) people should follow the rules, be loyal to society, and accept their fate.

On social-psychological issues, the views of most ancient philosophers were largely similar. Women were generally encouraged to participate in social affairs.

However, most scholars were against equality between men and women and maintained that women should perform traditional roles in the family and local affairs. Slavery was viewed as part of life, an inevitable component of social stratification. Astrology was also popular as a way to predict future and to protect from misfortunes.

Conclusion

Although merciless invasions, natural disasters, and countless reconstructions destroyed or dramatically altered most of the physical foundation of early civilizations, new generations could preserve core elements of their ancestors' intellectual life. Many important questions about psychology had been already asked in the distant past. Many great theories about human behavior and experience developed during the early stages of human civilization. They were later advanced, forgotten, and revived again. Centuries later, we turn yet again to the ancient legacy.

Summary

- Early psychological observations began to emerge in written folklore, religious scriptures, and paintings. Although these observations seem grossly incomplete today, they allow us to study people's knowledge about sensations, emotions, desires, dreams, will, and other experiences.

- Most information today is available from sources traced back to the ancient Near East, ancient Greece and Rome, the Middle East, and North Africa; these are commonly referred to today as the roots of Western civilization. Non-Western written sources came primarily from Central Asia, India, and China.

- Greek thinkers made a remarkable contribution to philosophy and science by developing original views of the principles of human behavior and experience. Their views laid a strong foundation for the further development of global psychological knowledge. There are at least five major areas of influence: (1) the study of the soul, (2) the teachings about the mechanisms of human cognition, (3) the suggestions about the biological foundations of mental activities, (4) the initial inquiry in the fields of clinical psychology, and (5) the rich observations of social behavior.

- Like the Greek tradition, both Indian and Chinese ancient traditions developed an extremely sophisticated view of behavior, emotions, thought, and other mental activities. Both Indian and Chinese schools, as well as the Greek school, developed remarkable worldviews of the individual, social roles, cognition, and the ability of people to control the outcomes of their behavior.

- Roman scholars preserved and strengthened the traditional Greek views of the soul, its structure and functions. Roman philosophers also turned their attention to moral behavior, self-restraint, and moderation. They emphasized the importance of reason and patience, goodwill and hope.

- The Scholastic tradition of psychological knowledge developed, to some degree, as a symbolic alliance of Christian theology and the Greek philosophy.

- Arabic, Middle Eastern, and Central Asian scholars played a crucial role in preserving knowledge originated in the ancient Greece. Moreover, scholars working within the Islamic tradition produced an original and complex knowledge about psychological activities; they also studied anatomy and acknowledged the connection between the brain and mental processes; they explained the basic mechanisms of memory, perception, imagination, and thinking. Like Greek, Roman, Indian, and Chinese scholars, they emphasized the importance of moderation, rational choice, and strong moral values as guides of human behavior.

Key Terms

Atomism

Caritas and cupiditas

Emanation theory

Epistemology

Holism

Hylomorphism

Idealism

Material monism

Materialism

Melancholy (often melancholia)

Scholasticism

Subjective culture

Theology

Psychology During Mid-Millennium Transitions

15th to the End of the 18th Century

> The soul and the body fall asleep together. As the motion of the blood is calmed, a sweet feeling of peace and quiet spreads through the whole mechanism.
>
> *Julien Offray de La Mettrie (1748)*

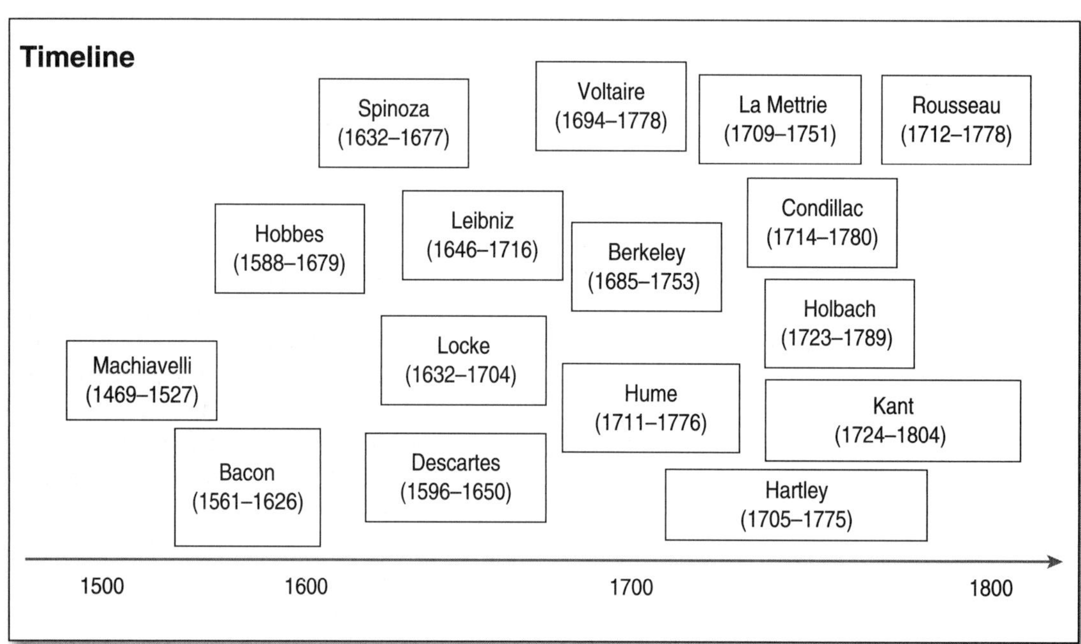

CHAPTER OUTLINE

During the Middle Ages, most people didn't live beyond age 50; they knew little about their own bodies; physicians were few, and they were incapable of curing most diseases; the mentally ill were ostracized and isolated. Trying to make sense of their own psychological world, people maintained superstitions and beliefs in the immortal soul and divine guidance. Common were beliefs in magical powers, astrology, extrasensory perception, distance healing, the evil eye, and the possibility of communication with the dead. The responsibility for misfortunes and illness was frequently attributed to devils and witches.

We like to think that in the 21st century we have overcome the "naïve" psychological beliefs of the past. We see ourselves as a civilized, reasonable, science-based civilization. But is this really true? Have people living today moved beyond what they believed 500 years ago? Have we abandoned superstitions, beliefs in supernatural forces, paranormal abilities, and distant healing? Not quite yet.

In Europe, Asia, and America, tens of millions of people continue to seek help from faith healers to heal physical and psychological maladies.

Surveys (Fox News and Gallup) in the United States reveal that 24 percent of the surveyed believe in the existence of witches, and 40 percent believe that people on this Earth are sometimes possessed by the devil.

In Sierra Leone, West Africa, local hunters do not call each other by name because they are afraid that the devils might identify them for later harm.

In Morocco, as in many other traditional communities in Islamic countries, scores of people believe in demons or *jinni* who, if disturbed, can become enraged and then possess someone's body and take revenge on that person's psyche.

In Russia, millions of people routinely talk about positive and negative energies radiating from other people that cause either good or harm.

In some areas in Malaysia, folk healers treat people suffering from "demonic possessions" by sprinkling the possessed with holy water and sacrificing a small animal in an attempt to pacify the offended spirits.

All over the world today, people believe in talismans and amulets, small objects that allegedly bring luck or protect from physical harm or evil spirits. Many people are apprehensive about particular numbers: a lot of Christians avoid numbers 666 and 13, and many people in Southeast Asia repulse number 4. Some people believe that when a black cat crosses your path, something bad could happen. Others have faith in horoscopes and plan their lives according to certain positions of the stars. Have our beliefs changed significantly since 500 years ago?

True, most of us are free from the power of superstitions and false beliefs that were common in previous centuries. Witches are no longer burned at the stake, and people are not brought to criminal court for insisting that the Earth is round. Yet the history of psychology reveals that in many instances certain understandings of our own psychological world have not changed much in the past several hundred years.

Social scientists often call the remarkable transitions that began 500 years ago in Europe a revolution, something that fundamentally changed the course of human civilization. We should understand the transitions of the late 15th to the 18th centuries not as a "giant leap forward" but as a continuous acquisition of new knowledge. Because this transformation continues today.

Transitions From the Late 15th to the End of 18th Century

The earliest prototypes of modern nation-states began to appear in the middle of the previous millennium. In Europe these new states included France, England, the Netherlands, and Spain, and later Sweden, Russia, and Poland. By the end of the 15th century in the eastern part of Asia, the powerful Ottoman Empire had gained strength after defeating the Byzantine Empire and had spread from Turkey to Iran, and from Egypt and northern Africa to Spain. Continual religious divisions and endless territorial wars devastated Europe and contributed to the economic depression of the 16th and 17th centuries. Kings and queens possessed enormous power, but the revolutions in England and the Netherlands signaled the beginning of the gradual erosion of royal authority.

This mid-millennium period was also the time of spectacular overseas journeys to new lands. Marco Polo, Christopher Columbus, Vasco da Gama, and Ferdinand Magellan introduced "new worlds" to Europeans. Chinese merchants had traveled and settled as far as Africa and the Arabian peninsula. The voyages let people gather and share new information. For example, European scholars exchanged scientific ideas with the Ottoman Turks and learned from them, among other things, the art of public administration.

While there is no universally accepted theory to explain the global complexity of mid-millennium transitions, historians generally agree about Western civilization. They describe this period in terms of three fundamental developments: the Renaissance, the Reformation, and the scientific revolution. These developments transformed psychological knowledge.

Renaissance

Renaissance means rebirth. The Renaissance stretched from the 14th through the 16th centuries in the Italian states and in the 16th century in the northern European countries of France, England, and Holland. Historians associate the Renaissance with the reintroduction of major elements of Greco-Roman antiquity in arts, sciences, and education. Many rediscoveries of antiquity were influenced, in part, by the archeological findings and the surfacing of previously unknown scientific manuscripts. These manuscripts had been brought to the West by the influx of Byzantine scholars who had fled the advancing forces of the Ottoman Empire and the fall of Constantinople in 1453.

The Renaissance is commonly contrasted with the so-called "dark ages"—the medieval period frequently described as stagnant and inert in terms of social changes and scientific advancements. The famous Swiss art historian, Jacob Burckhardt, wrote in *The Civilization of the Renaissance in Italy,* released in 1860, that the Renaissance was largely about innovation, secularism, enthusiasm, rationality, and people's acknowledgment of the importance of the code of good manners and honor. In contrast, during the "dark ages" most people lived in the captivity of their own naïve beliefs mixed with fear, illusion, and prejudice (Burckhardt, 1860/2002). Such broad generalizations are inaccurate. People and society did not rapidly evolve from "not knowing" to "knowing," or from fear to confidence. The Renaissance period was a time of continuous transition affecting the scope and quality of science-based knowledge and common beliefs.

The renewed interest in antiquity sparked people's interest in science. It was becoming increasingly diverse, breaking through the barrier of *theology, formal logic,* and *geometry*—the main subjects of most medieval universities. An anti-Scholastic mood grew. Aristotle's unchallenged authority in philosophy had been weakening after scholars turned to Plato and Lucretius, Stoicism and Epicureanism. Interests were shifting from formal logic to ethics and social theory. The search for the recipes of happiness was in style.

The Renaissance also brought about change to the institutions of higher learning. Universities were increasingly available to ordinary people, although most universities were profoundly discriminatory against women and people of lower social classes. More scientific debates were taking place outside traditional academic institutions. Many ordinary people with no formal academic or religious titles were making serious contributions to science.

Although Europe is viewed as the cradle of the Renaissance, scholarly knowledge was developed within other cultural traditions as well. In the Ottoman Empire— including Persia and the Middle East—mathematicians, philosophers, physicians, historians, and poets flourished. Persian and Arabic languages remained the major means of communication in education, science, poetry, and bookkeeping in the vast area between Spain on the west and Himalayan Mountains on the east. As in Europe, scholars in central Asia accepted many fundamental ideas of the Greek thinkers. Psychological knowledge in the Middle East, Iran, and Mediterranean Africa was developed within both religious and secular traditions.

To many Renaissance scientists, the theorems of mathematics and the rules of mechanics appeared as capable of explaining the functioning of the human body and mental functions.

By the 17th century, however, one significant difference had become apparent. While Middle Eastern thought was becoming increasingly connected to theology, Western science—including the views of psychology—had challenged theology and the doctrines of the Catholic Church in particular.

Reformation

The most significant change that affected the powerful position of the Catholic Church in Europe was the Reformation. Fueled by dissatisfaction with the religious doctrines and selfish practices of the clergy, the leaders of this movement challenged the authority of the church in all spheres of life. The religious teachings of Martin Luther (1483–1546) inspired the birth of the Protestant branch of Christianity. Luther's teachings also encouraged people to question authority and assume individual responsibility. As the advancing Reformation movement grew in Europe, religious faith was becoming increasingly a matter of individual conscience. This contributed to the fundamental belief in the possibility of individual freedom (Spielvogel, 2006). Individualism as a cultural phenomenon, with its emphasis on responsibility, gradual savings, choice, and privacy, has its roots in the Reformation period. Many prominent scholars began to see individuals as independent thinkers driven by practical reason (Gergen, 2001).

The Protestant Reformation called upon men and women to read the Bible and participate in religious services together. This new religious doctrine, in theory, had opened doors for joint education of boys and girls. Hundreds of Protestant schools were open across Europe, accepting children of both sexes. In practice, however, the religious reforms did not bring substantial changes in the position of women in the church and in society in general. Although the voices supporting equality between the sexes grew stronger, most scholars believed in natural inequality between the sexes.

Overall, many scientists began to challenge the monopoly of religious authorities on knowledge and truth. Latin as the language of scholarly communication, a position it had held for hundreds of years, gradually declined. In their writings, scientists began to use own national languages.

Scientific Revolution

Another major turning point in the development of Western civilization was the scientific revolution. The 17th century was the age of new scientific societies and academies sponsored by the powerful rulers. The invention of new machines and instruments such as the telescope, the microscope, and other devices of measurement stimulated an avalanche of new discoveries (see Table 3.1). For the educated, the mysterious and unpredictable quality of nature was unfolding into something clear and quantifiable. The Earth appeared as a round object that rotated around the sun, as did other planets (as Copernicus had theorized in 1543).

Table 3.1 Scientific Discoveries of the 16th and 17th Centuries: Selected Examples

In 1543, Nicolas Copernicus theorized that the Earth rotated around the sun.
In 1621, Johannes Kepler established that the celestial orbits were not circular but elliptical.
In 1638, Galileo Galilei introduced his theory of inertia.
In 1641, William Gilbert published his theory of magnetism.
In 1628, William Harvey collected evidence about blood circulating in the body and in 1651 formulated the main principles of embryology.
In 1687, Newton articulated the laws of motion.
In 1665, Robert Hooke first reported to the world that life's smallest living units were "little boxes." These were later known as cells.

The impact of Isaac Newton (1643–1727) on science was remarkable. His discoveries of the laws of motion inspired many thinkers to accept the view that these laws were applicable to all physical bodies in the natural world. The axioms and theorems of mathematics appeared as capable of explaining the miracle of life, the functioning of the human body, and mental functions. During the time of Newton, many materialistic suggestions of the Greeks appeared correct: small elements comprise the structure of living tissue and physical objects.

Although printing had been invented earlier in China, one of the greatest technical achievements of the 15th century in Europe was the independent invention of the printing press of the moveable type. In 1455 (in some sources in 1437), Johannes Gutenberg began to produce books using this type of the press. The invention of moveable type meant that more books could be printed in less time and for less cost.

ON THE WEB

Read about Francis Bacon (1561–1626), a remarkable philosopher and public administrator, and his contribution to science and psychology on the book website.

Change was coming to interpersonal communications. Among upper classes of society, reading and writing were in vogue. It was fashionable to correspond by letter. Established scientists maintained continuous correspondence with the educated nobility, including queens and kings. It was a matter of prestige for a young scientist to exchange lengthy scholarly letters with established intellectuals or aristocratic thinkers.

The scientific revolution was a time of renewed interest to gender. Yet the vast majority of scientists tended to maintain the traditional view of the roles of men and women in society. Before the beginning of the 15th century, very few women were allowed to choose the life of a scientist. Social customs required a woman to get only elementary education and play a home-based role of a mother and wife. The law did not allow women to enroll in most universities. Gradually, however, more women were able to break societal resistance. Many prominent families were willing to allow their daughters to spend significant time at school, attend lectures, and engage in scientific investigation and writing. Most of these women were, of course, aristocrats inspired by the opportunities for secular learning. The most popular fields to explore were education, literature, music, history, and fine arts. There were a few female philosophers, astronomers, and zoologists. Yet women were generally discouraged from studying medicine. The best they could do was to pursue knowledge and develop skills as pharmacists or midwives. Although changes in the social climate were taking place and more upper-class women would receive advanced education, science was still considered a field suitable for men only.

ON THE WEB

Read about Margaret Cavendish (1623–1673) and her life and work on the book's website.

The mid-millennium transitions were significant and dynamic. In Europe, all forms of life were affected by profound political, economic, social, and religious changes. The evolving human needs pushed forward advanced psychological knowledge, which began, albeit slowly, to turn toward many applied areas of education and health (Smith, 1997).

Psychology in Mid-Millennium: What People Knew

How did psychological knowledge develop? First, we briefly discuss psychological knowledge developing in the fields of science. Then we turn to religion and then take on popular beliefs.

Scientific Knowledge

From the 16th through the 18th centuries an increasing number of scholars believed that people were part of the natural world and were an equal species in the animal kingdom. People learned new facts about biology and physiology, health, and psychological processes—especially sensation and emotion. Rational thinking, based on investigation and education, appeared as the key to human advancement (Vande Kemp, 1980).

The greatest minds of that period—Copernicus, Galileo, Newton, and Kepler—believed that the secrets of nature were coded in mathematical formulas. Mental life appeared explicable. What was previously seen as spiritual or divine was increasingly understood as mechanical, chemical, or as functioning as a reliable machine. Still, scientific knowledge was frequently inaccurate. For instance, it was commonly accepted around the 16th century that the brain's functions were localized in the ventricles that contained brain fluids, and the shape and size of these ventricles had something to do with the way the brain functioned. Galen's teachings dominated medicine prior to the 16th century. His works were mandatory for medical students. Treatment was based on Galen's assumption about the imbalance of the humors, which could be detected by observing the color of human urine.

New discoveries in physiology (cadavers were dissected in medical schools at that time) came with the work of William Harvey (1578–1657) from England. Like most scientists at that time, Harvey made comments about psychology. He believed in the existence of a general processing mechanism, called common *sensorium.* It was located in the brain and helped to distinguish between different qualities of sensations. He described the brain as a sensitive root to which a variety of fibers attached, one of which was able to see, another to hear, a third to touch, and a fourth and a fifth to smell and taste. The *sensorium* itself could induce certain emotional states that influence the incoming sensations. For example, people could be excited or agitated to such a degree that they could not even feel pain or discomfort. In one of his writings on biology, Harvey made an interesting observation about the exceptional memory of uneducated shepherds (Harvey, 1628/1965). He also speculated about gender psychology. In his 1651 book, *Essays on the Generation of Animals* he wrote that both men and women have to provide "matter" for their offspring. However, men provide an "active matter" that brings activity and power. Women, on the other hand, provide a more "passive" agent. These views of gender were, of course, highly speculative (Harvey, 1651/1965).

For many educated minds of that time, the physical world, including the human body, resembled a functioning mechanism. One of many scientists who explored the idea about the motorized nature of human bodies was La Mettrie (1709–1751). His most famous book, *Man a Machine,* was published in 1748 and later released in many languages. He claimed that mechanical laws are good enough to explain complex human behavior. We return to La Mettrie and his studies later in this chapter.

A noteworthy example of how educated people approached the study of human behavior comes from the written observations of Girolamo Cardano, a 16th-century doctor and scientist. Notice his passion for detailed self-observations.

CASE IN POINT

Girolamo Cardano was a true example of the Renaissance scientist: an educator, physician, mathematician, and optimist with a curious mind.

Girolamo Cardano (1501–1576). Cardano (known also as *Jerome Cardan)* was born in Pavia, Italy. A gifted physician, clever mathematician, and astrologist, he was a true example of the Renaissance scientist: an educator, enthusiast, and optimist with a curious mind. Cardano wrote a detailed autobiography (a relatively common practice among scientists), filled with meticulous details about his activities and psychological experiences. He described scrupulously his daily events, including meals, drinks, physical exercises, lectures he delivered, and even the process of peer voting for his academic and medical degrees. The reader also finds Cardano's thorough observations and reflections about his psychological world: thought process, doubts, and anxieties. For example, not only did he describe his own powerful addiction to gambling, but he also suggested a self-therapy to reduce his addictive cravings. Girolamo Cardano provided an interesting account of therapeutic techniques, such as self-inflicted physical pain to reduce more serious psychological disturbances. Small pain or irritation, he believed, would overtake psychological anguish caused by a more serious disturbance. He also described different parenting styles. Cardano gave detailed accounts of an inconsistent or ambivalent parental style in the child's upbringing. He also described his own life stages—an early detailed account of psychological changes taking place during the life span. He strongly believed in determinism and suggested that every small decision people make today influences their future.

Cardano's autobiography is an amazing example of relentless optimism (despite his physical problems and tragic life events) and confidence. "Whenever my personal affairs have been in a state nothing short of desperate, I have been swept up on a wave of Fortune," he wrote about his life (Cardano, 1576/2002, p. 147). Cardano, as many of his contemporaries, believed in the possibilities of self-improvement. He left detailed instructions about discipline, dieting, stress reduction, healthy lifestyle, and psychological coping with misfortunes.

Yet he carried many other beliefs common in his times. He maintained that people's behavior and experiences could be influenced by the location and movement of stars. He believed in superstitions and attributed much to omens. Although he was a scientist and experimenter, Cardano also believed in magic and the existence of paranormal powers, and extrasensory perception (Cardano, 1576/2002).

Many scholars of the time offered their views on certain stable patterns of behavior and thinking, today labeled *personality traits.* The natural makeup of the body, the temperament (understood according to the teachings of ancient Greeks such as Hippocrates) was a source of stable psychological activities (addressed often as the "character" of the soul). According to such views, the soul imitates the complexions of the body. Some people are choleric: they are active, ambitious, and wrathful. Other people are sanguine: they are even tempered and kindly. The melancholics are commonly depressed, envious, but creative. And, finally, the phlegmatics are slow and slothful.

Physicians began to make detailed observations of psychological abnormalities. As an example, Robert Burton in England published in 1621 the book called *Anatomy of Melancholy* devoted to anxiety and mood problems. Later editions of the book are readily available today (see Figure 3.1). Burton identified specific environmental

Figure 3.1 *Anatomy of Melancholy* published in 1621 was one of the earliest books devoted to anxiety and mood problems.

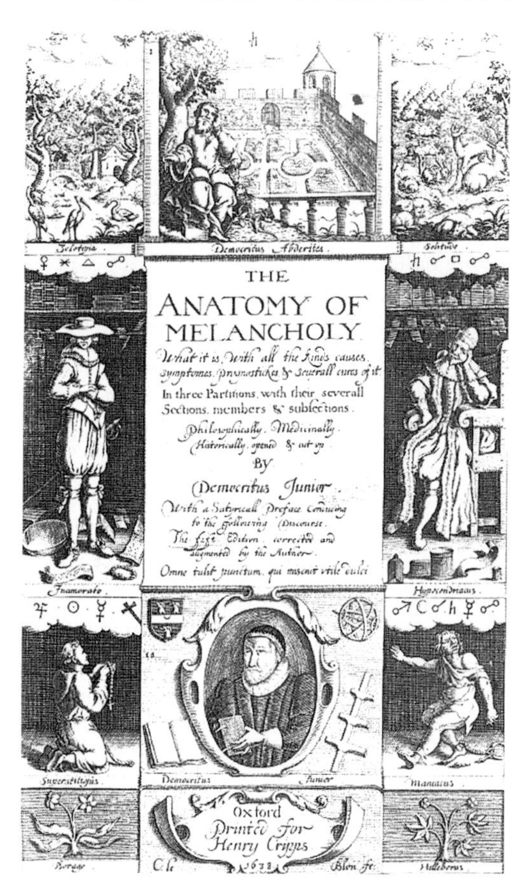

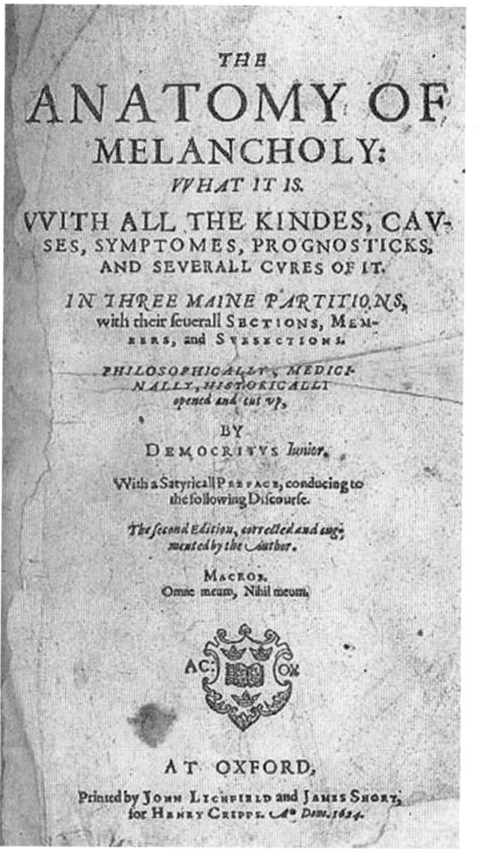
THE
ANATOMY OF
MELANCHOLY:
VVHAT IT IS.
VVITH ALL THE KINDES, CAV-
SES, SYMPTOMES, PROGNOSTICKS,
AND SEVERALL CVRES OF IT.
IN THREE MAINE PARTITIONS,
with their seuerall SECTIONS, MEM-
BERS, and SVBSECTIONS.
PHILOSOPHICALLY, MEDICI-
NALLY, HISTORICALLY
opened and cut vp.
BY
DEMOCRITVS Iunior.
With a Satyricall PREFACE, conducing to
the following Discourse.
The second Edition, corrected and aug-
mented by the Author.
MACROB.
Omne meum, Nihil meum.
AT OXFORD,
Printed by JOHN LICHFIELD and JAMES SHORT,
for HENRY CRIPPS. Ano Dom. 1624.

factors such as rigorous diet, consumption of alcohol, biological rhythms, and passionate love as forces contributing to persistent sadness. During his time, melancholia was commonly considered a condition typical in noblemen, artists, thinkers, and other intellectuals who expressed exceptional compassion about people and relationships. It was frequently labeled as "love sickness" (Gilman, 1988). Burton discussed causes and symptoms of melancholy and introduced some treatment ideas, including suggestions about changing a person's lifestyle and redirecting sad thoughts.

Psychological knowledge was also developing outside the realm of science. Organized religion remained a powerful institution promoting the religious view of human behavior and psychology. Science was a growing challenge to organized religion, which had held for centuries an uncontested monopoly on knowledge. Religious officials and religious scholars wanted to preserve their high social status and exercise their moral authority fully.

Religion-Based and Folk Knowledge

Throughout history, religious authorities and secular scientists were typically in different "camps" trying to reach for people's hearts and minds. Although the Protestant elites had abandoned much of the Catholic theology, religious leaders agreed that new scientific discoveries were a direct challenge to religious scriptures. Despite the fundamental changes in science and education, ordinary people had extremely limited knowledge about biology, anatomy, or medicine. Superstitions frequently prevailed over science. Most common folk views of mental phenomena were often rooted in religious postulates, to the acts of God or the devil.

For example, sleepwalking disorder is defined today as repeated episodes of rising from bed during sleep and walking about. Five hundred years ago, people who displayed these symptoms were commonly called lunatics; allegedly, they had been molested by the devil. During the night, a sleepwalking individual becomes vulnerable because the devil could wait for this moment to molest again. Such behavior is likely to take place during certain phases of the moon. Other alterations of consciousness (labeled in translations as delirium) were also interpreted as the result of the evil work of the devil, who snatches away the senses of certain individuals who then become delirious.

The church accepted the explanations of St. Augustine (see Chapter 2) that the devil disguised himself everywhere: in colors, sounds, smells, and even in angry conversations. Evil desires were the imposition of the devil's will upon people, especially on witches (see more about witchcraft later in this chapter). **Mysticism**, a belief in the existence of realities beyond perceptual reflection or scientific explanations but accessible by subjective experience, remained a very important element in the lives of the Christian and Jewish communities in Europe and in the Muslim communities of the Middle East and North Africa.

Mysticism was not only part of folk beliefs. Mystic experiences were considered divine and, therefore, appreciated and even sought by many people of faith. Acceptance of mysticism was reflected in the Sufi tradition in Islam, the Kabbalah tradition in Judaism, and in the Christian tradition as well. Ignatius of Loyola (1491–1556), the founder of the Society of Jesus (known as the Jesuits), published a book under the title, *The Spiritual Exercises.* The book described 370 exercises by which people could advance their individual willpower to serve the will of God. For example, the book teaches how to use meditation and focus on specific experiences of the past as well as imagination about the future. During meditation, a person can focus on his or her own sinful behavior or imagine painful experiences that he or she can encounter in hell. Mystic experience was a common subject of debates among Islamic scholars. The soul could not be studied by science. Persian thinker Mulla Sadara (1571–1641) in his teachings, for instance, separated the natural sciences from **metaphysics**, the branch of philosophy that examines the nature of reality, including the relationship between mind and matter. He believed that experience should be studied within metaphysics.

Witchcraft. The term witchcraft refers to the alleged practices or arts of witches: the acquisition of supernatural power, sorcery, enchantments, and sexual contacts with evil spirits. Witchcraft is depicted in scores of contemporary horror films. In the United States and many other countries where Halloween is celebrated, many children and adults are dressed like witches. Black hats, pointy noses, black hair, screechy voices—all these are the stereotypical and comical attributes of a witch. However, a few hundred years ago, everything associated with this image wasn't a joke.

Belief in witches was widespread in Europe in early medieval society and continued through the scientific revolution. Earlier in the 15th century, the pope had sent Jacob Sprenger and Heinrich Krämer, two Dominican monks, to investigate witchcraft. As the result of their work with written sources and personal accounts of other people, they published a book entitled *The Malleus Maleficarum,* commonly known as *The Hammer of the Witches* (published in the late 1400s; the exact year is disputed). From this book and several other sources, we learn that 400 and 500 years ago, both Catholic and Protestant communities across Europe witnessed a great number of witchcraft trials. The alleged witches were sought, hunted down, and persecuted. Records show that women, particularly older ones from lower social classes, were significantly more likely than other people to be prosecuted for witchcraft. In fact, about 80 percent of all the accused were women. Why?

One of the reasons is that women were believed to be inferior to and weaker than men and thus were vulnerable to the wicked intentions of the devil. The victims would face charges such as contact with the devil and performance of inappropriate sexual activities that included night orgies. There were also charges against witches for causing sickness in neighbors, dangerous thunderstorms, droughts, floods, and even business deals that went wrong. One of the accusations against witches was their alleged use of wax dolls (prototypes). Acceptance of the idea of the possibility of casting spells via dolls is one of the oldest and universal cross-cultural beliefs, known in Babylon, ancient Egypt, ancient Greece, India, and Rome. This custom also was found among the native tribes in America, Africa, Japan, Russia, and China and in many other places. In many places in Europe at the time, the use of wax dolls was associated with witchcraft and was criminalized.

Witchcraft was part of human folk tradition supported by religious beliefs. From the evidence accumulated in printed sources, including *The Malleus Maleficarum,* we

ON THE WEB

Religion, Witchcraft, and Gender. Find out why in the Middle Ages so many female witches were "discovered" but only a few males.

can infer that the work of the devil, and witchcraft in particular, was attributed to psychological and behavioral symptoms such as delusions, hallucinations, or manic episodes.

Of course, there were individuals who did not believe in witchcraft. Many powerful and educated people put pressure on governments so that by the end of the 17th century the number of witchcraft trials in Europe had fallen significantly. Educated people began to reject the idea of a spirit possession. More people were turning to scientific explanations of human activities, referring to the functioning of the brain as a source of unusual or abnormal phenomena that had been previously explained by supernatural factors.

In Chapter 6, we take a closer look at how scientific psychological knowledge about mental illness progressed. Yet, we also will find that even as late as in the 19th century, speculations about the sources of unusual psychological phenomena, labeled as madness, involved persistent references to "evil forces."

CASE IN POINT

Who Invented the Term *Psychology*? Who was the first to employ the exact word *psychology*? The first appearance probably occurred around 1506 when a Croatian humanist and poet named Marco Marulic (1450–1524) used this term in a manuscript. Critics disagree about Marulic. They say that we know about this alleged manuscript from someone called Božičević-Natalis, who published a treatise, *Life of Marko Marulic From Split.* It has also been commonly assumed that German Protestant reformer Phillip Melanchthon used this term in his writings in the late 1530s, but his authorship is also questionable because of the allegedly inaccurate translations of his works made in the 1800s.

Other historians posit that the first author to use the term *psychology* in a book title was Rudolf Goeckel (also known as Rudolphus Goclenius). In 1590, he published a collection of articles related to human behavior entitled *Psychology on the Improvements of Man* (Goclenius, 1598/1976). Four years later, in 1594, Otto Casmann (1562–1607) published another book with the word *psychology* in its title: *Psychologia Anthropologica.*

No matter who claims the original authorship, the term *psychology* remained virtually unknown to the general reading public and was not used frequently until the 18th century. Only then, beginning probably with the German philosopher Christian Wolff and the French scholar Denis Diderot, the term received more attention from a broader reading audience.

Sources: Boring (1929); Krstic (1964); Yakunin (2001)

ON THE WEB

Did playwrights of the 16th century contribute to psychological knowledge? Check the book website.

Overall, during mid-millennium transitions, more individuals started to pay greater attention to themselves as unique persons, carriers of their own distinct individualities, feelings, and thoughts. Yet, various superstitions, including beliefs in witchcraft, continued to be part of their lives. The 16th through 18th centuries produced many intellectual giants, including philosophers, scientists, and physicians. The teachings of these intellectuals influenced the world of science and made a significant impact on contemporary views of psychology and behavior in general.

✓ CHECK YOUR KNOWLEDGE

The term *renaissance* means rebirth. Rebirth of what?

What are the main points of Robert Burton's *Anatomy of Melancholy*?

What is mysticism?

The Impact of Scholars and Their Theories

The term "a Renaissance scientist" refers not only to a particular historic period but also to a scholar's academic orientation rooted in a wide scope of research interests. You will notice how broad these interests were. First we turn to the studies about the spiritual and the material. Then we examine humanism and scientific rationalism. After that we discuss the works of the most remarkable scholars of the period lasting from the 1400s to the early 1800s.

Epistemology: Understanding the Psychological Experience

What were the scholars' views of epistemology? How advanced were their understandings of cognition and other psychological activities? What were their approaches to the mind-body problem?

Opinions about the mind-body problem reflected at least three traditional philosophical views: materialism, dualism, and idealism. Some scholars chose to defend materialism—the view about the existence of one material substance such that the spiritual was considered part of the material world, thus understandable through the objective methods of science (Smart, 2001). Others accepted **dualism**, the tradition that claimed the existence of "parallel" spiritual and material realities. A third school of thought, idealism, emphasized the soul as primary and independent of the body and the main source of knowledge (see Table 3.2).

Please note that theoretical views are not easily catalogued and neatly packed in boxes of materialism, dualism, and idealism. Besides, scholars frequently maintained mixed views of epistemology and psychology that combined different views together.

Table 3.2 Materialism, Dualism, and Idealism: Views of Basic Psychological Activities

Questions to Address	*Materialism*	*Dualism*	*Idealism*
What is the relationship between body and soul?	Body is primary substance; soul is a function of the body.	Body and soul are independent but interacting substances.	Soul is the prime substance independent of the body.
How does the mind work: innate ideas or empirical data?	Empirical data are received through sensory organs; there is nothing in the mind that hasn't been there prior to sensations.	Empirical data are received through sensory organs; innate ideas exist.	Sensations cannot give a confirmation of the outside world; innate ideas exist.
How do human sensations work?	Sensation is a physiological process, a reflection of reality.	Sensation is a physiological process.	Sensation is a physiological process but is directed at itself.

We use these general categories to critically evaluate them and see how these views affected the development of psychology on the later stages.

Views of Human Behavior

At least two distinct views of human behavior dominated scientific thought during the mid-millennium period. One view, labeled **humanism,** emphasized the uniqueness of the subjective side of the individual: the sense of freedom, beauty, and moral responsibility. Humanism was based on the renewed interest in classical antiquity and the humanities. Supporters of **scientific rationalism**—the view that focuses on the mechanical character of the universe and human beings as the consequence—were critical of humanist views, which they considered only a fashionable trend. Humanists, in their turn, argued that science simply ignored certain features of human existence, including empathy, honor, or hope.

Humanists. The humanist outlook gradually found many supporters among writers, educators, and philosophers. New literary genres appeared that included letters, memoirs, romantic confessions, and detailed biographies and autobiographies. A new type of hero was emerging in literature and performing arts: a person of creative endeavors, an independent thinker, who is an artist and poet. The proposed ideal individual was a humanist—a person of virtues, knowledge, and passion.

The human element in behavior was clearly separated from the divine. The works of humanists centered around three major themes: dignity, independence from the intellectual authorities (i.e., religious institutions), and human frailty. Humanism carried the belief in the supremacy of the individual in the pursuit of individual goals for the sake of common good. An important scientific development of this period was the debate about the sources of human behavior. Humanists believed that individuals were generally free to exercise their will and follow their desires.

Scientific Rationalists. Supporters of scientific rationalism believed that human beings are part of the universe and thus are orderly and predictable. According to this belief, people using mathematics and physics would eventually understand the nature of psychological processes. Moral behavior was also guided by the principles of mechanics: people choose actions that bring satisfaction and avoid destructive. Self-preservation and self-interest, as in animals, were often suggested as the main generators of people's actions.

Humanists criticized rationalists and turned to history, literature, and rhetoric instead of science. In search for the roots of human motivation, many thinkers turned to observations of people's actions and applied them to various aspects of human activities, including politics and warfare. Consider the case of Niccolò Machiavelli (1469–1527), a political philosopher and writer who emphasized the importance of self-interest in human actions. He believed that people are driven by self-interest; he also maintained that such motivation was normal, natural. Machiavelli has made an important contribution to our views of human motivation. One of his favorite subjects is the individual acting in accordance with practical goals. He wrote that human beings are seldom motivated by kindness or compassion. Instead, they seek mostly wealth, status, and power. He wrote about what we call today *cynicism*—a general distrust of the moral integrity or professed motives of others, especially the powerful. To achieve their goals, people have to recognize their own shortcomings, especially negative emotions, and to learn more about other people's weaknesses to take advantage of them.

You can easily find Machiavelli's translated works in your school library.

✓ CHECK YOUR KNOWLEDGE

What is dualism?

Compare humanism and scientific rationality.

In contemporary books on history of science and philosophy, René Descartes (1596–1650) appears as one of the most influential philosophers of all time. Scores of philosophers who lived after him used his work as a source of either inspiration or criticism. What was so special about his teachings? How can we evaluate his impact on psychological views?

René Descartes: The Rational Thinker and the Cartesian Tradition

The focus of Descartes' approach to science (this approach is commonly called "Cartesian") outlived its creator and influenced several scientific branches and

ON THE WEB

Read René Descartes' brief biographical sketch on the book's website.

methods, including introspection, one of the most popular methods of psychology at the end of the 19th century. At least three areas of Descartes' teachings had a valuable impact on scientific psychological views: his theory of cognition, his intriguing descriptions of animal spirits, and an elegant concept of automatic reactions or reflexes.

"I think, therefore I am." Although Descartes valued skepticism and doubt, his overall view of knowledge was optimistic. He was certain that the external world existed and that human beings could make the right impression of it. In his view, God is perfect and does not deceive humans in their quest for accurate knowledge. If a person continues to have doubts about the accuracy of human experience, the act of doubting exists. Therefore, anyone who thinks should exist too. *Cogito ergo sum* (I think, therefore I am)—the famous phrase coined by Descartes—reflects one of his most fundamental assumptions about the nature of human existence.

Descartes also believed in innate ideas. Unlike animals, which have sensations and act like sophisticated machines responding to changes in their body and surroundings, human beings have souls. Sensations help individuals to gather knowledge. However, the human soul does not consist of sensations alone. There are fundamental innate ideas, such as extension, implanted in it before it is affected by external signals. These ideas are not learned. Human beings are born with them.

Animal Spirits. One of Descartes' books, *The Passions of the Soul* (1646/1989), is particularly interesting to psychologists. Written in 1645–1646, this remarkable volume reflected on extended correspondence between a 50-year-old Descartes and Princess Elisabeth of Bohemia, an educated woman in her mid-twenties (she is remembered today mostly because of her correspondence with Descartes). In this book, Descartes discussed a common belief at that time that the human body contained **animal spirits**—light and roaming fluids circulating rapidly around the nervous system between the brain and the muscles. (We sometimes use this term in our ordinary conversations when we talk about being in "high" or "low," "good" or "bad" spirits: when we are feeling sad or angry, or feeling great.) The animal spirits move along the nerve channels and come into contact with the brain. Because of this contact, affective states in the soul, or passions of the soul, are triggered, strengthened, or weakened. Descartes distinguished six basic passions: wonder (surprise), love, hatred, desire, joy, and sadness. All other passions represented different combinations of the original spirits. The passions, according to Descartes, influenced the soul to will or want certain actions. For example, fear is a passion that moves the soul to generate a response in the body.

René Descartes also believed that the soul was completely different from the body but functioned closely in parallel with it. In *The Passions of the Soul,* Descartes hypothesized that some part of the brain should serve as a connector or doorway between the soul and the body. He singled out the pineal gland (also called today *epiphysis*) in the

Figure 3.2 Descartes Believed That the Pineal Gland Served as a Connector Between the Soul and the Body

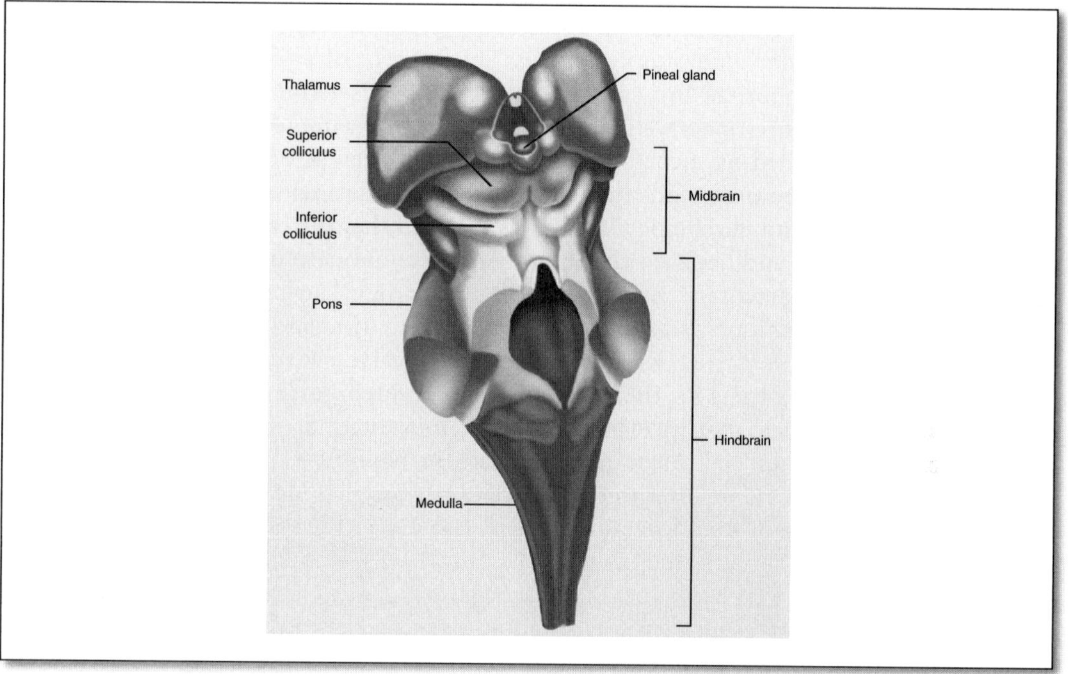

center of the brain as the connector between the soul and the body (see Figure 3.2). Signals go from the ear or from the eye to the pineal gland through animal spirits. The soul moves the gland and "pushes" the animal spirits toward the pores of the brain. Thus, different motions in the gland cause various passions. These motions are based on God's will: people are supposed to want and like things that are useful to them. Nevertheless, distortions could occur: animal spirits that move freely around the body could distort the commands from the pineal gland. People had to learn how to control their passions. Otherwise, passions could result in negative consequences such as illness (Clover, 1998; Sutton, 1998).

Automatic Reactions. Descartes developed the ideas about automatic bodily reactions as responses to external events. These views undoubtedly contributed to the general reflex theory later advanced in the 19th century. According to Descartes' theory, external motions, such as touch or sound, reach the endings of the nerves and thus affect the flow of animal spirits. The heat from the fire affects a spot on the skin and then sets in motion a chain reaction process. The spirits reach the brain through a tiny cavity and then are sent back to the muscle that moves the hand away from the fire (Descartes, 1662/2000). Such a simple description of the reflex action explained the nature of automatic reactions that do not necessarily require a thought process.

Briefly, what was Descartes' contribution to psychology? From the 21st-century standpoint, many of Descartes' ideas about psychology appear unsophisticated, naïve, or simply untrue. The concept of animal spirits has become only a metaphor used in casual conversations. His assumption about the pineal gland did not resonate well even in the minds of his immediate followers and was quickly rejected as incorrect (Gaukroger, Schuster, & Sutton, 2000). However, taken in the context of his time, his teachings made a remarkable contribution to physiology and psychology. Descartes believed that the brain resembled a working machine and believed that mathematics could help in understanding of the brain's fundamentals. In the 20th century, Alan Turing (see Chapter 12), a founder of computer science, advanced mathematical biology based on those initial ideas of Descartes (Kirkebøen, 2000). Descartes' writings about animal spirits served as a basis for the development in contemporary theories of emotions, especially those that incorporate cognitive evaluations into affective processes. Indeed, a sound of music may generate in us either joy or displeasure: it all depends on how we interpret that music! His original ideas about reflexes served as a foundation for more advanced physiological theories that were developed more than 200 years after his death (Kenny, 1968). Ivan Pavlov, the Russian physiologist who won the Nobel Prize in 1904, was said to have installed a sculptured bust of Descartes at his research laboratory as a sign of his personal respect for the great thinker.

Descartes was a rationalist, believing in the power of innate ideas. But, most important, René Descartes was among the first scientists who began to understand the soul as a functioning machine. Rational and divine, the soul in the minds of many scientists was above and beyond any scientific investigation. Descartes dared to challenge this view. He considered the body and physiological processes as mediators between the nature and the soul and assumed that the laws of math and mechanics could explain the most complicated processes of the mind. Descartes' teachings undermined theology. No wonder the religious authorities considered his books dangerous.

Many European thinkers at that time supported a holistic view in the study of human behavior and experience. One such thinker was Benedict de Spinoza.

Monism of Benedict Spinoza

The central element of the teachings of Benedict Spinoza (1632–1677) is substance: all existence is contained in one substance, which can be named differently, such as nature, universe, or God. We may understand it as consisting of two key attributes: extension (objective) and thought (subjective). Spinoza believed in universal rules governing everything taking place within the universe. In the material world, there is a hierarchy of objects, with God as an infinite substance and the highest

IN THEIR OWN WORDS

René Descartes. *I now notice that there is a vast difference between [being asleep and being awake], in that dreams are never linked by memory with all the other actions of life as waking experiences are. . . . But when I distinctly see where things come from and where and when they come to me, and when I can connect my perceptions of them with the whole of the rest of my life without a break, then I am quite certain that when I encounter these things I am not asleep but awake.* (translated by Cottingham, Stoothoff, & Murdoch, 1984)

Here Descartes makes interesting observations about consciousness and its altered states, such as sleep. He writes about self-awareness, attention, and comprehension of the connectedness of things around him as the criteria for being awake. This is an example of self-observation. About 200 years later, a new method based on self-observation, called introspection, would become very popular in early psychological laboratories. We address this topic in Chapter 4.

substance. Human beings were part of nature and were the carriers of the two attributes, objective and subjective. The human mind corresponded to the world of material objects. Ideas and objects were two sides of the same substance: nature (Spinoza, 1677/1985).

Geometry and Psychology. Spinoza believed that a scholar should act as a mathematician, unbiased and rational. He admired the precision and logic of geometric formulas and thought that mathematics and geometry could be applied to the study of mental activities, emotions in particular. This made Spinoza a distinct contributor to the study of emotions (Davidson, 1999).

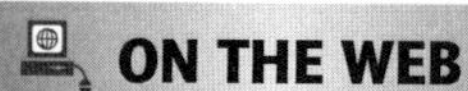

ON THE WEB

Read Spinoza's brief biographical sketch on the book's website.

Spinoza believed that the external events that contribute to self-preservation are associated with pleasure, and the events undermining self-preservation are associated with pain or displeasure. People too often follow their impulses and become virtual slaves to their wishes (a view formulated long before Spinoza by Socrates and the Stoics in ancient Greece and Rome). Spinoza believed that people lose freedom because they are trapped in the continual search for gratification of their wishes without knowing why they do so. To avoid this endless quest for pleasure, people should know more about the causes of their own actions. This knowledge can make them relatively free. Why? Because people are capable of understanding their emotions and wishes and are also capable of restraining them and forming a reasonable view on what is possible in their lives and what is not.

Spinoza's views of individual knowledge appear quite modern. Consider, for example, his recurrent assertion that our rational understanding of choices and possibilities help us to avoid mistakes. Of course, Spinoza did not invent this therapeutic principle. Nevertheless, an interesting parallel can be drawn between Spinoza's prescriptions and some contemporary principles of cognitive-behavior therapy aimed at understanding of the real reasons behind people's actions (Farmer & Chapman, 2007). Although contemporary therapeutic techniques are very diverse, their underlying idea may not be that different from Spinoza's assumptions: people have to understand the causes of their behavior; they have to understand the sources of their pleasure and suffering and, based on this knowledge, reevaluate their lives.

Now we turn to another remarkable scholar, Gottfried Leibniz, who was Spinoza's contemporary, just 16 years younger. They lived hundreds of miles apart and maintained radically different lifestyles; Spinoza lived in seclusion, while Leibniz served at many royal courts. They met briefly, not long before Spinoza's death, and discussed their philosophical ideas (some historians say that Leibniz could have used some of Spinoza's ideas without giving him credit, but these are just assumptions). Yet they both defended the view of **rationalism**, a position in epistemology also shared by Descartes: reason is the prime source of knowledge; the thinking mind, not sensations alone, should provide justification of truth.

Monadology of Gottfried Wilhelm Leibniz

Like Spinoza, Gottfried Wilhelm Leibniz (1646–1716) developed a holistic view of nature and human beings. According to his view, the universe is made up of an infinite number of spiritual forces called **monads**—windowless entities—each reflecting the state of every other according to the established principle of harmony. A monad is not dimensional but contains within itself the potential of all the properties that it will exhibit in the future, and it also contains the marks of all the properties it had in the past. One of Leibniz's ideas was that everything in this dynamic world is rooted in the past but is also "pregnant" with the elements of the future. Speaking in today's terms, for example, your behavior at this moment is determined by your experiences and your plans.

According to Leibniz, the soul has an infinite number of monads and therefore perceptions. Monads can perceive, and the soul possesses "little perceptions" that are not conscious but could become so because of memory and attention (called *apperception*). While listening to the roar of the waves on the beach, he wrote, we do not hear the sound made by every wave or pebble. What we hear is a composite sound of many "little" sounds. The concept of little perceptions also helps us to understand the nature of personality: people gradually develop numerous individual habits and characteristics that, when combined, make a distinct individual personality (Leibniz, 1670/1951). The soul possesses several areas of knowledge distinguished by the strength of apperception: clear knowledge, fragmented knowledge, and unconscious knowledge. Leibniz is one of the first scholars to have identified a category of unconscious psychological phenomena.

Like Descartes, he believed in the existence of innate ideas because he felt it was impossible to derive certain abstract ideas directly from experience. Such ideas are not necessarily conscious; they could exist in the form of a potential: an inclination for reasoning, such as in planning work or anticipating something that has not happened before and has no analogy to past experience. People have an advantage over animals: the latter have no reason and can only move from one idea to another by association.

Leibniz was a supporter of **psychological parallelism**. This view suggests that physical and mental processes are set to develop in parallel courses. Imagine a pair of clocks showing the same time when, in fact, they work absolutely independently from each other. Parallelism was a view shared by many psychologists later in the 19th century. Leibniz's ideas provided theoretical foundations for a number of psychological theories in the fields of human development, perception, and unconscious processes. Leibniz philosophy also influenced major theoretical postulates of psychoanalysis, which we examine in Chapter 8.

Descartes, Spinoza, and Leibniz represented philosophy and science of continental Europe. The British Isles produced their own remarkable generation of scholars. We discuss next the views of Hobbes, Locke, Berkeley, and Hume and their impact on psychology.

✓ CHECK YOUR KNOWLEDGE

What are the animal spirits according to Descartes?

What is rationalism as a point of view shared by Descartes and Spinoza?

What is psychological parallelism?

Materialism and Empiricism: Thomas Hobbes

Thomas Hobbes (1588–1679) gained an excellent reputation as a specialist in optics, mathematician, prolific translator of the classics, and a writer on legal and religious issues. Born in England and educated at Oxford, Hobbes was a loyal supporter of the monarchy and served, at one point of his career, as a tutor to the future king of England, Charles II. Hobbes continued to be active until his eighties, but he was in poor health, suffering from symptoms resembling Parkinson's disease. Refusing to stop his work, he dictated his thoughts to his secretary (Ewin, 1991). Hobbes maintained innovative materialist teachings and believed in the power of human experience. At the same time, he developed conservative views of the monarchy and societal order. These were two distinct parts of his scientific legacy. Let's begin with his materialists views.

Materialism. Hobbes believed that the essence of human behavior is in physical motion and that the principles of Galileo's mechanics could explain sensation, emotions, motivation, and even moral values. The same principles could be used to describe society. Hobbes agreed with the Greek materialists, Democritus and Epicurus in particular, who gave distinct mechanical descriptions to mental processes. Sensations, in Hobbes's view, were complex internal motions in the body that were caused by the movement of the external object. Thinking was a process of movements in the brain. He believed that dreams occurred because the body accumulated experiences or motions within it so that at night these motions continued. According to Hobbes, free will was also the result of mechanical processes. Complex voluntary movements helped people gain pleasure and avoid pain. Because of the law of inertia, sensations resulted in imagination or thinking. Like Plato and Aristotle, Thomas Hobbes evoked the term *association* to explain the functioning of the mind. Unlike René Descartes, however, who emphasized the importance of higher mental processes, Hobbes believed that associations explain all psychological processes, from simple sensations to complex thought processes and rational behavior.

Empiricism. As you remember, René Descartes understood the soul as separate from the body, a distinct entity. Thomas Hobbes, to the contrary, understood the soul as mechanical movements in the body. This was a reductionist view, which gained significant popularity in that period. **Reductionism** is an approach to explaining the nature of complex processes by reducing them to the interactions of their elements or underlying processes, such as psychological functions are described as simple physiological reactions or reflexes.

Hobbes criticized the Cartesian teachings about innate ideas that exist prior to experience. He laid foundations for the empirical branch of epistemology and psychology and supported **empiricism,** the scientific belief that experience, especially sensory processes, is the main source of knowledge. Supporters of empiricism emphasized the importance of direct experience, as opposed to abstract thinking. Hobbes maintained that human judgment should be guided by science because scientific knowledge is neutral. People's opinions are unreliable because they tend to be biased.

Social Views. One of Hobbes's greatest concerns, according to his own account, was the social and political chaos in England. Hobbes lived in the 17th century, the time of the most dramatic social upheaval in England's history. The civil war deeply divided the people for many years. Only the strong survived the turmoil.

Witnessing the chaos, Hobbes claimed that human nature is extremely selfish; self-preservation is the main driving force behind human action. Self-interest, according to Hobbes, was the essence of love, pride, and self-esteem. This view was not necessarily original in the history of thought. However, Hobbes gave these ideas a new life by applying them to the events he had personally witnessed or learned about. This view had many supporters then and now. A handful of contemporary scholars, for example, believe that self-preservation was an important mechanism of evolution responsible for the development of many psychological features such as compassion, care for the weak, and even sacrifice in the name of the group (Kurzban & Houser, 2005; Ridley, 1998). However, Hobbes's suggestion about human selfishness was always received in history with a measure of skepticism. Many of his critics remain hopeful that violence and ignorance are not necessarily inseparable elements of human existence.

Thomas Hobbes believed there is no immaterial substance such as the soul, and physical processes are only the accounts of mental functions. Voluntary behavior is a purely mechanical movement. People move toward sources that give pleasure and avoid anything that gives displeasure. In a way, this is selfish behavior. Yet, according to Hobbes, if people are capable of learning, they can understand their mutual obligations and thus act responsibly toward one another.

Another independent thinker, humanist, and critic whose writings appear in his many essays on education and knowledge was John Locke.

The Empiricism and Liberalism of John Locke

An outstanding figure in English science, John Locke (1632–1704) was a man of many talents: a philosopher, medical researcher, teacher, economist, and political scientist. Many of Locke's writings criticized authoritarianism, which made him a respected figure in the liberal political circles. He is also considered today a major contributor to psychological views of the 17th century.

John Locke distinguished two processes in human experience: sensation and reflection. He believed that complex ideas arise from simple ones because people can observe them and reflect on them. Locke was a supporter of empiricism. His ideas became a foundation of studies of consciousness in the 19th century. According to Locke, reflection is not an independent source of ideas. Reflection contains nothing that has not previously been in our sensation (King, 1991). Children's minds are formed as a result of their interaction with the world. In the *Essay Concerning Human Understanding* (1690/1994), John Locke criticized the doctrine of innate ideas (the views defended by Descartes and Leibniz). If ideas were inborn, they would have been known to every human—adults and children alike—as well as both smart and feeble-minded individuals. In addition, he argued, if these ideas did exist, every person would carry the same moral beliefs. However, this is not the case in reality. Locke believed that the child's mind is a "clean board," or in Latin, **tabula rasa**. Experiences can be recorded in the mind in a fashion similar to the way in which teachers use a piece of chalk to write on the board.

Following a tradition in epistemology, Locke continued to distinguish between the primary and secondary qualities of things. Primary qualities are inseparable from the body and reflect the qualities of objects; these included extension, motion, number, or firmness. Secondary qualities, such as color or taste, exist only in sensations. Why do certain motions produce sensations of sweetness (when we taste, for example, water in a glass) or loudness (when we hear the sound of a wave)? One of the explanations that Locke gave was that God had decided to connect perceptions in the brain to physical motions outside human bodies. Locke was deeply convinced that education was the solution to many societal problems. He believed that moral values could be taught to children: the child ought to develop good feelings about the right moral acts and negative feelings about immoral behavior. He considered positive emotions to be important in education because they help children to learn better.

Locke was a materialist who believed in the cause-and-effect relationship between the body and soul. Not everyone in England shared the same view. Nicolas Malebrance (1638–1715), for example, believed that a spiritual substance has no contact with material bodies. Ralph Cudworth (1617–1688), an English philosopher known as a member of the "Cambridge Platonists," also maintained that knowledge is not gained through sensation; it is obtained through the mind grasping eternal truths. However, one of the most remarkable scholars representing these and similar views was George Berkeley, whose ideas we next discuss.

George Berkeley: Idealism and Empiricism

In the 18th century, **deism**, the belief that God has created the universe but abandoned earthly affairs afterward, became increasingly popular among the educated European elites (Smart, 2001). Deism encouraged a scientific worldview. However, despite the development of the scientific theories of cognition—including the works of Descartes, Spinoza, Hobbes, and Locke—science could not produce a unifying theory explaining how the mind worked.

George Berkeley (1685–1753) took advantage of this situation. An Irish religious scholar and representative of empiricism, he believed that experience, especially as it concerned the sensory processes, was the major source of knowledge. However, Berkeley challenged the views of Thomas Hobbes and John Locke and developed an intriguing approach to epistemology. This approach found support among scholars who were disenchanted with materialism.

☞ CASE IN POINT

Berkeley's Visit to America. George Berkeley was among many people who visited America in the 18th century as missionaries. As an aspiring man in his thirties, he spent almost 3 years between 1728 and 1731 in the colonies (America was a British colony at that time), attempting to put forth an ambitious project to build a seminary for the sons of colonists and Native Americans in Bermuda. Berkeley had settled with his wife on a farm near Newport, Rhode Island. The colonies, at that time, were considered by visitors to be hopelessly provincial lands, not a desirable place to settle for a long time. During his stay in America, Berkeley met with many American intellectuals (such as Samuel Johnson, the first president of King's College–Columbia University today) who later became prominent figures in education and science. Unfortunately, contrary to what had been promised to Berkeley, his missionary project was not funded by the Parliament in London. Berkeley was obviously disappointed and decided to leave America. Before sailing back to Europe, he donated his farm to Yale College, now Yale University, and divided his library between the colleges at Harvard and Yale.

To Exist Is to Be Perceived. To understand Berkeley is to comprehend his famous principle: to exist is to be perceived (*esse est percipi* in Latin). Berkeley's position as an idealist was close to the main postulates of **solipsism**—the theory claiming the self as the only entity that can be known and verified.

Solipsism was not a new theory. Similar ideas existed in several Eastern philosophical traditions, including Taoism and Buddhism. These philosophies claimed that experience is a product of reflection and language; experience is not necessarily caused by the physical reality of objects. Berkeley developed these and similar ideas further. How do we know that the desk in this room exists? We know it by looking at it. We can touch it and knock on it to hear the sound. In other words, we could prove the existence of the desk by using our sensations. But this also means that, as far as this argument goes, no matter what we do, we always use our sensations to prove the desk's existence! Therefore, every object requires a perceiving mind. Berkeley did not deny the existence of the world. To avoid confusion, Berkeley included God as an ultimate observer: the world exists so long as God observes it.

At age 25, Berkeley produced *Principles of Human Knowledge.* Berkeley did not make the distinction between primary (size, motion, number, firmness) and secondary qualities (such as color or taste), because even primary qualities, according to him, can be perceived subjectively and differently. What seems hard to one person could be perceived as soft to another (Berkeley, 1710/1975). Berkeley claimed that visual ideas are only signs of tactile ideas. When we hear a word, he argued, we think of the object this word represents. The word itself is not the object. In a similar fashion, if we see something, such as a table, we think of a corresponding idea of the table. But, as the word is not an object, the thought of it is not that object either.

How can we develop knowledge about the world if the only reality we deal with is ideas? If the existence of things is in question, how can we learn about the objects and their connections? For Berkeley, there is no problem here. He believed that although there is an unknown substance behind the sensations, an individual is still able to learn to coordinate ideas generated by various sensations to judge length, shape, scope, intensity, or magnitude. These properties are immediately perceived only by touch. The ideas of one sense become signs of ideas of the other senses. We learn about ideas as well as their connections. For Berkeley, science became a system of natural signs. The scientist is one who puts ideas in a systematic manner. In a way, an active mind is a guarantor of the existence of the world.

Berkeley also wrote about "visibles" and "tangibles," the smallest indivisible points of experience. These were later called *sensory thresholds.* Empirical studies of thresholds were conducted in the 19th century by several scientists, including Wilhelm Wundt, a founder of experimental psychology.

Further Development of British Empiricism: David Hume

In many textbooks, for chronological reasons, David Hume's psychological views are almost always discussed next to theoretical views of George Berkeley, and this text is no exception. Yet the lives of these two scholars, the ultimate goals of their writings, their lifestyles, and even the circles of people they were attached to have been noticeably different.

ON THE WEB

Read David Hume's brief biographical sketch on the book's website.

David Hume (1711–1776) stated that individuals do not have any strong reasons to believe in the existence of the external world. He was also skeptical about people's ability to understand the causes of their actions: they mistakenly believe that the future should resemble the past, but they do not have supportive evidence. For example, in our mind, if B follows A, this fact contains no information about the connection between these two events. Only mental impressions are perceivable. These mental impressions are connected by association, custom, or habit. For example, because of the conjunction of heat and flame in our experience, we expect the one (heat) to follow from the appearance of the other (flames of a fire). We are accustomed to observing objects or events in a single, flowing sequence of perceptions. We know that spring comes after winter, but this does not mean the winter is the cause of the spring (Hume, 1777/1987).

Naturalism and Instrumentalism. Hume contributed to psychology by developing pragmatic views in the fields of **naturalism** and **instrumentalism**. Naturalism refers to the view that observable events should be explained only by natural causes without assuming the existence of divine, paranormal, or supernatural causes such as "magic" or "evil eye." Instrumentalism applied to Hume's works means that human action is reasonable as long as it justifies this individual's goals. To better explain naturalism and instrumentalism, let's consider the way Hume approached a delicate subject: suicide. Described primarily in literary pieces and folk stories, suicide appeared in the eyes of his contemporaries as a consequence of an extreme, irrational passion. From a religious point of view, suicide was a terrible sin, for only God makes decisions about life and death. Almost 120 years before the French sociologist Émile Durkheim (1887/1997) provided the first systematic scientific investigation of this phenomenon, David Hume, in the essay *On Suicide* challenged religious doctrines on suicide. He wrote that suicide is a natural event that shouldn't be condemned. The lives of people depend on the same laws as the lives of animals, he wrote. And these are all subjected to the general laws of matter and motion. The life of a person is of no more greater importance to the universe than that of an oyster. According to Hume, if there is no crime in diverting the waters of a river, there shouldn't be a crime found in suicide. Death from suicide is as natural as death from a predator or an infection. There is no decision of God represented. Hume wrote sarcastically that if the clergy saw suicide as a rebellion against the Creator, then all our attempts to alter nature, build bridges, and cultivate the ground should be called rebellion against God as well (Hume, 1777/1987). Hume's position made a significant impact on humanistic psychology and psychological theories of individual choice.

Hume also criticized the religious interpretations of immortality. "Nothing in this world is perpetual," he wrote (Hume, 1777/1987, p. 597). He rejected the concept of innate ideas. Neither the body nor the mind possesses any sensation before birth, nor do they after death—a belief that was significant because it was contrary to most fundamental religious teachings and most people's beliefs of the time. Hume hoped that people would assign less religious mystery to the actions of the soul and understand human behavior and mental life as habits and associations.

Hume was against divorce. He used several psychological arguments to justify his opposition. For example, his major concern was the fate of children of divorce. He also suggested that marriage should not be based on feelings alone. It is true, he wrote, that the heart of the man naturally strives for liberty and should hate everything to which the heart is confined. On the other hand, individuals are capable of friendship, which is a sedate affection, "conducted by reason and cemented by the habit" (Hume, 1777/1987, p. 189). If people understand that separation is easy, they are likely to pursue easier escapes from marriage instead of working on their relationships. If there is no sense of stability, husbands and wives would likely pursue their own selfish interests. This is quite a contemporary observation, as you can see.

Hume's Views of Personality. In addition to his fundamental works on epistemology, Hume wrote a number of essays on human behavior. In these works, he developed views of an individual's personality. For example, in four essays on ancient Greek and Roman philosophies, Hume described four personality types:

1. The Epicurean displays elegance and seeks pleasure.
2. The Stoic is a person of action and virtue.
3. The Platonist is the person of contemplation and philosophical devotion.
4. The Skeptic is the person of critical thinking.

Creating categories and clusters was a general trend in social sciences of the time. Hume also wrote about national character, a psychological and behavioral profile typical in people of a nation. Hume believed that social factors such as government policies, customs, resources, and relations with the neighbors are far more critical issues influencing character than climate or geographical location. The social status and wealth determine the behavior of individuals. A soldier and a priest, for instance, who both live in the same natural environment, may be completely different in terms of their characters because they had different moral upbringings. He stated that the uncertainty of the lives of soldiers makes them lavish, generous, and brave. They may appear ignorant because their lifestyle requires more action and less intellectualization than that of a priest. Hume also believed that revenge is a natural passion of mankind, but he felt it is most dominant in priests and in women. He stated that these two groups are deprived of the immediate release of anger and, consequently, seek out other venues to release their tension.

ON THE WEB

Who are more honest: the Swiss or the Irish? Who is funnier: a Frenchman or a Spaniard? Read more about Hume's writings on national character on the book's website.

Hume's views were critical of organized religion and its doctrines. He understood the possible ramifications that could follow the publication of his blasphemous ideas about the soul, individual choice, and independent thinking. The church was strongly against such views, and Hume could have faced legal persecution. However, he found support among powerful European elites. Despite serious moral, political, and legal challenges imposed by the religious authorities, more people of power at that time were willing to critically examine religion and acknowledge the importance of individual choice.

Hume was a scholar of many interests approaching psychological issues from various positions including philosophy, natural and political science, and even geography. This tendency to pursue multidisciplinary interests was a common practice. Hume inspired many of his followers by the scope and independent nature of his ideas. Other philosophers earned their reputation by studying their subjects in depth. David Hartley's role in psychology has been determined by his association theory that attempts to describe how the human mind worked.

Development of Associationism: David Hartley

The son of a clergyman, David Hartley (1705–1775) had lost his parents by the age of 15. Because of this tragedy, he matured earlier than did most of his peers. He decided to pursue education and to dedicate his life to medicine. His scientific interests, nevertheless, remained very broad. Hartley liked mathematics and wrote on a variety of topics in education, sociology, and psychology. He was the author of *Observations on Man, His Frame, His Duty, and His Expectations,* published in 1749. This book is an excellent literary and scientific attempt to combine science and spirituality, physiology and moral psychology. This book gradually received a wide recognition in Europe and the United States.

Physical Associations Explain Mental Activity. Hartley believed that sensation is the consequence of a pulsation of the microscopic elements inside the nerves. Pleasure, according to his assumptions, is the result of regular vibrations. Pain, on the other hand, is the result of intense and violent vibrations. These vibrations leave physical marks in the brain, which should be a foundation for memory. People must remember pleasant and unpleasant events. Memory helps people to avoid unpleasant situations and pursue more pleasant outcomes. Such marks, or ideas, are associated with many others to form complex associations that help individuals to function properly. For example, a person's heart will beat faster when she encounters something that has caused her fear in the past. Such reactions can become automatic: they take place without lengthy contemplation and are caused by the associative processes in the body and brain.

Hartley's ideas seem to resemble the position of René Descartes on reflexes described earlier. However, unlike Descartes, who believed in the existence of higher mental functions of a nonmaterial nature, Hartley believed that physical associations could explain practically all mental activities of an individual. Through the physiological connections of neural impulses in the brain, any sensation or muscular movement stimulates other sensations and movements. Abstract ideas are complex associations. Most of the things people do during the day are automatic: we don't think too much about how to hold a fork or how to open a door. Yet there are activities that can be more complex than a set of learned responses. Hartley called these activities "decomplex actions" (emphasizing that they derive from complex actions) that involve the association of movements with perceptions in one or more sensory modalities (Hartley, 1749/1999). Hartley's ideas were developed later in the 19th century by other notable scholars, including James Mill and John Stuart Mill, who were the founders of a psychological school called "association psychology."

Personality. Hartley offered an original view of personality. He distinguished six clusters of features or traits, and divided them into two groups. The first group includes imagination, ambition, and self-interest. The second group includes sympathy, theopathy, and the moral sense. *Imagination* refers to objects as sources of pleasure or displeasure. *Ambition* is the realization of one's own status in the eyes of other people. *Self-interest* manages the demands of imagination and ambition. *Sympathy* refers to the feelings of other people. *Theopathy* refers to the individual's moral sense and connection with spiritual issues such as religion. Even though Hartley's theory of personality is based on theoretical assumptions, it shares common ground with trait theories of personality developed in the works of Gordon Allport, Raymond Cattell, and others in the 20th century. Like in Hartley's writings, these theories state that individuals possess relatively stable and unique characteristics that influence behavior.

The next philosopher on our list did not write specifically about psychology. Yet his interests focused around human cognition: perception and thinking in particular. Critics commonly evaluate his work as a symbolic passage or "bridge" between the rationalist and empiricist traditions in philosophy of that period.

Connecting Rationalism and Empiricism: Immanuel Kant

Immanuel Kant (1724–1804) was a German philosopher (although to be precise, he lived in East Prussia and died long before the unification the German states in 1871) commonly viewed as one of the most influential thinkers of all times.

Innate Categories. Kant believed that we, as humans, could never understand the order of the world by making observations and relying on our senses alone. We make numerous mistakes when we try to explain the world and ask general questions about the causation, God, nature, the soul, happiness, and so forth. To reduce confusion, people have to switch their attention from general inquiries about the world to the study of specific phenomena.

Each individual has innate abilities to understand reality from a preprogrammed position. To illustrate this Kantian view, please answer this question: What is time? You may say it is an interval between two events. So, what is an interval then? According to Kant, time and space are the innate concepts (or categories) that are not learned. They are "installed" in us. Speaking in contemporary terms, a category is software allowing us to see the world as three-dimensional and organized in periods. If we had the preexisting concept of space as two-dimensional, we would have never seen this world in three dimensions! The ideas of Immanuel Kant, especially those related to the possibility of knowledge prior to experience, remained popular for many years among so-called mental philosophers (see Chapter 4).

Our experience is important, however. The external world provides the material that we sense. The world makes sense to us because we have innate "tools" to comprehend it. Although we can understand the world around us thorough the kaleidoscope of events, we can never understand its true nature.

Moral Values. Kant created a unique theory of moral behavior. This is a philosophical theory. However, it influenced many later psychological theories of human behavior. Kant was trying to find one unifying principle for moral actions, rejecting ideas popular at that time that morality is relative and depends on the interests of people. Although the discussion of the philosophical foundations for his moral philosophy is beyond our task, we underline that Kant's views echoed the ancient "Golden Rule": act according to your rational will but assume that your action, to be considered moral, should become a universal law for others to follow. He believed that such a moral imperative should be innate, which means, in contemporary terms, that all human beings should have a natural predisposition for moral behavior. Many years later, founders and supporters of humanistic psychology and its many branches emphasize the moral side of human behavior and, like Kant, they celebrate moral act as a natural expression.

✓ CHECK YOUR KNOWLEDGE

What were Hobbes's views related to innate ideas?

Explain solipsism.

Explain naturalism and instrumentalism.

What was Kant's "Golden Rule"?

French Materialism and Enlightenment

After the end of the 16th century, France became the dominant economic and military power in Europe. By the end of the 18th century, the people of France had experienced dramatic social cataclysms that included the French Revolution. These events changed the French principles of government. They also brought about change in people's lifestyles, values, and beliefs. The events of the French Revolution laid a foundation for the development of the contemporary social climate of market capitalism. Although the church's ability to influence politics had diminished on all levels, the clergy was strong enough to influence science and to single out and punish atheism as well as anyone who attempted to promote it. One of such intellectual rebels was the Frenchman Paul-Henri Thiry.

Materialism of Paul-Henri Thiry

Much science of the time hoped to eliminate the mystery of human behavior. Emotions or thinking could be explained if one understood how the brain works. What is called the soul is merely the physical entity, which strives for physical pleasure and disintegrates when the body dies.

Paul-Henri Thiry (1723–1789), known also as Baron d'Holbach, maintained a similar point of view. Born in Germany in December 1723 and baptized under the name of Paul-Henri Thiry, Holbach was brought up from the age of 12 by his French uncle, Franciscus Adam d'Holbach. From him, Paul-Henri received his new last name, title, and substantial wealth in 1753. Educated at the prestigious University of Leiden, Holbach wrote numerous books and essays in which he defended the materialist view of psychological processes and revolutionary ideas about the necessity of change in society.

Paul-Henri Thiry believed that the brain is capable of producing within itself a great variety of physical motion called intellectual faculties.

In his materialist outlook, the brain is the center of all activities attributed to the soul. To understand how the brain works, scientists should put aside absurdities of religious doctrines and combine their efforts as physicians, natural philosophers, and anatomists (Holbach, 1770/1970). How does the brain function? It connects the nerves distributed through every part of the body. An impulse or motion occurs in the nerve, and this impulse modifies the brain. As a consequence, the brain reacts by sending impulses to bodily organs or limbs. The brain could act upon itself and become capable of producing within itself a great variety of motion called intellectual faculties.

Holbach translated into French scores of manuscripts on religion and political philosophy. He contributed nearly 400 articles to the famous *Encyclopédie* edited by philosopher Denis Diderot. The goal of the *Encyclopédie* was to sketch and summarize contemporary knowledge in the fields of arts and sciences and to make the knowledge accessible to a large audience. One of several distinct goals of the publication was to disseminate the idea of individual freedom and sovereignty of people over authority. In addition to his publications, Holbach was best known for hosting his famous *salon*—a common name for periodic "get-togethers" of people of social status and intellectual merit.

For psychologists, as for any scientists, it is essential to have the support of colleagues. It is also important to communicate ideas freely. Holbach's salon was known for its stimulating intellectual atmosphere of support, the role it played in the development of materialist and atheist ideas, and its contribution to the intellectual tradition of the French Revolution. The guests at the salon were prominent intellectuals, atheists, and ardent opponents of authoritarian power. Famous people as well as ambassadors from countries across Europe attended dinners served at the salon. Biographers mention many names on the salon guest list, including the American Ambassador Benjamin Franklin and the philosopher David Hume.

Another original contributor to materialist ideas and radical empiricism was Etienne Bonnot. We turn next to his views.

Sensationalism of Condillac

Etienne Bonnot, Abbé de Condillac (1714–1780), frequently referred today by his royal title, Condillac, had health problems as a child, so that by the age of 12 he still could not read. He advanced rapidly as a teenager and continued his education at the Sorbonne, the most prestigious university in France. He supported the materialist views and argued that sensations could provide all the information for all mental operations, including abstract thinking. The central idea of his *Treatise on the Sensations*, published in 1754 (Condillac, 1754/2002), was to convince the reader that reflection, which was an important element in other materialists' teachings, including John Locke's position, is based entirely on sensations. All mental operations and faculties, including memory, dreaming, and thinking, are special forms of sensation.

Trying to explain his views, Condillac presented a model or allegory: a statue (known to historians of science as the *Condillac statue*). Imagine, he asked, a statue that is passive at the beginning when it is not connected to the world. Then, the statue acquires the senses—one by one, from the most basic, which is smell, to the most precise, which is touch. After acquiring all of the senses, the statue obtains the distinction between the self, which is a collection of all sensations, and the non-self. Then understanding arrives. A set of focused sensations is called *attention*. An impression may remain even after the original object disappears. This impression is called *memory*. People attach labels or words to certain combinations of sensations. These words are called *ideas* or *concepts*, and they are supposed to bring clarity and order to people's knowledge. Thinking brings simple sensations into complex ideas. Humankind's progress is reflected in the improvement of thinking. (See Figure 3.3.)

Figure 3.3 Acquisition of Knowledge, According to Condillac

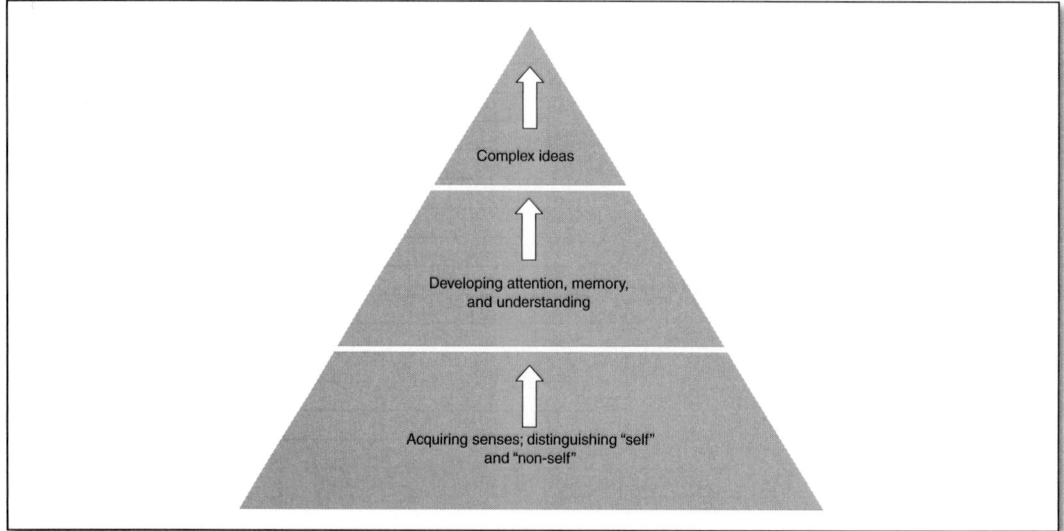

As a member of French and Prussian academies of sciences, Condillac developed a theory of education. He suggested that the stages of the child's development resemble the stages of the development of humankind, so that they go from simple and unsophisticated to more complex and mature. He believed that children should be educated according to the skills they develop at each stage and that teachers should adjust their methods accordingly. These ideas were further advanced in evolutionary and cultural theories of human development put together later in the 20th century. (We examine these theories further in Chapter 5.)

Mechanism of La Mettrie

Although his father wanted him to be a priest, Julien Offray de La Mettrie (1709–1751) chose a career in medicine. He later interrupted his work as a physician and turned to philosophy. La Mettrie was especially proficient in anatomy and gradually developed materialist views to explain the functioning of the soul. He supported the ideas of **mechanism** suggesting that almost everything about human beings can be effectively explained in mechanical terms. The most notable work of his was *Man a Machine,* the book, in which he defended a view that a human being is just a complex machine. Each tiny fiber or part of a living body moves by a particular principle. People are trained to perform simple and complex tasks in the same way that animals are trained to look for food and protect themselves. A geometrician, according to La Mettrie, learns to perform the most complicated calculations in the same way as a trained animal learns to perform tricks. Even the most complex forms of communication may be reduced to simple sounds or words that pass from one person's mouth to another person's ears. The differences between animals are based on their structural organization. Most observations made by La Mettrie were interesting but speculative. As an example, he drew parallels between the size of an animal's brain and aggressiveness: animals with smaller brains tend to be fiercer. Creatures with intelligent behavioral reactions show less instinctive behavior.

Published in 1748, *Man a Machine* brought La Mettrie enthusiastic support of many readers. His critics, however, believed that the book was a gross simplification of facts. Religious authorities saw it as a disrespectful attempt to besmirch the church by excluding the very idea of the soul as a divine entity. It was an unusual case when some scientists joined theologians and religious officials—including Calvinists, Catholics, and Lutherans—in their condemnation of the book (Vartanian, 1960; Wellmann, 1992). Some supporters of secular science did not like the extreme reductionism of La Mettrie's theory: explaining phenomena on one level in terms of phenomena on a lower, seemingly less complex level. Unable to work under the fire of criticism, La Mettrie left France to seek a safer and more tolerant social environment. He found protection and financial support at the royal court of Frederic the Great, King of Prussia, who later wrote in the eulogy dedicated to La Mettrie, "A good man and a wise physician."

IN THEIR OWN WORDS

La Mettrie on Dreams. *The soul and the body fall asleep together. As the motion of the blood is calmed, a sweet feeling of peace and quiet spreads through the whole mechanism. The soul feels itself little by little growing heavy as the eyelids droop, and loses its tenseness, as the fibers of the brain relax; thus little by little it becomes as if paralyzed and with it all the muscles of the body. . . . A single fright in the midst of our dreams makes the heart beat at double speed and snatches us from needed and delicious repose, as a real grief or an urgent need would do.* (La Mettrie, 1748/1994)

Like most thinkers at that time, La Mettrie maintained sexist attitudes. He wrote that in women, passion is stronger than reason, and therefore women are prone to tenderness, affection, and quick feelings. Men have solid brains and nerves and, therefore, have stronger personality features and more vigorous minds. Because women generally lack education, men have better opportunities to demonstrate strength of mind and body. Men are more grateful, generous, and constant in friendship. As if he attempted to bring some balance in the description of men and women, La Mettrie mentions women's beauty as their superior feature (La Mettrie, 1748).

As you can see, scientific ideas and secular views frequently coexisted with stereotypical judgments. However, it is incorrect to assume that French scholars maintained reactionary views of social life. Quite the contrary, France gave to the world many progressive-minded philosophers, like Voltaire and Rousseau.

Moral and Social Development: Voltaire and Rousseau

Another remarkable French thinker and writer, Francois-Marie Arouet de Voltaire (1694–1778) remains in history as one of the most influential representatives of the French Enlightenment. He believed that human beings have a potential for moral behavior rooted in respect and kindness to other people. Voltaire did not believe that there should be an idea or principle of morality innate in the soul. People are not born with the idea that they must be righteous and virtuous. Education and experience make people who they are.

Perhaps the most remarkable views of education and the development of children appear in the writings of Jean-Jacques Rousseau (1712–1778). He openly glorified the very early stages of human civilization, the view endorsed today by some cultural anthropologists and psychologists (Shiraev & Levy, 2009). Rousseau even coined the term, "**noble savage**" suggesting that people were essentially good when they lived under the rules of nature, before modern civilizations were created. Those rules, in his mind, stood for honesty, reliability, and spiritual freedom. The institutions of modern civilization, the church and the state in particular, degraded and suppressed these features in people. When Rousseau repeatedly suggested, "Let us return to nature," he did not mean that people should abandon all the advantages of civilization, including scientific and technological advancements. He wanted to eliminate prejudice and corruption of the society (Rousseau, 1762/1997). He applied this principle of freedom to the process of learning. Children, according to Rousseau, should develop their own activities and feel free during learning because the will of the teacher imposed on the child affects the child's education in a negative way. The teacher's work should consist of preparing the conditions that would help the child to develop internal potentials. Teachers should be friends with children, and teachers should be motivators in the classroom and not dictators.

✓ CHECK YOUR KNOWLEDGE

La Mettrie's views are frequently called *reductionist.* Why?

What did the term "noble savage" stand for?

Assessments

The social and political changes in western Europe occurring between the 15th and 18th centuries went hand in hand with changing views of human behavior and psychology. Previously referred to as functions of the timeless and divine soul, psychological activities were increasingly often understood as processes available for observation and scientific investigation. Theories varied about the connections between mental and physiological activities: supporters of dualist, materialistic, and idealist views were making intriguing but dissimilar assumptions about the mental and physical worlds. Although these assumptions were largely theoretical, they laid a solid foundation for future psychology as a scientific, experimental discipline.

The humanist tradition in the arts, education, and science emphasized the subjective side of the individual: the sense of freedom, beauty, and moral responsibility. Both 17th and 18th centuries gave to the world an incredible lineup of scholars who shared an optimistic view of the individual. It was the time of renewed interest in self, individuality, rational choice, privacy, individual skills, and other capacities distinguishing human beings. Psychological knowledge accumulated during this period—within the humanist or scientific traditions—was becoming increasingly free of prejudice, discriminatory beliefs, or speculative assumptions. Knowledge about human emotions, thinking, desires, decisions, and so on was becoming more practical, useful, and based on empirical facts. The ideas of Descartes, Spinoza, Hume, La Mettrie, and many others signified the beginning of a new era in research. A human being, a feeling, thinking, and reasoning individual, was becoming the center of attention. Many scholars hoped to discover fundamental universal laws of science governing psychology. They preferred research models borrowed from physics and mathematics.

The Renaissance period signified the change in the scope and quality of knowledge. By the beginning of the 16th century, the Reformation movement had significantly changed not only the religious practices and beliefs but also the overall social climate in Europe. The scientific revolution challenged the traditional beliefs of human behavior, life and death, and the divine nature of the soul. The ideas about nervous energy and vital "spirits" in the body, and their assumptions about the functioning of glands and blood circulation, would echo many years later, in the 20th century, in biochemistry and neurophysiology.

However, we shouldn't understand this period as the time of unlimited progress and humanism. Psychological knowledge remained vastly speculative. It was heavily influenced by many competing philosophical approaches and traditions. Scientific knowledge remained out of reach for the vast majority of people, and most forms of education continued to be elitist, that is, available only to the members of the upper class. Despite the progress made by a few scholars in their understanding of psychology, the advanced knowledge did not change predominant popular perceptions about the nature of the soul and the mechanisms of psychological activities. Common sense, practical knowledge, along with superstitions, guided millions of human beings in their daily activities.

Despite the significant advancement of secular ideas, it is also wrong to believe that atheism prevailed in science. The main target of criticism of many enlightened people was religion as a social institution with the unlimited power of the clergy. Religious beliefs, meanwhile, were part of most people's existence. Many intellectuals combined religion and science in their explanations of human behavior and psychological phenomena. Some used religion to clarify the very reasons for human existence. For Benedict de Spinoza, for example, God was nature and nature was God. This position is often referred to as *pantheism.* Others, like the German philosopher Immanuel Kant, borrowed religious concepts to explain moral behavior. Despite an increasing independence from organized religion, leading scholars of this period were religious individuals and, almost without exception, mentioned God in their manuscripts. (See Table 3.3.)

Despite the emerging calls against social discrimination, psychological knowledge was routinely used to justify the existing social order. Rational explanations were given to ethnic stereotypes and suggestions about superiority of large social groups over others. Scientific justifications were provided in support of inequality between men and women. Jean-Jacques Rousseau, for example, a remarkable figure of the French Enlightenment, along with his progressive views of society and equality maintained that men should be strong and active and women should be weak and passive when they are engaged in relationships. Rousseau's biased views of gender relations were quite typical for the time.

Studies of psychological abnormality also produced many erroneous conclusions. From the contemporary standpoint, many descriptions of particular abnormal symptoms appear too vague and biased. The descriptions often contained prejudice against people with "outrageous" psychological symptoms.

Table 3.3 The Role Assigned to God in Selected Scientific Teachings

Scientists	*Role of God or Divine Entity in Psychological Processes*
René Descartes (1596–1650)	God is supremely good and serves as the proof that people are not deceived in their knowledge.
Thomas Hobbes (1588–1679)	If the roots of the sensation process are difficult to explain, we can refer to God as a creator of ideas and physical motions.
George Berkeley (1685–1753)	God is the ultimate observer, a guarantor of the existence of things that cannot be proven by sensations.
Benedict Spinoza (1632–1677)	God is nature and nature is God. Knowledge of God is the highest good for a human.
Isaac Newton (1643–1727)	God created the world based on rational and universal principles. God governs all things and knows everything.
John Locke (1632–1704)	God explains the nature of secondary qualities in human sensations.
Voltaire (1694–1778)	God has implanted the idea of morality in our souls.
David Hartley (1705–1775)	There is a special personality feature, theopathy, that refers to the individual's connection with the spiritual issues such as religion.

Conclusion

Psychological knowledge during mid-millennium transitions developed within two main traditions. On the one side, psychology was embracing science, a fast-moving enterprise serving society's need for reliable empirical knowledge. On the other side, psychology reflected the society's old cultural and moral foundations (Kendler, 1999). Psychology as an independent scientific discipline was taking its first steps. Yet these steps were becoming steady and firm.

Summary

- The global complexity of mid-millennium transitions is described in terms of three fundamental developments: the Renaissance, the Reformation, and the scientific revolution. Rational, scientific thinking, based on investigation and education, appeared as the key to human advancement.

- Although during mid-millennium transitions, more individuals started to pay greater attention to science, various superstitions, including beliefs in witchcraft, continued to be part of their lives.

- Opinions about the mind-body problem reflected at least three traditional philosophical views: materialism, dualism, and idealism. At least two distinct views of human behavior dominated scientific thought during the mid-millennium period: humanism and scientific rationalism.

- René Descartes was among the first scientists who began to understand the soul as a functioning machine. He considered the body and physiological processes as mediators between the nature and the soul and assumed that the laws of math and mechanics could explain the most complicated processes of the mind.

- Benedict Spinoza believed that people have to understand the causes of their behavior; they have to understand the sources of their pleasure and suffering and, based on this knowledge, reevaluate their lives.

- Gottfried Wilhelm Leibniz's ideas provided theoretical foundations for a number of psychological theories in the fields of human development, perception, and unconscious processes.

- Thomas Hobbes believed there is no immaterial substance such as the soul, and physical processes are only the accounts of mental functions. Voluntary behavior is a purely mechanical movement. Experiences can be recorded in the mind in a fashion similar to the way in which teachers use a piece of chalk to write on the board.

- John Locke distinguished two processes in human experience: sensation and reflection. He believed that complex ideas arise from simple ones because people can observe them and reflect on them.

- George Berkeley emphasized that although there is an unknown substance behind the sensations, an individual is still able to learn to coordinate ideas generated by various sensations.

- David Hume approached psychological issues from various positions including philosophy, natural and political science, and even geography.

- David Hartley believed that sensation is the consequence of a pulsation of the microscopic elements inside the nerves. Such marks, or ideas, are associated with many others to form complex associations that help individuals to function properly.

- Immanuel Kant's ideas views of moral behavior remain influential in social sciences today. His ideas about the possibility of knowledge prior to experience remained popular among mental philosophers.

- Holbach's materialist outlook was based on the idea that the brain was the center of all activities attributed to the soul. For Condillac, all mental operations are special forms of sensation. La Mettrie supported the ideas of mechanism suggesting that almost everything about human beings can be effectively explained in mechanical terms.

- Voltaire believed that human beings have a potential for moral behavior rooted in respect and kindness to other people. Education and experience make people who they are, according to Jean-Jacques Rousseau.

Key Terms

Animal spirits
Deism
Dualism
Empiricism
Epistemology
Humanism
Instrumentalism
Mechanism
Metaphysics
Monads
Mysticism
Naturalism
"Noble savage"
Psychological parallelism
Rationalism
Reductionism
Scientific rationalism
Solipsism
Tabula rasa
Witchcraft

Psychology in the Laboratory

Psychology will gain greatly in clearness and accuracy by using the methods and conceptions of physics and mathematics.

E. Cattell, first meeting of the American Psychological Association, 1892

All such machinery out of the way—and I cannot help thinking that Professor Titchener sometimes allows the dust of his machinery to obscure his vision.

J. M. Baldwin's reply to Titchener, 1895

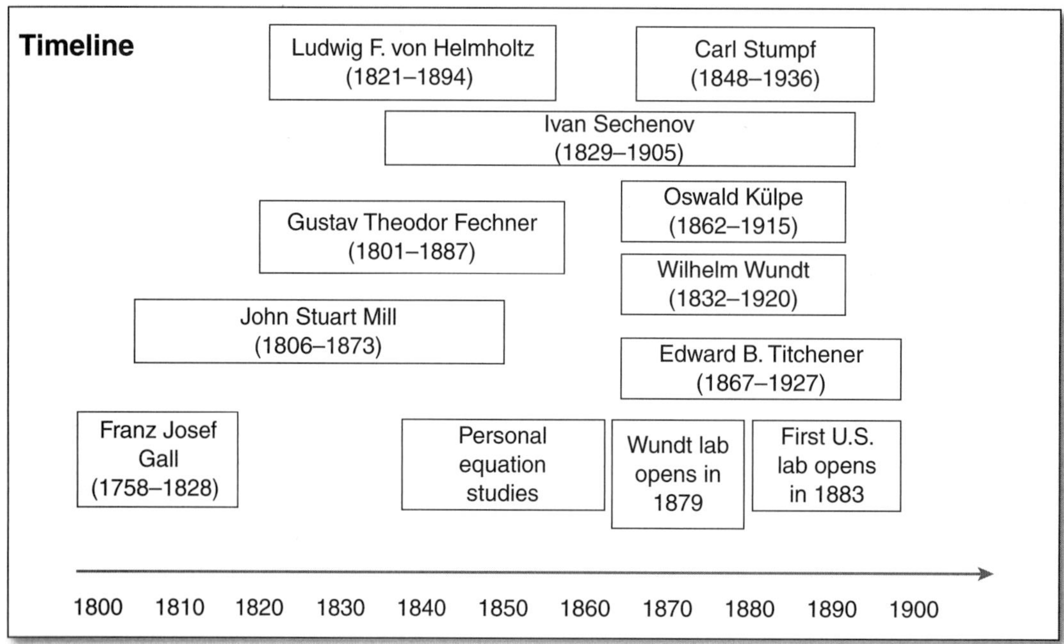

CHAPTER OUTLINE

In 1889, George Paxton Young, the University of Toronto's philosophy professor, passed away. Looking for his successor, the university invited applications from qualified candidates. It was seemingly a standard procedure of selecting the best individual suited for the job. Yet the process of replacing of G. P. Young turned into a controversy. Two finalists had emerged: James Baldwin, an American and a Princeton graduate, and James G. Hume, a Canadian and a Toronto native. Some professors involved in the selection process argued that only research and teaching qualifications of a candidate should determine the final vote. Baldwin seemed to be a favorite in this case: he had already earned a degree, some teaching experience, and great written recommendations. Baldwin believed in evolutionary theory and experimental psychology. Hume was different. He was a speculative philosopher studying moral aspects of behavior. He was suspicious of the aspirations of the evolutionary theory. Nevertheless, many professors argued that Hume was a better candidate simply because he was a Canadian. They insisted that a public university in Canada should hire a Canadian native! Hume appeared to some a more traditional and secure choice. Others disagreed. The debate about a teaching position became intertwined with contentious arguments about America's cultural dominance, Canadian nationalism, religion, and the proper place of science in public education.

Finally, a compromise was reached: both candidates got the job! Their academic paths converged for a brief moment. Soon after the hiring, the university's main building, University College, was seriously damaged in a fire. Baldwin turned this adversity into an opportunity: he insisted that the new building should include a permanent psychology laboratory—just the 12th in North America and the first in the British Empire (Canada was formally a part of it). This event was a formal inauguration of Canadian experimental psychology, and Baldwin later became a significant figure in North American psychology rooted in experiments and evolutionary theory. He was also an important contributor to the American Psychological Association (APA).

He founded and edited most important psychology journals: *Psychological Review* (with Cattell) and *Psychological Bulletin.* Probably, if Baldwin could have stayed in Toronto longer, the psychology lab would likely have become one of the leading research centers in North America. After Baldwin's departure, the laboratory continued to be productive for some time. However, there was no scientist of Baldwin's caliber and enthusiasm to match his effort.

Hume, on the other hand, remained extremely skeptical about psychology as an experimental discipline and continued to advance his opposition to evolutionary theories. Hume chose to teach psychology as in a traditional way, discussing abstract theoretical issues related to the work of the mind. He couldn't accept psychology as an experimental discipline. While Baldwin, an experimentalist, is commonly credited today as a leading world psychologist of the end of the 19th century, Hume's name is practically absent from philosophy and psychology textbooks. He was a representative of an "old" psychology that was rapidly pushed away by the new generation of psychologists-experimentalists.

Sources: Green (2002, 2004)

Transitions of the 19th Century

In the 19th century, Europe and North America were going through significant social and economic changes. Industrial capitalism was replacing the traditional economy based on farming and handicraft. England and then Germany established themselves as the industrial leaders in Europe, achieving the highest standards of living in the world. Other countries, including the United States, Canada, France, and Belgium, were not far behind in their improving socioeconomic conditions. People were moving in great numbers from villages and small towns to big cities. The educated middle class was on the rise.

Resources and Infrastructure

The 19th century was the time of rapid transformation of education and science. New medical and technical schools appeared in England, France, Russia, the German states, and many other parts of the world. Governments, industrialists, and bankers began to make long-term investments in university research and scientific and technical education. German companies were among the first to invest in laboratory science through major universities. American and other national businesses adopted similar investment strategies later.

In the middle of the 19th century in Europe and North America, secondary and university education was increasingly available to middle-class families. Many liberal thinkers believed that education was a great opportunity to enlighten people. Conservatives also thought that mandatory education would promote self-discipline and respect for authority. But most important, demands of developing industries and the growth of government bureaucracy required skilled and educated workers. As a result, by 1900 adult illiteracy was practically eliminated among young adults in countries such as Great Britain, France, Germany, Sweden, Norway, and Denmark.

Social Climate of the 19th Century

Two trends in the developing social climate of the 19th century were particularly relevant to psychology as a developing discipline. The first one was the tradition of materialism and realism reflected in so-called **mastery values**—the belief that individuals using the power of science and technology must exercise full control over society, environment, and their own bodies. Ambition and high self-esteem were important individual traits associated with the mastery values (Schwartz, 1994). It seemed that the individual was approaching an ultimate dream "to conquer nature to his use," as Prince Albert of the United Kingdom said in the opening statement of the 1851 Great Exhibition in London. The scientific and economic achievements of the 19th century led many social commentators to believe that society, despite problems, was on the right path toward progress and prosperity so long as it endorsed rationality, science, and technology.

Not everyone embraced mastery values, of course. A competing intellectual climate was rooted in the traditions of idealism and **romanticism.** While idealism was associated with religious views of mental life, romanticism was a comprehensive viewpoint of society and human behavior based on the idealistic enchantment with the individuality, spontaneity, and passion. Romanticism did not deny reason; rather it downplayed the importance of rationalism. In literature, romanticism glorified the power of emotion and imagination, intuition and inspiration, beauty and brilliance. Popular mystery novels and horror stories stimulated the interest of the educated circled toward veiled, hidden features of the human psyche. Stories involving dreams, hypnosis, the altered state of consciousness, uncontrolled impulses and instincts were in high demand.

How did all these developments affect psychology? Mastery values embraced scientific investigation of mental phenomena. Romanticism strengthened popular interests to mental life too. Yet there was a price to pay. The interest in psychology often grew at the expense of scientific knowledge. Most people who rejected mastery values and scientific pragmatism did not want science to touch the delicate fabric of human souls.

Academic Tradition of the 19th Century

In 19th-century Europe and North America, materialism was increasingly popular. Many young scholars accepted the idea that physical forces were responsible for everything mental, spiritual, or ideal. They believed that physics, biology, and math could explain the most complicated psychological processes (Farber, 2000). In university courses, human beings were increasingly often portrayed as part of the natural world (discussed in Chapter 5). Theoretical speculations about the nature of psychological process gave way to more advanced forms of scientific research involving experimentation and sophisticated forms of observation (Green, Shore, & Teo, 2001). In medicine, careful self-reporting and recording of symptoms became a widespread method of collecting data (Wampold & Bhati, 2004).

The growth of materialist thinking did not necessarily mean the end of speculative analysis related to the mental processes (Boring, 1929). In fact, Catholicism and Protestant religions witnessed a period of revival at that time. The advancement of the materialist tradition in science and the growing influence of mastery values encouraged many educated opponents to reject experimental science in the delicate world of spirituality and consciousness. Materialism also appeared to be a vulgar way to present human beings as driven by primitive impulses (see Table 4.1).

Table 4.1 Psychology: Social, Economic, and Cultural Contexts of the 19th Century

Contexts	*Main Features*
Resources and infrastructure	Rapid industrialization and urbanization of society Sustained technological progress Massive migration and development of new forms of communication Initiation of mass public education
Social climate	Mastery values against the values of idealism (associated with religious beliefs and practices) and romanticism (a social climate embracing individuality and passion)
Academic tradition	Secularization of social sciences and life sciences Increasing investments in research and education

What People Knew About Psychology: An Overview

By the 19th century, scientific knowledge that was previously confined in universities and available only to a small layer of society's elite became accessible to many people. Psychology as a subject of studies developed within at least two fields. One was experimental science, including physics, biology, physiology, or medicine. The other was so-called mental philosophy, to which we turn later.

Scientific Knowledge. What did the typical educated individual of the second half of the 19th century know about psychological phenomena? Most likely he or she would call them "psychic" or "mental" activities. A popular university textbook published in the United States introduced, for example, four clusters of such activities, including sensation, emotion, intellect, *and* volition. Educated people were aware that *sensation* involved vision, hearing, touch, taste, and smell in addition to temperature, organic (associated with internal organs), and muscular sensation. *Emotion* referred to fear, anger, and surprise; this term also referred to astonishment, curiosity, aesthetic feelings, love, sympathy, and jealousy. *Intellect* was described through perception, memory, association, imagination, the discursive process (which we call thinking today), and the self. *Volition*, an unusual topic in today's psychology textbooks, dealt with various movements, including reflexes and impulsive, instinctive, and ideational movements (Wright, 2002).

People knew about the localization of the brain functions. Experimental data and clinical observations suggested that specific parts of the brain were responsible for particular aspects of behavior. Significant progress was achieved in understanding the basic mechanisms of human sensation, particularly vision and hearing. Studies of Johannes Müller, Ludwig F. von Helmholtz, and their followers brought a revolutionary change to scientific knowledge: psychological processes have been explained in seemingly clear terms of physics and biology. Many physiologists of the early 19th century maintained the belief that although the brain carried the most important intellectual functions such as thinking, emotions were largely localized in other parts of the body, such as in the internal organs. The logic behind this assumption was that the brain and nervous system react to the signals coming from the outside world directly, while emotions accompany actions.

Most educated people distinguished between conscious and unconscious processes. The experiments on snakes conducted by English physician and physiologist Marshall Hall (1790–1857) sparked the debates about the reflexes and whether or not the reactions of animals were conscious. Hall believed that there was nothing conscious in the spinal reflexes of animals. His critics argued that consciousness was a function of the whole nervous system, and therefore spinal reflexes were conscious too. Gradually, however, the view that spinal reflexes were unconscious became prevalent in physiology. Consciousness became a phenomenon associated with psychology. Psychology was frequently referred to as a science that examined voluntary conscious processes.

ON THE WEB

Do you want to know what classes psychology students took in the 1880s? Take a 19th-century undergraduate psychology quiz on the book website.

Popular Beliefs. Across countries, people's confidence in the ability of science to explain "mysterious" phenomena was growing. Educated people were gradually abandoning beliefs in witches and demons, evil eye, and magic. Yet knowledge about psychology was very limited and the interest in mystifying phenomena was common. Ironically, new scientific facts about the brain, the nervous system, and the functioning of sensory organs rejuvenated people's interest in mysticism. Take hypnosis as an example. By the end of the 18th century, public interest in hypnosis declined significantly after the scientists had proven repeatedly the absence of so-called animal magnetism (see Chapter 1). Yet in the 19th century, hypnosis was again in the center of attention because of new discoveries in the field of physiology of sleep. (In Chapters 6 and 8, we return to hypnotic phenomena, the interest in which was inspired in the late 1870s by the French doctor Charcot and his followers.)

The growing interest in **spiritualism** and **clairvoyance** was also a significant development of the 19th century. A fashion, a trend, and a faith—spiritualism was a belief that the living could correspond with the deceased through special channels of communication. As an example, in 1848 American newspapers carried reports about the Fox sisters from the state of New York who had allegedly communicated with the dead. The newspapers called the Fox sisters *mediums,* or people who served as spiritual bridges between the two worlds. Scores of people around the United States, Great Britain, and other nations began to explore possibilities of communication with the dead though the means of mediums. In all times, human imagination has no limits.

Clairvoyance was also fashionable. A term originated in the French language meaning *clear seeing,* it stood for the supposed extrasensory power of an individual, that is, the power to see or feel objects or events that could not be perceived by the senses or measured objectively. There have been numerous reports of clairvoyance in many parts of the world. Most stories related to individuals predicting death, disastrous events, or other happenings that otherwise could not have been anticipated. The novelty of the "clairvoyance obsession" of the 19th century was its apparent scientific background. Some people believed that science could discover that seeing through walls was possible!

☞ CASE IN POINT

Folk Beliefs Yesterday and Today. One hundred and fifty years ago, many people believed in extrasensory perception and other supernatural abilities for a certain reason. Scientific literature was hardly available to most readers. Compulsory public education was at its early stages. Folk beliefs in mystical phenomena had deep cultural roots reinforced by religion and custom.

Have our beliefs changed significantly? You are likely to be surprised when you learn about some beliefs held in the 21st century. A 2005 national poll revealed that 55 percent of American adults believed in "psychic or spiritual healing or the power of the human mind to heal the body" (Gallup, 2005). The percentage of those who did not believe was much lower—26 percent—and the remaining 17 percent were not sure. In another survey, 57 percent of Americans said they believed that "psychic phenomena occur," that there are such things as ESP (extrasensory perception) or telepathy or other experiences that cannot be explained by normal means. Thirty-four percent said they did not believe in these (CBS, 2002; Shiraev & Levy, 2009).

Phrenology: Between Science and Popular Beliefs. There is no a clear dividing line between scientific knowledge and popular beliefs. Scientific views of today may be deemed unscientific tomorrow. Likewise, popular assumptions may receive scientific support. **Phrenology** will remain in the history of psychology as a highly controversial theory: both its creators and supporters sincerely believed that phrenology was an undisputed science. Many educated people perceived phrenology (called initially *cranioscopy*) as an intriguing theory that made sense: it connected the size and shape of the brain with human behavior and the individual's personality. Yet its opponents maintained that phrenology was a pure hoax that had nothing to do with science.

The originator of phrenology, Franz Josef Gall (1758–1828), was born in Baden, a German land. In his youth, observing his fellow students, he had noticed that the size and shape of the boys' eyes were connected, as he thought, with their ability to memorize. Later, as a physician, Gall decided to investigate how the brain's size and shape affect behavior and complex psychological functioning. He needed empirical facts. First, he studied subjects in prisons and mental asylums. He later examined his friends and acquaintances. Observing their behavior, he compared certain habits with the physical characteristics of the head. Gall's logic was plain: the skull's architecture should tell a trained specialist a lot about the brain structure underneath the skull. Gall divided the brain into two large groups and 37 zones representing emotional characteristics (such as desire to live, reverence, or imitation) and intellectual characteristics (such as order, calculation, and comparison). He used seemingly solid scientific hypotheses. He tried to connect two variables: the skull's characteristics and the actual behavior of individuals. He claimed he had found these connections.

However, most scientists, doctors, and biologists reviewing Gall's work believed that he had erred. It was a cognitive error called today the *self-fulfilling prophecy.* In the context of science, this error represents the impact of personal expectations of scientific results: if you want to see a certain result you are likely to see it (Levy, 2009). For example, a phrenologist suggests that one enlarged area of the skull should indicate a person's benevolence. Then this researcher will make every attempt to describe this person as benevolent! The facts inconsistent with the expectations will be ignored. As a result, only some facts will be selected to support the expectations, while other observations will be ignored.

ON THE WEB

Find more information and illustrations about phrenology on the book website.

Despite criticisms, phrenology gained popularity among ordinary people in Europe. As you remember from Chapter 3, some French scholars of the 18th century moved to German states to seek refuge from censorship in France. The irony of Gall's case was that, in reverse, he was struggling with an opposition in Austria, where he worked, and sought support and protection in France. There he found many supporters, including Johann Caspar Spurzheim (1776–1832.) In the 1820s, the two published popular editions of their scientific research accompanied by pictures of the skull indicating how to read measurements and judge people's intellectual and behavioral features.

Gradually, phrenology turned into a popular movement, with dozens of phrenology societies formed in Europe and the United States. As an example, the *American Phrenological Journal* was established in 1838. Overall, 124 volumes of the journal were published before the last issue in 1911. Later in the 19th century, phrenology became a big business: people were willing to pay money to get evaluated. The popularity of phrenology was in part due to Gall's personal connections. Many powerful people close to the royal circles believed in Gall's work and supported him. They saw him as a doctor, scientist, and, perhaps, entertainer (which he had never wanted to become). In the history of psychology, the case of phrenology remains one of most colorful examples of uneasy interactions between scientific and popular knowledge.

Values. In 1845 a group of four young German physiologists, students of the physiologist Johannes Müller, signed a pact promising to each other to maintain the scientific view of physiological processes and battle against the theories endorsing the existence of religious or spiritual forces. This pact signing may appear childish to some of us. Yet, to these young physiologists it was a statement in their ideological struggle against **vitalism,** the view that life processes cannot and should not be explained as physical and chemical phenomena (Boring, 1929).

As you remember, value-based knowledge is different from popular beliefs because it represents a set of coherent principles and ideas (see Chapter 1). Powerful elites accepting these values could promote one type of research and shut down others. In the 19th century, for example, many university professors opposed secular values and resisted the advancement of scientific materialism. This resistance was not just a reflection of individual dislikes for certain theories. This was an ideological battle for dominance between education and science. Franz Gall, as an illustration, was under attack from his fellow doctors. But the strongest opposition to his theory came from the religious authorities; they accused phrenologists of being disrespectful to religion. As a result, Gall was prohibited from lecturing in Austria.

Many university professors believed that only Christian religion could provide answers to the questions about psychology. Consider the case of the renowned Russian physiologist Ivan Sechenov (1829–1905). One of his most fundamental works was first published in the medical journal *Meditsinsky Vestnik* in 1863. The proposed title of his new book was *An Attempt to Introduce Physiology as the Basis of Psychic Processes.* First, government censors told Sechenov to change the title: they thought it was offensive to many people's spiritual feelings. Sechenov obeyed, and the book appeared as *Reflexes of the Brain* (1876/1965). But his troubles persisted. After the book was released, the critics still considered its contents detrimental and offensive to public morals. Some critics turned to personal insults and threats. As a result, Sechenov was indicted (although the charges were dropped later under public pressure). When Sechenov was told he needed to hire a defense lawyer, he replied that he did not need one. He argued that his best defense would be to show a dissected frog to the judge, so that the judge could see how reflexes worked (Nozdrachev & Pastukhov, 1999).

IN THEIR OWN WORDS

Ivan Sechenov on Psychological Activities. *The infinite diversity of the external manifestations of cerebral activities can be reduced ultimately to one phenomenon that is muscular movement. Does a child laugh at the sight of its toy, does Garibaldi smile when they expel him for overwhelming love of the fatherland, does a girl tremble at the first thought of love, does Newton create world-governing laws and inscribe them on paper—everywhere, in every case the ultimate fact is muscular movement.* (Sechenov, 1876/1965)

The impact of ideology on psychology varied from country to country. Although by the 19th century, theology was giving up its positions across European and North American schools, the developments in Great Britain were different. University authorities and many scientists did not share the ideas of German and American philosophers and physiologists who saw the future of psychology in an experimental laboratory. As a result, in Great Britain, research funds were not allocated to support experimental psychological laboratories. As we will see shortly, such labs grew rapidly in Germany, Austria, the United States, Russia, and Canada.

Legal Knowledge. Using legal rules, authorities pass judgments about certain aspects of human behavior. As an example, a few psychologists supported the social movement in the United States and Canada to legally abolish alcohol. One of the early Canadian philosophers-psychologists, David Hume from the University of Toronto, besides teaching and writing was actively involved in campaigns to prohibit alcohol in Ontario (Green, 2002). However, anti-alcohol views of these psychologists were rooted in their moral beliefs rather than on the research they have conducted. At that time, most psychologists accepted and justified widespread practice of state-sponsored involuntary isolation of individuals deemed insane or mad. Homosexuality and masturbation were openly condemned and were considered a form of abnormal behavior that required treatment (sometimes mandatory).

However, before the end of the 19th century psychologists did not represent a major social force, and their impact on the law was insignificant. Most scientists interested in psychology were engaged in a debate about the fundamental nature of psychological processes.

✓ CHECK YOUR KNOWLEDGE

Explain mastery values.

Explain the main assumption of phrenology.

What was the main point of Sechenov's *Reflexes of the Brain*?

Why did spiritualism and clairvoyance remain popular in the 19th century?

Physiology and Philosophy: Two Academic Schools

The Impact of Mental Philosophy

Imagine yourself in 1860. You are a student enrolled in a major university in the United States or Europe. You take a college course in psychology. Who is your teacher? Most likely, he will be an ordained Protestant minister. He (and there were almost no female professors up until the early 20th century) would emphasize the importance of theological understanding of the soul. His lectures would be about reason, causes of mental acts, creation of the soul, the vital force of the soul, the willpower, and so on (Farr, 1988). He would support idealism and reject experimentation. You would also hear about the ideas of Immanuel Kant, especially those related to the possibility of formal knowledge prior to experience (Fuchs, 2000.)

Some other mental psychologists would teach psychology from the standpoint of association theories. Most influential in this area were ideas of the British philosopher John Stuart Mill (1806–1873) and his father, James Mill. Association theories considered sensations as a foundation of human experience and rejected the idea of the existence of innate mental concepts. As a philosopher, J. S. Mill understood human knowledge based on the principles of mathematics and logic and derived by generalization from sensory experience. People have sensations and ideas, which are copies of sensations. The mind is a stream of ideas. If the stream is composed of drops, we must, of course, consider the drops as elementary foundations of the stream. The question is, How do these elementary foundations organize together? The answer was, A previous contact between two ideas is the explanation for the organization! One idea not only could evoke another, because they have been previously connected, but also generate in a person a belief in such a connection. We hear thunder, for example, and think of lightning. The two ideas are entirely distinct and separated because they have been produced by different senses. Yet we not only think of thunder when we see lightning, but we have no doubt that the lightning has caused the thunder. Thus, in our mind, we have countless connections representing a stream of thought. This stream is held together by the fact that the thoughts have previously occurred together. They have established an association.

Despite the remaining influence of mental philosophy, more scholars turned to experimental research inspired by the recent accomplishments in science and, particularly, physiology.

The Impact of Physiology

For most physiologists of the time, the nervous system was a sophisticated conductor of nervous impulses. What was the nature of the nervous impulse? Some researchers turned to physics and particularly to the electric current, which, as it was assumed, had something to do with the way the nervous system functions. Physiologists began to conduct experiments on animal tissue. Luigi Galvani (1737–1798), after stimulating a frog leg by electrical discharges and watching it move, provided the evidence that the nerve impulses were electric. Luigi Rolando (1770–1831), based on experimental studies, proposed that the cerebellum was functioning as an electric battery, generating energy for the whole brain. Marshall Hall (1790–1857), a physician of Scottish descent, conducted experiments on decapitated animals such as snakes to show that they would move if the nerves' endings were stimulated. Gustav Fritsch (1837–1928) and Eduard Hitzig (1839–1907) from Germany used electrical currents to stimulate various parts of the cerebral cortex in animals and described motor responses. Charles Bell (1774–1842) in England and Francois Magendie (1785–1855) in France discovered and described various fibers in the spinal cord. They put forward a surprising hypothesis that nerves conduct electric impulses only in one direction, a discovery that has become an essential foundation for reflex theories. Bell was also the first to distinguish sensory and motor nerves. Santiago R. y Cajal (1852–1934) of Spain suggested the direction of travel of nervous impulses in the brain. He became a Nobel Prize-winner in 1906. Camillion Golgi (1843–1926) of Italy created a brand-new method of staining individual nerves and cell structures, the method that allowed scientists to discover new structures in the nervous system.

Experimental research was closely associated with new theoretical inquires. Johannes Müller (1801–1858) from the University of Berlin, the leading physiologist at his time, published a detailed handbook in which he presented a comprehensive picture of anatomy and physiology (the eight volumes were published between 1833 and 1840 in German and were soon translated in English). Russian physiologist Ivan Sechenov (1829–1905), after completing his postgraduate work with Johannes Müller, claimed in his publications that psychological processes are cerebral mechanisms or reflexes. Sechenov considered that cerebral reflex activity arose from stimulation of peripheral sense organs, modulated by several brain centers, including the midbrain, and was the source of voluntary actions. In another publication, an article titled, "Who Should Develop Psychology and How," he insisted that only physiologists (not philosophers!) could understand the whole complexity of the psychological world of the individual. The subjective world was portrayed as a pure physiological activity. Another prominent Russian physiologist, Ivan Pavlov, enthusiastically supported such views and developed his own theory of reflexes (discussed in Chapter 7).

Other researchers were interested in localization of functioning of the nervous system. French anatomist and natural historian Pierre Flourens (1794–1867) operated on the brain and spinal cord tissue in pigeons to see how the place and extent of damage would affect the animals' behavior. He described the function of the cerebellum and cerebral lobes involving vision and hearing, remembering, and willing, speech, motor, and sensory centers. Eduard Hitzig and Gustav Fritsch in 1870 found experimentally the motor areas in rabbits and dogs. Paul Broca in 1861 made a discovery of the speech center on the third frontal convolution of the left cerebral hemisphere. Hermann Munk in 1881, using the results of other studies and describing the results of his own studies, identified the visual center in the occipital lobes.

Gradually, the mystery of the nervous impulse was fading away thanks to experimental physiology and its new branch—neurophysiology. Ludwig F. von Helmholtz (1821–1894), a German physicist by education and training, made a remarkable impact on neurophysiology. He measured the speed of nervous impulses, which he registered as approximately 90 feet per second. By the 1870s physiologists showed that neurons functioned according to the all-or-none principle: the strength by which a nerve responds to a stimulus is not dependent on the strength of the stimulus. Approximately at the same time, the membrane theory of nerve conduction appeared. These discoveries had a very important impact on psychology. A psychological process now appeared measurable too.

ON THE WEB

Read Ludwig von Helmholtz's brief biographical sketch on the book website.

Sensory Physiology. Discoveries in anatomy and physiology have stimulated research in the area of physiology of sensory processes including vision, hearing, and taste. Studies of acoustics and optics were quite advanced at that time. Physicists and physiologists had already developed sophisticated knowledge about eye convergence, binocular vision, color blindness, and the afterimages described as persistence of sensation after the cessation of the stimulus. Thomas Young (1773–1829) of England in 1801 described the effect of central and peripheral vision. In the middle of the 19th century, the studies of dark and light adaptation took place and showed that the retina of the eye contained areas different in terms of their sensitivity. The sense of touch was described as being organized in three subcategories of pressure sensations, temperature sensations, and sensations of locality. The Czech researcher Jan Evangelista Purkinje (1787–1869) observed experimentally the psychological consequences in visual experience after stimulation, including application of pressure and electrical current to the eyeball.

Ludwig F. von Helmholtz made a significant contribution to physiology of optics and acoustics. He believed that perception contained experiences not immediately present in the stimulus, such as in cases of visual illusions. These experiences are hard to resist: they can act unconsciously, that is, they are beyond an individual's ability to control. For example, we may be aware of an optical illusion; however, we are "tricked" by this illusion anyway. Helmholtz also noticed that some people are capable of self-observation while others are not. Therefore, specialists who study perception in university laboratories should train other people to become first-class observers.

Charles Bell developed a theory stating that different nerves could produce different sensations. Johannes Müller believed that the nervous system contains unique kinds of energies related to different forms of sensation. (These views found some support in a contemporary concept of specific nerve energies.) According to Müller's theory, people are not aware of the objects around them. They are aware of their own nerves, which serve as mediators between the outside world and the mind. Both Bell and Müller believed in the existence of a special sensory device in the brain called *sensorium*, which is capable of receiving and combining certain qualities transmitted through nerves. Prominent experimental physiologists entertained beliefs developed in ancient Greece: the ideas about sensorium and the views of primary and secondary qualities.

✓ CHECK YOUR KNOWLEDGE

What was the overall impact of physiological studies on psychology?

Early Measurements in Psychology

A few apparently insignificant events in history may become its turning points. History contains examples of some seemingly ordinary observations triggering significant changes in science. In psychology, several historic events have had a special emblematic meaning. We think of them today as turning points in the development of psychology as a scientific discipline.

Mental Chronometry

Several historic occasions help us today separate the "old" psychology from the "new" one. As you remember from Chapter 1, there are some scientific events that we describe as important not only because they have an immediate significance but also because of the way these events have been interpreted later.

The Personal Equation Studies. The firing of a young man named David Kinnebrook in 1794 from the British Observatory at Greenwich is such an emblematic event in the history of psychology. Kinnebrook was a research assistant to the astronomer Navil Maskelyne. The astronomer had noticed that his assistant was persistently late identifying the passage of a star across a marking in the telescope. The work that Maskelyne was doing was related to the calibration of the Greenwich clock. Today many of us are unaware of why mechanical watches and clocks (do you have one?) show the time with such a remarkable precision. Within the whole day-and-night cycle the small hand makes the full circle twice and the big one makes 24 circles. More than 200 years ago the clocks were calibrated based on the registration of the movements of the stars, known as *stellar transits.* That is why the precision of the measurement was crucial. However, the margin of error with which Maskelyne's assistant would notice a star crossing a certain wire was about 8/10 of a second. Such substantial measurement errors were unacceptable, and Kinnebrook was fired. Although his boss hired him again a few years later to do some computational work, David Kinnebrook did not live long enough to tell his version of the story: he passed away in 1802 at the age of 30 (Mollon & Perkins, 1996).

This story could have easily been forgotten. Yet German astronomer Friedrich Wilhelm Bessel (1784–1846) described this seemingly obscure event in a scholarly astronomical journal. The article drew the attention of a few astronomers. As a result, they decided to measure individual differences themselves using the same method that was used in the Greenwich Observatory. The existence of remarkably consistent differences in measurement between any two observers had been established in several experiments and was labeled as **personal equation**. More details were found with the passage of years. Similar observations were made in Ireland, Germany, and England: the observers were prone to commit a persistent error; the significance of the error varied based on the conditions of observation. By the 1860s, the personal equation phenomenon received several explanations. Some critics, including Bessel, suggested that because the speed of transmission of the nervous impulse was instantaneous, the problem was within the mind: something was slowing down when a person was attempting to combine various impressions and then come up with an answer. Others believed that the key was in a delay occurring in the nerves, particularly in the reflex time, in the ear or in the eye. Other physiologists suggested that the answer was in the physiology of the retina of the eye. Yet others argued that people involved in measurement had different levels of attention as a factor determining clear perception: the more attention is paid the "clearer" perception is.

This was the beginning of experimental studies of the **reaction time**. The main finding of these studies was that personal psychological characteristics such as attention or anticipation could significantly affect reaction time and behavior in general.

Gustav Fechner was physicist, philosopher, writer, poet, and scientist who wanted us to enjoy the beauty of his carefully crafted experiments.

Psychophysics. Have you read publications by Gustav Theodor Fechner (1801–1887) in German or translated into English? If you have, you were likely to find his works difficult to follow, too technical, and even boring. This is not the way Fechner wanted to be remembered. He was a dedicated physicist, inspired philosopher, and a motivated writer and poet. He was a great experimental scientist who wanted to enjoy the beauty of carefully crafted experiments designed to support some of his philosophical views. Fechner first took a medical degree but later changed his interests to mathematics and physics. He published several works on electricity. Working at the University of Leipzig, he later began to study color perception and after-images, for which he was conducting experiments on self-observing the sun through special glasses. As the result of this experimentation, he damaged his vision and took three years off because of his disability. However, he recovered against mostly pessimistic medical predictions. Partially due to his amazing healing, he turned his interests to philosophy and psychology. He remains in the history of science as a founder of **psychophysics**, which he defined as an exact science of the functional relations of dependency between body and mind.

Fechner continued the tradition of Johann Frederick Herbart (1776–1841), who used applied mathematics in the studies of mental activities. He also based his research on the findings of Ernst H. Weber (1795–1878), professor of anatomy at Leipzig University. Weber showed in his experiments that when an individual is asked to describe his perceptions of different weights placed on his hand, the smallest perceived difference between two weights could be described as a ratio between these two weights. He later found that this same principle was true for visual estimation of the lengths of lines and the auditory description and estimation of the pitches of tones. Weber formulated the concept of just-noticeable differences: a just-noticeable difference in a stimulus is proportional to the magnitude of what the original stimulus was. Weber noted his findings an important principle but he did not described them as a law. Fechner did.

In 1850, Fechner suggested a possibility that subjective estimations of measurements such as weight or length may develop in an arithmetic series in response to a geometric series of physical changes. Later he found the supporting evidence in experiments on weights, visual brightness, tactile perception, and visual differences. He graciously called this finding "Weber's Law," referring to the research made by his predecessor.

CASE IN POINT

Fechner's Law. The essence of this law was that if the intensity of a sensation may increase in arithmetical progression, the stimulus must increase in geometrical progression. Fechner's law states that the magnitude of a subjective sensation increases proportional to the logarithm of the stimulus intensity:

$$S = k \log I$$

where S = subjective experience, *I* = physical intensity, *k* is a constant.

Fechner (1860/1966) believed that sensation could not be measured directly. People could assess sensations in relative terms by comparing them to other sensations. Signals or physical stimuli, however, are measurable. For example, it is possible to measure exactly the strength of a visual signal. The researcher could also measure a difference between two kinds of stimuli that produce a different sensation, either stronger or weaker. Fechner also noted the difference between absolute and difference sensitivity that is commonly referred to as *absolute* and *difference thresholds.*

Fechner's main work, *Elements of Psychophysics,* was published in 1860. He was a careful experimenter. If numbers, he argued, could represent sensations, psychology might become a science founded on the rules of mathematics.

Measurement of Memory. Another seemingly insignificant event took place when a virtually unknown young German man named Hermann Ebbinghaus purchased a used book written by Fechner. This purchase affected experimental psychology in a significant way.

Hermann Ebbinghaus (1850–1909) was among the first scientists to conduct experimental studies of memory and learning. He was born into the family of a merchant near Bonn, where he attended university and studied history and philosophy. He served in the military, as did most men at that time. His dissertation, which he defended at the age of 23, was about philosophical aspects of the unconscious. He did not have a stable income and spent several years traveling to France and England and tutoring. Even without a professorship and a salary, without an access to experimental equipment of prestigious university labs, he still was able to make a significant contribution to experimental psychology.

Ebbinghaus applied a new experimental approach to study memory. He used himself as a subject, gathering data for more than a year (1879–1880), and then replicating the entire procedure (1883–1884) before publishing the results. He designed a method known in psychology as the method of **nonsense syllables.** Ebbinghaus designed a list of words containing two consonants and one vowel, words that would have no apparent meaning in the German language. Altogether he individually drew a list of 2,300 syllables. To assure that material was learned to the approximately same degree from test to test, Ebbinghaus introduced the method of *learning to criterion:* the subject repeated the material as many times as was necessary to reach a certain level of accuracy. With the use of his method, Ebbinghaus obtained a remarkable set of results (see Table 4.2). Ebbinghaus's most important contribution was the use of the methods of natural science to study memory. His experimental procedure was simple: there were independent variables that the experimenter could manipulate and also measurable dependent variables. The experimenter could observe and record all kinds of relations between the variables.

Table 4.2 Major Findings by Hermann Ebbinghaus

Findings	*Brief Descriptions*
The learning curve	The time required to memorize an average nonsense syllable increases sharply as the number of syllables increases.
Learning trials	Distributing learning trials over time is more effective in memorizing nonsense syllables than massing practice into a single session.
Practicing	Continuing to practice material after the learning criterion has been reached enhances retention. A small amount of initial practice, far below that required for retention, can lead to savings at relearning.
Primacy and recency effects	Early and late items in a list are more likely to be recalled than middle items.
Associations	Contrary to the prevailing philosophical position, Ebbinghaus observed that items exceeding this span, namely those separated from each other by more than the limit of five intervening syllables, could nonetheless become directly associated.

Source: Ebbinghaus (1885/1964)

What was the significance of the early measurement-based studies in psychology? Fechner and Ebbinghaus were among the first researchers to abandon speculative approaches to sensory processes and memory. They started experimentation. Like an experiment-oriented chemist, a psychologist knew that the key to success was in working with ideally clean experimental conditions. Hermann Ebbinghaus and others wanted to study "pure" memory, untouched by the disturbances of the experience and environment. To avoid the impact of unwelcome noise and other distracting influences, psychological research should have been confined to the quiet atmosphere and physical isolation of research centers located within private facilities or on the grounds of public universities.

✓ CHECK YOUR KNOWLEDGE

What is the personal equation related to reaction time?

Why did Ebbinghaus use nonsense syllables for his study?

First Psychological Laboratories

What has psychology to do in a laboratory? German experimental psychologist Hugo Münsterberg was asked this question most frequently when he was visiting New England. Other questions received from the American hosts were about the weather in Europe and why people in Germany didn't play American football (Münsterberg, 1893). This curiosity is easy to explain: most Americans did not travel across the ocean. In terms of psychology, experimental investigation was perceived as nonsense. But soon enough most American psychologists would not imagine the development of their discipline outside psychological laboratories!

Germany's Social Climate

Experimental psychology emerged first in Germany. Why did Germany play such a leading role? Several reasons come into play. One was the infrastructure of German society in the middle of the 19th century. At that time, Germany was a conglomerate of many smaller states competing against others in many areas, including the arts, education, and sciences. After political unification of German lands in 1871, the new country preserved its university-based research infrastructure. The national university system was also decentralized, unlike in France, or consolidated under the influence of a major school, such as Oxford in England or the University of St. Petersburg in Russia. In addition, an education reform of German universities gave students and professors a greater academic freedom, which stimulated a variety of studies. Economic factors played a significant role too. Germany at that time was becoming the most economically advanced country in the world, surpassing Great Britain. German universities in the 19th century received better funding than institutions of higher education and research in other states.

One hundred and thirty years ago, most experiments took place in an isolated mini-universe of a psychology laboratory. The corridors of university buildings were now filled with sounds of rings, snaps, and chronoscope whirs. White sheets of paper have been filled not with theoretical discourses about the nature of a willful act but with numbers organized in rows and columns describing the reaction time of a subject. The sign on the door, "Psychological Laboratory," implied that a loud conversation nearby was not welcome.

The Wundt Laboratory in Germany

Today we associate the birth of experimental psychology with the name of the German scholar Wilhelm Wundt (1832–1920). Psychology undergraduates first come

ON THE WEB

Read Wundt's brief biographical sketch on the book website.

Wilhelm Wundt was founder of the first psychological laboratory in Leipzig, Germany. Thirty-three American and scores of students from other countries worked on their doctoral degrees under Wundt's supervision.

across his name at the very beginning of an introductory course. Usually, there is not much said or written about his theoretical views and the results of his research. Most facts are about *how* he conducted his studies. This is exactly how history treated Wundt: his theory was neglected relatively quickly (what is twenty years for history)? Yet the impulse he gave to experimental psychology lasted for a long time.

Who was this person who became a universally respected figure in the history of psychology?

Wundt's academic career might appear ordinary: he was advancing his education, moving from school to school, receiving teaching appointments, and writing papers and books. Nevertheless, these apparently "dry" facts reveal a series of accomplishments that played a crucial role in the development of psychology as an independent science. The significance of his work for future psychology lies in his specific actions and accomplishments that are difficult to appreciate without taking them in a greater social and cultural context of the time. Before explaining his psychological views, let's turn to his specific academic achievements (Nerlich & Clarke, 1998), which are summarized in Table 4.3.

Table 4.3 Wilhelm Wundt's Academic Accomplishments

Accomplishments	*Brief Descriptions*
A new research program for psychology that became a model to follow	According to this method, the researcher had to carefully observe his own experience as a response to a physical stimulus. Wundt's method involved evaluations of quality, intensity, and duration of such experiences.
The first psychological laboratory on the university campus in Leipzig	No one before Wundt was capable of undertaking a project of similar scale and significance. His lab (founded in 1879) and the Institute for Experimental Psychology (founded in 1894) in Leipzig became a precedent for others to look at, admire, and repeat.
The academic study of scientific psychology in Europe	In 1874 he wrote *Principles of Physiological Psychology.* He created a doctoral program in experimental psychology. In 1879, Wundt assisted his first graduate student at "pure" psychological research. Many prominent psychologists of the early 20th century have been his graduate students or worked in his laboratory. In 1881, he started the journal *Philosophische Studien* (*Studies in Philosophy*), which became an early academic publication for psychology research. In 1883, he taught the first course titled experimental psychology.

Inside Wundt's Laboratory. Learn more about the laboratory from the book website.

According to Wundt, psychology was becoming a laboratory-based science of experience. The researcher was supposed to carefully measure psychological elements according to their quality, intensity, or duration.

Among the students involved in Wundt's laboratory, few earned a PhD at Leipzig; most of them came for one or two semesters to study the experimental techniques and then returned back to their schools. It is an irony that only few of his students and fellows shared Wundt's theoretical views. Nevertheless, almost all of them would share the passion for experimental research cultivated in the Leipzig laboratory. Among his students were Germans Oswald Külpe and Hugo Münsterberg (who later taught at Harvard), the Russian behaviorists Vladimir Bekhterev and Ivan Pavlov, as well as American students, including Stanley Hall ("father" of developmental psychology in America), James McKeen Cattell, Lightner Witmer, and Wundt's main translator from German to English, E. B. Titchener. Altogether, according to the archives at Karl Marx University in Leipzig, Germany, 33 American students have worked on their doctoral degrees with Wilhelm Wundt as a supervisor (Benjamin, Durkin, Link, & Vestal, 1992).

Laboratories in the United States: A Comparative Glance

In the late 1880s, psychological laboratories had been established by Ebbinghaus at Berlin, Müller at Göttingen, Münsterberg at Freiburg, Götz Martius at Bonn, and Alfred Lehmann at Copenhagen, Denmark. Not everyone rushed to open psychology labs, however.

Resistance to Experimental Psychology. In other parts of Europe, the process of transformation of psychology into a true experimental discipline was relatively slow, which should not be surprising. Psychology had to deal with many serious obstacles impeding its development. Let's mention just two: financial and ideological.

Who pays the bill? Unlike the traditional mental philosophy taught in major schools, new experimental psychology required significant investments. Like in chemistry or biology, researchers needed equipment, facilities, spare parts, and salaries for technicians, researchers, and their assistants. Most universities were government funded, and most administrators were not particularly eager to finance new (and seemingly controversial) research. In the mid-1800s, private funds available to psychologists were scarce. Potential donors could not foresee practical use of psychological research in a lab.

The second obstacle was cultural-ideological. For many administrators in European universities, psychology was not their "favorite daughter." Physics, chemistry, and engineering departments expanded rapidly, and funds were allocated to support basic science. Many university officials were also reluctant to fund psychological experimentation on moral grounds. While supporting the theoretical study of the mind, they were unwilling to endorse new research laboratories. Critics argued that the laboratory-based teaching resembled industrial production: you enroll, learn how to push buttons and take measurements, then you do some statistics, then you write a paper, and then . . . graduate. In addition, experiment-oriented psychology departments had an enrollment problem: many students who contemplated psychology as a career field had almost no training in physiology or math and did not like any kind of laboratory work associated with wires and buttons (Calkins, 1892).

America's Different System. In the United States, psychologists found a more favorable environment. A combination of public financial support, tuition, and private donations created an infrastructure with available resources for experimental research and training of future psychologists. Two great psychologists, Stanley Hall and James Cattell, were among the first returning American students who, after studying with Wundt, brought back their experiences and aspirations.

The first laboratory of psychology was organized by G. Stanley Hall at the Johns Hopkins University in Maryland early in 1883. Like Wundt, Hall had a wide range of interests not limited to psychology. He studied and published in the fields of philosophy, pedagogy, the lifespan, religion, and sexuality. Following the example set by Wundt, Hall established a journal called the *American Journal of Psychology.* As president of Clark University in Massachusetts, the second newly founded graduate school in the United States, Hall established a psychological lab there in 1889. James Cattell formally opened a psychology lab in 1887 at the University of Pennsylvania.

The organizational problems that Hall or Cattell faced were relatively similar. Besides trying to secure funding for salaries and equipment, they had to allocate available rooms and repair, design, and outfit them. Then they had to purchase illustrative models (handmade replicas with detachable parts of the brain, eye, and ear) showing the students how the brain, nerves, and sensory organs worked. Posters with the anatomical diagrams and the histological samples appeared on the walls. Labs had to have specially designed equipment. Many skilled craftsmen, including mechanics, carpenters, and electricians, would create devices for psychology labs.

Hugo Münsterberg in 1893, as an illustration, described a variety of instruments needed for a psychology laboratory at Harvard University. He listed a pipe organ, a collection of tuning forks, pipes, resonators, and so on to be used for psychological acoustics. Color-mixers, prisms, apparatus for after-images and color blindness, were purchased to study psychological optics. Complex gadgets to measure touch and temperature sensations and instruments to study movement and pressure were also bought (Münsterberg, 1893). Certainly, not every university could afford a psychology laboratory. Some schools did not have sufficient funding, or psychology professors could not draw enough students to their classes.

ON THE WEB

See a brief description of most significant psychology laboratories in the United States born between 1883 and 1893 on the book website.

Laboratories Outside Germany and the United States

As you remember, Wundt's laboratory in Leipzig hosted students from all parts of the world. Two groups stood out in terms of the number of visitors: Americans and Russians (Cattell, 1928). Other countries used their own intellectual resources to create psychology laboratories.

Labs in Russia. Russia's more centralized system of higher education, compared to German or American systems, was slow to accept innovations. However, due to the strong, world-class tradition in physiological and medical research, Russian government-run medical schools and universities had sufficient funding to send dozens of talented academics to study abroad. In Russia, the young doctor Vladimir Bekhterev established the first psychological laboratory in 1886. During his study in Leipzig, Bekhterev was truly impressed with the organization of experimental methods.

In his new laboratory, he began to measure motor reactions, emotional manifestations, and other behavioral responses of healthy individuals and mental patients. He kept detailed protocols of measurements and observations. To illustrate, Bekhterev studied the impact of fatigue on learning and memorization. He measured verbal communications and persuasion. He also studied how "neuro-psychological tone" (mood symptoms) affected the quality and accuracy of visual perception (Bekhterev, 1888). (We return to his pioneering work in Chapter 7.)

Labs in France. Psychology in France took a different path. The French psychological tradition in the end of the 19th century was focused in the study of so-called mental pathology. It was a new branch based on systematic observations of abnormal psychological symptoms. Most research took place in hospitals or mental asylums. These institutions were built to isolate and treat individuals whose behavior deemed persistently inappropriate or dangerous. Starting in the 1870s, scores of publications appeared in France dealing with pathological phenomena in psychology (Moser & Rouquette, 2002; Nicolas & Charvillat, 2001).

What were the reasons for such an interest to pathology? In the 19th century, the French system of higher education was significantly centralized. University departments had little interest in creating psychology laboratories or hiring full-time psychology professors. There were very few new positions offered for professors. A young individual with a doctoral degree in psychology had a very difficult time finding a job unless he or she had clinical training. Those who taught psychology, for the most part, delivered courses related to psychopathology, which seemed to be a more practical discipline (Nicolas & Ferrand, 2002).

The second reason was that in French-speaking countries, and especially in France, a PhD obtained in Germany was not accepted as an equivalent to a French doctoral degree. As a result, it would have been unreasonable for young researchers to travel to Germany to obtain academic degrees there (Brooks, 1993.) The practice of rejecting foreign countries' degrees continues today everywhere, including in the United States. Some such restrictions, probably, make sense. However, rejection of foreign degrees may also reflect the system's attitudes of superiority and protectionism and resulted in unfair judgments about the quality of education in other countries. A large number of universities outside the United States provide first-class education and superb training for their graduates, including psychology majors. The college selection system in many countries is extremely competitive, allowing these universities to accept best national candidates. However, when they move to the United States, students have to take many classes again.

Labs in Canada. In Canada the first experimental psychology laboratory was established by an American, James Baldwin, a graduate of Princeton University (Green, 2004). Early experiments in this lab concerned different conditions affecting reaction time, sensory thresholds, color perception, color blindness, color aesthetic, time reactions, discrimination of geometrical figures, letters, and rhythmical intervals. As a rule, psychologists conducted experiments on each other. They also studied family members. James Baldwin, for example, studied language development using his own small children as subjects (Wright, 2002). Baldwin encouraged studies of any psychological phenomena that was "ripe" for experimental investigation but rejected hypnotism or telepathy for the same reason: no exact experimental methods existed for such research (Baldwin, 1892; 1895a). Significant help to the laboratory was given by Dr. A. Kirschmann, a new head of the department of psychology in 1894. He had been Wilhelm Wundt's assistant during his studies and work in Leipzig. Early in the 20th century, a psychology major was available at McGill University in Montreal; a graduate degree was available there in 1910 (Ferguson, 1982).

Labs in China. In China, in the end of the 19th century, psychology as a college subject or research discipline was at its very early stage. Psychology classes were not taught at institutions of higher education. It sounds unusual for a psychologist or philosopher trained in the West, but for centuries, Chinese thinkers did not make the body-mind relationship a top problem to study and contemplate about. The change took place on the institutional level first.

After the devastation of the second Opium War of 1860 against Western powers, Chinese rulers came to a realization that the country needed a fundamental change. China needed to modernize its economy. Most important, China needed a new educational system. Scores of Chinese students and scholars were sent overseas to study and collect new experiences. As a result, many Chinese students who had studied in the West or Japan brought back notes, memories, and books about a new subject: psychology. In 1889, Yan Yongjing translated a Japanese version of an American textbook written by Joseph Haven and called *Mental Philosophy* (1882). This is regarded as the first Western psychology book published in China (Higgins & Zheng, 2002; Kodama, 1991). In 1917 Peking University established China's first psychological laboratory under the supervision of Yuanpei Cai (1868–1940). It shouldn't be surprising: Yuanpei Cai had studied experimental psychology in Germany under Wundt's general supervision.

Labs in Other Countries. Psychological labs were appearing in other countries. Alexius Von Meinong (1853–1920) established the first psychological laboratory in Austria in 1894 at Graz University. The experimental facilities were well equipped according to the standards of that time. A few years later the University of Innsbruck also had an experimental psychological laboratory. And at the end of the 19th century experimental psychology began its development at the University of Vienna (Rollett, 1999). The first psychological laboratory in Argentina was founded in 1898 at the National College in Buenos Aires. Historians believe it was the first lab in Latin America (Ardila, 1968, p. 567). In Japan, the first psychology laboratory was opened at Tokyo University in 1903 and the second one, which resembled labs in Germany and North America, was opened at Kyoto University in 1907 (Sato & Graham, 1954, p. 443).

Table 4.4 provides a comparative summary of early psychology laboratories and research in nine countries during the late 19th and early 20th centuries.

Table 4.4 Experimental Psychology in Selected Countries

Country	*Experimental Laboratories*
Argentina	H. G. Pinero founded the first psychological laboratory in South America at the University of Buenos Aires in Argentina in 1898.
Austria	A. von Meinong (1853–1920) at the University of Graz founded the first Austrian psychological laboratory in 1894. In 1897, the Psychological Institute of the University of Innsbruck was opened.
Belgium	Georges Dwelshauvers (1866–1937) founded three laboratories of psychology, the first one at the Free University of Brussels in 1897. Dwelshauvers spent the summer semester of 1889 in Leipzig and conducted experimental research under the supervision of Wilhelm Wundt.
Canada	James Baldwin founded the first laboratory at the University of Toronto. He pursued two main goals: to provide demonstrations for the undergraduate courses in psychology and to run a center for advanced research in experimental work.
China	In China, at the turn of the 20th century, psychology as a scientific discipline was taught in some pedagogical institutions. Only in 1917, under the supervision of Yuanpei Cai, Peking University established China's first psychological laboratory.
France	The French psychological tradition in the end of the 19th century was founded on the study of mental abnormality. The French Society of Psychology was founded in 1901.
Great Britain	The first English psychological journal *Mind* was established by Alexander Bain in 1876; experimental psychology developed slowly due to institutional and ideological restrictions imposed by the academic establishment.
Italy	The first laboratory of psychology in Italy was established at the University of Rome in 1885.

(Continued)

Table 4.4 (Continued)

Country	*Experimental Laboratories*
Japan	Yujiro Motora (1858–1912) and Matataro Matsumoto (1865–1943) were early founders of Japanese psychology. After visiting labs in Germany and the United States, Matsumoto designed the psychological laboratory of Tokyo University in 1903 and at Kyoto University in 1907.
Romania	Psychology as an independent academic program was introduced to Romania in 1922 at Cluj-Napoca by Florian S. Goanga, a student of Wilhelm Wundt.
Russia	In 1886, physician and therapist Vladimir Bekhterev founded the first psychological laboratory at the Kazan University. He also established a new scholarly journal, *Review of Psychiatry, Neurology, and Experimental Psychology.*

Sources: Abbott (1900); Blowers (2000); David, Moore, & Domuta (2002); Green (2004); Nicolas & Charvillat (2001); Rolett (1999), Sato & Graham (1954)

Little more than 100 years ago, psychological studies were moving within the confinement of laboratories. Most of them were located on university grounds and supported by government and small but increasingly common private funding. What was the psychological theory at that time? How did experiments influence theory?

✓ CHECK YOUR KNOWLEDGE

Why was experimental psychology often resisted at universities?

In the Laboratory: Psychology in Search of Its Own Identity

In this section, first we examine the views of Wilhelm Wundt and his contemporaries in Europe. We turn next to theoretical studies of American and other psychologists working in the late 19th century and the beginning of the 20th century.

Wilhelm Wundt's Views

Today, Wilhelm Wundt remains one of the most prominent psychologists of all times. Besides his role in organizing the first experimental laboratory and an institute, and bringing up hundreds of inspired students, what was Wundt's theoretical legacy?

Let's examine his views in several steps. First, we consider his views of the body and mind interaction. Second, we study the concept of psychological compounding. Third, we take a closer look at the method of experimental inspection. And finally, we inspect his assumptions about so-called higher mental processes.

Theoretical Background: Body and Mind. Wundt believed that every physical event has a mental counterpart, and every mental event has a physical corresponding event. This was not a new position. Previous chapters in this book have described various theories of psychophysical parallelism or correspondence between mental and physical components. Yet the theory of parallelism of the 19th century was somewhat different from its earlier forms. Wundt was a scientist who not only carefully observed psychological phenomena (the scientists before him did exactly the same) but who also believed in the possibility of experimental measurement.

Wundt believed that to study the mind experimentally there must be measurable variables available to the researcher. Here he made a fundamental assumption: such measurable variables should be the "products" of (a) sensory activities and (b) movements, both functionally related to physiological processes. Indeed, a sensory process is a physiological process; a movement is a physiological process as well. There are physical processes corresponding to the mental processes of thinking or will. Every psychological experiment, therefore, is also a physiological one (Wundt, 1904). This was the formulation of the Wundt's **physiological psychology.**

Wundt named three goals for psychology. The first was the analysis of elements of consciousness. The second was finding the manner of connection of the elements. And the third goal was the finding of the laws of this connection. The general goal of psychology thus becomes the analysis of mind, consisting of simple elements, the analysis of quality of such elements, and the finding of the ways that determined the order of these elements.

Psychological Elements and Compounding. Wundt's approach to psychology was relatively simple. Consider an illustration. Once you study something complex, it is absolutely appropriate for you to look inside this complexity and find out what those small elements are. Now let's assume that the act of thinking or feeling is complex. How could one divide an act of thinking or feeling into something "smaller" yet available for examination? Wundt offered an answer: the mind could be described as a collection of formal elements with certain measurable attributes such as quality, intensity, and duration.

British philosopher John Stuart Mill also wrote about deconstructing mental operations into mental elements. However, Mill's ideas were largely speculative. Wundt was willing to test his ideas experimentally. According to Wundt, *sensations* as elementary parts of experience are activated by signals stimulating sense organs and producing responses in the brain. The other set of elements of experience was *feelings*. They accompany sensations. Feelings are distinguished by three characteristics, such as pleasantness and unpleasantness, strain and relaxation, and excitement and calm. The process by which elements connect was called **psychological compounding.**

Thinking about the organization of psychological compounding, Wundt suggested the general laws of cause and effect in psychology. For example, during the compounding process, elements are combined together in new forms according to the law of creative synthesis. According to the law of psychological contrast, opposites mutually reinforce each other. Overall, the process of organizing mental elements together received the name **apperception,** or the active (selective and constructive) process of attention (see Chapter 3). Wundt suggested that mental elements, like chemical elements, when they are associated together produce something new, something that does not resemble the original elements.

Experimental Introspection. One of Wundt's accomplishments (and what is also his most significant scientific liability) was the method of experimental introspection. Based on this method, psychology was becoming an experimental science of experience. The researcher was supposed to carefully measure psychological elements according to their quality, intensity, or duration. Then the observations should have been recorded on paper. Wundt's famous work, *Principles of Physiological Psychology,* published in 1873 and 1874 and based on his lectures, laid down four conditions for the successful experimental introspection. In a way, these rules look quite contemporary:

1. The observer should be in a position to observe the phenomena under investigation.
2. The observer should be in a state of anticipatory attention.
3. The experiment should be repeated.
4. The conditions under which the observed phenomena occur should be determined through variation of the experimental conditions.

One important feature of the method was that the researcher was studying his own experiences, or, if we express it in the appropriate way according to Wundt, the *elements* of his own experiences.

Wundt did not want to see the experimental study of sensations or feelings as the only method for psychology to develop. He asked a question: If I can use experimental introspection to examine my immediate experiences by breaking them up into elements, will it be also possible for me to analyze complex psychological processes such as friendship, pride, or feeling of solidarity with other people? A person of relentless scientific curiosity, Wundt could not escape the temptation to study psychological phenomena of a "higher" level.

"Second" Psychology. Wundt turned to the study of so-called higher mental processes, the field frequently called Wundt's *second psychology.* (The first one was his physiological psychology.) He wrote a 10-volume *Völkerpsychologie,* published in stages between 1900 and 1920. The title of this book is difficult to translate precisely. At various times it was translated as *Folk Psychology, Social Psychology,* or *Cultural Psychology.* Each version reflects something, but not everything, from the original title. According to Wundt, large social groups, such as Catholics, Poles, or Germans, for example, carry cultural representations of individual experiences. These experiences are incarnated in the brain and the nervous system and appear in the form of myths, fairy tales, and beliefs, which can be studied by scientific methods (Wundt, 1916).

IN THEIR OWN WORDS

Wilhelm Wundt About Folk Psychology. *We may add that, fortunately for the science, there are other sources of objective psychological knowledge, which become accessible at the very point which the experimental method fails us. These are certain products of the common mental life, in which we may trace the operation of determinate psychical motives: chief among them are language, myth and custom. In part determined by historical conditions, they are also, in part dependent upon universal psychological laws; and the phenomena that are referable to these laws form the subject-matter of a special psychological discipline, folk psychology.* (Wundt, 1904)

As an example, every language has a grammar structure different from other languages. The order with which words are placed in certain spots in a sentence is a custom. This custom should reflect the way people understand their social environment. However, if an individual speaks a language, this means that this individual follows a particular custom and thus acquires a specific order of thinking. Wundt paid attention to the positioning of words in Greek and Latin. Both languages, for example, are relatively loose, compared to the positioning of words in German. The German language, according to Wundt, requires discipline, precision, and order. Thus, people speaking German since childhood had to become prone to discipline and orderliness.

Wundt also developed the idea of stages of cultural development. He believed that people as a social group developed from the primitive level to the totemic, through the age of heroes and gods, to the age of modern humans. The main goal of his comparative studies was to find facts helpful in understanding psychological processes. Psychology should study these facts. Customs and myths, like language, are facts that are available for people to study objectively through unbiased observation (Greenwood, 2003).

Wundt's Impact on Psychology. It is a rare introductory psychology textbook today that has no references to Wilhelm Wundt. He was the most prominent psychologist of the 19th century and the founder of the first experimental laboratory. As an innovator, he helped psychology to gain confidence and become an independent discipline. He trained hundreds of aspiring individuals who later developed psychology as a respectable academic field around the world. He helped to free psychology from the old-fashioned frame of mental philosophy. Wundt stood on a solid educational background: he developed expertise in both philosophy and natural sciences. As psychologist, he used facts from history, physiology, anthropology, medicine, and psychophysics. His contemporaries truly respected him.

Nevertheless, his theory was short-lived. Despite hundreds of pages he wrote on a variety of subjects from psychology to history, from medicine to anthropology, from physiology to physics, almost all his works were out of use in a few years after they had been published. Basically, none of his theoretical views has passed the test of time.

Wundt was interested in the laboratory as a process, an innovation. It may sound strange, but he was not a dedicated laboratory experimenter. James Cattell, Wundt's onetime assistant, recalled that his boss used to walk through the laboratory after the lecture, always courteous and ready to answer questions. However, Wundt usually limited any discussion to 5 or 10 minutes (Cattell, 1928). His contemporaries mentioned that Wundt was not in particularly friendly relations with influential German scientists and seldom tried to secure academic support for his theories. However, there were many psychologists in history who had limited social skills and yet their theories remain very influential today.

Wundt remains in the history of psychology as a pioneer who brought psychology into the confinement of the university lab. Psychology began to acquire its own identity within science. He set an example for others to follow. The students studying at Wundt's lab had brought up their own followers, who became mentors to a new generation of psychologists. In a way, we are all students of Wundt, students who have quickly forgotten many details of his theory. His legacy (see Figure 4.1), nevertheless, is here to stay.

Figure 4.1 Wundt's Legacy

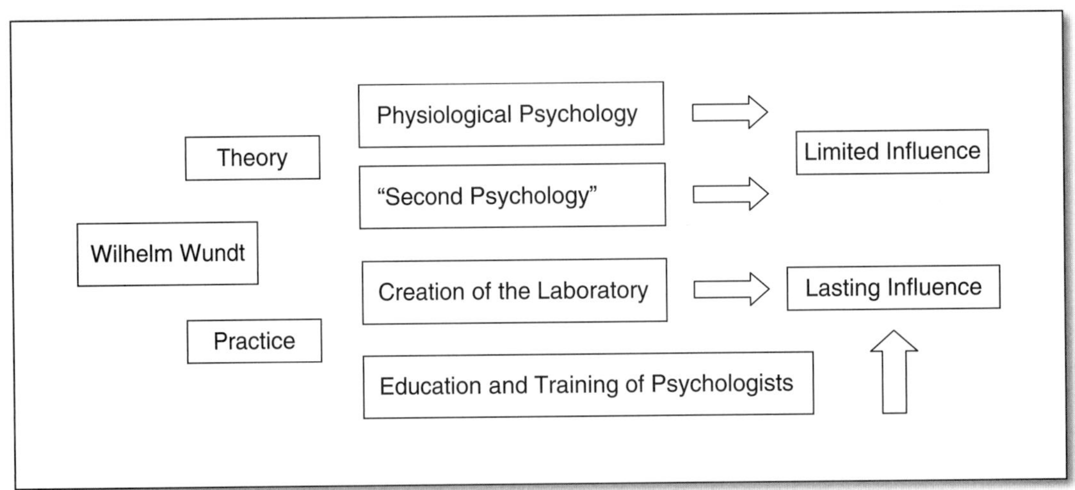

✓ CHECK YOUR KNOWLEDGE

Explain the experimental introspection of Wundt.

What was Wundt's "second psychology"?

Wundt's Contemporaries: Empirical Psychology

At the time when Wundt was organizing the first laboratory, psychology was still primarily a theoretical science. However, to be a theoretician did not mean to reject psychology as a science based on empirical studies.

Franz Brentano and Act Psychology. One of such scientists was Franz Brentano, a German of Italian origin. He was a transitional figure in 19th-century psychology. He wrote about the nature of sensation, optical illusions, hearing, and psychology as a science. Brentano's *Psychology From the Empirical Standpoint* (1874/1995) was his most important work. He believed in an independent, empirical psychology, but not in experimental one.

ON THE WEB

Read Brentano's brief biographical sketch on the book website.

Brentano belonged to so-called *act school* in psychology, which affected to some degree psychoanalysis of the 20th century. To understand act psychology we should try to answer the question: What is psychological? Brentano's answer was, Anything that is about imminent objectivity. What is imminent objectivity? Psychological phenomena should be understood as acts. If one person hears a sound of a thunder, then the sound itself is not mental. The impact of the act of hearing is psychological. But hearing is impossible without something that produces thunder and a person who hears it. The sound exists in the act of hearing.

Brentano divided the acts into three categories. The first is associated with sensing and imaging. The second is associated with judging, such as accepting or recalling. And the third is associated with psychological phenomena such as hating or loving. For example, believing that it rains and believing that it snows are intentional states of the same psychological mode (namely, believing), but they have different objects. In contrast, believing that it rains, desiring that it rains, and being angry that it rains are intentional mental states that have the same object, but each represents that object in a different psychological mode. We must always bear in mind that the psychical phenomenon is active. As Brentano illustrated this point, if an individual perceives, believes, desires, loves, or hates, this individual is likely to feel this way *about something!* This something (which may not actually exist) is the intentional object of the respective mental state. Intentional mental states can, therefore, exist as special types of relations between the person and the object of the mental state. (See Table 4.5.)

Table 4.5 Psychological Acts According to Brentano

Psychological Acts	*Descriptions of Acts*
Ideating	Sensing, imaging. For example, *I see, I hear, I imagine.*
Judging	Accepting, recalling, or proceeding. For example, *I acknowledge, I reject, I perceive, I recall.*
Loving-Hating	For example, *I feel, I wish, I resolve, I intend, I desire.*

What was Brentano's contribution to psychology? Brentano's call to consider psychological phenomena as acts was not entirely original. Philosophers studied the process of interaction between the perceiving subject and the outside world for a long time. Yet Brentano wrote about psychological acts beyond cognition. He proposed a new and complex approach to psychology involving the individual and his or her environment. Many years later, the idea of the individual engaged in the process of active interaction with the environment would become central in humanistic and similar theories examining an individual as a carrier of values in specific social and cultural environments (Bronfenbrenner, 1979; Maslow, 1970).

Ideas of Carl Stumpf. To understand better the early views of a new academic discipline called psychology, we now turn to the life and work of Carl Stumpf (1848–1936). Another contemporary of Wundt, Stumpf grew up in an educated family of professionals involved in medicine, law, and education. At the University of Würtzburg he studied philosophy and the law. He became Brentano's student. He taught in several European schools before getting an appointment at the prestigious Friedrich-Wilhelm University (known today as Humboldt University of Berlin) in 1894.

In his lectures, Stumpf presented all mental states as divided into two broad categories: intellectual and affective. His main contribution to psychology was his cognitive-evaluative theory of emotions (Searle, 1983; Stumpf, 1907). He was among the first to make a serious evaluation of the impact of knowledge on emotional experiences. According to Stumpf, an emotion is a passive affective state caused by a belief and attached to the content of a person's cognitive experience. Take envy, as an example. This emotion occurs in person X as an evaluation of disapproval of the fact that person Y has something that X doesn't have. Furthermore, the evaluation is based on the belief that X should have the object and Y should not. Almost forgotten in the first half of the 20th century, his ideas were further developed in studies related to the role of cognition in emotions. Contemporary cognitive therapies are based on the assumption that certain individual thoughts have a negative impact on a wide range of emotion-related problems (Reisenzein & Schönpflug, 1992).

Stumpf suggested that emotions could not exist without mediating cognitions or beliefs. Opposing Wundt's theory, he stated that feelings are not elementary emotions but rather sensations of a special kind, like sensations of tones or colors. Wundt did not accept these ideas and, in turn, criticized Stumpf's theoretical work. Disagreements between them became personal.

Relationship With Wundt. Reading about the history of psychology, you will find many examples demonstrating the impact of personal relationships on academic research. Friendship between two scientists would frequently stimulate new studies and generate original ideas. Alternatively, mutual animosity would frequently distract scientific research. In our case, Carl Stumpf's attitudes toward Wundt were not likely to have played a significant role in Wundt's research: Wundt was a more visible figure than anyone else at that time. Their academic paths crossed, however. Remember that in 1894 Stumpf received an appointment to teach in Berlin. This position was supposed to be offered to Wundt, but it wasn't for a number of reasons, most of them related to personal objections of a few key decision makers (including the prominent physiologist Helmholtz). Academic positions are not always offered to the best scientists or lecturers. Many other personal and financial factors influence such decisions. As a result, Stumpf spent almost 27 years as professor of philosophy and director of the Institute of Experimental Psychology in Berlin, the German capital. Wundt continued his work in Leipzig.

Regardless of the fact that Stumpf taught in the capital of Germany and Wundt was working at a somewhat peripheral school, Wundt's name and research remain in the history of psychology while Stumpf is known only to a few professionals. Why? Both Wundt and Stumpf were administrators interested in experimentation, and both were in charge of research institutes. Stumpf, however, was primarily a philosopher interested in psychology. Wundt was a psychologist eager to create an original school and active in recruiting his followers. Stumpf, on the other hand, was interested mostly in theory and did not conduct research to address his critics (Reisenzein & Schönpflug, 1992).

A "New Breed" of Researchers. Psychology's history preserves some names and nearly erases others. The lives and work of George E. Müller (1850–1934) and Oswald Külpe (1862–1915) demonstrate the different impacts of psychologists on the development of the young discipline. Consider the case of George Müller, a promising young scholar who after studying philosophy and history at the University of Leipzig, at the age of 23, released his first serious study on attention. After 1881, he worked at the University of Göttingen, south of Berlin. He had a fine research laboratory and taught many students but never gained prominence as an original researcher, because for the rest of his life he worked at advancing experimental studies that were initiated by someone else. For example, Ebbinghaus first initiated research on memory. Müller developed ideas of Fechner, conducting measurements in the fields of psychophysics. Müller also studied the mechanisms of vision, developing the views of the physiologist Karl Hering. Müller never wrote a serious book in psychology. Nevertheless, his role in the history of psychology is illustrative. Like Wundt, he was a psychologist of a new breed, an experimental researcher. Wundt, Müller, and many other psychologists with similar attitudes were changing the academic tradition in and around psychology.

Oswald Külpe had a relatively similar biography: like his teacher, George Müller, he showed early interest to history and philosophy studying under the supervision of Müller. Külpe met Wundt and at one period served as his research assistant in Leipzig. Like Wundt and Müller, he developed passion for experiments. In 1883, as a professor, he wrote *Outline of Psychology*, a textbook that his contemporaries praised for its clear style and argument. It was translated in 1885 in the United States (1885/2008). In 1894, he accepted the chairmanship position at Würtzburg University. In short, his research biography is somewhat ordinary. Nevertheless, the name of Oswald Külpe appears in most psychology textbooks. What was his role?

Külpe proposed the idea of *imageless thought*, a new concept in psychology at the time. Thinking was already a favorite topic in philosophy. Yet Külpe's contribution was in the method of studying thought processes. He brought thinking under the magnifying glass of experimental research. Wundt, his boss at one point, brought immediate experience as the experimental variable studied in a laboratory. Külpe as a researcher went further. He suggested that studying experience after an actual experiment could bring valuable data. To show the usefulness of this suggestion, Külpe began to ask his research subjects— most of them were students or fellow researchers—to recall and then analyze their experiences that had occurred during the experiment. This method received the name *systematic experimental introspection*. Külpe would ask a subject, for example, about how he came to certain conclusions while performing mental tasks such as comparing weights. One of the assumptions was that thinking process could occur without "mental" elements. In other words, decision making could involve some kind of imageless thought. For instance, subjects who have been comparing weights A and B often could not provide any coherent description about how they had made a judgment about which weight was heavier, A or B.

The idea about the existence of an imageless "element" of mind was very appealing to many psychologists. Having been impressed with Külpe's ideas, many of them began to investigate thinking experimentally. A new path of psychological studies appeared: first perception and thinking, and later attitudes, decision making, learning, intelligence, and language. All became common areas of the experimental psychological investigation. We return to these studies in the following chapters.

Structuralism in the United States

Structural psychology or **structuralism** is the term invented by its critics and other observers who thought of structuralism as a special school in psychology. In general, a structuralist psychologist studied an individual by paying attention to elements of this individual's experience that are further irreducible. Further, a structuralist studies complex experiences in the context of these irreducible elements (Calkins, 1906).

Titchener's Views. In the history of psychology, the term *structuralism* is usually associated with the name of Edward B. Titchener (1867–1927). He shared basic theoretical ideas with Wundt, who was Titchener's mentor, and believed that the nature of psychological phenomena is in mental elements, those elementary "bricks" from which the larger mental structures are created. The problem was to identify how these complex structures were formed. This was a difficult question. According to the British school of associationism (tradition originating from John Locke), the answers to the question were found in the associations: the mechanisms combining "simple" sensations into something more complex and meaningful. But who directs those associations? Titchener did not answer this question. He turned to the study of mental elements suggesting that the most appropriate task for him was to examine the nature of the elements and their associations. To investigate what force organizes those elements could be a task for others to pursue.

ON THE WEB

Read Titchener's brief biographical sketch on the book website.

Because of Titchener's influence, psychology strengthened its position as a legitimate discipline and a university major. He published numerous articles and several books. The most remarkable was, perhaps, *Experimental Psychology: A Manual of Laboratory Practice,* released in four volumes at the very beginning of the 20th century. While at Cornell University, he rebuilt and redesigned the research lab while making many tools and gadgets with his own hands. Of course, his students were available to help.

Titchener compared psychology to biology and especially to morphology, or the study of biological structures such as muscle tissue. Using this analogy, he wanted to build experimental psychology as an exact counterpart of modern biology. The primary aim of the experimental psychologist has been to analyze the structure of mind, to unravel the elemental processes from the tangle of consciousness (Titchener, 1898). Titchener, like Wundt, believed that psychology was the science of conscious experience at a measurable period.

How could a researcher examine such conscious experiences? Consciousness consists of elements: sensations and affections. The task of the psychologist is to describe these elements and learn how they interconnect. In the process of observation, a scientist should not use common labels, such as, "I see the table and it is brown." Instead, the scientist should describe the elements of his or her conscious experience. The observer, of course, must know what to observe. Sensations as mental elements have four basic characteristics: quality, intensity, duration, and clearness. If a researcher, for instance, studies attention, this experimenter should detect whether attention increases or decreases. Affections are likely to be pleasant or unpleasant.

Psychology should not deal with phenomena unavailable for observation. Titchener, therefore, paid little attention to child or comparative psychology because he did not believe in the possibility of experimental observation there. Observation, however, is not just a simple process of looking "inside." Titchener warned against the common misperception about his method: you don't just look inside yourself and then report your observations. He called this type of introspection *unschooled introspection.* Introspection as a true research method should develop as a result of rigorous training. Titchener believed in repetition of experiments and wanted total isolation of experimental conditions from outside intrusions.

IN THEIR OWN WORDS

E. B. Titchener on the Essence of His Approach. *The primary aim of the experimental psychologist has been to analyze the structure of mind; to ravel out the elemental processes from the tangle of consciousness, or (if we may change the metaphor) to isolate the constituents in the given conscious formation. His task is a vivisection, but a vivisection which shall yield structural, not functional results. He tries to discover, first of all, what is there and in what quantity, not what it is there for.* (Titchener, 1898)

ON THE WEB

The Introspection Method.
M. W. Calkins, the first woman president of the American Psychological Association (1905), in one of her works published in 1915 gave a detailed description of the introspection method she learned from Titchener. Read more about this method on the book website.

On the personal level, his students reported that he did not interact much with his colleagues around the country. Nevertheless, because of the growing power of the publishing business and the tradition of using textbooks for college education, his works caught the attention of many psychologists. Internationally, by the end of the 19th century, the English language was becoming more popular than French, German, or Spanish. Published in English, Titchener's books and articles (he published 176) were available at many universities around the world.

Titchener's Legacy. Titchener was a talented researcher. He believed in psychology as an experimental science. This was a popular and growing view among psychologists. On the other hand, opposition to his research grew too because of his loyalty to introspection. He refused to revise the method of introspection and was critical to newly developing behavioral studies. He believed he was supporting a new psychology. It turned out he was supporting the "old" introspective psychology. Practically none of his numerous followers (the number of people who obtained doctoral degrees from him was 54) continued his theoretical tradition.

If you happen to visit Cornell University, ask any psychology major where Titchener's laboratory was. She or he will likely say that they don't know. Address this question to psychology professors at Cornell. Only few would give a correct answer (I have asked and I have the proof). Still, Titchener's brain is prominently displayed in a jar filled with formaldehyde near the psychology department as a symbolic reminder about a person who once was an innovator and groundbreaker.

The American Psychological Association: The Beginnings

When in 1889 a group of European psychologists tried to identify a national organization representing their American counterparts, they couldn't find one. There was a small organization called the American Society of Psychical Research; however, the focus of its studies was telepathy and other extrasensory phenomena. Psychologists in a large country such as the United States with a number of premier universities and psychological laboratories (the number of which was 20 by 1892) did not have a national organization. The necessity to form such an association was evident. The American Association for the Advancement of Science (AAAS) (which was founded in 1848) no longer could satisfy the professional interest of so many scholars representing so many academic backgrounds. By the end of the 19th century, many academic associations had appeared in the various fields of science.

ON THE WEB

Read more about American scientific associations in the 1880–1890s on the book website.

Historically, the U.S. government was not directly involved in academic affairs, although it assisted in the foundation and development of universities. Therefore, the initiative to form a national research association should have come from psychologists themselves. Although several psychologists took that initiative, most recognition was given to G. Stanley Hall. His effort and aspirations resulted in the creation of the American Psychological Association.

Hall's role was controversial, however. He was a great researcher who had contributed significantly to the development of several branches of the discipline. He was a skilled and demanding administrator. Yet on the other hand, his contemporaries portrayed him as a controlling, at times capricious and intolerant person who wanted to promote his own agenda regardless of other people's objections (Sokal, 1990). Quite often, his ambitious plans paid off. When Joseph Jastrow from the University of Wisconsin started to discuss possibilities for psychologists to contribute as a group to a special section about technology at the World Columbian Exposition (Chicago 1893), Hall decided to pursue a more ambitious goal: to form a national association. In July 1892, a small group of psychologists joined Hall in Worcester, Massachusetts, for a preliminary meeting.

☞ CASE IN POINT

The Founding Members of the American Psychological Association. In response to an invitation issued by President G. Stanley Hall of Clark University, a preliminary meeting of psychologists from various institutions was held at that university in Worcester, Massachusetts, on July 8, 1892. Among the invited were Professor Fullerton of the University of Pennsylvania, Professor Jastrow of the University of Wisconsin, Professor James of Harvard University, Professor Ladd of Yale University, Professor Cattell of Columbia College, Professor Baldwin of the University of Toronto.

In December 1892 at the University of Pennsylvania, the first annual meeting of the American Psychological Association took place, representing 31 original members (18 had attended the first meeting). The composition of the association was diverse and included psychiatrists, philosophers, experimental psychologists, and experts in education (called pedagogists). They were all men. The average age of the members was 35, with the most mature 54 years old. The members shared enthusiasm about their discipline and promised mutual support. Hall was elected president and delivered his first presidential address. Table 4.6 contains the list of the presenters at the meeting and a brief description of their topics.

Table 4.6 Proceedings of the American Psychological Association (1892–1893)

Name	*Issues Discussed at the First Meeting*
Stanley Hall Clark University	Topic: *History and Prospects of Experimental Psychology in America.* (The Presidential Address)
J. McKeen Cattell Columbia College	Topic: *Errors of Observation in Physics and Psychology.* (Psychology will gain greatly in clearness and accuracy by using the methods and concepts of physics and mathematics.)
Herbert Nichols Harvard University	Topic: *Experiments on Pain.* (Certain parts of the body are sensible of pain only, in response both to temperature and to mechanical stimulation. There must be special pain nerves.)
E. A. Pace Catholic University	Topic: *Tactile Estimates of Thickness.*
Lighter Witmer University of Pennsylvania	Topic: *Some Experiments Upon the Aesthetics of Simple Visual Forms.*
Joseph Jastrow, University of Wisconsin	Topic: *Experimental Psychology at the World's Fair.* (Paper described the plans of the Section of Psychology of the Department of Ethnology at the World's Columbian Exposition. The typical instruments for demonstration included devices to study movements and sensations.)
Herbert Nichols Harvard University	Topic: *Certain Illusions of Rotation.*
W. L. Bryan University of Indiana	Topic: *Note Upon the Controversy Regarding the Relation of the Intensity of the Stimulus to the Reaction-Time.* This paper was only given in part, and abstract has not been furnished.
E. C. Sanford Clark University	Topic: *Minor Studies at the Psychological Laboratory of Clark University.* (A report upon six studies made under his direction by students of psychology at Clark University.)
Hugo Münsterberg Harvard University	Topic: *The Problems of Experimental Psychology.* (Münsterberg was a guest of the meeting. He suggested that psychology was rich in decimals but poor in idea—an early call for practical applications of research.)

Source: APA (1892)

ON THE WEB

The book website contains information about APA's budget. See the materials related to Chapter 4.

During the early years after its establishment, the membership in the American Psychological Association grew, as well as its reputation. Membership reached 127 by the year 1900, and its budget rose to $2,770 by 1901. The annual fee was from $1 to $3; a psychology professor at the time earned from $1,000 to $7,000 a year.

There were a few problems, however, related to internal "turf battles." As you remember, some psychologists perceived G. Stanley Hall negatively. They rejected his authoritarian style, including his arbitrary decisions about publications in the *American Journal of Psychology*. He was the owner of the *Journal* and could, of course, make all executive decisions. Nevertheless, the members of the association believed that if the journal was to become the main publication for the American Psychological Association, the decisions should be collegial (Ross, 1972). To emphasize his disagreement with his critics, Hall did not participate in the second meeting in New York. Although he continued to publish his journal, another psychological periodical, *The Psychological Review,* appeared in 1894 as the result of efforts of psychologists Cattell and Baldwin. In the same year, the association adopted its constitution emphasizing the goal to promote psychology as science.

The APA's Role. The American Psychological Association was initially a group without real power. The association could not get involved directly in psychologists' teaching and research. It could not enforce its own recommendations. Nevertheless, during its first formative years, the American Psychological Association served several important functions. It became an important symbol of psychologists' group identity. Psychology was developing an institutional structure, which is a very important asset in dealing with financial, business, private, and government institutions. The organization gave psychologists a great opportunity to communicate about their research in the most efficient way. The members maintained regular correspondence by mail and participated in joint projects. Circular letters (such as an announcement mailed to multiple recipients) were becoming very popular. The members of the association now could present themselves to the larger community of American scientists. This was an important contribution to psychology's reputation.

✓ CHECK YOUR KNOWLEDGE

What was so-called act psychology?

Which school proposed the concept of imageless thoughts?

Titchener's approach is called structural psychology. Why?

Assessments

Psychology as a discipline did not have a straightforward development. Many scholars and educated people in the 19th century believed that psychology was not a science like physics or biology. Early studies by Fechner and Ebbinghaus challenged this skeptical point of view. Studies in the fields of psychophysics and memory demonstrated both the elegance and power of scientific hypotheses and numbers. Fechner was among the first who introduced methods of measurement. Since then, psychology was increasingly seen by its supporters as an experimental discipline, just like basic sciences. The only serious difference between them was that psychology turned to experiments later. Professors teaching and doing research in psychology continued to debate about the main subject of this discipline. The emphasis on experimental research was growing. Moving into the laboratory was an important step that helped psychology to earn its initial reputation of a serious, legitimate university discipline.

Astronomers of the 19th century gave psychologists maybe unexpected but very valuable empirical materials about reaction time. Doctors and physiologists made new discoveries connecting mental processes to specific areas of the brain and specific physiological processes. The "new" psychology was becoming predominantly nonideological and increasingly free of theological doctrines (Fuchs, 2000; Kosits, 2004).

The prominent historian of psychology Edwin Boring in his famous *History of Experimental Psychology* wrote that psychology as a discipline appeared first; psychologists came later. From the beginning, psychology as a science was a collective creation. Representatives of a wide range disciplines participated in its process. Almost all of them were not psychologists by education. In their late teens and twenties they studied science, medicine, or philosophy. Fechner was known as a physicist "converted" into a philosopher. Helmholtz was a physiologist interested in physics. Ebbinghaus was a philosopher. Wundt was train in philosophy and physiology. Bekhterev was a doctor. Müller was a physiologist. Brentano was a philosopher. This list can be easily continued. However, all these and many other "psychologists by training" were instrumental in psychology's rapid development as an experimental science. While quite many people at the end of the 19th century associated psychology with paranormal and mysterious phenomena, hypnotism, extrasensory abilities, and mind reading, many researchers working in private and public universities began to turn to science for facts and reliable methodology.

The last quarter of the 19th century and the beginning of the 20th century was the time when several countries established national associations of psychologists. Many universities institutionalized the discipline by creating academic positions and departments, sponsoring journals and professional societies. Psychology was establishing its own research and educational tradition.

However, an obvious weakness of psychology emerged by the end of the century: psychology did not produce widely acclaimed theories that would have given a broad theoretical view of the discipline, it methods, and applications. There were several attempts to create such theories. The works of Wilhelm Wundt and

Were early experimental psychologists unfocused, eclectic? Join the discussion on the book website. See the materials related to Chapter 4.

William Titchener are the examples. Nevertheless, Wundt's theory had never brought him a global support outside his laboratory in Leipzig (his method did). Titchener's theory was short-lived too.

Conclusion

When many psychologists began to use scientific experimental method in the 19th century, this was indeed the beginning of psychology's quest for independence. Committed to developing a laboratory-based science modeled after physics, many university-based psychologists hoped to discover fundamental laws governing psychology, similar to ones of other sciences. A quiet, isolated lab was viewed as the place to discover such laws. For some time, a researcher confined in a basement of a university building was a role model for many psychologists. Such passion about experimental research was commendable. However, by turning away from applications, by emphasizing "pure" research, psychologists very often put themselves in a very awkward position (Driver-Linn, 2003). They wanted to be recognized as scientists. Yet, using a highly technical language of experimentation, some psychologists distanced themselves from a potentially supportive and curious public.

Summary

- The 19th century was a time of rapid transformation of education and science. New medical and technical schools appeared in many countries. Two trends in the developing social climate of the 19th century were particularly relevant to psychology. The first one was the tradition of materialism and realism reflected in so-called mastery values. The second one was rooted in the traditions of idealism and romanticism.

- Most scientists interested in psychology were engaged in a debate about the fundamental nature of psychological processes. Physiology and mental philosophy offered different answers.

- Studies in mental chronometry and psychophysics, especially the works of Ernst Weber and Gustav Fechner, provided a foundation for experimental psychology.

- Fechner and Hermann Ebbinghaus were among the first researchers to abandon speculative approaches to sensory processes and memory. They started experimentation and offered mathematical equations to measure experience such as sensations.

- Ebbinghaus suggested an experimental approach to memory untouched by the disturbances of the experience and environment. It was a growing belief that, to avoid unwelcome noise and other distracting influences, psychological research should be confined to the quiet atmosphere and physical isolation of research centers located within private facilities or on the grounds of public universities.

- Wilhelm Wundt is recognized as a founder of experimental psychology. He founded the first psychology lab in 1879 in Leipzig. Many similar laboratories were later organized in several countries around the world.

- Wundt named three goals for psychology. The first was the analysis of elements of consciousness. The second was finding the manner of connection of the elements. And the third goal was the finding of the laws of this connection.

- Franz Brentano wrote about psychological acts beyond cognition. He proposed a new and complex approach to psychology involving the individual and his or her environment.

- Carl Stumpf, among others, examined the role of cognition in emotions and created the cognitive-evaluative theory of emotions.

- Oswald Külpe conducted experimental studies of perception and thinking and designed the method of systematic experimental introspection.

- Edward Titchener worked on experimental psychology that was designed to analyze the structure of mind, to unravel the elemental processes from the tangle of consciousness.

- G. Stanley Hall and some of his colleagues are recognized as creators of the American Psychological Association. It became an intuitional structure and an important symbol of psychologists' group identity. The organization gave psychologists a great opportunity to communicate about their research in the most efficient way.

Key Terms

Apperception

Clairvoyance

Experimental introspection

Mastery values

Nonsense syllables

Personal equation

Phrenology

Physiological psychology

Psychological compounding

Psychophysics

Reaction time

Romanticism

Spiritualism

Structural psychology or structuralism

Vitalism

Muskulärer Typus

5 Psychology and the Mass Society at the Beginning of the 20th Century

The union of the mathematician with the poet, fervor with measure, passion with correctness, this surely is the ideal.

William James (1892)

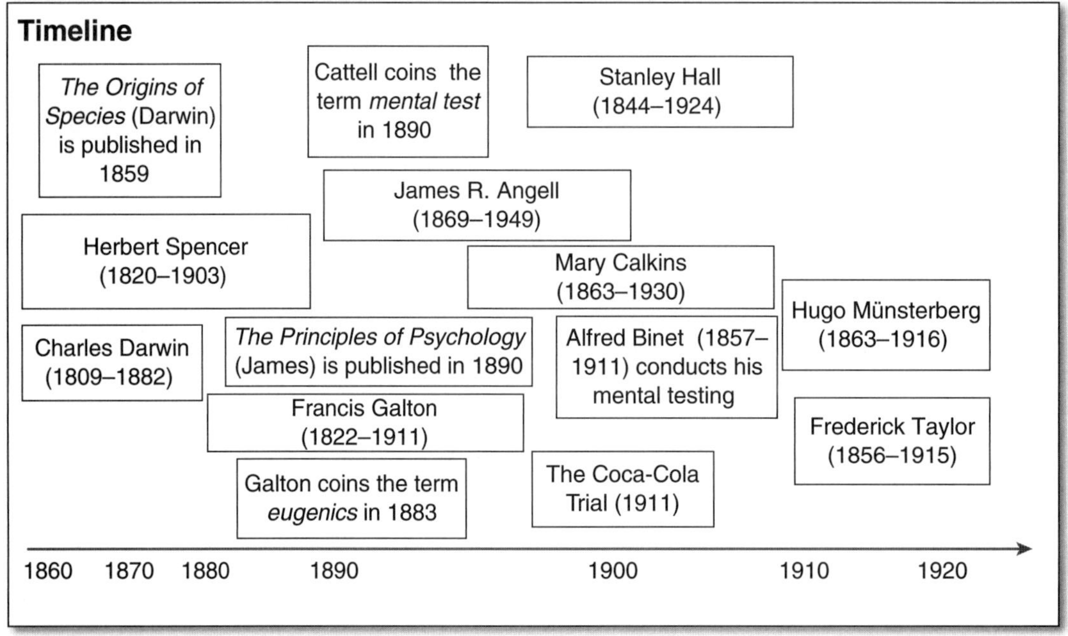

CHAPTER OUTLINE

Taking their first steps away from quiet campus laboratories, psychologists turned their attention and efforts to everyday problems. They began to work at schools, factories, and health care facilities. Probably for the first time in history, the science of psychology was used in government litigation. In 1911, in a highly publicized court case, the U.S. government accused Coca-Cola of adding caffeine to its beverages. Caffeine was believed to be a hazardous "added" substance, and the government wanted Coca-Cola to stop this practice. To defend itself in court, Coca-Cola hired psychologist Harry L. Hollingworth to conduct research and testify about the effects of caffeine. As a result of a carefully crafted series of experiments, Hollingworth provided the evidence that caffeine did not affect behavior significantly. This was one of the earliest instances of a large corporation hiring a professional psychologist to give scientific testimony. Two years later, in 1913, the science of psychology was used in a highly publicized litigation case in Russia. Vladimir Bekhterev, a well-known therapist, was hired to testify as an expert in a murder trial in which a Jewish man was accused of a ritualistic killing of a Christian boy. Bekhterev conducted, as he called it, a "psychological expertise" of the circumstances of the crime. He provided evidence for the jury showing that the crime under investigation did not fit the behavioral profile of a ritualistic murder. His testimony helped to acquit the accused man. Bekhterev demonstrated the importance of observable and measurable facts and the usefulness of psychological investigation in a court case (Bekhterev, 1916/2003). Slowly but surely psychological research was coming out of the laboratory to be used with real-life problems. Psychology was emerging as a young and promising field. But was it ready to deliver its promise?

The Social and Cultural Landscape

Did you know that the words *automobile, airplane,* and *mental test* became part of the English vocabulary approximately at the same time? These words symbolized the changes taking place in many countries, primarily in Europe and North America, at the turn of the 20th century. A series of interconnected developments have influenced psychology's future: economic expansion went hand in hand with political transitions and fundamental changes in education and professional training. How did psychology benefit from these developments?

Modern Mass Society

Historians refer to the transitions of the late 19th to the beginning of the 20th century as the emergence of "mass society" and "modernity" (Hall, Held, Hubert, & Thompson, 1996). It was a period of a steady industrial growth, substantial material improvements, and deep societal and educational changes (Winks & Neuberger, 2005). Traditional, mostly rural, community-based social infrastructure was rapidly disintegrating. Mass education, mass information, and mass consumption were emerging as the distinct attributes of the new century.

Economic and Political Transitions. It was a period of rapid economic expansion in Europe, North America, and Japan. Industries were booming, creating millions of new jobs. A new middle class was emerging, including people involved in service, law, education, medicine, and government administration. In 1910, 25 percent of all employed Americans were white-collar workers. Psychology's research facilities, funding sources, and employment opportunities were improving. Psychology was under pressure to prove its usefulness as a practical science.

Economic expansion was inseparable from political transitions. It was a painful period of change from a system dominated by hereditary elites, discriminatory laws, and traditional customs to various forms of mass political participation. Women began to gain equal rights with men. They were allowed to own property and vote in an increased number of countries. Governments were under pressure to adopt social reforms to satisfy the demands of increasingly influential political movements and parties. Many psychologists began to see their greater role as social "whistleblowers" and "engineers" who had the capacity and obligation to detect social ills and improve society for everyone's sake.

Expansion of Education and Training. In the second half of the 19th century, industrial nations began to require mandatory education for all children regardless of origin and social status. At least three reasons explained the growth of education: a consensus among the elites about the necessity of schooling, widening acceptance of science as a source of social progress, and the increasing demands of industries for educated and skilled professionals. Primary education was first offered to boys and girls under the age of 12. The age limit was expanding gradually.

Higher education was changing too. Governments and businesses began to allocate substantial funds for colleges and universities. For example, wealthy Russian industrialists and financiers subsidized the construction of new educational and research facilities, including the Institute of Psychology in Moscow (Yaroshevsky, 1996). Japanese government was sponsoring scholars to study abroad and foreigners to come to Japan to teach. The Chinese government sent students abroad and began to push Western subjects in local universities. By 1905 there were as many as 8,000 Chinese students in Japan. In the United States, the Morrill Act of 1862 provided federal money and land (so-called land-grant funds) to create new schools across the nation. Private universities grew too. Overall, higher education became ever more affordable to middle-class families. Colleges opened the doors to children of small businesses owners, merchants, engineers, government clerks, and teachers.

Higher education was also changing from within. German universities were the first to use the system of elective classes. North American schools followed the trend. This meant that students now could choose specific classes according to their own preferences and the demands of the emerging job market (Charle, 2004). This new elective system was obviously good news for psychologists. More students wanted to take psychology courses, so more universities offered such classes, and more psychologists were employed by universities.

The educational and political changes were inseparable from the changing social climate. It was not a smooth transition, however. It was a struggle between an old, traditional social order and innovations of the emerging society of consumers.

Changes in the Social Climate

The changes of social climate embraced quite a few, at times paradoxical, developments reflecting a broad diversity of perceptions and values. Several of these contradictory changes deserve to be mentioned here: increasing attention to practicality, acceptance of social bias, progressivism, changing perceptions of women's roles, and irrationality.

Practicality. Examples of the movement toward practicality were evident in all areas of life. Four developments converged to make practicality a major force for change. First, people were leaving traditional communities of small towns and villages and moving to large metropolitan areas. Second, the emerging new social customs and democratic laws encouraged the rule of common sense and reason. Third, math and science won a growing influence in school curricula. Fourth, the expanding market encouraged individual effort, initiative, and competition. These developments rippled through the many different areas of life. In the social area, acceptance of practicality meant embracing the notion that personal or professional success was a measure of an individual's value: the capable become successful; the incapable fail.

Travel and the rapid expansion of interpersonal communications (including telephones connected through wires) enhanced the common belief that people as well as nations are not all the same: some are successful, while others are incapable of achievement. To many, this bias was a normal outcome of life.

Embracing Bias. A massive colonial expansion in Africa and Asia let many people of colonial powers to believe that some civilizations were "inferior" because of their "innate" inability to compete with "higher" cultures. For many Westerners, almost anything created in the West, including social standards, was desirable. However, the educational traditions, family norms, food practices, and customs found in other lands were viewed as deviations or peculiar developments (Shiraev & Levy, 2009). Nationalistic sentiments flourished. In *The Foundations of the 19th Century*, published in 1899, English social philosopher Houston Chamberlain urged Europeans to defend their superior culture from foreigners. According to Chamberlain, only the German race was capable of defending the Western world from the new "barbarians," including Asians, Africans, and the Jews. This book was a best-seller. As we will see later, psychology was frequently used to provide justifications for racial and ethnic inequalities.

Yet not everyone at that time eagerly embraced such biased views.

Progressivism. Many educated individuals were increasingly convinced that to improve the lives of people, government and concerned citizens should engage in a deliberate, planned intervention in many areas of society. Today we commonly call such a planned intervention "social policy" and consider it a necessary part of government's responsibilities. Now imagine yourself living 120 years ago. Any kind of social policy was, in fact, a radical innovation in government's functioning (Flanagan, 2006). Supporters of **progressivism** genuinely hoped for different, civilized forms of industrial production and wealth distribution, with guaranteed pay, a shorter workday, disability insurance, and affordable health care. An increasing number of psychologists embraced progressive values. For psychology professionals, progressivism meant an opportunity to apply scientific knowledge to many spheres of life. Progressivism also emphasized the importance of applied psychological knowledge in three areas: health care, education, and social services. Consequently, from the beginning of the 20th century, a growing number of psychologists began to identify themselves with social reformers who were pursuing the expansion of the government's role in social life. They also hoped for the increased importance of psychology as an applied field.

Changing Perceptions of Women. Progressive ideas were inseparable from a changing cultural perception of women's role in society. Women were entering the labor force in significant numbers. Social scientists challenged the conventional assumptions about women's exclusively submissive and nurturing role in society. Educated psychologists read the works of well-known progressive thinkers. The popular English philosopher John Stuart Mill (1806–1873) was particularly admired among progressive-minded scholars. His historic essay, *On the Subjection of Women* (1869/2010) advocated gender equality, claiming that the differences between men and women were the product of social customs.

Nevertheless, social and political inequality between men and women in industrial nations remained considerable. Most universities outside the United States were reluctant to admit females. Progressive and egalitarian ideas were continually challenged by old-fashioned bias and even irrationality.

Irrationality. Life in the early 20th century wasn't all about progressive ideas, reason, and peace. The new century witnessed growing skepticism about the ability of human beings to handle their own affairs. To many intellectuals, the rapid industrial and urban changes signaled a forthcoming gloom and doom. Like today, when we discuss humans' destructive impact on the environment, 100 years ago people were worrying about technical progress going out of control. In philosophy, literature, and the performing arts, destructive irrationality became a common theme.

What did these changes mean for the development of psychology? Overall, the increased popularity of progressive and egalitarian beliefs was a positive trend allowing psychologists, both men and women, to increase their role in studying and, eventually, addressing social problems. Progressivism also helped to link together theoretical knowledge and practical issues. Yet the promotion of the progressive agenda did not win overwhelming societal support. Ethnic, racial, and gender biases, acceptance of irrationality—all continued to influence psychology for some time.

Having briefly addressed the emerging social climate of the early 20th century, let's turn to the development of science and technology and their impact on psychology.

✓ **CHECK YOUR KNOWLEDGE**

What was progressivism related to psychology?

Advances in Natural and Social Sciences and Their Impact on Psychology

The beginning of the new millennium brought breathtaking new discoveries and accomplishments in a variety of scientific disciplines. Consider just a few.

Scientific Discoveries

In physics, the discovery of radioactivity by French scientists stimulated the development of nuclear physics. Roberto de Moura of Brazil publicly demonstrated a radio broadcast of the human voice in 1900. Successes in theoretical engineering brought to the world the automobile and the airplane. In medicine, the triumph of germ theory of disease helped to cure millions of people. Studies of pathology of the brain and nervous system, the brain chemistry, and new morphological discoveries advanced the knowledge about the brain's functions. Impressed with the advancement of science, psychologists were eager to improve their own research methods and strategies (see Table 5.1).

Social sciences were actively adopting the scientific method. Sociologists began to switch from speculative discussions to empirical observations, measurements, and statistical methods of analysis of societal trends. Cultural anthropologists traveled to faraway places to provide detailed record of the intricate lives of indigenous groups. Human culture appeared as a complex system with many interconnected functions. Mainstream economists turned to calculus to describe the basic mechanisms of economic production, trade, and consumption. From discovery and interpretation of facts, science was turning increasingly more toward practical applications of knowledge.

Table 5.1 Scientific Disciplines Contributing to Psychology

Scientific Disciplines	*Scientific Developments*
Physics and chemistry	Discoveries in the fields of electricity, radio, thermodynamics; discoveries of new chemical elements, and forms of energy were rapid and astonishing. Psychology adopted the use of the scientific method for its own experimental methods of data gathering.
Biology and medicine	Advances in general biology and physiology, including new discoveries of the mechanism of brain functioning and descriptions of brain pathology and new morphological structures, lead to the weakening of "mental philosophy" and the strengthening of theories advocating neurophysiological foundations of psychological activities.
Sociology and anthropology	Scientific studies included many new empirical theories about society, community, customs, indigenous cultures, socialization, religion, social mobility, urbanization, suicide, and group actions. Psychologists began to use the new and rich sociological evidence in their own studies.
Evolutionary theories	Natural selection principle emphasizing that a species evolves as a result of competition influenced the views of many psychologists. Psychological processes appeared as a series of adaptive mechanisms allowing individuals to adjust to the changing environmental and social conditions.

Psychologists were direct witnesses of the advancement of science. Working on university campuses side by side, physicists, chemists, engineers, biologists, and sociologists, most academic psychologists also wanted to advance their studies following the three common, accepted by many university scholars, paths:

1. They wanted to advance psychological knowledge through the use of objective methods.
2. They were increasingly concerned about promoting their knowledge thorough peer-reviewed publications and scientific conferences.
3. They were increasingly concerned about the practical application of their work.

This was a period when psychologists were studying, comparing, and embracing the natural science and social science traditions applied to their discipline. Both traditions put a premium on objectivity of the gathered facts. The natural science tradition placed an emphasis on biology and physiology, while the social science tradition emphasized the importance of social factors in interpreting psychological processes (Driver-Linn, 2003). Scores of psychologists, as publications of that period suggest, considered knowledge as a practical tool necessary to improve people's lives. This kind of psychological progressivism was influenced by the ideas of utilitarianism and pragmatism.

Utilitarianism and Pragmatism

A major impact on the debates about the role of psychology was made by two schools of thought: **utilitarianism** and **pragmatism.** The first is associated with Scottish philosopher, economist, and social scientist, James Mill (1773–1836) and his son John Stuart Mill. Supporters of utilitarianism maintained that the value of an object or action is defined by its utility or usefulness. Utilitarianism focuses on the consequences of a behavioral act. An action is "right" if it tends to promote happiness—not only that of the person who commits the act but also of everyone affected by this action. But what if actions promote happiness on the one hand but inflict pain on the other? Thinking in contemporary terms, an illegal drug, for instance, is supposed to bring temporary joy to a drug user. If so, should we all support the use of illegal drugs? The answer is "No." Why not? Because a drug might cause a temporary pleasure, yet the long-term effects of the drug on the individual are devastating. Not everyone understands this. Only education could help people know what is good for them. Mill believed that well-informed people would be able to determine which actions are in their own best interest (Mill, 1863/1998). Many psychologists embraced utilitarianism as a guiding principle of their research.

Pragmatism, as related to the scientific tradition, has at least two meanings. A broader definition refers to a way of approaching situations or solving problems that emphasizes practical applications and consequences. In a narrow sense, pragmatism refers to a specific philosophical school. John Dewey (1859–1952) was an American philosopher, psychologist, and educational reformer whose ideas have been greatly influential in the United States and around the world. Dewey was one of the three central figures in American pragmatism, along with Charles Sanders Peirce, who coined the term, and psychologist William James, who popularized it (James, 1909/1995). Supporters of this view believed that facts do not stand apart from thought. Facts depend on thought. Language is the means by which people acquire knowledge. Applied to psychology, these assumptions meant that the world is not perceived passively (as structuralists maintained). Human perception is, in effect, an active manipulation of the environment! In *The Reflex Arc Concept in Psychology* (1896) Dewey argued that the organism interacts with the world through self-guided activity that coordinates and integrates sensory and motor responses. Dewey's views had been influenced by G. Stanley Hall (see Chapter 4 and also later in this chapter), from whom Dewey acquired the appreciation for the experimental method and practical knowledge.

Many psychologists working in universities in the United States and Europe shared the utilitarian and pragmatic ideas. Although very few questioned the importance of applied knowledge, debates started about whether psychologists themselves should become practitioners and work directly with schools, hospitals, government offices, and industries. If they should, would they have enough knowledge and skills to make a difference in the "real" world?

More Psychologists Become Practitioners

Psychology enthusiasts had little doubt that their discipline was ready to serve its progressive role. Three goals had to be pursued.

1. To attract more students to take psychology classes or select psychology as their major, psychologists had to be concerned about the public visibility of their research. Therefore, psychological studies and their results should be understandable to ordinary people. Without television or the Internet, the best possibilities for promoting psychology were the newspapers and popular journals that were increasingly available for the general reading public in the early 20th century.

2. Psychologists had to earn reputation and status among private businesses and financial corporations. Psychologists needed to show that their research had serious practical applications. This could secure new private funding and employment opportunities.

3. Because of government's increasing involvement in education, business regulations, military training, health and child care, government could be a potentially generous sponsor of new psychological studies.

Skeptics argued that psychology wasn't ready yet to offer practical solutions and should not assume responsibility for everything that happens in society. Some academic psychologists even ridiculed psychological articles in popular journals and newspapers and called their authors irresponsible attention seekers.

Were psychology and psychologists ready to give informed answers to the many questions that society posed to them? As we did in previous chapters, let's now examine what people—both educated and not—knew about psychology by the end of the 19th and early 20th centuries.

✓ CHECK YOUR KNOWLEDGE

Explain pragmatism and utilitarianism.

Psychology as a Scientific Discipline

What People Knew: Scientific Knowledge

Most educated people could make distinctions between voluntary and nonvoluntary processes, conscious and unconscious phenomena. Research provided by Hermann Ebbinghaus (described in Chapter 4) explained how memory worked. Psychologists also explained the reaction time (Cattell, 1885). It was common to divide sensory processes into categories according to the nature of sensation: visual, tactile, auditory, and so on (Baldwin, 1895b). The structuralist approach to the sensory processes introduced a relatively clear model involving simple elements connecting together into something more complex. Various association theories explained how people structured meaningful images, memories, and thoughts. Educated people also knew about inherited features passed on from parents to children (it was a common belief that the mother, not the father, was largely responsible for the transmission of such features). Researchers began to pay attention to the child's behavior. For example, Charles Darwin published a detailed observation of his own infants. He meticulously described various behaviors (he called them *reflex actions*), including sneezing, hiccupping, yawning, stretching, sucking, and screaming. He also described the development of vision, anger, fear, pleasurable sensations, shyness, spoken language, and even moral senses (Darwin, 1877).

At least three main areas of psychological research had emerged by the end of the 19th century.

Three Areas of Research in Psychology. The first was associated with experimental studies developed in the Wundt laboratory in Leipzig. Soon, similar experimental laboratories were created in the United States (1883), Russia (1886), Canada (1891), France (1889), England (1897), Japan (1903), and in many other countries (see Chapter 4). Like experimental physics or chemistry, psychological research by the end of the 19th century was confined in laboratories on universities' grounds.

The two other areas developed partially in response to growing social demands. One involved the measurement of individual development and psychological abilities. Many great scholars developed procedures for measurement and statistical interpretation of behavior and psychological abilities. Finally, in the third area, many psychologists were engaged in scientific studies of abnormal psychological symptoms and their treatment in clinical settings. There were talented enthusiasts, mostly university professors and physicians studying psychological disorders (we return to their studies in Chapter 6).

Most people, of course, did not take psychology classes in college and did not read psychological journals. What was the status of psychological knowledge outside universities and clinics?

Popular Beliefs

For the most part, people perceived fellow human beings as reasonable individuals pursuing rational objectives. Actions and feelings were increasingly associated with brain activities. People were gradually more aware of the impact of social environment on behavior. However, many accepted the view that heredity was mainly responsible for most antisocial and criminal acts. Also, the prevailing opinion was that women were generally inferior to men in their intellectual capacities and their ability to work under pressure and control their emotions. People usually believed in the existence of significant differences in mental abilities among different ethnic groups. Most people condemned homosexuality and masturbation as immoral and disgusting practices. Psychologists at that time did little to alter such attitudes. Moreover, most of them agreed with these views (Laqueur, 2004).

Values

Religion remained the main source of values for most people. Religious institutions were reluctant to endorse scientific studies of mental life in psychological labs.

Scientific pragmatism related to psychology was also a threat to long-established values of traditional communities. Evolutionary ideas were resisted partly because they virtually eliminated God and put competition as the most important causal force. James McCosh (1811–1894), president and a leading psychology professor at Princeton, 1868–1888, was certain that science and faith could find a harmonious unity in which religion would be given priority in explaining so-called higher mental processes. He believed that manifestations such as honesty, patriotism, or self-sacrifice could be explained only from a spiritual viewpoint (McCosh, 1871, 1880).

In Europe and North America, with the emergence of mass society in the end of the 19th century, many academic psychologists remained religious but only as followers of customs, such as holidays, or supporters of moral norms. Some developed an increasingly popular agnostic view of God (for an agnostic, existence of God is impossible to prove). Moreover, what could have been a peaceful coexistence between science and religion quickly became open intolerance. In the subsequent warfare between psychology and religion, psychology clearly became the aggressor. Although some prominent psychologists, such as G. Stanley Hall, hoped that his discipline would never rid itself of faith, these were just declarations. In the early 1900s, references to the divine power of God almost disappeared from psychological research literature (Maier, 2004). Interests shifted toward empirical studies of religious beliefs and experiences (Miller, 2004).

Legal Knowledge

Psychological knowledge was increasingly often used in legal decisions. Psychologists could make contributions to legal judgments about the mental competence of adults and children. Professional psychological expertise was taking its first steps in jurisprudence. Experts in human behavior were invited to conduct court-ordered psychological evaluations of the suspects or their victims, as you could see from the Coca-Cola case described in the opening vignette. Attempts were made to use psychological research to create and legalize official government policies and selective programs related to schooling, immigration, and employment. An underlying assumption of these policies was progressivism: society could be improved by scientific methods. However, despite reliance on science and progressivism, psychology was frequently silent about or even helped the government to legally discriminate against some categories of fellow human beings. For example, in the United States between 1907 and 1937, 32 states required sterilization of individuals with severe mental illness, disabilities, or severe retardation. People convicted of sex or substance-related crimes were often included in this category.

Psychology was rapidly pursuing ambitious practical goals and responding to the demands of the emerging mass society. What kind of changes took place in psychology's theory at that time?

ON THE WEB

Has psychology evolved as a science by changing its main research paradigms?

Read more about the emergence of a "new" psychology and its struggle with pseudo-psychology on the book website.

✓ CHECK YOUR KNOWLEDGE

Name the three areas of research in psychology in the end of the 19th century.

Functionalism: Connecting the Individual and the Social Environment

The developing approach in American psychology called **functionalism** gradually diminished the importance of structuralism, which focused on the elements of psychological experience. Functionalism, commonly associated with the name of William James, was focusing on the dynamic purposes of psychological experience rather than on its structure: mental states are interrelated and influenced by ever-changing behavior within a complex environment. The functionalist approach challenged the theories of Wundt and Titchener and the view of the psychological experience as comprised of independent elements or independent powers. John Dewey, who was influenced by William James, maintained, using an analogy, that having a detailed knowledge of the geography of a country cannot explain this country's history; similarly, psychology cannot draw its conclusion from the knowledge of the abstract elements of experience (Dewey, 1884).

According to the functionalist approach, it is impossible to consider psychological phenomena as isolated from the environment in which they take place. Psychologists should study experiences only in relation to other experiences and the situational contexts in which they occur (Calkins, 1906). There must be a complex dynamic connection between the individual and the social surroundings. As an illustration, a structuralist studying speech is likely to examine the alphabet and the ways different letters are combined into sounds, words, and then sentences. Conversely, a researcher with the mind of a functionalist is likely to examine the sentences and the person's use of language in various situations. A shift to practical, real-life application is obvious.

ON THE WEB

Read William James's brief biographical sketch on the book website.

William James in 1890 published *The Principles of Psychology,* which became one of the most popular psychology books of his time.

William James's Views of Psychology

The Principles of Psychology was a 1,200-page journey into the depths of three fields: philosophy, physiology, and psychology. Personal observations accompanied research data. The book's author, William James (1842–1910), a professor at Harvard University, described psychology from the position of functionalism: it was the science of mental life focusing on its phenomena (such as feelings, desires, cognitions, reasoning, and decisions) and on the conditions in which these phenomena take place (James, 1890/1950). This was an innovative approach that was based on a combination of three basic methods of research.

First, James did not abandon the traditional structuralist method of introspective observation. Second, while emphasizing its inaccuracy, he also endorsed the experimental method, which added measurement to introspection. The third method was comparative. James believed in the necessity for psychologists to expand the scope of their research and gather comparative data from animal, abnormal, and developmental psychology. This comparative method would examine the origins of psychological processes, their interdependence and combinations, and different levels of functioning. James believed that to understand how the mind functions, psychologists should examine the thinking processes of all animal species all types of humans, including infants, the mentally and physically disabled, criminals, and savages (this was the common label for tribal hunter-gatherer groups).

James proposed an original theory of emotions. He challenged the common view among psychologists that emotions were first felt and then caused bodily reaction. He wrote that many people commonly assume that the sequence is simple: someone loses money, and this makes them sorry and then they cry. In James's theory, the relationship is reversed. We feel sorry after we cry. We experience anger because we engage in a fight; we are afraid because we tremble. James believed that emotions are tied in with a person's bodily expressions and simply cannot exist without them. Although this view of emotions was later regarded as simplistic, James was among the first to connect the situation, behavior, and physiological response in a complex picture of emotion.

☞ CASE IN POINT

Emotions and Physiological Reactions. The history of science provides quite a few examples of scientific discoveries or theories made by two scientists at the same time but independently from each other. Among the most well-known examples in psychology is the case of the James-Lange theory of emotion. Carl George Lange (1834–1900) was a Danish physician who, like William James, suggested that emotions could be closely linked to physiological reactions and even caused by them. Unlike James, however, Carl Lange held a more radical view. He thought that reactions related to constriction or dilation of blood vessels in the body are, in fact, emotions. What happens when a hot-tempered patient is splashed with cold water? This person will probably calm down. The power of cold water is likely to subdue the "outbreaks of passion." Lange also gave an example of the impact of chemical substance on emotions: bromide of potassium, for instance, would paralyze the vasomotor (related to blood vessels) apparatus, which would eliminate fear, anxiety, and similar uncomfortable emotions. When vasomotor functions are suspended, the individual cannot become festive or sad, or anxious and angry (Lange, 1885a/1912, 1885b/1922). Carl Lange also noted the psychological effects of lithium on behavior and emotions. Although his work in this area of physiology or emotions was nearly forgotten, lithium is widely used today to treat the symptoms of bipolar disorder.

ON THE WEB

Learn more about William James's book *The Principles of Psychology.*

See the Table of Contents and complete text on the book website.

James's Psychology as a Practical Discipline

Should we regard William James as the creator of functionalism in psychology? Probably not. James was a significant figure but not the sole creator of an academic discipline or a new field of science. So, what is his place in psychology?

First, James was an influential psychologist occupying a prestigious position at a prominent university when psychology was establishing itself as an academic discipline and profession. He wrote an influential textbook. Second, and most important, his name is forever connected with the development of psychology as an applied, practical discipline. James believed that knowledge serves a pragmatic purpose because it allows individuals to develop a cohesive understanding of life (James, 1909/1995).

James's interests were extremely diverse, ranging from experimental psychology to studies of telepathy, from psychic experiences to the psychological analysis of war. He was criticized by his contemporaries for doing too much in too many fields. Like today, many psychologists of the past believed that it was imperative for psychology to earn its reputation outside universities. Popular writers, including William Atkinson and Henry James (William James's brother), held that psychology should become more familiar to ordinary people. Yet many psychologists maintained that by exploiting popular issues, psychologists could send a distorted message that psychology was less about science and more about entertainment.

IN THEIR OWN WORDS

Views of War. William James hoped to elevate psychology's reputation and suggest its applications in many fields of life. Following you will find a quote from a speech about war that James gave at Stanford University in 1906. He did not live long to witness the devastation of World War I, which began in 1914. Yet he already warned the audience of a potential danger of a global conflict. He believed that wars among nations were caused by psychological reasons: exaggerations of threats and self-generated fear. Today these ideas of James are frequently used in publications on international relations (Betts, 2005).

And when whole nations are the armies, and the science of destruction vies in intellectual refinement with the science of production, I see that war becomes absurd and impossible from its own monstrosity. Extravagant ambitions will have to be replaced by reasonable claims, and nations must make common cause against them. I see no reason why all this should not apply to yellow as well as to white countries, and I look forward to a future when acts of war shall be formally outlawed as between civilized peoples. (James, 1906)

William James was not the only psychologist who raised the banner of functionalism and encouraged practical applications of psychological research. Among several influential names, at least three deserve mentioning: James Angell, Harvey Carr, and Mary Calkins. The psychological views of John Dewey (who like Angell and Carr was associated with University of Chicago), another prominent figure of that time, are discussed later in this chapter.

Advancing Functionalism: James Angell

One of the most prominent supporters of the functionalist approach was American psychologist and educator James R. Angell (1869–1949). He defended the clear functionalist view that psychology should be engaged in empirical investigations of the functioning of the human nervous system in various environmental conditions (Angell, 1907). Accepting the pragmatic view of behavior and psychological functions, he maintained that psychological functions and behavior evolve by adapting to complex challenges of the environment. Angell explained, for example, a person's habit formation as a gradual learning of useful movements and elimination of useless ones. At first, when we form a habit (for instance, riding a bicycle or learning a foreign language), conscious efforts are necessary and useful. We follow instructions and remember mistakes and try not to repeat them. After practice, however, the habit proceeds without conscious effort. Why? Consciousness has already played an important function at an earlier stage of habit formation. After a habit is formed, a conscious effort is no longer needed.

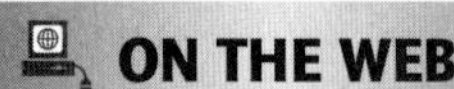

ON THE WEB

Read James Angell's brief biographical sketch on the book website.

Read also the *Time* magazine cover story (June 15, 1936) about Angell on the book website.

One of Angell's students at the University of Chicago was Harvey Carr (1873–1954), who eventually succeeded his mentor's position as chair of the psychology department. Carr developed Angell's functionalist ideas in a milestone textbook published in 1925, at the time when functionalism was accepted as a mainstream view of psychology in many countries. But before this happened, psychologists made a serious effort to promote functionalism and distinguish it from the influences of structuralism.

Structuralism and Functionalism: Critical Evaluations

While the new functionalist ideas gradually gained recognition and popularity among psychologists, a few prominent psychologists, such as Titchener, did not want to give up their theoretical positions.

Criticisms and Comments on the Two Theories. Criticism against functionalism was coming from several positions. One critical argument was methodological (Kugelmann, 2001). The functionalist approach was criticized for lack of experimental rigor. Another argument was that functionalism had brought nothing new to psychology's theory. As Titchener wrote, referring to himself, structural psychologists (sometimes called *morphological*) were already very much interested in the problem of structure and function. Memory, recognition, imagination, conception formation, judgment, attention, apperception, and volition (which we are likely to call *will* today) are not abstract elements but the function of an organism (Titchener, 1898).

Titchener also believed that functionalists had unfairly exaggerated the differences between functionalism and structuralism. This view was shared by E. G. Boring, one of Titchener's prominent students. He believed the alleged struggle between functionalism and structuralism was imaginary because there were no real enemies in this battle. He recalled many years later that, unfortunately, people often misinterpret the history of psychology by paying too much attention to labels and clichés. It was also true that Titchener adopted the term *structural psychology*. However, he abandoned the term quickly because he did not want his psychological views to be perceived as narrowly focused and preoccupied too much with psychological elements (Boring, 1929). Some graduate students called themselves "structuralists" at the beginning of the 20th century, but there were only a few of them. To Boring as well as to some other psychologists, the theoretical positions of structural and functional psychologists did not appear mutually exclusive. One such psychologist was Mary Calkins.

Calkins and Self-Psychology. One of the prominent psychologists of the turn of the century, Mary Calkins (1863–1930), believed that both structural and functional approaches could coexist and complement each other. A true psychological theory should involve description of function that involves references to structural elements, just as the functions themselves involve structure. As a theoretical compromise, she offered a theory in which both structural and functional psychology could supplement each other. In her paper, "A Reconciliation Between Structural and Functional Psychology" (which was her presidential address to the American Psychological Association), Calkins maintained that psychology was supposed to become the science of "selves" (Calkins, 1906).

Psychology of the self is closely related to its environment, both physical and social. Calkins's self-psychology had three founding concepts: the self, the object, and that of the self's relation or attitude toward that object. A conscious self is a complex set of (a) structural elements and (b) relations of self to environment. The self is described on two levels or dimensions: the first is contents of consciousness, and the second is the environment in which the content unfolds. As an illustration, an individual's perceptional experiences appear as a conscious process of sharing the experience of a number of other selves. An individual's imagination, in this context, is his or her unshared experience. Calkins also referred to emotions as passive experiences. The characteristics of will and faith were active components in her theory because they describe an individual involved in goal-directed activity.

The self is both structural and functional. It contains many elements, but they should be seen in totality, in unity. The self is also unique to each individual and discrete (I am "I" and you are "you"), but at the same time continuous in time (my own self at this moment and 10 years ago are the same). But the structure and function are united in a paradoxical, contradictory way: my own self 10 years ago is also different from what is self now, because the self is constantly changing, developing a set of unique relations or attitudes with its environment. Calkins was among the first who started to use the term *attitudes* to describe the complex interaction between the individuals and their surroundings. A few decades later, attitude as a complex evaluation of self and surroundings will become one of the central concepts of rapidly developing social psychology.

Mary Calkins's career deserves special attention because it is emblematic of the role that women played in psychology at that time.

Struggle for Recognition of Women. Calkins was born on March 30, 1863, in Hartford, Connecticut, to the family of a Presbyterian minister. She attended Smith College and received degrees in philosophy and classics in 1885. Two years later she was offered an opportunity to teach Greek at Wellesley College, where she also was appointed to teach psychology, although she hadn't had formal training in this discipline.

Calkins wanted to continue by enrolling in courses at Harvard University. Her experience at Harvard was typical of the time. Most universities then did not admit women. Special petitions were filed on Calkins's behalf that required decisions on the level of the university president. The reluctance of the administration was justified by referring to a long-term tradition of accepting men only. They told Calkins that a woman would become a distracting factor for the exclusively male audience. After a delay, she was finally allowed to attend classes. She took classes at Clark University and Harvard University (where she attended a class taught by William James).

After Harvard, by 1891, Calkins had returned to Wellesley College and set up a psychological laboratory there. During her long professional career, she wrote hundreds of papers in the fields of philosophy and psychology, including four books. By 1905, she was named president of the American Psychological Association. In 1918, she became president of the American Philosophical Society.

ON THE WEB

Read more about Mary Whiton Calkins, her life and work on the book website.

In 1905, Mary Calkins became the first female president of the American Psychological Association.

In 1902, Calkins and three other female scholars had completed enough coursework to obtain graduate degrees from Harvard. However, university authorities cited formal regulations of the school (again, the regulations did not allow women to be officially enrolled) and refused to award the degrees. Instead, they suggested a compromise: the women would receive their academic degrees from Radcliffe College on the basis of Harvard's recommendation. (Radcliffe was started as a women's school. The Harvard faculty taught the courses at the two buildings designated for Radcliffe.) The women were told that although the degrees would not be from Harvard, yet unofficially they somehow would. Several colleagues urged Calkins to take the degree, but she declined. She wrote in her memoirs that by accepting the discriminatory practices of that time, she would have prolonged injustice. She believed that the Harvard degree must be open for women (Calkins, 1930). Her ultimate dream was realized only in the 1960s when almost all private universities in the United States, including Harvard, started to admit women.

In the history of psychology, Mary W. Calkins will forever remain a courageous woman who stood for principles and preferred to struggle for justice and equality at the expense of her scholarly degrees and other personal gains.

In sum, functionalism accepted the fundamental view that psychological processes should be regarded as adaptive mechanisms allowing individuals to adjust to changing environmental and social conditions. Few other theories could complement this functionalist view better than evolutionary theory.

✓ CHECK YOUR KNOWLEDGE

What did William James bring to psychology?

What was William James's view of war?

Did Mary Calkins finally graduate from Harvard?

Evolutionary Ideas in Psychology

The ideas about continuous adaptation, interaction between the individual and environment, and hypotheses about gradual transformation of behavior and psychological functions have been advanced by evolutionary theories developed in the works of their pioneers, Charles Darwin and Herbert Spencer.

Evolutionary Theories

The evolutionary theory had a remarkable impact on science in general and psychology in particular. Although Charles Darwin (1809–1882) has never been recognized as a psychologist, his theory caused fierce debates about the developmental aspects of human behavior and the role of evolution in the advance of mental functions. Darwin's theory directly influenced various branches of psychology, including comparative, educational, and developmental. Because most students today have an opportunity to examine Darwin's theory in different courses, we focus primarily on his views specifically related to psychology.

Charles Darwin's Views. Raised in an affluent English family, young Charles Darwin tried to pursue several opportunities and careers, including medicine. Darwin attended Oxford University to study religion. His passion for natural sciences prevailed, and he spent most of his time studying geology, botany, zoology, and archaeology. He was fascinated with the writings of Robert Edmund Grant (1793–1874), a doctor and biologist who furthered the development of the theories of French naturalist Jean-Baptiste Lamarck (1744–1929) and of Erasmus Darwin (Charles Darwin's grandfather) about

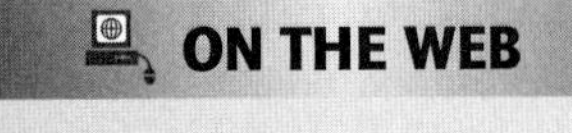

ON THE WEB

Read Charles Darwin's brief biographical sketch on the book website.

evolution of species by acquired characteristics. Darwin also was impressed with **homology,** the theory that all animals have similar organs and differ only in complexity. A 5-year sea voyage on the ship called the HMS *Beagle* provided the young scientist forever with a great possibility to study a rich variety of geological features, fossils, and living organisms and meet a wide range of people, both native and colonial.

One of the most important psychology views of Charles Darwin was that living organisms had evolved in time. This view challenged the prevailing **creationist approach** to species that explained the creation of the universe and of all living organisms as an act of God. However, Darwin was not the first scholar to maintain an anti-creationist view. In the 19th century, philosophers, anthropologists, and biologists had already exchanged ideas about so-called transmutation of species (which we now call evolution). Robert Chambers (1802–1871), for example, anonymously published the book *Vestiges of the Natural History of Creation,* presenting a cosmic theory of transmutation. It suggested that everything currently in existence had developed from earlier forms: the solar system, Earth, rocks, plants and corals, fish, land plants, reptiles and birds, mammals, and finally, the humans. Because of the book's anti-creationist stance, it was labeled immoral (which is a partial reason why the author had decided to conceal his real name). However, many intellectuals and people of power, including Abraham Lincoln and Queen Victoria, read his outstanding and daring book.

Darwin's original contribution was a theory that explained how evolutionary change took place. Darwin published in 1859 his famous book, *The Origins of Species,* in which he maintained that due to natural variations some organisms are more likely to survive than others. Those who survive pass on their advantageous characteristics to their offspring. Over many generations, those characteristics that promote survival become dominant. He named this process **natural selection,** thus emphasizing that a species evolves as a result of competition, which serves as a filter preserving the organisms that have advantageous characteristics. Darwin also proposed that the principle of natural selection could be applicable to human beings as well. In the two-volume *The Descent of Man and Selection in Relation to Sex* published in 1871, Darwin introduced the concept of evolution of human culture and attempted to give evolutionary explanations to the differences between the human genders and races.

Although the name of Charles Darwin is forever associated with the evolutionary theory, another English scholar, Herbert Spencer, has made no less significant contribution to social sciences and psychology by applying evolutionary ideas directly to society and human beings.

Herbert Spencer's Views. Educated at home in mathematics, natural science, history, and languages, Herbert Spencer (1820–1903) began his first serious intellectual endeavors by studying phrenology (see Chapter 1). He drew the concept of society as a living organism in which interdependent, specialized structures serve diverse functions. Later he switched his interests to writing and commenting on economics, politics, biology, psychology, sociology, and other disciplines. In 1853 he received a large inheritance from his uncle and continued to write as an unaffiliated scholar. He had no official teaching position and held no university degree. However, he had great personal connections among the English elites that helped him to publish and promote his ideas. In 1848 Spencer became the sub-editor of *The Economist*, an important financial weekly in London read primarily by the upper middle class. He interacted with most famous people and leading intellectuals of Europe.

What distinguishes Spencer's ideas? He was an ardent believer in human freedom and free market capitalism. He maintained that people's success is based on their ability to withstand challenges and adapt to their environment. Spencer coined the phrase "survival of the fittest." To succeed, people have to adjust to surrounding conditions: environmental, social, and political. They also should create opportunities to change such conditions. Innovation, experimentation, or calculated risk—all these behaviors change society. People who are incapable or unwilling to adjust would eventually lose. Spencer saw competition as a natural, healthy phenomenon, the behavioral foundation of societal progress. Spencer viewed human adaptation as the increasing adjustment of inner subjective relations to outer objective relations. Some psychological functions, such as spoken language, are preserved simply because they are useful, while the functions that are deemed useless tend to lose significance and eventually disappear. Spencer and his numerous followers who shared his views of free competition and survival of the fittest were called social Darwinists. In fact, Spencer's theory of evolution preceded Charles Darwin's main work. Spencer wrote an essay called *The Developmental Hypothesis* in 1852 (Spencer, 1852/1891), about 7 years before Darwin's book *The Origin of Species* was released (Darwin, 1859). However, as it has been mentioned, Spencer's views were largely theoretical and speculative. Darwin was a natural scientist who based his theory on factual, empirical evidence. Therefore, Darwin's ideas appear today as scientifically more sound than Spencer's theoretical assumptions.

ON THE WEB

Take a quiz about Spencer's life and views on the book website.

Read more about his afflictions and their influence on his work.

ON THE WEB

Read Herbert Spencer's brief biographical sketch on the book website.

General Impact on Psychology

The writings of Charles Darwin and Herbert Spencer—widely circulated around the world in original English and translations—encouraged many psychologists to accept a broader view of psychology. Psychological processes appeared as adaptive mechanisms allowing individuals to adjust to the changing environmental and social conditions. Evolutionary theories have encouraged scientific imagination and offered a series of intriguing assumptions. For instance, if human beings and animals have the same natural origin, as evolutionary theories stated, then by studying animal behavior a researcher can learn more about humans! Next, if a child's individual development is a "product" of evolution, then by studying a developing child we can study the origins of human civilization! More, if human society can be explained by several universal principles of natural selection, then psychologists can study these principles and offer scientific "recipes" to improve society! Functionalists embraced evolutionary ideas eagerly.

Overall, the impact of evolutionary views on psychology was both significant and controversial. On the positive side, Darwin's and Spencer's theories stimulated the research in several new fields of psychology, including developmental and comparative. Psychologists sharing evolutionary views saw a natural connection between animal and human behavior and emotions (Darwin, 1872). Humans were commonly viewed as representatives of a stage in the course of evolution. Social scientists began to write about social instincts (Tarde, 1903). New psychological theories of childhood and adolescence began to emerge. Psychological functions could be traced through evolution and also through observations of an individual growth of a child (Baldwin, 1902). Overall, research was shifting to the study of adaptive functions of emotions, thinking, consciousness, and learning. As we will read in Chapter 13, evolutionary theories influenced contemporary evolutionary psychology, which explores the ways in which complex evolutionary factors affect behavior and experience.

On the other hand, evolutionary ideas encouraged quite a few researchers to assume that the principles of natural selection could be used to improve human society. As a result, radical approaches emerged as camouflaged forms of racism and discrimination against women, ethnic minorities, and the mentally disabled.

Social Engineering. The controversial impact of evolutionary ideas was especially noticeable in the development of the principles of **social engineering**, a general concept to describe the use of science by the government or other social institutions to improve society through policies. (See Figure 5.1.) Quite a few psychologists believed that most important principles of natural selection should be used to improve society through social engineering. It was a mixture of social progressivism and evolutionary views. These ideas grew out of good intentions: scientists genuinely wanted to improve the human race by the means of evolutionary science. What if, for example, as Spencer

Figure 5.1 Assumptions About Psychology's Role in Social Engineering

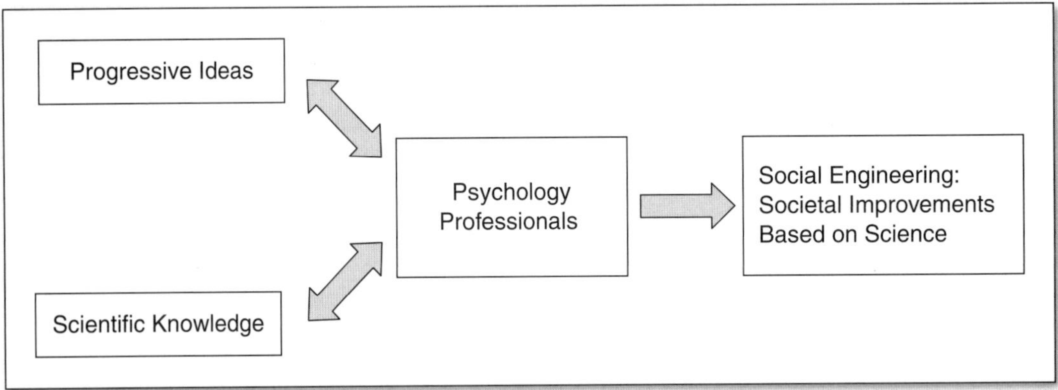

mentioned, society fought overpopulation by limiting the birth rates of people whose intellectual capacities were below average? If smartness is hereditary, then by the means of natural selection the human race could soon increase its intellectual potential. Smart people would gradually replace the "stupid" in government offices, plants, factories, and schools. What is wrong with this plan? History will show that the mixture of social progressivism and evolutionary ideas could lead to unwanted and even disastrous consequences. The ideas of Francis Galton are remarkable in this regard.

The Impact of Francis Galton. One of the pioneers of social engineering was Francis Galton (1822–1911). He was confident, for example, that proper selection of partners in marriage would improve society. Galton, a half-cousin of Charles Darwin, was a British poly-scientist. He conducted research in mathematics, anthropology, climate studies, statistics, biology, and psychology. Altogether he published more than 300 papers and several books, and he was awarded with the title of a knight, the highest honor for a British subject. One of his main works, the book *Hereditary Genius,* was published in 1869 and remained popular for half a century (Galton, 1869).

Francis Galton believed that mental features of people could be advanced through a special selection process.

Impressed with Charles Darwin's *The Origin of Species,* Galton became particularly interested in the studies concerning the breeding of domestic animals. He believed that acquired characteristics are inherited and attributed this to *gemmules,* certain particles in the body. He even conducted a series of experiments transfusing blood from different breeds of rabbits and examining the characteristics of the offspring. His assumption was wrong, as he realized. Later Galton studied the evolutionary principles applied to humans. Galton believed, by analogy, that mental features of people could be advanced through a special selection process. As an example, he suggested that by selecting men and women of rare and similar talent and mating them, generation after generation, an extraordinarily gifted line of people might be developed. Similarly, great moral features such as honor or kindness could also be bred (Galton, 1875).

Galton was engaged in a wide variety of projects. He wanted to study facts, compare them, and make logical conclusions from the established evidence. He examined the facts related to the work of missionaries sent to the tropics to find out why their health was deteriorating. He was interested in the effects of religious prayer on health. He also looked at the longevity and the rates of mental illness among heads of states. Galton also wanted to find whether banks holding funds for religious organizations manage to avoid financial ruin more successfully than banks holding money for non-religious enterprises (McCormick, 2004). The results were inconclusive.

Francis Galton believed that entire nations could be evaluated from the evolutionary view. For example, he thought that North American settlers originate from the most restless, antagonistic, and combative class of Europeans. During many generations, to avoid persecution, scores of people who disagreed with oppression and discrimination were leaving their homes for America. Peasants, merchants, and workers, who hated the tyranny of the elites, and the disgruntled elites themselves, were looking for new opportunities. Potential criminals also eyed the "new world" as the place to be. New immigrants to North America varied in their social status and occupation: some were looking for an opportunity to escape from an abusive society while others were eager to find new opportunities. Despite their differences, most new immigrants had a few features in common: a restless character and a rebellious spirit. Therefore, most Americans by nature are prone to business and adventure. They were defiant toward and impatient with authority. Many of them were religious, but many could tolerate fraud and gambling. Americans are as generous as they are violent (Galton, 1869).

As engineering is based on fundamental knowledge of mechanics and physics, psychology too can provide, according to Galton, important facts to government so that public officials use this knowledge to improve society.

The Birth of the Eugenics Movement. Galton coined the term **eugenics** in 1883. It was the name of a theory that proposed a way of improving society by improving people's hereditary features. In *Inquiries in Human Faculty and Its Development* Galton (1883) wrote that individuals of a distinguished merit or social rank who marry other distinguished individuals should receive financial incentives so that they would have more offspring. On the opposite side, individuals with socially unacceptable features should be discouraged or prohibited to have children.

Galton's ideas received wide recognition. A few radically minded researchers and writers, including famous authors George Bernard Shaw and Herbert Wells, hailed Galton's ideas. Eugenics societies began to emerge around the world. Argentina, Austria, Brazil, Canada, China, Finland, France, Italy, Japan, Mexico, Norway, and Sweden had eugenics societies involving scholars and influential politicians. Calls were made to create policies regulating marriage and allowing sterilization of "unwanted" individuals, including those with psychological and physical disabilities, but especially immigrants and criminals (Ludmerer, 1978). There were a few, such as American psychologist Henry H. Goddard (1866–1977), who saw eugenics as a means to promote and maintain the superiority of the white race.

In Germany in 1905, Dr. Alfred Ploetz founded the German Society of Racial Hygiene, which reflected a widespread interest of the public to improve, as people believed, the hereditary qualities of the Germans (Weiss, 1987). It took less than two decades for eugenics to gain reputation and appear as a legitimate and well-funded scientific field. By the 1920s various German textbooks already had incorporated ideas of heredity and the importance of racial hygiene to maintain the purity of the German nation against immigrants and religious minorities. In many other countries, eugenics was used to justify discriminatory policies (Kevles, 1985).

The enthusiastic support by some psychologists of social engineering and eugenics illustrates the mistakes and setbacks that psychology had to go though in its past. Fortunately, psychologists tended to be quick learners and drew powerful lessons from their own mistakes. Overall, psychologists were driven by ambition rooted in the desire to apply their knowledge to real-life problems. Psychologists hoped to improve society and help people have healthy and productive lives. In this quest, psychologists developed several new fields within their discipline.

✓ CHECK YOUR KNOWLEDGE

Explain the phrase "survival of the fittest."

Explain the main theoretical assumption of eugenics.

Why was the impact of evolutionary views on psychology controversial?

New Fields of Psychology

By 1902, many philosophers and some theory-oriented psychologists withdrew from the American Psychological Association. Although each had personal reasons for leaving APA, they were theorists united by their dissatisfaction with the new, practical orientation of psychology. Psychologists were pursuing their own interests in education, clinics, industries, and social institutions. They were looking for direct application of their research (Münsterberg, 1913). Several fields of research looked especially promising: studies of mental abilities (measuring intelligence, for example), social problems (studying poverty or crime), and gender studies.

Studies of Mental Abilities

The impact of Francis Galton on science is not limited only by his theoretical studies of heredity. Galton's studies of mental abilities, which he defined as the psychological functions associated with social success, also had a significant impact on psychology of the early 20th century. To find empirical evidence about the causes of social success, Galton examined reference books, biographical lists of prominent individuals (all of them were men), including politicians, military commanders, writers, and artists—the "chief men of genius" as Galton described them. He designed a questionnaire, a new research tool at that time, and sent it out to 190 Fellows of the Royal Society, the most prestigious academic association in Great Britain. At the time of Galton's study, such requests were rare, and the response rate was very high. Based on the received answers, Galton tabulated characteristics of the respondents' families, including birth order, the occupation, and origin of their parents. He found that greatness (again, identified very broadly as social success of an individual) is transmitted by inheritance: a talented person in one generation has a higher probability to have talented children (Galton, 1869). Galton also recognized the importance of social factors. In particular, he was aware that the individuals born to parents of social prominence have more opportunities in life than do the children of "ordinary" parents. Galton wrote about, for instance, a custom among young German professors to marry the daughters of senior professors. In his view, this was a selection process: people of high intellectual capacity were likely to have intellectually advanced children.

To advance his research of the interaction between natural and societal factors, Galton turned to the studies of twins. He was the first who conducted an empirical study on this subject. He wanted to see if twins who shared the same natural features become different when raised in dissimilar environments. Again, he used a questionnaire and sent it to known twins or to people in close relations to twins. The 13 groups of questions asked about similarities and differences between the studied twins, and Galton used the responses as factual information. (To increase the sample, he also asked the respondents to suggest the name of a twin they knew who would be likely to respond if Galton wrote to this person.) After analyzing more than 80 returns, Galton described the results of his study in a paper, "The History of Twins," published in 1875. He provides a descriptive analysis of the observations and pointed at many similarities between twins. In some cases the resemblance of body and mind had continued unaltered up to old age, notwithstanding very different conditions of life. Of course, there were differences between twins: handwriting, for example. Still, Galton's overall conclusion was that the impact of nature was stronger than the influence of environment. As an analogy, he used the example of the cuckoo, the bird brought up exclusively by "foster mothers." However, the cuckoo never adopts behavior and singing of its foster parents: nature dictates the cuckoo to sing its song and not to chirp and twitter.

ON THE WEB

Visit the book website to read more about contemporary twin studies.

Galton's research was truly remarkable in the context of the time. He was among the first to attempt to measure intelligence. To him, individual differences in intelligence were assumed to be primarily a function of heredity (Galton, 1880). He used an original survey method and cared exclusively about factual materials and verifiable observations in his respondents' answers. Unfortunately, Galton's sample was too small and thus was nonrepresentative of the general population (the people who answered the questions were exclusively from the upper class) to make broad generalizations about the impact of nature on twins. Nevertheless, Galton's research provided groundwork for further studies of intelligence and differential psychology.

Early Mental Tests. Psychologists began to develop new methods of measurements of individual traits in the context of statistical averages and other measures. These studies found important applications in schools and professional evaluation. Several prominent researchers contributed to the area of mental tests.

ON THE WEB

Read James McKeen Cattell's brief biographical sketch on the book website.

James McKeen Cattell (1860–1944) was an influential researcher, organizer, and practitioner. He stressed quantification and ranking in psychological measurements. He studied in Leipzig under Wundt's supervision and taught at Columbia University for 26 years.

There he organized a psychological laboratory. He was editor of *Science*, which became one of the leading American scientific periodicals.

Cattell coined the term *mental test* in 1890. By this term he meant the procedures used to measure "mental energy" of the participants of psychological experiments. Attention was paid to the difference between (a) an individual's performance and (b) the performance of large populations on the same test. The goal of such measurements was mostly educational: Cattell believed that university counselors would use mental testing to make speedy assessments of students' potentials and give reasonable advice about their future. He first began to administer tests in 1894 to students at Columbia University, where he worked as professor. In the early 1900s many universities and private businesses began to ask professional psychologists to help them with assessments of students and potential employees (von Mayrhauser, 2002). The popularity of mental tests grew; so did the professional skills of psychologists who designed and applied such tests. One of these talented professionals was Charles Spearman.

Growing Sophistication of Tests. Working in the field of measurement of mental abilities, Charles E. Spearman (1863–1945) suggested the existence of a general factor of intelligence (often known today as the *g* factor). Spearman found that, according to his measurements, various types of psychological processes, including hearing, vision, touch, and so on, are somehow related, and there is a constant measure to indicate such a relationship (Spearman, 1904). As a scientist, he wanted to find practical applications for his findings. He thought that children's high scores of mental abilities at school should be correlated with their professional accomplishments in the future. Spearman also wanted to find correlation between general intelligence and specific psychological characteristics, such as force of will, physical constitution, honesty, or zeal. Although he was passionate about these hypotheses, he later realized that many such correlations probably did not exist: a highly intelligent person could be also dishonest, for instance. Spearman remained hopeful that his research would convince school administrators of the importance of regular mental testing in schools. His desire was shared by scores of other psychologists.

ON THE WEB

Read Alfred Binet's brief biographical sketch on the book website.

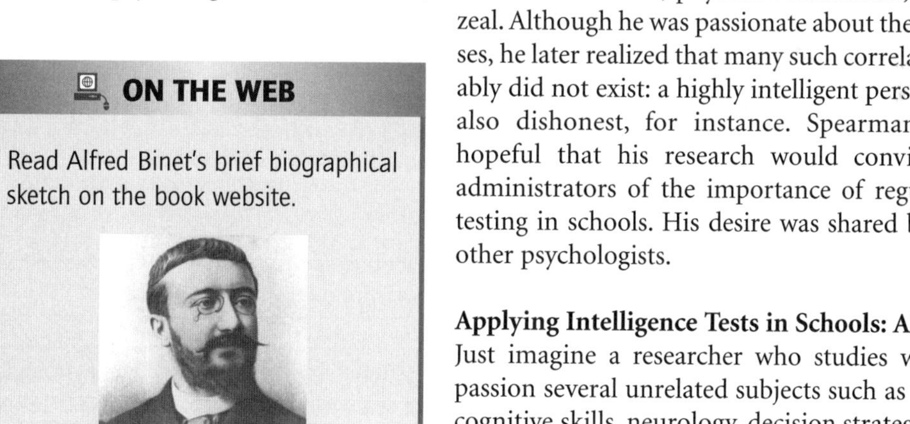

Alfred Binet had diverse research interests but is remembered today mostly as a creator of a groundbreaking method to study intelligence.

Applying Intelligence Tests in Schools: Alfred Binet. Just imagine a researcher who studies with similar passion several unrelated subjects such as hypnotism, cognitive skills, neurology, decision strategies of chess players, memory, child development, attention span, and suggestibility. That was Alfred Binet (1857–1911), who in the 21-year period following his changes in career, published more than 200 books, articles, and reviews in the fields of experimental, developmental, educational, social, and differential psychology. And this is just a short list of his interests. Despite Binet's extensive research interests and wide breadth of publications, today he is known mainly for his contributions to the studies of intelligence.

Binet's main contribution to psychology was his research of mental abilities of children. Directing the Sorbonne's Laboratory of Experimental Psychology, Binet supervised a dissertation of a young man, future psychiatrist Theodore Simon (1873–1961). Their interaction sparked a very productive collaboration that lasted for several years. Binet and Simon proposed a method based on questions directed to a child and instructions that she or he had to perform. Both the answers and actions of the child were recorded and then evaluated. Binet and Simon assumed that children develop specific knowledge and could fulfill certain tasks, such as comparing shapes or doing multiplications, only at a certain age. It was almost impossible to expect a 4-year-old girl to execute a task easily performed by a 10-year-old. Based on this logic, Binet and Simon designed an interesting research strategy: to study whether a child, by answering a set of specially designed questions and by performing tasks, could perform on the level of his or her peers of the same age. If that is the case, then the child would have "average" mental skills. If the child answers the questions designed for older (and more advanced intellectually) children, this child would have "higher" mental skills than his or her peers. Similarly, and this was the main task for the researchers to pursue, if the child persistently scores below the standard level, then this child is likely to belong to special group, which was labeled "retarded" (see Table 5.2). In sum, the

Table 5.2 Description of Tasks for Age Groups (selected sample)

Age	*Required Tasks*
3	Shows nose, eyes, and mouth. Repeats two digits. Enumerates objects in a picture. Gives family name. Repeats a sentence of six syllables.
5	Compares two weights. Copies a square. Repeats a sentence of 10 syllables. Counts coins of the same value. Arranges two pieces in a combination.
7	Distinguishes right hand and right ear. Describes a picture. Executes three tasks at the same time. Counts several coins of different value. Names four colors.
9	Gives change from 20 *soups* (French currency). Names the months of the year. Understands the questions about calendar. Recognizes all the pieces of money in use.
12	Resists suggestion when an obvious mistake is made. Uses three given words in one sentence. Says more than 60 words in three minutes. Defines abstract terms such as *charity, justice*, and *kindness.* Puts the words of a sentence in a proper order after they have been mixed.
15	Repeats seven digits. Gives the rhymes to a word. Repeats a sentence of 26 syllables. Interprets a picture. Solves a problem from several facts.
Adults	Reconstructs a triangle after it has been cut in two pieces. Gives difference in meaning of abstract terms. Solves a question concerning the role of the president.

Source: Binet and Simon (1911; English transl. 1913)

purpose of the testing method was to compare children's mental abilities relative to those of their average peers (Fancher, 1985).

Binet and Simon designed 30 tests arranged roughly in ascending order of difficulty. This became an early version of so-called Binet-Simon test. To begin, children should have accomplished the easiest tasks, such as following a lighted match with their eyes or shaking hands with the examiner (which, as we know today, is not necessarily common in all cultural groups; some kids might not know how to shake the hand of another person). Then children take on more difficult tasks. For example, 15-year-olds were expected to explain the following situation:

My neighbor has just received some singular visitors. He received one after the other: a doctor, a lawyer, and a priest. What is going on at my neighbor's?

Certainly, the child undergoing testing should have known what priests, doctors, and lawyers do. The researcher expected the child to interpret this situation in this way:

The neighbor was ill and, therefore, he invited a doctor; the doctor said the illness was dangerous; thus, the neighbor invited the lawyer to take care of some legal issues and the priest to perform some religious rituals.

In other, more difficult tasks, adults, for example, were supposed to explain differences in meaning of two abstract terms, such as laziness and idleness. In another task, an adult was asked to tell the difference between a king and a president (Binet & Simon, 1911).

The construction of the Binet-Simon test shows the sophistication of the requirements of psychological testing a century ago. The task selection process, for example, was based on observations of children in natural settings. After the tasks were assembled, Binet and Simon tested their measurement on a sample of 50 children, 10 children per five age groups. Then the researchers began to use their test in schools, hospitals, orphanages, and asylums to identify retarded children (Siegler, 1992). For the practical use of determining educational placement, the score on the Binet-Simon scale would reveal the child's mental age (descriptions of which appear in most introductory psychology books published in the United States today). Before Binet died in 1911, the scale was revised several times based on new sampling data.

Binet and Simon recognized the limitations of their research. They warned against over-reliance on pure measurements and called for the use of qualitative methods to complement quantitative research of mental functions. Binet also warned against quick generalizations about the hereditary causes of differences in test scores between children of different social backgrounds. He did not recommend his method to diagnose emotional or behavioral problems in children (Siegler, 1992). Binet's approach to testing has had a lasting influence on the work of an entire generation of psychologists in many countries. Mental testing gave them seemingly unlimited opportunities to apply theoretical research to school education, skill evaluation, and professional selection.

Scholars After Binet. One of many examples of Binet' intellectual influence is the work of German-born psychologist William Stern (1871–1938). A student of Ebbinghaus, he received a PhD in psychology (1893) from the prestigious University of Berlin and spent most of his years teaching in Germany before he moved to the United States in

1933 as a refugee. He worked and finished his career at Duke University. Influenced primarily by the work of Binet, Stern reviewed research in the field of measurement of mental abilities and came up with an idea of expressing intelligence test results in the form of a single number, the mental quotient (known today as the *intelligence quotient*, or IQ): the ratio between the mental age of the child and the child's biological age (Lamiell, 2009). Stern was also known for his theory of personality, his applied research, and his work on individual differences, which he undertook later in life.

Another scholar who admired Binet's work was Lewis Terman (1877–1956). He took the scale used in the Simon-Binet test and standardized it using a large American sample. Terman spent 33 years of his academic career (20 of them as head of psychology) at Stanford University. That is why a revised and perfected Binet-Simon scale soon was abbreviated to the Stanford-Binet (it is also called the Stanford-Binet Intelligence Scale). Terman adopted Stern's ideas about quantitative measure and developed further the idea of intelligence quotient: the ratio of mental and chronological age multiplied by 100 (White, 2000).

Besides the famous association of his name with IQ, Terman's other research is less known to today's students but remains a noticeable contribution to the history of psychology. Terman, for example, conducted retrospective studies trying to figure out the mental age of prominent individuals (when they were children) based on their own autobiographical recollections (Cox, 1926). As he expected, the estimated IQs were very high, above 150. Terman also initiated in 1921 one of the earliest longitudinal studies of intellectual giftedness; this investigation continued for many years after his death. He wanted to know how children scored high on intelligence tests at school would turn out as adults. Like many psychologists of that time, he emphasized the important role of inheritance in intelligence. Yet the results of this inquiry were inconclusive (Klein, 2002). Terman, however, expressed many progressive ideas. He believed, for example, that children should be assessed early in life to identify those children with superior intellectual abilities so that they could take more advanced classes taught by specially trained teachers.

The social climate of the early 1900s created a favorable environment in which individual skills and merit were increasingly seen as a legitimate measure of social success. We will see later how the measurement of intellectual skills was widely considered as an appropriate way to distinguish "capable" people from others.

Mental Tests: Possibilities and Concerns. In 1896 the American Psychological Association established the Committee on Psychical and Mental Tests. The goal of this committee was to promote and coordinate research in the field of physical and mental statistics (i.e., measurement of psychological, anthropological, and behavior characteristics). In 1897 the APA allocated $100 for the committee, which was a substantial amount of money then, primarily to type copies of tests and cover administrative expenses (Sokal, 1992). Testing was introduced in education and professional training. Psychologists were gradually earning respect among other professionals. Unfortunately, many problems associated with mental tests gradually became apparent.

First, psychologists could not reach an agreement about which tests should be used by schools and businesses. Moreover, they also were in frequent disagreement about the major goal of mental testing. Some suggested the testing was necessary for establishing norms, the averages for the general population. Only then could individual differences be examined. Others believed that mental tests should be used for specific issues (and without reliance on norms), such as helping a person in education or job placement.

Second, serious concerns were raised about nonpsychologists, or people with little knowledge of research methodology, using mental tests to make assessments. It was a growing problem because many educated individuals, such as parents, teachers or school administrators, considered the administration of mental tests an easy enterprise that could be done by anyone. Leading psychologists, including Robert Yerkes (1876–1956), president of the American Psychological Association, warned about the popular misperception of testing and called on psychologists to undergo special training before they administered the tests (von Mayrhauser, 2002). Other psychologists went further and demanded that the administration of tests should take place only in special "psycho-educational" clinics that would offer a wide range of diagnostic services (Wallin, 1924/1955).

Third, reliability and validity of mental tests were problematic. Psychologists found, for example, that the scores on some mental tests correlated poorly with the scores of overall academic performance of students. Furthermore, some professionals began to believe that mental tests should allow the government to reduce crime and poverty by selecting people with low test scores and isolating them from society. This was obviously not the policy that psychologists wanted to establish with their mental tests (White, 2000).

Despite these difficulties, a growing number of professionals were convinced that psychology could offer useful tools of assessment of individual skills and behavior. One of several promising fields for psychology to offer helpful applications was child development and education.

✓ CHECK YOUR KNOWLEDGE

What were Galton's twin studies about?

Who coined the term *mental test* and what did this term mean?

Why is the Stanford-Binet Intelligence Scale called by this name?

Child and Educational Psychology

By the turn of the century, more than 30 states had adopted compulsory education for children. By 1915 there were approximately 12,000 high schools in the United States, with 1.3 million students enrolled. State and private colleges and universities began to sponsor summer schools for adults. Correspondence courses emerged, allowing students for the first time in history to receive educational materials and submit their coursework through mail. These were early prototypes of contemporary online education (as you understand, professors couldn't post the lecture materials and grades on the Web yet). States and private individuals began to donate money for public libraries, which played an increasingly important role in education. For example, American industrialist and philanthropist of Scottish descent Andrew Carnegie paid for 2,500 public libraries across America for the cities and towns that allocated the land for such libraries and paid for their maintenance. Newspapers became affordable to most people, and millions of Americans began to read daily papers and weekly magazines. Illiteracy was curtailed significantly.

New Approaches. For decades, most teachers believed that rigorous discipline, drill, and repetition should be the key factors in influencing academic success of the child. Some professionals even referred to the studies of Ebbinghaus on memorization to emphasize the special importance of repetition and effort (Young, 1985). Ongoing socioeconomic changes and increasingly popular progressive views had a significant impact on educators' attitudes. The progressive viewpoint related to education was based on an assumption that children should receive a variety of opportunities and equal choices at school so that they could develop their intellectual and emotional potential fully. It was argued that children should be given more freedom and creativity in the classroom. Previously held beliefs about the importance of restriction and punishment in learning were challenged. Teachers began to attend local and regional gatherings to learn from each other and other professionals. In 1894 the University of Pennsylvania organized a special series of courses for public school teachers, which later became regular across the country (McReynolds, 1987).

John Dewey, mentioned earlier in the chapter, became one of the most influential writers about children's education. He believed, for example, that children need guidance, not punishment, and that a child's potential should be facilitated by special educational and psychological means. Yet Dewey has earned a reputation not only as a theorist but also as a practitioner.

School Psychology Movement. In 1896, John Dewey established a University Elementary School at the University of Chicago. This school also served as a research facility for classroom observation and testing. Known as the Dewey School, or the Laboratory School, it soon attracted national attention. The School of Education at the University of Chicago began to teach educational psychology to its graduating teachers and specialists in elementary and secondary schools as well as in colleges. In 1899 the Chicago Board of Education established the Department of Child Study and Pedagogic Investigation. It was one of the first psychological centers in the United States in the public school system. The department was mainly involved in body measurements (such as measuring height, facial proportions), psychological assessments, studying of specific educational problems, and training teachers. By 1914 there were 19 similar centers, or clinics, as they were called, in the United States (Wallin, 1924/1955).

Psychologists focused their interests in several practical fields. Some psychologists, following the research tradition of Binet in France, began to conduct psychological assessments of children's intellectual skills and assisted in students' placement at school. Others were interested in psychological intervention, counseling, or teachers' training. Yet other psychologists focused primarily on working with talented and gifted children. This work was the beginning of what would be called the **school psychology movement**, a collective attempt by some professionals in the United States and Canada to bring psychology into the classroom and to use psychology in developing solutions to specific educational problems.

Notice a paradox, however. The American Psychological Association did not give recognition to school psychology until much later in the century. The main argument was that school psychologists are preoccupied with practical problems and did not contribute much to the fundamental psychological science, its theory, and major methods. Psychologists working at schools were frequently viewed as lacking fundamental psychological knowledge.

☞ CASE IN POINT

Psychologists in Action. In 1911 Helen Bradford Thompson (1874–1947) became director of the Bureau for the Investigation of Working Children, which was formed after the passing of the Ohio child labor law in 1910. The child labor law gave the state some limited legal control over children until the age of 17. In fact, the law enabled psychologists to investigate the development of children who were employed but not attending school. Under the direction of Helen B. Thompson, the bureau conducted a 5-year follow-up study, investigating the mental and physical differences between 750 children in school and 750 children who had left school to go to work at the age of 14. She discovered that being away from school affected the child's intellectual development in a profoundly negative way. The findings of this study inspired her to support compulsory school attendance for children. In her numerous articles and speeches, she argued for the child's systematic education.

Despite the lack of support at the time, looking back at that period today it is appropriate to suggest that many specialists working in the field of school psychology movement have made serious contributions to psychology. They were both theorists and practitioners aware of the role that psychology should play in education. One such significant contributor was G. Stanley Hall (1844–1924).

Recapitulation Theory of G. Stanley Hall. The founder of the first psychological lab in the United States, G. Stanley Hall also served as the first president of the American Psychological Association. Among most substantial accomplishments of Hall's long career was his two-volume book, *Adolescence: Its Psychology and Its Relations to*

ON THE WEB

Read G. Stanley Hall's brief biographical sketch on the book website.

G. Stanley Hall maintained that the growing child naturally repeats the development of humankind. Hall was the founder of the first psychological laboratory in the United States.

Physiology, Anthropology, Sociology, Sex, Crime, Religion, and Education (Hall, 1904). Judging by the title alone, a reader could anticipate that Hall considered psychology a multidisciplinary field with boundless social applications. At least three elements of his theory are noticeable. First, Hall embraced evolutionary theory and considered human behavior as a never-ending process of adjustment to changing social conditions. The nervous system and the brain are products of evolutionary and historical developments. Second, he called on psychologists to study childhood and adolescence within a specific social context. Third, he was among the first in psychology to pay special attention to adolescence as a stage of human development.

According to Hall, the growing child repeats the development of humankind and that development is a natural change from one stage to another. This theory, called the **recapitulation theory,** relies heavily on evolutionary views. The child's development advances through critical periods. Children develop to their full potential if they are not forced to follow constraints but allowed to go through the stages freely. Before the age of 6, for example, the child is unable to make sophisticated theoretical judgments, is insensitive toward religion, and cannot make value judgments. There is no reason at this age to teach the child sophisticated moral theories. At 8, at the next stage, formal learning should begin. The child is ready to understand moral issues such as kindness, love, and service for others. The next stage is adolescence. During this stage, the body and psychological functions undergo reconstruction. Hall believed that here coeducation should be discontinued and boys and girls separated because they cannot optimally learn in the presence of the opposite sex. During adolescence, new sensations are formed and new associations are created. As a result of these rapid changes, confusion builds. This is a stage of rapid mood changes, inner conflicts, and behavioral turmoil. In a way, adolescence is a new birth (see Table 5.3).

Table 5.3 G. Stanley Hall's Developmental Stages

Early childhood (from birth to 6–8 years)	The child is not ready for formal education; the child is unable to reason, is insensitive toward religion, and cannot make value judgments.
Childhood (from 6–8 to 13–14)	Formal learning should begin; yet the child's brain is not at full size and weight. The child is ready to deal with moral issues such as kindness, love, and service for others.
Adolescence	Rapid reconstruction of psychological functions. This is the time of emotional and behavioral turmoil. Coed education must be discontinued at this stage.

In his research, Hall used experiments, tests, interviews, and observation. Some of his observations led him to make erroneous assumptions, however. He maintained, for example, that certain racial and ethnic groups are less advanced than others due to differences in their natural development. Hall compared African Americans as a group with adolescents, emphasizing their emotionality and relatively weak intellectual skills. Justifying separate education of boys and girls, he insisted that both genders play different evolutionary roles, and it was only natural for schools to set different school curricula: boys should learn primarily math and science, and girls should learn arts and crafts. Although Hall's theories exhibited prejudice, he did not practice it. He accepted many women into his graduate program and helped the first black student, Francis C. Sumner, to obtain a PhD in psychology (see Chapter 10).

Stanley Hall's impact on psychology was noticeable. He was among the first to focus on the child's behavior in everyday situations: at school, at home, or during play (Goodchild, 1996). He was a pioneer in studies of adolescence. Overall, his theory of developmental stages influenced many contemporary views of psychological development that emphasize the crucial role of cultural and social contexts in the child's development. Although most psychologists around him were interested in the child's learning deficiencies, and behavioral and psychological problems, Hall's attention was primarily in the fields of normal behavior. He studied the factors contributing to academic achievement and successful adjustment. A growing number of practicing psychologists also began to focus on in-depth studies of the child's successful learning and exceptional cognitive skills.

✓ CHECK YOUR KNOWLEDGE

What was the school psychology movement?

Explain the main idea of recapitulation theory.

Industrial and Consumer Studies

Psychologists offered a seemingly powerful tool for solving many work-related, organizational problems: the test. Psychologists' message to businesses was clear: allow professionals to conduct tests and they would make necessary scientific evaluations that could help in many organizational and professional decisions. Many businesses and government offices turned to testing methods to select and evaluate individuals for particular professions. Testing the working adults wasn't an invention of American or French psychologists. In China, for example, an evaluation system had existed for centuries. As early as in the 1830s British officials familiar with this system encouraged the British East India Company to use the Chinese system as a method for selecting employees for business or government work overseas. By the turn of the 20th century, the governments and businesses in France, Germany, the United States, and Russia followed this trend. The popularity of testing for employment purposes grew in many other countries.

Why did the testing method receive such an enthusiastic support? Psychologists insisted that through this method they could improve training and performance of employees. This was a right idea suggested at the right time. In the beginning of the 20th century, for example, the U.S. government and business management were very enthusiastic about the idea of efficiency of production. President Theodore Roosevelt (who was in office from 1901 to 1909) even declared work efficiency a national policy. The business community supported this policy: if a business makes more money, the employees also receive higher wages so that everyone benefits. Companies wanted to produce more at less cost and with a higher rate of safety for workers. Psychologists found a responsive audience to their suggestions that better knowledge of psychological factors at the workplace (such as fatigue, attention, motivation, etc.) could benefit production. The work of Hugo Münsterberg, whose name has been mentioned earlier in the book on several occasions, demonstrates the type and quality of such suggestions made by psychologists.

IN THEIR OWN WORDS

I found this to be a particular complicated act of tension by which the manifoldness of objects, the pedestrians, the carriages, and automobiles, are continuously observed with reference to their rapidity and direction in the quickly changing panorama of the street. (Hugo Münsterberg, 1913, describing his research on driving skills)

Work Efficiency in Münsterberg's Studies. The American Association for Labor Legislation was puzzled by the high number of accidents involving trains and street cars. Railway companies suffered substantial financial losses because of numerous accidents involving their motormen. The association asked Harvard professor Hugo Münsterberg to investigate this problem using the capacities of his psychological lab (Münsterberg, 1913). It was already known that fatigue and sharpness of vision could have been factors contributing to the accidents. Münsterberg was asked to investigate other factors and conditions and offer a method to select the most reliable employees.

Based on Münsterberg's request, an electric railway company provided him with groups of motormen: those with excellent records of performance, those who had very poor records, and those who were average. Münsterberg designed an experimental procedure that examined attention, ability to focus, make decisions, and some other abilities. Overall, the results of the experiments showed a high correlation between efficiency in the experiment and efficiency in actual service. The best motormen performed well in experimental procedures, while employees with poor records performed poorly during the experimental procedure. The experiments showed that the most successful motormen could predict most accurately the developing test situation. In the end, Münsterberg designed a numerical scale to evaluate potential candidates or employed motormen. For example, according to the test, if someone was making more than 20 mistakes on the test, this person should not be allowed to operate an electric car. The study also revealed weaknesses of the testing method: many individuals were extremely nervous during the experiment and couldn't perform well. Other individuals performed well during the experiment but on the job they applied riskier strategies, which they were reluctant to use during the experimental procedure in the lab.

Hugo Münsterberg made a contribution to psychology as a specialist in work efficiency. His passion for applied psychology and organizational skills translated into developing psychological studies of business management, efficiency, and work satisfaction. Working in San Francisco and Portland, Oregon, he designed questionnaires to select ship captains. In Boston, he improved the selection of trolley car operators. One of his most famous books, *Psychology and Industrial Efficiency,* published in 1913, brought him reputation and public appeal.

Psychology was gaining reputation through mass media. Special attention was paid to legal battles in which psychologists took part more frequently than ever before.

Psychologists in Litigation. Münsterberg (1912/2009) applied principles of experimental psychology to the administration of law, thus building foundations for **forensic psychology**, a discipline that applies psychological principles to the criminal justice system. He believed that judges, lawyers, and jury members needed experimental psychologists to improve the quality of their legal work. Private businesses found it important to use psychology for litigation purposes. In the 20th century, governments in industrial countries became increasingly involved in the regulation of consumer products (Benjamin, Rogers, & Rosenbaum, 1991). As mentioned at the beginning of this chapter, the U.S. government sued Coca-Cola for putting caffeine in the popular drink. Coca-Cola maintained that caffeine was harmless. The government lawyers disagreed.

"Enjoy a glass of liquid laughter"—that was the motto of Coca-Cola in the early 1900s. But the litigation was not a laughing matter. It could bring the company down. Coca-Cola authorities needed a perfect defense strategy, part of which was obtaining evidence about the impact of caffeine on human behavior. H. A. Hare, a physician and the head of Coca-Cola team of scientific experts, asked his friend James Cattell to help to study such impact. Cattell declined. The job was given to Harry Hollingworth, an aspiring young psychologist at Columbia University in New York (and a husband of Leta Hollingworth, whose work is described on the website). Many psychologists had ambivalent feelings about this type of work. On the one hand, financial compensation was substantial. On the other hand, many university psychologists considered these types of research as "selling out" to businesses. In response to their concerns, Coca-Cola agreed to three things: not to pressure the researchers, not to mention their names in advertisements, and to allow publication of the results in academic journals.

So, what was wrong with caffeine? At the beginning of the 20th century many doctors expressed concerns that caffeine had harmful effects on human health and behavior. Some physicians even considered caffeine a poison, with serious addiction-related features. One of most significant complaints against Coca-Cola was that the company was selling its product to children.

Hollingworth's research design was complicated: the study involved 10 major tests and many minor ones. Tests measured coordination of movements, speed, perception, associations, attention, judgment, color identification, mental manipulations, and reaction times of subjects who took different dosages of caffeine. It was a typical double-blind study (neither researchers nor subjects knew which of the subjects were given caffeine and which were not). The study was funded quite generously. Coca-Cola provided a salary to the principal investigator and his associates, including graduate students. Coca-Cola also paid for two apartments in Manhattan to conduct the experiments, a compensation for the 16 subjects selected for the study, and even some of their expenses. When the experiment was over, nearly 64,000 measurements had been obtained. Although the psychologists concluded that caffeine was harmful in large doses, an average consumer of Coca-Cola would not get that much caffeine even if he or she consumed large quantities of the drink. Hollingworth testified on March 27, 1911, and he was the ninth witness-scientist called by defense. He concluded that the experiment produced no evidence that caffeine was responsible for any detrimental effects in the performance of the study subjects.

The case was dismissed on legal technicalities. After the appeals, it was settled by Coca-Cola, which also agreed to reduce the amount of caffeine in the drink. Although the work of psychologists had no direct impact on the outcome of the court case, the results of this study gained widespread interest in the media and contributed to the reputation of psychologists (Benjamin et al., 1991). Harry Hollingworth had a long and successful career in applied psychology. One of its growing fields was advertisement.

Advertisement Studies. Hollingworth's career in applied psychology also included the study of the psychological aspects of advertisement (Hollingworth, 1913). He divided the process of advertisement into stages and studied individual behavior on each of these stages. Hollingworth studied the advertisements of several companies selling soap and facial products and provided psychological evaluations of their ads' effectiveness.

Another psychologist who gained reputation studying advertising was Walter D. Scott (1869–1955), who in 1901 was appointed assistant professor of psychology and pedagogy and director of the psychological laboratory at Northwestern University in Evanston, Illinois. In 1903, he published *The Theory of Advertising*, the first book in this field (Scott, 1903/2010). A few years later he published *Psychology of Advertising*, in which he laid down a set of scientific principles to predict the probable effectiveness of advertisement strategies (Scott, 1908/2009). Scott did experimental work for many agencies and manufacturers. For a 2-year period, for example, he experimented with the employment of salesmen, first for a tobacco company and then for other large organizations. He collected information about tobacco salesmen, starting from their first job interviews. He was interested in sales records, disciplinary problems, and so on. As a result, Scott designed tests measuring vocational aptitudes of people working in sales.

Interest in the new science of advertising grew rapidly. In 1916, Carnegie Institute of Technology organized a Bureau of Salesmanship Research, designed to understand how scientific knowledge could aid business. Professor Scott was granted a leave of absence to serve as its director, and soon, with the cooperation of 30 national companies, he undertook a study of their methods of selecting, developing, and supervising employees.

That was the beginning of an era of optimism about the unlimited possibilities of advertising and its impact on the consumer's behavior. Many psychologists and entrepreneurs believed that soon enough the universal mechanisms of persuasion would be discovered and businesses would learn how to use science to make better sales. Unfortunately, similar and seemingly good intentions to increase production efficiency resulted in theories and methods designed to convert people into obedient consumers and manufacturers.

Industrial Efficiency and Taylorism. Münsterberg, as you remember, believed that psychologists could help private businesses improve their efficiency and increase job satisfaction of their employees. Another enthusiast of industrial efficiency was Frederick Taylor (1856–1915), who believed that science could assist businesses in achieving this goal. His theory, however, is an example of how good intentions can result in disastrous, inhumane consequences.

Frederick Taylor was an engineer by education and occupation. In a collection of essays published in 1911, he emphasized that human effort in manufacturing was continuously wasted due to poorly planned operations, badly designed rules, and awkward movements of workers making products and operating machines. He also noticed that workers tend to perform more slowly than they could. He suggested two reasons for this. First, there was a natural inclination of people to do less when they are unsupervised. Second, people slow down because they talk to one another too much and learn bad habits.

Taylor's goal was to increase efficiency through training. He did not believe that great managers have natural abilities. Nobody is born with management skills: such abilities are learned. In his view, the best management should be based on science and rest upon clearly defined rules and principles (Taylor, 1911). According to Taylor, scientific methods of management should save time and effort. Taylor did not want to create sweatshops where workers endure abuse and suffering to achieve maximum production. He stated that he had great sympathy with those employees who are overworked. However, he felt more for those who were underpaid. His ultimate intention was to increase manufacturing efficiency and to make people happy: an efficiently run business should bring both material and moral satisfaction to the owner and the employee! Many industrial owners and managers accepted Taylor's ideas enthusiastically and uncritically. They began to require workers to follow the rules suggested by Taylor. Everything was regulated: every operation, movement, and step. Every break was reduced to a minimum. Conversations among workers on anything unrelated to work were disallowed.

Soon, however, the euphoria about the Taylor's method evaporated. Both managers and workers hated the labor camp atmosphere created by the method. Taylor's system ignored the role of individual motivation, pride, and interpersonal relationships at the workplace and focused exclusively on production. As psychologists gradually realized, an individual's well-being, the sense of comfort at the workplace, and good relationships with coworkers and management are far more important for efficiency than stopwatch-controlled movements and the worker's fear of underproducing.

In addition to conducting studies in industrial, consumer, and manufacturing fields, scores of researchers turned to the emerging and lingering social problems associated with rapidly growing cities: overpopulation, poverty, and crime.

✓ CHECK YOUR KNOWLEDGE

What was Münsterberg's main area of research?

What kind of experiments did Harry Hollingworth conduct during the famous Coca-Cola trial?

What did Frederick Taylor try to achieve?

Psychology of Criminal Behavior

An emerging field of research, called *criminology*, attempted to explain why crime takes place. Sociologist Émile Durkheim (1858–1917) considered social alienation produced by the collapse of the traditional family as the main reason for a host of problems associated with urban life. Durkheim referred to the social ills of the modern society as the main source of crime. Significant scholarship has also focused on biological and psychological features contributing to criminal and antisocial behavior. Cesare Lombroso (1835–1909), an Italian physician, became renowned worldwide for his attempts to describe and explain criminal behavior as rooted in individual factors. In 1876 he published in Italian a pamphlet setting forth his theory of the origin of criminal traits. An English translation of his book, titled *Criminal Man*, was published in 1911 after his death.

Lombroso believed that most violent criminals have a biological predisposition, which is an *atavism*, a reversion of behavior to some earlier developmental stages when theft, rape, and pillage contributed directly to male reproductive potential. Lombroso also argued that heredity interacts with environment to produce individuals with various potentials for criminality. These views brought his book popularity and respect (Gibson, 2002). Other views were quite speculative. Table 5.4 displays, for example, Lombroso's ideas about some typical features of a criminal.

Another book, *The Female Offender* (1895/1959), translated and published in English (coauthored with Guglielmo Ferrero) was based on his observations of female criminals and women of deviant behavior, such as prostitution. The book was published with many editorial cuts. Publishers at that time imposed censorship on any references to genitals, homosexuality, and even female breasts (Rafter, 2003). One of Lombroso's contributions to psychology was his belief that criminal behavior has different types: some individuals have serious predispositions to break the law and be violent, others are less predisposed, yet others would break the law but without resorting to violence (a certain prototype of what we now refer to as *white-collar crime*).

Table 5.4 Criminal Physiognomy

Skin	Criminals' skin commonly displays scars and lesions on the elbows and temples.
Face	High cheekbones are the most salient characteristic of criminals; the jaws are also overdeveloped.
Tattooing	Tattooing frequently reveals obscenity, vindictiveness, or cupidity.
Beard	Beards are typically scanty in criminals.
Ears	The ears of criminals are often of abnormal size or stand out from the face.
Nose	In thieves the base of the nose often slants upward.
Height	Criminals are rarely tall; they are likely to be under medium height.

Source: Lombroso (1911)

Lombroso's work was criticized during his lifetime. His critics generally underestimated his position about social factors affecting criminal behavior and focused instead on views of biological factors in criminality. Overcoming criticisms, psychology of deviant behavior began to gain ground as a discipline.

Despite rapid advances in many branches of psychology, most of them remained primarily male dominated and male oriented. Gender studies in psychology were at the very early stage of their development.

Gender Psychology

A contribution to early gender studies was also made by G. Stanley Hall. He wrote about the differences in the way adolescent boys and girls are educated in their families. He believed that marriage and maternity should be the supreme interest of women and warned about some unwanted psychological consequences if a woman chooses a different path in her life (Hall, 1904). His work is an example of how psychology was used to serve the traditional societal views of the family and the woman's roles in it.

One of the true pioneers of psychological studies of gender was Helen Bradford Thompson (1874–1947). She was an active and relentless supporter of gender equality. Ironically, in psychological literature her research often appears under the name Wooley, which she accepted after marriage. She studied neurology and philosophy, common subjects for psychology majors, and received a doctoral degree from the University of Chicago in 1900. James Angell supervised her dissertation, entitled *Psychological Norms in Men and Women.* Using undergraduates as subjects, she conducted experiments on motor ability, skin and muscle senses, taste and smell, hearing, vision, intellectual faculties, and affective processes (Thompson, 1903). Contrary to popular expectations, she found no significant gender differences in her measurements.

Individual differences in scores, as she showed, could have been easily contributed to different experiences of the involved subjects. She was known as a women's rights activist and was a member and chairperson of the Ohio Woman Suffrage Association (Scarborough & Furumoto, 1987).

Leta S. Hollingworth (1886–1939) was known for her work with intellectually gifted children. She also performed pioneering psychological research of women. In the early 1900s, there were two commonly held beliefs regarding women. First, it was generally accepted that women go through a stage of reduced mental capability during menstruation. Based on this belief, many employers would not hire women because they believed it was not possible for them to be as productive and reliable as men every day in the month. Hollingworth empirically tested this belief and found that women's performance on cognitive, perceptual, and motor tasks was consistently similar to that of males. The second premise that sparked the interest of Hollingworth was the variability hypothesis, which at the time asserted that women were more similar than men as a group; furthermore, men had a wider range of talents (as well as defects) than women. To test this hypothesis, in a large study, Hollingworth examined 1,000 male newborns and 1,000 female newborns and found no greater inherent variability in males compared to females.

ON THE WEB

Read more on the book website about Leta S. Hollingworth (1886–1939) and her studies of gifted children.

✓ CHECK YOUR KNOWLEDGE

What was criminology?

What is the variability hypothesis related to gender?

Assessments

Why did psychology undergo such a rapid development in North America and Europe but not in many other parts of the world? Several factors contributed to this advancement. The first one was economic. The rapid industrial development in the end of the 19th century was accompanied by unprecedented wealth accumulation in a number of countries including the United States, Canada, and Europe. Having taken care of basic economic problems, governments and private businesses began to increase their investments in science and education. Although psychology was not on the short list of the most demanding recipients (compared to chemistry, engineering, and medicine, for example) of such investments, funding became increasingly available for this young and promising discipline.

The second reason was structural. Psychology as a scientific discipline could not develop without a vast educational and research base provided by colleges and universities. The United States took leadership in advancing higher education at the end of the 19th century. Although historically, the most prominent universities had been located in Europe, America soon surpassed them in funding, number of students enrolled, and the scope and quality of education and research provided there. Both public and private universities in North America flourished (Rudolph, 1990). Continuously and increasingly, after 1890s, many European psychologists would come to work and teach in the United States, and not the other way around.

The third, and very complex, reason was educational. The reforms of elementary education and the advancement of compulsory schooling of children in many countries created an avalanche of logistical problems related to proper placement of students, their evaluation, training of teachers, and counseling. Psychologists seemed to be capable of offering educational assessment tools to satisfy the demands of national educational systems.

The fourth reason was professional. Private businesses and government institutions were expanding; they were in continual need for new trained and competitive workers and civil servants. Educational and professional assessment became urgent necessities and psychologists were seemingly ready to offer tests and other evaluation methods. New possibilities of applied studies in production, management, advertisement, and consumption of products appeared. Also new possibilities for psychologists emerged in litigation, criminal investigation, training, and assessment.

Psychology was limiting its ties with philosophy and embracing views of both natural and social science traditions. Functionalism, with its emphasis on development, change, and practicality, gradually replaced the classic, laboratory-based structuralist views. Evolutionary theories were increasingly popular. Yet some psychologists accepted them uncritically. Mental testing was becoming a common trend in education, business, and government service. The first differentiation of psychology took place in the beginning of the 20th century and involved the development of educational, child, industrial, and other fields of psychology.

Conclusion

The developments of the early 20th century strengthened an important moral position of psychologists: their scientific optimism and societal progressivism—both increasingly popular among theorists and practicing specialists. Psychology was also moving in the fields of mental illness, its diagnosis, and its treatment. It was no longer a priest, a shaman, or a fortune teller who was expected to heal psychological symptoms. In Chapter 6, we turn to the development of clinical psychology.

Summary

- The emergence of "mass society" and "modernity" was associated with steady industrial growth, substantial material improvements, and deep societal, political, and educational changes. Women began to gain equal rights with men. Industrial nations began to require mandatory education for all children. Governments and businesses began to allocate substantial funds for colleges and universities.

- The beginning of the new millennium brought new breathtaking discoveries and accomplishments in a variety of scientific disciplines. At least three main areas of psychological research had emerged by the end of the 19th century: experimental studies, measurement of individual development and psychological abilities, and scientific studies of abnormal psychological symptoms and their treatment in clinical settings.

- Functionalism focused on the dynamic purposes of psychological experience rather than on its structure: mental states are interrelated and influenced by ever-changing behavior within a complex environment. William James saw psychology as the science of mental life; he focused on its phenomena and on the conditions in which these phenomena take place. James also proposed an original theory of emotions. Among influential psychologists at that time were James Angell, Harvey Carr, Mary Calkins, and John Dewey, who studied and wrote on a variety of theoretical and applied problems.

- The writings of Charles Darwin and Herbert Spencer encouraged many psychologists to accept a broader view of psychology. Psychological processes appeared as adaptive mechanisms allowing individuals to adjust to the changing environmental and social conditions. The controversial impact of evolutionary ideas was especially noticeable in the development of the principles of social engineering and eugenics.

- Francis Galton was among the first to attempt to measure intelligence, which he believed was a hereditary function. To him, individual differences in intelligence were assumed to be primarily a function. Galton conducted early studies of twins.

- James Cattell, Charles Spearman, and Alfred Binet's contribution to psychology was their research of mental abilities of children. Mental testing gave psychologists seemingly unlimited opportunities to apply theoretical research to school education, skill evaluation, and professional selection.

- Psychologists began to conduct research in the areas of education, learning, advertisement, professional training, work skills, work productivity, business management, criminal behavior, and many others. Early steps were taken to advance developmental and gender psychology. Despite mistakes and excesses, psychology increasingly often accepted its progressive role in society.

Key Terms

Creationist approach (also called creationism)

Eugenics

Forensic psychology

Functionalism

Homology

Natural selection

Pragmatism

Progressivism

Recapitulation theory

School psychology movement

Social engineering

Utilitarianism

Clinical Research and Psychology at the End of the 19th and Beginning of the 20th Century

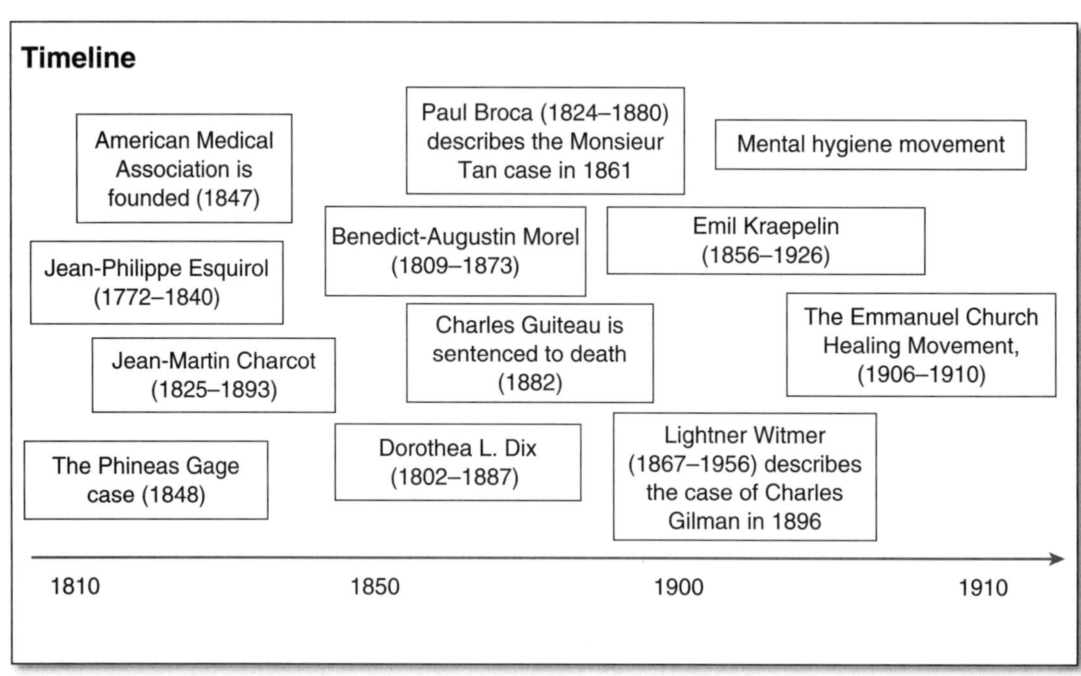

CHAPTER OUTLINE

On July 2, 1881, Charles Guiteau shot and mortally wounded President James Garfield. Then the killer said calmly, "I did it. I will go to jail for it; Arthur is President, and I am Stalwart!" The entire country was in shock. Newspapers discussed a possible conspiracy. Religious commentators held that the assassination was a payback for America's sinful behavior and impiety. Many Americans, however, believed that the shooting had been the work of a lunatic. In the mind of an average person, lunatics act irrationally. They are different from normal people. They are dangerous and unpredictable. Guiteau appeared to be one of them.

Who was this "lunatic" and murderer? What caused his murderous act? The details about Guiteau's past were sketchy. His late mother had a kind of "brain fever." (Most likely, they were postpartum symptoms.) Did her illness affect her son? She died when Guiteau was young. Did her early death cause her son's mental instability? Did his harsh and neglecting father trigger his anger? Was it a venereal disease Guiteau had contracted in his youth? How did this illness affect his brain? He was a member of a religious community practicing free love; did he become insane because of that involvement? Obviously, Guiteau had a rough past. Probably he had a serious mental illness. Most people believed, however, even before the trial started, that Guiteau deserved death.

The trial began in November and continued until January 1882. The medical experts commissioned for the hearings were sharply divided about definitions of insanity and guilt. Some felt strongly that Guiteau was insane and, therefore, could not understand his murderous act. They recommended clemency and serious medical treatment. Other experts testified that Guiteau was mentally ill but not insane; he was competent to tell right from wrong during his crime. Yet others argued that he was sane during the crime but became insane later, lost his mind, and could not understand the court proceedings. This debate about his illness, sanity, and guilt did not last long. After listening to the arguments of the experts, the jury found Guiteau guilty and sentenced him to death. Very few argued against the death penalty. Many educated people saw mental illness as a form of moral deficiency. Guiteau was executed 6 months later.

Society's interest in mental illness rises after tragic events. Many years later, the murder of John Lennon in 1980, the attempted assassination of President Reagan in 1981, or the massacre at Virginia Tech University in 2007—each committed by a lone gunman—renewed spirited discussions about mental illness, insanity, treatment, and causes of extreme violence. Although with years passing, science brings new information about possible causes of psychological abnormalities, today, like 100 years ago, we continue to debate this subject.

Back in 1881, people's experience with mental illness was very limited. Society was only about to embrace a new medical field called psychiatry and a new field of studies and practical work called clinical psychology.

Sources: Freedman (1983); Paulson (2006); Rosenberg (1989)

In the first five chapters we traced the development of major ideas in psychology before the beginning of the 20th century. Now we examine knowledge related specifically to mental illness. At least two categories of specialists contributed to the development of knowledge about mental illness. First, there were physicians. Second, there were university-based psychologists.

What People Knew About Mental Illness

Across cultures and times, people commonly referred to mental illness as something grossly atypical, off-putting, and undesirable within a person's mind. This "something" caused persistent behavioral problems or odd manifestations. Mental illness was somewhat opposite to physical maladies, which were identifiable body-related abnormalities such as a skin lesion or broken arm, for example. The causes and mechanisms of mental illness were far more difficult to spot. Mental illness appeared as an unpredictable and painful pattern of actions, emotions, and thoughts coupled with a person's inability to reason or act rationally.

How did psychology as an emerging discipline develop knowledge about mental illness? What kind of problems did psychologists face at that time? To answer these questions, we examine first the state of knowledge about mental illness at end of the 19th century.

Scientific Knowledge

Several common categories of mental illness already existed. Notice how imprecise these categories were. In the next sections, we start with madness and then review neurosis, hysteria, affective disorders, eating disorders, and substance-related problems.

Madness. The label **madness** (also called *insanity* or *lunacy*) referred to symptoms of two kinds: either gross excessiveness or overwhelming deficiency of certain features in an individual's behavior and experiences. First, this term described aggressive, violent behavior and dramatic emotional outbursts. Second, it concerned an individual's profound lack of will, desire, or emotion. General descriptions of these symptoms appear in various written accounts in different periods and cultures (Foucault, 1965). More specific descriptions began to come into view about 200 years ago. Physicians Philippe Pinel (1801) in France and John Haslam (1810) in England provided detailed accounts of individuals exhibiting mostly withdrawn behavior: diminished speech, no interest in joyful activities, and lack of emotional attachment. Their thinking was disorganized. They paid little attention to personal hygiene. Many of them reported hallucinations and bizarre ideas. Individuals developed these disturbing symptoms as young adults and never improved. German doctor Karl Kahlbaum (1828–1899) and his student Ewald Hecker (1843–1909) labeled such symptoms *hebephrenia*. Kahlbaum also introduced the term *catatonia* to describe rigid and peculiar postures and the profound lack of speech. These and other similar descriptions were vague. They provided nevertheless valuable information for the 20th century's studies of schizophrenia. Another significant development in the history of psychology was the study of symptoms labeled in the 19th century as neurosis and hysteria.

Neurosis. Most descriptions of **neurosis** referred to an individual's persistent, overwhelming anxiety and avoidant behavior. These symptoms were different from madness in one important way: most neurotic patients were aware of their problems and usually acknowledged the oddness of their symptoms. At the end of the 19th century, physicians already recognized several kinds of neuroses. *Anxiety neurosis,* for example, referred to a person's persistent worry, restlessness, and inability to focus. *Phobias*—excessive and inappropriate fears—and especially agoraphobia (an abnormal fear of open or public places), originally described by German physician Carl Westphal in 1871, also drew the attention of clinicians.

A key development of the time was the identification of a general type of neurosis called *neurasthenia*: a disorder characterized by persistent feelings of weakness and general lowering of bodily and mental tone. G. M. Beard, who coined this term in *American Nervousness* (1881), wrote that the nervous system has a varying *tonus,* which is either *sthenic* (strong) or *asthenic* (weak). Neurasthenia soon became a fashionable diagnosis for all kinds of neurotic conditions. It was convenient to believe that neurotic symptoms originate from a person's mental weakness or nervous oversensitivity or both. Doctors considered neurasthenia a valid medical diagnosis. Patients received a new label for their emotional problems.

Hysteria. French physician Jean-Martin Charcot (1825–1893) focused on a specific category of symptoms: psychological and physical complaints without an identifiable anatomical defect of physiological malady. He called such symptoms **hysteria.** Although physicians knew about these symptoms for centuries, the knowledge was fragmented. Charcot, on the other hand, had continuous access to patients assembled in Salpêtrière Hospital in Paris. He and his followers conducted unique and systematic observations. In the book *Clinical Lectures on Certain Diseases of the Nervous System,* translated and published in the United States, he described symptoms including muscle spasms, involuntary movements, panic attacks, refusal to eat, stomach disturbances, and immobility without any symptoms of muscular atrophy (Charcot, 1888). He believed that the symptoms of hysteria related to the weak nervous system. In his view, people with weaker nervous systems were more susceptible to hysteria than others.

Studies suggested several forms of hysteria. For example, American doctor Morton Prince (1854–1929) described patients with chronic physical symptoms such as fatigue or pains. These patients could pay attention to one area of their consciousness while losing attention to others. Prince also indicated that some individuals, especially those with history of psychological trauma, could assume different personalities.

In his famous book *The Dissociation of a Personality* (1905/2007), he described a form of hysteria that could be compared today to the dissociative identity disorder.

Another French physician, Pierre Janet (1859–1947), also suggested that hysteria could be caused by a person's *traumatic memories* about an episode experienced in the past. These memories continue to disrupt the person's life, causing various unpleasant symptoms. Janet accepted the idea about weakness in the nervous system as a root cause of hysteria. He also coined the term *psychasthenia* to describe the lack of cohesiveness in the nervous system resulting in symptoms such as excessive fears and anxiety, coupled with ritualistic actions and thoughts (Nicolas, 2002). These symptoms received a common label *neurosis of obsessional states* (which is close to contemporary definitions of obsessive-compulsive disorder). As you can see, hysteria and neurosis referred to somewhat similar psychological symptoms.

Affective Disorders. Symptoms of what we know today as **mood disorders** attracted physicians' attention for centuries. Historically, certain states of human mood were recognized as abnormal if they satisfied two important conditions. First, the symptoms should be profoundly different from normal mood fluctuations such as periodic capricious behavior or temporary sadness. Second, such fluctuations should be frequent or long lasting. In the English language the most common term for long-lasting sadness was *melancholy.* It originates from the Greek *melas* (black) and *khole* (bile, the liver-generated bitter liquid stored in the gallbladder). Many scholars two or three centuries ago regularly associated sadness with the function of the liver, gallbladder, or the spleen, thus connecting psychological and bodily symptoms (La Mettrie, 1748/1994).

ON THE WEB

On the book website, read about various historical accounts of mood disorders.

In the United States, Benjamin Rush (1745–1813), the founding figure of American medicine, used the term *tristimania* to describe his patient's symptoms of exaggerated and prolonged sadness. Karl Ludwig Kahlbaum (1843–1899) in Germany described the symptoms characterized by alternating mood swings from mild depression to mild euphoria and termed such symptoms *cyclic insanity* or *cyclothymia.* Henry Maudsley (1835–1918), the renowned British physician, coined the term *affective disorder.* In the 20th century, this term became common but yielded later to a more contemporary *mood disorders.*

Eating Disorders. Descriptions of symptoms of excessive fasting appeared in publications several hundred years ago in Europe, Africa, the Middle East, and Asia (Keel & Klump, 2003). Theories about causes of such symptoms varied: brain damage, weight obsession, or even fraud. Other observers believed that the cause was possession by supernatural powers (Winslow, 1880). Most experts in the 19th century viewed causes of excessive fasting as deriving from nervous conditions. In 1874 William Gull introduced the term *anorexia nervosa* when describing four cases of adolescent girls with deliberate weight loss through self-starvation (Habermas, 1989). Symptoms of bulimia appeared less common. There were isolated cases involving individuals exhibiting binge eating after a period of restricted food intake. Unlike cases of **anorexia**, which involved mostly women, most documented cases of bulimic symptoms before the 20th century involved men (Keel & Klump, 2003).

ON THE WEB

Learn about the symptoms of "holy anorexia" on the book website.

Substance-Related Problems. The first scientific reports and systematic clinical observations of substance effects began to appear about 200 years ago. Most of them described alcohol-related problems. In the 1800s, morphine addiction also attracted the attention of physicians. In early scientific reports published in European and American journals, morphine addiction was viewed mostly as a person's character flaw or bad habit (Berridge & Edwards, 1981). The widespread use of morphine as a pain medication caused addiction and misery in tens of thousands of patients. By the end of the 19th century, the term *morphine addict* was already well known.

One hundred and fifty years ago, society maintained predominantly tolerant attitudes about opiates and cocaine, and the use of these substances in Europe and other parts of the world was extensive. However, views of these substances were changing. Take opium as an example. Once considered a recreational product, opium was gradually earning a negative reputation. Journal publications began to warn about the harmful consequences of habitual opium use, which could result in a person's dependency and a host of emotional problems (Eaton, 1888). Attitudes about cocaine changed too. Although many people at the turn of the 20th century believed that cocaine could produce nothing more than mild intoxication, several reports already suggested harmful effects, including hallucinations, delusions, and depressive symptoms. A doctor concluded hopelessly in a 1914 op-ed in *The New York Times* that cocaine use could become so strong that no force or law could stop it (Williams, 1914). Despite numerous reports about the harms of substance use, there were no scientific guidelines about how to prevent or treat this problem.

Overall, most observations of abnormal symptoms were imprecise. Similar labels routinely applied to different symptoms. Likewise, doctors would give different labels to similar warning signs. For example, the term *idiocy* stood for a wide range of developmental problems. It could also be labeled as *lunacy* or *dementia.* During the 19th century, the term *insanity* applied to a wide range of symptoms, including severe forms of alcoholism, fire setting, compulsive theft, senility, and many others (Quen, 1983). Scientific knowledge borrowed heavily from popular assumptions and beliefs about mental illness.

ON THE WEB

Read more about assumptions about medical use of certain addictive substances on the book website.

Popular Beliefs

Popular views of mental illness developed within specific social and cultural conditions of countries and regions. At least three trends of general beliefs about mental illness became common.

First, mental illness became a special explanatory category for those individuals whose behavior was out of the ordinary and difficult to explain by understandable causes. If someone was insane, then he or she must be different from other people. If someone commits a heinous crime for no apparent reason, then it would be a form of madness that drove this individual to commit the crime.

Second, having a mental illness often meant being an outcast. Across cultures the public maintained an overall negative perception of mental illness. People commonly ostracized the mentally ill, avoided them, or displayed intolerance against them.

Third, people had broad expectations that some forms of mental illness were curable. Plants, roots, leaves, and other natural substances frequently served as remedies to treat abnormal psychological symptoms. Ritualistic acts, meditation, and prayer were also common therapeutic methods. Some folk methods were effective, of course, but most were not.

Gradually, due to emerging mass education and the media, more people began to understand mental illness not as a mysterious state but rather as a medical condition. People were also changing their views of abnormality itself. Take, for example, cultural views of sexuality. The traditional widespread belief that women, not men, should be troubled by their sexual feelings was in doubt. More educated people accepted the idea that sexual feelings are a natural part of female experience. More people were willing to discuss, understand, and reevaluate sexuality from a more tolerant perspective. Books on previously forbidden topics appeared on bookstores' shelves. One of them was by physician Edward B. Foote (1829–1906), who published *Plain Home Talk,* a book related to marriage, love, and healthy sexuality (Foote, 1896). Society was gradually changing its views of many aspects of human behavior.

However, various religious and social rules continued to identify "appropriate" behaviors and psychological experiences and contrast them with "deviant" and "abnormal" ones.

Ideology

For centuries, across most cultures, religious views of mental illness were based on the idea that psychological abnormalities must have been caused by some evil possession, curse, or a person's lack of religious commitment. Mental illness was seen as God's payback for an individual's inappropriate actions, shameful desires, or some kind of perversity. This curse may last for generations. In addition, feelings of insecurity associated with substantial social and economic changes in the 19th century and the dissolution of the traditional society in Europe and North America led many people to believe that mental illness was the result of their deviation from the established good path of quiet, traditional life (Shiraev & Levy, 2009).

Yet the scientific outlook was gaining strength. An analysis of manuscripts published between the late 17th and the early 19th centuries in Europe, for example, shows a general decline in religious explanations for insanity and a corresponding advance in the science-based description and interpretation of mental illness (Ingram, 1998).

Legal Knowledge

With the increasing role of government in social affairs of modern society, legal rules became gradually more important, especially in democratic states. Authorities began to discuss mental illness in legal terms. The case in the opening vignette, related to the assassination of President Garfield, as many commentators admitted, underlined the necessity to have clear legal rules about mental illness. Authorities also needed legal rules to justify specific societal policies related to the mentally ill. Among these policies were at least three: mandatory social isolation, educational placement, and forced sterilization.

Social isolation was a widely acceptable practice for dealing with the undesirable. Some psychologists in the late 1800s supported compulsory isolation of people with serious mental defects. Legal authorities accepted as reasonable the practice of putting people in specially organized facilities. As you remember from Chapter 5, compulsory education of children established by the beginning of the 20th century gave authorities in several countries the right to decide on the child's placement (to decide whether a child should receive special education). The label "mental retardation" now required a legal definition. Furthermore, a certain level of mental capacities became an official standard for accepting or rejecting some categories of immigrants to the United States. Psychological knowledge influenced the law. Serious debates, however, continued around the legality of forced sterilization of people with serious psychological problems. Supporters of the eugenics movement (see Chapter 5) believed that the law should allow and mandate such sterilizations. Others began to raise their voices in defense of the legal rights of the mentally ill.

In 1868, the Association of Medical Superintendents of American Institutions for the Insane adopted a series of recommendations related to legal status, responsibilities, and the rights of the mentally ill. There were other professionals who believed that mental illness was not a legal issue but rather a social or moral problem. As an illustration, two American physicians, Clifford Beers (1876–1943) and Adolf Meyer (1866–1950), attempted to change legal policies and subsequently public perception of mental illness. Beers, in the book *A Mind That Found Itself*, described his own experiences in a mental facility as a patient and emphasized the necessity to change the inhumane practices in such places (Beers, 1907). Meyer insisted that people with symptoms of severe mental illness were patients, not outlaws to be forced into prisonlike isolation.

Overall, clinical practitioners and researchers of the late 19th century had inherited important knowledge about psychopathological symptoms, their variety, and severity. Disagreements grew about causes and treatment of such symptoms. Like in biology or chemistry, specialists in the fields of mental illness began their advancement in the areas where they could collect and interpret new empirical data. One of the main questions was about the causes of mental illness.

Table 6.1 Terminology Referring to Mental Illness in the 19th Century

Patients	Lunatics, feebleminded, the insane, the distracted, the distempered in mind, fools
Custody places and treatment facilities	Asylums, madhouses, jails, almshouses, fools' houses
Therapists	Alienists, medical superintendents, neurologists, psychiatrists

✓ CHECK YOUR KNOWLEDGE

Name the most important differences between madness and neurosis.

Which psychological symptoms were called *sthenic* and *asthenic*?

Society and Psychopathology

Massive social and economic transitions of the late 19th century brought significant changes to the lives of many people, especially in the industrial nations. Life expectancy of the general population had increased. In western Europe and North America, life expectancy was 55 years, in contrast to 45 years in the rest of the world. One of the reasons for the improvement was a fundamental change in health care. It was an era of new surgical procedures, immunization, and anesthesia. Great discoveries in brain anatomy and physiology allowed scientists to associate particular behavioral and psychological functions with specific regions of the brain.

Many specific changes that took place by the end of the 19th century have had a profound impact on how society began to understand mental illness, its causes, and its treatment.

Social Climate and Psychopathology

Public attention to mental illness grew significantly in many industrial nations. Several interconnected reasons exist for this. First, there was an apparent increase in incidences of mental illness. Second, the process of medicalization of mental illness and deviance (understanding them primarily in medical terms) stimulated new methods of medical treatment. A new social category called "mental patients" emerged. Third, ongoing scientific discoveries brought a possibility to explain mental illness in a scientific manner. And finally, the booming newspaper and magazine publishing business provided a very effective way to disseminate sensational information about the most unusual and dramatic cases involving individuals with psychological problems. Let's discuss these points in some detail.

Sex, Drugs, and Alienation. Historians in the United States and Europe documented a significant increase of incidences of mental illness at the end of 19th century. Archival reports show that the number of patients in private and state psychiatric clinics in Germany, Russia, the United States, and Great Britain grew 5–10 times over just several decades. By 1910 Germany had 16 psychiatry clinics in universities, nearly 1,500 psychiatrically trained physicians, and more than 400 private and public mental asylums (Shorter, 1997). At least three factors contributed to the rising numbers of registered cases of mental illness.

First, the 19th century was the time of a considerable increase in the number of patients with neurosyphilis, a venereal disease associated with slowly progressive and destructive infection of the brain or spinal cord. Most people contracted this infectious illness through unprotected sex outside marriage. The early symptoms included constant headaches, irritability, depressed mood, confusion, and movement problems. Many patients were secretive about the illness and remained untreated until the appearance of secondary symptoms, including progressive personality changes, memory loss, and decreasing ability to make judgments.

A second serious problem of that time was the rampant substance abuse sweeping cities and towns in Europe, North America, and some countries in East Asia. The most abused substances were alcohol, cocaine, opium, and morphine. Scores of people in increasing numbers turned to liquid and powdered drugs to ease stress of their daily lives, reduce pain and anxiety, or simply feel high. Most of them didn't know about the dangerous addictive nature of the substances and devastating psychological consequences of their abuse. Scores of people with severe symptoms of addiction ended up in prisons and mental facilities.

The end of the 19th century also signified the occurrence of a third and new psychological phenomenon: alienation. Today we commonly call it stress or daily hassles. Prominent writers and social scientists, including Émile Durkheim in France, Karl Marx in Germany, Mark Twain in the United States, and Fyodor Dostoevsky in Russia, wrote about the devastating pressure of the big city, the faceless reality of big factories and apartment buildings, and a lifestyle of continual production and consumption. Continuous stress and the lack of family or community support were two important factors that probably affected large groups of individuals at that time.

Changing Attitudes About Mental Illness. A significant sociocultural shift in attitudes about mental illness also took place in this period. A person with painful or dangerous emotional and behavioral symptoms was increasingly often seen as a patient who needed professional treatment. For years, the immediate family took primary responsibility for people with severe psychological problems. In an emerging social climate of individualism, a growing number of families did not want to keep a relative with serious psychological problems at home. There was an emerging belief that individuals had the fundamental right to enjoy freedom, happiness, and pain-free existence. Anything, such as a sick family member, that prevented an individual from pursuing pleasurable goals should be avoided (Boring, 1929). A psychological problem, as a result, was often framed as an "anomaly" that should have been corrected. As a result, mental health care was considered a necessary social institution, like many others, including schools, law enforcement, or sanitation services.

There is a connection between psychological individualism, on one hand, and the way we define mental illness today, on the other. Individualism, in a psychological sense, is based on two principles: *utilitarianism* (anything useful is good) and *hedonism* (rational, goal-directed behavior of human beings is bound for pleasure). Furthermore, a rational individual is entitled to experience joy. Any obstacles diminishing happiness or causing suffering should be reduced or eliminated. This individualistic attitude probably stimulated the heightened attention to mental illness as a threat to happiness. In other words, mental illness in Western culture has become defined as something that prevents an individual from being happy.

Do you believe that we, as humans, are entitled to be happy? Alternatively, if there is no such entitlement, then mental illness ceases to be an abnormal phenomenon because it becomes part of our experience. Which view would you support and why?

Medicalization of Abnormal and Deviant Behavior. At the end of the 19th century, medicine was becoming a rapidly growing profession. Many specialists began to see persistent violence, sex crimes, homelessness, or chronic drug abuse as medical, not social, problems. Therefore, they thought, these problems required attention of medical professionals. This was a period of **medicalization** of abnormal and deviant behavior. Medicalization of behavior reflected the way many people understood mental illness. Consider an example. Since the inception of war, military commanders have had to deal with soldiers' fears on the battlefield. Excessive fear was often labeled cowardice and soldiers' complaints about serious emotional problems were called *malingering.* These were punishable offenses, especially during wartime. Psychology, however, had brought the term *shell shock* to describe serious psychological symptoms of traumatic nature associated with battlefield experiences. Now many doctors insisted that people who exhibit these symptoms deserve medical attention, not punishment (Lerner, 2003).

Institutionalization of Treatment. Professional groups representing the interests of health care specialists began to organize in many countries. Several medical organizations had already been established, including the American Medical Association (1847) and the British Medical Association (1860). Two main goals appeared most important for them: to impose comparable standards on medical education and training of physicians, and to provide general guidelines for the work of medical professionals.

Mental health care workers had their own professional associations as well. In 1844 the Association of Medical Superintendents of the American Institutions for the Insane was created. The *American Journal of Insanity,* the predecessor of the *American Journal of Psychiatry,* appeared in the same year. In 1892, this organization changed its name to American Medico-Psychological Association and again in 1921 to the American Psychiatric Association (the name retained today). Similar medical-psychological associations emerged in many countries.

Hospitals widened the practice of clinical assessment of patients based on the advanced knowledge of anatomy and physiology. To train physicians, Germany, the United Kingdom, France, the United States, Austria, and Russia, among others, began to move away from the system of apprenticeship. This traditional system required future physicians to spend several years learning skills and obtaining knowledge directly from their mentors. Now the focus was on medical schools attached to universities. The Johns Hopkins University School of Medicine in Baltimore established a 4-year graduate program, which quickly became a model for similar medical schools around the world. In Russia, the government sponsored several medical academies to train physicians for military and civil service. Medical schools for women appeared in several countries, including the United States, Russia, and Great Britain. The female Medical College of Pennsylvania was founded in 1850; the London School of Medicine for women was established in 1874. In 1887 the Women's Medical Institute opened its doors in Russia.

Specialists studying mental illness generously shared their knowledge with colleagues regardless of their nationality or professional affiliation. There were few restrictions on international travel, and international conferences became commonplace. From 1818 to the end of the 19th century the or approximately major 50 journals appeared in Europe and the United States dedicated to **psychopathology**.

As we saw in Chapter 5, the advancing 20th century had brought remarkable opportunities for university-based research psychology. Experimental, industrial, and educational psychology were gaining reputation and respect in society. Clinical psychology, however, had a more difficult history. Today approximately one half of professional psychologists in the United States participate in clinical practice, clinical research, or related teaching. Yet the early development of this field took place in the atmosphere of fierce and often unfair competition with medical establishment, which was claiming its sole right to interpret and treat mental illness. To understand the development of clinical psychology better, we look first at the "turf battles" around mental illness.

The Turf Battles

Although the early 19th-century textbooks on medicine already had chapters on psychiatry, mental illness appeared as a special category of illness only in the mid-1800s (Zilboorg, 1941). To study and treat mental illness, doctors wanted to establish their own independent and fully legitimate field of medicine. A growing number of university psychologists also wanted to study and treat psychological abnormalities. The question was, Who should conduct clinical research, diagnose, and treat mental illness? Medical doctors claimed that they, not psychologists, should have this exclusive right. Although psychiatry in the 19th century was not a fully legitimate branch of medicine, physicians had already established a precedent of treating the mentally ill (Perrez & Perring, 1997).

Licensing. Medicalization of treatment in industrial nations also meant that doctors were supposed to be *licensed*, or given the legal right to practice medicine. Clinical psychologists wanted equality; they too claimed their right to apply and receive licenses. They faced, however, serious opposition from two sides: medical doctors and psychologists themselves. Why did this dual opposition occur?

An important reason that medical professionals were unhappy with psychologists was financial. Psychiatrists wanted to limit their professional competition and exclude from it nonmedical specialists. In fact, under pressure from medical associations, psychologists were pushed away from clinical facilities in several countries. As late as in 1917, the New York Psychiatric Society published a report about the dangers of involving psychologists in medical evaluations and practice. A common practice was established: psychologists were allowed to conduct tests and make limited assessments, but the power to interpret the tests and make recommendations to patients belonged to licensed medical professionals.

Physicians also wanted psychologists out of medical research. Why? In most countries, including the United States, governments had some but limited control over medical facilities. Physicians had more freedom to experiment with various treatment procedures and, subsequently, with health of the patients. Many discoveries were made by chance or surreptitiously, when doctors assumed roles of researchers and tried to determine the effects of certain procedures on their patients. This approach drew criticism from psychologists who believed that clinical practice lacked rigorous scientific background: without carefully planned experiments doctors were prone to commit errors, thus endangering their patients. Doctors frequently (and mostly unfairly) brushed off these criticisms and believed that psychologists should remain in universities, not in clinics.

Many academic psychologists did not want to see clinical psychology as an independent field within the psychology discipline. Some university-based researchers were unhappy with the clinical psychologists. Their clinically oriented colleagues were considered guilty of committing two sins. First, they were seen as intruders into the medical field, the area beyond a psychologist's competence. Second, clinical psychologists were perceived as defectors who left traditional research psychology. The debates about the role of psychologists in diagnosis and treatment of mental illness continue today.

These turf battles affected research and clinical practice. Yet both moved forward. Specialists began to offer more sophisticated concepts of classification, causes, prevention, and treatment of mental illness.

✓ CHECK YOUR KNOWLEDGE

What is alienation as a perceived cause of mental illness?

Explain the phenomenon of medicalization of deviant behavior.

What were so-called turf battles in the field of mental illness about?

Understanding Mental Illness

In contrast with the observational procedures designed by Wilhelm Wundt (see Chapter 4), clinical researchers were less interested in the structure of perceptions or feelings of a self-observing individual. They focused on the patients' abnormal symptoms and their classifications (Taine, 1870). They attempted to collect, categorize, and make a systematic description of various symptoms treated as empirical facts (Nicolas & Charvillat, 2001). In the 1800s, specialists continued to identify two major clusters of mental abnormalities: madness and "nervous" dysfunctions.

Classifications of Mental Illness

The first group of abnormalities was madness or insanity, the labels attributed to extremely bizarre, sometimes violent, and unpredictable behaviors. Madness was further categorized in subgroups based on the duration and intensity of its symptoms. In contrast, nervous dysfunctions represented in disturbances and deviations from normal, usual behavior: persistent and overwhelming anxiety or sadness, difficulty sleeping, absence of appetite, constant fatigue, and so forth (Gilman, King, Porte, Rousseau, & Showalter, 1993).

In the middle of the 19th century, several new categories of mental illness appeared in French, German, Russian, American, and British scientific literature. Guillaume Ferrus (1784–1861), for example, distinguished three categories: *temporarily idiotism, acute dementia,* and *stupidity.* Karl Stark (1787–1845) recognized three categories: *dysbulia* (disturbance of mood), *dysthenia* (anxiety symptoms), and *dysnoesia* (dysfunction of perception and thinking). These categories then were matched with "hyper" symptoms (exaggerated emotions and dramatic actions) and with "low" symptoms (withdrawal). David Skae (1814–1873) focused on sources of mental illness. He recognized *moral idiocy* and *chronic masturbations.* He also distinguished *sthenic* (strong, active symptoms), *asthenic* (weak, inactive symptoms), and *idiopathic* (related to unknown causes) groups. Henry Maudsley (1835–1918) offered a classification that included disturbances of emotion (depressions in particular), affective insanity, and disturbances of imagination.

The list of such classifications can be easily continued. Yet the history of psychology distinguishes one German-born scholar and clinician who used this outcome-based approach as the most significant contributor to the contemporary classification of mental illness. His name was Emil Kraepelin.

Emil Kraepelin offered an early scientific classification of mental illness, which included 15 categories or groups.

Classification by Emil Kraepelin. Emil Kraepelin (1856–1926) made the most significant attempt to organize mental illness along the lines of a number of distinct categories. Kraepelin was a hard-working researcher trained in experimental psychology at the Wundt laboratory in Leipzig. But unlike Wundt, Kraepelin did want to study elements of psychological dysfunctions (remember that Wundt assumed the existence of psychological elements, the most basic modules of experience). Kraepelin's strategy was purely clinical: he wanted to know how the symptoms of mental illness develop and whether or not patients recover or remain chronically dysfunctional.

Kraepelin, as well as many of his colleagues, traveled across Europe searching for work. He found a teaching and clinical position at Tartu University (it was in Russia then; today it is in Estonia) in 1886. There he began to keep detailed records of his patients' histories. Over the years, he recorded small and big changes in patients' symptoms and created a large database. As an innovative development, Kraepelin kept track of some of these people even after they left hospital. He was interested in the course of illness and the circumstances affecting the symptoms.

As a result, Kraepelin offered a classification of mental illness, which included 15 categories or groups. An important category in his classification was *dementia praecox,* with symptoms resembling today's schizophrenia. Kraepelin further divided this category into three subgroups. One was called *catatonia.* The key symptoms were severely inhibited behavior activities. Another category was *hebephrenia,* characterized by inappropriate emotional and behavioral reactions. The third category was *paranoia,* characterized by delusions of grandeur or persecution. Kraepelin was among the first who put together the symptoms of melancholia and mania under an umbrella of an illness, called *circular insanity,* in which manic and depressive symptoms would alter each other; it was later renamed *manic-depressive illness.* The symptoms of this disorder together with schizophrenia became widely recognizable by the vast majority of practitioners and researchers at the end of the 19th century. (See Table 6.2.)

Table 6.2 Emil Kraepelin's Classifications of Mental Illness

Category	*Some Examples and Symptoms*
Infection psychoses	Delirium and psychotic symptoms believed to be associated with infection or fever
Exhaustion psychoses	Chronic nervous exhaustion, acute confusional insanity
Intoxication psychoses	Acute intoxications, chronic alcoholic intoxication, morphinism, and cocainism
Thyroigenous psychoses	Cretinism
Dementia praecox	Disturbances of orientation, thought, attention, emotion, and will; hallucinations. Appears in three forms: hebephrenic, catatonic, and paranoid
Dementia paralytica	Disturbances of thought, judgment, memory, conduct, speech, and emotions. Appears in several forms
Organic dementias	Associated with organic problems, including multiple sclerosis, cerebral tumor, cerebral apoplexy or trauma
Involution psychoses	Melancholia (with symptoms of guilt, nihilism, disturbances of thought, etc.) and senile dementia
Manic-depressive insanity	Manic states, depressive states, and mixed states
Paranoia	Querulent insanity: abnormal suspicion and accusations
Epileptic insanity	Mental disturbances associated with epilepsy including delirium, somnambulism
Psychogenic neurosis	Hysterical insanity manifested as changes in character, hypochondriasis, or showy behavior; traumatic neurosis

Category	*Some Examples and Symptoms*
Constitutional psychopathic states (called also insanity of degeneracy)	Nervousness, compulsive insanity (included phobias and tormenting ideas), impulsive insanity (including the impulse to kill, impulse to tramp, pyromania, and kleptomania); contrary sexual instincts
Psychopathic personalities	Born criminals (moral insanity), the unstable, the morbid liar and swindler, the pseudo-querulants (having tendencies of false accusations)
Defective mental development	Imbecility and idiocy (a more intense degree of imbecility)

Source: Kraepelin (1883)

ON THE WEB

You can examine psychological dysfunctions that were identifiable by the early 20th century on the book website.

Kraepelin's classification symbolized the advancement of a medical model of classification of mental illness. He was interested primarily in the symptoms, how they occur, and whether or not these symptoms are curable. This knowledge would allow him to presume with some confidence whether a patient would recover from illness and how soon. This classification has become an early foundation for the contemporary classifications of mental illness.

✓ CHECK YOUR KNOWLEDGE

What strategy did Kraepelin pursue in his classification?

What was *dementia praecox* in the Kraepelin classification?

Approaches to Mental Illness

At the end of the 19th century, there existed at least two general schools of thought about mental illness. According to the first one, mental illness is best explained if we turn our attention to the brain and nervous system, their structure and functioning. The main cause of any mental illness is, therefore, natural or organic. There should be identifiable structural abnormality or dysfunction in the work of the brain (Osborne, 2001).

The second school of thought emphasized the importance of social and psychological factors contributing to mental illness. Supporters of this point of view were in agreement about the biological foundations of mental illness. Nevertheless, the environmental and psychological factors also played a very important role in contributing to mental illness. The competition of these two traditions influenced, to some degree, the debates about the roles and responsibilities of psychologists and medical doctors.

The first, the biomedical approach, had a long history. The ideas that observable psychological dysfunctions have underlying physiological mechanisms began to appear in various medical publications as early as in the 1700s. William Battie, an English physician, wrote in *A Treatise on Madness* (1758/1962) that muscular spasms of the blood vessels in the brain cause obstructions and compressions of the nerves, which in turn could cause various emotions and sensations that manifest as symptoms of mental illness. He would give his patients special anti-spasm substances such as asafetida. In 1793–1794, Vincenzo Chiarugi, an Italian physician published a three-volume book *On Insanity and Its Classification* (1793/1987) in which he claimed that abnormal psychological symptoms could be the result of brain lesions. Russian professor I. I. Enegolm wrote in his 1815 book, *A Brief Observation of Hypochondria and Its Treatment,* that serious depressive symptoms must be associated with dysfunctions of internal organs in the body.

Approximately at the same time, Benjamin Rush (1745–1813), one of the most prominent American contributors to the studies of mental illness (also a signer of the Declaration of Independence and a chemist, writer, and educator) published a textbook in which he noted dysfunctions in blood vessels as causes of abnormal psychological symptoms (Rush, 1812/1979). Henry Maudsley (1835–1918), a practicing British doctor and editor of the prestigious *Journal of Mental Science,* strongly considered nervous disease as the cause of various forms of psychopathology (Maudsley, 1870). Practicing German psychiatrists such as Wilhelm Griesinger (1817–1868) actively promoted a similar view. He believed that physicians should be familiar with the symptoms, but also they have to understand the anatomical and physiological nature of psychological dysfunctions.

Inevitably, in their search for causes of mental illness, researchers' attention turned to specific areas of the brain and particular physiological mechanisms.

Localization of the Brain Functions. In England, Thomas Laycock (1812–1876) published *Mind and Brain,* in which he described the functioning of the brain from an evolutionary view (Laycock, 1860/1976). He wrote that the lowest levels of the brain and spinal cord are the oldest in evolutionary terms and are responsible for simple reactions. The middle level of the brain, including the cerebellum, is responsible for more complex motor activities. The frontal lobes are the latest product of the evolution and are responsible for thinking. The top portions of the brain, however, are the least organized and are more vulnerable to environmental influences. For example, a toxic agent affecting the frontal lobes diminishes their ability to control impulses generated by lower portions of the brain. Such an approach identifying higher and lower centers became popular. Research by another English neurologist, J. H. Jackson (1884), suggested that higher centers regulated advanced and rational behavior, while lower centers were responsible for primitive, childish, or antisocial actions. Most neuroscientists thought of a direct link between the structure of the brain and stable behavioral traits. Many psychologists also shared this view, which, in part, inspired later research about the integrative function of the brain (Sahakian, 1968).

Neuropathology was becoming an attractive academic field and provided new methodologies. Among the most intriguing was the **clinical-pathological method.** The supporters of this method compared clinical observations of a patient's abnormal symptoms with the reliable data about brain pathology, most likely obtained during an autopsy on the patient's brain. Unusual psychological behavior appeared as something that had to do with the body, the brain, or the nervous system as the result of either structural damage or malfunctioning (Taves, 1999). A few spectacular cases drew special attention.

The case of Phineas Gage has become one of the most prominent episodes in the history of psychology and psychiatry.

☞ CASE IN POINT

The Case of Phineas Gage. On September 13, 1848, Phineas Gage, resident of New Hampshire, had suffered a severe head trauma in an accidental explosion at the site of his work. As a result of the powerful blast, a 3-foot-7-inch-long tamping iron weighing almost 14 pounds went under the man's left cheekbone and exited through the top of his head, landing about 90 feet behind him. Although the left side of the front of the brain had been smashed, the man survived and after more than 2 months of hospital treatment returned home. Phineas had a strong desire to go back to work. He claimed that he had fully recovered after the accident. However, people around him were skeptical. His behavior and emotional expressions had changed dramatically. Prior to the disaster he had been a smart, reliable, and efficient worker, a foreman with good leadership skills. After the trauma, he became erratic and rude. He was often impatient, displaying grossly capricious or stubborn behavior. He lost his ability to plan ahead and control his impulses, which made him unable to work with people.

This case provided evidence that the destruction of certain brain areas could seriously affect important psychological functions. Because of its unusual circumstances, this case continues to make an impact on many people's interest in psychology and the functions of the brain (Macmillan, 2000a, b). You will find today at least four or five book titles about this case in our leading online bookstores.

Theodor Meynert (1833–1898), a German physician, attempted to create a precise localization theory according to which researchers and doctors would be able to find cause-and-effect relationships between pathology of certain areas of the cerebral cortex and various psychological dysfunctions. Meynert, like many colleagues of that time, used a microscope to find the underlying roots of pathological symptoms in the brain cells (Seitelberger, 1997). Meynert discovered that certain convolutions of the cerebral cortex should be responsible for language comprehension (Whitaker & Etlinger, 1993). One of the most prominent of Meynert's students was Carl Wernicke

(1848–1905), who at the age of 26 published a book on *aphasia* in which he described the symptoms related to the loss of comprehension of spoken language and the limited ability to speak. He showed that an apparently insignificant damage of the brain, due to a stroke as an example, could become the cause of serious psychological dysfunctions, such as a patient's inability to understand spoken language. This discovery brought him wide international recognition at a very early age.

Yet probably the most prominent research case revealing a remarkable connection between brain pathology and psychological functioning was presented by the French doctor Paul Broca (1824–1880). He showed that the loss of speech, or aphasia, without the paralysis of the organs of speech is tied to lesions of the third frontal convolution of the brain. This did not mean that the frontal lobes were exclusively responsible for speech. The ability of an individual to speak is based on several brain functions. The problems in the left hemisphere only indicated that an individual was not capable of producing language, concluded Paul Broca in his 1865 article.

☞ CASE IN POINT

The Case of Monsieur Tan. Monsieur Leborgne was admitted to Bicêtre Hospital in Paris at the age of 21. By that time he had already lost the use of speech. He could no longer pronounce two or more syllables, which he usually repeated twice at a time. He could hear well, yet the most common reply to questions was "tan, tan" accompanied by dynamic gestures. Therefore, people around him–and he had spent 30 years in the hospital–called him by his nickname, Monsieur Tan. At the time of his admission, he had no other serious symptoms. Yet some years later he began to lose the movement of his right arm and the lower body. Eventually, he became partly paralyzed. Most of his intellectual skills were declining. In April 1861, Dr. Paul Broca saw the patient for the first time, shortly before the patient's death on April 17 of that year. The autopsy revealed, besides other abnormalities in the brain, a large cavity the size of a chicken egg in the frontal lobe of the left hemisphere. Most likely, it was chronic and progressive softening of the second and third convolution of the superior part of the left frontal lobe. This finding gave Broca strong evidence that the pathology of the frontal lobe was probably the cause of the patient's loss of speech.

The Phineas Gage incident and the cases described by Wernicke and Broca, along with many other clinical cases, continued to attract the attention of researchers. The assumption that psychological functions are closely related to the anatomy of the brain, as the clinical-pathological methods showed, gained numerous and enthusiastic supporters among specialists of many countries (see Table 6.3).

Critical Lessons. Many supporters (called sometimes *anatomists*) of the clinical-pathological method believed that the neuroscience was near a major breakthrough in

Table 6.3 Discoveries of the Links Between Brain and Behavioral Abnormalities

Antonine-Laurett Bayle 1822	French physician among the first to link psychological symptoms of neurosyphilis to a chronic inflammation of the meninges in the brain
Marie-Jean-Pierre Flourens 1824	Provided the first experimental demonstration of localization of function in the brain; higher mental functions operate together, spread throughout the entire cerebrum
Pierre Paul Broca 1861	Reported finding a superficial left frontal lobe lesion during postmortem examination of the brain of an aphasic patient
Gustav Theodor Fritsch and Eduard Hitzig 1870	Provided evidence that circumscribed areas of the cortex are involved in movements of the limbs; findings established electrophysiology as a method for the experimental exploration of cortical localization of functions
Carl Wernicke 1874	Described physiological causes of memory and speech loss; described the effects of toxins and substances on emotions and behavior
David Ferrier 1876	Localized the centers for smell, auditory functions, and vision in the brain
Hermann Munk 1878	Described visual cortex in the occipital lobes
Santiago Ramón y Cajal 1894	Established basic principles of the functioning of neural connections. The nervous system is made up of billions of separate nerve cells

Sources: Broca (1861); Ferrier (1873); Flourens (1824); Fritsch & Hitzig (1870); Munk (1878); Wozniak (1992)

explaining mental illness. The brain appeared like a complex machine with interconnected parts, each playing its own role in psychological functioning. Different brain centers seemed to be responsible for different mental functions. The task appeared easy: to identify specific dysfunctions in the brain and relate them to a psychological abnormality observed in behavioral or psychological terms.

This point of view, however, was as simplistic as it was inspiring. It was an example of *reductionism* in science: the attempt to explain a complex set of facts, ideas, behaviors, or structures by another, simpler set, such as anatomy or physiology (see Chapter 3). Unintentionally, some enthusiastic anatomists even returned to the assumptions of phrenology (Franz, 1912).

The critics of this reductionist view warned that the even the most compelling clinical facts, such as the case presented by Broca, gave no warrant to believe that each part of the brain was responsible for discrete behavioral or psychological function. To dismiss the reductionist assumptions, researchers continued to show evidence that an apparently similar brain abnormality in two different patients did not necessarily result in similar psychological symptoms. Moreover, similar pathological symptoms are not necessarily caused by the same pathology of the brain. Many years after Broca's historic observations, experts continued to argue about the neuropsychological abnormalities underlying the loss of speech in that and similar cases. For example, there are patients diagnosed with similar brain pathology but with different psychological symptoms: some people lose their ability to speak yet they continue to read and write well (Fox, Kasner, Chatterjee, & Chalela, 2001).

One critical lesson we learn from the localization theory is that it correctly suggested that particular brain areas are associated with certain general behavioral and psychological functions. But we have to keep in mind that these brain centers do not operate independently, and their functions are continually influenced by the activities in other parts of the brain.

Not only the brain, but the entire nervous system began to attract attention of scientists. Despite differences among them, they believed that if the nervous system does not function properly it should cause abnormal psychological symptoms.

The Nervous System. Almost 300 years ago, Charles Perry, an English physician of broad knowledge and remarkable travel experience, published a treatise *On the Causes and Nature of Madness* (1723), claiming that mental illness was a mechanical defect of the whole nervous system that affected its functioning. Later, in 1740, George Cheyne in *An Essay on Regimen,* published in England, wrote about the existence of nervous illnesses that had to have a general physiological background. He wrote in his 1755 book about a special kind of nervous disorder based on deficiencies of human secretion.

Perry and Cheyne and many of their followers believed that, like the body in general, the nervous system functions within a set of parameters. Any serious deviation away from such parameters could cause psychological problems. This type of reasoning echoed the early scientific theories incorporating the idea of body *spirits* or nervous fluids (see Chapter 3). Such spirits, allegedly, went through the blood vessels or nerves, mixing with other body fluids, and, eventually, resulting in an individual's emotional states. The scientific concept of fluids and spirits did not survive past the 18th century, but the principles on which it was based did. The idea of the nervous system being "out of balance" remained extremely popular (Sutton, 1998). Today, for example, several key ideas of Chinese and Japanese holistic treatment—the importance of the balanced interaction of the body, the mind, and the environment—have regained popularity among many researchers and practitioners (not mentioning millions of ordinary people around the world).

Nervous Fatigue. In the 19th century, ideas about exhaustion of the nervous system as a cause of abnormal psychological symptoms also became fashionable. An individual experiencing persistent stress is at risk of developing a nervous illness. Hence, any measures that soothe the body should change the psychological symptoms as well. In Europe, recreational centers near mineral water resorts became major attractions. People shared a view that the combination of mineral water, relaxing atmosphere of a resort, proper dieting, and moderate physical exercises all together could provide remarkable healing for their emotional problems. Places such as Bath in England, Wiesbaden in Germany, Karlovy Vary in Bohemia, or Miveralnye Vody in Russia became hugely popular among both aristocracy and the growing middle class. So-called nerve and spa doctors gained recognition.

Why were these water resorts popular? The idea that the nerves need rest appeared reasonable and even scientific. Advertisements about famous spas were frequent in magazines and newspapers—increasingly accepted sources of information at that time. More people in developed nations began to have vacations from work. More people could afford short (a few weeks) and even extended trips (a few months) to such resorts. Furthermore, people felt comfortable discussing their psychological problems and explaining them as nervous exhaustion. Problems related to the nervous system appeared to have a better public acceptance than anything labeled "mental illness."

Contemporary health psychology has accumulated evidence that absence of significant stressors, regular relaxation, proper dieting, and physical exercises together have a positive influence on the body and subjective well-being (Lewis, 2001). We all know how important it is to get away sometimes from the stress-prone environment of daily lectures, pressing responsibilities, and deadlines. However, water resorts, despite their relative effectiveness in reducing stress and anxiety, could not provide a cure for many other forms of psychological dysfunctions—particularly serious ones, including severe anxiety problems, bipolar symptoms, chronic delusions, or depression.

More specialists began to look into hereditary factors in a search for knowledge about psychopathology.

The Hereditary Approach. Many researchers turned their attention to hereditary factors of mental illness, especially its serious forms. Their assumption was that certain forms of mental illness ran through generations.

Prominent French physician, Benedict-Augustin Morel (1809–1873) coined the term **degeneration,** referring to a generational regress in physical and psychological traits. As a physician, he had examined many case histories of mental retardation. He looked at the conditions of the families and paid special attention to the cases involving poverty, physical illness, and substance abuse. Morel claimed that particular behavioral and psychological traits should have been the result of hereditary transmission. Some of his critics claimed incorrectly that Morel believed that specific abnormal traits were inherited. Actually, his conclusion was not that crude. According to his views, people acquire only susceptibility of their nervous system to behavioral and psychological disturbances or deficiencies. These susceptibilities become symptoms if the person lives in constant poverty, suffers from violence, receives little care, or is exposed to alcohol or other substances. His conclusion was that with no social support or medical care, such individuals weaken their own heredity and transfer these weakened traits to their offspring. As an illustration, if a grandfather had some disturbing psychological symptoms, his son or daughter should have more significant mental symptoms if their social conditions remain poor. Next, their children living in similar conditions were likely to develop severe retardation and contribute to the ultimate infertility of the fourth generation (Morel, 1857/1976). Morel's views gained reputation in France and in other countries and remained influential for several decades.

Sensationalism associated with crime and bizarre behavior helped certain theories become popular. Richard von Krafft-Ebbing (1840–1902) wrote the book *Psychopathia Sexualis*, in which he provided a detailed analysis of human sexuality. Published in 1886, the book stated that madness was a form of psychological degeneration and the most important cause of criminal behavior. The degenerates either have no sexual feelings at all, according to Krafft-Ebbing, or their sexuality is clearly abnormal. These individuals cannot control their impulses and, therefore, turn to different forms of anomalous sexuality. He described several pathological categories of sexual behavior, including self-exposure, masturbation, and homosexuality—all clear attributes of degeneration in his view.

Psychopathia Sexualis serves today as an example of how a scholar could easily misuse science to pass on moral judgments and prescriptions. Claiming that the degenerates are engaged in masturbation and homosexuality, he automatically assumed that these forms of sexual behavior are "bad" by definition and, for example, anyone who masturbates is a sick individual in need of medical treatment. Don't forget that in the 19th century (and even much later), masturbation was widely considered a form of pathological behavior or even a serious chronic affliction that required therapeutic intervention or, sometimes, physical punishment. In publications and public speeches of that period, most doctors, psychologists, and psychiatrists routinely labeled masturbation and homosexuality as forms of degeneration and pathology. Do you think that there are some types of behavior today that we consider pathological but future generations might consider normal?

The conclusions of the degeneration theories went beyond their initial and modest research objectives. To some people, these theories seemed to answer a difficult question about why violence, alcoholism, and homelessness existed: heredity. Therefore, the only effective way to tackle these problems was to prevent some people from getting married and having children. Government-mandated sterilization was the way to deal with some forms of mental illness and deviant behavior (Pick, 1989). Others believed in social isolation. American Henry Goddard, in *Feeble-Mindedness: Its Causes and Consequences* (1916), proposed mandatory social isolation for the mentally retarded so that the biological makeup of the general population would eventually improve. Supporters of these and similar views belonged to the so-called **social hygiene movement**, an eclectic conglomerate of intellectuals and health care professionals whose beliefs were driven by a mix of Darwinism, progressivism, social engineering (see Chapter 5), and, unfortunately, prejudice.

However, we should understand the social hygiene movement in the appropriate cultural context. Morel's idea of degeneration related to social behavior was not new. Many intellectuals in the end of the 19th century feared that society seemed incapable of changing society through education and care. Many scholars began to question the very possibility of societal progress: there were people, in their view, who were not capable of improvement. Therefore, the belief that science had finally found a remedy for many social ills offered a form of social protection. It gave communities justification to get rid of the mentally disabled, the afflicted, and the deviant. In fact, it was a psychological justification of "social cleansing." One of the lessons of history is that many educated people, despite all their good intentions invested in social engineering, could not foresee its resulting faults.

By the beginning of the 20th century, when the idea of heredity as an important cause of mental illness began to take shape, an alternative school of thought was also advancing. Many researchers and medical practitioners turned to the study of social and psychological factors causing and contributing to mental illness.

Social Approaches. Edward Shorter, in *A History of Psychiatry* (1997), wrote about a long-lasting intellectual tradition to explain mental illness as a result of societal problems. Poverty, systematic abuse, injustice, traumatic events—all could have long and profound effects on an individual's emotional stability, thinking, and actions (Goldney & Schioldann, 2002). The challenge was to explain how social factors affected mental illness. In the history of medicine this approach was labeled *romantic psychiatry.* Some supporters of this optimistic and idealistic view were social progressives who believed that the remedy against mental illness was social change. Others maintained a less dramatic view and focused only on moral factors of treatment.

An early representative of this approach was Jean-Philippe Esquirol (1772–1840). He believed that dramatic or difficult events in an individual's life could trigger distressful psychological symptoms. Introducing statistical methods to clinical studies, he proposed that the most frequent cause of mental illness was emotional. He even classified psychological causes of emotional abnormalities such as extreme anger, excessive love, and financial worries. Echoing Esquirol's views, Johann Christian Heinroth (1773–1843), professor of psychiatry in Leipzig (Saxon, Germany), in his 1823 *Textbook of Mental Hygiene* suggested that people's passions can drive some of them to extreme despair or moral corruption. If extreme passion prevails, the individual stops acting rationally. Moral rules should guide the afflicted to overcome their psychological problems (Shorter, 1997, p. 31).

Another French scholar, Émile Durkheim (1858–1917), an influential sociologist and anthropologist, described social and psychological factors influencing suicidal behavior. He proposed several types of suicide based on social conditions an individual's responses, thus making suicide a behavioral phenomenon available to scientific investigation.

CASE IN POINT

Suicide Acts According to Durkheim. *Egotistic suicide* takes place when an individual feels lonely, abandoned, or mistreated. Such individuals also assume that their deaths would have a positive impact on a particular cause. They kill themselves in an attempt to draw the attention of other people.

Altruistic suicide is committed for the sake of the group to which the person belongs. It can be a result of group pressure or the desire to earn reputation. For example, *hara-kiri* (self-disemboweling) or *seppuku* (assisted suicide using the same means as hara-kiri), practiced in Japan until the mid-20th century, are examples of the altruistic suicide: individuals die to save their reputations. In the past, some devout Hindu widows killed themselves out of customary practice. In Western cultures there was an unwritten military code requiring officers (especially of a senior rank) to commit suicide in case of extremely dishonorable conduct.

Fatalistic suicide takes place when the individual loses hope. As they did 100 years ago, contemporary accounts of suicide contain scores of cases in which events, such as a debilitating illness, monetary loss, sexual infidelity of a loved one, triggered suicidal behavior.

And finally, *anomic suicide* (anomie means "without norms") occurs at times of rapid societal transitions. Durkheim, in fact, drew special attention to a new, stress-prone industrial society and urban culture taking shape at the end of the 19th century in Western Europe.

Source: Durkheim (1897/1997)

Psychological Causes. Many scholars and physicians also turned to psychological factors of mental illness. German physician Alexander Haindorf (1782–1862) was among the first to suggest that a serious cause of mental illness, along with physiological reasons, was an inner conflict within an individual. Ernst Feuchtersleben (1806–1849) considered mental illness a result of developmental problems: mental states that are normal but not fully developed. Friedrich Groos (1768–1852) defined mental health as a state of harmony between the natural forces and behavior of an individual. When a natural force is blocked, an illness ensued. Physical and psychological symptoms influence each other. Anxiety can cause high blood pressure, which may elevate an individual's worry.

Anatomy, physiology, and social sciences advanced scientific knowledge about mental illness and its roots. From a practical standpoint, at least three major questions required answers. First, who should diagnose and treat mental illness? Second, what kind of treatment should be used to help the suffering? Third, who could provide resources for research, diagnosis, and treatment of mental illness?

Figure 6.1 Views of the Causes of Mental Illness in the Early 20th Century

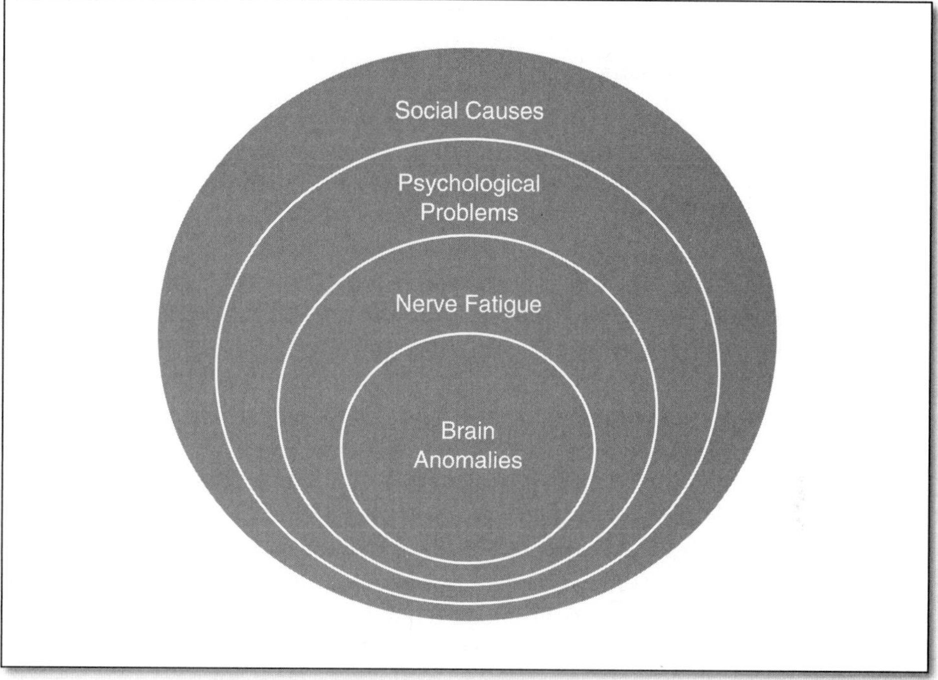

✓ CHECK YOUR KNOWLEDGE

How did Morel understand degeneration?

What was the social approach to mental illness?

Explain the clinical-pathological method in studies of psychological disorders.

Early Attempts at Treatment

It was widely recognized in the early 20th century that medical doctors trained in the fields of behavioral and neurological problems should play a major role in diagnosis and treatment of mental illness. Psychologists gradually accepted the assisting role, helping physicians in gathering information about the symptoms of psychological dysfunctions, their dynamics, and outcomes. But after establishing their right to diagnose mental illness, psychiatrists could not offer effective treatment for most of the recognized psychological dysfunctions. It was a paradox: biology and physiology provided new knowledge about the functioning of the brain and nervous system. However, this knowledge provided little help in a practical sense.

In addition, the number of doctors specializing in mental illness was very insignificant considering the growing demand for treatment. Across industrial countries, the scope of state-sponsored medical services was very limited. The few private facilities were out of reach for most people. Clinical studies depended mostly on small university salaries, insufficient hospital budgets, and the relentless enthusiasm of early specialists. Most mental patients with the most severe symptoms were confined in so-called mental asylums.

Where to Treat? Asylums

A typical asylum was a detached building or a gated compound with several dwellings inside. Patients in most cases could not leave the facility without permission. Surveillance and head counting was part of the staff's many responsibilities. Strict regulations controlled patients' everyday activities: eating, sleeping, working, and recreation. Special logs contained information about each patient's habits, conversations during the day, friendliness with patients and staff, and even requests made. According to a common assumption, discipline and orderliness were essential for the successful operation of an asylum. Most early facilities were large enough to accommodate many hundreds of patients. There were also smaller facilities for a few dozen patients.

Facilities to take care of the afflicted or orphans existed for centuries in countries such as China (Mungello, 2008, p. 47). Asylums for the mentally ill began to appear a few hundred years ago. Britain began to build asylums in the late 1700s. Russia started similar projects in the first half of the 19th century. In the United States, the first asylums opened in Philadelphia, Williamsburg (Virginia), and New York City. Other countries, including Canada and South Africa, began to build asylums later in that century (Louw & Swartz, 2001). The United States and Great Britain maintained a largely decentralized system of asylums. In most European countries, however, central governments played a crucial role in the creation, financing, regulation, and maintenance of mental institutions. Who would end up in such institutions? These were primarily people diagnosed with insanity or serious disability due to alcohol addiction or mental retardation.

Asylums served several important but controversial functions. First, they incapacitated some violent individuals, thus providing relief for their families and communities. However, many mental asylums soon became virtual stockpiles for people who, often unwanted and abandoned by their families, had no capacity to get out. In addition, besides hosting people with severe psychological symptoms, asylums attracted scores of swindlers, petty criminals, or other social misfits. Some asylums' practices became at odds with practical matters. For example, some British asylums had an open door policy, allowing most of their patients to check themselves out and leave anytime they wanted. This policy certainly created many unforeseen problems: some patients were too dangerous to let free.

Second, asylums were supposed to provide treatment. A common assumption was that by isolating some troubling individuals, society would be able to provide cure and thus address the problem of the mentally ill. In some cases, temporary social isolation, regular physical exercises, scheduled day activities, and modest diet provided relief to patients. In most other cases, patients showed little or no signs of improvement. Overcrowded conditions and lack of effective therapeutic methods worsened patients' symptoms. Segregation by gender, race, social class, linked to unequal treatment, was also a widespread practice. Reports describe, for example, facilities in the United States and India in the middle of the 19th century that were designed to avoid mixing of patients of different racial backgrounds. Although humane treatment for all patients was required, patients of lower social classes were commonly placed into overfull and less resourced facilities (Grob, 1994).

Third, asylums gave medical professionals a unique opportunity to collect empirical data about a wide range of symptoms of mental illness and test various methods of treatment. Yet without clear understanding of mental illness, without systematic observation and other reliable methods of data collection, most studies did not produce significant results.

Overall, most early asylums promised shelter, food, and security for their inhabitants. The main goal of the asylums was to provide humane and individualized treatment to each patient. It turned out to be a daunting task. The rapidly increasing numbers of patients in each facility made an individualized approach to treatment nearly impossible (see Table 6.4).

Table 6.4 Functions of Mental Asylums in the 19th and Early 20th Centuries

Incapacitation	Asylums served the function of incapacitation. The asylums incapacitated violent individuals who were considered to be dangerous to self or others, thus providing some relief for families and communities. However, asylums became a convenient depository for unwanted individuals who were no longer capable of exercising their rights.
Isolation	They isolated individuals who were deemed embarrassing, difficult, or unacceptable, thus creating a societal impression that the problem of the mentally ill has been somehow addressed.
Research	Asylums provided the opportunity to gather empirical information about mental illness and to conduct experiments on the effectiveness of treatment methods. Yet the methods of data collection were often unreliable.
Treatment	Some asylums offered a range of treatment procedures, typically limited to work, exercise, or diet. Unfortunately, specialists did not agree on the major principles and methods of treatment.

How to Treat?

In 1763, French physician Piere Pomme recommended chicken soup and cold baths as remedies against fatigue and emotional emptiness. Although chicken soup as a prescription did not win approval of physicians in later years, cold baths did. In fact, patients with violent or manic symptoms were frequently put, against their will, into such baths. As you recall, physicians were relatively free to choose any method of treatment and study its effectiveness. Curiosity guided many experimental procedures. Doctors frequently followed some common assumptions. For example, scores of physicians agreed with a popular idea that the human body needs "cleaning" to rid itself of troubling psychological symptoms. Therefore, laxatives became a widely used prescription against a variety of symptoms. Some doctors even combined cold baths, laxatives, and bloodletting as a way to clean the body of harmful elements—whatever they were.

Many physicians routinely conducted dangerous experiments on their patients, prescribing substances such as opium or morphine. Searching for the right medication, doctors also relied on chance or intuition. Only a few experiments achieved notable results. Danish psychiatrist Fritz Lange reported that in the late 1800s he and his colleagues routinely used lithium in the treatment of affective disorders. They erroneously believed that lithium salts could correct abnormal uric acid levels and treat the symptoms of mania and melancholia (Schioldann, 2001). Although their explanations about the physiological effects of lithium use were wrong, lithium later was recognized as an effective drug to treat symptoms of bipolar disorder.

Other physicians, in search for remedies, turned to drug-free methods of treatment. Some therapists returned to orderliness. For example, Ernst Horn (1778–1848), a German military doctor in charge of a hospital facility for the mentally ill, believed that discipline and clarity of instructions given to the patients could drastically improve their conditions and, therefore, their mental states. The patients should not spend their time without a purpose. They should be involved in the organization of the day, which eventually would return them the ability to control their symptoms and their lives. Other therapists chose other methods.

Moral Therapy. It was generally assumed that some forms of mental illness result from serious misfortunes in a patient's life. Therefore, to return to a normal mental state, the patient should experience compassion and trust. Gradually, through learning and hope, he or she could restore the lost qualities of good behavior. This kind of treatment received the label **moral therapy**. In most cases, the method had little to do with moral issues. However, because this treatment was an alternative to physical restraint and isolation of patients, the term remained in use for some time.

Followers of this view maintained that to achieve cure, the mentally ill should restore their ability to reason. To achieve reason, special conditions should be created in clinical facilities. French doctor Philippe Pinel (1745–1826) was an early advocate of compassion in treatment. He believed that severe limitations on patients' freedom affect their dignity and worsen the chances for cure. In Italy, physician Vincenzo Chiarugi (1759–1820), in a book (1793/1987) emphasized the importance of humane treatment of patients placed in mental asylums. He practiced this method in his clinic in Florence.

Dorothea L. Dix advocated the rights of the mentally ill and called for their humane treatment in asylums.

In the United States, human rights advocate Dorothea L. Dix (1802–1887) led a campaign to create civilized conditions of individuals living in mental asylums. She traveled across the United States to inspect the facilities in which mental patients were kept. She reported about the inhumane conditions in which the afflicted spent their lives abandoned by their family members. In part because of her advocacy, the federal government in 1855 funded the Government Hospital for the Insane located in Washington, D.C. The asylum was the first large mental facility of this kind in the United States (Wilson, 1975).

Besides offering patients relative freedom, supporters of moral therapy offered classes about good habits and personal hygiene. Some promoted religious education. Other asylums introduced painting, music, gardening, or carpentry. In France, Guillaume Ferrus (1784–1861) worked under Pinel at the Bicêtre Hospital in Paris. Serving later as general inspector of asylums, he introduced occupational therapy, a kind of moral treatment through work. Although he believed that the causes of mental illness are in the brain, some people become weak because they face tough circumstances. Therefore, work under supervision can restore some patents' confidence and might eventually reverse their abnormal symptoms. Russian clinician P. A. Butkovsky (1801–1844) also believed that because mental illness is a disruption of sensory processes, a structured environment of the asylum should help to restore the balance of sensations (Yaroshevsky, 1996).

More specialists tried to study and use specific forms of treatment based on education, discussion, or persuasion. They believed that if mental illness occurs as a result of past misfortunes or serious personal disruptions, then the patient should be able to recover from his or her maladies with the help and advice of a caring specialist.

Mental Therapeutics. Ideas about psychological methods as a form of therapy developed rapidly. The assumption was that a suffering individual should go through reeducation, a kind of psychotherapy that allowed the patient to develop new skills and get an insight into his or her mental illness. At least three areas of professional interests emerged. One was the study of the patient's past: detailed knowledge of the patient's personality, habits, or problems should help therapists to make helpful therapeutic decisions. The second area of interest was the study of interactions between the patient and the therapist. The third area was the study of the patient's individual capacities for understanding and self-improvement.

Supporters of mental therapy saw the weaknesses of the existing asylums. They believed that asylums sheltered too many people with severe and incurable symptoms.

While there, people with curable symptoms could not find a healthy psychological environment for communication and self-improvement. Hopelessness decreases chances of recovery from illness. This was an important assumption that is still accepted today.

More professionals believed in the therapeutic power of dialogue and persuasion. For example, if a patient displays persistent anxiety, a friendly discussion with a therapist would help to address some of the patient's worries. Other clinicians turned to different forms of persuasion. One of the remarkable trends in clinical psychology was the reemergence of mesmerism and hypnotism as methods of treatment. As you remember, Anton Mesmer (see Chapter 1) claimed that many illnesses, including mental illness, arose from the disruption of the normal flow of an invisible fluid called *animal magnetism*. A well-trained physician, according to Mesmer, could learn to locate the blocks that were causing the disruption of the flow of the fluid, and by touch or massage remove the blocks, thereby curing the patient (Schmit, 2005). Mesmerism, first overwhelmingly rejected by scientific circles, regained its popularity in Europe and the United States (Quinn, 2007). Some physicians and amateur enthusiasts made public demonstrations, delivered lectures, and promised treatment for a variety of symptoms. People who conducted such sessions often called themselves "psychologists" or "mental healers." Many of their clients reported improvements in their chronic pain symptoms, sleep, or disappearance of headaches. Did these people really feel better? One hundred and fifty years ago there were no solid experimental methods to verify the claims of these individuals. Today we know, however, from introductory psychology classes about the power of the placebo effect: people believe they get better because they want to feel better.

A somewhat similar phenomenon, hypnotism, also gained popularity in Europe and America. Described by a Scottish physician James Braid (1795–1860), the phenomenon was called first *nervous sleep*. Braid coined the concept *neuro-hypnology*, or in a shorter version, **hypnology**: the study of causes and effects of nervous sleep. Witnessing the demonstrations of mesmerism, Braid in his 1843 book *Neurypnology; or, The Rationale of Nervous Sleep,* suggested that nervous sleep in some people was caused by a paralysis of the muscles of the eyelids (Braid, 1843/2008). An English doctor, John Elliotson, *explained* nervous sleep as superconcentrated memories (1843). Charcot in France made an observation that people susceptible to hypnosis are likely to have symptoms of hysteria, suggesting the common cause of these two phenomena. Some therapists proposed further that hypnotherapy could be used to persuade patients to abolish their symptoms of hysteria.

The early use of the term *psychotherapy* is frequently associated with hypnology. Two Dutch therapists, Frederik W. van Eden (1860–1932) and Albert W. van Renterghem, who in 1887 opened a clinic in Amsterdam called the Clinic for Psychotherapeutic Suggestion, used hypnosis as a method of treatment. In the United States, Boris Sidis (1867–1923), trained as a psychologist and a doctor, published *The Psychology of Suggestion,* in which he gave a detailed account of hypnosis as a medical method (Sidis, 1907). In France, Hippolyte Bernheim (1840–1919), whose work had an impact on the young Sigmund Freud (Chapter 8), began to use various forms of suggestion with his patients. He was among the early specialists to use *talk therapy*, which was gaining popularity in many countries. In Japan, for example, a therapeutic procedure called *Morita* was practiced after 1917 to treat serious anxiety-related problems. The procedure involved psychological isolation, inner reflections, and talk therapy combined with physical exercises (Hendstrom, 1994). Some patients suffering from anxiety or depressive symptoms sought help in specially organized retreats where they could dedicate themselves to reflections and spiritual healing (Reynolds, 1983).

At about the same time as Wilhelm Wundt in Leipzig was conducting sophisticated laboratory experiments, clinicians turned to the study of the effects of various treatments, particularly hypnosis (Wampold & Bhati, 2004). For example, Russian doctor Vladimir Bekhterev (1857–1927) used hypnosis to treat some behavioral problems and attempted to provide evidence of therapeutic success. He believed that during hypnosis, specific forms of energy exchange take place between a therapist and a client.

In sum, two important changes took place at the turn of the century. First, science produced reliable knowledge regarding a wide range of psychological symptoms. People began to recognize problems such as chronic emotional tensions, melancholia, or sleep problems as a special kind of psychological problems treatable by professionals. Second, more of these professionals began to work outside mental asylums. Increasingly, educated and well-to-do people would seek help from a medical professional working in a private office and offering treatment based on persuasion and reasoning.

✓ CHECK YOUR KNOWLEDGE

Describe the basic functions of mental asylums.

What was moral therapy?

Describe the hypnology method.

First Psychological Clinics and Clinical Psychologists

The life and work of an American psychologist serve as a remarkable example of the trials and tribulations of early clinical psychologists. Lightner Witmer founded one of the world's first psychological clinics at the University of Pennsylvania in 1896, at a time when psychology research labs were opening in several schools across the United States. He was also interested in research, but above all he wanted to develop a new field of psychology dedicated to helping people in need.

Lightner Witmer and Early Clinical Psychology. Witmer (1867–1956) was among an early group of psychologists who took their doctorates under the supervision of Wilhelm Wundt. Witmer studied at the Leipzig laboratory right after James Angell had left and almost at the same time that Edward Titchener was there. Upon returning to the United States, Witmer became a member of the American Psychological Association (McReynolds, 1987). In July 1896, he designed and delivered a special course of lectures on methods of working with children with serious behavioral, physical, and psychological problems. This was an early prototype of a more advanced clinical course offered a year later. An informal inauguration of clinical psychology took place (McReynolds, 1996).

Witmer faced significant organizational and personal difficulties. Medical doctors dominated the clinical field and, as you remember, generally rejected the role of psychologists as clinicians. Most psychologists remained in the experimental or theoretical fields, working for universities and studying healthy subjects. On the personal level, Witmer had problems with several leading psychologists. For example, he criticized William James, a renowned authority in psychology at that time, for his excessive attention to mysticism and paranormal phenomena. Although Witmer's criticisms were legitimate, the tone of his comments was disrespectful. This caused a negative reaction from many psychologists who knew about this conflict.

Witmer didn't mind facing such challenges and conflicts. As a scientist, he vigorously defended academic freedom—the fundamental liberty of a scientist to speak and conduct research. In June 1915, Scott Nearing, a young economics professor at the University of Pennsylvania, was dismissed from his position for his radical anticapitalist political views. Witmer put aside his academic work and joined other colleagues to protest the actions of the authorities (Witmer, 1915). Their civil efforts were unsuccessful, yet the case received national coverage and raised awareness about academic freedom in American schools.

ON THE WEB

Read Lightner Witmer's brief biographical sketch on the book website.

Lightner Witmer worked with children with serious behavioral, physical, and psychological problems. He founded one of the world's first psychological clinics at the University of Pennsylvania in 1896.

Witmer was among early psychologists to use the terms *clinical psychology* and *psychological clinic.* Today these words sound almost ordinary. Yet 100 years ago they were unusual. Witmer used them to promote, as he believed, a new profession for psychologists. In his clinic, Witmer saw people who were referred to him frequently from schools and sometimes from medical facilities. Most cases involved children with speech delay, learning problems, motor coordination issues, and hyperactivity. Witmer believed that psychologists should first use careful observation of the symptoms and then conduct experimentation to examine the effectiveness of therapeutic procedures. The end result would be procedures to improve children's skills and overcome their bad habits (Witmer, 1907a).

Clinical psychology in the United States developed in the 20th century in the ways Witmer had generally anticipated. First, he wanted the field to be free of abstract speculations. He was interested in facts and observable behaviors. Second, he wanted psychology professionals not to cause emotional harm by the use of their methods (Witmer, 1907a). He also wanted clinical psychologists to begin to work in tight collaboration with physicians, teachers, and other professionals, focusing on children's academic and behavioral problems (Routh, 1996). Witmer performed several professional roles at once, a practice common today. He had to provide direct services in clinical settings and in private practice; he had teaching responsibilities; he supervised treatment by other professionals. He also had to do administrative work and research.

IN THEIR OWN WORDS

Although clinical psychology is clearly related to medicine, it is quite as closely related to sociology and to pedagogy. . . . An abundance of material for scientific study fails to be utilized, because the interest of psychologists is elsewhere engaged, and those in constant touch with the actual phenomena do not possess the training necessary to make the experience and observation of scientific value. (Witmer, 1907a)

Witmer believed that individuals have the tendency and the capacity to surpass expectations, to develop their abilities and potentials to the fullest. This was one of the antecedents of a concept of self-improvement and self-actualization developed later in humanistic theories. Witmer also called for a careful interpretation of test results. He believed that statistical numbers could conceal a true personality of a human being. Instead, Witmer emphasized the importance of a detailed clinical observation and cared about the development of observational skills in his students.

Early Clinical Observations. In an 1896 article, Witmer described the symptoms that today are labeled as *autistic disorder.* It was the case of a 7-year-old boy who was born to well-educated parents but never learned to articulate fluently and clearly. His attention span was very short, but he would string buttons and play with toy balls for a long time. The boy had an acute sense of smell and was particularly attracted to music. He could repeat from memory most of the tunes he had heard. Yet he was capricious and impatient.

Witmer was also among the first to describe a case of *dyslexia,* recognized today as a learning disability. Another clinician, Pringle Morgan (1862–1934), described similar symptoms about the same time in the United Kingdom (Morgan, 1896). Witmer, however, did not publish his study until 1907. This was the famous case of Charles Gilman, which is also known as the "case of chronic bad spelling."

☞ CASE IN POINT

The Case of Charles Gilman. Charles Gilman was a boy of average intelligence and fine reasoning and spoken skills. He had no difficulty remembering the sounds of letters and geometric figures. He did well in science and history. However, his reading and spelling abilities were deficient. When he was reading, he had to examine every word letter by letter, combining them into sounds and then pronouncing the entire word. Mistakes were rampant. For example, he would say "saw" instead of "was."

(Continued)

(Continued)

Witmer labeled these symptoms as *visual verbal amnesia* and designed a treatment program for the boy. The program started in 1896 and consisted of weekly visits to his clinic and daily work with the Charles's schoolteacher. The goal of this program was to teach Charles to identify words without spelling them. After several months of treating the boy in clinic, Witmer recommended Charles to continue his exercises at home. Though he never achieved reading proficiency, by 1903 Charles improved his reading skills significantly so that he could read almost any text. Unfortunately, Charles died of tuberculosis in January 1907 (Routh, 1996; Witmer, 1907b).

Witmer's impact on clinical psychology in the United States was significant. He introduced a new profession. Overcoming resistance, clinical psychologists began to work relatively independently but close to psychiatrists and educational specialists. He also defined clinical psychology as a new research discipline allied with university-based psychology. He conceptualized, organized, and carried out the first program to train clinical psychologists in the United States. Witmer also founded and edited *The Psychological Clinic*, a journal dedicated to the new profession. But most important, the realization of his idea that psychologists should use their knowledge to help people in special circumstances is, perhaps, Witmer's greatest contribution to psychology.

Assessment and Research. Biographical facts provide great examples about the work psychologists performed at that time. Assessment and psychological research were becoming the two main professional activities of clinical psychologists in the early 20th century. For example, William Healy (1869–1963), director of the Juvenile Psychopathic Institute of Chicago (founded in 1909), and his wife, Augusta Bronner (1881–1966), provided regular assessments and psychological recommendations for the children, adolescents, and their parents. In Japan, the Department of Justice after 1916 sponsored studies related of mental health of inmates (Uyeno, 1924, p. 226). In France, Pierre Janet (see his studies of hysteria earlier in this chapter), occupying a prestigious position at the Sorbonne University, noted the differences between the work of a psychiatrist and a psychologist. Psychologists, in his view, should take into consideration the wide range of factors affecting mental illness and focus on hereditary circumstances, educational factors, and life events. Psychiatrists should be both psychologists and physicians who provide cure using all methods, including surgery and medication. Here Janet assigned psychology a major role to assessment and description of mental illness.

American psychologist Henry H. Goddard (1866–1957) was actively engaged in raising awareness about mental illness and advocated improvements in education of students with learning problems. He became famous for his studies of **feebleminded children**, the term used to describe children with serious developmental problems identified today as mental retardation. He served as director of research and head of a laboratory for a training school in New Jersey for boys and girls with such developmental problems. He supported the hereditary approach to mental skills. One of his books, *The Kallikak Family,* became famous because of its controversial conclusions. He claimed in his book that he had found strong empirical evidence of the hereditary foundation of both mental retardation and giftedness (Goddard, 1912/1950). Later he retracted his finding and interpretations due to methodological errors.

Most clinical psychologists worked for universities. As professors, they tried to introduce students to the new profession. Many universities began to offer psychology courses with a clinical emphasis. The University of Illinois, for example, offered psychology students practical observations at the newly open hospital for the "insane, deaf, and dumb, and the blind." Clinical psychologists also drew attention from the media.

The Emmanuel Movement. Very few ideas in psychology achieved such resonance and created so much controversy as the views and practices of **Emmanuel Church Healing Movement.** It was a social movement and therapeutic practice that turned the attention of millions of people to psychology and its practical applications. Lasting from 1906 to 1910, this popular movement was partially responsible for the subsequent rapid development of psychotherapy in the United States. Initially started as a local cooperative venture between Boston physicians and Episcopalian ministers, the movement continued as an experiment in helping people. Who needed this help? They were primarily the poor, the afflicted. There were also ordinary people looking for advice and assistance. What was the method of treatment? People learned how to gain access to their psychological problems through the power of scientific knowledge and religious faith (Caplan, 1998a).

One of the movement's founders was Elwood Worcester (1862–1940), who obtained a doctoral degree in the Leipzig laboratory in Germany. Back in the United States, he worked as a chaplain and a psychology professor. He was convinced that mental illness has both psychological and spiritual causes. A rector of the Emmanuel Church in Boston, he and his assistant Samuel McComb, with the help of other colleagues, developed an approach involving two steps: (1) clinical assessment and (2) spiritual advice. Worcester and McComb offered free advice to help any person with either personal (for example, a loss in the family) or psychological problems (for example, excessive anxiety or substance abuse).

As a treatment, they frequently used hypnosis and relaxation training. They believed that after the mind takes greater control of the body, spiritual advice should be given to address the specific problems of a client. In 1908 Worcester, McComb, and Coriat published *Religion and Medicine: The Moral Control of Nervous Disorders.* In its final form, the treatment program was organized around three main activities: (1) free weekly examinations in a medical clinic; (2) a weekly class taught by physicians, clergymen, and psychologists; the topics included physical health, mental health, and spirituality, and (3) private sessions during which the minister conducted talk therapy (Worcester et al., 1908/2003).

These sessions received considerable coverage in the press. Eager to provide sensational stories, journalists often distorted the facts or focused on gaffes and blunders of the founders of the method and their followers. To combat these distortions and misconceptions, Worcester and McComb had to spent considerable time attempting to correct the media's mistakes. They published many articles and went on a lecture tour across the United States and Europe (Caplan, 1998a).

Criticisms of the Movement. Protestant leaders, fearing that moral power was slipping away from the church, were skeptical of the movement. They feared that many people would accept Christianity only because it provided immediate psychological relief. Most physicians and psychologists criticized the method too. Their main argument was that religious authorities, even those with academic degrees in psychology, should not administer therapy. The continuing conflict between science and religion in Western culture contributed to the scientists' displeasure with something they saw as a religious intervention into the fields of science. Hugo Münsterberg, an authoritative psychologist at that time, believed that physicians have more knowledge and skill to deal with psychological problems than any other specialists. Good intentions, in his view, should not allow a nonprofessional to intervene into the delicate world of another human being.

Psychologists who criticized the Emmanuelle movement also hoped to turn attention to themselves as legitimate providers of psychological healing. The movement inspired many professionals to take a closer look at their capacities and turn to practical applications of theory (Abbott, 1988). Twenty years earlier, most of them would have stayed away from offering clinical assessment and therapy (Calkins, 1892). In the early 20th century, however, many psychologists realized they could offer analysis and treatment based on science (Caplan, 1998b). The Emmanuel movement was only one but still an important event that altered the nature of clinical psychology and psychotherapy as a profession in the United States.

✓ CHECK YOUR KNOWLEDGE

What functions did psychological clinics play in the early 20th century?

What was the Charles Gilman case about?

What was the Emmanuel movement?

Assessments

Before the end of the 19th century, most individuals with persistent psychological problems but manageable behavior remained under the care of their families. Clinicians created a great variety of theories about the nature of mental illness. Despite the existence of asylums, only a small portion of individuals with severe psychological problems ended up there. Some of them stayed with their families; others tried to survive on the streets, often confronting physical violence and psychological abuse. Traditionally, people maintained a very discriminatory and negative attitude about those unfortunates whose emotional manifestations were difficult to understand or whose behavior was profoundly different from established norms.

However, by the end of the 19th century, people in most industrial societies had witnessed the rise in the number of mental patients in asylums. Many reasons for such changes existed: the rapid growth of the cities, the spread of neurosyphilis, the change of the structure of the rural traditional family, changes of folk beliefs about the causes of mental illness, the growth of individualism, birth and development of welfare policies, and progressive attitudes of many medical professionals and psychologists about society's obligation to take care of the weak.

Many medical doctors during that period believed that they had established a new field of medicine called *psychiatry* that could take care of mental illness. Psychiatrists would use science and medical methods to treat their patients. This new profession could also bring a stable income. It was a common belief that the knowledge about brain anatomy and pathology should be sufficient enough to explain the nature and dynamics of mental illness within psychiatry. It was an incomplete view, however. Without knowing the complex dynamics of brain physiology, without understanding of the role of individual psychological and social factors in mental illness, psychiatrists alone could not explain and treat abnormal symptoms successfully.

It was also the time of the birth of clinical psychology as a discipline and profession. Psychologists who believed in studying psychological aspects of mental illness had to find something to prove that their research findings were correct. This stimulated both theoretical and applied research in psychology. Not only research laboratories but also clinical facilities began to provide psychologists with empirical information about behavior, its deviations, and a variety of abnormal psychological symptoms. Overcoming resistance of the medical establishment, psychologists were also vocal supporters of science-based assessment of therapeutic effectiveness.

The early 20th century had strengthened an important moral position of psychologists: it was their scientific optimism and societal progressivism—the attitudes increasingly popular among researchers and practicing specialists alike. It was no longer a priest, a shaman, or a fortune teller who was expected to heal psychological symptoms. It was now a professional, educated, trained, and licensed, who could use both science and compassion to understand and treat people in need.

Conclusion

The 20th century brought a twofold belief, widely shared in the Western countries, that incorporates knowledge from several scientific fields. First, mental illness was a form of an underlying physical or neurological illness worsened by certain life events and experiences of the patient. Second, the science-based clinical method was the only reliable one in providing diagnosis and suggesting cure for the afflicted.

Summary

- At the end of the 19th century, mental illness appeared as a painful pattern of actions, emotions, and thoughts coupled with inability to reason or act rationally. Clinicians recognized several general categories of disorders, including madness, neurosis, hysteria, affective disorders, eating disorders, and substance-related problems. Having a mental illness often meant being an outcast.

- Public attention to mental illness grew significantly in many industrial nations. Authorities began to discuss mental illness in legal terms. A new social category called "mental patients" emerged. The process of medicalization of mental illness and deviance (understanding them primarily in medical terms) stimulated new methods of medical treatment. Ongoing scientific discoveries brought the possibility of explaining mental illness in a scientific manner.

- Psychology's role in the understanding and treatment of mental illness was not recognized readily. Many psychiatrists and university psychologists opposed psychology's involvement in clinical research and therapy. Psychologists gradually accepted the assisting role, helping physicians in gathering information about the symptoms of psychological dysfunctions, their dynamics, and outcomes.

- Among many classifications of mental illness, the outcome-based approach of Kraepelin remains the most significant contribution to the contemporary classification of mental illness.

- At the end of the 19th century, at least two general and interconnected schools of thought of mental illness existed. According to the first one, mental illness is best explained in terms of structure and functioning of the brain and nervous system. The second school of thought emphasized the importance of social and psychological factors that contributed to mental illness.

- Mental asylums remained the major centers for treatment of mental illness. Most early asylums promised shelter, food, and security for their inhabitants. The main goal of the asylums was to provide humane and individualized treatment to each patient. It turned out to be a daunting task. The rapidly increasing numbers of patients made an individualized approach to treatment nearly impossible.

- Witmer's impact on clinical psychology in the United States was significant. He defined clinical psychology as a new research discipline allied with university-based psychology. He conceptualized, organized, and carried out the first program to train clinical psychologists in the United States.

- Clinicians offered a variety of views on treatment of mental illness. The approaches ranged from water treatment to work therapy, from moral support to reeducation. Attempts at healing such as the Emmanuel movement in the United States offered psychological and spiritual methods of treatment.

- Psychologists began to understand the clinical significance of their knowledge about the subjective world of an individual. They could examine specific problematic symptoms related to memory, reasoning, and learning skills. Psychologists began to analyze individual circumstances that contributed to illness and affecting treatment.

Key Terms

Anorexia

Clinical-pathological method

Degeneration

Emmanuel Church Healing Movement

Feebleminded children

Hypnology

Hysteria

Madness

Medicalization

Mood disorders

Moral therapy

Neurosis

Psychopathology

Social hygiene movement

7

The Birth and Development of the Behaviorist Tradition

> Psychology is the science of the intellects, characters and behavior of animals including man.
>
> *Edward Thorndike, 1911*

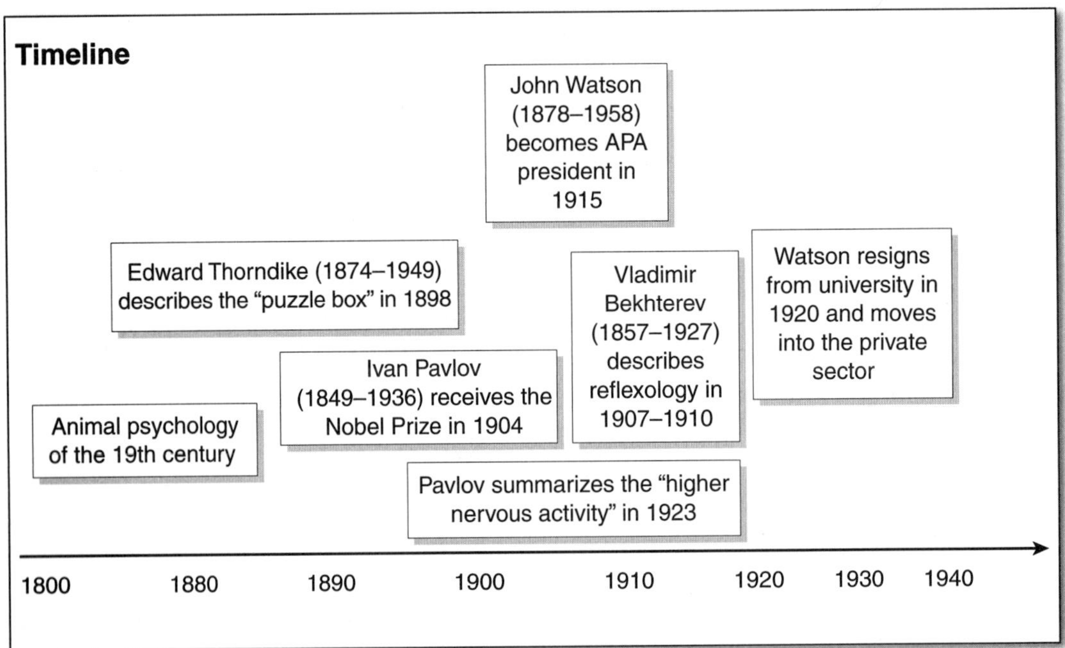

CHAPTER OUTLINE

There is a miniature park in the northern part of St. Petersburg, a large Russian city located on 100 islands connected by 300 bridges. Far away from major tourist attractions, the park is surrounded by the massive walls of the Institute of Experimental Medicine. If you ask a security guard to let you in the park, you will see an unusual monument: a bronze dog on a marble pedestal decorated by a sculptural relief that depicts several doctors standing by an operating table. This monument, known as *Pavlov's Dog*, is a symbol of gratitude to all the dogs used in medical, physiological, and behavioral experiments. Increasingly often since the 19th century, physiologists and then psychologists began to use animals in experiments. First, they used mostly worms, insects, fish, frogs, rats, mice, and birds. Later they added rabbits and cats. They also used thousands of unnamed dogs of all ages, breeds, and sizes. Today's medicine can cure many forms of cancer, diabetes, infectious diseases, and AIDS partly because of the experimental use of animals. Many life-saving medications are tested on animals first. But was it necessary for psychologists and behavioral scientists to use animals in their studies? Opinions differ. Some people say "no" because animal suffering should not be the price of scientific curiosity. Others argue that the research conducted on animals helped to find cures for many devastating psychological problems, including depression, phobias, panic attacks, and addictions. The debate continues, and both sides have a point. Nevertheless, regardless of our views of experimentation on animals, this research is part of

history. Animal research was a foundation for the development of experimental biology, physiology, and psychology. The 20th century's psychology, which we will examine in this and the following chapters, is heavily rooted in experimental studies involving animals.

If you have a chance to see this statue one day, come during a quiet hour, look at the dog intently, and smile. The locals say (they claim they have witnesses) that the bronze dog should wag her tail as soon as she sees you smiling. After all, they say, this is a learned reflex.

The Social Landscape: The Right Time for Behaviorism?

The term *behaviorism* appears self-explanatory. Anyone remotely familiar with psychology could associate it with behavior, action, or movement. Those with more knowledge would likely recall the famous "stimulus and reaction" idiom. Of course, this association is somewhat superficial. Behaviorism is based on the incredibly rich psychological tradition, which is both complicated and contradictory. It embraced studies ranging from animal experimental research to measurements of reflexes in children and adults and to early therapies.

Behaviorism gained strength in the beginning of the 1900s within a favorable social climate. The rapidly developing industrial societies needed technocrats—educated and skilled individuals expected to make a difference in society by creating useful objects and services. Social progress was increasingly seen as rooted in modern technology and a scientific understanding of life. A psychologist had to be a successful researcher capable of explaining psychological problems and improving people's lives.

The 20th century and its materialistic overtones brought new debates about the possibility of describing the "subjective" in untainted behavioral terms. Although a long tradition in psychology stemming from Locke, Berkeley, and Wundt emphasized the importance of consciousness, many psychologists hoped to interpret consciousness differently (Boring, 1929). The teachings of La Mettrie, the amazing Frenchman who had described behavior of humans and animals in mechanical terms (Chapter 3), became popular again. Many psychologists turned to measurement of behavior. Simple reactions and movements as well as complex social performances were addressed through mathematical formulas. Researchers' logic was simple: we may have difficulty explaining pain, but we can measure a person's behavioral responses to painful electric shocks.

Several developments contributed to early behaviorism.

- **Success of Animal Psychology.** The success of animal psychology was among the major factors stimulating behaviorism. Many researchers studying animals believed in a principle of continuity: both humans and animals represent one natural world and must be subject to similar laws. William James, you may recall, believed that human consciousness is a stage in a long process of evolution of the neurological structure of the organism.

- **Accomplishments of Physiology.** The success of general physiology in the 19th century encouraged many psychologists to turn to physiology of the brain and the nervous system. The researcher looked for measurable facts that are subject to verification and further experimentation. Similarly to physics, which studied the atom, psychologists hoped to find physiological "atoms" of human behavior.

- **Search for New Methods.** A growing number of psychologists treated introspective self-reports as unreliable methods. These methods could provide interesting results and rich descriptions—but they were imprecise. A true scientific experiment should not be at the mercy of a person's memory, attention, or some linguistic uncertainties. Psychology as an experimental science should turn to a new generation of experimental methods.

IN THEIR OWN WORDS

John Watson, whose role in psychology is examined later, wrote sarcastically imitating a typical introspection report: "This, as a whole, consists of gray sensation number 350, of such and such extent, occurring in conjunction with the sensation of cold of a certain intensity; one of pressure of a certain intensity and extent, and so on."

Source: Watson, 1913; cf. Sahakian, 1968, p. 454

Animal Psychology

To understand difficult, complex phenomena, a scientist should seek the simplest explanations. This principle, known in science as **parsimony**, became a working rule for many researchers. They argued that animals and humans should be subject to similar laws. Hunger and thirst, for example, are universal drives that activate behavior in many living organisms. Humans, like animals, look for safety and comfort and try to keep away from pain.

By the 1890s, several universities in Europe and North America had scholars studying animal behavior from a comparative perspective. Laboratories appeared in the United States, including at the University of Chicago and Harvard. In 1911 the *Journal of Animal Behavior* was founded (renamed in 1921 the *Journal of Comparative Psychology*). Most of the researchers in this field supported principles of evolution and developed experimental, laboratory-based methods involving observation combined with some experimentation. Small research laboratories created in various parts of the world helped scientists to conduct simple behavioral observations and experiments. Researchers used paper and pencil to draw sketches and record their detailed observations of animal habits, movements, responses, and communications.

Animal and Comparative Psychologists

When in 1973 two Austrians, Karl von Frisch (1886–1982) and Konrad Lorenz (1903–1989), together with Nikolaas Tinbergen (1907–1988) from the Netherlands, shared the Nobel Prize, this event became perhaps the highest recognition ever of studies of animal behavior. This scientific award was also an informal recognition of thousands of lesser known comparative psychologists who had been making their contribution to science for many decades. Although the term *comparative psychologist* became widely accepted in psychology only in the 20th century (Johnston, 2002), systematic studies go further back in history. Who were these researchers, what did they study, and what methodologies did they use?

Supporting Anthropomorphism. Better known today as the early ethnographer of Native American culture, Lewis Henry Morgan (1818–1881) was also a passionate student of animal behavior and animal psychology. Morgan rejected the scientific usefulness of the instinct concept. He believed that this concept didn't add anything new to the science of animal behavior. Instead, Morgan argued that animals, like humans, possess many mental abilities, such as reason, creativity, and moral judgment. Portraying animal behavior in human terms is called **anthropomorphism**. For instance, he conducted his own comprehensive observations of the behavior of the American beaver. Morgan was fascinated with the ability of this small animal to build sophisticated dams. Humans, he argued, also build similar river dams and other complex dwellings.

Morgan introduced a scale of development of species, which placed human beings on top of the scale. He argued that although humans have significant mental advantage over animals, the differences are based on the sophistication of their habits and the difficulty of their projects. Animals create relatively simple things, but humans are capable of more complex projects. Humans know more, do more, and have superior reasoning abilities. Morgan argued that animals too could develop their mental abilities if they had access to special training. However, as a religious man, Morgan also believed that the differences between animals and humans are caused by divine creation and not necessarily by evolution (Johnston, 2002).

Morgan attempted to provide serious evidence in support of his anthropomorphic ideas. Unfortunately, the quality of his research method could not support his theory. He used detailed observations of animals; in addition, he used unconfirmed, anecdotal evidence obtained elsewhere. He wanted to see animals acting like humans, and he saw what he wanted to believe. He wasn't alone in his beliefs.

George J. Romanes (1848–1894) was a British physiologist who introduced the term *comparative psychology.* Not affiliated with any university, he conducted animal research using his own private lab. He met and developed friendly relationships with Charles Darwin. One of the most remarkable works of Romanes was *Animal Intelligence,* published in 1882. The book was based on numerous observations and clearly defended the anthropomorphic view.

Today we hear stories from pet owners about the astonishingly "smart" behavior of their pets: some say that their dogs understand college football and figure skating, others tell stories about their parrots' ability to maintain an intellectual conversation, and still others rave about their cats' sense of humor. We should doubt such interpretations. However, both Morgan and Romanes were uncritical of similar stories and accepted cases about supersmart pets as scientific evidence. Romanes describes animals as driven by sophisticated emotional dilemmas. Imagine a dog trained not to eat food placed nearby (you can train the dog to do this after a series of exercises). The dog is permitted to pick up food as soon as the experimenter gives verbal permission. Romanes labels this example as clear evidence that animals, like humans, have fortitude and patience. Not everyone, of course, supported the anthropomorphic approach.

In Search of Similarities and Differences. An American historian, physician, and naturalist, Joseph LeConte (1823–1901) wrote about various topics, including geology, but many of his ideas referred to behavioral psychology. He maintained that animal learning does not involve rational thought. Adaptive behavior serves an evolutionary role: the most adaptive habits allow animals to survive. In Britain, C. Lloyd Morgan (1852–1936) attempted to describe animal behavior in objective terms, without biased evaluations. He insisted that anecdotal evidence produced by passing observers could not become scientific facts (Murchison, 1930). C. L. Morgan also believed in the principle of parsimony, which attempted to describe even the most complex animal behavior in biological terms—for example, habit formation. His work was characterized by the use of careful, detailed examination of verifiable facts.

Jacques Loeb (1859–1924), a German zoologist and experimenter who spent many years in the United States, was the most noteworthy advocate of the mechanistic view of psychology. He introduced so-called tropistic theory, or **tropism**. In his view, various forces—physical, chemical, biological, and social—all influence living organisms. Tropism stood for a physical and chemical reaction of orientation of the organism in a field of force. Favorable conditions of this field stimulate specific types of behavior. Unfavorable conditions suppress other types of behavior. Loeb was against using psychological terms in descriptions of animals. Behavioral equivalences should come into their place. As an example, *reception* should replace *sensation. Resonance* should replace *memory.* Consciousness in his view was little more than the ability of an organism to gain behavioral options as a result of experience (Wozniak, 1993a).

Unlike L. H. Morgan, who never served as a professor, John Bascom (1827–1911) was a professional scholar and educator, and also president of the University of Wisconsin. In 1869 he published *Principles of Psychology,* in which he considered the human mind as a part of the natural world. Sensation, perception, memory, and imagination are not only human phenomena; they also typical, in his view, in some animals (Bascom, 1869). However, complex animal activities should be explained in simple behavioral terms. Imagine that a cow learns to open a gate. First, the cow accidentally rubs its head and horns against the door. The latch gets loosened somehow. If this process is repeated, there must be a connection occurring between the act of rubbing and its results, which is the gate opening. Bascom argued that animals lack reason, and this separates the human mind from the animal mind. Reason allows humans to think about the future, whereas animals are restricted to the present. Their behavior is based mostly on instinct.

Comparative psychologists understood the limitations of their research. They were aware, to some degree, about inaccuracies in their assumptions and comparisons. Most of them accepted the evolutionary ideas of Darwin and Spencer and believed in the adaptive nature of animal behavior. Some of them were deeply religious and yet did not allow their religious attitudes to influence their research. They wanted to find out as much as possible about animal behavior and to use this knowledge to learn more about humans. As a rule, most early studies involved observations in natural conditions. More often, however, researchers began to use so-called invasive experimental procedures. One of these researchers was Edward Thorndike.

The Impact of Edward Thorndike

As a representative of a generation of American scientists educated after the Civil War, Edward Thorndike (1847–1949) was optimistic, ambitious, and innovative. He belonged to a new and growing category of psychology professors who were simultaneously heavily involved in research and teaching. He maintained socially progressive views that science could and should transform society. He believed that after psychologists established facts about useful and harmful acts, they would be able to prescribe moral behavior (Kendler, 2000). Today, if he were alive, Thorndike could have identified himself with several academic disciplines but probably would not have refused to be called an "animal psychologist." Although he studied animals, his research interests included (to name a few) statistics, math, educational techniques, and social psychology.

ON THE WEB

Read Edward Thorndike's (1874–1949) brief biographical sketch on the book website.

One of Thorndike's passions was math. Not only did he like to "crunch" numbers and solve math problems, but he also believed that a true psychologist must know mathematical methods very well: math was a key to understanding behavior. He liked the certainty of observations, the clarity of statements, and the emotional detachment from the object of studies. Thorndike said on many occasions that the truth is found only in empirical facts and not in the feelings of the researcher. Conversely, he was very impatient in trying to apply research findings to everyday problems. He warned applied psychologists not to rely on their common sense as a substitute for rigorous academic research. Applied psychology requires serious experimentation and knowledge in the basic sciences. He even called experiments in physics "child's play" compared with what a psychologist should undertake to examine behavior in experimental situations (Thorndike, 1935).

The Puzzle Box. In 1898, Thorndike published a monograph describing studies of the behavior of cats and chickens. It was not just another book on animal behavior. Thorndike introduced a new experimental method. His research animals were placed inside a "puzzle box," which was a specially designed cage or enclosure. An animal could escape by tripping a latch mechanism that opened a door or lifted a small barrier. Using this method, Thorndike observed and measured the behavior of his experimental animals. How did he measure it? Instead of describing creatively the animal's actions (which was common practice for most researchers), he applied three procedures. First, he counted the number of trials attempted before each animal escaped from the box. Second, he measured the time that the animal took to escape. Third, he measured habit formation. Placing the same animal in the puzzle box 10, 20, 40, or more times, he observed how long it would take the animal to acquire a habit.

He began to use a concept called the **learning curve.** In theory, it should take a cat a lot of time to escape from the box in the first place. Then, with each trial, the cat was supposed to spend less time and make fewer trials before a successful solution was found. Thorndike proposed the principle of connectionism: there must be links between situations and responses, and they must be connected somehow. Any complex behavior can be studied as a combination of many interconnected elements. Therefore it is possible to study elements or acts to understand a more complex picture of behavior. In a way, Thorndike's strategy resembled somewhat the logic of Titchener, which called for the study of mental elements. The difference between Titchener and Thorndike in this case is obvious: the "elements" under examination are verifiable facts, not subjective experiences.

Thorndike found that the animals in puzzle boxes, unlike what some "observational" animal psychologists described, did not necessarily show brilliance in solving problems. Most animals, attempting to get out of a puzzle box, initiated chaotic action. It was a kind of trial-and-error behavior. Even after they formed a useful habit, their behavior still involved many futile efforts and useless movements. Thorndike dismissed the earlier assumptions of some researchers about the unique ability of animals to imitate behavior: in his experiments, chickens, cats, or dogs could observe animals escaping from the puzzle boxes, but they did not form new habits based on pure observation (Thorndike, 1911).

How do animals and humans learn? Thorndike believed that neurons adapt to different learning experiences: the useful actions are retained on the physiological level, and harmful actions are avoided. For a successful learning process, several conditions should be present. First, the connection between the situation and a response should be strong. For example, if an animal escapes from the box, it should receive food as a reward. Second, the time between the impact of the situation and a response should be short. If it takes ten seconds for a cat to learn how to escape from the box, then this habit is likely to be retained and formed in a matter of approximately five minutes. Third, an animal should be ready to connect the situation and response (in the traditional language, the animal should "comprehend" the situation). The experience of an animal, its familiarity with the experimental situation, the quality of the reward, the presence of distracting signals or noises all may affect learning.

Laws of Learning. Based on his experiments, Thorndike identified and described several major principles of learning. For several decades already, psychologists had been looking for universal principles regulating human behavior. Some ideas received recognition. For example, the so-called Spencer-Bain principle stated that the frequency or probability of a behavior increases if it is followed by a pleasurable event and decreases if it is followed by a painful event (Boakes, 2008, p. 8). Meanwhile, many new speculative assumptions appeared in the form of short-lived hypotheses or theories. Thorndike was a step ahead of most of his peers because his theoretical assumptions were not based on speculation: he provided his own rigorous experimental research. What were these laws of behavior? Consider an illustration.

Describing the *Law of Effect,* Thorndike maintained that of several responses made to the same situation those accompanied or closely followed by satisfaction are likely to be learned. When the same situation occurs again, the response associated with satisfaction will likely follow. The state of satisfaction means that the animal tries to repeat the reactions that have caused satisfaction. Dissatisfaction produces an opposite effect. Discomfort means avoidance of that situation. Satisfaction and discomfort are nothing but favorable or unfavorable circumstances in the lives of an individual or an animal. Thorndike believed that the law of effect explains how people form harmful habits. For example, overeating and alcohol intoxication bring immediate satisfaction to many individuals. Yet they don't realize that long-term consequences of these habits can be devastating (Thorndike, 1911).

Labeling these observations a "law" of behavior seems too unsophisticated today. We shouldn't forget, though, that Thorndike's main research goal was not about discovering some unknown or obscure features of behavior. He wanted to prove or disprove some commonsense assumptions about animal and human behavior with the help of thorough experimental research.

Contributions of the Early Animal Research. Observations of animal behavior and experimental studies made an important contribution to the development of both the theoretical and experimental branches of psychology not only in industrial nations but also internationally. Despite the diversity of research goals and the profound differences in the methods used, these studies encouraged psychologists to consider humans and animals similar in principle but different in complexity. The differences between them were clear, yet they were not profound. Humans were more sophisticated than primates, monkeys were more advanced than dogs, which in turn were more sophisticated than rabbits, and so forth. These assumptions, of course, appeared offensive to many supporters of the spiritual branch of mental psychology. Several conclusions of comparative studies irritated some professors who rejected the evolutionary theory. Yet the social climate of the 20th century was generally favorable for the development of comparative psychology. More psychologists than ever believed that animal research could help in understanding the complexity of human behavior.

Comparative psychologists first used primarily noninvasive techniques such as observation or simple learning exercises. Thorndike's puzzle box was clearly a new method. Thorndike used a commonsensical and quite attractive approach: give an animal a problem to solve and then study and measure whatever you see in the process. Thorndike was one of many experimental psychologists at that time. However, because of the sophistication of his experiments and the persuasive power of the statistical material to support his findings, his work is widely considered a pioneering study in animal psychology and behaviorism.

✓ CHECK YOUR KNOWLEDGE

Explain anthropomorphism.

What was the puzzle box, and how did it work?

Explain the learning curve concept created by Thorndike.

Studies of Reflexes

Being relatively isolated from the European academic world because of the language barrier and a relative geographic remoteness, Russian basic science meanwhile was making substantial advances and taking leading world positions in chemistry, physics, and biology. Experimental studies of reflexes by Russian doctors and physiologists were already in an advanced stage by the beginning of the 20th century. In physiology, a remarkably competitive research tradition was forming. Despite the great diversity of theoretical views within the school, it was unified by at least three important principles. First, the researchers embraced the concept of *reflex,* which stemmed from the teachings of René Descartes and of the physiologists of the 19th century. Second, they were dedicated to rigorous empirical research based on experimentation and a thorough gathering of facts in the fields of physiology and observable behavior. Third (and this is a very important fact in the history of psychology), many of these researchers wanted to use their physiological findings to better understand human psychology and its behavioral manifestations.

Here we turn to the legacy of two remarkable scientists and individuals: Ivan Pavlov and Vladimir Bekhterev. Their experimental studies and theoretical work took place earlier or at the same time as major behavioral experiments of American psychologists; their work helped to build a solid foundation for behaviorism in the 20th century.

The Work of Ivan Pavlov

The son of a priest from a province, he was one of the world's most influential scientists and the first Russian ever to win the Nobel Prize. Today many people would probably refer to his research as a study of dogs. Fewer people would say that

Read Ivan Pavlov's (1849–1936) brief biographical sketch on the book website.

he studied conditioned reflexes using experimentation on salivary glands, and even fewer would mention that he conducted experimental studies of the functioning of the central nervous system. In fact, Pavlov called his research an objective study of the **highest nervous activity** (i.e., physiological activities of the brain's cortex). On many occasions Pavlov equated the highest nervous activity with behavior. Pavlov was a doctor, a physiologist, and a psychologist. Although later in life he didn't like the label "psychologist," he nevertheless, at the very beginning of his career, titled his Nobel Prize-winning speech *Experimental Psychology and Psychopathology on Animals.*

Salivary Glands. Most of the initial work on reflexes was conducted within the Institute of Experimental Medicine and Women's Medical Institute in St. Petersburg, Russia. Pavlov and his assistants first distinguished themselves worldwide for their study of the digestive system. Brilliant experimenters and skillful surgeons on Pavlov's team successfully used a new method: they surgically installed various fistulas in the bodies of animals (they used primarily dogs) without a major disruption of all physiological processes in the digestive system. By establishing fistulas in the ducts of the salivary glands, Pavlov was able to carry out experiments on the physiology of these glands. By using live animals, he was able to show, without the destruction of the live tissue, how the digestive system works. Pavlov used practically normally functioning animals and collected the secretion into a vial on the outside of the animal. A dog with a surgically implanted fistula could live almost a normal life, from 10 to 15 years. All the dogs were healthy and kept in decent conditions. For his research, Pavlov received in 1904 the Nobel Prize. These experiments, however, lead Pavlov to observe something that directed his subsequent research and to which he dedicated his entire career.

Salivary glands begin to function and produce saliva as soon as food or any other substance touches the receptors of the mouth. This was the physiological reaction that Pavlov had studied initially. Furthermore, Pavlov began to learn how different amounts of food and various substances affected the work of the salivary glands. In the process, he and his colleagues also noticed that the glands could function even if food did not touch the receptors in the mouth. The presence of laboratory assistants, the smell of food about to be given to dogs, the sight and sound of the metal plates in which food was supposed to be placed—these and many other conditions could produce the salivary response in the laboratory dogs. At the beginning of his research, Pavlov attached a special term to this kind of phenomena: "psychic secretion." He even used this term in one of his lectures in 1900. It certainly sounded psychological. The food was a few feet away and yet the glands were working as if they had to react to the touch of meat or bread. But very soon Pavlov switched to the physiological terminology. He began to make use of the concept of a reflex, which was a popular but loosely defined concept at that time.

Reflexes. Pavlov's biggest inspiration was the work of Ivan Sechenov (1829–1905), a widely respected scientist of the 19th century. Pavlov used Sechenov's three-component understanding of the reflex: a state of excitement in the nerve, the psychological stage in the middle, and the ending motor reaction. Sechenov, whose work is described in Chapter 4, published his famous *Reflexes of the Brain* (1865/1976), in which he used his own experimental data and claimed that so-called psychological processes are nothing more than cerebral mechanisms, or reflexes. In 1873, Sechenov also published an article, *Who and How Should Develop Psychology,* in which he called psychology "a sister" of physiology (a younger one) who should learn from the knowledge that physiology provides. Animal psychology and human psychology should be studied by similar methods.

Pavlov transformed Sechenov's theoretical attempt to discover the reflex mechanisms of psychological activity into an experimental theory of conditioned reflexes. In Pavlov's view, any "psychic" (the term used 100 years ago) process in the brain is a physiological response, an activity related to a specific signal or stimulus. The stimulus causes an electric reaction in the brain, which goes through the nervous system and multiple connections and affects the work of the salivary gland. Pavlov believed that all the unknown processes in the brain should be studied by objective methods and that physiology was the most suitable field for this work.

Unconditioned and Conditioned Reflexes. In 1903, at the 14th International Medical Congress in Madrid, Pavlov described his basic ideas about reflexes. He suggested two categories of reflexes. In the case of salivary response, the reflexes of the first category are associated with the direct influence of a substance on the receptors within the mouth. This category received the name **unconditioned reflexes**. They are inborn: dogs do not learn how to salivate when the food enters their mouth. Altogether, unconditioned reflexes provide for the most basic biological functions: food (search and consumption), sex, and self-protection.

The reflexes in the second category appear only under certain conditions, which later gave them their name, **conditioned reflexes**. They were also called "acquired reflexes" in the early works. Pavlov wanted to emphasize that at least two special conditions must be present for the formation (or the acquiring) of the conditioned reflex.

- The first condition is a specific situation, or a specific environment in which the reflex is formed.
- The second condition is the existence of the underlying unconditioned reflex.

The reflexes of the second category don't exist without those of the first one. For example, as Pavlov explained, nobody taught you when you were a child to quickly move your arm away from a flame. This reaction comes after very little thought, because you are in pain. Compare this to your reaction as an adult when you touch an object that you know is very hot. Most likely you'll cautiously extend your arm, touch the object quickly, and then quickly remove it because you anticipate pain.

PAVLOV'S EXPLANATIONS OF REFLEXES DEMONSTRATED ON SALIVARY RESPONSES

Unconditioned Reflexes. The reflexes of this category are associated with the direct influence of a substance on the receptors within the mouth. They are inborn: dogs do not learn how to salivate when the food enters their mouth.

Conditioned Reflexes. Also called "acquired reflexes," they occur under two conditions. The first is a specific situation, or a specific environment in which the reflex is formed. The second is the existence of the unconditioned reflex.

A reflex is an elementary psychological phenomenon, which, at the same time, is a physiological one. Pavlov believed that he could investigate—exclusively by experimental means—the most complex interrelations between an organism and its external environment. A conditioned reflex also functions according to the principle of temporary connection. This indicates that connections in the brain are only temporary, transitory. If a situation changes, such connections may change as well. Imagine that you are conditioned to fall asleep quickly in your own bed. Now imagine you have to travel and sleep on the plane. Many of us in this situation will have a problem falling asleep.

What conditions are necessary to form a conditioned reflex? Certainly, there must be a simultaneous or closely related coincidence of the signals of the first and second categories: the bell is ringing and the food is given. But this is not enough. Other conditions must be present.

- The internal state or condition of an animal or a person is crucial for the formation of the conditioned reflex. Hunger, or the absence of such, sleep deprivation, anxiety, and many other factors affect the development of the reflex.
- Another condition is the presence or absence of external distractive signals.
- The third condition is the quality of the signal: its characteristics and the meaning of the signal in the experimental situation.

Pavlov noticed that a dog could respond with animation when somebody came into the experimental room. But there was no saliva produced. However, if the dog saw an individual who fed this dog all the time, the dog began to salivate immediately. These are basic orientation reflexes, which Pavlov called informally "*what is that?*" reflexes. A new or unusual signal may disrupt the formation of a conditioned reflex. Can you think of practical applications? For many years and in many countries, pediatricians told parents that children should not listen to the radio or watch television during meals. Why? It distracts their attention ("what is that?" reflexes are activated), and therefore saliva is not released properly, which affects the whole digestive process.

CASE IN POINT

Eating and Watching Television. Did your parents or grandparents tell you not to watch television during meals? It was a popular point of view among many parents that watching television could distract or interrupt the digestive process, and that was obviously not good for health. However, if we use our knowledge about conditioned reflexes, we could easily argue that television might be good for digestion. Why? Watching television is paired in the first place with eating food. Therefore every time you turn on a TV set, the saliva is instantly released in your mouth and you are ready to digest the food. According to this interpretation, television does not "distract." It stimulates digestion. Which interpretation, prohibitive or permissive (or neither), sounds plausible to you?

Reflexes are complex reactions. The organism constantly produces a variety of responses to different signals. Which signals could form a reflex and make the gland release saliva? Experimenters used a whistle, a metronome, and a lightbulb. In all cases, the second category of reflexes was produced (Orbeli, 1961). On the one hand, when a dog is conditioned to salivate in the presence of a plate with food, the dog produces a complex positive movement reaction. On the other hand, an experimenter could produce a negative movement reaction from a dog, which then doesn't produce saliva but shows clear behavioral symptoms of fear or discomfort. Pavlov concluded that many conditioned reflexes should allow animals and humans to successfully adjust to the changing environment. For example, a fearful reaction may take place sometime before a dangerous situation occurs: a dog sees a person who was a source of discomfort previously (this person produced a loud noise). The dog runs away to avoid further discomfort.

The use of the method of conditioned reflexes allowed Pavlov to study the sensory system of animals. For example, many of us know that dogs have very poor color vision. How do we know about this? Obviously, dogs cannot tell us. Pavlov showed experimentally that, while forming reflexes, dogs could not differentiate between a green light and a red light and other colors. This was an indication that color vision in dogs was limited. He also found that sound signals do not work well with frogs. In addition, he found tremendous differences in animals' ability to detect sounds, forms, shapes, and other experimental signals. For example, dogs differentiated sounds much better than human beings did.

Pavlov believed that he was entering a new and exciting area of research, the field in which he had really wanted to work from the beginning of his scientific career. He was switching his attention to the study the "higher" nervous system.

Associative Connections. Pavlov applied the term *association* to physiological processes. Instead of speculating about "mental associations," as many psychologists did, he introduced the concept of physiological associations. How is a conditioned reflex formed, and where is that association?

First, there are areas of excitement within the nervous system and the brain. If, for example, two areas of excitement appear at the same time, then a connection may be established between these two zones. This means that when one zone is activated, the other zone is activated as well. For conditioned reflexes, Pavlov used the term *lock*: when two areas of excitement are connected, they are locked together in some way. This connection could exist for some time but may be only temporary.

The organism is in constant search of new locks because it must adjust to constantly changing conditions in its environment. From Pavlov's standpoint, the locks in the brain or conditioned reflexes are basic physiological mechanisms of mental processes. Imagine, for example, that a person is experiencing an excessive amount of anxiety for no apparent reason. In Pavlov's terms, the center of anxiety in the brain is overexcited. Coincidentally, a thought (also a physiological reaction in Pavlov's terminology) crosses the mind of this individual about the necessity to wash his hands. Thus anxiety and the thought of washing hands are now locked together. This is a physiological foundation for constant hand washing, which can be a symptom of obsessive-compulsive disorder. Remarkably, more than sixty years after Pavlov's death, clinicians studying obsessive-compulsive disorder continued to develop similar ideas about brain locking and its impact on behavior, including compulsive habits (Schwartz, 1997).

Pavlov identified language as a form of communication, the **second signaling system**, in contrast to the first signaling system (such as, e.g., the sight of food). The words are just sounds before a person or an animal forms associations that represent the meaning of those words. We can say to a dog, "Shake," and teach it to lift a front leg. Soon the dog will learn how to "shake." If we say the same word to other untrained dogs, they will not respond (they might bark at us instead). The words used in the language serve as signals to other signals that form conditioned reflexes.

Excitement and Inhibition. To explain how the brain develops conditioned reflexes, locks, and unlocks, Pavlov used a well-known (at that time) concept of physiological **excitement** and **inhibition**. He proposed that the principles of excitement and inhibition could explain the complex functioning of the nervous system. He thought he was very close to finding the scientific key to understanding human behavior.

His assumption was that a nonstop process of excitement and inhibition regulates our life. These are two interconnected processes constantly following each other and manifesting in sleep and awakening, stress and relaxation, or pleasure and sadness. Their interplay is the essence of the activities of the higher nervous system. Patience is an example. We can stay away, for instance, from a delicious cake in the refrigerator. However, we know how tasty it is and how easy it is open the door and take a big bite. Something keeps us from opening the door. This "something" is a promise we give to ourselves or some other condition that serves the role of an inhibiting signal. Take, as another example, the reaction of panic. In dangerous situations some people lose self-control and act erratically because they are influenced by excitement. Others, influenced by inhibition, freeze. Still others do not panic and show very responsible behavior. Their inhibition and excitement are balanced.

Excitement and inhibition influence each other. This process is called **induction.** On the one hand, excitement related to one type of behavior may inhibit other behaviors. Inhibition in one part of the brain may, on the other hand, excite other parts of the brain and activate them. In today's terms, for instance, if you are texting a message you may not hear what somebody is verbally telling you at that moment. Excitement and inhibition can clash. A dog can develop a conditioned reflex and salivate even when an unpleasant signal is used to train the dog, such as a mild electric shock. Because the animal is hungry, the excitement of the center of hunger in the dog's brain, as Pavlov believed, inhibits the activity on the pain center. Instead of running away, the dog salivates. Pavlov suggested that such "collisions" take place almost constantly in our lives when a signal associated with joy is paired with a signal associated with pain or suffering. In such situations one activity is inhibited and another is likely to be carried out. For example, some of us can spend tedious, long hours waiting in line to buy tickets to see a popular performer: the "suffering" during the waiting period is inhibited by an anticipation of the excitement during the forthcoming show.

Generalization and Differentiation. How do both excitement and inhibition work? Consider an example. One of the research assistants in Pavlov's laboratory was trying to develop a conditioned reflex based on touch. A dog's skin was tickled in one area (the belly), and then food was given immediately. Soon the dog salivated as soon as the experimenter tickled the dog's belly. The assistant quickly found that as soon as the reflex was formed, the dog responded to tickling regardless of the place the stimulation was applied: the belly, the leg, the tail, the ear. These results were surprising. Pavlov believed that this was a mistake due to the sloppiness of the assistant. However, Pavlov realized a few days later that he was wrong. At the beginning of the formation of any reflex, the reaction tends to be very generalized: the animal tends to respond to any sound or touch regardless of where it was applied. After a period of training, the differentiation takes place and the animal learns how to respond to only specific signals. Generalization and differentiation according to Pavlov are two sides of the process of excitement and inhibition. These processes are evolutionarily useful: quick learning is essential for survival.

Pavlov knew about many new discoveries related to the localization of the brain functions. However, he supported a holistic approach to behavior and its physiological regulations. He frequently imagined the brain's cortex as a colorful field with radiating waves of energy.

Characteristics of the Nervous System. Pavlov offered a remarkable behavioral interpretation of the nervous system's dynamics. He began to interpret the dynamics of the nervous system from a standpoint of three functions: strength, balance, and agility.

The **strength** of the nervous system is a reflection of the functional ability of the neurons to maintain the state of activation or excitement without developing self-protecting inhibition. The strong nervous system is capable of responding to strong, frequent, or unexpected signals. The responses can be measured: a weak stimulus causes a weak response, and a strong signal causes a strong response. The weak system replies differently: a weak signal may cause a strong response, and a strong signal may cause a nonresponse reaction. However, the weak nervous system is incapable of sustaining long and strong signals. It is very sensitive and exhausts itself quickly. The **balance** characteristic refers to equilibrium between excitement and inhibition within the nervous system. The system may be balanced or unbalanced: it is either biased toward excitement or toward inhibition. Finally, the **agility** characteristic refers to the quickness of the activation of excitement or the quickness of change between inhibition and excitement. There are types of nervous systems based on a combination of these features. People develop what Pavlov called a "character," which is based on the type of the nervous system interacting with the environment (see Table 7.1).

Table 7.1 Types of the Nervous System According to Pavlov

<table>
<tr><td rowspan="3">Strong</td><td rowspan="2">Balanced</td><td>Agile</td><td>Strong, balanced, and agile type. Inhibition and excitement are balanced. The person adjusts quickly to the changing conditions and can stand up to difficulties. Commonly makes quick decisions and changes strategies when necessary.</td></tr>
<tr><td>Inertial</td><td>The person is typically calm, slow, can resist pressures; can handle difficult situations by ignoring them or taking carefully planned decisions. Changes in behavioral strategies are difficult to make.</td></tr>
<tr><td>Imbalanced</td><td colspan="2">Strong, imbalanced type in which excitement dominates over inhibition. Explosive and temperamental, feisty and energetic. Can stand up to difficulties but often cannot control emotions and may lose self-control frequently.</td></tr>
<tr><td>Weak</td><td colspan="3">Experiences difficulties under the pressure of difficult circumstances including lack of time. Highly sensitive to external signals and has a hard time making quick decisions or choices.</td></tr>
</table>

Pavlov and his followers believed that after they were able to explain the functioning of the nervous system, they would discover the most fundamental laws of human behavior. Every detail of the theory seemed to be falling into its proper place. Compare two types of people, for instance. There are those who are constantly in a hurry; they are talkative, explosive emotionally, and very temperamental. There are others who are slow; they do not talk much, and they do not make decisions without serious thinking. Why are these two people different? Each has a certain type of nervous system. The first type is strong and imbalanced; the other type is strong, balanced, and inertial. Physiological patterns now apparently predicted behavioral types! However, what appeared theoretically clear was difficult to measure in reality. Specifically, the most challenging and eventually impossible task was to measure the strength, balance, and agility of the nervous system (see Chapter 1).

Mental Illness. One of the characteristics of mental illness, according to Pavlov, was the individual's inability to form new reflexes: he or she uses old reactions when some new behavior is necessary. Another condition that could trigger the development of mental illness is a combination of contradictory signals that create confusion or conflict in the individual. In most cases, a healthy person is capable of differentiating signals. In other cases, a person finds this difficult to do. This may cause psychological problems. Moreover, signals could be extremely strong, thus causing a constant "what is it?" reflex. Sometimes, an "ultra-paradox phase" is achieved when a weak signal causes a very strong reaction or when a strong signal causes a very weak reaction or nothing at all.

Pavlov believed that it would be possible to create experimentally the conditions resembling psychological dysfunctions by generating confusing signals and creating conditions of extreme pressure on the nervous system. In his view, a collision of excitement and inhibition is one of the most obvious examples of how mental illness is formed. Contemporary studies of stress and stress-related illnesses partially support Pavlov's assumption (Resick, 2001).

Social Behavior. In 1923, Pavlov published his famous *The Twenty-year Experience*, which summarized his studies and applied his theory to social behavior. On many occasions he indicated that the term *higher nervous activity* referred to behavior. Therefore one could use reflexes to describe all kinds of behavior including love, crime, educational progress, revolution, or even violence. The conditioned reflexes are very sophisticated devices that people use when they adjust to changing conditions of their lives. At the beginning, as children, we learn relatively simple reflexes, and the conditions become more sophisticated as we grow older. To adjust to them, we try to anticipate an outcome and thus develop complex reflexes of *purpose* that make our behavior goal directed. There are reflexes of *freedom* that allow us to make our own judgments and take responsibility for our actions.

☞ CASE IN POINT

Science and Politics. Throughout his career Pavlov did not participate in politics. Nevertheless, he supported the Communist revolution of 1917 in Russia, hoping that it would bring change and eliminate the old, corrupted, and inefficient political system. The grim reality of the revolution changed his views. His savings were confiscated. He had to share his large apartment with other families that were moved in by the authorities. The Russian civil war virtually halted his teaching and research. In 1922, without funds, research staff, and any hopes for improvement, Pavlov wrote a petition to the head of the government, Lenin, asking for permission to leave and move the lab overseas. His petition was denied, but the government began to generously finance the laboratory and its employees. It was an attempt to retain Pavlov, a renowned scholar and a symbol of Russian science. The government built new research facilities and purchased equipment for the lab. He was permitted to travel freely, and he visited the United States in 1923.

(Continued)

(Continued)

Despite the government's sponsorship, he remained openly critical of the Communists and their policies. Pavlov was a deeply religious man and resented the Communist government's closure of the Russian churches, confiscation of church property, and the state-sponsored harassment of believers. When the Soviet government began the campaign of "cleansing" the universities–firing professors, researchers, and staff who were not of working-class background–he spoke openly against the government's intrusion into academic affairs. He also refused to accept Marxist philosophy as a theoretical foundation for his studies. He warned about the dangers of the so-called slavery reflexes in people who, for the fear of losing their jobs, would do anything the government ordered them to do (Golubovsky, 1998; Shnol, 1997).

Animal Research. Pavlov was aware of the negative reaction of some people to his research on animals. He received many letters asking why animals had to suffer to satisfy a scientist's research interests. Pavlov frequently addressed this question during his public lectures. He always maintained that he had no easy feelings when he had to operate on a dog or cat. However, he believed that this was necessary to do for the sake of science, medicine, and, above all, people. Pavlov told his critics to overcome their ignorance and tone down their emotions. Today, of course, the photographs of the experimental dogs in the Pavlov laboratory may cause a critical reaction. Critics may argue that Pavlov did not directly save a human life: for example, his research has not created a lifesaving medication. We have to understand, nevertheless, that his research was done according to the law and based on customs of that time. He paid serious attention to the well-being of his research animals. They were kept in clean facilities, with plenty of food and decent care available to them.

The statue at St. Petersburg University is dedicated to all the cats used in experimental research in physiology.

Pavlov and His Role in Psychology and Science. In his Nobel Prize lecture, Pavlov said that one of the major goals of science was to understand human psychology using objective methods. Pavlov's ultimate goal as a researcher was psychological, as he stated on many occasions. The dogs, the fistulas, the salivary glands, the conditioned reflexes—everything served to help him pursue his main goal: understanding objectively the mechanisms of human behavior. The salivary gland was a very functional and practical physiological device; it was a convenient bridge between the concealed world of the brain and visible, measurable responses.

For Pavlov, his work was a two-stage process. He wanted to use his theory of conditioned reflexes to study the types of nervous systems. But before moving to the second stage, he thought he must first advance his physiological theory. (In one of his works, titled *A Letter to the Young Generation,* he wrote that even "two lives" for a researcher are not enough to accomplish his modest plans.) Pavlov sincerely believed that he was near a great breakthrough in physiology and psychology. He believed that the model of the reflex could explain the most complicated forms of behavior.

The experiments on dogs helped Pavlov comprehend the impact of physiology on behavior. He clearly understood that the complexity of human life couldn't be reduced to simple reflexes. But he had to begin somewhere; he had to study the "elements." The next step in his program would have been the detailed investigation of the physiology of the sensory organs or, as Pavlov would call them, "analizators." Unfortunately, the development of the studies could no longer rely on his methodology, which had been revolutionary in 1900 but was not so in the 1920s. New generations of neurophysiologists and psychologists began to examine the mechanisms of sensory systems using different, more sophisticated equipment and methods.

ON THE WEB

Read more about Pavlov's research and popular culture on the book website.

For today's critical observers, Pavlov's shortcomings are obvious. Measuring physiological characteristics in certain parts of the brain, he did not take into consideration that different parts of the cerebral cortex might function differently. An organism may show signs of strength in one receptor (e.g., the tactile receptor) and at the same time show weakness in another (e.g., taste). The second substantial weakness of Pavlov's theory was that, although his model of the three basic characteristics of the functioning of the nervous system was simple and attractive, physiologists have not been able to show specific physiological mechanisms in the brain that would stand for the strength, balance, and dynamics of the nervous system.

✓ CHECK YOUR KNOWLEDGE

Explain Pavlov's conditioned and unconditioned reflexes.

What were Pavlov's characteristics of the nervous system?

How did Pavlov understand mental illness?

Reflexology of Vladimir Bekhterev

Another remarkable researcher whose life and work contributed to the behavioral tradition of the 20th century was Vladimir Bekhterev (1857–1927), a physician, professor, neurologist, poet, and psychologist. Unlike Pavlov, besides research and lectures he was actively engaged in outpatient and inpatient therapeutic work and legal consulting. He was a supporter of women's educational rights and children's welfare programs. He was a dedicated promoter of psychology in newspapers and magazines. Like Pavlov, he lived in the transitory period between the 19th and 20th centuries, which was marked by rapid social developments and brewing political tensions. It was, at the same time, a period of great scientific discoveries.

ON THE WEB

Read Vladimir Bekhterev's (1857–1927) brief biographical sketch on the book website.

Objective Psychology. Bekhterev was already an accomplished clinician and researcher when he turned to psychological studies. Most of his early work was in the fields of physiology and the anatomy of the nervous system. From the late 1890s on, Bekhterev published several articles based on his observations of symptoms of hysteria and neurosis. He believed that to study psychology, scientists should never use personal feelings, likes, or dislikes (Strickland, 1997).

Bekhterev sought a theoretical model to explain the interaction between the body and the mind. He rejected the introspection of the Wundt school. In his view, the only alternative was an objective psychology that focused on behavior and physiological processes taking place within the brain and the nervous system (Bekhterev, 1888). Bekhterev became convinced that anything called "psychological" or "subjective" was, in fact, a kind of physiological process in the brain and nervous system. If the nature of both subjective and physiological processes is one, he continued, there should be a founding substance or force that is responsible for the manifestations of both processes. What was that unifying force?

For Bekhterev, the most suitable was the concept of energy. He endorsed the popular assumption at the time about energy conservation: energy does not disappear but transforms from one form to another. Applied to physiology and psychology, the function of the sensory systems of the human body is a transformation of external energy into a kind of internal energy. Bekhterev believed that he could explain all psychological processes as transformations of energy accumulated in the brain and nervous system (Bekhterev, 1904).

The next step for Bekhterev was to develop new, objective methods to register and measure behavior. Between 1907 and 1910, in several steps, Bekhterev published one of his most significant works under the title *Objective Psychology.* The monograph described the principles of **reflexology**, a new term that he began to use first sparsely and then consistently after 1912 (Schniermann, 1930; Yaroshevsky, 1996). Two central concepts of Bekhterev's theory were reflex and adaptation.

Reflex and Adaptation. In line with functionalist assumptions, Bekhterev accepted the idea that living organisms have the capacity to alter their behavior under the changing circumstances of the environment. Most important, an organism preserves some alterations. Every reaction is based on two influencing factors: one is the specific impact of the environment, and the other is the inner condition of the organism. This inner condition is determined by hereditary factors and the experience of the organism, which is related to age and education.

Two principal actions underwent a serious change during the evolution from plants to animals: *attack* and *defense.* The complexity of these actions depends on the scope and quality of the experiences of a species or of human beings. Plants, for example, are exposed to limited experience because most of them cannot move. Animals have greater experiences and therefore develop a more sophisticated repertoire of aggressive and defensive actions. Furthermore, animals are not the same. Worms and fish live in less advantageous environmental conditions than the animals above the ground. Differentiations of organs should profit the organism because they allow both animals and humans to respond better, or to adapt, to the environmental changes. Energy is stored in some modified fashion by past experience; it is put into action by a stimulus affecting the organism. Bekhterev called this type of stored energy *consciousness* (Frost, 1912).

Two Types of Reflexes. Bekhterev defined two types of reflexes. The first was called *innate reflexes,* which are stimulated by the body. Reflexes of the second type are trained or acquired with experience. They are called the *associated reflexes.* For example, when a person's hand is placed on a very sharp object, an innate defensive reflex is activated and the hand is pulled back: if this reaction does not happen, the hand is cut and the person is hurt. An associate reflex in this case will be the common reaction of cautiousness when we handle sharp objects: an association is already created to avoid pain.

As a practicing medical doctor, Bekhterev saw many patients and knew well the brain's anatomy. He believed that the innate reflexes are regulated primarily by means of the spinal cord and the subcortical structures of the brain. The associated reflexes are regulated by means of the cerebral cortex, with some participation of the subcortical-level structures. Reflexes can be inhibited, that is weakened, or become less observable. The process of thinking, for example, as Bekhterev stated is, in fact, inhibited speech reflexes. American psychologist John Watson would maintain a relatively similar view, which is examined a bit later in this chapter.

Reflexology. Already a well-known physician, Bekhterev (1918/1933) dedicated the rest of his life to a new scientific discipline. He called it reflexology. One day, as he hoped, reflexology would become a universally accepted discipline. As a result of almost two decades of work, he published *General Principles of Human Reflexology* in 1918, which underwent three editions during Bekhterev's life. Each new edition was expanded to include new research data.

Bekhterev maintained that general laws of reflexology are also part of some universal rules governing nature. On the level of human reflexes, these fundamental rules are energy conservation, constant variability, mutual effectiveness, cycles, economy, adaptation, synthesis, function, inertia, compensation, evolution, selection, relativity, and some others. Take, for example, inertia. In physics, the law of inertia manifests as an object in rest or in uniform motion. On the level of behavior, inertia appears as something unchanging, such as rigid thinking, laziness, stubbornness, or apathy. Bekhterev understood that these general laws might appear as simplistic or even reductionist. But these verbal descriptions, he thought, should help understand better the principles of reflexology.

Energy transformation is the main mechanism by which to describe physical and biological processes. How does the energy transformation process work in psychology? The energy of an outside stimulus affects the receptors. This energy could be mechanical, thermal, or chemical. It is transformed in the receptors into molecular energy of the colloidal formation of the nervous tissue. A nervous current then occurs. The energy is conveyed through fibers to the brain centers. It is processed in these centers and sent to the muscles and glands. There the energy transforms again into a variety of forms, including mechanical, which makes muscles move; chemical, which makes glands release certain substances; or thermal, which results in an increase or decrease of body temperature.

The nervous energy also accumulates in the centers, most likely in the cerebral cortex of the brain. Bekhterev called this accumulation of energy in the brain "emotions." When the energy affects action after a delay, people label this "process thinking." Bekhterev was certain that what was called a "psychological process" was based on the same physiological mechanisms of energy transformation as any other behavioral process. Overall, in the context of his theory, the process of energy transformation was, in fact, the reflex (see Figure 7.1).

Collective Reflexology. Bekhterev applied the reflexological principles to the study of group behavior. His *Collective Reflexology* was one of the earliest books in social psychology (Strickland, 2001). Reflexology can describe group behavior in the same way it describes an individual's behavior. Group activities, for Bekhterev, were special kinds of social reflexes. He coined the special term **collective reflexology**, or the study of the

Figure 7.1 Reflexology: The Energy Transformation Process

Energy → Receptors → Molecular Energy → Fibers → Nervous Centers

Energy Transformation → Muscle Reactions

Accumulation of Energy (Emotion)

Delayed Energy Action (Thinking)

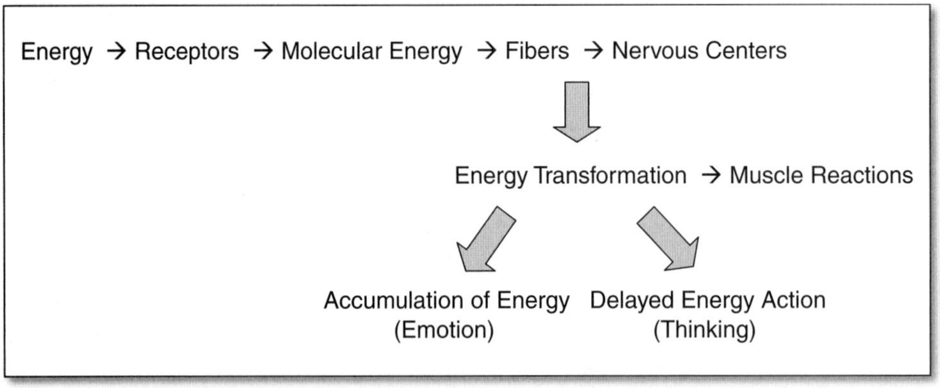

emergence, development, and behavior of groups that display their collective activity in unity. Collective reflexology, to which Bekhterev dedicated almost ten years of his life, investigates ways and forms of collective reflexes (Bekhterev, 1921a/2001).

Social reality, in the forms of words, symbols, and other signals, transfers from a group to an individual. This is a kind of measurable energy transformation. Among several measurable features are group sensitivity, observational skills, group mood, creative activities, focus of attention, and decision making. Bekhterev also offered a variety of specific methods (including experimentation and surveys) to study group actions. He believed that collective reflexology, as a scientific field, should introduce instructive principles or laws to explain social groups, crowds, and even the social processes of an entire nation. For example, Bekhterev described a positive correlation between grain prices and the number of reported thefts (Bekhterev, 1921a/2001). He described 23 such laws, including the law of conservation of energy, the law of equal and opposite reaction, the law of inertia, the law of reproduction, and so forth.

☞ CASE IN POINT

Bekhterev's Views of Immortality. Bekhterev used the concept of energy transformation to discuss death and immortality. He argued that physical death extinguishes forever the existence of the body. Trying to cope with the mystery of death, many people turn to religion, a great source of hope. Many believe in the resurrection of the dead, a concept that denies physical extinction. However, in his view, science can provide the most profound justification of immortality. According to the principle of energy conservation (the principle he defends in most of his works), energy cannot disappear without a trace. It cannot appear without being caused by another source of energy (Bekhterev, 1919/2001b). Human internal energy transforms into the energy of muscles and behavior. A living person transforms energy around him or her. When a person dies, the body decomposes and ceases to exist. The decay of the body leads to decomposition of the organism into simple elements. Yet life is not over. It transforms into new forms of energy, into the thoughts and actions of other people. This is, in fact, the life cycle of immortality (Dobreva-Martinova & Strickland, 2001).

Suggestion and Hypnosis. Bekhterev was among the first to use hypnosis to treat behavioral problems (Chapter 6). He believed that during hypnosis specific forms of energy exchange take place. Although public demonstrations of hypnotic effects were common in the early 20th century, they were done largely for entertainment and profit: hypnotists traveled from town to town demonstrating their skills to paying audiences gathered in a small theater or a hotel ballroom. Bekhterev distanced himself from such entertainers. He believed that hypnosis should be used exclusively for therapeutic purposes (Bekhterev, 1903/1998).

At first, his colleagues reacted negatively to his hypnotic studies. After years of research, Bekhterev showed that some patients produced behavioral improvements after undergoing hypnotherapy. In particular, Bekhterev was involved in the treatment of alcoholism. There is archival footage of a session filmed in the 1920s in which he talks about the harmful effects of drinking to a small audience—all his patients presumably under hypnotic suggestion during the filming (Yaroshevsky, 1996).

Bekhterev published a series of works on suggestion, hypnosis, and telepathy. He viewed these phenomena as caused by the underlying energy-transformation process. Among the best-known studies of this kind were Bekhterev's experiments involving dogs. By 1921, within a 20-month period, Bekhterev and colleagues conducted more than 1,200 measurements of the impact of telepathy on dogs' behavior. The researchers claimed that their experiments proved the existence of telepathy. In their view, it was the process of dissemination of the special "shining" type of energy released from one person and influencing another.

Traumatic Emotions. As a doctor, Bekhterev was among the first in psychology to acknowledge and treat problems related to emotional traumas. War, he wrote, affects not only soldiers but also civilians. He reported a significant increase in anxiety and depressive symptoms in the Russian army during the war against Japan in 1904. The symptoms included diminished motivation, general slowdown in cognitive functions, and difficulty making decisions. He also noticed an increase in the number of diagnosed cases of hallucinations and delusions among military personnel during World War I (1914–1918). His explanation was that the traumatic events of war could exacerbate preexisting weaknesses in the brain. Extreme situations could trigger the development of abnormal symptoms such as epileptic seizures, hysteria, and severe deterioration of memory. He described long-term effects of war on soldiers and officers who had to spend years in trenches, away from their homes and families, under the constant threat of death or injury (Lukova, 1992). Contemporary data supported Bekhterev's early observations: there were increases of the reported cases of psychological disorders in the military during the U.S. wars in Vietnam, Afghanistan, and Iraq (Seal, Bertenthal, Miner, Sen, & Marmar, 2007).

A Civil Servant. Bekhterev believed that a scientist has an obligation to speak publicly about social issues. He also believed that a democratic environment was the best for a person's psychological health. He publicly defended civil freedoms. He supported the idea of the unification of the Slavic nations (such as Poland, Slovakia, Bulgaria, Croatia, etc.) to create a healthy social environment for the people of similar cultures. Bekhterev was vehemently against religious and gender discrimination. He spoke against quotas (widely practiced at that time) that restricted access of ethnic minorities to education and employment (Bekhterev, 1916/2003). He applied the rules of scientific ethics to his research and consultations. Serving as an expert in a highly publicized murder trial (see Chapter 5), Bekhterev demonstrated the importance of objective, unprejudiced professional testimony.

Bekhterev contributed to programs fighting homelessness among children. He believed in musical education as a way to teach moral values (Moreva, 1998). He hoped to defeat alcoholism. He was in constant search of new methods of treatment for alcohol and substance-related problems. He supported the decision of the Russian government to stop selling alcohol during the war in 1914.

Some historians believe that Soviet dictator Stalin played a role in Bekhterev's sudden death in 1927. Bekhterev, reportedly, saw Stalin for a clinical evaluation and diagnosed him with paranoia. This diagnosis, if it were to become public, would have damaged the reputation of the dictator. However, contemporary sources, including interviews with his relatives, indicate that there is no evidence of Stalin's involvement in Bekhterev's death (Bekhtereva, 1995).

In *Collective Reflexology*, Bekhterev relies on his own and eyewitnesses' accounts of the events that shook Russia in 1917. It was a time of revolution, street battles, rallies, violence, and great uncertainties. He applies the idea of energy and reflex to explain crowd behavior (Osipov, 1947). In Bekhterev's view, like a person having mood swings because of an imbalance in the body's neuropsychological energy, large social groups go through similar disturbances. The group energy levels can be high or low. Revolution and violence are caused by high energy levels boosted by many people's desire to commit their individual energies to a common cause. Bekhterev and many scientists before and after him became witnesses of important social events, and they often recorded their observations. Violence, war, crime, social justice, and abuse have always been favorite themes for psychologists to debate. There are no rules that compel or prohibit psychologists from making commenting about social events.

To what degree and when should psychologists, from your point of view, make social and political commentaries?

Thinking about your current psychology professors, whose social and political commentaries would you like to hear and why?

Bekhterev's Impact. Even a short description of Bekhterev's accomplishments is impressive. He was a founder of the first Russian experimental psychological laboratory in 1886, organized just a few years after Wilhelm Wundt opened his renowned research facility in Leipzig. Like William James in the United States, Bekhterev impressed his contemporaries with his many works in the fields of psychology, psychiatry, philosophy, and history. Bekhterev made a distinct effort to challenge subjective psychology and to promote a new, objective psychology free from introspection.

Bekhterev placed human behavior in the center of experimental studies and, like Ivan Pavlov, considered reflexes as the "pillars" of human activity available for the most objective empirical scrutiny. Bekhterev introduced the principle of energy transformation to explain the correspondence between physical and psychological processes. As a physiologist, he studied and described several brain centers, and his name now appears in many brain atlases and anatomy textbooks. As a physician, Bekhterev examined many patients with neurological and psychological dysfunctions. He laid the foundation for experimental social psychology. He established several research institutes and scholarly journals. Bekhterev delivered public lectures and raised funds to help homeless and abused children. His name is on one of Moscow's streets and on the building of a respectable health institution in St. Petersburg, Russia.

Bekhterev was among the active promoters of the idea that science must study the individual from a complex, multidisciplinary perspective, in the center of which he hoped to see his reflexology. The propensity to seek a general, unifying theory of psychological studies and the desire to create a universal branch of science related to the individual continued to influence the minds of many psychologists during his lifetime.

Nevertheless, for decades Bekhterev and his work remained mostly unknown to the majority of American psychiatrists and psychologists. Bekhterev obviously was not in the psychology mainstream: in 10 randomly selected major introductory psychology textbooks published in the United States in 2008, the name of John Watson is mentioned 47 times, the name of William James is referred to 67 times, and Pavlov is mentioned 56 times. But there are no references to Vladimir Bekhterev; there are only brief comments about reflexology. But by the end of the 20th century the international audience began to rediscover Bekhterev. Substantial portions of his works were finally translated into English (Strickland, 2001). He is credited for his contribution to the behavioral tradition and his almost zealous dedication to experimental methods in behavioral studies. If translations of Bekhterev's works had been made in the 1920s, his behaviorist contemporaries in the United States would likely have immediately supported his views.

Bekhterev was a product of his time. He was both a progressive scientist and a carrier of old prejudices. He was against the death penalty but considered masturbation a serious psychological disorder. He demanded attention to the homeless but passionately stood against homosexuality. He defended the dignity of his alcoholic patients but did not hesitate to drop occasional sexist remarks.

Bekhterev, as were a few of his followers and contemporaries all over the world, was a distinct reductionist who genuinely believed that psychology could be described in pure behavioral terminology. Another remarkable scientist shared similar views. His name is forever associated with behaviorism and its early developments: John Watson.

✓ CHECK YOUR KNOWLEDGE

Name two central concepts of Bekhterev's theory.

What was collective reflexology?

How did Bekhterev understand immortality?

The Behaviorism of John Watson

In the early 20th century, many scientists came from middle-class families of modest means. Pavlov and Bekhterev were among them. In the United States, social changes were rapid and sweeping. The social elite were giving up their exclusive societal status and access to higher education. Wealthy families from New England or New York were no longer the predominant sources of students entering major universities and graduate programs. Social mobility, as history frequently shows, is a crucial factor of societal progress.

Behaviorism: The Beginnings

John Watson, the most prominent representative of behaviorism, was born in South Carolina. He grew up in the rural country of the American South, which was undergoing multiple transitions after the Civil War. People were moving in large numbers from farms to towns and cities. They were looking for jobs, education, improved living standards, and better opportunities. This move reflected a significant demographic, socioeconomic, and cultural change in America at the end of the 20th century.

Watson attended Furman University, a small Baptist school, which he graduated from in 1899 with a master of arts degree. He chose the University of Chicago for his advanced studies. His mentor, James Angell, ignited Watson's interests in animal and comparative psychology. Watson received a PhD in 1903, which made him the youngest holder of a doctorate psychology degree at that university. At Johns Hopkins University he began to work under James Baldwin, a top psychologist of that time and a cofounder of *Psychological Review*, an authoritative professional journal. Unfortunately, Baldwin had to resign from his professional posts because of a scandal that stemmed from his alleged sexual misconduct. The young John Watson suddenly found himself in charge of psychological studies at Johns Hopkins with an influential journal under his supervision.

The Approach. From the beginning of his career, Watson, like Lloyd Morgan, tried to avoid anthropomorphism in his observations of animals. Since his early studies in Chicago, Watson accepted Jacques Loeb's idea that human beings are more likely to be organic machines. As a professor at Johns Hopkins University, Watson began to work hard to develop a new kind of experimental psychology that would identify behavior and measurable signals as the only two significant variables worth examining.

ON THE WEB

Read John Watson's (1878–1958) brief biographical sketch on the book website.

One of Watson's first research projects was a study of the behavior of the white rat. He wanted to see a correlation between the ability of rats to learn and the structure of their brain. The number of connections in the brain was assumed to have something to do with the learning capacity of rats. A Swiss-born neuropathologist, Adolf Meyer, who later became Watson's colleague at Johns Hopkins University, suggested some ideas for Watson's studies. In one of these experiments reported in 1906, Watson compared the behavior of normal rats with similar rats whose brains had been surgically damaged to affect their vision, smell, and touch. Many psychologists considered such experiments cruel and unnecessary. As most scientists involved in animal research, Watson dismissed these criticisms as based on ignorance. He believed that scientists should conduct unpopular experiments if the studies advance science.

Focus: Behavior. Two views distinguished Watson's approach to behavior. First, he considered behavior as actual movements of the body: legs and arms, glands, specific muscles. Like Thorndike, Watson saw any complex behavior (such as playing a musical instrument) as containing numerous smaller behavioral elements. This "elementary" approach to understanding complex actions was different from the way most comparative psychologists described behavior.

The second distinct feature in Watson's approach was that he did not accept the concept of purpose in behavioral studies, as some other psychologists did (McDougall, 1912). A purpose, in his view, is not a cause of behavior. Only signals or stimuli could determine an individual's next step. Later supporters of behaviorism would disagree with this assumption and attempted to study purpose from an objective, empirical standpoint, as Chapter 11 discusses. Watson rejected the idea of purpose, which he believed was part of old subjective psychology. True psychology, according to his vision, should be built on gathering observable facts about animals and humans, which both adjust to the environment by means of heredity and habit. He presented his views in a series of articles and lectures. This series was not just a summary of his research. It was a manifesto, a declaration of purposes and methods of a new scientific discipline: behaviorism.

The Behavioral Program. In 1915, Watson unexpectedly became president of the American Psychological Association (APA). Some psychologists who voted for this relatively little-known person thought of him as hard working and ambitions. Others viewed him as too inexperienced to lead a national organization. To some degree, Watson's election was a sign of unity within the APA, which was not in the best organizational shape at that time. American psychology suffered a serious blow to its reputation when the APA declined an opportunity to host the 11th International Psychological Congress. This decision about Watson was made for two reasons. The first was the sudden resignation of James Baldwin, the chair of the Congress. The second was the inability of several factions within the organization to find a substitute for Baldwin. Psychologists preoccupied with their own ambitions could not cooperate well. Therefore Watson's presidency was a compromise. The elected post brought him wider recognition and provided a convenient venue for his ideas.

Watson defined psychology as the science of human activity and conduct. Simplicity was a key to success of this discipline. There are three **founding principles of behaviorism**:

- stimulus and response (behavior is a set of responses to specific signals);
- habit formation (behavioral responses become useful and retained); and
- habit integration (simple reactions develop in complex acts).

In 1915, Watson reported to the APA about two Russian scientists, Bekhterev and Pavlov, who had developed new methods and theories to study behavior. He discussed the nature of Pavlov's conditioned reflex and the perspectives open to psychology if it turned to study reflexes. Watson praised Pavlov but believed that Bekhterev's methods of studying and measuring motor reflexes were more suitable for further experiments. Measuring conditioned reflexes, as Watson predicted, psychologists could finally achieve their goal: to describe and control human behavior (see Table 7.2).

Table 7.2 John Watson's Objectives

Psychology should become an experimental branch of natural science. All the speculations about the mechanisms of "the mind" and "consciousness" should be put aside.
All experiments should be verified and controlled. Specifically, introspection should be ruled out as a method of scientific investigation.
Psychology should resemble biology, which studies and discovers natural laws applied to all living organisms, including animals and people.
The ultimate goal of psychology should be to describe, predict, and control human behavior.
To achieve these goals, psychology must embrace behavior as the subject of studies. Moreover, the study of behavior should become an independent science.

Watson's *Psychology From a Standpoint of a Behaviorist* became one of the most popular psychology books ever (Watson, 1919). It was translated into many languages. It is very easy to read: Watson wanted to make psychology an attractive subject, especially to students. Years later he commented that, unfortunately, in several places, he had overdramatized some of his arguments. For example, he wrote that the process of thinking is nothing more than an "inner" or subvocal speech. Despite the book's relatively easy written style, it contains a great variety of examples and provides suggestions about how to apply psychological knowledge to real-life situations.

From the behaviorist view, psychology should be an experimental branch of natural science. Like Bekhterev and Pavlov, Watson believed that introspection was a useless method. Consciousness should be an exclusive problem for philosophers to examine. Psychology's goal was to develop principles to explain, predict, and control behavior (Wozniak, 1993b).

Behaviorism: Applications

Serving as the head of a laboratory at the John Hopkins Medical School, in the clinic of Adolf Meyer, Watson began observations of infants. The idea was to find out more about how certain maladaptive habits—formed mostly in infancy—become sources of mental illness during adulthood.

Mental Illness and Deviance. Watson was now describing the behavior of infants exclusively in terms of conditioned reflexes. Watson believed that the causes of both mental illness and deviance were in maladaptive habits (Watson, 1916). To him, mental illness was a kind of *habit disturbance.* He didn't reject the developing clinical psychology. He interpreted abnormal symptoms differently than most clinical psychologists did. Symptoms of hysteria or neurosis, defensive reactions, guilt, irrational fears—all these and scores of other symptoms were maladaptive reflexes. How did they develop? There must have been a situation or condition in the past, an emotional trauma, physical or sexual abuse, masturbation, or something else that triggered the development of a dysfunctional habit. This habit, in a chain reaction, caused the development of other progressively maladaptive habits.

Watson applied the reason of behaviorism to the issue of human values and deviance. He believed that social values are learned according to changing social standards. If an individual has a problem adjusting to societal norms, then behaviorism will be able to provide special methods of training and correction to teach good habits to that individual. Several prominent thinkers, among them Walter Lippmann and John Dewey, shared similar views. Social deviance and crime, in their view, take place because of the acts of a few socially untrained individuals. These persons did not have an opportunity to learn how to act according to society standards. Psychologists, in Watson's opinion, were capable of providing treatment through special programs funded by the government. Subsequently, new behavioral habits will be formed, and this will result in crime reduction.

☞ CASE IN POINT

Analyzing What Psychologists Said and Meant. The following statement by John Watson is frequently quoted. Read it carefully.

Give me a dozen healthy infants, well-formed, and my own specified world to bring them up in and I'll guarantee to take any one at random and train him to become any type of specialist I might select–doctor, lawyer, artist, merchant-chief and, yes, even beggar-man and thief, regardless of his talents, penchants, tendencies, abilities, vocations, and race of his ancestors. I am going beyond my facts and I admit it, but so have the advocates of the contrary and they have been doing it for many thousands of years.

If you have not already noticed, in the last sentence he admits that he is putting aside his research principles; he is going "beyond" his facts. Many critics accused him of putting his beliefs above facts. What does this statement really mean? Most probably it means that he didn't have research data to support this statement. He simply *believed* that he was right. Education was everything. There is no such thing as "bad" behavioral heredity. Abnormal conditions produce deviant behavior. Change conditions and you will change behavior. He also meant that he could make his beliefs compete against the beliefs of supporters of the hereditary factors of human behavior.

Emotions. John Watson, as did many psychologists of his time, divided emotions into three categories: love, fear, and rage. He considered them as conditioned responses or habits learned during childhood. To him, emotion formation was a process of habit formation. To examine it, Watson turned to infant behavior. In 1920, in experiments conducted together with his student and future second wife, Rosalie Rayner, he studied the development of conditioned reflexes on a nine-month-old baby named Albert B. The experimenters wanted to show that emotions created in a laboratory were retained later in life (Watson & Rayner, 1920). Watson paired, for example, unconditioned stimuli that should cause initial alarm and fear in the child (such as a very loud noise) with live animals and objects that initially did not cause any emotional reaction. In fact, he repeated what Pavlov and Bekhterev had done earlier, studying conditioned reflexes. In his experiments, Watson attempted to develop fears and long-term phobias in children. These experiments became among the best known in psychology of all time. An interesting fact: For generations, psychologists didn't know the real name of the boy (who was frequently called in textbooks Little Albert) until a group of researchers established after archival search and interviews that he was probably named Douglas Merritte. He died in 1925 from a serious illness (Beck, Levinson, & Irons, 2009). Today, similar experiments on infants are considered unethical by the APA. First, Watson did not ask the boy's mother's permission to use her son in the experiments. Second, as you know, psychologists may not cause unnecessary distress in their subjects. But in the 1920s, experimental psychologists were not required to follow these rules.

Watson later applied his views of emotions to advertising. He suggested that selling a product is about generating certain emotions in a consumer. Imagine that you are a manufacturer and distributor. You have to make the consumer worry or feel happy—it all depends on the product or the circumstances. Without emotions, according to Watson, the buying capacity diminishes. Emotions guide consumers, regardless of their gender or nationality. In Watson's terms, it does not matter if a consumer buys a painting, a sword, or a plowshare.

Watson applied his knowledge to an advertisement technique known as "testimonials." In such testimonials, people appear on the pages of magazines or on billboards and tell stories or make comments about a product or service. Businesses had been already using this method for some time, but Watson refined it and tested its effectiveness. For example, he helped design a series of ads for Pebeco toothpaste. In those ads, a smoking woman worries about the negative impact of cigarettes on her teeth (which is a fearful reaction) but finds the solution in the toothpaste; if used frequently, the toothpaste should keep the woman attractive (a reaction of love).

Other Applied Work. Watson always sought new assignments and accepted new offers as an applied psychologist. Even a short list of his projects is impressive. In 1916 he served as a consultant for an insurance firm in Delaware and two railroad companies. He proposed a new course, Psychology of Advertising, at Johns Hopkins University. In advertising, he studied dissimilar subjects such as customer brand loyalty and the central and peripheral route to persuasion. Watson pioneered much of the work on personnel selection. He used performance tests to select customer representatives. After

World War I he did research for the Western Union Company conducting employee evaluations. In 1919 he worked for the United States Social Hygiene Board to investigate the effect of motion pictures specially produced to educate the public about the dangers of sexually transmitted diseases. In 1920 he cofounded the Industrial Service Corporation to conduct research in the field of industrial psychology. He also studied smoking habits (Watson, 1922). In 1921, Watson began to work for the J. Walter Thomson advertisement agency making $25,000 a year, which was five times his salary at Johns Hopkins (Buckley, 1994). He said on a few occasions that he did not regret leaving his university career for good.

The Media. Watson was a prolific writer and liked to publish in popular magazines. In 1907 he published an article for the *World Today* on human evolution and the possibilities of animal research in understanding an individual's behavior. In 1910 he published an article for *Harper's* about the new science of animal behavior and the enormous practical benefits that this new discipline should bring. The *New York Times* enthusiastically reviewed his major book *Psychology From a Standpoint of a Behaviorist.* At that time it was a very unusual endorsement for a psychology monograph. This glowing review was an indication of John Watson's popularity and the growing reputation of psychology.

ON THE WEB

See the list of Watson's publications in the newsletter by J. Walter Thompson Company (1922–1929) on the book website.

However, Watson's critics always maintained that he was more an enthusiastic leader and polemist than a diligent scholar and thinker (Boring, 1929). One criticism was Watson's desire to publish in nonscientific magazines. Watson defended his work vigorously: he published there because psychology needed a greater exposure to the average person. On other occasions, he diminished the significance of his popular publications. He argued that there was nothing wrong with a psychologist's desire to earn some money.

Unfortunately, as soon as Watson became a popular author, his life was exposed to the public. Every detail of Watson's nasty divorce (he had an extramarital affair with his student) was scrutinized. The divorce proceedings had given him, in today's language, the scandalous status of some Hollywood celebrities. Watson obviously wanted to avoid such an embarrassing exposure, but he couldn't. However, after he resigned from Johns Hopkins, his life outside the academic world didn't slow his writing and publishing. He published in *Harper's*, the *Nation*, the *New Republic, Liberty, McCall's,* and many other journals and periodicals. The prestigious *New Yorker* issued his profile. A short list of titles of some of his articles published in the 1920s and 1930s indicated the shift of his interests to the area of pop psychology: *The Weakness of Women, Can We Make Our Children Behave? The Heart or the Intellect?* and *Are Parents Necessary?*

Watson never regretted his decision to pursue this type of work. He liked attention and enjoyed his ability to influence people. His desire to publish in mass media was also rooted in his bitterness toward the academic community, which, he believed, had abandoned him during his bitter divorce.

Watson's Paradoxes. Watson had a very volatile personality and an almost unpredictable personal life. It was paradoxical in many ways. Constantly attracted to women, he dated many of them yet had difficulty expressing interpersonal emotions. Even his own children commented that they hardly remembered their father showing any signs of affection. He loved his children but also thought that they distracted him from his research and teaching. His family relationships were constantly strained. He married early. His first wife was Mary Ickes, a student whose family did not like Watson because of his rude manners, alleged promiscuity, arrogant attitudes, and lack of money. His in-laws also disliked that he was from the South. His good friends liked his strong ambition; his critics called this ambition careerism. He always complained about his lack of money and free time. However, he bought property in Canada for a summer home, which he built himself. He was ambitious but did not accept an offer from Harvard University, apparently for financial reasons; he thought the offered salary was low. He craved privacy at the same time that he allowed others, including his mentor, James Angell, to intervene in his marital affairs. According to his contemporaries, including Robert Yerkes, he had a bad habit of looking for trouble and a gift for getting things done. He believed he was involved in too many projects, yet he was always looking for new deals as if they were new adventures. He wanted to serve his country in a war but didn't like his experience in the military service. He called it a nightmare. He did not like anything that would limit his behavior but liked social order. He was serious in his academic aspirations and almost childish in his daily habits. He was a hedonist and a much disciplined experimental scientist. In short, he was a normal human being.

Why Was Watson's Behaviorism Popular?

In the midst of his career, Watson undoubtedly used his public positions as the APA president, professor of psychology at Johns Hopkins, and editor of several influential journals to promote his work, and behaviorism in particular. Even when his career as an academic psychologist was cut short in 1920, Watson continued to be an active writer, corporate researcher, and promoter of his views. By the time he stopped conducting academic research in the 1930s, behaviorism had become a major influential force in American psychology. What were the reasons for this success?

Support. Watson was by no means the first to criticize introspection and mind psychology. He wasn't the first to exclude consciousness from his research. He did not pioneer the concept of reflex in psychology. He wasn't the first to propose that animal and human behavior should be subject to the same laws. Watson was not even the first to use objective, experimental methods to study behavior or to invent experimental methods of measurement. However, his role in the history of psychology was significant. Watson's ideas were simple, understandable, and attractive to many psychologists. He gave psychologists inspiration and built their confidence as researchers and practitioners. It was his personal enthusiasm that sparked the interest of others. He influenced a large audience ready to accept and follow his ideas.

Simplicity. One of many empirical findings that John Watson produced was that practicing a behavioral response should increase its frequency. Practice allows a person to keep useful movements and neglect useless ones. One good example of such practice is repetition of movements or words. He provided the results of experiments to support this finding. But what was particularly innovative in this "discovery"? Watson's findings about human behavior were almost commonsensical. However, like Thorndike, Watson converted the language of "common sense" into the language of experimental research. Instead of describing self-observed feelings, behaviorists turned the attention toward learned reactions, reaction times, emotional responses, skills to discriminate between signals, and so forth. Watson described the results with amazing clarity and tremendous enthusiasm, showing where and under which circumstances research should be applied to education, therapy, work, and other areas.

Inspiration. Watson was an enthusiastic researcher. He emphasized the great potential that behaviorism would have in the future. He believed that his methods would bring new possibilities to psychology and society. He wanted to capture the imagination of the general public, inspire his senior colleagues, entice new followers, and encourage students to study psychology. To many people, behaviorism appeared as a straightforward and simple theory in a confusing world of complexity. It was an unambiguous statement of clarity in a world of ambiguity. It was also an honest promise of confidence in a world of skepticism.

Controversy. Many of Watson's scientific ideas have been controversial. This brought him many supporters: many people enjoy challenging the establishment, whether it is a government policy or a widely accepted academic theory. His social views were no less controversial. Watson believed that the function of the family would gradually diminish and society would eventually create a system of social nurseries for children. In the new social institutions, as he hoped, all the mothers would learn the science and the specific rules of behaviorism related to childrearing. He believed that behaviorists would teach people to avoid parental mistakes. It is important to say that Watson later abandoned this idea of community-based childrearing. At the end, he considered it impractical.

Practicality. Watson believed that the university-based psychology was moving away from the real problems of society. Watson also believed that the universities he knew provided little teaching of the skills that psychology students would actually need in the real world (Herrnstein, 1967). He believed in applied psychology. His critical view was not necessarily an accurate reflection of the actual situation (university psychologists cared about practical applications and did a lot to improve practical skills of psychology graduates). Watson wanted to emphasize that psychology could have done more to contribute to education, health care, professional training, and many other areas of life.

✓ CHECK YOUR KNOWLEDGE

Name three founding principles of behaviorism.

How did Watson explain mental illness?

How did Watson understand emotions?

Assessments

Despite the enthusiastic support of many students and professors, the criticisms of behaviorism were focused and relentless. Supporters believed it was a new and truly scientific approach free of abstract speculations. Behaviorism promoted positivism and endorsed moderate pragmatism. Reflexology and Pavlov's experimental methods were solid alternatives to introspection. John Watson's response to introspection was his method of direct observation and measurement of behavior and its elements. Thorndike, Pavlov, Bekhterev, Watson, and scores of their followers chose laboratory conditions to study behavior. They brought statistics to support their measurements. Critics portrayed behaviorism as reductionist, simplistic, and methodologically weak.

Many critics considered some initial behaviorist assumptions ridiculous: that consciousness is bodily reaction, that seeing is eye movement, that emotion is chaotic instinctive reaction, and that thinking is internal speech (Calkins, 1913). Critics also argued that Watson's belief in conditioned reflex, the idea that inspired him early in his career, soon became his theoretical dogma shielded from critical evaluations. Many disagreed with Watson's dismissal of consciousness as a useless psychological concept (Bode, 1914). Bekhterev's reflexology and Pavlov's views of reflexes came under attack for similar reasons. Pavlov's opponents maintained that the conditioned reflex was an important physiological model; however, it was not the conceptual foundation to explain the complexity of human behavior. Pavlov's daring claims that physiology should take over psychology was rejected in psychology departments.

Overall, the response of psychologists to Watson's "new" psychology was mixed: the experimental method was praised, but his theoretical arguments weren't (Titchener, 1914). Some supporters suggested that animal behavior was indeed a key to human psychology. Many psychologists, especially the functionalists, shared the idea that psychology as an academic discipline that should focus less on theory and provide more practical tools and specific methods to influence behavior. Nevertheless, only a handful of Watson's and Pavlov's followers in psychology accepted the idea that psychology must abandon consciousness altogether and switch to behavioral or physiological models.

Accepting certain points of John Watson's position about psychopathology, many psychologists disagreed with his radical evaluations of mental illness. Even his colleague and boss Adolf Meyer believed that behaviorism brought the views of psychopathology back 200 years, when mental illness was considered nothing more than a physical impairment in the brain tissue. Watson, in his typical dismissive manner, replied that bringing back "subjective" experiences as the focus of psychopathology, as Meyer had insisted, would push science even further backward, straight to the "dark ages." But these were just emotional arguments. Even Watson's supporters believed that his position on psychopathology was mistaken.

Conclusion

In 1910, psychologist Robert Yerkes from Harvard University asked a sample of leading biologists and physiologists to answer a few survey questions. He asked the researchers to define psychology and identify its place as a science. Yerkes reported the results of his survey in an article, *Psychology in Its Relations to Biology.* The obtained and published results were not encouraging for psychologists (Yerkes, 1910). Some biologists viewed psychological processes as a form of energy resulting from brain activity. They suggested that as soon as biology and physiology were sufficiently advanced, psychology would disappear—it would no longer be needed. In fact, this was a point of view close to what Ivan Pavlov believed. Other biologists maintained, as the survey results revealed, that psychological processes and consciousness in particular could not be studied with the techniques of natural science at all. Yerkes, as a psychologist, was disappointed with such a gloomy assessment of psychology. In his article, he offered a modest compromise. In his view, psychology should maintain its status of a science. To achieve this, it should accept two kinds of methods: objective and subjective.

His opinion was left almost unnoticed. During this time another innovative intellectual wave was inspiring, and provoking, the minds of psychologists on both sides of the Atlantic Ocean. It was the wave of psychoanalysis, the method and the theory that plainly declared the possibility, and the necessity, of studying "the subjective" by objective methods of observation and analysis.

Summary

- Behaviorism gained strength in the beginning of the 1900s within a favorable social climate. A psychologist had to be a successful researcher capable of explaining psychological problems and improving people's lives. Behaviorism made such promises.

- Early behaviorism developed in the works of comparative psychologists. Most of them accepted the evolutionary ideas of Darwin and Spencer and believed in the adaptive nature of animal behavior. They wanted to find out as much as possible about animal behavior and use this knowledge to learn more about humans. Comparative psychologists first used primarily noninvasive techniques such as observation or simple learning exercises.

- Thorndike's work is widely considered a pioneering study in animal psychology and behaviorism. He created the "puzzle box" to study the behavior of animals experimentally and statistically.

- Behaviorism received a boost from the work of physiologists. Ivan Pavlov believed that one of the major goals of science was to understand human psychology using objective methods. Pavlov's ultimate goal was to understand objectively the mechanisms of human behavior. Pavlov's central concept was the conditioned reflex, which should underline all aspects of human behavior and experience.

- Another physiologist, Vladimir Bekhterev, made a distinct effort to challenge subjective psychology and to promote a new, objective psychology free from introspection. Bekhterev introduced the principle of energy transformation to explain the correspondence between physical and psychological processes. He also believed that science must study the individual from a complex, multidisciplinary perspective, in the center of which he hoped to see his theory of reflexology.

- John Watson supported the behaviorist view that psychology should be an experimental branch of natural science. Like Bekhterev and Pavlov, Watson believed that introspection was useless. Psychology's goal was to develop principles to explain, predict, and control behavior by objective methods. Watson's ideas were simple, understandable, and attractive to many psychologists. He gave psychologists inspiration and built their confidence as researchers and practitioners.

Key Terms

Agility

Anthropomorphism

Balance

Collective reflexology

Conditioned reflexes

Excitement

Founding principles of behaviorism

Highest nervous activity

Induction

Inhibition

Learning curve

Parsimony

Reflexology

Second signaling system

Strength

Tropism

Unconditioned reflexes

The Birth and Development of Psychoanalysis

Psycho-analysis is my creation.

Freud, 1914/1957

One psychoanalysis or many?

Wallerstein, 1988

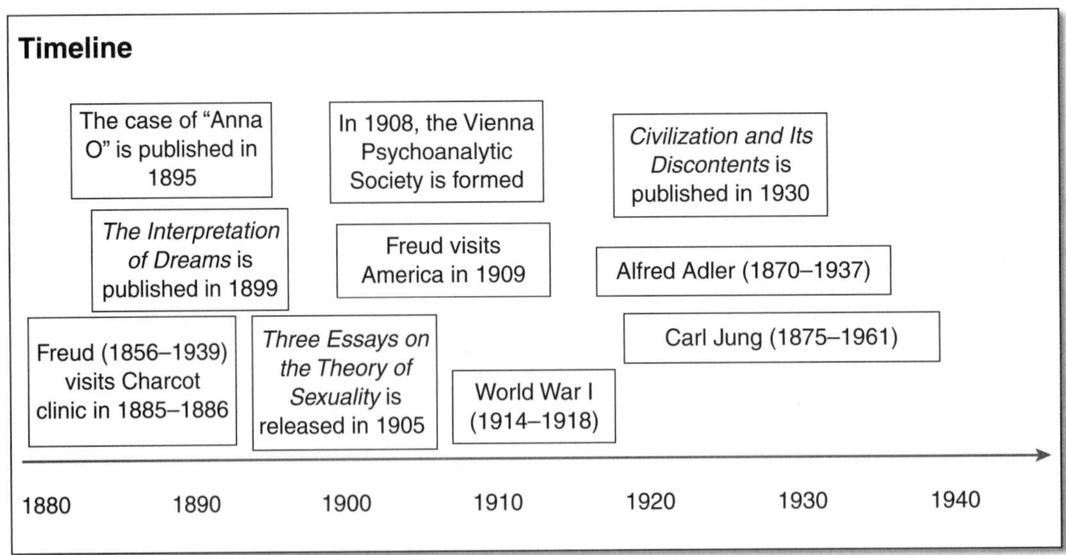

CHAPTER OUTLINE

At the entrance of the Sigmund Freud Museum in Vienna, Austria. Freud lived, wrote, and saw patients there for more than 45 years.

A roundtrip ticket to Vienna—$700. A room in a hotel in the Alsergrund district—€120. An early morning walk using a city map to Berggasse 19—free. Admission charge for the museum—€7. A poster, a pen, and a book—€30. A chance to see the apartment of one of the most influential psychologists of the 20th century—priceless.

If you ever have a chance to visit the capital of Austria, you should stop by Berggasse 19. This is an ordinary-looking building indicating its significance only by a giant, red, vertical sign that reads, "Freud." There are few such places on earth where you feel the nerves of human civilization mysteriously intersecting. Neither grandiose nor arrogant, it stands like a humble and silent witness of history. The stones of the building have heard the music of Mozart, Beethoven, and Strauss as they were first played. Vladimir Lenin, the future leader of the Communist revolution in Russia, and Adolf Hitler, the notorious tyrant, walked nearby just 100 years ago. They could have passed Freud's house many times. It was in Vienna, at Berggasse 19, where Freud wrote most of his books. The psychoanalytic tradition, or psychoanalysis, as we will address it for convenience, is possibly the most scrutinized and controversial in the history of psychology. Supporters of psychoanalysis say that it has contributed immensely to the knowledge of human behavior and psychology. The most ardent critics maintain that psychoanalysis was a significant setback in the history of psychology, a collective delusion brilliantly disguised in a fake academic uniform. Who is right? Was psychoanalysis a remarkable product of its time, or was it a giant hoax willingly followed by a crowd of enthusiasts? Was it a reliable therapy method or simply a moneymaking machine providing a nice living for therapists? Was it all about money after all?

If you ever find yourself near Berggasse 19, just visit the museum. The fee is not small, yet the museum is crowded every day. Only a few dead psychologists today continue to generate both money and debates. Freud is one of them.

What is *psychoanalysis*? Which associations will come to a person's mind when he or she hears this word? Many people produce such ideas as "Freud," "unconscious," "the couch," or "dream interpretation." Psychology majors will add to the list "the Oedipus complex," "libido," "death wish," "the id, the ego and the superego," "defense mechanisms," or "resistance." Some would make much longer lists of associations. Psychoanalysis has brought many words to the active vocabularies of many languages. The most famous person associated with psychoanalysis is likely to be Sigmund Freud, its founder. Many people will also recall the name of Carl Jung and his analytical psychology and terms such as *archetypes* and *introversion-extraversion*. Some could name Alfred Adler and the terms *individual psychology* and the *inferiority complex*.

This chapter examines the origins of psychoanalysis and some milestones of its developments late in the 19th century and in the first quarter of the 20th century. The focus of the discussion will be on Sigmund Freud, Alfred Adler, and Carl Jung. The further development of psychoanalysis and its branches is traced later in the book.

The Social and Scientific Landscape

The general mode of thinking of the growing middle and upper-middle classes in Europe and North America during the close of the 19th century was that the world had reached its desired stability and that they lived in a new era of progress and innovation. The first fourteen years of the 20th century gradually changed these attitudes. The increasing sense of uncertainty and elevated anxiety suddenly plunged society into a state of despondency during World War I (Spielvogel, 2006). How did these events affect science and psychology in particular?

Early Globalization. The period before 1914 is frequently compared to the globalization of the 21st century (Betts, 2005). International borders seemed to be disappearing. Trade barriers were easing, and commerce grew rapidly. Many Europeans could travel around the continent without visas. Telephones, telegraphs, daily newspapers, popular magazines, indoor plumbing, orders by mail—all brought a relative and increasing comfort to the daily lives of many people. The Ottoman Empire and Imperial Japan were trying to modernize their economies and social infrastructures. Old customs and fashions were changing. The traditional way of life was under pressure from almost every direction. Higher education was available to a greater number of people. Studies and research abroad were common, and psychologists traveled freely across borders. Publishers found it profitable to invest in social science books. Psychological literature was popular. But these developments were only one side of the ongoing changes.

Nationalism. Paradoxically, the first fifteen years of the new century was also a period of boiling nationalism and blind militarism. Many intellectuals and the uneducated alike openly acknowledged their national identities. To say with pride, "I am a German"—or

"Japanese," "French," "Austrian," or "Russian"—was increasingly popular. Strong national and ethnic identification was also a source of negative feelings against other nationalities. Sigmund Freud, a staunch opponent of violence, was proud to call himself an "Austrian" and expressed negative feelings against "barbarous" Russians, who were on the other side fighting against Freud's home country, the Austro-Hungarian Empire, during World War I.

Scientific Perplexity. In science, new alternative views of nature developed rapidly. The emerging area of quantum physics challenged the traditional Newtonian understanding of the world as a mechanical unity. The seemingly undivided atom now contained numerous particles. Albert Einstein formulated the basic principles of the theory of relativity (Einstein, 1905). Time and space, according to the theory, are not absolute, but relative to the observer. Matter appeared as a form of energy. In the social sciences, it was the time when Max Weber (1904/2003) published his famous *The Protestant Ethic and the Spirit of Capitalism,* which conveyed to the general reader the values that are at the core of the modern capitalist society: hard work, gradual savings, and moderation. It was also the time when Émile Durkheim (1897/1997) revealed the social causes of suicide and Otto Weininger (1903/2009) discussed human bisexuality and the roots of sexual attraction. Social scientists portrayed life as complex, organized, and multiphased. The theme of the irrational quintessence of human existence reemerged. This idea wasn't new in philosophy. During this time, however, it gained support among many educated and young readers. It was the time when Friedrich Nietzsche (1844–1900) authored a philosophical system based on the idea that irrational forces dominate human motivation. The rationality of capitalist society, its reliance on orderliness, in his view, was a sign of weakness and future defeat. Only the strong and the power-driven should rule the world.

Creative Perplexity. Artistic imagination and the scope of creative genres appeared limitless. This was the time of impressionism, cubism, symbolism, abstract painting, and conceptual poetry, an era of bold experimentations with form, sound, and color. On the one hand, artists challenged the traditional canons of art and the rules of self-expression. On the other hand, proportions and shapes served two masters at the same time: beauty and practicality. Functional architecture and efficient furniture were in style. This was the beginning of the mass consumption of art and art-oriented fashion. Psychologists were finding their way into advertisement. Pop psychology flourished with the advancement of printed media. But a sudden turn of events took place in 1914.

The War. The battles of World War I (1914–1918) took more than 19 million lives and left another 21 million wounded worldwide. The United States alone suffered 116,000 dead in two years, twice as many as in the entire Vietnam War sixty years later. Most European psychologists and some American counterparts served in the war as doctors, engineers, and officers. They witnessed the physical destruction of cities and the collapse of ideals. Historians refer to young people living through World War I as the "lost generation." They experienced the cruelty and irrationality of their fellow human beings. It became common to discuss the forthcoming end of human civilization. The experiences of the war led to a global collective trauma. World War I had seriously undermined the belief of social scientists and psychologists in the ability of human beings to achieve self-management and prosperity (Morawski, 2002).

These were the years of optimism and doubt when the founders of psychoanalysis developed their major ideas. New ideas must start somewhere.

Sources of Psychoanalysis

Sigmund Freud (1856–1939), the founder of psychoanalysis, has influenced scores of followers. But who influenced Sigmund Freud? Freud had few "mentors" in his earlier career. But they triggered the young doctor's interest in the nervous system, mental illness, and unconscious processes.

The Unconscious. Did Freud discover unconscious processes? No, he did not. The idea of hidden forces inside human beings entertained the most brilliant minds of philosophy, including Leibniz (remember his ideas about the soul's containing experiences from the past and future) and Kant (recall his intriguing ideas about the sources of moral judgments). Another influential philosopher, Arthur Schopenhauer (1788–1860) emphasized the deeply irrational nature of human love. He emphasized that reason is weak before powerful desires and will. German thinker Karl R. E. von Hartmann (1842–1906) claimed that the unconscious was the supreme and comprehensive ground of all human existence. World-famous writers such as Henrik Ibsen from Norway and Fyodor Dostoevsky from Russia scrupulously explored the depths of the human unconscious mind. Neurologist Paul Flechsig discussed the physiological foundations of unconscious processes (Jones, 1953). Some psychologists turned to experimental studies of below-threshold stimulation and telepathy in their attempts to find scientific validity for these processes. William James, a leading figure of American psychology, studied dream experiences. The intellectual tradition examining unconscious processes has a long and rich history (Keegan, 2003).

Sexuality. Was Freud the first to turn to sexuality as a research subject? No, he wasn't. Sexuality was already a subject of research and publications by the time Freud began his research. For example, in the 19th century, Richard von Krafft-Ebbing wrote *Psychopathia Sexualis* (1886), in which he provided a detailed analysis of human sexuality. Based on many interviews with private patients and criminal defendants, he described sexual drives and sexual deviance, including human homosexuality, which was widely recognized as an abnormal and even illegal behavior. The book became a best-seller in many countries. Books by Henry H. Ellis (1894/1929) discussed sexual characteristics of men and women and the causes of homosexuality (Ellis & Symonds, 1897/2006).

Psychological Energy. Was Freud the first to research "psychological energy"? No, he wasn't. Freud developed his initial ideas from the concept of energy conservation. Physiologist Johannes Müller was among his inspirers. Freud's works also echoed to some degree the ideas of activity addressed by Leibniz and the act psychology of Brentano. Freud reflected the main energetic ideas of hedonism, a school of thought claiming that the main energy source of human activities is pleasure (Boring, 1929/1950). German physiologist Ernst von Brücke (1866) influenced Freud's ideas about animals and humans as energy systems.

Psychological Resistance. Was Freud the first to encounter and describe the mechanisms of psychological resistance? No, he wasn't. Clinicians were already aware of situations in which a patient was reluctant or unable to discuss his or her psychological problems with a therapist. Freud also learned from Pierre Janet (see Chapter 6), whose terminology Freud used and developed. What Janet called *psychological system*, Freud labeled *complex. Moral fumigation* became *catharsis.* Janet used the term *restriction of consciousness*; Freud called it *repression* (Ellenberger, 1970; Janet, 1924).

So what was Freud's innovative role if he used already known ideas? Like Watson in behaviorism, Freud put these and many other ideas together in a new, comprehensive, and creative way. Freud used his personal qualities to promote his ideas. He worked relentlessly collecting and analyzing reports from his patients. He published articles, small brochures, and books. He sustained harsh criticisms, but he attracted several followers. Soon his theories fashioned an international movement. With every year passing, his ideas captured the imagination of more people.

✓ CHECK YOUR KNOWLEDGE

The terms *scientific perplexity* and *creative perplexity* of the early 20th century refer to what?

Explain the term *psychological resistance.*

Sigmund Freud and Psychoanalysis

Sigmund Freud was born in 1856 in Freiberg in the Austrian Empire (today the city is in the Czech Republic). His parents were Jewish and his native language was German. He was an excellent student, and he chose to study medicine in college. As a specialist in neurology, in 1885–1886 Freud visited the famous Charcot clinic in France where he learned firsthand about hypnosis. He became *Privatdozent* of the University of Vienna, which gave him the right to lecture on a part-time basis. In 1886 he married Martha Bernays and began private practice. His reputation as a specialist grew. In 1891 he moved his office, which also was his apartment, to Berggasse 19, the famous address in Vienna forever associated with his name. In 1908 a group of his close friends and followers formed the Vienna Psychoanalytic Society. Similar societies began to form across Europe. Freud's reputation grew further after his visit to the United States in 1909.

ON THE WEB

Read more about Freud's biography, his associates, and his personal idiosyncrasies on the book website.

Sigmund Freud probably did not anticipate that his theory and therapeutic method would become among the most influential and controversial in psychology's history.

World War I virtually destroyed his private practice. Most scientific journals were closed and scientific gatherings canceled. By 1918, Austria, defeated in the war, experienced especially severe social and economic difficulties, which certainly affected Freud's life and work. During this time he continued to write, and his private practice gradually reemerged. International psychoanalytic congresses began to congregate again in 1918. Freud's daughter, Anna, was accepted as a member of the Vienna Psychoanalytic Society in 1922 and became a prominent psychologist. Freud attended his last congress in 1922, after which his illness (he had cancer of the mouth) did not allow him to travel or attend many public gatherings. He was in a state of constant physical discomfort due to numerous operations and the necessity to wear a prosthesis in his mouth. In the 1930s, anti-Semitism in Austria became an official government policy. Freud's books were prohibited, and he lived under virtual house arrest until his emigration in 1938 to London, where he died a year later.

Birth of Psychoanalysis

Some events in a scientist's life become turning points. In Freud's case, such an event was his meeting with Jean-Martin Charcot (see Chapter 6). During his visit to Paris in 1885–1886, Sigmund Freud spent more than a month studying brain pathology with a microscope at Charcot's laboratory. This type of research did not particularly fascinate Freud. He was more interested in hypnosis and its medical use. Heretofore only studying hypnosis from books, he could now observe hypnotic sessions firsthand in the clinic. Although Freud's spoken French was limited, he saw therapists at work and had direct access to clinical cases.

Freud admired Charcot's enthusiasm and dedication to research. Yet he criticized Charcot's assumptions that hypnotic states could be produced only in individuals with hysteric symptoms. Here Freud sided with scholars who considered hypnotism as a result of suggestion, which meant that an average person was susceptible to hypnosis. Freud even translated the work of Hippolyte Bernheim, a supporter of similar views, in German. Freud made a presentation to the Vienna society of physicians, claiming that hypnosis could be induced not only in women (as it was widely thought) but also in men. Critics considered these ideas unconvincing. From that moment, Freud would face relentless criticisms continuing for more than 50 years of his professional career. To some, criticisms of their work are discouraging. To others, critical comments become a source of inspiration. Freud was this latter type of individual.

Approaching Psychopathology. As a physician-practitioner, Freud wanted to develop his own, unique approach to mental illness and its treatment. If successful, this approach could build his professional reputation and subsequently bring more paying patients.

One of his early assumptions was that some clues about a patient's symptoms could come from sources that are not usually under clinical observation. For example, a person's fantasies, dreams, or funny remarks may produce some fascinating information about the inner world of the individual. At about the same time, Freud also began to think about the importance of the human body as an ultimate source of pain and pleasure. In the 19th century, the educated public was aware of the connections between various parts of the body and various psychological effects. Some therapists in the West were already using acupuncture methods (practiced in Japan, Korea, and China) to treat chronic pains. The erogenous zones drew the particular interest of scholars. Yet at this time there wasn't much scientific research in this field, only speculation. Freud also became interested in human sexuality, and especially infantile sexuality. He wrote about the effects of masturbation on neurosis. He also hypothesized about the negative impact of contraceptives (they put pressure on the spontaneity of intimate relations) on the moral and psychological well-being of an individual.

These were just disjointed ideas and thoughts. Freud wanted to assemble a psychological theory to explain the causes of mental illness. This was an ambitious, but not unique, task. Many scholars and physicians hoped to create their own theories too. What probably made Sigmund Freud successful were his professional skills and work ethics. Freud was a stubborn and hard-working scholar who studiously collected clinical observations, which he liked to write up in great detail.

The First Famous Case. A break came unexpectedly. In the 1895 book *Studies on Hysteria*, he presented the case of "Anna O" (the book was written together with Josef Breuer, who had disclosed this case to Freud). This was the most prominent inaugural case that launched the whole theory of psychoanalysis. The authors did not reveal the real name of the patient, which became known years later. She was Bertha Pappenheim. Twenty years of age, she was suffering from a complicated set of symptoms including headaches, anxiety attacks, poor vision, and partial loss of sensations and movements. The symptoms worsened and included hallucinations, problems with speech, and distortions in self-awareness. The most remarkable aspect of this case was that when, during a therapy session, she was able to talk about her symptoms with the therapist, many of her symptoms would diminish. In short, the symptoms were "talked away." It was a kind of *catharsis*, a liberation from something that bothered her.

But what was that "something"? Freud and Breuer proposed that the main reason for her symptoms was a trace of unsettling memories that she was trying to suppress. These memories have been apparently associated with her early sexual experiences. This was the turning point in the creation of psychoanalysis. Freud assumed that the early traumatic experiences, primarily of a disturbing sexual nature, might become causes of mental illness. In a snapshot, sexual conflicts within individuals accumulate unreleased energy, which then manifest in a variety of pathological symptoms.

The main question was how to identify these traumatic experiences and conflicts. Freud knew that patients become resistant as soon as they were led to talk about their sexual experiences. What method could help the therapist find the deeply buried causes of the disturbing psychological symptoms? Later describing his method, Freud liked to use the archaeology analogy. The memories of a patient are like the artifacts of an ancient city. As a careful archaeologist, the therapist collects hidden, unrecognizable pieces one by one. After months of work, a silhouette of the city appears. In therapy, the only "artifacts" that Freud could use were the memories of his patients. As such, this information had only limited value: patients were mainly unaware of the meaning of their memories. Here the therapist steps in. As a careful guide, slowly the therapist takes three steps: (a) collecting the reported reflections, (b) analyzing them, and then (c) interpreting them to the patient. It was an imaginative construction and reconstruction of the person's experiences (Le Poidevin & MacBeath, 1997). This was the method Freud began to call **psychoanalysis** (in English translations it appeared as "psycho-analysis" for more than 50 years).

ON THE WEB

Who were Freud's most famous clients? Learn about them from the book website.

The initial method included the procedure called **free associations.** (The method of free association is labeled thus on an apparently inaccurate translation from German, in which the term means "free occurrences," as if the patients reproduce thoughts and images that "occur" in them freely.) Again, the procedure was like an archeological excavation of an ancient city. The patient was asked to make a chain of associations, starting from a word suggested by a therapist and then naming anything that came to mind. In the relaxed therapeutic atmosphere, the patient was supposed to reveal some valuable associations and images, which, as Freud thought, could help him understand the patient's traumatic past. Some patients went on easily. Others manifested serious resistance: their associations weren't instantaneous; they chose carefully what to say and how. Their resistance continued to interest Freud. Could these resistances reveal the patient's real but hidden problems?

Freud's *Studies on Hysteria* received only lukewarm reception from his contemporaries (Kavanaugh, 1999). However, it introduced an innovative way of understanding traumatic events and their role in pathological symptoms. This work also suggested a method to trace these disturbances. Now Freud needed empirical evidence to advance his theory.

The Seduction Hypothesis. Seduction is the enticement, without force or threat, of another person into sexual relations. What Freud actually meant was not enticement but rather sexual abuse during childhood. He thought of abuse as the prime source of the psychological problems of an adult. When Freud was almost forty years old and had ten years of clinical experience, he admitted that he had been wrong that sexual abuse was the prime cause of psychological problems. Freud changed his mind about the seduction hypothesis also because of the pressure of the academic community. Although sexual abuse was common (Jackson, 2000), many people of power continued to deny the very fact of its existence. Then as now, many authoritarian governments censor information and research about sexual behavior, sexual abuse, and sex crimes. In Freud's case, insufficient evidence and the pressure of the academic establishment pushed Freud to abandon his hypothesis. This topic, however, later became one of the most important fields of psychological research and therapeutic efforts (Gleaves & Hernandez, 1999).

Sources of a Neurosis. Freud's lack of success with the seduction hypothesis did not discourage him. He turned to the patient-therapist communication. What if the words conveyed to the therapist are not actual feelings and memories but specially coded messages? Why would patients code them? Do patients do it deliberately because they are embarrassed? Freud believed that there must be an internal processor that distorts these messages. This "censor" alters the memory contents so that they become less frightening to the patient. To explore his assumptions, Freud turned to the memories of his childhood dreams and fantasies. He believed that he should be honest with himself without experiencing embarrassment.

To most of us, childhood memories have either entertaining or nostalgic value. To Freud, early memories were the most precious sources of information. He suggested that children, craving love and comfort, develop sexual attachments and fantasies about their parents. These fantasies are coupled with jealousy toward their siblings. Later in life, children repress their sexual fantasies and jealousy, which surface in many peculiar forms including dreams, jokes, and even pathological symptoms. These were key principles of his developing theory (Freud, 1901/2009b).

As a practicing doctor, Freud was concerned less about the actual symptoms of his patients and more concerned with the history or etiology of the reported cases. In his mind, sexuality and early childhood experiences were the causes of most neurotic symptoms. Fears experienced in the past contribute to symptoms of hysteria. Problems with sexual pleasure produce symptoms of obsessional neurosis. Freud began to assemble the pieces of the jigsaw puzzle of his theory.

Development of Psychoanalysis

The Interpretation of Dreams, published in 1899, and *Three Essays on the Theory of Sexuality*, released in 1905, reveal the complexity of Freud's developing theory. In these books, he formulated the classic ideas about the Oedipus complex, repression, and the struggle between wishes and defenses. For the contemporary student, these books also represent a unique opportunity to look into European society and the family at the turn of the 19th century, including the most intimate moments in the lives of men and women of the upper class.

Wish Fulfillment. Structural psychologists before Freud studied people's recollections of their dreams in terms of their frequency, recency, and vividness (Calkins, 1892). Freud wanted to find a connection between a dream's content and an individual's past experiences. Freud assumed that dreams represent **wish fulfillment**, a symbolic attempt to realize an unfulfilled desire. Every dream has two contents. One is easily describable, which is called the *manifest content* (because it is manifested or presented as a story). The other is the *latent content*, the meaning of which is hidden because of its traumatic or shameful nature. A small girl does not experience shame, and therefore most of her dreams reveal her actual wishes: to play with a toy, eat candy, or feel safe. Older children, adolescents, and adults have already learned the meaning of shame. To them, their dreams distort their repressed wishes. Here Freud makes an important suggestion. The most significant wishes of an individual are infantile and sexual in nature; society prohibits them, and they are therefore concealed in the "basement" of the unconscious mind and are unavailable for the mind's rational evaluation. What kind of shameful sexual wishes do people develop?

The Oedipus Complex. The **Oedipus complex** is the key postulation of psychoanalysis. This exact term in the English translation was coined many years after Freud suggested this phenomenon, which remains one of the most controversial ideas in psychology ever. Oedipus is a character who appears in several ancient Greek poems. According to a common plot, he became king after he killed his father and married his mother, although unknowingly. Learning later about this horrific act of incest, Oedipus blinded himself. What did this myth give to psychological theory?

Freud suggested that boys and girls mature differently: both develop emotional attachment to their parents; however, the boys are attached to their mothers, and girls are attached to their fathers. These conflicting attachments create a foundation for future psychological problems and influence every element of the family's functioning. The siblings compete against each other for the affection of their parents. Bound by social restrictions, they must repress their infantile feelings—which society deems indecent—and act by the rules of society. Here Freud dared to challenge most traditional assumptions about the family as a socioeconomic unit bonded by obligations and the law. Instead, he claimed that the family relationships are also mediated by unconscious, incest-related memories.

What was the significance of the Oedipus complex in the future development of an individual? People always try to avoid pain and seek pleasure. Pain and pleasure are the first feelings to remain in memory. We try to secure pleasurable moments in the memory and return to them in hopes of repeating them. However, only a few can be repeated. Two reasons exist for this. First, society restricts many pleasure-related activities by imposing moral values. Second, some pleasurable memories are deemed shameful. The infantile memories associated with the Oedipus complex are both shameful and wrong. Therefore they must go away. Where do they have to go?

Repressed Desires. To answer this question, Freud turned to the idea of **unconscious** processes. He defined *unconscious* as mostly repressed desires and memories. Unconscious is not something that is forgotten but can be later remembered, which is termed *preconscious*. The unconscious is a reservoir of guilty wishes and indecent thoughts. The desire to reexperience some of these thoughts is matched by a powerful force that keeps them inside. What keeps the desires inside is conscience, a moral guardian, which develops under the pressure of social norms. The repressed memory says to us, "This event happened." The conscience replies, "No, it did not." In contemporary terms, think of someone attempting to explain an embarrassing or inappropriate act and saying, "I don't know how it happened; I felt like it wasn't *me* doing it," as if the person is trying to suggest that the real "he" or "she" could not have done the act being described. Freud argued that the dynamics of the unconscious mind are similar to the act of denial. The content of the unconscious reservoir is filled early in life, and the power of the conscious mind keeps these memories repressed.

ON THE WEB

Did Freud write nonacademic, popular books? Check the book website.

Freud liked the publicity he was getting but always wanted to achieve a higher goal: to understand human psychology fully as a scientist, and not simply as a clinician. Understanding mental illness as a reflection of an imbalance within the nervous system, he wanted to create a study of mental functioning that involved a quantitative analysis of the nervous energies. He also wanted to use clinical observations to apply them to the analysis of "normal" life. Freud turned his attention to individual cases.

Individual Cases: Dora, Little Hans, and Rat Man. *Three Essays on the Theory of Sexuality,* released in 1905, provides a detailed overview of Freud's psychological theory, which is based on the assumption that a major source of psychological illness are cultural restrictions imposed on sexual behavior. This book heralds the beginning of the **libido** theory, which Freud constantly modified throughout his academic life. At that time, Freud interpreted libido as a form of sexual expression common in both women and men (English & English, 1958). The 1905 book also advanced Freud's earlier position about infantile sexuality. The center of his focus was an unresolved sexual conflict in a patient's early childhood.

The book presented three case studies of patients that Freud saw, analyzed, and treated. The case of Dora (Ida Bauer), an 18-year-old woman, is a complicated conglomerate of devastating emotional problems set against the background of the troubled life of a young girl. Because of Dora's resistance, she couldn't comprehend the solutions offered by her therapist and left treatment prematurely. The next case, universally known as the case of "little Hans" (Herbert Graf), is perhaps the second most acclaimed story (after the Anna O. case) that received wide international recognition. Hans's parents tried to raise their son according to Freud's advice. They didn't use coercion, engaged their son in conversations, and recorded his stories about his dreams. At the age of five, little Hans developed a phobia of the animal type: he grew increasingly afraid of horses. His parents were puzzled about the source of his phobia. After conducting several analytic sessions with little Hans, Freud offered an explanation. In his view, the boy had developed a strong erotic attachment to his mother as well as aggressive intentions against his little sister, who was seen as a competitor for their mother's love. In Hans's world of fantasy, his father was a competitor too; yet Hans had to love and respect him. Fearing punishment for his aggressive impulses,

Hans developed **castration anxiety** and related to it a fear of horses. In its original formulation, castration anxiety meant the irrational fear of the loss of the genitals.

Even at that early age, Hans was able to understand the meaning of some of his inner conflicts, such as his aggressive thoughts about his sister. Such realization, according to Freud, eventually helped the boy to overcome his phobia. Was it a successful therapeutic intervention, or did this little boy simply outgrow the phobia, as many children do without any therapeutic intervention? We don't know for sure (see Figure 8.1).

Figure 8.1 The Stages of Phobia Progress According to Freud

- A child has infantile attraction to his mother as a source of comfort and safety.

↓

- At the same time, the child carries negative, aggressive wishes against his father and a sister, both seen as obstacles threatening his affection for his mother.

↓

- Aggressive wishes as well as affection toward mother are socially inappropriate. The boy represses these wishes into his unconscious.

↓

- Unable to surface back to the boy's conscious mind, the incest wishes manifest themselves in the form of a phobia and other anxieties.

The third case of the Rat Man (Ernst Lanzer) was about the emotional obsessions of a 29-year-old man. (The Rat Man was, of course, a pseudonym given because of one of Lanzer's embarrassing dreams involving rats.) Today we would call his problem a serious obsessive-compulsive disorder. His symptoms included constant fear of self-injury, persistent and disturbing aggressive thoughts, and excessive urges to do something inappropriate. During the therapeutic sessions, Freud explained to this patient the nature of his anxieties as being based on infantile fears (such as the death of his father). One of the most important points in the therapy was that Freud persuaded Lanzer that love and hate could coexist and that he should accept even the most embarrassing thoughts. As soon as Lanzer accepted the interpretation of his impulses, he found a way to gradually get rid of his compulsions.

ON THE WEB

Learn more about the Freud's stages of infantile sexuality from the book website.

Advancing Psychoanalysis

The popularity of psychoanalysis as a therapeutic method developed rapidly. Many therapists used Freud's ideas and earned respectable sums of money. Many analysts in

Austria and Germany spoke several languages and received cash-paying foreign patients, especially from France, the United Kingdom, and even the United States. Psychoanalysis was becoming a fashion trend among the people of the upper and upper-middle class.

The Psychoanalytic Movement. As early as 1902, in Freud's apartment in Vienna, a group of a few followers began to gather on Wednesdays to discuss case reports, history, culture, and dreams and to eat and . . . smoke. (During one of the early gatherings they discussed the psychological impact of smoking.) In 1908 the Vienna Psychoanalytic Society was formed. A similar group was created around the same time in Berlin. The American Psychoanalytic Association appeared in 1911. The London Psychoanalytic Society was established in 1913.

The Vienna society was an informal gathering of people that shared similar interests. It was also a pseudo-political group, a loose professional union trying to establish its own respectable position within psychology and psychiatry. This was the beginning of the global psychoanalytic movement. Critics saw the Vienna Psychoanalytic Society as a tightly controlled political unit protecting the original Freudian ideas. They believed that this society was a sect, a cohesive unit of single-minded plotters carrying selfish ideas of domination in science. This simply wasn't true. In fact, from the beginning of these meetings, its members engaged in heated debates.

Freud's first and only trip to the United States gave a significant boost to the psychoanalytic movement. In September 1909 Freud delivered a series of lectures at Clark University in Worcester, Massachusetts. His talks received widespread coverage in the press. The reaction was mostly positive, mixed with excitement and enthusiasm. Psychoanalysis was presented as the latest scientific breakthrough from the European continent. Eminent American psychologists gave animated reviews. Freud's ideas generated considerable and growing public curiosity. Critical articles appeared shortly thereafter. Freud and other psychoanalysts received passionate support, especially among nonprofessionals. As historians admit, Freud delivered in America far more than a few lectures at Clark University. He brought a new idea that spread across an entire continent (Caplan, 1998b).

☞ CASE IN POINT

Freud's 1909 American Tour. *How many people accompanied Freud to America?*

There were two additional people: Carl Jung and Sándor Ferenczi.

How did they get there?

By ship. All together the round-trip tour across the Atlantic Ocean took 16 days.

Who paid for the trip?

G. Stanley Hall arranged the sum of $750 for Freud. Ferenczi paid his own expenses. Jung arranged his own invitation.

(Continued)

(Continued)

Who invited Freud and why?

It was G. Stanley Hall, president of Clark University in Massachusetts. Sigmund Freud was awarded an honorary doctor of laws title. An innovator and great organizer, Hall not only wanted to reward the Austrian psychiatrist but also desired to promote the name of the newly founded university. Besides Freud and Jung, there were more than two dozen invitees for the occasion.

Did Freud deliver his five lectures in English?

No, he did it in German.

How did Freud evaluate his trip to America?

He was surprised to see the attention and interest people paid to his visit and his theories. Unlike in Europe, he felt that people treated him as an equal. He met with William James, who thought that psychoanalysis was a good addition to functional psychology. Yet, according to Jung, James found Freud a little bit uncritical and obsessed with his theory. Freud generally disliked American mercantilism and America's fascination with money, yet he didn't hesitate to ask Hall to raise his honorarium before he had agreed to visit the United States.

Therapists' Tactics and Ethics. Freud changed his therapeutic techniques continuously. In the beginning of his independent work, he tried hypnosis but soon stopped because he realized that the method was ineffective. Then he tried to use the method based on the patient's supervised "confession": Freud's role was to try to persuade his patients to reveal (please, tell me!) their intimate and embarrassing secrets. This technique didn't work well either. Then he focused on catharsis, the method based on the release of tension and anxiety by reliving the incidents of the past. The patient had to overcome resistances to explain and eventually understand the sources of his or her own psychological problems. This method showed only a marginal success. Then Freud began to actively use dream interpretation and free association. Later he included in his system the analysis of **transferences**. This was the term he used to describe the process by which patients shift emotions applicable to another person onto the psychoanalyst. For example, when a patient feels hostility toward her therapist, this could be interpreted as an original, infantile anger against her father that is being transferred to the therapist. Overall, Freud's theoretical views and his therapeutic techniques remained interconnected: changes in his theoretical views influenced his method, which in turn influenced his hypotheses.

A careful researcher, Freud also remained a dedicated doctor who set high standards for other clinicians. Between 1911 and 1915, Freud outlined some important rules of doctor-patient interactions. For example, before taking a patient, a therapist must determine if his or her case is within the therapist's knowledge and competence.

The patient should pay on time (however, Freud accepted quite a few patients for free). Sessions ought to be scheduled for six times a week. He insisted that a therapist must be an excellent listener. During sessions, no topic should be avoided. The patient should be encouraged to say anything that comes to mind. The therapist must focus on everything that disturbs the progress of therapeutic work, including a patient's resistances and transferences. The treatment must be founded on trust, and the therapist must not disclose to others any personal information obtained during sessions. There must not be any personal affairs between therapists and their patients. Many of these ethical rules and requirements remain in force today.

☞ CASE IN POINT

Paying for Psychoanalysis. In 1923, Freud had some wealthy patients willing to pay $50 a day for his services. Although the average rates he charged then were lower, he was earning a significant income. Jung, his follower, charged fees not only for his individual sessions but also for group lectures and seminars. Sometimes business proposals to psychoanalysts were more than generous. Freud once received an offer for $25,000 to come to Chicago and conduct a psychoanalytic investigation on behalf of a newspaper for a murder trial. How much would this sum buy those days? Let's compare. A cup of coffee then was less than 50 cents, a bathing suit in the United States would cost $8.50, a vacuum cleaner around $40, and a pair of women's top-notch dress shoes would go for $50.

Metapsychology Attempted. Freud's critics maintained that his theory was too speculative. He believed that physiology and the basic sciences eventually would prove him right. In an unfinished work, *Preparatory Essays on Metapsychology*, prepared around 1915, Freud turned to the concept of instinctual energy, a relatively common topic of debates at that time (recall that Bekhterev in Russia and other psychologists introduced similar ideas). Instinctual drives direct people to seek gratification. Defenses or repressions create blocked gratifications, which do not disappear but remain preserved within the nervous system. In contemporary terms, "out of sight" should not mean "out of mind": the images and the memories are all preserved in different forms. How long could the nervous system keep the repressed energy? Not forever. Freud believed in the principle of energy conservation defended in the 19th century by physiologist Alexander Bain (1818–1903). This meant that that the nervous system should somehow discharge surplus energy or excitation. This discharge is pleasurable and should have an impact on all activities of an individual.

Later in that period Freud formulated the concept called the **unconscious** (appearing as a noun this time, not an adjective)—the activities not open to direct conscious scrutiny but influencing conscious process and behavior. This was a complicated dynamic of wishes and drives fighting against restrictions, logic, and delays of gratification of these wishes. To counterweight the powerful impulses on the unconscious, there must be another mental construct capable of passing moral judgments and restrictions. Here Freud offered a new concept called the **ego**—the aspect of the human psyche that is conscious and mostly in touch with reality.

How do the unconscious and the ego function? Freud formulated and described two major mechanisms that regulate their activities: the **pleasure principle** and the **reality principle**. The first principle is the demand that an instinctual need be immediately gratified. The second principle is the realization of the demands of the environment and the adjustment of behavior to these demands. Driven by the pleasure principle, people cannot postpone their desire to gratify their immediate wishes. Controlled by the reality principle, they continue to live in the state of constant delay of their desires.

The War Reflections. World War I had a deep impact on Sigmund Freud, his family members, and his colleagues. The war affected his practice and writings. His worldview became increasingly pessimistic. It seemed to him that educated and prosperous Europe had attempted suicide. Millions of people had perished in trenches, many more had died of diseases and starvation. Unemployment, inflation, crime, and food shortages—they all appeared as a collective suicide. The years after 1914 provided Freud with ample evidence to contemplate the reasons behind self-destructive behavior. He adopted the concept of the **death wish** (often labeled as death instinct or death drive)—the repressed instinctual tendencies that lead toward destruction.

ON THE WEB

Read about the roots of the Freudian idea of the death wish on the book website.

According to Freud, people have a repressed desire to destroy and kill. Because this wish is not culturally sanctioned, people try to experiment with one another to see what death is. Some people voluntarily and cheerfully participate in violent acts. Is this a manifestation of the repressed death drive? Besides the *death drive*, called **Thanatos**, Freud introduced the idea of the constructive *life drive*, called **Eros**. Eros defines all the tendencies that strive toward the integration of a living substance. Eros is about birth, creation, building, preserving, and loving. It manifests in love, friendship, courtship, altruistic help, kindness, and the creative work of artists, among other things. Eros is responsible for the survival of the individual. The psychic energy of this instinct was called libido. Initially, libido was used as a synonym for "sexual energy," the most important aspect of the life instinct. People who are in love, individuals who cure patients, design clothes, write songs, or draw pictures—all are influenced by their libido.

Thanatos stands for striving for destruction, humiliation, pain, and death. It manifests in violence but also in offensive jokes, jealousy, envy, feistiness—in anything that involves competition and advancement at the expense of others. This is a biological instinct based on natural, self-preserving drives of an organism: you must kill or, otherwise, you will be killed. The individual displaces internal aggression upon external objects, other individuals, or social and ethnic groups. Why do we slam the door when we are angry? Why do people enjoy watching horror movies? Why do many people rubberneck to glimpse a car accident? In contemporary terms, these are all indirect indications that the death wish exists and affects our behavior. After describing the competing instinctual drives, Freud began to understand life as a conflict between these two primal drives, between the creative and the destructive forces.

☞ CASE IN POINT

On the Professional Language of Psychoanalysts. Are you overwhelmed already by the number of special terms that Freud introduced? A distinct feature of psychoanalysis is its language and a wide range of special, even technical, terms. A psychoanalyst could easily recognize her colleague-analyst in a stranger just by a brief verbal exchange. Psychoanalysts' professional language is a symbol of their status, a source of their professional identity, a unique way to distinguish self from others, and, frequently, a source of self-esteem.

From the early days of psychoanalysis, many of its educated followers believed that they had access to something that laypeople did not. Psychoanalysts, as professionals, were capable, as they believed, of understanding the deep-seated individual problems hidden in the murky waters of unconsciousness, covered with a thick layer of resistance. Only trained psychoanalysts could finally reveal the "truth" to their patients and ordinary people alike. Something that was shameful yesterday appears today differently: "*It is not your bad luck; it is your repressed fear of your mother!*" A social phenomenon is finally explained: "*Why do people run for political offices? Because they are insecure and narcissistic individuals who are secretly craving their parents' love.*"

The language of psychoanalysis is straightforwardly brutal. A woman's close friendship with another woman could be interpreted as a reflection of her infantile homosexuality. A simple slip of the tongue during dinner could be translated as an unconscious hostility toward the host. A verbal fight between a mother and her daughter could be interpreted as the daughter's repressed fascination with her father and the resulting death wish directed against her mother. A student's tardiness could be interpreted as a hidden hostility against the professor. And your high GPA could be a projection of your narcissism.

It is difficult to agree with these and many other psychoanalytic interpretations. Defenders of psychoanalysis often underline that critics misinterpret its vocabulary. Certainly, if by "death wish" one means a person's desire to die, this interpretation may be sheer nonsense. But if one means a person's envy of other people's status and privileges, then this interpretation makes more sense.

Freud had passed the age of sixty when he published one of his fundamental books, *The Ego and the Id* (1923/1990b). In this book and in some of his other, earlier publications, including *Beyond the Pleasure Principle* (1920/2009a), he laid out the structural system of his psychology, the system that today appears familiar to many educated people all over the world.

The Id, the Ego, and the Superego. An individual's psyche is comprised of three levels (parts). The most primitive part of the personality is the **id.** This term was borrowed (and modified) from German philosopher Friedrich Nietzsche. The id is the component of the psyche that contains inborn biological drives (the death wish and the life instinct); the id seeks immediate gratification of its impulses. The id, like unmanaged will, operates exclusively according to the pleasure principle. It represents a constant struggle between love and destruction.

Making compromises between the id and the environment is the ego, which is guided by the reality principle. During an individual's development, the ego starts within the id but gradually changes to accept reason. Not every feature of the ego is conscious. A growing child faces an increasing number of regulators restricting the child's behavior, emotional expressions, and thinking. The especially harsh and unexplainable restrictions are applied to the child's sexual interests (they are innocent and guided by the pleasure principle at first). Soon children see their parents as objects of love and aggression. Almost immediately, the children find that many of their emotional attachments are inappropriate, and they transfer the feelings into themselves. Instead of being close to parents, the child learns how to act like his or her parents. This moment launches the development of the **superego**, the moral guide with unconscious features. This guide tells us what we should and should not do. Among the first lessons children learn is what they have to wear and under which circumstances they should cover certain body parts. Nakedness almost automatically launches the powerful emotion of shame. Overall, the superego, transmitted to the child through parents, represents the values and the customs of society.

Increasingly often, Freud turned to the study of society and its culture. He pursued two major goals. The first one was to search for the societal sources of psychological conflicts within individuals. The second was a daring attempt to apply the main principles of psychoanalysis to history and the social sciences.

Psychoanalysis Reflects on Society

Many psychologists today believe that they, as professionals, should not comment publically on topics—including social and political—that are beyond their professional expertise. Many others disagree. They believe in the progressive mission of psychology and feel confident that psychologists, as citizens, can write about social and political affairs. Freud belonged to the second group. From the beginning of the 20th century, he began to publish articles and books dedicated to a wide range of phenomena of social life: history, anthropology, linguistics, education, ethnography, and politics. Moving in the fields of history and anthropology was a bold move. His critics maintained that he wasn't academically competent enough to do so.

We should try to understand, however, Freud's frame of mind. He truly believed that psychoanalysis was a genuine scientific method and a reliable scientific theory of human functioning. As such, this scientific theory should be applicable to many areas of life. For example, in *Civilization and Its Discontents* (1930/1990a), Freud wrote that the cause of most social problems is psychological: people don't know how to be happy when they face too many choices.

There was another reason that stimulated Freud's attempts to contribute to the social sciences. Freud's popularity was enormous. He received invitations and solicitations from popular magazines and newspapers from many countries. Very often, newspapers and magazines asked him to comment on social and moral issues. Religion remained a very popular topic.

Religion as an Analysant. An **analysant**, in psychoanalytic vocabulary, is a person undergoing psychoanalysis. In more common terminology, it is a therapeutic patient or client. A committed atheist (he did not practice Judaism but acknowledged his Jewish identity), Freud didn't hesitate to discuss and criticize religion. He used psychoanalysis as a method to examine religion as if it were one of his patients. Freud wanted to explain the birth and development of religion in history. In his mind, religion had brought too much misery and hostility in the past.

In his letters, Freud wrote excitedly to his close follower and friend, Carl Jung, that he believed that psychoanalysis could uncover the source of religious beliefs. People embrace religion to address their unconscious sense of helplessness. Religion is also needed so that people accept the order and restrictions passed on to them by their parents. This assumption—in a modified form—was brought back to life in the 1960s. Theorists such as Herbert Marcuse (1898–1979) creatively combined the ideas of communism and psychoanalysis to justify youthful rebelliousness against capitalism and religion. In his early notes, Freud also described religion as an obsessive neurosis. He found parallels between religious ceremonies and rituals and similar actions in his neurotic patients. Human behavior in both religious and neurotic contexts addresses internal anxieties and serves a protective function. Soon, however, Freud moved into the fields of speculative history, a loose system of assumptions about the origins of human civilization.

One of his famous works in this field is *Totem and Taboo* (1913/2010). Freud wanted to investigate and describe the process by which our "savage" ancestors accepted culture and religion. Culture begins with restrictions. To be a human meant to obey the societal taboos. Animals, Freud argued, have no such taboos. Freud presented an intriguing and energetic description of how culture and religion first appeared and grew out of early fears and compulsive behavior. His story involves assumptions about the "universal sin" committed by sons who kill and eat their father, thus creating the foundation for an eternal fear and guilt present in all their descendants. To compensate for their guilt and fear, people turned to magical thinking and cultural prohibitions such as fear of incest (sexual relations between close relatives). As a symbolic desire for safety, people also created totems, prototypes of religious symbols—objects with alleged magical or holy powers.

In *The Future of an Illusion* (1927/1990c), Freud further developed the ideas about the psychological foundations of modern religion. For a child, religion becomes a continuation of fantasy. Adults also maintain religion as an extension of their infantile fantasies. Here Freud echoed the famous idea by German philosopher Ludwig Feuerbach (1804–1872), one of the main supporters of an anthropological view of religion. Feuerbach suggested that religion is an external projection of the individual's ultimate needs for love, understanding, and acceptance. Freud viewed religion as a restraining force limiting human choices. As a result, an individual is trapped in a maze of fears and superstitions. Freud argued that the fear of eternal damnation prevents people from thinking rationally and thus questioning the existing social order. Infantile fears perpetuated by religious beliefs generate human passivity or, sometimes, irresponsible and destructive acts. Some people accept religious intolerance and violence as a reflection of their own infantile fears and insecurities.

Freud explained history and society in psychological terms. He believed that psychoanalysis as a scientific method could eventually replace religion and liberate people from their irrational anxieties. Later in life, Freud modified his critical view of religion. In *Moses and Monotheism* (1939/1955), Freud shifted toward a much more positive view of religion as an institution. He continued to explain religious behavior as a kind of neurosis. However, more than ever, Freud recognized and stressed the constructive and positive psychological effects of religious beliefs capable of protecting a person's dignity, bringing hope, and promoting kindness (Meissner, 2006).

Some readers may find a few of Freud's statements about religion questionable. Although he was an atheist, he always promoted tolerance and acceptance of other people's religious beliefs even though he disagreed with them. He was critical of religious dogmas because he believed that they impede a people's search for truth just as infantile fears prevent a patient from finding the source of his problems. Freud's atheism, like a therapeutic procedure, was about self-doubt and self-analysis.

Psychobiography. Freud believed that the rules regulating the activities of human beings are universal and therefore applicable to the behavior of historic figures. One of the most famous of his cases was Leonardo da Vinci, a genius artist and scientist born in the 15th century (known to many people as the creator of the *Mona Lisa*). Freud took some biographical facts and gave them distinct psychoanalytic interpretations. In Leonardo's case, Freud noticed that the artist, born out of wedlock, grew up without his father for the first few years of his life. After his father married another woman, he adopted his five-year-old son. To Freud, this case of a child's having a mother and a young stepmother is particularly revealing. Freud was convinced that Leonardo's creativity and enormous productivity were rooted in his repressed inner conflicts. Conflicts produced anxiety, which resulted in fantasy. Fantasy for us—adults—is a form of symbolic alteration of reality. Artists take a step further: to reflect on their fantasies, they use canvas and oil. In Leonardo's case, the *Mona Lisa*'s smile, according to Freud, reflects the artist's repressed love for his mother and stepmother.

Freud analyzed creative artists and other people of prominence. One of his analysants was U.S. president Woodrow Wilson (1856–1924), though Wilson was unaware of this. Freud's coauthored work on Wilson wasn't published until 1967, so Freud, who died in 1939, could not read the book's poor reviews. However, the genre of psychoanalytical biography flourished from the 1920s on. Scores of authors adopted Freud's view that not only historic figures but also literary characters could be subjects of psychoanalysis. The idea was, of course, intriguing. It continues to inspire creative minds today: just look at the large number of books published in the field of psychobiography.

Views of Women. Freud's views of women were controversial. Although most of Freud's patients were women, most of his original postulates related to males and were only later modified to describe women as well. Freud tended to see women as "failed" men because of their anatomical differences. Women do not have the anatomical organs that men have. According to Freud, girls tend to develop an envious reaction, which later manifests in some women in various forms of submissive behavior. Other women, to overcome envy, express constant hostility toward men. Nevertheless, Freud made equally bizarre assumptions about men (see the earlier section on infantile sexuality). He suggested that many boys tend to develop an irrational castration complex, which is a prime unconscious source of their indecisive and irresponsible behavior as adults.

Freud also considered women as sexually passive as compared with men. Freud thought that such passivity was the result of social inequalities and cultural restrictions imposed on women. Nevertheless, he disliked the feminist movement in Europe. He did not accept the feminists' radical idea of eliminating the traditional order of the family and society. Yet he encouraged women to have access to sex education, contraceptives, choices in marriage, and the right to divorce. He encouraged women who decided to become psychoanalysts to receive education and training. One of the best illustrations of his position was his enthusiastic support of the professional advancement of his daughter, Anna, who became a world-renowned psychologist. In general, Freud's views of women reflected the social climate of 20th-century Europe and the common assumptions of many psychologists at that time.

✓ CHECK YOUR KNOWLEDGE

What was the most prominent inaugural case that launched the whole theory of psychoanalysis?

What was the seduction hypothesis?

How did Freud view religion?

How did World War I affect Freud's views on human psychology?

Early Transitions of Psychoanalysis: Alfred Adler

Freud created a therapeutic method, a psychological theory, and an approach to social sciences. Most people working closely with Freud remained forever associated with the term *psychoanalysis*. Alfred Adler and Carl Jung are the most noteworthy of Freud's disciples and rebels (Eisold, 2002).

Adler and Freud

Sigmund Freud began cooperating with Alfred Adler (1870–1937) in 1902 when Adler joined the weekly gatherings in Freud's apartment. They never became close friends, but Adler accepted most of the original ideas of psychoanalysis. Disagreements between Adler and Freud began early. These were small points of difference at first. Adler, for example, emphasized the importance of the relationships among siblings, not only that between the parents and the child. Then Adler began to question the validity of the claims that sexuality dominated human life—one of the central points of Freud's psychoanalysis. In 1911, Adler resigned his position as presiding officer of the Vienna Psychoanalytic Society. Later he gave up his membership altogether. Adler was also stripped of his editorial responsibilities in the main psychoanalytic journal. The decision to separate was mutual. Until the end of his days, Freud maintained that Adler's ideas were harmful to psychoanalysis. Freud also described his former follower as having paranoid ideas. Adler accused Freud of being power-hungry and authoritarian.

ON THE WEB

Read Alfred Adler's brief biographical sketch on the book website.

Alfred Adler was Freud's follower who later disagreed with his mentor and developed a new theory known as individual psychology.

ON THE WEB

Visit the site of the International Association of Individual Psychology using the link on the book website.

Evolution of Adler's Views

Alfred Adler was born near Vienna on February 7, 1870. His father was a middle-class Jewish grain merchant. Young Alfred's health was poor, and he had to overcome numerous physical difficulties as he grew up. He went to medical school, became a doctor, and established practice in Vienna. In 1902, Adler began to attend the weekly meetings in Freud's home.

Organ Inferiority. In *Study of Organ Inferiority and Its Psychological Compensation* (Freud first praised this work published in the 1907), Adler accepted

Freud's assumption that the body is the source of desires and pleasure. Adler then moved in a different direction and stated that the body may also become a source of pain or dissatisfaction. One of Adler's central concepts is **organ inferiority**. This is not exactly an accurate term because it refers not only to organs as such (the eye, the hand, the heart, etc.) but also to various sensory and physiological systems, including the nervous system. The term stands for a wide range of difficulties that become impediments. They can be physical or psychological. They appear at birth but may develop later in life. For example, a short boy is unable to reach something on a shelf; children tease him for his lack of height and reject him in their games. Similarly, a child with a mild learning disability, an obvious weakness in the classroom, may feel embarrassed for being slow and suffer abuse from his peers. In this case, that child's learning disability is his organ inferiority. According to Adler, a physically defective organ or a malfunctioning system send signals to the brain that suggest something is wrong or insufficient. The body then needs to compensate for an emerging insufficiency and to find energy resources to address the problem.

Based on lengthy observations of children, Adler concluded that organ inferiority appears in individuals who are physically weak and have relatively poor adaptation skills. These children attempt to overcome the discomfort and negative experiences caused by their perceived inferiority. This is called **compensation**. The process of compensation is not a steady process of improvement and growth. It can help as well as create problems. The compensating child could develop aggressive, self-destructive, or other negative tendencies.

Alternatively, some children may turn to fantasies. Adler uses the Cinderella fairy tale as an example of a childish expectation of a better outcome, a form of personal liberation from humiliation and pain caused by her stepmother. Children tend to develop their own ideal world of fantasy, in which they finally achieve redemption. Being preoccupied with fantasies, the child may become increasingly withdrawn and, unfortunately, suffer more because of the constant abuse from other children. All in all, the compensatory behavior frequently results in the child's retention of the bad habits and psychological problems. The child sees the whole world as hostile. Even family members become enemies.

After Freud grew critical of the inferiority ideas, Adler began to drift away from him as a researcher and colleague. Adler no longer accepted the view that sexuality was the most decisive factor to determine an individual's behavior and psychological problems. In his view, people with the symptoms of neurosis could have experienced an emotional trauma in an early stage of their development. However, their trauma was the result of some organic or bodily defect or imperfection. If this is the case, then an individual's life is a relentless attempt to compensate for that initial imperfection. These attempts may cause the development of abnormal psychological symptoms. In other words, any neurosis is a person's failed attempt to compensate for an infantile imperfection (see Figure 8.2).

Figure 8.2 Alfred Adler's Views of Compensatory Behavior

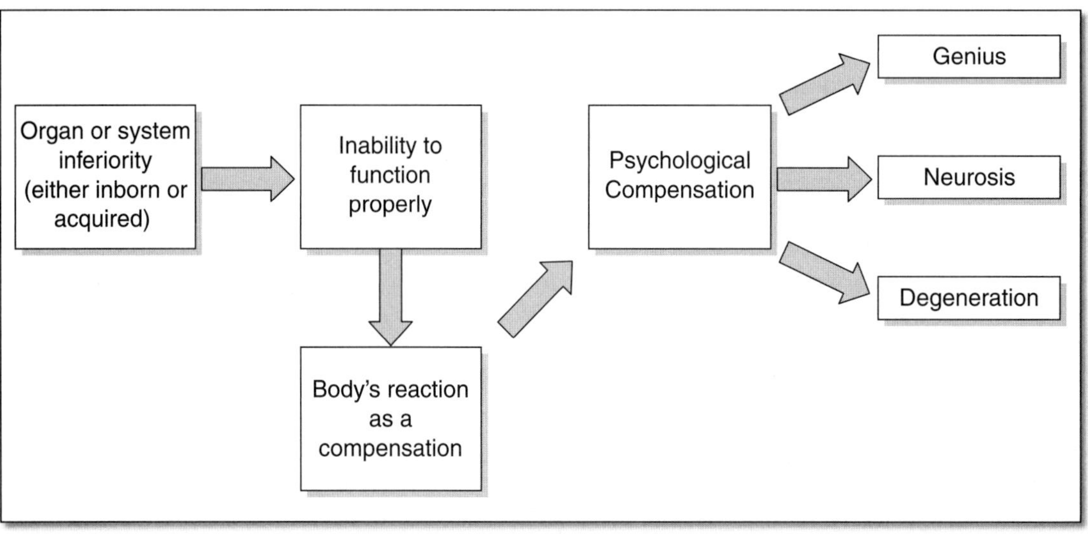

Degeneration, Neurosis, Genius. There are three outcomes of an individual's compensatory efforts. In the case of *degeneration,* the attempted compensation is unsuccessful. The person falls out of the normal course of life and is unable to adjust to social requirements. The *genius* achieves exactly the opposite result. Compensation brings success and delivers a new life free from pain of inferiority. The third outcome is *neurosis.* This happens when an individual is bouncing back from success to failure. As an illustration, imagine for a moment a woman with heart problems; she brings attention to herself because she really needs help, care, and compassion. Later, however, to prolong care and to continue to enjoy the compassion of other people, she may perpetuate the existing heart problem or refuse to admit that her heart condition has improved. This is not a case of deliberate lying or malingering—simulation of one's symptoms to get benefits. This is done without conscious effort. Physical deficiency brought the feeling of psychological deficiency: she feels that she now suffers more than anyone else, that she doesn't deserve to suffer alone, that no one understands her and her feelings, and that the world around her is mean, cold, and unresponsive. These feelings, accurate or false, according to Adler, are components of a neurosis.

Organ inferiority manifests in a variety of ways. A boy performing poorly at elementary school is labeled "lazy" and "stupid." Could these names affect the boy's feelings and actions? A teenage girl suddenly discovers that she is not beautiful compared with her peers. Why? A mean person told her that she has a big nose and big ears. Suddenly the girl looks in the mirror and sees that the allegations about her "ugliness" were true. As a result, she changes psychologically. Once an outgoing and happy girl, she becomes anxious and withdrawn. She loses interest in activities she previously enjoyed. She turns to fantasies. In her dream world, she becomes a supermodel, creates her own fashion line, and returns to her school to confront her peers, who turn out to be, of course, big losers. The fantasy is a temporary substitute for real action. In cases of degeneration, such fantasy ultimately becomes "reality," thus making the individual incapable of social functioning. Some people withdraw deeply in the world of dreaming. Others may turn to guns to address their violent fantasies against their abusers. Adler described children who compensate by engaging in violent acts. This is an example, which Adler described as *protesting behavior*, which can manifest in many ways and in people of all ages.

Although Adler acknowledged inequality between men and women, he also believed that mistakes of the history of civilization must be corrected. However, as a man of his time, Adler accepted the long-established construction of gender roles. He believed that women's protests against sexism and discrimination were wrong because, in reality, as he insisted, it was a protest against women's natural roles as mothers and caregivers.

ON THE WEB

Adler used the life of Johan A. Strindberg (1849–1912)—one of the most prominent Swedish cultural icons of the modern era—to portray a typical neurotic character. Learn more about this case on the book website.

Individual Psychology

Adler was particularly impressed with the work of Hans Vaihinger, who published the book *The Philosophy of As If.* In this book the author maintains that people live primarily by a fiction that does not correspond with reality (Vaihinger, 1924/1952). People believe that the universe is orderly, and that might be a fiction. Yet people put aside this idea and behave as if the world were orderly. Similarly, people create God, ignoring the idea that God could be a fiction as well.

Why do people create and live by falsifications? One of the reasons is that we tend to live by expectations: to achieve a goal we have to believe in it. We have to know how to achieve it. These assumptions motivated Adler to identify his own field of interest in psychoanalysis. While Freud was interested in the past of his patients, Adler assumed that people are motivated primarily by future expectations. By forming future expectations, people put together their fictional final goal, called *self-ideal.* This is the unifying principle of an individual's personality. One of the central themes of Adler's therapeutic method is the search to understand a person's hidden motives.

Self-ideal can be achieved if an individual engages in **striving toward superiority**, an assumption that Adler formulated in 1930. A person striving for superiority does not necessarily want to dominate, as some critics incorrectly interpreted this point of Adler's theory. Individuals strive for security, improvement, and control in all activities they undertake. They win or make mistakes—it doesn't matter. This is the great upward drive, as Adler put it. The human feeling of imperfection is never ending. But people constantly find a solution to this problem by using the imperatives "Achieve! Arise! Conquer!" (Adler, 1930).

Social Interest. The idea of striving to superiority was not Alfred Adler's discovery. Friedrich Nietzsche (1901/1968) wrote about *will to power* as a core motivational force.

French psychiatrist Charles Féré (1852–1907) believed that the feeling of joy stems from the feeling of power. Powerlessness, conversely, generates sadness. But Adler viewed the power drive as a response to feelings of inferiority. He later modified his position, adding another important motivational feature to his explanatory system: **social interest**, or the desire to be connected with other people. Adler realized that, while a person strives for self-advancement, this process is not set in a vacuum. We, as people, have to take into consideration other people and their interests (which are, ultimately, their own strivings for power). Social interest is the desire to adapt positively to the perceived social environment. There are three major and interconnected social ties appearing in social interest.

The first social tie is *occupation*. People are engaged in different activities to provide food, water, safety, and comfort. People then create division of labor. *Society* is the second tie. People join different groups based on their occupation or other interests. The third tie is *love*. People are attracted to one another. The division of labor and social requirements influence love.

People create their own **style of life**. This concept is helpful in summarizing Adler's views. Each style of life forms in stages. First, a growing individual tends to develop an inferiority complex. Second, an individual establishes a goal to overcome this inferiority, which involves compensation. Compensation may manifest in behavior or imagination. Pursuing goals of compensation, an individual strives toward superiority and self-enhancement. There are right decisions and mistakes on this path. This quest for superiority involves an individual's engagement in social life and the establishment of social ties. All together, these elements will present a unique style of life for each individual.

From the beginning of his career, Alfred Adler made relentless attempts to reach a broader audience, popularize psychology, and explain it in nonacademic, lay terms. He specifically mentioned that individuals and society together form a dynamic structure. When conditions change, social ties tend to change as well. So do our individual perceptions of them.

IN THEIR OWN WORDS

Alfred Adler: "No experience is a cause of success or failure. We do not suffer from the shock of our experiences—so-called trauma—but we make out of them just what suits our purposes."

✓ CHECK YOUR KNOWLEDGE

What were the main disagreements between Adler and Freud?

What are *degeneration, neurosis,* and *genius* in Adler's theory?

Explain social interest in Adler's theory.

Early Transitions of Psychoanalysis: Carl Jung

Carl Jung is frequently called the "crown prince" of psychoanalysis. At some point in 1908 Freud truly believed that Jung would become his successor. For several years Jung was a firm and loyal supporter of Freud, his theory, and his method. He showed his support publicly at many formal and informal professional gatherings. In letters, Freud used to address Jung cordially as "dear friend and colleague." Their short-lived friendship and eventual breakup have become one of the most discussed cases in the history of psychology.

Freud and Jung

The son of a Protestant preacher, Carl Jung (1875–1961) suffered from anxiety and obsessive symptoms early in life. Carl was imaginative and creative, showing early interest in self-analysis. After getting a medical degree in 1900 from the University of Basel, he worked in a mental asylum in Switzerland. In 1907, Jung began his six-year collaboration with Sigmund Freud. Freud hoped initially that Jung would apply the basic ideas of psychoanalysis to psychotic behavior, an area of Jung's expertise. In particular, Freud urged Jung to analyze dreams of psychotic patients in the same way he, Freud, analyzed dreams of neurotic patients. Knowing about Jung's interest in mythology, Freud also wanted Jung to apply the concepts of libido and repression onto the world of folklore.

ON THE WEB

Read Carl Jung's brief biographical sketch on the book website.

Carl Jung was probably the most influential student and later critic of Freud's views. Jung's legacy is being constantly rediscovered and reevaluated in today's psychology.

ON THE WEB

Visit the International Association for Analytical Psychology using the link on the book website.

Promoting an "Heir." Freud promoted Jung's candidacy for the leadership position in the newly formed international psychoanalytic movement. Expectedly, critics were displeased with this "princely" status given to Jung, a little-known 35-year-old Swiss. Yet the new status of Jung was a compromise. Why? The vast majority of psychoanalysts at the beginning of the century, and particularly in Austria, were Jewish. Because Jung was Christian and from Switzerland, his leadership role was supposed to symbolize that psychoanalysis was a true multiethnic, international movement (Hayman, 1999). Freud, in his letters, emphasized that Jung was very important to the movement because of his Christian background, young age, and non-Austrian origin. Freud and Jung established cordial interpersonal relationships. For several years, they exchanged letters, discussed cases, and explored each other's theoretical ideas (Eisold, 2002).

CASE IN POINT

Communication Between Psychologists. Today's e-mails, texts, and tweets have brought new components to the interaction among psychologists. The number of our daily contacts is unprecedented. Interpersonal communication among psychologists has always been crucial for the development of the discipline. In the early 20th century, scientific journals and conferences were the main sources of new research information. However, personal, handwritten letters played a special role in psychology. Many important facts in psychology's history are obtained from personal correspondence. These letters convey the history of the psychoanalytic movement, which was also a complicated story of interpersonal relationships, informal meetings, romance, jealousy, mutual betrayal, remorse, and neglect. Letters between Sigmund Freud and Carl Jung are a fine source of such information. They also provide information about Freud's and Jung's theoretical views. They tell about their developing and then deteriorating friendship. It is emblematic that Sigmund Freud, when he decided to break up with Jung, wrote that his friendship with Jung was not "worth the ink." They ended their personal correspondence in 1913.

Meanwhile, at some point during their cooperation, Jung tried to convince Freud that the unconscious contains not only infantile memories but also relics from early human history. He argued that to understand the delusions of a schizophrenic patient, an analyst should examine the delusions as ancient "memories" of humankind. Jung insisted that the causes of hysteria do not originate in early childhood experiences. They have a hereditary, somatic origin. Psychosis (Freud did not explain the nature of delusional symptoms) brings people directly into confrontation with the unconscious, which is filled with mythological symbols. Here Freud realized that Jung was attempting to change the original concept of psychoanalysis. Freud took it personally. This was the beginning of a growing tension between the two.

The Split. Jung was hesitant to embrace the Freudian concept of sexuality and libido. He considered *mental energy* a better term. When in 1912 Jung visited Fordham University in the United States during a series of lectures about psychoanalysis, he significantly de-emphasized the importance of infantile sexuality and practically denounced the sexual origin of neurosis. He was also critical about the Oedipus complex, which was, as discussed earlier, a very important element of the Freudian system. Jung also started to downplay the efficiency of psychoanalytic therapy. Fascinated with mysticism and spirituality, Jung wanted to incorporate the ideas of Eastern philosophy, theology, and mythology into his theory. In 1913, Jung was already giving lectures about his own *analytical psychology,* which he thought was different from the Freudian theory.

These proposed innovations bothered Freud, who wanted to keep his original theory unaltered. Scientific disagreements affected their mutual irritation. It turned into intolerance, as Jung admitted later (Jung, 1961). Jung began to see Freud's relations with other psychoanalysts, including with Jung himself, as if they were psychoanalytic sessions with patients. Freud was upset at what he saw as Jung's betrayal of the entire psychoanalytic movement. Soon Freud let his grievances out. The end of the friendship and academic cooperation between Freud and Jung was painful for both of them. It was perhaps one of the most significant professional "divorces" in psychology.

Finally, Freud asked Jung to resign from his position as president of the International Psychoanalytic Association. By this time, Jung had little interest in running an organization. In April 1914, he resigned and withdrew from active work in the movement (Eisold, 2002). The uncrowned prince of psychoanalysis would never be king. He turned now to build his own theory and to attract a growing posse of dedicated followers.

Forming the Ideas

Much later, in 1935, Jung wrote in a letter that his analytical psychology had its roots in the Christian Middle Ages, Greek philosophy, and alchemy. Why such a strange combination?

The Roots. Jung believed in the existence of prehistoric memories, the significance of which we grossly underestimate (Drob, 1999). He wasn't the first one to explore this topic. Adolf Bastian (1826–1905) from Germany had earlier introduced the concept of inherited "elementary thoughts." Bastian wrote that we don't know much about these elementary thoughts, but we can infer information about them from studying folklore or dreams (Köpping, 2005). Jung was also impressed with the works of William James and the Swiss psychophysiologist Theodore Flournoy (1900/1994), who was interested in spirituality, mediums, and unconscious processes. Flournoy wrote about giving psychological interpretations of the reincarnation beliefs common in Hinduism. Jung was also inspired by English poet and artist William Blake (1757–1827), who believed that humanity could overcome the limitations of the five senses and turn to intuition and fantasy as sources of knowledge.

In one of his earlier works (Jung & Hinkle, 1912), Jung began to explore the idea that human dreams contained a special type of experience beyond conscious awareness. He thought of dreams as a multistory house in which the basement represents the most fundamental and ancient features of dreams. Contradicting Freud, Jung proposed that dreams do not necessarily reflect unrealized wishes but rather mythological stories and images from the experiences of our ancestors. Fantasy, too, like a dream, serves a connecting role between our ancestors and our life at this moment.

Collective History. One of the most important elements of Jung's theory was the belief that there must be an impersonal layer in human psyche, different from the individual unconscious, which he called the **collective unconscious.** It is inherited and shared with other members of the species. Jung agreed with Freud that the individual unconscious consists primarily of repressed ideas. But the content of the collective unconscious consists of **archetypes**, or images of the primordial (elemental, ancient) character. People, according to Jung, share similar ancestral experiences. These archetypes manifest in three universal ways: dreams, fantasies, and delusions. Jung believed that certain delusions reported by his patients (like a belief that the son has wings or a fear of being swallowed by an animal) resemble mythological images of the past. Our ancestors accepted them. In modern times, however, they are treated as abnormal symptoms.

☞ CASE IN POINT

Jung's View of Symbols. Jung believed that the collective unconscious appears through symbols (Jung, 1964). In dreaming, for example, the symbols are produced spontaneously and unconsciously. Symbols also constitute the unconscious aspects of our perception of reality. Can you remember everything that happened to you today, every minute? If you say "no" this is because you have lost your conscious awareness of your memories. However, you still remember on the level below the threshold of consciousness. Your memories may manifest on the symbolic level. Because there are so many things beyond the range of human understanding, people constantly create and use symbols, including symbolic words, to represent concepts that people cannot define or fully comprehend. For example, what symbolic meaning do numbers have? Jung referred to even numbers as "feminine" (associated with harmony and growth) and odd numbers as "masculine" (associated with power). In this view, the Trinity in Christianity is thus a masculine symbol. Jung also believed that Christianity has created a culture emphasizing masculinity over femininity. Chapter 12 examines a different view of numbers provided by cognitive psychology.

Analytical Psychology. In 1913, Jung began to use the term **analytical psychology** to distinguish his views from Freud's ideas. Analytical psychology wasn't a set of cohesive postulates tested in empirical studies. As practically all psychoanalytic theories are, it was a set of assumptions connected by a string of logic. He provided two sources of information to support his hypotheses. The first one was composed of fairy tales, myths, and legends. The other was his clinical practice. Jung asked his patients to record their dreams. Then he analyzed and interpreted them. Dreams, in his view, could represent wish fulfillment on the one hand. On the other hand, dreams were also symbolic representations of archetypes.

An initial point of the Jung's disagreement with Freud was the method of free association. Jung believed that analysants should pay more attention to the content of each dream to understand the dream's symbolic meaning rather than turn to free associations, which could lead the analyst far away from the dream. Jung modified and developed the method of free association, calling his own method simply the "association method." The principal difference was that Jung presented his clients with specific words, for which they called out anything that came to their mind spontaneously.

The analyst then would scrutinize these associations and look for (a) a particular pattern of responses or certain words appearing repetitively, (b) the effort with which the patient gives these associations, and (c) the emotions and behavior accompanying associations such as nervous laughter, fidgeting, or other reactions.

☞ CASE IN POINT

Imagine that you are swallowed by a giant animal. Does this idea scare or fascinate you? Jung believed that fear of being swallowed is one of the universal human fantasies related to death and rebirth through the act of eating. Jung compared the dreams and fantasies of his patients with different fairy tales. He turned to several such tales. One was the famous Red Riding Hood story in which the wolf eats the grandmother, who is later rescued by the huntsman. Jung also considered ancient myths in which the sun is swallowed by a sea monster. The sun rises again in the morning. The story of Jonah in the Christian tradition and of Yunus in the Islamic tradition both contain the plot element in which a man is swallowed by a giant fish but then rescued. We can find many similar examples. In the *Adventures of Pinocchio*, by the 19th-century Italian author Carlo Collodi, the little wooden puppet is also swallowed by a giant fish and then escapes. In the famous Russian fairy tale by Kornei Chukovsky, a giant crocodile swallows the sun. The distressed people then force the crocodile to spit out the sun. In the film trilogy of *Pirates of the Caribbean*, Captain Jack Sparrow is swallowed by a giant sea beast in the second film, only to reappear in the third.

Could you suggest other tales involving the act of swallowing and rebirth reappearance? Using these examples, supporters of Jung maintain that the similarities in these stories are based on the common human archetypes: we all share similar fears and fascinations. Critics of Jung's views disagree. They say that children (and adults as well) hear such stories about beasts swallowing a character first and then develop fantasies and fears related to these stories, not the other way around.

ON THE WEB

Read more about the famous case of Mandala in Jung's interpretations on the book website.

Archetypes. Recall that archetypes are images of the primordial (elemental, ancient) character. Most contemporary students say that the general idea of archetype is relatively easy to grasp (despite the lack of scientific validity to support it, which is discussed later). However, there is considerable confusion about specific issues related to archetypes. In fact, Jung's position evolved throughout his career. Therefore it will be fruitful to focus on several basic features of archetypes. How do they manifest? Let's give examples.

An archetype called the *shadow* contains the unconscious aspects of the self. In a way, the shadow in Jung's theory resembles the id in Freud's psychoanalysis. The shadow acts according to its instinctual forces. It manifests in a person's attachments, aggressive acts, fears, avoidant behavior, and so forth.

Another archetype is labeled *persona,* a symbolic mask appearing in the collective unconscious to convince or trick other people into the belief that the carrier of the mask is playing a particular social role. The persona represents an individual's public image (the word *persona* comes from a Latin word for "mask"). Jung used the label "personal man" to refer to individuals who identify themselves with real or imaginary social roles. Such identification can be productive and healthy; it also can be pathological when the person suffers from a split between his or her "real" personality features and his or her actual social roles. Imagine a woman, for example, who tries continuously to present herself to others as rich, independent, and arrogant (unconsciously playing the role of a fashion supermodel or heiress). Playing this role could be hurtful because this woman invests so much energy to appear as someone she is not.

Men have an inherited collective image of the feminine human essence called *anima.* In contrast, every woman has an inherited image of masculine essence, called *animus.* These two archetypes are primarily unconscious masculine and feminine psychological qualities. Every individual possesses anima and animus, the fundamental unconscious feminine and masculine features. These archetypes, according to Jung, provide an unconscious guide to our romantic behavior. People often fall in love without a rational reason because the real guides of their feelings and subsequent behavior are their archetypes.

Jung maintained that his theory could help individuals become aware of their archetypes. This, Jung believed, can be accomplished through an interpretation of cultural symbols, dreams, and fantasies (Jung, 1929/1967). These cultural symbols appeared to Jung consistently across similar cultures and times. If people produce comparable images and artifacts, then it is safe to assume that they have similar mental patterns preserved in today's generation.

Therapy. In the world of rationality, individuals fail to recognize their archetypes. These unrecognized archetypes, however, may appear in the form of neurotic symptoms (Jung, 1929/1967). Therapy could provide an individual with a way to shake off pathological symptoms.

What were the goals of Jungian therapy?

- The first goal of therapy was to teach patients how to learn their neurosis. Patients do not necessarily cure their own neurosis; exactly the opposite is true. Neurosis provides a cure to patients who acquire the skills to understand it. One of the differences between Freud and Jung is that the founder of psychoanalysis attempted to eliminate neuroses in his patients. Jung, conversely, attempted to help his patients come to terms with their neuroses.

- The second goal of Jungian therapy was balance restoration. Using the concept of energy conservation, Jung believed that the mental energy in us is limited, and if we pursue one activity, other activities receive less energy.

- The third goal was **individuation**. This is not pursuing tangible results, such as getting into graduate school. Individuation is the process of fulfilling an individual's potential by integrating opposites into a harmonious whole, by getting away from the aimlessness of life (the condition most of his patients were suffering from, according to Jung). Psychopathology is disorganization. Sanity is harmony.

To achieve these goals, a therapist should guide an analysant through four stages in the therapeutic process: (a) confession (the analysant reports his or her experiences), (b) elucidation (the therapist helps the analysant understand the meaning of his or her symptoms), (c) education (the analysant learns how to get out of the state of misery), and (d) transformation (the analysant achieves changes). See Figure 8.3.

Figure 8.3 Jung's Views of Psychotherapy

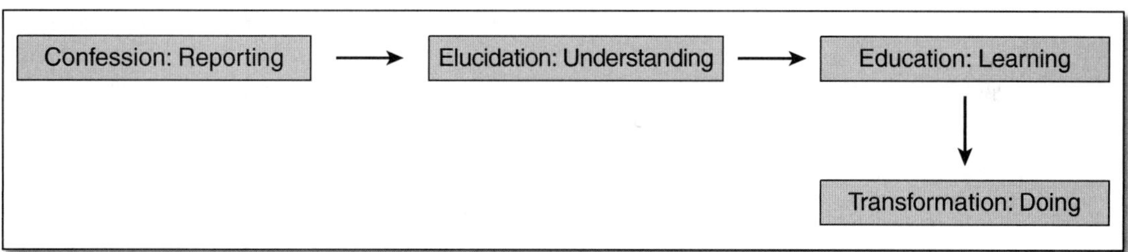

Scores of people from many countries sought his treatment. They paid significant sums of money and settled in hotels near Jung's lakeshore residence, devoting weeks and months of their lives to therapy. Most of them, as you can imagine, were wealthy. They wanted, and had the luxury, to follow the instructions of a mysterious and charismatic Swiss. Many supporters as well as critics compared this massive group of followers to worshipers who had found a new religion and a new "prophet." Jung didn't like such comparisons. He reminded his analysants that they, not Jung, had to uncover the secrets of their souls. His role was simply to provide guidance. From two thirds to three fourths of his patients were 30- to 40-year-old women, who were well-educated and for the most part married. Jung suggested that the reason for this therapeutic gender gap was that women were better analysants than men.

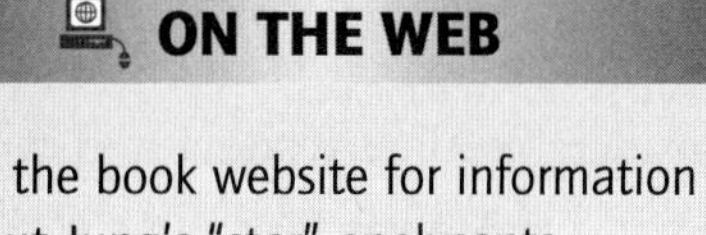

ON THE WEB

See the book website for information about Jung's "star" analysants.

In addition to individual sessions, Jung also offered lectures and seminars attended by many of his patients, who could receive an abbreviated course of his analytical psychology. At the end of his career, Jung wanted to represent the analytic moment as its own legitimate headmaster. He became more conciliatory to the views of Sigmund Freud and offered some suggestions to unify therapists working in the fields of analysis.

Psychological Types. Jung did not conduct laboratory experiments. He preferred to do theoretical analysis and support it with clinical observations. He used this method to create his theory of psychological types. Published in 1921 (it was translated in English in 1924), the book was based on the immense number of references to present-day and ancient authors. The idea of psychological types came to Jung earlier in his career when he compared the experiences of patients with schizophrenia with those of patients with hysteria. The hysteric patient attaches his or her energy to other people, which is an act that Jung termed *extraversion*. Conversely, most schizophrenic patients turn energy back to themselves, which is an act he named *introversion*.

Introverts turn their attention and interest to themselves. This is a source of strength, because they seek internal resources to solve problems and achieve success. Extraverts frequently miscalculate their options because they are too optimistic and don't see potential problems around them. Introverts make mistakes too, because they often see things from a gloomy, pessimistic perspective. Extraverts may start a business project because they see potential rewards and seldom anticipate failure. Introverts will not start the same project because they don't anticipate any rewards and see difficulties ahead. Both types often come to the same result using different ways of thinking. Jung believed, however, that introverts have a harder time in contemporary society than extraverts. To an introvert, the world is too challenging, pushy, and annoying, demanding that everyone march in unison. These critical perceptions are uncommon in the mind of an extrovert. Extroverts agree that the world is demanding, but who says that it shouldn't be?

ON THE WEB

Was Jung an extravert? Learn more about Jung's types of personality and his views of himself and other people on the book website.

Jung warned about paying too much attention to psychological categories and overemphasizing the importance of psychological typology. Human beings are unique individuals with distinctive individual qualities, strengths, and weaknesses. Nevertheless, such classifications should help psychologists in their theoretical and practical work. Moreover, these classifications should also help recognize psychological variations among individuals. Knowing an individual's "personal equation" should therefore help professionals in their clinical practice.

Expanding Theory

In the 1920s and later, Carl Jung spent considerable time reading and writing about issues related to general social science, history, literature, religion, and ethnic studies. In the number of works he produced in that period, a few have particular interest for the history of psychology.

Critics of Ethnocentrism. Jung was among the first psychologists to criticize the ethnocentric worldview of Western psychology. He confronted a widespread opinion of the time that the European type of thinking was far superior to Asian or African types of thinking and that the psychoanalysis of Sigmund Freud had finally allowed European psychologists to look inside the depths of the mental world and to share this knowledge with other people. Quite the opposite was true, according to Jung. Europe is only a peninsula on the Asian continent, he liked to point out. Europeans, in fact, were merely catching up with other ethnic groups whose psychological world has been richer and more complex than Europeans had thought. Furthermore, Europeans had almost rejected the world of the supernatural, mythological beliefs, and unconscious experiences.

Jung deserves special recognition today because he was able to show similarities in cultural experiences, and he encouraged psychologists to understand and appreciate them. Both college graduates living in large cities such as New York, London, or Berlin and individuals living in tribal areas discuss their dreams and fantasies. The only difference between the college-educated people and the tribal people is that the former are dismissive of, and the latter pay more attention to, their imagination. In contemporary terms, a person who catches an infection and becomes ill may explain this as a result of bad luck during the flu season. A person from a traditional culture would explain this as sorcery, a malevolent act committed by an evil force. Both these people believe that the infection is only the means to deliver harm. In both cases, each individual is satisfied with his own explanation. On the one hand, people in remote African tribes believe in evil spirits, ghosts, and gods, which most Europeans consider misleading perceptions. On the other hand, we make similar misleading judgments, blaming, for example, our parents for our own mistakes or believing that some people wish you ill when, in fact, they don't. Jung was a cultural relativist who believed that people of all civilizations have common psychological features (Shiraev & Levy, 2009).

Psychology of Religion. Like Freud, Jung defended the anthropological view of religion. He believed that religion is a product of human experience. People tend to create collective images and beliefs, and then act as if those images are real. Religion is one of those powerful images. Freud interpreted religion as the manifestation of an individual's libido and fear. Jung, however, had a different view. According to him, the concept of God is rooted in archetypes. In the course of centuries, people developed images and memories related to the existence of something that has a life of its own, something fundamentally different and independent from a person's life. These archetypes are preconditions of the God concept.

Jung echoed to some degree the views of the prominent German philosopher Friedrich Nietzsche (both Jung's and Nietzsche's fathers were Protestant pastors who died relatively young, but this is probably not what attracted Jung's interest in Nietzsche). Both viewed religion as a very important path to self-understanding: by studying religion, people could discover their inner selves.

Jung hoped that the Eastern type of thinking would be gradually accepted in the West. The Western world, according to Jung, was based on rationality and needed to be in touch with a deeper view of self and other cultures. Contemporary psychology today has generally accepted Jung's encouragements to develop an inclusive, cross-cultural approach to psychological knowledge.

✓ CHECK YOUR KNOWLEDGE

What were the main disagreements between Jung and Freud?

Explain three main goals of Jung's therapy.

What is the collective unconscious?

Assessments

Mainstream university-based psychology developed unsettled relations with psychoanalysis. Psychologists today tend to acknowledge yet downplay psychoanalysis's impact on psychology. Although most introductory textbooks dedicate from 5 to 10 pages to the teachings of Freud and his immediate followers, the overall attitude about their impact is mixed. Two opinions coexist:

- Early psychoanalysis had a notable impact on psychology. Psychoanalysis paid serious attention to the unconscious side of human experience. It focused on early childhood. Psychoanalysis also justified sexuality as a legitimate research topic. Psychotherapy became a mainstream method of treatment. Psychoanalysis helped scores of medical professionals and psychologists legitimize their new profession.

- Psychoanalysis grossly exaggerated the impact of sexuality on individual development and interpersonal relationships. It overemphasized the importance of early childhood and unconscious phenomena in an individual's life. As a theory and therapeutic method, psychoanalysis was not scientific. It drew conclusions from a vague research base with little possibility of controlled experiments and correlational studies.

Let's consider some of these arguments in detail.

Attempts to Find a Physiological Foundation

Supporters generally considered psychoanalysis a natural science and believed in the principle of energy distribution within the nervous system (Slife, 1993). Their argument was somewhat clever. When Isaac Newton presented the laws of gravity, no one could see gravity. People saw only gravity's effects, such as apples falling to the ground. Psychoanalysis is a science concerning the laws of mental energy. Can we see it? No, but we can detect its effects. Freud, Adler, Jung, and their followers wanted to build a solid physiological background for their theories. Freud, for instance, held that there are different groups of neurons (the receiving, transmitting, and distributing types) responsible for attention and defense (the terms are compatible to Pavlov's excitement and inhibition). Some recent studies measure the impact of psychoanalytic therapies on bodily responses (Goldberg, 2004). Others consider psychoanalytic principles as sophisticated software coordinating physiological activities of the brain (Meissner, 2006).

Unfortunately, a few attempts to identify biological mechanisms of psychoanalysis were inconclusive. Psychoanalysts paid little attention to human physiology and biology. Therefore most critics maintain that psychoanalysis is a speculative theory best resembling mental philosophy or theories of associative psychology of the 18th and 19th centuries.

Evolutionary Science Remains Skeptical

Psychoanalysis has a problem with evolutionary theories. Jung appeared to be the most ardent defender of the idea that some psychological characteristics (collective unconscious) should be based on the common ancestry of human beings. But was there any evidential support for his ideas? Contemporary evolutionary and archaeological studies identify one common geographical origin of the entire human species (Oppenheimer, 2003). Most probably, our ancestors appeared first in Central Africa and later spread in three different directions. However, these findings provide little evidence to support the collective unconscious concept. We have no evidence so far that genetically transmittable mechanisms of our unconscious experience exist.

Researchers also debated for some time one Jungian assumption that the historical and cultural development of human beings appears in the individual's developmental history (Ritvo, 1990). Does the mind of a developing child resemble human cultural history? Such theories had been popular before Jung's publications, such as the recapitulation theory of G. Stanley Hall (see Chapter 5). Today, we have no evidence that people carry in their memory the inborn unconscious images from different historic periods.

Was It an Effective Treatment Method?

How many patients did psychoanalysts cure? From the start, psychoanalysts including Freud came under criticism because their clinical reports did not provide solid facts about their cure and improvement rates, remission cases, or returning patients. To learn more about psychoanalysis, a few psychologists back in the 1920s became "clients" themselves to observe and report the effectiveness of the method. The reported results were mixed: some observers said that the method was effective, but not completely. Others were unimpressed but remained generally positive about the method's potentials. Critics considered such reports as proof of psychoanalysis' failure. Many prominent psychologists maintained dismissive views.

However, many effects of the psychoanalytic method are difficult to measure directly. Take the phenomenon of self-cure, for example. Like patients 100 years ago, many people today want to learn psychoanalysis as a technique of self-improvement. Unable to receive sufficient help from clinical professionals, or embarrassed to disclose private information to another person, some people turn to psychoanalysis as an attempt at self-cure. Psychoanalysts encouraged this type of learning. Contemporary studies show that the desire to cure or improve self without turning to a professional continues to be a powerful reason why many people buy psychology books or take psychology classes (Campbell, 2006).

Methodology Is the Weakest Link

For many years after the inception of psychoanalysis, researchers continued to struggle with the basic question of what exactly constitutes a "fact" in the psychoanalytic process (Siegel, 2003). Freud, Jung, Adler, and scores of their contemporaries were more creative and sophisticated storytellers than careful collectors of unbiased empirical facts. See, for example, how Sigmund Freud built his theoretical discourses (see Figure 8.4). First, an analyst collects and records observations from his or her own experience or from a clinical case. Then the analyst compares the selected facts from several cases. Relevant literature is a useful source of information. Next, the analyst interprets the selected facts from a psychoanalytic perspective. A psychoanalytic conclusion follows, and this is constructed as fact. Freud paid attention to infantile conflicts of sexual nature. Adler focused on an individual's unconscious effort to compensate for deficiency and inferiority. Jung turned to dreams and suggested their links with ancient myths and cultural artifacts.

Figure 8.4 Working With Research Data: Freud's Experience

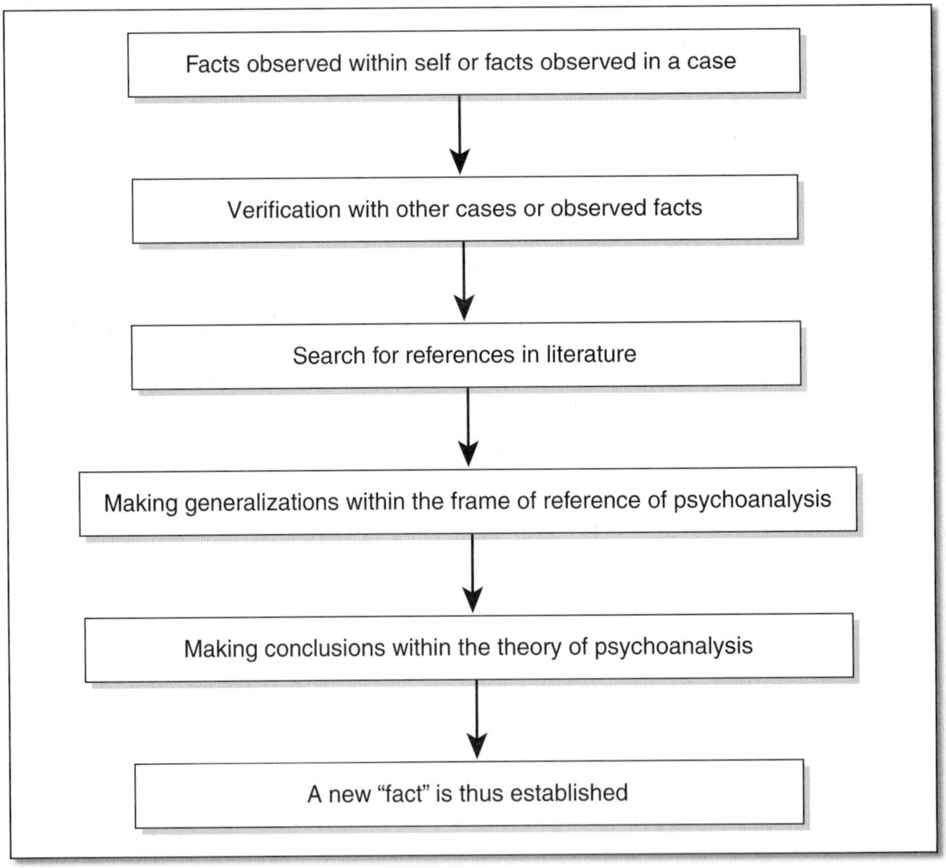

Facts observed within self or facts observed in a case

↓

Verification with other cases or observed facts

↓

Search for references in literature

↓

Making generalizations within the frame of reference of psychoanalysis

↓

Making conclusions within the theory of psychoanalysis

↓

A new "fact" is thus established

Early psychoanalysts embraced a form of self-fulfilling prophesy. They constructed their own facts to support their theory (Levy, 2010). Their method of gathering information resembled the principle "I see only what I like to see," which is probably suitable for creative artistic expression but not for unbiased scientific research. For example, scores of new historic and archaeological facts continuously challenged many Freudian assumptions. However, on several occasions, he insisted that a psychoanalyst was entitled to choose any theories suitable to support his own assumptions and reject those that disproved them (Dufresne, 2003). Although Freud always presented himself as a scientist, he did not send his works for independent peer review and had little interest in publishing in psychological journals, except those under his control.

☞ CASE IN POINT

An Illustration. The following is a sample of critical epithets used by some American and European psychologists and psychiatrists to describe psychoanalysis (Esterson, 2002; Gay, 1998; Hornstein, 1992; Shorter, 1997).

grotesque, weird, sheer nonsense, uncanny, religion, idiotic, uncomprehending, deplorable, "old wives psychiatry," wildly conjectural, unproved, improvable

Conclusion

Despite fundamental problems associated with his theory, Freud remains one of the most prominent representatives of modern thought. Because of his influence on the minds of many people, he is frequently compared today with the most prominent thinkers of the recent past—naturalist Charles Darwin, economist Karl Marx, and physicist Albert Einstein. Adler and Jung also remain in the ranks of the most well-known minds of the past century. The overall cultural impact of psychoanalysis was enormous. Works of Freud, Adler, and Jung have affected many writers, journalists, theater critics, artists, and millions of people interested in the history of religion, the theory of arts, cultural studies, linguistics, and anthropology.

Psychoanalysis drew sharp criticism. However, both its critics and its supporters agree about at least one of its features: the *epistemological optimism* of psychoanalysis, or "know yourself better!" In the view of psychoanalysts, you as a person have to find your own problems, and you have to seek your own solutions. To implement these solutions, you have to use your individual effort, self-knowledge, and critical thinking. Psychoanalysis produced a new and distinct approach to treatment and self-understanding.

At the time of general medicalization of mental illness (see Chapter 6), psychoanalysis became a profession, a prestigious specialization within medicine and psychology. Practicing psychoanalysis meant earning money, finding research opportunities, and enjoying recognition. To justify their treatment method, therapists had to constantly rationalize and defend psychoanalysis. This stimulated the creation of new professional groups, journals, and the constant quest for legal and political support. Psychoanalysis as a profession soon began to resemble a social institution.

The founders of psychoanalysis wanted to originate a new science based on advanced scientific methods. Yet the method is a major weakness of psychoanalysis. As the prominent psychologist and former president of the American Psychological Association Edwin Boring (1929/1950) wrote, "It is not likely that the history of psychology can be written in the next three centuries without mention of Freud's name and still claim to be a general history of psychology. . . . [P]erhaps, had Freud been smothered in his cradle, the times would have produced a substitute. It is hard to say. The dynamics of history lacks control experiments."

Psychoanalysis too lacked its own control experiments.

Summary

- Among several sources of psychoanalysis were studies of unconscious experiences, sexuality, psychological energy, and psychological resistance.

- One of Freud's early assumptions was that clues about a patient's symptoms could come from the sources that are not usually under clinical observation. Freud's *Studies on Hysteria* outlined some principles of his approach to mental illness, including the method of free associations.

- The *Interpretation of Dreams*, published in 1899, and *Three Essays on the Theory of Sexuality* revealed the complexity of Freud's developing theory. In these books, he formulated the classic ideas about the Oedipus complex, repression, and the struggle between wishes and defenses. Freud assumed that dreams represent wish fulfillment, or the symbolic attempt to realize an unfulfilled desire.

- The Vienna Psychoanalytic Society was formed in 1908. Similar groups began to emerge in several countries. In 1909, Freud's first and only trip to the United States gave a significant boost to the psychoanalytic movement.

- World War I had a deep impact on Sigmund Freud, his family members, and his colleagues. The war affected his practice and writings. His worldview became increasingly pessimistic. He adopted the concept of the death wish as the repressed instinctual tendencies that lead toward destruction.

- Freud made a contribution to personality theories by describing the id, the ego, and the superego. He became a successful therapist and popular commentator on social and cultural issues.

- One of Freud's close followers was Alfred Adler, who later distanced himself from his mentor. Adler developed a theory based on Freudian ideas but rejected Freud's views of sexuality. Adler explored the view of organ inferiority and compensation and suggested three outcomes of an individual's compensatory behavior: degeneration, neurosis, and genius. Adler's individual psychology embraced the ideas of social interest, striving toward superiority, and styles of life.

- Carl Jung is frequently called the "crown prince" of psychoanalysis. Chosen as Freud's successor, he later distanced himself from his mentor and criticized him. Jung developed the ideas of analytical psychology, collective unconscious, archetypes, and psychological types. He was an early champion of cross-cultural psychology.

- Despite popularity and advancement as a therapeutic method, psychoanalysis only partially resembled a scientific theory and method. Critics pointed out its ethnocentrism, the lack of experimental validity, and selective attention to facts.

Key Terms

Analysant	Free associations	Social interest
Analytical psychology	Id	Striving toward superiority
Archetypes	Individuation	Style of life
Castration anxiety	Libido	Superego
Collective unconscious	Oedipus complex	Thanatos
Compensation	Organ inferiority	Transferences
Death wish	Pleasure principle	Unconscious (adjective)
Ego	Psychoanalysis	Unconscious (noun)
Eros	Reality principle	Wish fulfillment

The Paths of Gestalt Psychology

The educational processes, even within a small educational unit like the family, depend to a high degree on the spirit of the larger social body in which the persons are living.

Kurt Lewin, 1936

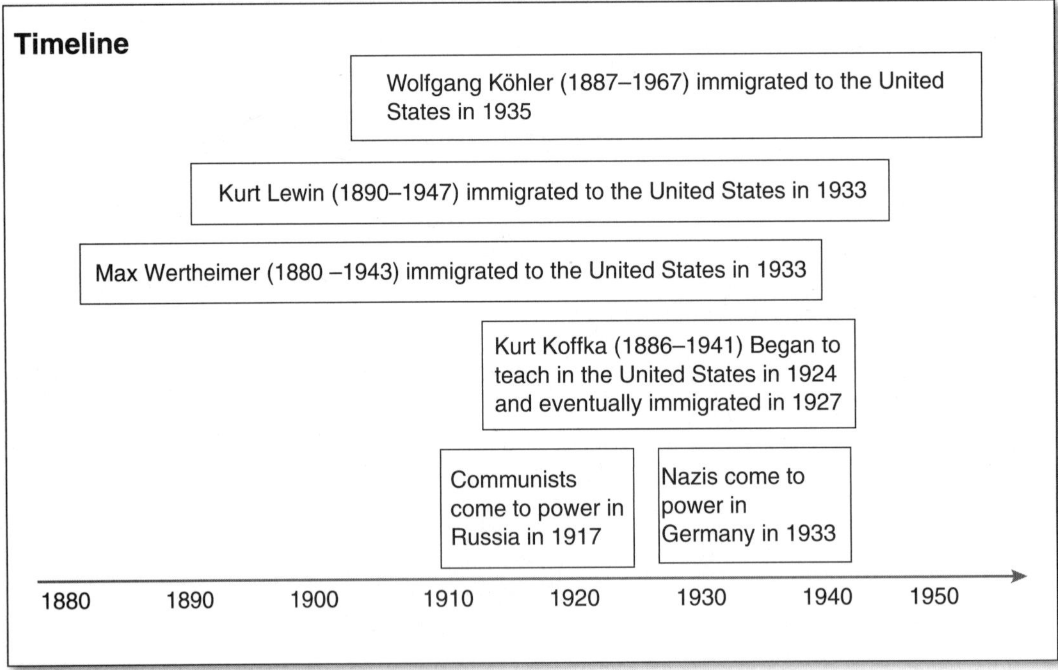

CHAPTER OUTLINE

Freddie Adu is a Ghana-born American professional soccer player. At the age 19 he became a member of the U.S. national team. At that time he was 5 feet 6 inches tall, and he weighed 160 pounds. Did you know that 85 percent of his body—the chemical composition of which is similar to your body—is oxygen? Miley Cyrus (otherwise known as Hannah Montana) is a superstar singer and actress. At the age of 15, her height was 5 feet 4 inches, and she weighed about 100 pounds. In fact, almost 11 percent of her body—and your body as well—is hydrogen. When Cristina Fernández de Kirchner became president of Argentina, reporters described her as being tall and in great shape. What reports didn't mention is that almost 2 percent of her body weight is chlorine and that 1 percent is sodium. The same proportion of sodium and chlorine is in every person's body. In fact, the bodies of all human beings are comprised of the same proportions of chemical elements. Almost 70 percent of an average human being is water.

Now imagine that an alien scientist from a faraway civilization is making a chemical analysis of human bodies living on the earth. Will the composition of all chemical elements inform this scientist about the unique personalities of the three persons mentioned earlier? Will the quantities and weights of organic molecules tell the detached stranger about the meaning of human life, their misfortunes, happiness, and suffering? Will this scientist, by studying the composition of carbon and magnesium in the body, grasp the meaning of your passion for music or cooking? A soccer player, a singer, a politician, a professor, or a student—we are inimitable small universes. A unique combination of molecules in our bodies is not just a sum of chemical elements.

This chapter deals with a branch of psychology called Gestalt psychology, a remarkable theoretical and experimental school whose main and original thesis was quite modest. Gestalt psychology stated that there are patterns of our experience that cannot be explained by the comprising elements, no matter how sophisticated our analysis of these elements. Probably, most people who have superficial knowledge about psychology may anticipate that Gestalt psychology was mostly about different forms and shapes. Such an interpretation is acceptable, but only partially. Gestalt theory constantly evolved to win a broader appeal and, ultimately, widespread acceptance. Through the years, its principles influenced social, developmental, educational, clinical, and many other branches of psychology. The founding "parents" of Gestalt psychology shared similar fates. Most of them had to leave their country to start a new life and career in the United States.

The Social Landscape After the Great War

World War I lasted four years (1914–1918) and caused global devastation. In Europe and Asia, the German, Austro-Hungarian, Ottoman, and Russian empires collapsed. New governments had to deal with massive economic and financial problems. Brief periods of stability and growth were followed by frequent downturns and crises. Unemployment and inflation became chronic problems. The Great Depression caused new problems. Economic difficulties contributed to social instability. Strikes were frequent in the United States and across Europe. Claiming the restoration of social order, authorities in Spain, Germany, Russia, and Italy turned to authoritarian policies and restricted civil liberties. Alternatively, governments in many democratic countries, including the United States, had turned to active involvement in economic and social policies. Despite global economic and political instability, the world was constantly trying to find its way to stability and progress.

Psychology and Society After the War

After the war, psychology as a profession and an academic discipline counted significant losses. Witnesses recalled that many universities in Europe were empty because most professors and students had been called into active duty or had volunteered (Katz, 1952/1968). Many of them would never return from the battlefield. The university-based European psychology was in worse shape than that in the United States or Canada. Immediately after the war, European governments had little money for funding universities. Private subsidies to schools declined. Psychology was given a lower priority than chemistry, physics, engineering, and other fields. The situation began to improve only by the mid-1920s.

Social Climate. Social and political instability in the 1920s and 1930s affected the lives of millions of people. Political authorities in many countries began to establish and expand their control over science and education. This was not the kind of government policies and regulations that existed in almost every society. It was a direct government intrusion into education and science. Nazism and communism were two major government ideologies of the post–World War I period that directly affected the development of science, university education, and psychology in several countries.

History shows that governments could successfully impose an ideology on any academic discipline. Psychology was not an exception. After the end of the civil war in Spain in the late 1930s, the regime of General Franco imposed a theological, scholastic framework on Spanish psychology. It was imperative that psychologists remain true Catholics and fight against inappropriate tendencies in life (Kugelman, 2005). Religious and government authorities decided what was appropriate to fight against or study in psychology.

In Germany, psychology had been increasingly influenced by Nazi ideology, which was a mixture of nationalism and racism. The government ideologues in charge of German universities believed that psychologists must provide research to train the younger generations to become physically and mentally strong, to learn the

Nazi principles, and to defend the German state as soldiers. The official policy was to focus on applied fields that could be used in professional and military education. As a result, many theoretical psychological disciplines in Germany by the mid-1930s were eliminated (Kressley-Mba, 2006). Many German psychologists served later in the military and performed diagnostic services for officers and soldiers (Geuter, 1987). In Germany, after the expulsion of minority and liberal-minded professors, academic psychology became an obedient servant to the government of the new German Reich (van Strien, 1998). The leaders of the Nazi Party and obedient industrial leaders became prime sponsors of German psychology. They demanded research results and theories advancing the goals of the repressive state. Most psychologists in Germany became servants of the oppressive political system that delivered scholarly "facts" about the supremacy of the Aryan character, the effectiveness of racist educational doctrines, and the importance of strong leadership in people's lives (Geuter, 1987). The Nazi "racial hygiene" program supported by some scientists in Germany was an act of genocide. The 1933 Law for the Prevention of Congenitally Ill Progeny was aimed at individuals with symptoms of schizophrenia, epilepsy, bipolar disorder, or alcoholism (Weiss, 1987). Based on eugenics, this law led to the forced sterilization of 350,000 patients diagnosed with schizophrenia. Sterilization was soon replaced by physical extermination. Overall about 70,000 German psychiatric patients were killed by the Nazis (Müller-Hill, 1988).

Nazism and Science. National Socialism, or Nazism, was a racist ideology claiming the universal supremacy of the Aryan race and the German people's right for domination over other, inferior peoples and nations. Nazism was rooted in German nationalism, intolerance for minorities, and militarism. It claimed that scientists and educators must surrender their personal interests and pledge their unconditional support to the state and its leadership. Nazism became the official ideology in Germany in 1933. Every German educator and scientist had to pledge allegiance to the German leader, Adolf Hitler. Psychologists as well as other scientists were not allowed to use non-German literature in their research and teaching. Authors of non-Aryan origin were banned and their books burned. University professors—if they remained loyal—were considered part of the national "organism," the carriers of Nazi ideology (Harrington, 1996). The "new" German psychology was supposed to serve the interests of the state and promote the new social order—an unsettling blend of racism, obedience to authority, prejudice against minorities, and mysticism (Koenigsberg, 2007). Those professors who refused to follow orders were physically eliminated.

Nazi ideology also identified the principal enemy of the German people: the Jews. Because many psychologists whose work and ideas are described in this chapter were Germans of Jewish origin, it is important to address this question openly: Why did the Nazi government target the Jews? How did anti-Semitism affect the fate of the Jewish scientists and the development of psychology?

Since the Middle Ages, the European Jews had not shared equal rights with other citizens. Most states allowed them to live only in limited areas. They could not occupy government positions, marry Christians, or pursue advanced academic degrees.

Political reforms of the mid-19th century gave all ethnic and religious groups in Europe equal rights. Successful businesses owned by the Jews grew. Many of them pursued careers in medicine, science, the arts, and politics. Jewish families moved into big cities. By 1880, for example, Jews made up 10 percent of the population of Vienna. At the same time, data suggest that they comprised almost 40 percent of the city's medical students and almost one fourth of its law students (Spielvogel, 2006). By the end of the 19th century, many Jews were entering the field of psychology after most universities began to limit the discriminatory hiring practice against minorities.

However, history teaches that at that time of economic uncertainty and social instability, minority groups, as a rule, become the target of discrimination and violence. The postwar difficulties provided fertile ground for the outbursts of antiminority attitudes and anti-Semitism. Moreover, under the influence of Nazi ideology, Jews, as well as other minority groups, became the convenient targets of violent attacks. After Hitler's ascendance to power in 1933, the anti-Jewish campaign in Germany became an official policy. Nazi activists targeted schools and universities in Germany, harassing Jewish professors, disrupting their lectures, and interfering with their research. Jews were subsequently expelled from all public posts and state universities. In private institutions they were forced to resign under threat of death.

German psychology had played a leading role in European and world psychology since the middle of the 19th century. However, the ideological "cleansing" of German science that had begun in the 1930s and the forceful expulsion of scores of professors all delivered a tough blow to psychology as an academic discipline in Germany.

Communism and Science. The ideology of communism is rooted in the fundamental ideas of German philosopher and economist Karl Marx and his followers. Communist ideology had become the backbone of the government policies of the newly formed Soviet Union in the early 1920s. Marxism, in the eyes of the procommunist scientific elite, was supposed to be the basis on which scientists could create their theories and design specific methods of investigation. In light of this reasoning, according to the official government doctrine, the only "true" scientific psychology was the one based on Marxist principles.

Three such principles refer to psychology. The first one was materialism and the emphasis of the primary role of physiological processes over "resulting" psychological phenomena. The second was ideological: psychology must serve the interests of the working class. And the third one was historical determinism: human psychological functions are the products of social developments.

The implementation on these principles to university psychology brought some unfortunate results. First, the Soviet authorities saw psychology as a "useless" discipline that could add nothing new to biology or physiology. They presumed that a scientist educated in neurophysiology, for example, should explain psychology better than anyone else. Second, the officials in charge of Soviet science believed that history and biology are the only disciplines necessary to explain human behavior. Therefore, there was no need to have psychology as a separate discipline. Following this logic, the government's actions in the Soviet Union seriously limited the development of psychology after the mid-1920s and eventually resulted in its official dismissal as a discipline. Communist governments in other countries, unfortunately, used the same strategy. Psychology was seen as a reactionary Western discipline designed to undermine biology and history and as such was practically banned. The situation began to change only in the 1960s.

Nazism as an ideology and policy affected millions of lives. After the end of World War II, it was condemned and outlawed in Europe. Communism, however, survived for a long time and was able to affect science and psychology in many countries.

Politics and Psychology. How did these developments affect psychology? Most psychologists mentioned in this chapter were German. Almost every one of them, as well as scores of German scientists, had to seek safety overseas. Many scholars wanted to leave the Soviet Union as well. However, the government would not allow it.

Most of immigrants to North America never went back to their home countries. Although their decision to leave was an act of desperation, it was also a rational choice. The United States and Canada experienced significant economic difficulties at the time of the Great Depression, yet it offered tremendous scientific and teaching opportunities, possibilities for private grants, and decent living conditions. Most important, North America gave them academic freedom.

We begin our study of Gestalt psychology by reviewing briefly its main principles and theoretical roots. Then we discuss the term *gestalt* and its origins. Next, the life and works of two great psychologists, Max Wertheimer and Kurt Koffka, reveal how the early studies—conducted under the Gestalt paradigm—interpreted and explained human perception and memory. The research and publications of another great representative of this school, Wolfgang Köhler, reveal the innovations and contributions of Gestalt psychology to the areas of thinking, decision making, learning, and general behavior. Finally, the remarkable life and work of Kurt Lewin and his colleagues and followers show the maturation of Gestalt psychology and outline its many applications in the studies of personality, motivation, social perception, and group dynamics.

✓ CHECK YOUR KNOWLEDGE

How did Nazism affect psychology as an academic discipline?

Why did Communist ideologues consider psychology a useless science?

Principles of Gestalt Psychology

Originating in Germany at the beginning of the 20th century, Gestalt psychology gradually earned recognition around the world. Its original principles were well received by university-based psychology. Gestalt theory is sometimes compared to a protest or revolt. In fact, there was not much of a revolt or confrontation. It was a new experimental and theoretical approach mostly critical of Wundt's views and the introspective psychology of the 19th century. Certainly it was a challenge to traditional German psychology

(Köhler, 1959). It was also critical of the experimental psychology of mental elements promoted by Titchener in the United States. However, Gestalt psychologists did not focus specifically on criticisms of the past. They moved psychology forward.

Three features of this forward progress stand out. First, the psychologists supporting Gestalt theory believed that they were offering something new: novel principles, an innovative understanding of known facts, and the explanations of perception that had been overlooked by previous research in psychology. Second, they demonstrated a range of new psychological phenomena previously hidden from scientific psychological investigation. Third, they suggested a general psychological doctrine that explained and investigated a whole new range of psychological and behavioral phenomena.

If we turn our attention to the beginning of the 20th century, we easily recall that approximately at the same time two other approaches—behaviorism and psychoanalysis—were gaining strength and acceptance by challenging traditional psychology. Behaviorism was critically concerned with the old, traditional methods and principles of psychology and its emphasis on subjective, conscious processes. Thorndike, Watson, Pavlov, and others believed that by studying reflexes psychologists would be able to explain the rich complexity of human behavior. Psychoanalysis was also based on the rejection of traditional psychology that paid little attention to a massive layer of psychological phenomena. Psychoanalysts turned to the field of unconscious processes, which was focused on the dynamic relations between various elements of human motivation. Freud, Jung, and Adler, as well as most behaviorists, also believed that their research would have universal value and broad applications.

But what was the uniqueness and originality of Gestalt psychology? What was new in its approach to psychological phenomena?

Main Ideas

Unlike behaviorists, psychologists developing Gestalt psychology accepted consciousness, yet they rejected the structuralists' fragmentation of consciousness into mental elements. The fundamental assumption of Gestalt psychology is that there are units or "wholes" in individual experience and, as it was added later, behavior, which are not determined exclusively by composing parts or elements. Similarly, the parts of a unit are better explained by the intrinsic nature of the whole. (Remember the example that opened this chapter.)

Now, how can we understand this "whole"? It is a pattern, a complete entity, a totality of characteristics. Does it make sense? In fact, for years the most challenging task for students of Gestalt psychology was to describe precisely the nature of the "whole." To illustrate, when we look at a coworker, we don't perceive her as a combination of different elements such as her hair, sunglasses, business suit, and cell phone. We see her as a colleague. When a mother looks at her daughter, she sees her child, not a sum of facial elements and body parts in her sight. In very general terms, Gestalt psychology presumes that experience and behavior is organized not from separate elements but rather from these organized wholes.

The Label. *Gestalt* does not have a single or exact translation from German, the original language of the founders of this theory. *Gestalt* has several meanings including "form," "shape," "manner," or "essence." It is something that represents elements put or placed together and defines their togetherness. Some followers of Gestalt psychology even argued that this label was the product of the imagination of its critics, who tended to attach simplistic labels to something they didn't understand well (Boring, 1929).

A label is, in most cases, a simplification that distorts the complexity of the thing the label describes. Some psychologists, such as the behaviorists or psychoanalysts in the early 20th century, didn't mind various verbal tags attached to their research. A distinctive name can help identify and distinguish your work from the work of other psychologists such as "structuralists." The term *Gestalt* had its own history of gradual acceptance. At first, only a few critics and reviewers used it to describe the research of several German psychologists who were studying perception. Later commentators and critics simply became accustomed to the term *gestalt.* Other terms, such as *holism* or *holistic psychology*, did not survive (Boring, 1929).

In which theories did Gestalt psychology find its original assumptions?

Theoretical Roots

Like behaviorism or psychoanalysis, Gestalt psychology was not developed in a theoretical vacuum. Several intellectual traditions had a significant influence on the originators of Gestalt psychology.

Philosophy. The first theoretical line of influence was mostly philosophical. Many German intellectuals in the 20th century accepted philosopher's Georg Hegel's (1770–1831) call for the development of a holistic view of nature, human life, and history. A single element is impossible to understand without studying its multiple connections with other elements and its environment. When a scientist studies a particular element of reality, this is an act of separating that element from the whole of reality. A living person is not just a sum of body parts or chemical elements within it. A nation is more than the summation of its citizens. Gestalt psychologists, most of whom had studied philosophy, adopted this general holistic philosophical position in their psychological studies (Kendler, 1999).

The second line of thought was rooted in epistemology. The Austrian physicist and philosopher Ernst Mach (1838–1916) argued that space and time are specific forms that cannot be explained by their elements. Thus, if people see the geometrical form of a circle, in addition to sensing each individual element of the drawn line, people sense a circular "space form" as well. If a person hears a melody, the person perceives a "time form" in addition to the tone sensations of the melody. Mach, in fact, reformulated the classic idea of another prominent German philosopher, Immanuel Kant, who stated that time and space were both special, innate forms of cognition (Chapter 3). The human mind, in most cases, is ready to perceive a circle or a straight line or to prefer the architecture of a beautiful building to that of an ugly one. Such mental categories of form and space are not only the product of our experience but are probably common in every human being. They are thus universal and inborn.

Physics. How do these forms function within our experience? To answer this question, some scientists turned to early 20th-century physics, which had become another source of knowledge and inspiration for the founders of Gestalt psychology. Some psychologists turned to chemistry for theoretical explanations and also for its clear examples. For instance, we can easily imagine that everything consists of atoms that are joined together in different combinations. Nevertheless, we don't see these atoms, molecules, or their combinations. What we see are the different things that are made from these elements. We can learn a lot about the elements of a whole but most likely will not be able to understand the whole by simply observing its elements without the knowledge about how such elements are connected. Another attractive idea was the physical concept and model of the *field*. This was understood as a dynamic system in which a change in one part affects the other sections of the field. The idea of the field allowed psychologists to imagine time, space, and force in somewhat measurable terms for the first time.

Psychological Research. Another line of influence was associated with experimental psychological research. In 1890, Christian von Ehrenfels (1859–1932) gave the name *gestalten* to visual psychological states, the main properties of which cannot be reduced to the sum of their parts. Future Gestalt psychologists were also aware of the work of Edgar Rubin (1886–1951), a Danish psychologist. Interested in figure-ground relations, he conducted research with so-called ambiguous figures. He showed that complex depictions could be seen from two different perspectives, one from the ground perspective and the other from the figure perspective. But most people tend to distinguish the figure first. The figure always dominates experience and covers the ground, which we tend to distinguish after the figure. Very rich evidence came from various experimentations with so-called **reversible figures** such as the Rubin vase, a figure in which you can see either a white vase on a black background or the black profiles of two human faces on a white background. Psychologists noticed here that if you ask a person to describe his or her individual sensations or the elements he or she discerned during the process of viewing the figure, practically everyone will describe the colors, the lines, and the contours in a similar way. Yet people can form two distinctly different perceptions using the same elements of their experience.

Today most of us know about ambiguous figures. The Internet provides spectacular examples of ambiguous figures and visual illusions. But we have to understand that 100 years ago such pictures were an incredible innovation. Using them, Rubin was among the first to provide illustrations that showed the relationships between figure and ground in human perception.

Psychologists began to seek similar psychological patterns in other types of perception. David Katz (1884–1953), for example, conducted studies of touch as well as color vision (Arnheim, 1998). By the end of the first decade of the 20th century, psychologists had accumulated a rich set of empirical materials in the area of hearing and musical perception. They established, for instance, that chords and melodies, the shape characteristics of visual objects, and the roughness or the smoothness of tactual impressions could be examples of psychological states—gestalts—different from and superior to those of the materials of which they consist. If the physical stimuli or elements change but the relations among them remain constant, the qualities taken as a whole remain about the same (Köhler, 1959).

ON THE WEB

Learn more about Rubin's vase and other visual paradoxes on the book website.

Imagine that you are listening to satellite radio. You just heard a great new song. Now you try to recall the melody of this song. You want to download this melody as a ringtone on your cell phone. You go on the Web and listen to several samples before finding the one you are looking for. You make a few clicks and buy this ringtone. The question is, how did you recognize this particular melody? In its original sound on the radio, the melody was a combination of different sounds produced by a synthesizer, drums, a guitar, and a human voice. On your cell phone, the sound of the melody is completely different, yet you recognize the original melody heard on the radio. From the standpoint of the psychology of mental elements (remember Titchener's research), this could be a difficult situation to explain: the musical elements in the song, on the radio, and in the ringtone are completely different, but you hear the same melody. Gestalt psychology offers a different explanation. You remember the melody not simply because your memory stores a sequence of distinct sounds. Rather, you remember the melody as a "whole," and each musical note is part of the complete gestalt of the melody (Wertheimer, 1925/1938).

Psychologist and philosopher Oswald Külpe and his studies of imageless thoughts conducted at the University of Würtzburg (see Chapter 4) also had a considerable impact on Gestalt psychologists. As discussed earlier, Külpe proposed the method of systematic experimental introspection to study so-called imageless thoughts. These were hard-to-grasp mental processes that allowed the subjects to make judgments and solve problems. People were reaching conclusions without dividing their decision-making process across specific mental elements such as sensations and feelings. Külpe's ideas became a theoretical foundation for Gestalt psychology's theory of thinking and decision making.

The "Actors." According to Edmund Boring, in *A History of Experimental Psychology*, Gestalt psychology had three principal founders: Max Wertheimer, Wolfgang Köhler, and Kurt Koffka. Although many other psychologists worked on similar problems, these German names clearly stood out in history. A fourth psychologist—Kurt Lewin—is discussed in this chapter as well for his role in the development of Gestalt psychology and its broad applications.

The aforementioned psychologists were of a similar age. They knew each other well and worked together during the same period. They all shared the understanding that their field, called early Gestalt theory and labeled later Gestalt psychology, was rooted in the original studies of the "wholes" given in experience (Koffka, 1922). Köhler frequently used the pronoun *we*, referring to Wertheimer, Koffka, and himself. Kurt Lewin did not hesitate to mention the names of his three predecessors in his publications. These psychologists also shared a similar fate: born in different parts of Europe to German-speaking parents, they all ended up in the United States, where they continued and ultimately finished their careers (see Table 9.1).

There are at least three identifiable stages in the history of Gestalt psychology. Initially, Gestalt psychologists were interested in the studies of perception as well as shapes, contours, and geometrical forms (van Campen, 1997). Afterward, their research interests widened to include memory, problem-solving behavior, motivation, and learning. Later, Gestalt psychology continued in applied fields including education, management, advertisement, therapy, and professional training.

Table 9.1 The "Grand Masters" of Gestalt Theory: Wertheimer, Koffka, Köhler, and Lewin

Name	*Main Career Highlights*
Max Wertheimer (1880–1943)	The oldest of the four. He is regarded as the originator of the theory and is frequently quoted by his followers. Suggested main theoretical principles and conducted early empirical studies. Immigrated to the United States in 1933 and worked there until his death in 1943.
Kurt Koffka (1886–1941)	Most productive as writer, and most enthusiastic promoter, of the original ideas of the Gestalt psychology. Began to teach in the United States in 1924 and eventually immigrated in 1927. Died in 1941.
Wolfgang Köhler (1887–1967)	Best known for his studies of problem-solving behavior. Occupied the most prestigious teaching position at Berlin University. Vigorously opposed the Nazi government and its policies. Immigrated to the United States in 1935. Had a productive career and elected in 1956 as president of the American Psychological Association. Died in 1967.
Kurt Lewin (1890–1947)	Most well-known promoter and innovator of the original ideas of Gestalt psychology. Immigrated to the United States in 1933. Created a unique dynamic theory and laid foundations for social psychology.

Studies of Perception in Gestalt Psychology

We begin our analysis with the description of the earlier studies that had brought Gestalt psychology its name and earned it initial recognition and respect. These studies were related primarily to perception and were associated with the names of Max Wertheimer and Kurt Koffka.

Max Wertheimer. Few psychologists can be called "pioneers." Max Wertheimer (1880–1943) was one of them. He initiated the early experimental studies in this field and put together a set of theoretical ideas, which he and his colleagues would test later. He was born in Prague (the capital of the Czech Republic today) in 1880 to German-speaking parents of Jewish descent. He studied in several schools and finished at the University of Würtzburg under the direction of Oswald Külpe (see Chapter 4). He obtained his PhD there in 1904. He chose an academic career, which he started at the University at Frankfurt. There in 1910 he met Kurt Koffka and Wolfgang Köhler at a laboratory in the Psychological Institute. Their professional relationships resulted in a very productive scholarship. Wertheimer had spent almost 30 years as an active researcher and professor in Germany. However, in 1933, after the Nazi Party came to power, he left the country. Until his early death in 1943, he worked in New York at the New School for Social Research.

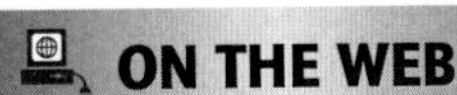

ON THE WEB

Read Max Wertheimer's brief biographical sketch on the book website.

Wertheimer recalled in one of his publications how he had arrived at his initial theoretical assumptions (Wertheimer, 1925/1938). He was puzzled by the arguments of Ehrenfels (mentioned earlier) about people's perception of music: we can listen to a melody performed on different instruments, but we can still recognize the melody. How can all the elements in a melody change and yet we perceive it as the same one? Wertheimer believed that every individual note or sound is experienced as part of the entire melody. That is, the melody as a whole comes first. What is given to the individual by the melody does not arise as a secondary process from the sum of the sounds. Instead, what takes place in each single part already depends on what the whole is.

Notice that this assumption was a departure from a traditional point of view in psychology that stated that an individual's experience should be understood as the complex sum of multiple experiences or elements. Wertheimer, however, looked at psychological experience from a different direction: perceptual elements do not "bundle" together, as the mainstream experimental psychology maintained at that time. Most probably, he assumed, they integrate together forming new images and new structures. The mind does not consist of a bunch of sensations associated with one another.

Wertheimer did not work alone. He had graduate students and colleagues whose assistance and advice he sought. Two young scholars who were among Wertheimer's subjects in his early experiments on perception of movements and who became his collaborators for many years to come were Kurt Koffka and Wolfgang Köhler.

Kurt Koffka. If Wertheimer was a pioneer of Gestalt psychology, then Koffka was a spokesperson. Kurt Koffka (1886–1941) was born and raised in Berlin. There he studied philosophy at the University of Berlin, the most prestigious school in the country. At the age of 18, he spent a year at the University of Edinburgh in Scotland. Koffka completed his doctoral research in psychology in Berlin. His research topic was on musical perception and rhythms. Carl Stumpf, a key German experimental psychologist at that time, was one of his mentors. Koffka met Wertheimer at Frankfurt in 1910, which marked the start of their productive collaboration. Because of his impressive scholarship and English proficiency (recall that he studied in England), in 1924 Koffka visited the United States and served as a visiting professor at Cornell University and then the University of Wisconsin. Later he moved to America permanently. He worked for Smith College in Massachusetts and held other research appointments, including one at Oxford University, until his early death at the age of 55.

Koffka's impact on psychology was significant. First, he attempted to systematize the initial ideas of Gestalt psychologists into a coherent theory. Second, he expanded the field of research from studies of perception to other fields and, most important, developmental psychology. Third, his knowledge of the English language and his international contacts were helpful in making Gestalt psychology a recognizable approach globally. Koffka was the principal promoter of Gestalt theory in North America (Koffka, 1921/1924). With the help of American psychologist Robert Ogden, Koffka introduced Gestalt psychology

ON THE WEB

Read Kurt Koffka's brief biographical sketch on the book website.

in the United States in 1922 via a paper in *Psychological Bulletin* (Henle, 2006). His other works were translated into English as he began to teach and conduct research in the United Sates.

Gestalt Principles of Perception

The beginning of systematic research in the fields of Gestalt psychology began around 1912 when Wertheimer published an article on the so-called **phi-phenomenon**. Wertheimer explained this phenomenon as the observable fact of pure motion when two images are projected in succession. This is a perceptual illusion in which two stationary but alternately flashing lights appear to be a single light moving from one location to another. His experiments described in the article showed that, although there was no physical motion in the experimental objects presented to participating subjects, they consistently reported the experience of some type of movement. In sum, the subjects did not see elements changing their place or spatial position, but movement was registered in their experience anyway (Wertheimer, 1912/1961).

☞ CASE IN POINT

The Stroboscope. An entertainment device called a stroboscope inspired Wertheimer to study the perception of motion. What was a stroboscope? In 1832, Belgian physicist Joseph Plateau and his sons introduced the phenakistoscope ("spindle viewer"). Simon von Stampfer of Vienna, Austria, who called his invention a stroboscope, also invented it independently in the same year. The device uses the persistence of motion principle to create an illusion of motion. Although this principle had been recognized by the Greek mathematician Euclid and later in experiments by Newton, it was not until 1829 that this principle became firmly established by Joseph Plateau. The stroboscope (or phenakistoscope) consisted of two discs mounted on the same axis. The first disc had slots around the edge, and the second contained drawings of successive action, drawn around the disc in concentric circles. Wertheimer later used a different model of stroboscope, called a tachistoscope. The tachistoscope displayed an image (usually by projecting it) for a specific amount of time.

There was something that happened in the individual experience that was difficult to explain using the principles of traditional experimental psychology. The main thesis taught in German universities at that time was that all psychological facts (not only those in perception) consist of unrelated inert elements. The mind, from the traditional view, was a builder that collected multiple elements of experience, like bricks, and put them together in an organized fashion under the laws of association. Wertheimer considered this explanation unacceptable. In his view, if one follows the traditional psychological approach, human life, apparently so colorful and so intensely dynamic, becomes a frightful bore (Köhler, 1959). The young psychologist wanted to challenge the traditional understanding of human experience.

Wertheimer and his followers began to see this traditional picture from the opposite direction. The process of perception was about the mind—a "builder" producing something new, something fundamentally different from the assemblage of these elements. The main postulate introduced first by Wertheimer was that what takes place in each single part already depends on what the whole is (Wertheimer, 1925/1938). Several psychologists, including Koffka and Köhler (described later), agreed and shared similar views. One of their targets of criticism was introspection.

As discussed earlier, disappointed with introspection and rejecting it altogether, behaviorists moved in a different direction. They believed that they could eliminate the problem of subjectivity if they moved away from perception and thinking and focused on measurable behavioral variables instead. Behaviorists created their own laboratories and experimental methodologies. Gestalt psychologists probably remained in the same psychological laboratories, but they changed the principal approach to psychological studies. They began to call their basic observational data "phenomena," as compared with the "elements" of the traditional psychology.

Let's provide an illustration that Gestalt psychologists commonly used in their publications and lectures. When you see, for example, a human face for just one second you don't usually engage in a lengthy analysis of the lines, contours, and shades on the picture. Your immediate experience indicates that you are seeing a human face. In everyday situations, we look at a human face and say, "This is a face." And after we make this judgment, we pay attention to different features of the face: the eyebrows, the nose, the lips, the cheeks, and so on. Now look at these two faces:

Almost all of us instantly recognize these faces as a "child" and "woman" without analyzing every facial detail. Gestalt psychologists believed that this is the way our perception works.

Which one of them is a picture of a child and which one of a woman? This will be a very easy task if our vision is not impaired. Under most circumstances, we can distinguish the child's face on the left from the adult's face on the right. Moreover, we make this judgment quickly. How much time did it take you to give the answer? But could you tell how you made that judgment? Did you analyze the facial features carefully, going back and forth several times from one picture to the other? Probably not.

If we ask an experienced artist or a computer graphic designer to take time and explain the differences between the facial features of an adult and a child the answer will probably be that the typical face of a baby will have a larger head and bigger eyes in proportion to the face, a somewhat rounder facial contour, plumper cheeks, and a shorter, smaller, and turned-up nose. However, when we see such faces in our daily encounters, do we really go over the detailed list of these features? No, we make a judgment almost instantly. If you look at a person sitting near you or listen to his or her voice, you can almost instantly and relatively accurately (of course, there are exceptions) identify that person's sex and even approximate age. If you like cars, you can often identify a car's make without looking at the logo on the hood. You can instantly tell the taste of orange juice from apple juice. There is something general, primary, and integrated in our perception that is the core of experience.

To summarize briefly, about 100 years ago, Gestalt psychologists showed in their experimental research that it is not the elements but the integrated and constant patterns or "wholes" that are likely to be the fundamental features of our psychological experience. A psychologist from the Wundt laboratory was likely to report, "I perceive a pattern of sensations that usually occurs when I am engaged in the perception of a woman's face." A Gestalt psychologist would likely put it very simply, "I see a woman." Gestalt ideas were a significant departure from the ideas of the traditional psychology of perception.

Structure and Organization. If there are general patterns of human experience, there must be some rules according to which these patterns function. The terms *structure* and *organization* became focal points for the Gestalt psychologists, although the meaning of these terms had little to do with structural psychology. Describing the structure and organization of perceptual gestalts, psychologists received their inspiration from the basic sciences, including mathematics, physics, and biology. Stimuli have a certain structure and are organized in a definite way, and it is to this structural organization, rather than to individual sensory elements, that the organism responds. Gestalt psychologists introduced the **Gestalt laws**, or several general principles that refer to perceptual functioning (see Table 9.2)

Critics maintained repeatedly that Gestalt psychology hadn't formulated its major principles and laws clearly, including the idea of the "wholes." Why does an individual's experience use these particular laws but not others? And where in the brain are these gestalt mechanisms? To address these criticisms, the originators of Gestalt psychology frequently referred again to physics and physiology.

Table 9.2 Selected Gestalt Laws and Their Description

Gestalt Laws	*Description*	*Illustration*
Law of Proximity	We perceive elements that are closer together—compared with other elements—as a coherent object.	
Law of Closure	We perceive a coherent object by enclosing a space and completing a contour and ignoring gaps in a depiction.	
Law of Similarity	We perceive elements that appear similar as part of the same form or continuing pattern.	
Law of "Good Form"	We organize stimuli into as "good," or "cohesive," a figure as possible (which is symmetrical, simple, or familiar to us).	
Law of Figure and Ground	We perceive a stimulus or a figure as separate from its ground.	
Law of Common Fate	We perceive elements with the same moving direction as a unit.	

For example, while explaining the uncertainty associated with the definition of the "whole," they argued that when the concept of energy was first introduced in physics, it was confusing. For decades, its meaning was confused with force in traditional mechanics. And what did the physicists do? They continued to work hard and conducted their research until they came up with clarifications about energy, identified several types of energy, and suggested ways in which to measure them. Likewise, the concept of gestalt is probably unclear. Nevertheless, in science, there is no other recourse but to continue research and debates (Köhler, 1959).

Turning to physiology for help, most Gestalt psychologists argued that the brain and the external world are probably organized in the same fashion (Helson, 1987). Whatever makes three dots appear as a triangle or four dots appear as a square is due to their structure. Gestalt psychology as a theory suggested unity of stimuli and their physiological configurations. Because perception follows the law of physical dynamics, there are supposed to be some "fields" or wholes in the brain containing neurons that correspond with the dynamic characteristics of perception. In other words, physiological processes in the central nervous system are likely to be linked with the laws of perception. The external object, its content, and the psychological act are somehow unified. The phenomena that people experience and the underlying processes in the brain are correlated; such a correlation called **isomorphism**.

Gestalt psychologists dared to link psychology to physics and physiology, as they believed in the universality of scientific laws. Subsequently, supporters of Gestalt psychology, after formulating the main principles of organization of perception, attempted to apply these principles to thinking, learning, and behavior in general.

✓ CHECK YOUR KNOWLEDGE

What does the term *gestalt* mean?

What is the difference between introspection and the methods used in Gestalt psychology?

Explain the main principles of Gestalt psychology by looking at something or somebody right in front of you.

From Perception to Behavior

Gestalt psychologists believed that thinking, like perception, needed a substantial reevaluation. Also like perception, the process of thinking is rooted in the mechanism of evaluating the entire situation. Wolfgang Köhler's studies explain these ideas in detail.

Wolfgang Köhler. Born to German parents in Reval (now Tallinn, the capital of Estonia), Köhler (1887–1967) studied in Germany at Tübingen, Bonn, and Berlin. At the age of 22, he earned his PhD under the supervision of Carl Stumpf (see Chapter 4). His research topic was the psychology of sound. In Berlin he also studied with the famed physicist and developer of quantum theory, Max Planck. As discussed previously, Köhler later became acquainted with Wertheimer and Koffka. In 1913, right before the war, Köhler was sent to conduct research on animal cognition in Tenerife (the largest of the Canary Islands off the northwestern coast of Africa). However, he became trapped there during the war (the islands were blockaded by British ships) and, as a result, remained there for almost six years. One of the outcomes of his research was his famous book *The Mentality of Apes*, released first in German in 1917. In 1922 he became a professor at the University of Berlin. In 1925 he came to the United States as a visiting professor at Clark University. There he met many prominent psychologists and made a very positive impression on them. This would help him later to secure employment in America when the political situation in Germany had deteriorated.

The Psychological Institute of Berlin University in Germany maintained its reputation as a stronghold of European experimental psychology. Wolfgang Köhler served as the director of the institute, and Max Wertheimer worked as a professor there. Their status gave them great research opportunities. The school attracted the best students from German-speaking lands, and the pull of international students was always impressive (Henle, 1978). These facts plus the growing reputation of Gestalt psychologists provided the necessary conditions for their theory's continued development.

Köhler actively promoted the idea of psychological holism: every aspect of human behavior should be understood in multiple contexts and from many viewpoints. Yet behavior is not a combination of different actions, just as experience is not a combination of perceptual elements. From the beginning of our lives, we process information and act holistically.

ON THE WEB

Read Wolfgang Köhler's brief biographical sketch on the book website.

Wolfgang Köhler worked within the Gestalt tradition and focused on problem-solving behavior and thinking. He served as President of the American Psychological Association in 1967.

Decision Making and Learning. According to Köhler, decision making, as a process involving a selection from alternatives, is about "grasping" the relations between two elements. It involves the act of comparison. An animal does not simply respond to the absolute properties of a stimulus, as John Watson and behaviorists would have suggested. An animal responds to a signal relevant to its surroundings.

One of Köhler's many contributions to psychology was his study of animal intelligence. Köhler studied animals in conditions resembling their natural habitat (contrary to behaviorists, who studied them mainly in laboratory conditions). In particular, one of his most significant accomplishments was the study of **insight**. In the English language, *insight* is commonly interpreted as the ability to see into a situation and understand its "inner" nature. Sometimes this word is used to indicate a sudden, intuitive perception or the ability to grasp useful information in a given situation. The study of this phenomenon was a significant development in psychology because it introduced an innovative model of learning. It was different from the most traditional psychological models involving repetition of a habit or popular behaviorist models emphasizing conditioning (Pavlov's theory) and trial and error (Thorndike's work).

To simplify, imagine an experimental situation. A cracker is placed near a monkey. The monkey cannot reach the cracker because it is too far from the monkey's cage and the cage door is locked. Several bamboo sticks are scattered around the cage. They are all relatively short, yet if two sticks are put together, they will be long enough to reach the cracker. However, the monkey has never done anything like this before. The animal, in behavioral terms, has not developed a habit of reaching for food with the help of a self-made device. Köhler observed that, in many cases, animals' behavior in this experimental situation was based on trial and error, exactly what behaviorists suggested. Frequently, after several attempts, a monkey would put two sticks together and get the food.

Köhler, however, saw more to these trial-and-error sequences. In his view, the right decision was always reached after some lucky "accident" during the monkey's seemingly disorganized series of manipulations with the sticks. What was that lucky accident? At first, these manipulations with the sticks did not have a clear connection with a desired goal: the monkey was just holding them. However, after connecting a pair of sticks together, the monkey suddenly "realizes" that this new device is a convenient tool to get the food placed outside the cage. This sudden realization involves the reflection of the entire situation. First, the monkey connects two sticks together. Second, the monkey remembers about the food outside the cage. Third, the monkey assesses the distance between the cage and the food. The problem is solved: the double-stick technique is used "intelligently" (Köhler, 1917/1925).

As you can see from this example, the first important characteristic of insight is the animal's reflection of the whole layout of elements in the field. The second important feature of insight-based solutions is that they are a perceptual reconstruction of the task. Köhler maintained, contrary to Thorndike's assumptions, that the learning process is not necessarily gradual. It is very quick, almost instantaneous. The third important feature is that insight-based learning can be transferred from one problem or situation to other situations and tasks. For example, a chicken can learn to receive food from a white card but not from a black one. Whenever a white card is shown next to a black card, the chicken approaches the white card but not the black one. When this chicken is presented with any pair of cards in which one was lighter (but not white) than the other one, the chicken would prefer the lighter one. Similarly, chickens trained to prefer the darker color, when presented with a parallel choice, chose a new, darker color. This phenomenon was called **transposition**, the ability to transfer one's initial experience to new circumstances (Köhler, 1917/1925). We respond to the relationships among the stimuli in a situation, not to separate stimuli. These results, Köhler maintained, proved that what the chickens had learned was a relationship between two experimental objects, two colors.

Transposition serves an important evolutionary function, such as learning certain emotional reactions like fear. Köhler observed that animals stay away from strange-looking objects when they see them for the first time. For example, he conducted experiments wearing a cardboard mask of an African demon and made the frightened laboratory monkeys run for cover. Probably the novelty of such a situation requires the animal to respond with caution or to hide. Transposition in this case plays an important role in survival (Köhler, 1959).

Errors in Learning. Reading about these and other experiments with animals, some people may assume that the animals were quick to resolve problems and to learn. In fact, in most experiments, animals produced mistakes and errors leading to failure. Sudden "understanding" of the situation did not necessarily lead to successful decisions. Köhler identified at least three types of errors that appeared in experimental situations with chimpanzees. The first type was "good errors." These are nearly correct solutions containing mistakes that prevented the animal from making the right decision. The second type of mistake was making completely inappropriate actions that apparently make little sense (instead of placing one box on top of the other, the monkey destroys both boxes). And the third type of mistake was based on behavior previously learned by the animal. In the past, these behaviors were successful, but in a new situation they didn't work. Such observations made more than ninety years ago find further support in contemporary studies.

Professor Robert Sternberg showed in experimental studies that many successful and allegedly smart individuals (this is how other people would describe them) with a long history of success are prone to make foolish mistakes. Why do they make such errors? Köhler's explanations are valid today: for example, "smart" people have a tendency to believe that if they made many successful decisions in the past (based on insights), they will make only great decisions in the future. In Gestalt terminology, these individuals develop a permanent insight, which might lead them to failure in new situations. They must always learn from new situations and view their experience critically (Sternberg, 2004).

Values. Debates about the relative nature of knowledge and moral judgments have a long history. Philosophers always argued that anything one person considers "good," other individuals may consider "evil." The values we attach to events and behavior are relative to our own experience. Gestalt psychologists challenged this view. They suggested that because of the perceived congruency between the physical world and our reflection of it, there must be a degree of objectivity in human values. Koffka believed that value is an attribute of an object or events (Harrington, 1996). Science is capable of predicting future events. Knowledge leads to expectations, and the pursuit of these expectations may have either positive or negative value. Köhler also believed, especially in the later stage of his career in the United States, that psychological research is more than experimental studies and theoretical work. Psychologists, in his view, are capable of describing moral principles that ought to guide human conduct (Köhler, 1938). Overall, Köhler argued that science cannot exist without a value attached to it. Together they create a gestalt—a foundation of our knowledge.

The main ideas that Gestalt psychologists proposed in their publications and lectures sparked discussions and brought them new supporters. One of the most remarkable psychologists who applied Gestalt principles to motivation, development, and individual and group behavior was Kurt Lewin.

✓ CHECK YOUR KNOWLEDGE

What are three important features of insight-based learning?

Where did Köhler collect the data for his book *The Mentality of Apes*?

Advancements of Gestalt Theory

Earlier studies in Gestalt psychology focused on perception and thinking processes. In the 1920s and later, more specialists turned to the area of group behavior and the interdependence of the individual and the group. Mathematics, physics, and geometry appeared suitable to explain such interdependence.

Field Theory of Kurt Lewin

From the beginning of his academic career, Kurt Lewin (1890–1947) wanted to learn about the internal and external sources of human motivation. Born in Germany in a small town near Posen (today Poznan, a city in western Poland), he attended two universities consecutively before transferring to the University of Berlin to pursue a doctoral degree in psychology. He was wounded while serving in the military in World War I. He obtained a PhD, as the original Gestalt psychologists did, under the formal supervision by Carl Stumpf. Lewin expressed an interest in many disciplines, including philosophy and theory of science (Ash, 1992). He was also interested in behavioral studies and Marxist theory, especially in Marx's approach to social justice and equality. Lewin embraced behaviorism but subsequently grew dissatisfied with it (Zeigarnik, 1988). Studying motivation, Lewin combined his interest in psychology with his passion about science, math, and geometry. His research career was interrupted in 1933 when he had to leave Germany in fear for his life. Using help from his American colleagues, he secured private funds to work at Cornell University; the Iowa Child Welfare Research Station; and, after 1944, the Massachusetts Institute of Technology, where he established the Research Center for Group Dynamics.

ON THE WEB

Read Kurt Lewin's brief biographical sketch on the book website.

Kurt Lewin, as many psychologists of his generation, had a productive career after immigrating to the United States. Lewin's research influenced the early developments of social psychology.

Topology. Working in America, Lewin wanted to create a new theory of human behavior. He turned to geometry and **topology**. The latter is the complex study of the properties of geometric figures and spaces in terms of their connectedness, continuity, and orientation. Topology in Lewin's view helps to describe an individual's actions, intensions, arising conflicts, and puzzling dilemmas. Circles, lines, squares, and vectors are used to model, explain, and even predict behavior. Lewin called his new theoretical system *psychodynamic*, emphasizing the active, changing nature of psychology. In today's psychology, this term has a variety of different meanings.

Lewin's research was rooted in formal logic, precision, and quantitative facts. Colorful examples and illustrations are plentiful in his publications. Yet when you open any of his papers or books, you will often find columns of formulas and layers of graphs. Lewin genuinely believed, as did many psychologists at that time (behaviorists in particular), in the existence of specific laws of human behavior describable in mathematical equations. Unlike many behaviorists, Lewin acknowledged the existence of motives as goal-directed, internal forces. Yet he was convinced about the existence of certain mental states that represent the purpose of human behavior.

Lewin turned to carefully crafted experimental procedures, which imposed retesting and controlled evaluation of their results. He began to use film recording for his experiments. He initiated detailed filming of children in their natural conditions. Recorded thus, a child behavior was documented, observed by independent reviewers, and measured. Today video recording of experimental situations is common. However, eighty years ago such techniques were innovative and inspiring: adherents believed that filming allowed a psychologist to measure behavior with the accuracy of a physicist.

Field Theory. The **field theory** was Lewin's approach to combine the main principles of Gestalt psychology and topology (Lewin, 1943). According to field theory, the acting and thinking individual is a part of a dynamic field or interdependent forces. This individual is also a part of **hodological space**, which is a finitely structured space; its parts are composed of certain regions, and direction and distance within this space are defined as paths. In Lewin's theory, life appeared as a giant diagram with opposing forces, energy fields, obstacles, goals, conflicting interests, supportive aids, and obstructive opponents. To understand or predict someone's behavior (Lewin label it "B"), the researcher must understand the psychological state of a person (labeled "P") and of the psychological environment (E). In this system, P and E are interdependent variables. Behavior becomes a function (labeled "f") of an individual's personality characteristic and of specific environmental or situational conditions.

$$\mathbf{B} = f(\mathbf{P}, \mathbf{E})$$

When first presented in Lewin's book *Principles of Topological Psychology*, published in 1936, this idea attracted the support of many psychologists who saw in it a way to measure behavior. According to field theory, an individual behavior depends on the characteristics of the present field at a particular moment. An individual's goals (no matter how a psychologist understands them) and past experiences (behaviorists describe them as reflexes or habits) are all fit into the field characteristics of the moment. To describe the field, Lewin introduced terms such as *life space*, *field*, *existence*, *locomotion*, *force*, *valence*, *goal*, *conflict*, *interdependence*, and many others. As an illustration, these terms and their brief interpretations are presented in the following list (Lewin, 1944).

- *Life space* is the totality of facts that determine the behavior of the person or a group. It consists of regions; objects, including persons; goals; and other factors that influence the person's behavior.
- *Field* is a space within which forces operate.
- *Existence* refers to anything that has a demonstrable effect on an individual or a group. To exist is to be included in one's life space. Being aware of your own interest, for example, is to include this interest in your own life space and to be aware of it.
- *Locomotion* refers to a position at different times. Any psychological phenomenon or behavior can be represented as a specific locomotion.
- *Force* is a manifestation of energy by a person that must be defined in terms of the whole field. Power refers to the possibility of using force.
- *Valence* is the property of an object in a region in the life space according to which the object is sought or avoided. Positive valences initiate approach; negative valences produce retreat or withdrawal. Tension is an empirical syndrome indicating a need. When the goal is achieved, the tension is zero.
- *Goal* is a force field where all forces point to the same region.
- *Conflict* refers to the overlapping of at least two forces. Internally, opposite forces cause frustration.
- *Interdependence* stands for the interconnectedness of the elements of life space through tension and force.

The environment, according to Lewin, can be objectively measured in terms of direction (left, right, up, or down) and distances. To get from point A to point B, a person should overcome various barriers. Each barrier has a different strength. A greater effort is needed to overcome a strong barrier. There are conflicting forces in the field. Force is defined through three properties: direction, strength, and point of application (as in physics it is indicated by an arrow). See Figure 9.1.

Force Field Analysis. Using the concept of **force field analysis**, Kurt Lewin provided a framework for looking at the factors or forces influencing an individual's behavior in a particular situation. Every act can be viewed as an interplay of forces either moving an individual toward a goal (helping forces) or blocking his or her movement toward a goal (hindering forces).

For instance, very often the solution is very close, yet we have to wait or use a different path to reach a goal. Imagine that you come to a store at 7 p.m. to buy a pair of gloves. Unfortunately, the store is already closed for the day. The gloves you like are just a few feet away from you. Yet you don't break the window to get in and get the gloves.

Figure 9.1 An Illustration of Lewin's Field Theory

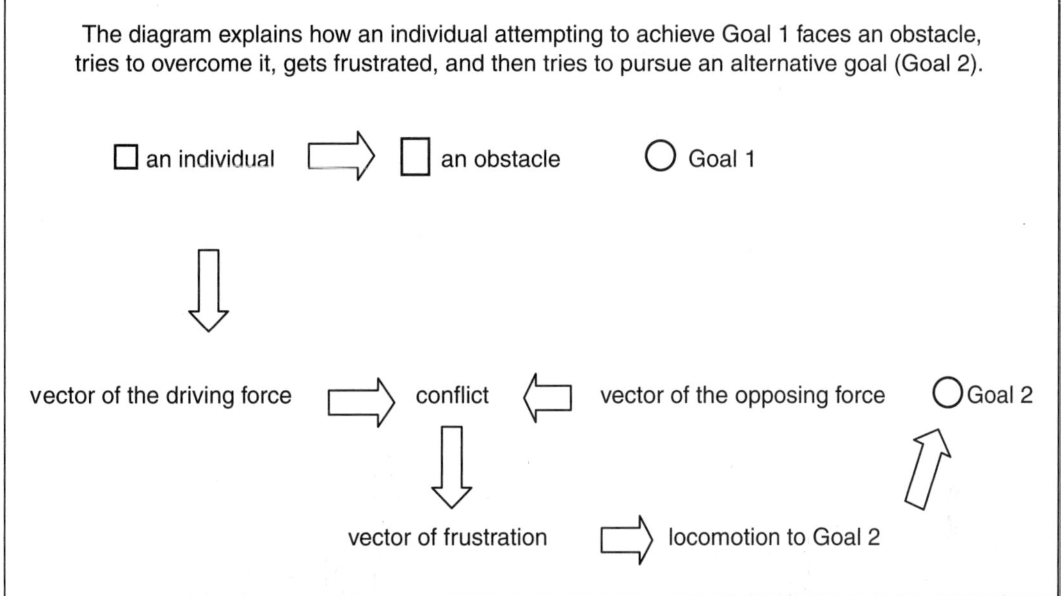

Instead, you go away and return to the store the next day. You approach this little problem in the most efficient way because you not only understand the whole situation—the store is closed and the gloves are not available—but you are also able to recall and apply appropriate legal restrictions (you may not break in if the store is closed) and social rules (the store will be open again tomorrow) to interpret this situation. By following these rules, you actually have moved away from the object (a pair of gloves) that you wanted to get. The forces of "reason" were more powerful than the desire to buy the gloves. Some illustrative examples of the force field analysis appear in Table 9.3.

As this illustrates, Lewin wanted to achieve a degree of formalization and mathematization of psychology (Lewin, 1951/1997). He always emphasized the importance of finding strong empirical support for his theoretical assumptions. His assistants and students often provided such support.

The Zeigarnik Effect. Bluma Zeigarnik (1900–1985) was born in Lithuania (at that time, a part of the Russian empire). She moved to Germany in 1924 as the spouse of a Soviet trade official. She was interested in philosophy and psychology and hoped that the German language would help her to study her favorite subjects. She chose a class taught by Max Wertheimer. Almost immediately she became fascinated with Gestalt psychology. She also attended Lewin's seminars and soon began to do research under his supervision. As a foreigner, Zeigarnik couldn't work as a paid assistant. So she became a volunteer. A petite young woman, she was one of Lewin's best students. One day he asked her to substitute for him and teach a psychology class. When she

Table 9.3 Illustrative Examples About the Force Field Analysis

Sources of conflicts	People constantly choose between two positive valences (choosing between two great options), two negative valences (choosing between two punishments), and ambivalent two valences (both positive and negative outcomes).
Possession of an object	Ownership or control of something or somebody reduces their positive valence, and an individual (who is in control) begins to desire something else.
Anticipation of a reward or punishment	Increases or decreases valences between an individual and the outside world and may cause tension.
Differentiation of life space	Learning is about differentiating: we comprehend the complex forces and valences within the field, realize their interdependence, mark our individual borders, evaluate conflicts, and understand our frustrations.

Source: Lewin (1936, 1943)

appeared in the classroom, a few male students told her to leave the podium: they couldn't imagine that a young woman was their substitute lecturer (Zeigarnik, 1988).

IN THEIR OWN WORDS

The system was such that I could have taken any class I wanted. I attended a class taught by Max Wertheimer, after which—with my typical naiveté—I came to him and said that I liked his gestalt theory. Wertheimer replied with all seriousness: "I like it too." (Zeigarnik, 1988)

Lewin constantly suggested new research topics to his students. He could find unusual, puzzling elements in seemingly ordinary situations. Once chatting with his students in a coffee shop, Lewin asked a waiter to tell him what a couple of customers sitting in the corner had ordered. The waiter answered accurately from memory. Then Lewin asked the waiter to tell what a couple, who just paid and left, had ordered a few minutes ago. The waiter could not recall. Lewin speculated that waiters probably have a selective memory: they are interested in remembering only the orders from the people who have not paid yet. That means that the memory is active when a business transaction is unfinished. After a customer pays the check and finishes the transaction, the waiter loses the motivation to remember.

But was this explanation correct? Lewin offered Zeigarnik the opportunity to investigate this problem. She conducted a study of **unfinished actions** from 1924 to 1926.

She would give her subjects simple tasks such as copying from a book, writing some words, or making simple clay figures. Zeigarnik wanted one group of her subjects to complete all the assigned tasks. The other group was interrupted at various stages of the procedure. (Some participants even complained that they had had a very strange experimenter who didn't let them finish the task.)

Overall, Zeigarnik found that unfinished tasks were remembered much better than the finished ones. As a student of field theory, she explained this phenomenon as a state of tension that occurs in individuals whose locomotion toward a goal is interrupted. The tension within an individual continues and maintains memory. If a task is completed, the subject achieves satisfaction. Lewin found these findings interesting and included some of Zeigarnik's experimental results in his report to the 1926 International Psychological Congress. These findings, called the Zeigarnik effect, generated significant interest internationally and gave Lewin additional assurances that his theory could find experimental support.

Zeigarnik later became a well-known specialist in clinical psychology. She applied Gestalt principles and Lewin's force field analysis to her study of mental illness. In her view, a healthy individual is capable of understanding internal forces, such as desires, hopes, and attachments, and their balance or imbalance. An individual capable of seeing self critically is capable of handling his or her own problems. Therapy is necessary primarily for those who couldn't handle the process of self-regulation. She was convinced that psychological dysfunctions should not be viewed as a constellation of symptoms taken in the context of an individual's interactions (Zeigarnik, 1988).

☞ CASE IN POINT

Organismic: Psychology According to Kurt Goldstein. Students who attended Max Wertheimer's lectures in Berlin often visited a medical clinic run by Kurt Goldstein (1878–1965), a physician who adopted the early views of Gestalt psychologists (Gelb & Goldstein, 1918). During World War I, he was director of the German Military Hospital for Brain-Injured Solders. He continued to work as a physician and neuropsychologist until 1933, when he left for the Netherlands and later for the United States. One of his most famous works, *The Organism*, was published after he had left Germany. His approach was based on a fundamental assumption of Gestalt psychologists that an organism must be analyzed in terms of the totality of its whole behavior and its complex interaction with its environment. Mental illness, as he understood it, was a failure of the entire organism to respond properly to changing physical and environmental conditions. A recovery from mental illness was frequently related to the restored ability of the organism to reestablish the function of self-control (Goldstein, 1939/1963). He believed that mental illness is the dysfunction of an entire organism and not only one small area of the brain. One of Goldstein's roles in psychology was his influence on the views of Abraham Maslow, one of the most remarkable psychologists of the 20th century.

Leadership Styles. Lewin proposed an original approach to group behavior, which became an early contribution to social psychology (see Chapter 10). Group dynamics is about group interdependence. To understand how a group functions, one should study the properties of the field where group activities take place (Lewin, 1939).

Studying group behavior, Lewin introduced the concept of **leadership style**: the predominant type of communications established by the group leader. Initially, he conducted a series of observations of children's play groups. He found significant differences between two climates of interaction within these groups, which he called democratic and authoritarian. Later, Lewin and his colleagues agreed on a comparison of two kinds of teachers: one, a "typical" German autocrat; the other, a "typical" American nonautocratic person (Patnoe, 1988). Psychologists wanted to measure levels of group hostility, group tension, and group cooperation under these two types of teachers. In addition, they decided to see what happens if a teacher provides a third type of management: no guidance at all. Based on these and other studies, Lewin proposed three leadership styles.

The *authoritarian* style is established when the leader makes all the decisions. This person is controlling, directive, and demanding and shares with group members few explanations regarding group activities. The members are not allowed to choose their own courses of action. Roles are precisely assigned to the group members, and a deviation from group norms is punishable. Negative sanctions usually outweigh positive sanctions. Displaying the *democratic* style, the leader makes decisions after consulting with the group. The leader often allows group members to choose their own strategies. The democratic leader tries to share as much information as possible with the group members. Positive and negative sanctions are equally applicable (Lewin, Lippitt, & White, 1939). The third style was called *laissez-faire.* The leader does not try to exercise control over the group and gives group members only general instructions and advice. The group members are then expected to act on their own, choosing their own methods and strategies for actions.

Which of these styles is the most effective? Lewin and his colleagues believed the democratic style to be the best and most effective one. The label "democratic" was chosen for ideological reasons to emphasize the advantages of the democratic society compared to dictatorship. However, despite some obvious advantages, future studies showed that this style cannot always be ranked as the most desirable. For example, in emergency situations, as cross-cultural research has shown, the authoritarian style may be more effective than the other styles (Shiraev & Levy, 2009).

Field Theory and Learning. To be effective, the teacher should understand the situation in the classroom and pay attention to all the elements of the situation, including the subject of the lecture, the preparedness of the students, their motivation, the enthusiasm of the teacher, and so on. Then the teacher can analyze these elements using concepts of the field theory such as position, movement, or psychological forces (Lewin, 1942).

Lewin distinguished at least two types of learning. The first type is a change in knowledge, and it is based on repetition. For example, you study history and memorize important dates. The second type of learning is done by an individual capable of restructuring the situation to understand it better, to solve a new problem, or to achieve a certain goal. This type of learning, as you remember, was labeled as insight. One of the biggest problems associated with repetition, according to Lewin, is that it does not stimulate a person's motivation. A change in knowledge is more effective when students understand why they learn and how to apply this knowledge. Lewin was an active supporter of creative learning because it stimulates a student's motivation.

Lewin supported child-centered education, which places great emphasis on what the child wants to do as compared with what the child is compelled to do by the school curriculum. He believed that compulsory learning does not necessarily stimulate the student's interest in studying. Fear of punishment or relentless repetition can create the opposite reaction: students begin to dislike their education. Only when a student is given an opportunity to understand what and why he or she should study, the effectiveness is much greater.

Learning also depends on the student's mood, which is based on that person's views of the future and the past. The totality of an individual's views of his psychological future and past is called **time perspective**. A child lives in the perspective that includes only the immediate past and future and does not distinguish between hopes and reality, wishes and actual experiences. An adult functions in a different time perspective and thus tends to make more reasonable decisions. Teachers have to help their students to better understand their time perspective. Children living in difficult conditions such as orphanages (where they receive less care than their peers elsewhere) illustrate the difficulty in differentiating their environment, which often results in their slower learning.

A very important component of the learning process is **the level of aspiration**, which is defined as the degree of difficulty of the goal toward which a person is striving. Whether or not a person will become successful is deeply influenced by that person's wish to be so. In most cases, a person's history of successes and failures determines a particular level of aspiration. In turn, they also influence the expectation for the outcome of the future action and increase or decrease the level of aspiration accordingly (Lewin, 1942). On the one hand, good students, in general, tend to keep their level of aspiration slightly above their past achievement. On the other hand, less successful students tend to show excessively high or excessively low levels of aspiration. That is, the poor students have not learned to be realistic in evaluating their past achievements and failures and today's opportunities.

✓ CHECK YOUR KNOWLEDGE

What is topology?

Explain the Zeigarnik effect.

Explain three leadership styles according to Lewin.

Gestalt Psychology and Applied Problems

Gestalt psychologists began to participate in applied research upon their arrival in the United States. The New School for Social Research in New York City had a fund for the scientist victims of Nazi repression in Europe. Wertheimer found employment in this school and remained there until he died. He worked on applying Gestalt principles to learning and education in general. Like Lewin, he was against mechanical memorization, which was widely practiced in schools worldwide at that time. Besides working on educational problems, Lewin studied national educational systems, the use of persuasion in advertisement, the effects of prejudice, interpersonal relations and productivity of work groups, leadership in the workplace, and many other issues. He also worked on changing eating habits among American people to make sure that they ate less traditional but less expensive meat products. He also worked for the Office of Strategic Services on propaganda issues. He founded the Society for Psychological Study of Social Issues (SPSSI) and served as its first president. Lewin advised on work-related conflicts, and he also did research for the military during World War II. He believed in a progressive role of psychology and even suggested using psychological methods to select the best candidates for democratic leadership positions in the government. Levin conducted studies of group effectiveness and productivity, the psychology of rumors, and social perception (the area that examines how people perceive each other and themselves). For training and educational purposes, he established so-called T-groups, or short-term educational programs, a kind of collective training exercise. As members of a T-group, individuals could learn the basic habits of group communication, learn more about other participants and themselves, discuss group goals, and find different ways to improve the group's effectiveness. Such training groups became very popular after the 1950s and are used today in many countries in areas of education and professional training.

Stimulus to Other Psychological Disciplines. General principles of Gestalt psychology served as a theoretical foundation for several developing psychological disciplines. Social psychology was one of them. Lewin, for example, worked on theoretical and experimental aspects of this young discipline. His research of leadership became classical. Ideas of Gestalt psychology also influenced remarkable experimental studies of a Polish-born American psychologist, Solomon Asch, and an Austrian-born psychologist, Fritz Heider (whose work is discussed in Chapter 10).

Gestalt theory had an initial impact on clinical psychology and a theoretical and practical field commonly called in clinical psychology **Gestalt therapy**. One of the founders of this method was Fritz Perls (1883–1970), a German American doctor who left Germany in 1933. His theoretical principles are based on several assumptions based on the classic Gestalt theory. The structure of an individual's experience is a dynamic summary reflecting needs, hopes, strengths, and weaknesses. Both satisfied and unsatisfied needs interact like figures and grounds of perceptual experience. Psychological problems arise when the form and structure of this interaction process is distorted. Another point connecting Gestalt theory to Gestalt therapy is that the latter focuses more on the process of our experience than on its content. The emphasis is on what is being felt at this moment rather than on memories. In other words, Gestalt therapy focuses on a here-and-now method embracing immediate experiences rather than past recollections of other therapeutic methods (Perls, 1968). Overall, Gestalt therapy used only basic principles of Gestalt theory, and the connections between the two are limited to the ideas about the holistic nature of human experience, the disruption of its structure, and the emphasis on the actuality of the moment (Perls, Hefferline, & Goodman, 1951).

✓ CHECK YOUR KNOWLEDGE

What were the major differences between Lewin's research and the studies of Koffka and Köhler?

What is Gestalt therapy?

The Fate of the Gestalt Psychologists

The life and work of Gestalt psychologists represent in the history of psychology a telling case of brutal intrusion of oppressive government—armed by a dangerous ideology—into science and education. To be a scientist, one had to show loyalty to the ruling regime and be of the "right" ethnic or religious background. Is it possible to compare the discrimination against psychologists and other scientists in Germany between 1933 and 1945 and other forms of discrimination based on race, sex, or religion in other parts of the world and at different times?

Attack on Education and Science. We all are aware of examples of restrictions and obstacles that society used to block access to education for different groups of people. In the United States, for example, various formal restrictions and open segregation existed throughout a substantial part of the 20th century. Discriminatory practices of many universities in student admissions and hiring were common (Klingenstein, 1991). Women began to make advances and obtain a measure of equality with men in the first half of the 20th century, even though some private schools continued their policies of gender discrimination. In the 1920s and 1930s, black citizens, Catholics, Asians, and some other ethnic and religious minorities in the United States were not equal in terms of education and employment. In the 1920s, for example, many universities in the United States established quotas limiting the admissions of Jews in undergraduate and graduate programs (Synnott, 1986). Similar prejudice was routinely expressed against non-Protestant and non-white professionals, such as Catholics or blacks (Winston, 1998). Institutional policies and restrictions were reinforced by discriminatory attitudes of some professors. Edmund Boring, a leading psychologist and head of the psychological laboratory at Harvard wrote in his letters to colleagues about several unpleasant "Jewish" traits displayed by of some of his graduate students, which he thought would be unhelpful in their search for employment.

However, discriminatory practices that existed in the United States and other countries should not be equated with the racism and anti-Semitism that flourished in Germany in the 1930s. Fervent, blind racism was an official government policy forced on professors and students. After the Nazi Party claimed political power in Berlin, the government started an official policy of removing people of non-German identity from government and managerial positions, including teaching. Similarly, in the Soviet Union in the 1930s, the government began a policy of "cleansing," which attempted to rid the country of scientists and professors of non-working-class origin. As a rule, after losing their jobs, they were not allowed to leave the country.

Ethnic cleansing was the first major goal of the Nazi government on German campuses. The second major goal was to establish total control over research, lectures, and speeches. Any act of disloyalty was punished. Professors received orders to start every lecture with a Nazi salute: a fully stretched right arm pointing up and forward. Professors, especially those suspected of independent thinking, were required to take a public oath of loyalty to Adolf Hitler. University-based grassroots activists of the Nazi Party were allowed to conduct inspections in search of anti-German activities and to identify "unreliable" professors and students. Public harassments of professors and students became regular. Imagine yourself in that situation for a moment: your school allows some student activists appointed by the dean's office to conduct daily searches of your belongings, lecture notes, and computer files. If the inspector finds some "politically incorrect" notes, you are expelled from school. Furthermore, most probably, you will go to jail. This was exactly what was happening on German campuses after 1933.

One example of a Gestalt psychologist is a lesson in courage. Wolfgang Köhler, a Christian, spoke openly against these Nazi policies. He published a newspaper article in April 1933 criticizing anti-Semitic policy as immoral and barbaric. He stood up for his colleagues whose jobs had been terminated by recent Nazi orders. At that time, he received support from many colleagues and scores of other people. They wrote to him about the dangerous turn Germany was taking and the necessity to resist ideological attack against science and education. However, at that time a growing number of people were afraid to speak publicly. Many professors believed that politics was beneath them and that their responsibility was only research. Köhler, despite his brave efforts, felt increasingly insecure. There were many Nazi sympathizers among his students who regarded his criticisms of the government as treason, and he received death threats.

As detailed earlier, the four main Gestalt psychologists were able to escape death and emigrated from Germany. Their distinguished reputation was helpful in obtaining employment and permanent residence in the United States. They continued their work, teaching, and publications in America. Sadly, many of their colleagues, assistants, and graduate students who remained in Germany did not have the money or the academic reputation to secure employment in North America or other countries. Especially difficult were the lives of the many psychologists of Jewish or non-German descent. After 1933, the government in Germany began the policy of physical extermination of minorities (Henle, 1978).

American Schools. It would be a mistake to assume that universities in the United States were eager to invite foreign guests to work and stay there. In the 1930s, America was going through a tough period of severe economic depression. With state universities' budgets slashed and private endowments dwindling, most schools didn't have enough funds to support their own faculty and to maintain research facilities. Jewish immigrants arriving from Europe were not necessarily receiving a universally warm welcome. Many Americans continued to maintain prejudiced views of Jews as a group, attributing to them many negative personality traits. Early scientific polls conducted in the 1930s show that such prejudice was widespread and typical for a majority of Americans (Shapiro, 1992).

And yet many American private and state schools, together with the federal government in Washington, D.C., did a lot to help German scientists and those from other countries to escape genocide in Europe. Livingston Farrand, president of Cornell University, became chairman of the Emergency Committee in Aid of Displaced German Scholars and Scientists. As a result of this committee's work, many European scientists, including world renowned physicists Enrico Fermi and Albert Einstein, immigrated to the United States. One of many professors who received help from this committee was Kurt Lewin, who secured a two-year faculty appointment at Cornell University. He also received help from the Ford Foundation to develop his research programs in this country.

It is always important to realize that every psychologist is a unique individual with certain weaknesses and strengths, a personal history of relationships, academic rivalries, agreements and disagreements, endorsements, victories, and defeats. Not every Gestalt psychologist was embraced in America. Wertheimer and Koffka were often seen as "show-offs," and their behavior was seen by some as an example of academic snobbery and pretentiousness. Indeed, many German professors adopted a traditional style of academic overconfidence. Gestalt psychologists, unfortunately, were frequently perceived of as arrogant. Many American psychologists thought that their famous German counterparts tried to teach everyone how to understand "true" psychology. We shouldn't forget also that English was the second language for the newly arrived German professors, who, except Koffka, had to go through the difficult process of learning and advancing their oral skills (Ringer, 1969).

Some Americans believed that Gestalt psychologists such as Köhler paid too much attention to impressive demonstrations rather than psychological research. A mutual dislike between Harvard professor Boring and Köhler was an important personal factor that certainly affected the history of psychology. The German believed that as a research professor at Harvard, he should not have a heavy teaching workload: in Germany professors didn't teach as many classes per semester as Americans did. Boring, in turn, felt that Köhler was not as effective a scientist as he had been a few years ago (Sokal, 1984).

The success of Kurt Lewin in the United States is a contrasting example. His sparkling temperament, relentless enthusiasm, interpersonal charm, and generous attitude toward his students played a positive role in his growing popularity. He remained humble and appreciative even with those who disagreed with his views. Lewin was very informal with students, was frequently spotted with them in coffee shops, and invited them to his home for discussion. He was approachable and easy in his relationships with his colleagues. As some joked, he did not appear to them as a "classic" German professor: formal, dry, and incomprehensible.

Assessments

Some psychologists have compared Gestalt theory to a bright meteor lighting up the "dim sky of the perceptual theory" (Helson, 1973, p. 74). If we put aside metaphors, what place does Gestalt psychology occupy in psychology's history? What did it accomplish in the first half of the 20th century? Köhler (1959) was a bit pessimistic about the impact of Gestalt psychology on American and world psychology. Others, such as Boring (1929), believed that Gestalt psychology was very successful because it later became a natural part of psychology as a universal discipline.

Born in Germany, the Gestalt movement was rooted in a deep cultural and educational tradition of German universities. The tradition encouraged scientists to embrace theories, unifying principles, and general hypotheses and to work on empirical facts to prove and disprove such theories. Traditional experimental psychology with its theoretical arsenal could not satisfy the academic curiosity of a younger generation of psychologists. Wertheimer, Köhler, and Koffka initially formed a close-knit group with a large number of students, associates, and supporters. They possessed courage, determination, and creative thinking.

Holism as a Principle. Gestalt psychology is forever associated with the principle of holism. Although William James in the United States, Christian von Ehrenfels in Germany, and a few others had written about the qualities of the "wholes" before Wertheimer, he put the concept of wholeness in the center of his theoretical project. Other theorists and experimenters talked about the important of wholeness, unity, and totality. But Gestalt psychologists emphasized it as a central theme and studied it experimentally.

Interest in the Momentum. Gestalt psychology emphasized the importance of the present situation in all forms of psychological analysis. They paid attention to the forces and processes that are acting here and now. The actuality of the present was the major emphasis of their theoretical and experimental work. It was an innovative approach. Focus on "now" was a challenge to psychological doctrines, such as psychoanalysis, that focused on past experiences (Lewin, 1943).

Gestalt psychologists, of course, immediately exposed their views to criticism for not giving enough attention to people's past and future. Critics pointed out that Gestalt psychologists all but ignored an individual history and, unlike psychoanalysis, paid little attention to developmental issues. Although Lewin argued that the past as well as the future are already incorporated in the psychological field of "now," this particular weakness of Gestalt psychology was obvious.

Relations With Behaviorism. Gestalt psychology, unlike the fields that studied the elements of experience, welcomed behavioral data as valuable facts (Köhler, 1959). It complemented popular behaviorist orientation, which focused on behavior and reflexes occurring in the experimental lab. In fact, Gestalt psychology helped to soften criticism against behaviorists often accused of eliminating the issue of subjectivity from psychological research. Conversely, inspired by some findings of

Gestalt psychology, behavioral psychologists began to use the concept of purpose in their studies of problem solving (see Chapter 11).

On the one hand, Köhler's studies on animal learning were critical of behavioral concepts related to trial-and-error learning techniques. On the other hand, the concept of insight did not destroy the essence of the behavioral approach to learning. For instance, insight could have been interpreted as a rapid drop in a learning curve or as an animal's quick acquisition of a direct path to a goal.

Scientific Appeal. Gestalt psychology had its roots in experimentation, which certainly set it apart from other theoretical approaches. Köhler, for example, had a strong educational background in physics. As a student of the renowned, world-class physicist Max Planck, Köhler believed that physics contains the most important answers for biology. Furthermore, together with physiology, biology should enlighten psychology. The experimental foundation was easily accepted by many psychologists of the functionalist and experimental orientation (Köhler, 1959).

Although Gestalt psychology originates in the studies of perception, the founders of Gestalt theory hoped to expand their research further and apply it to various aspects of human life (Wertheimer, 1912/1961). Koffka believed that human beings, as well as all living organisms, are subject to the law of order. Everything functions in a particular direction and under a particular organization (Koffka, 1922). Once some major principles related to perception had been revealed, similar principles would prove to be relevant to other parts, such as memory, learning, thinking, and motivation. Lewin advanced the main principles of Gestalt psychology; applied them to the study of motivation, personality, and social psychology; and brought Gestalt psychology into the mainstream of psychological theory (Ash, 1992). Gestalt psychology was the first and is still the only coherent psychological theory to use physical fields as a working analogy. Lewin (1948) always liked to use analogies from the natural sciences, comparing, for example, the ground to a cultural environment and a figure to a subject of study.

However, later, as critics mentioned, Gestalt psychologists began to pay less attention to rigorous experimentation and to focus on theory and demonstrations. This, as critics maintained, certainly would be very nice for a popular lecture course but was not enough for a rigorous scientific discussion (Boring, 1929).

Cross-Cultural Validity. Gestalt psychologists—and this view was largely shared among supporters of functionalism in psychology—were aware that psychological studies should not be conducted in the isolated, sterile environment of a psychological lab. Emphasizing values, psychologists called for greater attention to important psychological factors such as interactions between an experimenter and a subject, existence of group goals, and social values affecting behavior. A major emphasis of Gestalt psychologists on the holistic universality of human experience and behavior led them to pay attention to various social factors affecting psychological research. Gestalt psychologists were aware of the cultural applicability of their studies. Specifically, Lewin was certain that an experimental result of a study of a child's behavior in New York City would be quite different from a similar experiment conducted with a different child living in a European city, not only because the two children were different but also because of the different social and cultural circumstances of their lives (Lewin, 1931). Overall, however, many studies conducted in the 1960s and later have shown that major Gestalt principles of perception appear valid in various cultural settings. Of course, the way our individual perception works is based on our age, physical and environmental conditions, education, lifestyle, and access to information. However, with several environmental conditions equal (e.g., educational level), the major characteristics of perception show a remarkable cross-cultural consistency. Many reading patterns, depth perception, perception of forms and shapes, and susceptibility to visual illusions remain relatively consistent across various ethnic, religious, and national groups (Shiraev & Levy, 2009).

✓ **CHECK YOUR KNOWLEDGE**

Explain holism as a major Gestalt principle.

What was a general view of Gestalt psychology toward behaviorism?

Conclusion

Gestalt psychology played an important role in the development of psychology. It was based on holistic assumptions, the natural science approach, and theoretical rigor (Ash, 1992). It was a theoretical field at the beginning, which changed gradually over the years due to evolving research interests, social circumstances, and social climate. The American period gave Gestalt psychology an opportunity to apply theory to practice. Since the 1920s, many psychologists in Japan also used the principles of Gestalt psychology (Sato & Graham, 1954), which had gradually lost its exclusive identification with Germany. Gestalt psychology became part of the mainstream psychology in the United States and in many other countries. Soon Gestalt theory lost its unique face as a distinguished field of psychology.

Lewin once wrote that the history of new theories frequently shows one similar trend. At first, the new idea is treated as pure nonsense. Then comes a time when more people begin to pay attention to the theory and specific objections or criticisms emerge. Finally, in the next stage, many scientists begin to claim that they had always accepted this theory. This usually marks the last state before general acceptance of that theory (Lewin, 1943). Gestalt psychology shared a similar fate. By the mid-20th century, the discussion about the main principles of Gestalt psychology had reached a point of their general acceptance.

If psychology were music, Gestalt psychology would have been jazz.

Summary

- During the economic and social recovery after the Great War, psychology as a discipline developed in some countries but suffered setbacks in others. In the Soviet

Union, the official ideology deemed psychology unscientific. In Germany in the 1930s, psychology had been increasingly influenced by Nazi ideology, which was a mixture of nationalism and racism. Key founders of Gestalt psychology lived in Germany but were forced to immigrate to the United States.

- The principle of holism is the foundation of Gestalt psychology. From a philosophical standpoint, holism in psychology was a logical continuation of a scientific tradition cultivated in German universities. Gestalt psychologists challenged a mechanistic, detached approach to scientific facts.

- The early studies of perception were associated with the names of Wertheimer and Koffka, who developed the key principles of Gestalt psychology. Their approach was a serious departure from traditional approaches defending elementary and association views. They introduced forms, perceptual groupings, and constellations in contrast to elements or static experiences. Köhler focused on thinking and decision making. He introduced and studied the concept of insight, an innovative model of learning.

- Earlier studies in Gestalt psychology focused on perception and thinking processes. In the 1920s and later, more specialists turned to the area of group behavior and the interdependence of the individual and the group. Lewin in his field theory combined the principles of Gestalt psychology, geometry, and topology. He also was the first to study leadership styles.

- After the 1930s, most psychologists had accepted postulates and unifying ideas first proposed by Gestalt psychologists about the importance of context; the interconnectedness of the elements of experience; the role of goal-directed behavior and purpose; and the understanding of an organism as a wholeness of interconnected functions, goals, and histories. The holistic principles of Gestalt psychology eventually became the mainstream principles of academic and applied psychology.

- It is an increasingly accepted view today that a person, either young or mature, develops in a complex and interconnected world. Psychologists began to pay serious attention, and continue to do so, to the creative interaction between biological and social factors shaping an individual's behavior and mind.

- The life and work of Gestalt psychologists also represent in the history of psychology a telling case of brutal intrusion of oppressive government—armed by a dangerous ideology—into science and education.

Key Terms

Field theory	Insight	Reversible figures
Force field analysis	Isomorphism	Time perspective
Gestalt laws	Leadership style	Topology
Gestalt therapy	Level of aspiration	Transposition
Hodological space	Phi-phenomenon	Unfinished actions

10

Theoretical and Applied Psychology After the Great War

Knowing reality means constructing systems of transformations that correspond, more or less adequately, to reality.

Jean Piaget

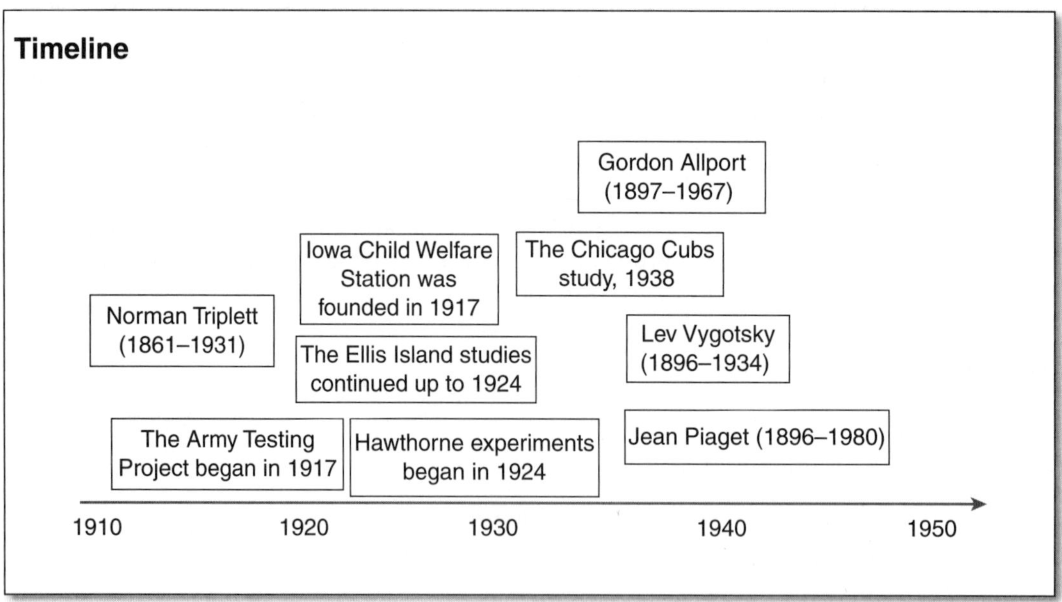

CHAPTER OUTLINE

After the United States entered World War I in 1917, the American Psychological Association (APA) established a special committee of prominent psychologists, including Edward Thorndike, John Watson, G. Stanley Hall, and Robert Yerkes, to discuss American psychologists' contribution to their country's war effort. Of course, by that time, many psychologists had been drafted and joined a 4 million-strong army. But the leading psychologists also believed that they, along with their civilian colleagues, could contribute to their country as researchers. One of the areas that they thought could have immediate impact was individual skill evaluation and personnel training.

Yerkes, president of the APA in 1917, cofounded and joined—together with well-known psychologists at that time, Terman, Thorndike, and Scott—the Committee on the Classification of Personnel in the Army. He took charge of a specially organized group of 40 psychologists to create a test to evaluate mental skills of the new Army recruits and active servicemen. On the basis of this test's measurements, the psychologists wanted to create categories of the recruits according to their mental abilities. Next, based on these categories, the scientists wanted to select and recommend the most capable individuals to serve in more advanced positions of responsibility and for future promotion (Yerkes, 1921). By the end of 1917, the government gave the permission to test all newly enlisted individuals in the U.S. Army. A psychological service specially organized for this purpose involved more than 400 people.

The Army Testing Project demonstrated that psychology was gaining strength and reputation as an academic discipline and applied field. Psychologists believed that they could offer practical recommendations based on research. Was the society ready to accept this professional advice?

In three previous chapters, we discussed how behaviorism, psychoanalysis, and Gestalt psychology shaped the emerging 20th-century psychology. But what was the state of theoretical and applied studies beyond these three main schools? This chapter will examine the general state of academic psychology in the first half of the past century. In terms of history, as you remember from Chapter 9, this period extends between the two world wars and during the period of economic and social instability of the 1920s and 1930s.

Society and Psychology

Before World War I, West European psychology played a leading role in the world as a theoretical, academic, and, in many respects, applied field. Full-time academic research before World War I had already been a rapidly growing new profession. Germany by 1913 had six times as many full-time researchers per capita as did the United States (Clifford, 1968). The postwar developments beginning in the early 1920s have changed this balance of scholarly power in favor of the United States.

America's influence. The number and size of colleges and universities in the United States grew rapidly (Rudolph, 1990). Many of them established and developed new psychology programs. The number of university-based departments of psychology in the United States had reached 34 by the end of 1914 and continued to increase steadily through the 1920s. By the 1930s, North America began to play a major role in world science due to at least three interconnected developments. Similar factors explain why the universities in the United States and Canada became growing centers of world psychology.

The first reason was economic. Unlike in Europe, there had been no military battles on American soil. At the same time, government's military spending boosted the development of many war-related industries and stimulated employment. The education and research—despite economic ups and downs—continued during the war with only insignificant interruptions. In contrast, the economic and social disruption in countries such as Germany, France, Russia, and Austria was considerable. After the 1920s, facing enormous challenges at home, many students and scientists in Europe and other parts of the world considered the United States or Canada as desirable places to live, study, and work. Gestalt psychology, as you remember, had its academic roots in Germany but blossomed in the United States.

The second reason was social. Governments of several countries increased their pressure on universities, forcing them, as it happened in the Soviet Union, Italy, Germany, and Spain, to become obedient institutions of the establishment. The official policy of anti-Semitism in Germany and Austria, as you remember from Chapter 9, forced many professionals to leave these countries. North America offered academic freedom and resources.

Third, despite economic difficulties of the Great Depression, the policies of the New Deal together with the tremendous efforts of millions of Americans had preserved the great standards of America's higher education in the 1930s. Psychological research continued.

Social Climate and Psychology

Some researchers remained disillusioned about the ability of humankind for self-improvement. However, many progressive ideas remained strong. They were based on an assumption that science could provide recipes about how to improve individuals and society.

In the 1920s, some psychology professionals turned their attention to **mental hygiene.** This first was a theoretical discipline and professional movement involving health care professionals, social activists, and charitable organizations. Their goal was to push for social innovations and healthy work conditions in a new atmosphere free from excessive stress, abuse, or discrimination. As a result, teachers would teach better, children learn faster, and workers produce more. Overall, the goal of mental hygiene was to create better conditions for the developing, working, and learning individual (Petrina, 2001). Progressive ideas also led to different types of initiatives.

Many people at that time believed that society could be bettered if it rid itself of "unacceptable" individuals. Research promoting social selection was well accepted. Eugenics and other ideas of genetic selection remained popular. Although some saw it as a discriminatory theory, others thought that, if applied correctly, eugenics should help in crime reduction, grade improvements in schools, and industrial work productivity. Increasingly often, criminal behavior and some behavioral problems such as violence, sexual deviance, and alcoholism were considered issues requiring medical treatment.

Further medicalization of deviance. Deviance stands for behavior that violates culturally established norms. In 1937, the Gallup Organization, a leading U.S. polling company, asked Americans about deviant behavior. Researchers wanted to know what people thought about societal deviance and how to address it. In one survey, 84 percent of Americans favored sterilization of "habitual criminals" and the "hopelessly insane" ("What America Thought in 1937," January 3, 1938). These responses reflected the popularity of beliefs in medical causes of certain behaviors. In a similar fashion, sexual problems, dysfunctions, and deviations from societal norms frequently were interpreted as medical issues. Many forms of sexual behavior received a clear medical-psychological evaluation and categorization. One of the main topics of research was homosexuality. The work of neurologist John Meaghers (1929) summarized the growing consensus among psychologists and psychiatrists about the "normal" nature of heterosexual behavior. On the other hand, professionals viewed homosexuality as largely pathological and requiring treatment. It is important to mention that most studies of sexuality were concerned primarily with male sexual behavior, and attention to female sexuality was insignificant until the 1940s (Spurlock, 2002). The lack of attention to gender studies reflected a global trend of continuing social exclusion of women and other groups.

Social Exclusion. Although the participation of women in American psychology after the 1920s was increasing, most women choosing a career in psychology faced significant obstacles. One was based on tradition. Many young women had to make choices between college education and marriage or between pursuing an advanced degree and academic career, on one hand, and having children on the other (men typically didn't face such a challenge). The second obstacle was a widespread gender prejudice in the workplace. Many employers did not hire women to teaching and research positions out of the belief that women would not dedicate themselves to work as much as men, who do not have to take care of their children and homes. The third obstacle was a relatively common practice to allocate women to assisting positions within applied psychology rather than to achieve the more prestigious academic appointments. Such obstacles reflected the long-lasting social belief about gender roles and responsibilities related to work and family.

Despite these social obstacles, women in the American Psychological Association (APA) in 1917 comprised 13 percent of its membership, a higher percentage than in any other American scientific society. Comparable figures for the British Psychological Society show that in 1921, women comprised 31 percent of the membership and 37 percent 20 years later (Wilson, 2003). By 1928, almost one third of the APA members were women. It took less than one hundred years from the inception of the APA when women members finally outnumbered men (see Table 10.1).

Table 10.1 Proportion of Women Members in the American Psychological Association

	Year				
	1917	1923	1928	1938	2005
Proportion (%)	13	18	34	30	53

Source: Wilson (2003); American Psychological Association (2009)

Universities across the world continued discriminatory practices based on race, ethnicity, and religion. You have read in Chapter 9 about the discriminatory practices in Nazi Germany and Soviet Union. In other countries, discriminatory practices against minorities were more subtle but still common. In North America, as you remember, it was an ordinary practice for professors to mention in their recommendation letters their students' ethnic, religious, or racial background. Such remarks were supposed to explain that a student might have some imbedded "weaknesses" associated with their origin. Many educated people continued to believe that the human races are fundamentally different and that equality among the races and ethnic groups was unachievable (Sawyer, 2000).

African American colleges were in most cases the only opportunity for Black students to study psychology because quite many schools at the time still practiced racial segregation (B. Holliday, 2009). Few African Americans were getting their college degrees in psychology at that time. The case of Francis Cecil Sumner (1895–1954) is exceptional. He was the first African American to obtain a PhD in psychology in 1920. A 24-year-old man, already a war veteran, he defended his dissertation, titled *Psychoanalysis of Freud and Adler,* at Clark University before the committee of several prominent psychologists, including G. Stanley Hall and Edwin Boring (Sumner, 1920). After graduation, Sumner had a long and successful career in psychology.

CASE IN POINT

Francis Cecil Sumner (1895–1954). As a boy, Sumner attended elementary schools in Virginia, New Jersey, and the District of Columbia. He was also homeschooled by his father. He enrolled at Lincoln University in Chester County, Pennsylvania, and finished as a valedictorian at the age of 19 with a B.A. degree with special honors in English, modern languages, and Greek. After receiving his second undergraduate degree from Clark University, Sumner appealed directly to G. Stanley Hall, then president of Clark, seeking graduate admission. He was accepted to study for a PhD in psychology (despite protests of some faculty not willing to admit a "colored man" as a graduate student).

Francis C. Sumner was the first African American to receive a Ph.D. in psychology in 1920. He was only 24 years old.

After serving in the military, Sumner was finally awarded a PhD in 1920. Following graduation, he was working as a professor for several schools and conducted research in the fields of education and educational psychology before accepting a position at Howard University in Washington, D.C., in 1928. One of his tasks was to start and develop a department of psychology there. As a result of his and his colleagues' lifelong efforts, Howard University became a supreme school providing education for African American and other minority students. The department of psychology at Howard University began to offer the PhD degree in psychology after 1972. By that time, about 300 African Americans had earned doctorate degrees in psychology from U.S. colleges and universities.

Source: Sawyer (2000); Bayton (1975)

Overall, despite some improvements, psychology in leading industrial countries continued to have a problem with diversity. Significant changes in this field began to occur only by the 1960s.

The State of Research

The multiplicity of views within psychology was spectacular. Students taking university psychology courses in universities in the 1920s–1930s learned about the "classical" experiments in psychophysics, intellectual searches of structuralists, and remarkable studies of child psychologists. The behaviorist orientation, because of its focus on measurement, was finding many supporters across the world. Psychoanalysis was acquiring its leading role in clinical psychology and making serious attempts to influence general psychological theory. Gestalt psychology was attractive and impressive because of its clear experimental orientation and solid intellectual background.

The debates about the nature of psychology continued. Some psychologists were inspired by quantitative research and wanted to see their discipline based exclusively on measurement. Others argued that without a coherent theory and qualitative studies, all measurements were fruitless. Some believed that psychology's future success must be rooted exclusively in biology and physiology. Others focused primarily on social factors shaping human behavior and the inner world. Scores of new psychology journals appeared (see Table 10.2). The continuous debates about psychology's role and method were so intense that some eyewitnesses described psychology's status in the 1930s as chaos (Hull, 1935; Jastrow, 1935). As a reaction to this perceived confusion, there were numerous calls to "unify" psychology under some guiding principle. This unified psychology would combine the study of both behavior and mind and would pay equally careful attention to biological and social factors influencing human behavior and experience (Dewsbury, 2002).

Table 10.2 A Sample of Professional Psychological Journals in the Early 1920s

Title	*Brief Description*
Journal of Experimental Psychology	Founded by John Watson in 1916. Focus: experimental research. Publishing was suspended after America joined the war. Continued in 1920.
Psychological Review	Focus: a wide range of theoretical articles and discussions.
Journal of Delinquency	Founded in 1916. Dedicated to studies of social behavior.
Psychobiology	Founded in 1917. Focus: an intersection between psychology and the biological sciences.
Journal of Applied Psychology	Dedicated to "psychotechnology" (the term used frequently one hundred years ago).
Schweizer Archiv für Neurologie und Psychiatrie	Founded in 1917 in Switzerland. Focus: mental illness, its diagnoses, and treatment.
Mental Hygiene	Founded in 1918. Focus: psychopathology, prevention, and treatment of mental illness.
Revista de Psiquiatria y Disciplinas Conexas	Founded in 1918 in Lima, Peru. Focus: discussion of psychoanalysis.

Title	*Brief Description*
Journal of Comparative Psychology	Focus: studies of mental function and behavior in any organism.
Archivio Italiano di Psicologia	Founded in 1919 in Italy. Dedicated to a wide range of research in psychology.
Japanese Journal of Psychology	Founded in 1926 in Japan. Dedicated to a wide range of research in psychology.
Journal of Abnormal Psychology and Social Psychology	In 1921, the *Journal of Abnormal Psychology* widened its research interests under the new title.
American Journal of Psychiatry	Changed its title in 1921 from the *American Journal of Insanity.* The change indicated the journal's new, broader vision on psychopathology.
Revue Metapsychique and Psychologische Forschung	Founded in 1921 in Germany under direction of Kurt Koffka. Dedicated to theoretical issues in psychology.
Psychologische Studien	Once influential journal directed by Wilhelm Wundt published its final volume in 1918.

Source: Griffith (1922).

Psychology Departments. Despite war-related interruptions, universities were open in most countries. A postwar educational boom affected psychology in a positive way. First, psychology laboratories and departments began to appear in a growing number of countries. Around the world, national governments were major sponsors of higher education and research. The direction of psychological research was determined mostly by the interests of their founders and early contributors. Most of them studied from the pioneers of European and American psychology.

In Romania, for example, an independent academic program in psychology was established in 1922 by Florian Ştefănescu-Goangă. He studied experimental psychology in Leipzig and focused on intelligence testing (David et al., 2002). The first psychology department in Australia was organized in 1921 (Taft & Day, 1988).

Chinese scholars turned to psychological studies of the "Western" type later than in many other countries. Historically, scholars there used Chinese philosophy to understand and explain human behavior and experience. Early Chinese psychology was heavily influenced by Japanese scholars. Gradually, the interests of Chinese scientists shifted toward psychological studies conducted in Germany and the United

States. Translations of texts in English and German began to appear in Chinese (Higgins & Zheng, 2002; Kodama, 1991). Some students could afford to travel to North America to study. In 1917, Peking University established China's first psychological laboratory. The Nanjing Higher Normal College opened the country's first department of psychology in 1920. A year later, the Chinese Psychological Society was founded and an academic peer-reviewed journal established (J. Blowers, 2000). Psychology's development was unfortunately interrupted in the 1930s when the boiling conflict with Japan had turned into the largest and most destructive war in Asia in the 20th century. In India, Calcutta University had its own department of psychology in 1915, although it was within the philosophy division (Pandey, 1969). About the same time, psychology departments began to appear in Pakistan (Heckel & Paramesh, 1974, p. 37). However, the main orientation of psychology in both India and Pakistan was mostly theoretical and philosophical, borrowing heavily from Western sources (Zaidi, 1959).

In France, as you remember from Chapter 6, clinical psychology was traditionally strong. Experimental studies of intelligence and theoretical work on personality theory brought a solid reputation to French psychologists. Influence of anthropology and history was remarkable. For example, Ignace Meyerson (1888–1983), an immigrant from Poland, developed historical psychology focusing on people's collective representations, memories, and images (Parot, 2000). Anthropological studies of language, thinking, and culture of indigenous people by French scientists Lucien Lévy-Brühl (1857–1939) and Claude Lévi-Strauss (1908–2009) have had a tremendous impact on psychology of the 20th century, especially on its cross-cultural and developmental branches. Another Polish immigrant, Waclaw Radecki (1887–1953), founded the first psychological laboratory in Brazil in 1923 and sparked the development of psychological research in that country. Some of his research was dedicated to selection of military pilots (Ardila, 1968, p. 567).

In Canada, the psychology program at the University of Toronto, led by Edward Bott, was the first program institutionally independent from philosophy (remember the case of James Baldwin from Chapter 4). In 1939, Bott became one of the founding members of the Canadian Psychological Association and its first president. During the first half of the 20th century, many Canadian psychologists embraced the principles of functionalism and holism, focusing largely on developmental aspects of human psychology. Clinical observations and longitudinal studies in real-life conditions received special attention. Contemporaries remember that both the faculty and students studying psychology at the University of Toronto shared an optimistic and progressive view of psychology: as a discipline, it could change society and improve the lives of individuals (Pols, 2002; Wright, 2002).

Experimental psychological research was burgeoning worldwide. Although many universities created psychological laboratories, experimentation at that time was in many ways a solitary enterprise. Typically, a professor would propose and then build an experiment. He or she would suggest, design, order, or assemble the necessary equipment. Then the professor would find, schedule, and run the subjects. Most of them were students. After collecting data, the professor would analyze and describe them and write a paper or report for publication (Hardcastle, 2000). A group of anonymous professors (peer reviewers) would read this paper and then recommend it or not for publication. This was becoming a standard international practice for most research publications. In clinical research, Ronald Fisher's publication of *The Design of Experiments* (1935/1971) was pivotal in terms organizing research around clinical trials. The concept of placebo control was introduced at that time to make sure that prior knowledge, expectation, vested interest, or other psychological issues did not affect the experimental procedure (Wampold & Bhati, 2004).

One of the most common methods of research in psychology remained testing. This method was also used for a variety of applied projects.

✓ CHECK YOUR KNOWLEDGE

What is medicalization of deviance?

Name at least three obstacles that American women choosing a career in psychology faced in the 1920s.

Psychological Testing

Psychologists believed that their discipline could offer scientific solutions to social problems. Psychological testing was a field of research where psychologists believed that they could evaluate, select, and train people for various purposes ranging from education to sports and business to manufacturing. Of all kinds of testing, research of mental abilities continued to attract attention of psychologists and their sponsors in government and private business. Measurement of mental abilities—the ways people solved problems presented in tests—appeared to many a legitimate and effective method serving an important medical and social function: to select people in categories according to their skills and potentials. In several European countries and North America, individual intelligence examinations had become a standard component of social policy in the first quarter of the 20th century (Petrina, 2001). The principles of mental hygiene also called for testing because it, as some enthusiasts expected, would eventually help society to solve the problem of crime and poverty (White, 2000). Scientific curiosity, progressive beliefs, and professional confidence guided many psychologists working on intelligence tests. Few of them expected to face significant difficulties in interpreting these tests' results.

The following cases should illustrate psychologists' genuine efforts, accomplishments, and setbacks in three fields of testing: military personnel, immigrants, and children.

The Army Testing Project

As you remember from the opening vignette, in 1917, a group of prominent American psychologists applied for and received permission to test all newly enlisted individuals in the U.S. Army. Especially organized for this purpose, psychological service began its work immediately. Psychologists developed two major tests: the **Army Alpha** for literate groups and the **Army Beta** for those who were illiterate, had very poor English written skills, or were non-English speakers, which overall were 40 percent of the recruits tested. Each test included several subtests. The Alpha test contained eight subtests on analogies, questions on everyday judgments, understanding of directions given, simple arithmetic problems, and so on. The Beta test included picture completion, drawing, and symbol recognition. The Beta test was also given to those who performed poorly on the Alpha test. Either one had to be administered in groups and should have taken no more than an hour. Overall, by the end of the war, more than 1,700,000 people had been tested. It was a project of previously unmatched proportions.

At least two problems appeared immediately. The first one was the implementation or practical use of the psychologists' findings. The existing military regulations and procedures did not allow the Army commanders to make decisions based solely on recommendations from psychologists. If a recruit, for example, was found to have exceptional analytical skills, neither psychologists nor supervising officers had the power to send that individual to work for the Army's headquarters. Similarly, psychologists could not keep that person off the battlefield simply because his IQ was too high. An ethical side of the problem also emerged: psychology tests could discriminate against people with low scores. The second problem was related to professional responsibility of military commanders. Many of them probably appreciated the testing work of psychologists. However, very few officers would agree to follow the recommendations of nonmilitary professionals, especially in the areas of promotion or placement. "Thanks, but no thanks" was a typical response of many military commanders, business managers, and educational officials regarding psychologists' recommendations. Today, psychologists often face similar problems in the workplace because many professionals in their areas believe that they are more competent than psychologists to make important decisions related to promotion, placement, or other personnel-related issues.

Overall, the results of the Army Testing Project did not bring significant changes to the way the military selected and placed its recruits. However, tests became an important supplementary source of assessment in schools and businesses. Tests were used to select, evaluate, and categorize students, jobseekers, applicants, and professionals. Public and private schools began to purchase intelligence tests and hire trained specialists to administer those tests among millions of schoolchildren. The result of the Army Testing Project also revealed several remarkable findings. One of them was the tremendous disparity in test scores among various groups of people.

Test Score Disparities. The project revealed that the average mental age of the Army recruits at that time was approximately 13 years, which was considered 2 years lower than the expected average mental age of the White adult population of the United States. Some attributed such results to insufficiency of the testing procedures. There were also those who believed that the test results revealed the gap between two distinct groups of American people: educated professionals and the uneducated from lower-middle-class and lower-class families. Yet others maintain that the project revealed the overall ineffectiveness of the American educational system.

The testing of Army recruits also showed that Blacks, Hispanics, and recent immigrants from Eastern and Southern Europe—as groups—scored significantly lower than other recruits. People from poor backgrounds also scored significantly lower compared to middle-class individuals. These comparisons prompted a heated discussion about the origins of such differences. Some believed that the differences were inherited, and therefore society had to accept the gap between the advanced and the less advanced. Others refused to accept the notion of the biological roots of intelligence and insisted that the differences in intelligence test scores are caused by disparities in education, differences in upbringing, and access to resources.

There were also serious debates about the validity of mental tests. Some psychologists insisted that intelligence could not be properly measured by a paper-and-pencil test, and a brief assessment could not measure and predict a person's ability to succeed in life (Lippmann, 1923). Intelligence has many forms and should be measured by more comprehensive methods. There was also an apparent cultural bias: White middle-class individuals were simply more familiar with the questions asked, and therefore their success had been already predetermined by their knowledge and experience. Other specialists turned to the results obtained from another large group of Army recruits: recent immigrants.

The Ellis Island Studies

By 1910, more than 20 percent of the American population was foreign born. In the beginning of the 20th century, the "traditional" wave of immigrants to the United States from Great Britain, Germany, and Ireland was strengthened by millions of individuals from Europe, including Italy and Greece, Poland, Hungary, Czechoslovakia, the Baltic regions, Ukraine, and Russia. Cheaper transatlantic fares resulted in approximately 10,000 new people arriving to the United States daily. Like today, one hundred years ago, Americans expressed different views about immigration. Although the general positive impact of immigration was acknowledged, many still believed that immigration had to be regulated. As a practical matter, some wanted to limit immigration of certain individuals. Many people believed that individuals with particular illnesses or deficient mental skills should not enter America. An 1882 immigration law excluded any potential immigrant who was "likely to become a public charge," and from 1907 onward, medical evidence could be cited to support immigration restrictions. Congress explicitly referred to "imbeciles" and the "feebleminded" as people who should be excluded from admission to the United States (Yew, 1980). Moreover, the U.S. Immigration Restriction Act of 1924 greatly restricted the entry of non-White persons. Special immigration stations were created to register the arriving immigrants and check their health. One such station was Ellis Island, near New York City.

CASE IN POINT

Ellis Island. The immigration station at Ellis Island was opened in 1892 to serve New York Harbor. The Department of Commerce and Labor was making decisions on the admission of immigrants, and special physicians appointed by the government advised the department. Potential immigrants traveling in first and second class received a brief examination on board ship in their cabins, but those traveling in third class were taken by ferry to Ellis Island to receive a more detailed inspection and questioning. Because of the numbers of people to be examined, the primary form of assessment was a line inspection, from which only selected individuals were detained for additional individual examination.

A particular issue with which the physicians at Ellis Island had to contend was the identification of "mental deficiency" (what today would be described as *developmental disability*). Three assumptions were commonly held at the time. First, the mentally deficient individuals were mostly responsible for social problems. Second, the mentally deficient could endanger the biological fitness of the nation. Third, immigrants from Southern, Central, and Eastern Europe contain high proportions of the mentally deficient. These beliefs led to political pressure to restrict immigration and mentally defective people from entering the country.

The station was functioning for almost 30 years. In 1924, Congress determined that the responsibility for screening potential immigrants would be delegated to the U.S. embassies or consulates overseas. The facilities at Ellis Island continued to be used as a detention center for deportees, but in 1954 they were closed completely. The Ellis Island Immigration Museum was opened in 1990. The current displays include examples of mental tests loaned by the Archives of the History of American Psychology at the University of Akron, Ohio.

Source: Richardson (2003).

In response to public alarm that the physicians at Ellis Island were failing to prevent mentally retarded people from entering the country, immigration officials turned to psychologists for help. The officials needed a simple but reliable method to identify the "mentally deficient." Henry Goddard (see also Chapters 5 and 6) believed that the Binet test, which he had translated from French, could be used to test the arriving immigrants (Zenderland, 1998). Howard A. Knox, an assistant surgeon at the immigration station, agreed and assembled a collection of tests, including the Binet test, a geometry test, and a test on knowledge of everyday issues. Each candidate for testing was selected from a sample of newly arrived. Most individuals taking the exams used the help of interpreters (Knox, 1913). What were the results of the testing? As an example, in 1913, on the basis of test results, more than 500 people had been deported from the United States as mentally defective. This represented a threefold increase in comparison with the number of people excluded in the 5 previous years without testing (Richardson, 2003).

The Significance of the Ellis Island Testing. It is important to underline at least two points of evaluation. First, researchers and practitioners as well as the general public believed that human intelligence was biologically determined and that mentally retarded people threatened society economically (through the costs of their institutionalization) and biologically (through their genetic impact on their offspring). Knox (1915) wrote in an article published in *Scientific American* that such selective screenings of immigrants were necessary for the country. Many prominent psychologists of that time, including Goddard, Woodworth, Cattell, and Yerkes, were active and enthusiastic contributors to the eugenics movement. Physicians and psychologists appeared as careful guardians of the nation's "purity." That was the prevailing social climate of the time.

The second point refers to the methodology of psychological research and its validity. In the 1920s, a growing number of psychologists began to realize the problem of the uncritical acceptance of psychological testing. The critics of the testing on Ellis Island believed that many people who had been identified there as mentally retarded could have been essentially normal. First, the critics objected to the idea of screening adult immigrants using tests designed initially for schoolchildren. Another argument was that the many of the newly arrived produced low scores due to a stressful environment of the testing. They were exhausted after a long trip. All of them were under a tremendous emotional pressure. Many of them were intimidated by the procedure that they had never encountered before. The critics also raised a very important issue: What if the tests have measured primarily culturally appropriate knowledge and not necessarily intellectual skills? The issue of cultural and social class bias in intelligence tests remains an important and controversial issue in today's psychology.

Testing of Schoolchildren

As in France and many other countries (see Chapter 5), compulsory education of children in the United States faced several challenges. Educational professionals dealt with a serious question: What do we do with children who seemed very difficult to educate? At the very least, they demanded a disproportionate amount of attention from their teachers. Although many states already had institutions to educate children with special needs, the questions persisted about the efficiency of such education (Zenderland, 1998). Another problem was related to procedures to identify these children. Many states turned to **mental surveys**—special measurements of mental capacities of a large population (most typically, children). In fact, such surveys became the tools to identify mental deficiencies based on individual scores and averages.

In the United States, for the most part, schoolchildren were tested according to local and state regulations to determine the children's mental "defectiveness" (a common term 90 years ago). Class and race were viewed as determinants of differences and were of particular interest. For example, in statewide mental surveys provided by the University of Indiana, psychologists tested all students in several counties and categorized them in three categories: subnormal, supernormal, and normal. If a child, on the basis of test scores, was identified as "subnormal," this would have automatically placed this child into a higher risk category. The teachers should have paid special attention to such children because they were believed to be predisposed to criminality, especially if they were from the low socioeconomic status families (Petrina, 2001).

Controversy. Mental surveys became a type of social practice mandated by the government and accepted by the management of schools, courts, and psychiatric and prison facilities. School authorities and teachers needed a reliable and relatively inexpensive method of measurement to improve the efficiency of mass education. However, psychologists at that time were not necessarily ready to provide such a method. Many people believed that intelligence was a person's ability to take and pass an intelligence test. If someone is incapable of earning a particular score on an intelligence test, this should mean that this person is also incapable of a certain level of education or professional training. If intelligence has something to do with heredity, as most believed, then intelligence tests should be used as a measuring device for the purpose of social engineering. Frequently, the results of such studies allowed school officials to discriminate against children who happened to score low on these tests.

Mental testing of the 1920s gave a new impulse to a century-long debate in psychology about the validity of measures and interpretation of intelligence scores (C. E. Spearman, 1927; Thurstone, 1938). At least two major points in psychologists' debates about intelligence testing emerged. First, what do intelligence tests actually measure? Second, how can it be proven that the test score was not influenced by factors such as motivation or emotional states of test takers?

Potential cultural bias of intelligence tests became an issue of constant concern. Later in the century, studies showed that an individual's test performance may not necessarily represent this person's cognitive potential in the future (Vernon, 1969). Moreover, factors such as language, test content, physical health, and motivation contribute to an individual's performance on tests (Sternberg, 2007). Unless intelligence tests accommodate the activities that people perform in their day-to-day life, the tests created in one social and cultural environment (upper-middle class) continue to be biased against other groups. There are many aspects of human intelligence, such as wisdom and creativity, that many tests are simply not designed to measure. Intelligence cannot be meaningfully understood outside its cultural context. As an example, cross-cultural research conducted over a few decades shows that intelligence is understood differently in various cultures. Studies also reveal that children may have advanced practical skills that are not recognized on academic tests (Shiraev & Levy, 2009).

Iowa Child Welfare Station. Some psychologists turned to studies of healthy children living and studying in ordinary conditions of their schools. Psychologists working in such research settings wanted to show the importance of environmental influences, education, upbringing, access to resources, and teaching skills in the development of the child. The goal was to find how the typical child develops and which factors contribute to this development.

An example of this kind of research was a massive project undertaken at the University of Iowa at the **Iowa Child Welfare Station.** The station, originally founded in 1917, was one of the first research institutions designed to study the behavior and skills of ordinary children under everyday conditions. On the basis of a series of studies in Iowa orphanages and adoptive homes, psychologists reported significant improvement in the IQs of those children who had been removed from their original environment (such as an orphanage) and placed in more favorable conditions, such as educated and economically secure families. On the other hand, psychologists showed that leaving children in dire environments would decrease their intelligence scores.

The Iowa Station is known for its contribution to the nature-nurture debate of the 1930s. Researchers working in the station challenged a common assumption that the child's development was a steady maturation and that biological, natural factors should play the crucial role in any child's development. Researchers at the station, in fact, developed and defended a genuinely progressive idea that deliberate, comprehensive, and psychologically sound "intervention" of qualified educators in the child's life should bring significant results. They thought that any girl or boy should be capable of major improvements in learning and behavior if only this child has opportunities and stimulating conditions (Cravens, 2002).

The finding that IQ could be changed by the deliberate effort contradicted the common assumption of that time that intelligence was in essence inborn and quite unchanging over an individual's life course. These research conclusions caused massive criticisms and accusations that psychologists at the station had deliberately manipulated their research results to prove their hypotheses. Most critics also suggested that the researchers were biased in their observations and, therefore, had committed serious methodological errors that affected the results of their studies (Herman, 2001). Nevertheless, these studies served as an important stimulus to the ongoing debate in psychology about environmental and natural factors in an individual's development.

Applied Psychology

Psychologists were becoming more confident in their ability to improve human behavior and society. They thought they could offer sufficient methods and procedures to identify individuals with special talents who were incapable of developing certain educational and professional skills. Psychologists argued that better selection procedures would allow the government to save both financial and human resources and businesses to hire people better equipped for successful professional activities. Such beliefs were enthusiastic and sincere.

Applied Research Around the World. Applied psychological research grew rapidly after the war. The development of testing instruments for the military stimulated the growth of industrial and organizational psychology in the United States, Great Britain, and Canada (McMillan, Stevens, & Kelloway, 2009). In England, France, and Germany, psychologists worked on selection of personnel for traffic jobs, telegraphers, and telephone operators. Sensory and motor functions, attention, intellect, memory, and character traits were studied. In Lithuania, psychologists in the 1930s studied vocational aptitudes of children and developed assessment devices to analyze professional skills of adults (Bagdonas, Pociūt , Rimkut , & Valickas, 2008).

Psychologists also participated in the diagnosis and treatment of war-related psychological problems. One of their areas of study was so-called *war psychosis,* the symptoms of which are likely to be labeled today *posttraumatic stress disorder.* In the United States, scores of psychologists participated in research sponsored directly by the government or by corporations using federal contracts. Postwar economic growth in many countries—although inconsistent—gave psychologists increasing opportunities to apply their knowledge in practical fields. Businesses would hire psychologists to conduct research and give recommendations about personnel selection, skill testing, or advertisement.

In Japan, clinical psychology grew rapidly in 1930s. Several child guidance clinics were established along with psychological services in prisons and courts under government's control (Sato & Graham, 1954, p. 448). The Japanese military employed psychologists to conduct psychological testing and assist in selection of the military personnel. Psychologists tested telegraph operators to measure their speed of receiving and sending messages, errors, and fatigue (Uyeno, 1924, p. 225).

In Europe, applied psychology found a new stimulus in the success of so-called **psychotechnics.** This term, coined by German psychologist William Stern (see Chapter 5), stood for the branch of applied psychology directed specifically toward treatment of human problems (Stern, 1903). He even compared psychotechnics to engineering. To be successful, engineers should know physics. Likewise, specialists in psychotechnics should know psychology (van Strien, 1998). Psychotechnics aimed at increasing both productivity and improving working conditions. Applied centers and laboratories engaged in psychotechnics grew rapidly across Germany, Sweden, Great Britain, the Soviet Union, and Spain, to name a few. In 1920, a big international conference on psychotechnics gathered in Switzerland.

IN THEIR OWN WORDS

William Stern in 1929: When 17 years ago I introduced the concept of the 'intelligence quotient' as a principle of measurement for intelligence tests, I had no idea that the IQ would become a world-wide formula and one of the most frequently used technical expressions in psychology in America. . . . But beyond that: Now countless batteries of tests have been developed, standardized, and put into practice to measure countless other psychological functions: spatial perception, manual dexterity, attention, suggestibility, knowledge, mathematical ability, character traits, etc., always with emphasis on the objective, quantitative population norm, with respect to which the individual case is then scaled (cf. Lamiell, 2009).

Hawthorne Experiments. In the 1920s, many psychologists and business managers agreed that science, if applied properly, could improve management's efficiency. The prospects of scientific management appeared promising. Under an educated guidance, businesses would become more productive and workers would make more money and feel satisfied. Governments and private companies began to sponsor research related to efficiency of management. Among the main questions were the following: What is an optimal method of business organization? How do working conditions affect productivity? How do we make sure that workers are not exhausted but remain highly productive?

A significant landmark of American industrial research was the **Hawthorne experiment**—which was, in fact, a series of experiments initially designed to investigate the effects of several improved working conditions on factory productivity. Later these experiments focused on human interaction within the work group. The experiments began in 1924. In collaboration with the National Research Council, the Western Electric Company conducted research at its Hawthorne manufacturing plant in Chicago. The plant produced telephones and their components (Gillespie, 1991).

The first stage of the research was about the effects of illumination on production and workers' comfort. To the experimenters' surprise, the level of brightness did not have any effect on productivity. Moreover, both experimental groups working in bright and badly lit rooms increased their production during the study! At that time, the researchers also noticed that the interaction among supervisors, workers, and researchers was having an impact on the workers' productivity. The experiment continued. Scientists examined how workers' rest intervals, lunchtime, refreshments, payment methods, and length of weekdays, workweeks, and vacations affected their efficiency and satisfaction. Again, whatever experimentation was applied, output went up. With either increasing or decreasing breaks, more frequent or less frequent payments, the workers' output and satisfaction in the studying samples steadily increased. Overall, regardless of the experimental conditions used, workers' productivity and morale were improving. The results were somewhat puzzling. What was the cause of such improvements?

To help with the results' interpretation, several additional researchers were invited to take part in the study. Among them were Elton Mayo (1880–1949), a native of Australia and professor of industrial research from Harvard Business School, his Harvard colleague Fritz Roethlisberger (1898–1974), Clair Turner (1890–1974) from the Massachusetts Institute of Technology, and several others (Trahair, 1984). They developed a series of in-depth interviews with managers and workers. The interviews were designed to study people's opinions within their "natural" work conditions (Hsueh, 2002).

As a result of these interviews, Mayo and his colleagues found that physical conditions of the factory, such as illumination or noise, played some role but not the most important one. A more important factor was the workers' personal satisfaction at the workplace. This satisfaction was not based exclusively on the size of their financial compensation. The workers also wanted to be included in the decision-making process. They wanted to feel important. They wanted to establish their own norms of production. Moreover, the researchers found that the employees tended to establish their own work "climate"—a set of informal rules helping or opposing certain managerial decisions. If the climate and managerial polices were on the same page, then the workers felt good and worked hard.

The Significance of the Hawthorne Experiments. The impact of these experiments on psychology and the social sciences was significant (Adair, 1984). Sure there were criticisms. Some critics claimed that the results of the experiment would give business owners and managers additional tools to exploit the working-class people and "squeeze" as much as possible from them by simply improving some informal relations in the workplace (Whyte, 1968). From the methodological standpoint, the opponents argued that the results of the experiment had been exaggerated by the participating specialists and the importance of certain psychological factors affecting productivity inflated. Other critics maintained that the Hawthorne experiments showed the inability of psychologists and social scientists to conduct valid experimental study: all the unpredictable factors played an unpredictable role in their experiment (Gillespie, 1991). Many others, however, evaluated this experiment positively.

First, the experiments used sophisticated procedures based on specially designed interviews. The Hawthorne researchers used a set of complex methods based on recording, documenting, and interpreting the worker's comments and actions (Hsueh, 2002). This study gave a significant boost to the interview method in studying group behavior and stimulated the development of social psychology as a discipline.

Second, the discovery of the **Hawthorne effect** was a significant development in applied psychology. The term refers to a positive effect of properly organized work relationships on workers' productivity and satisfaction. Many workers improved on a number of characteristics because both researchers and management paid attention to workers' needs during the experiment and treated them with respect.

Third, the results of this study showed that specific work conditions can affect productivity. Workers' attitudes also mattered: job satisfaction and output depended more on cooperation and a feeling of worth than on physical working condition (Mayo, 1933/2003). The experiment became an innovative study for an entire line of research related to human relations in the workplace and the theory of organizational behavior (Vaill, 2007). Contrary to Taylor's idea (Chapter 5) that only discipline and the precise organization of the workplace should guarantee high productivity, the Hawthorne experiments showed the importance of a good relationship between the workers and their managers and workers' involvement in some managerial tasks.

Success of this and other experiments built psychologists' confidence and brought them new research opportunities. One of such venues was sports.

Figure 10.1 The Hawthorne Effect

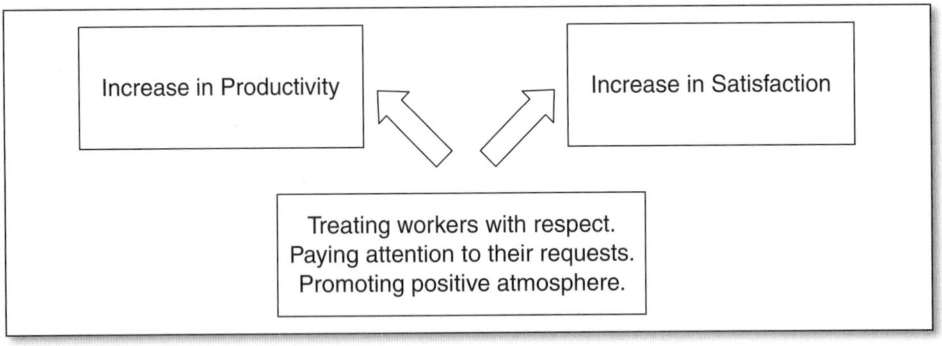

Early Sports Psychology. In the 1920s, professional sport was becoming a big business. More people were involved in sports advertisement, management, training, and selection of players for college and professional teams. For example, scientists from the research laboratory of Columbia University's psychological department wanted to create an effective method of evaluating new prospects for baseball teams. They obtained permission from the New York Yankees to test the recently acquired player Babe Ruth (one of the most celebrated American baseball players ever). The researchers studied his muscles, hearing, vision, movements, and reaction time to describe the differences between him and the average person (Fullerton, 1921).

Another study was conducted in 1938, when the management of the Chicago Cubs baseball team asked a group of researchers to give recommendations about how to improve the team's performance. The head of the project, Coleman R. Griffith (1893–1966) from the University of Illinois, is considered today a founder of sport psychology in the United States. Griffith was among the first professional psychologists to have been hired by a major league sports franchise. He was hoping to build a science-based training program. He and an assistant filmed the players' movements and measured their skills. They gave recommendations to the team management and produced many reports about this study (Green, 2003).

Despite the growing popularity of psychological research in many areas of life, the actual impact remained largely insignificant. Several reasons existed. Very often the results obtained by psychologists were too trivial. For example, to find that Babe Ruth had an excellent hand-eye coordination was to state the obvious. Baseball scouts and managers—without help from psychologists—could see, evaluate, and select young prospects based on how fast they threw the ball or how hard they hit it with a bat. Second, some professional coaches and managers saw psychologists as unnecessary detractors. Sport professionals believed that a trainer knowledgeable in psychology would be much more valuable to the sport than a professional psychologist with little knowledge of the sport. This opinion about psychologists continues to dominate among some coaches in college and professional sports.

Assessments. What was the real impact of psychological testing and applied research? Many businesses and government institutions benefited from testing and other types of applied psychological research. Organizations and firms wanted to test their employees and candidates on a variety of characteristics ranging from memory skills to accuracy of vision and aptitude to ability to work in stressful conditions. The growing demand stimulated psychological research. The popularity of tests had negative consequences too. Scores of nonpsychology professionals, impressed with the work of psychologists, began to design their own tests without proper understanding what such tests are supposed to measure and how to interpret them. Psychologists' efforts to explain the meaning of testing in applied research began a long time ago and continue today.

ON THE WEB

American Psychological Association Division 47: Exercise and Sport Psychology

✓ **CHECK YOUR KNOWLEDGE**

Name the difference between the Alpha and Beta tests.

What were the research goals of the Iowa Station?

What were the main lessons of the Hawthorne experiments?

Psychology developed as an applied and academic discipline. The following examples of developmental psychology, psychology of personality, and social psychology will show how theoretical studies constantly merged with practical, applied research.

Psychology of Development and Cognition

Lev Vygotsky's views of consciousness and the child's development continue to generate interest in the 21st century.

In the 1920s, studies within the behaviorist tradition portrayed the developing individual as an active learner acquiring reflexes, habits, and other responses to the changing environment. Psychoanalysis showed the complexity of the child's inner world and the dynamics of emotional transformations within the child's psyche. Gestalt psychologists emphasized the importance of studying children united with their psychological "field" or environment.

All these approaches, in fact, emphasized either adaptive or maladaptive interaction of the developing individual with the environment. Jean Piaget from Switzerland and Lev Vygotsky from Russia—two outstanding psychologists of the 20th century—maintained a similar view. Vygotsky's observations over parent-child interactions led him to a conclusion about an active and adaptive role of the child's adjustment to the changing conditions and demands of life. Piaget's theory emphasized the child's inner developmental mechanisms and their adaptive role. Both theories gained significant international recognition.

The Theory of Highest Psychological Functions

Lev Vygotsky (1896–1934) was born in 1896 in the Russian empire (Belarus today) to Jewish parents. He was homeschooled and showed a remarkable talent in various fields of social sciences and humanities. He received two undergraduate degrees: one in law from the prestigious Moscow State University and the other in history and philosophy from a smaller school. During the turmoil of Russia's Civil War in 1917–1920, he worked as a teacher and tutor. At that time, he began his theoretical research combined with his daily observations of his students. This would become his major research "style": unlike many psychologists of the time, he did not design rigorous experiments. He used observation, unstructured interviews, and simple procedures to test his hypotheses. He began to attend conferences and seminars where he could discuss his observations. During one such conference, he met with the director of Moscow's Institute of Psychology, a leading psychological research center at that time (Vygotsky reportedly had impressed everybody by delivering a 15-minute scholarly report without using a single written note). From 1924 until his early death from tuberculosis, Vygotsky worked in Moscow and several other cities. In 1933, Kurt Lewin made a stop in Moscow to meet, among other reasons, with Vygotsky and discuss mutual research interests. Vygotsky was a compassionate researcher who dedicated his short life to developmental and therapeutic work with children with special needs.

In general, Vygotsky's views represent a remarkable blend of philosophy, Marxism, evolutionary theory, and developmental and experimental psychology. Early in his career, he supported reflexology and behaviorism but later criticized them for the rejection of consciousness and subjectivity. He wanted passionately to unify psychology, divided at that time in many schools and subdisciplines. As most psychologists who hoped for such "unification," he believed that his own approach should become a major consolidating effort.

Psychological Tools. One of Vygotsky's important ideas was that speech is a mediator between an individual and the outside world. Speech is a special "tool," which our ancestors acquired in the process of evolution. Marxist philosophy paid special attention to work tools—from cutting stones to sophisticated machinery. Humans used these tools to transform the world and develop skills. In a similar fashion, Vygotsky believed, humans use speech. During evolution, a developing individual is, in fact, a speaking individual who uses language to change both the external world and "internal" psychological world as well. Vygotsky also believed that initially, the words are directed at transforming behavior of others. Later, individuals learn to regulate their own behavior—thus developing thinking and consciousness. But how do individuals use these tools and develop their inner world?

Vygotsky hoped to create a comprehensive experimental psychological program to examine these processes. He wanted to study children in their natural conditions: in the playroom or class, engaged in spontaneous conversations. He also believed that children with special needs, including blindness, severe hearing problems, and other disabilities, could provide dramatic insights into their developing minds. In 1931 (2002) he published *Development of Higher Psychological Functions,* in which he described the concept of symbols or signs as cultural tools or regulators of human development. A sign as well as a spoken or written word is a psychological tool with which humans build their consciousness. Before children begin to speak, they have already achieved a certain level of psychological development, which allows them to function and adjust to the environment. Using words and symbols, the child internalizes external contents and learns social rules (Vygotsky, 1931/2005). Vygotsky followed the ideas of Gestalt psychology that all psychological functions represent a cohesive system and develop together.

Every psychological function occurs as a result of communication among individuals. Then these communications are internalized. For example, why do children talk to themselves? Their speech is not an abstract process that accompanies a child's action, as many thought in that time. Talking to herself, for example, a girl is learning how to achieve a particular goal. At first, she thinks aloud. The girl later internalizes and transforms these words into thinking processes. She takes a tool and makes it her own, perhaps using it in a way unique to this child. For example, internalizing the use of a pencil allows the girl to use it very much as she wants it rather than draw exactly how the teacher explained (Vygotsky & Luria, 1930/2005).

Periods of Psychological Development. Vygotsky's research methods were largely observational. His students recalled that he had a habit of coming to the room where preschoolers played and sitting there for hours. After some time, the children in the room would stop paying attention to the man sitting there and began to act "naturally." This was exactly what Vygotsky wanted to see (Shedrovitsky, 2009). Most of his ideas came from such observations, like the idea about the child's developmental periods.

A child's development is not a steady process of a consistent, uninterrupted transformation and change. Periods of gradual changes are followed by the rapid transitions, sudden transformations, and crises. Vygotsky suggested five stages of such transformation occurring at birth, at the end of the first year, and then at the ages of 3, 7, and 13. In each stage, new situations and crises occur. Every new situation is a new source of development.

Parents and teachers have to understand the entire social situation surrounding the child. The goal of upbringing is not to emphasize a child's inabilities or deficiencies but to pay attention to what this child has already achieved or developed. Finding new potentials in a child is a top priority of an educator and parent (Vygotsky, 1933).

Zone of Proximal Development. In one of his most fundamental works, *Thought and Language,* published in 1934, Vygotsky introduces and develops the concept of **zone of proximal development,** understood as the difference between a child's learning progress with help or guidance and this child's learning achievement without guidance of an adult. Children usually have potential, a latent reserve for their intellectual growth. This means that the child is typically ready to learn more and understand better than a teacher or parent assumes. Vygotsky challenged a common belief that the child has to be prepared to understand certain concepts, so that a 3-year-old is not ready to study something that a 4-year-old is capable of knowing. In his view, the child can learn more if teachers or adults stimulate the child's intellectual advance within the zone of proximal development (Vygotsky, 1934/2005b).

Vygotsky thus argued that the task of education is not to offer something that the child is ready to perform. It is greater. Children as well as adults have hidden potentials that can be developed with some external help. Two tasks should be pursued here. The first one is to provide detailed information about what specifically each child's "zone" is: some kids may have a greater potential than their peers in some areas but not in others.

Second, both psychologists and educational specialists should create tasks, exercises, and even programs to assist children in developing their knowledge and skills.

Vygotsky originally developed the concept of the zone of proximal development to argue against the use of standardized tests as a means to gauge intelligence. Vygotsky believed that rather than examining what students already know to measure their intelligence, it is better to examine their ability to solve problems independently and with the assistance of an adult. Vygotsky's ideas emphasized the progressive role of psychology, especially in education. In his system, ideally, teachers and parents not only follow and accommodate children but also accelerate, improve, and enhance their potentials.

How can we summarize Vygotsky's work? When we study what a child can do alone, we study his or her yesterday's development. When we study what this child can do in cooperation, we look at the developments of tomorrow. This was a new, optimistic, and obviously progressive view of human development. Vygotsky believed that people have more talents hidden "inside" than they commonly think. His early death prevented him from implementing his ideas.

Vygotsky's Impact. Vygotsky's main research method was a combination of imagination and observation. Sure, in the world of sophisticated experimental procedures and measurements, the use of such unsophisticated methods was his liability. Despite this, his impact on psychology was substantial (Shedrovitsky, 2009).

Vygotsky believed that human beings could overcome many natural or social limitations to their psychological development. An individual in his view is not a sheer product of social environment—a popular thesis partially supported by behaviorists. To him, people are independent and active thinkers. He believed that education should involve the process of the child's interaction with teachers and peers and not necessarily memorization and repetition. Vygotsky's ideas resonated well among educational researchers working on advancing teaching techniques to stimulate the child's hidden or underdeveloped potentials (Bruner, 1960).

Vygotsky introduced the idea of cultural mediation. Every psychological function, thinking as an example, appears twice. First, it is an "outside" social activity or learning. Second, this learning is internalized as thinking. Human consciousness therefore should be understood in the context of interaction of an individual with the outside world. In fact, Vygotsky, in a symbolic way, placed the soul outside the human body! This was a new theoretical way to understand the most difficult question about the nature of consciousness. The essence of human consciousness is in its unity with the cultural environment (Vygotsky, 1934/2005b).

Vygotsky's views influenced many psychological and educational theories emphasizing social and cultural aspects of cognition and development. The ecocultural theories of the 1960s maintained similar views. Linguists used his ideas to understand the process of language acquisition and teaching foreign languages. His work related to stages of moral development found support in other modern theories. Vygotsky's views also found a reflection in so-called narrative therapy based on the assumption that an individual's identity reveals itself in certain symbols as short accounts or narratives about our life (Charon, 1993). To correct a person's psychological problem is to investigate such narratives and then restructure them to explain new potentials and possibilities for improvement. An externalization of a problem makes it easier to investigate and evaluate it. Vygotsky is also remembered as a founder of the field called in Russia *defectology*, elsewhere known as *special education* (Kotik-Friedgut & Friedgut, 2008).

Vygotsky died in 1934. But even when he was still alive and working, his opponents in the early 1930s began to accuse him of anti-Marxist tendencies and philosophical idealism. His view of consciousness as a product of individual-culture interactions contradicted the Marxist dogma that brain physiology is the only appropriate key to explain psychological phenomena. Vygotsky was labeled as an anti-Marxist disloyal to the government. After his death, his books were removed from libraries, and psychologists were discouraged to cite his works. Vygotsky's work appeared virtually unknown until the translation of *Thought and Language* (1934/2005b) was published in English in 1962 and later in other languages.

Another remarkable scientist who developed our understanding of the child's development and dynamic interaction with the environment and presented compelling experimental data to support his theoretical assumptions was Swiss psychologist Jean Piaget.

✓ CHECK YOUR KNOWLEDGE

What is cultural mediation in Vygotsky's theory of human consciousness?

What are the practical applications of Vygotsky's idea of the zone of proximal development?

Developmental Ideas of Jean Piaget

From his early days, Jean Piaget (1896–1980) was interested in a wide range of scientific disciplines, including biology and mechanics. At age 22, he had received his PhD in science from the University of Neuchatel in the French-speaking region of his native Switzerland. His interest in psychology grew when he began working for Alfred Binet's laboratory in Paris. He turned to developmental issues. Piaget was interested in how children construct thinking about themselves and the world around them. The birth of his own children gave him another opportunity to spend significant time observing them. During his long and productive career, Piaget worked at several universities but spent most of his life at the University of Geneva. He worked with several assistants who conducted more than a few projects simultaneously, thus providing Piaget with a constant flow of new empirical data.

Method. Like Vygotsky, Piaget wanted to study children in their natural surroundings: in nurseries, playrooms, and classrooms. He wanted to see how children build, draw, assemble, and take things apart (Piaget, 1926/1960). Piaget developed a new complex method based on several already existing methodologies. Specifically, they were naturalistic observation, psychometrics, and clinical interview.

How did he use his method? He asked children to solve certain problems or perform educational tasks. First, he would ask a child a standard question and record an answer. Then, he would ask the child additional, nonstandard questions based on the received responses. Borrowing from the clinical method (which he had studied early in his career), he began to emphasize several important elements of the interview. For example, he underlined the importance of giving full attention to the child, emphasizing listening, restraining form arguing, paying attention to what the child does, and helping the child to say what she or he wants to say (Mayer, 2005). Piaget's main task was not only to record and interpret the child's words but also see how the words and sentences relate to the task that the child performs.

Piaget wanted to show that a young child's cognitive processes are essentially different from those of adults (Piaget, 1926/1960). Children think and make judgments using different thinking principles compared to older children and grownups. The process of development goes in stages determined by the child's developing brain, skills, and social environment. However, the movement from one state to another is primarily a natural process. So what were these stages?

Stages of Development. In Stage 1, the *sensorimotor* stage, infants learn about their interaction with their immediate environment. Around age 1½, children develop the ability to hold an image in their mind beyond the immediate experience. During Stage 2, the *preoperational* stage, children acquire language, develop imagination, learn the meaning of symbols, and develop creative play. Children remain generally egocentric, which means they have a diminished capacity to see the world from another person's viewpoint. At this stage, lasting approximately until age 7, children tend to use incorrect assumptions about volume, amount, and weight. Children also tend to be animistic in their judgments or tend to believe in spiritual beings or actions.

At the third stage of *concrete operations,* children learn the rules of logic and begin to comprehend the laws of physics related to volume, amount, and weight. They become more mechanical in their judgments about nature and things around them. From ages 7 to 11, children acquire *operations* or logical principles to solve most problems. In this stage, the child not only uses symbols to make them represent something but can manipulate with those symbols logically. A child learns to classify and put objects in series or groups according to various rules. The final stage, *formal operations,* indicates the time when adolescents develop the ability to think abstractly. This involves using complex logical operations and hypothetical thinking.

In the process of intellectual development, one stage must be accomplished before the next can emerge. In each stage, the child keeps his or her cognitive abilities of the previous stage but forms new abilities of the new stage. The process may resemble construction of a building: Each new level is impossible to build without building the lower ones. As soon as the child has constructed the operations on a new level, he or she learns about more complex objects and performs more complex operations. Thus, children continually renovate the ideas they formed earlier.

Transitions between stages are not necessarily gradual. They tend to be rapid and radical. (Remember the rapid problem-solving process from the position of Gestalt psychology?) The time spent in a new stage is generally about developing, advancing, and refining the operations on this new cognitive level. A similar type of understanding of the rapid transition through the stages is also found in Vygotsky's work. Yet both psychologists differed in their views of the child's speech. Piaget used stage-based interpretation of the child's speech development. He proposed eight distinct categories of speech under two large categories: One was egocentric or inside oriented, and the other was socialized, which served as a way to communicate with the outside world. It was different from Vygotsky's view; he saw both these stages of the child's speech as socialized.

Cross-Cultural Applications. Do all children develop thinking and move through developmental stages in the way Piaget proposed? Summarizing results from a handful of studies, Dasen (1994) showed that the stage sequence—preoperational–operational–abstract thinking—appears to be similar across countries. Children tend to move from one stage to another as Piaget predicted. Nevertheless, psychologists were cautious about Piaget's other findings (Gardiner, Mutter, & Kosmitzki, 1998). Most of the critical comments were related to the methodology and procedures used by Piaget and his colleagues. For instance, researchers who conducted earlier cross-cultural studies of language development using Piaget's theory had only limited knowledge of the language studied. Maybe because of this liability, researchers preferred to use standardized tests and paid less attention to interviews with the studied children. Moreover, accurate birth dates of many children were not commonly available in many developing countries, so the accurate age of the child studied was not always known.

Genetic Epistemology. Piaget made a significant contribution to genetic epistemology—his favorite subject. **Genetic epistemology** attempts to explain knowledge (scientific knowledge in particular) from the standpoint of knowledge's history. Psychology plays a special role here because it explains the basic mind operations on which such knowledge is based. Piaget believed that human development is a process of adaptation to the changing contexts of life. Probably the most noticeable contribution made by Piaget was his idea of **assimilation and accommodation**—the two sides of the process of adaptation or learning. Assimilation is adopting operations with new objects into old mind patterns. Accommodation is modifying one's mental structures to fit the new demands of the environment. Assimilation and accommodation are both fundamentally biological processes and work in tandem helping individuals in advancing their understanding of the world.

Piaget's Impact. Piaget remains one of the most prominent psychologists of the 20th century. His original model of developmental stages has received significant support in further studies conducted over 50 years in different countries. Piaget's original ideas about the stage-by-stage development of children's moral values, political beliefs, and even geographical concepts have found applications in educational programs in many countries. Piaget's theory explains well how children deal with conservation of volume, weight, and amount.

Critics pointed out that Piaget provoked a temptation to interpret some higher developmental stages as more "valuable" than others. In reality, though, social success, satisfaction, and adaptation strategies, as well as certain activities and professions, do not require that the individual must function on the level of formal operations. It is also questionable whether the formal operational stage should be achieved by all adolescents in all societies. In both Western and non-Western settings, there are many healthy, happy, and successful individuals who are not that advanced on formal operational tasks (Byrnes, 1988).

Overall, both Piaget and Vygotsky have influenced a major shift in developmental psychology toward the child-centered approach. Their studies directed the attention of parents and teachers toward children's creativity, individual choices, and nonconforming attitudes. Critics of this approach agree that creativity is a desirable and noble goal, but to become a competitive member of today's society, the child has to learn a wide range of basic things, and it sometimes takes a difficult and tedious process of learning. The child's future life is not an endless process of creative play and amusement. Schools and parents should prepare children—in addition to being creative—to learn how to overcome difficult obstacles and invest their own discipline and hard work. In response, supporters of Vygotsky and Piaget maintain that creativity and discipline are not mutually exclusive phenomena, and educational programs can promote both imagination and orderliness.

✓ CHECK YOUR KNOWLEDGE

What was the essence of Piaget's interview method?

What is genetic epistemology?

Personality Theories

A growing number of psychologists in the 1920s began to pay attention to studies and problems focusing on individuality. As a result, personality psychology as a field grew rapidly in many countries (H. A. Murray, 1938).

Traditions and Approaches

By the end of the 19th century, early publications appeared examining unique aspects of the individual's self. Studies about individual memory styles, identity, or individual consciousness became more common. After the 1920s, psychologists interested in personality theory began to consolidate their research into a separate branch of studies different from psychoanalysis or educational psychology.

A significant interest in personality as a psychological problem emerged in France. A much celebrated tradition in French psychological literature was that the person was not a sum of parts, ideas, images, feelings, and memories. Me (or *moi* in French) stood for the reflection and ultimate integration of many experiences. This position was already reflected in the works of French psychologists Théodule Ribot, Pierre Janet, and Alfred Binet, whose names appeared earlier in the book (Lombardo & Foschi, 2003). In American scientific psychology, the notion of an individual's personality was introduced by William James in his influential book, *The Principles of Psychology* (James, 1890/1950). He referred to personality through the context of consciousness and individual memories.

Scientific vocabulary related to personality was changing gradually. Earlier in the 20th century, many used the terms *personality, character,* and *temperament* almost interchangeably. Approximately in the 1920s, American psychologists generally accepted the term *character* to describe the moral aspect of behavior. *Temperament* referred largely to biological factors (Danziger, 1997). Although disagreements existed about *personality,* this term increasingly often was used to describe the wholeness or totality of stable features of an individual. Starting in the early teens and continuing into the 1920s, psychologists devoted increasing attention to measuring personality, documenting its components, and theorizing about the form a mature personality might take.

Personality as a psychological phenomenon was described in both empirical (measurable) and social (descriptive) terms. Several scientific and social traditions had an impact on the studies of personality.

- First, it was the empirical and experimental tradition rooted in Galton's views and methods. Personality according to this view was not an abstract concept but a measurable combination of features and traits, some stable constructs of an individual's behavior and thinking.

- Second, it was the tradition of French clinical experimentation, based on methods distinguishing a fully functional personality from a dysfunctional, problematic, or pathological one.

- Third, it was a largely American tradition emphasizing the importance of moral features in an individual's behavior. Overall, the individual was viewed as a collection of stable, distinct, and measurable characteristics or traits, the sum total of which equaled his or her personality (Danziger, 1990).

From the 1920s onward, personality psychology emerged as a branch of scientific psychology. Already by 1940, personality had become a well-established category of psychological investigation (Nicholson, 1998).

The Trait Tradition

Through his publications, Gordon Allport (1897–1967) tried to create a new field of study dedicated to measurement of personality. He was born in Indiana and from the beginning of his life witnessed hard work, perseverance, and religious dedication of his parents. As a Harvard social ethics student, Allport had an opportunity to view the transformation in American social work close up. The principal hallmark of the "new" social work was a commitment to science. A formative experience for Allport was his postdoctoral fellowship in Germany in the fall of 1922. He was influenced by the works of German psychologist William Stern (1871–1938), especially by his attempts to give a classification to an individual's traits and behaviors. A holistic approach of Gestalt psychologists also influenced Allport (Nicholson, 2000). His fundamental work, *Personality: A Psychological Interpretation,* was published in 1937. Allport was very active in promoting his research. He wrote literature reviews, gave radio and magazine interviews, and wrote a psychology textbook. In 1939, he was elected president of the American Psychological Association (APA).

Allport argued that character and personality were distinct entities. Borrowing a distinction from John Watson, Allport maintained that character was a moral category; it referred to the self when viewed from an ethical perspective. Personality, on the other hand, referred to the objective self, the fundamental adjustment patterns that an individual had formed over the course of his or her experience.

Since graduate school, he repeatedly emphasized the "unique" quality of individuals. The study of personality should focus on the way in which traits join together (G. Allport, 1924). Allport believed, and this view was very popular, that experimental procedures and measurements (similar to intelligence testing) could bring psychology a new understanding of personality, free from speculations. Allport also argued that there was a stable core of traits in every person. This was an earlier assumption that later had grown into the contemporary **trait theory of personality,** which states that personality consists of a potent collection of qualities or traits. For Allport, individual conduct was largely determined by a relatively stable core of these inner attributes (G. Allport, 1937).

Allport's work on personality was a combination of research and a deep belief in social progressivism. Like many of his colleagues at that time, he believed that the solution to problems such as poverty, crime, and violence should be found in science, particularly in psychology. He understood, however, that psychology as a discipline does not change social institutions. It provides knowledge that may change an individual's traits and, subsequently, behavior.

Early Social Psychology

People often alter their behavior, emotion, and thinking when they act together. Big groups and crowds attracted the attention of many social scientists in the past. For the most part, studies in the fields of group behavior became the subject of *sociology,* a discipline studying structure and functioning of human society. Very often, however, social scientists were looking for explanations of group behavior in individual psychological mechanisms. Special attention was paid to instincts as universal mechanisms allowing dissimilar people to act in a similar fashion when they join in a group together. First publications on this subject appeared in the first decade of the 20th century. For example, the earliest Japanese book on social psychology appeared in 1906. The discourse in it was mostly theoretical (Hotta & Strickland, 1991).

Theories of Social Instincts

Supporters of the concept of instinctual behavior maintained that when joining a group, individuals become the living parts of a larger social organism, which has its own unique features and that can immediately activate people's instincts or other automatic responses. French psychologist Gustave Le Bon believed, for instance, that people acquire destructive instincts as soon as they join a crowd. In large groups, intentions of one person easily spread through the entire mob. According to Le Bon, therefore, it is natural for people in a group to act aggressively (Le Bon, 1896). Another Frenchman, Gabriel Tarde (1843–1904), wrote that the presence of other people activates imitation, a powerful human instinct. When people are surrounded by other human beings, they immediately begin to imitate the behavior of others, change their own behavior, and modify some individual psychological qualities (Tarde, 1903). The idea of the instinctual nature of social behavior was developed further by English scholar William McDougall (1908). He believed that most individual acts displayed in groups can be traced to initial instincts, such as parenting, self-display, or hoarding. Vladimir Bekhterev (1921/2001a), whose views were discussed in Chapter 7, wrote about the existence of special social reflexes, which are activated as soon as an individual joins a group. Like many of our individual reflexes, such as blinking, coughing, sneezing, and yawning, which are influenced by circumstances, social reflexes such as feistiness or stubbornness also are activated under certain conditions (Strickland, 2001).

These theories (and many others similar to these views) were based largely on assumptions and theoretical speculations. Only some of these ideas found empirical support in later research. Among them was the concept of so-called *de-individuation* in groups. When people assemble in a large group to perform an exciting activity, group members tend to become less careful, assertive, and attentive than they normally are. In addition, group members tend to become less critical in judgments and in subsequent actions (Lea & Spears, 1991). However interesting and sometimes intriguing, the early theories did not generate testable hypotheses and produced only few empirical studies. Most psychologists chose an experimental field to study human behavior in group conditions.

Experimental Social Psychology: The Impact of Other People

In the early days of experimental psychology, psychologists were aware of the potential impact of other people on an individual's performance during an experimental procedure. The original experimental procedures, as you remember, required somewhat "sterile" conditions: a subject must have performed an experimental task alone and away from noise, light, and other people. What would happen if the experimenter brought two or three participants to work on the same experimental tasks? Would this influence the subject's performance? A few empirical studies had already provided some answers to these questions.

The early groundbreaking experiments of American psychologist Norman Triplett (1861–1931) demonstrated that people perform tasks differently when they are in groups compared to situations when they have to perform alone. Triplett measured the performance of swimmers and cyclists and found that they showed faster times when competing against opponents than when racing for themselves (Triplett, 1898). Later studies in the 20th century provided new information about the specific impact of other people and measured these effects. Psychologists, for instance, found that people tended to perform certain simple motor tasks faster and more accurately when working in the presence of others than when in solitary conditions. Subjects also showed greater tolerance to pain when others watched them or were simply nearby. However, it was also found that in the presence of spectators or bystanders, people's memorization skills and attention span were likely to decline. In addition, group members also performed worse in many situations in which the experimental task was difficult and required mental concentration as compared to those experimental conditions in which they performed the experimental tasks alone (F. Allport, 1920; Bekhterev, 1921/2001a; Zajonc, 1965).

A significant event in the history of psychology was the publication in 1924 of *Social Psychology* by American psychologist Floyd Allport (1890–1978). His contemporaries considered the publication a symbolic beginning of a new experimental science of social psychology (Katz, 1979). Allport believed that although social situations change an individual's actions, all social behavior can be explained in terms of the principles of individual psychological functioning (F. Allport, 1924). People form habits that grow in their complexity to adjust to situational variations. In groups, the individual's behavior is influenced by the perception of others engaged in the same activity. This influence may take the form of social facilitation or social rivalry (Wozniak, 1997).

Studies of group influence by Muzafer Sherif (1906–1988) also had an important impact on social psychology. Born, raised, and educated in Turkey, Sherif received his graduate degrees in the United States. As a young scientist, he wanted to examine experimentally how people make judgments in groups and influence opinions and behavior of others. He designed experiments requiring group discussion and decision making. For example, a group was supposed to observe a motionless light in a dark experimental room. The group had to make a judgment about whether or not the light was moving. Although the light did not actually move, the group formed a collective opinion about this light's shift. After that, the group was very reluctant to change that opinion. This was an early experiment showing people form group norms—patterns of actions or judgments that influence the behavior of individuals later on. Sherif published his views in his famous book, *The Psychology of Social Norms* (Sherif, 1936). About two decades later, a Polish-born American researcher, Solomon Asch (1907–1996), conducted his illustrious research of social conformity—the process by which individuals modify their opinions and behavior to follow group norms. The necessity or desire to "fit" in the group overcomes people's perception and, very often, judgment abilities (S. Asch, 1952/1961). This research on conformity launched a massive surge of experimental studies of group behavior.

Expectedly, many followers of the psychoanalytic tradition made a contribution to social psychology in the middle of the 20th century. They tried to apply their theoretical approach to the study of human groups and society. We will mention two types of studies as an illustration. The first one refers to the theory and practice of psychotherapy. A Romanian-born American psychologist, Jacob Moreno (1889–1974), studied interpersonal influence and applied some of its principles to group therapy. His method, known as psychodrama, required participants to explore their own internal conflicts not through a private discussion with a therapist but through acting out their

ON THE WEB

Visit the American Society of Group Psychotherapy and Psychodrama.

emotions in front of one another. The presence of other people and interactions allowed most participants to explore their own inhibitions, release negative emotions, and learn about themselves in the permissive and stimulating atmosphere of psychodrama (Moreno, 1934/1977).

The other example refers to studies rooted in psychoanalytical theory but also incorporating testing and empirical research of individuals in social conditions. Studies of the *authoritarian personality* gained significant attention and sparked several waves of research later in the 20th century (Adorno, Frenkel-Brunswik, Levinson, & Sanford, 1950). One of the main assumptions tested empirically was that some individuals, because of their childhood experiences, form a stable pattern of individual and authoritarian traits. Such individuals are prone to mystical thinking and prejudice against particular social groups. They are obedient to authority figures, reluctant to innovations, and prone to anger and violence. The most remarkable conclusion of the study was that there are individuals who accept authoritarian methods and enthusiastically support political leaders who pursue order and impose limits on civil liberties. In other words, there are individuals themselves—because of their psychological features—who eagerly accepts limits on their freedom and accept social injustice.

Other studies in social psychology turned to the question about how people make judgments of various complex social situations.

Theories of Social Judgments

Early studies in social psychology focused on discrepancies of thinking and the reasons why people make decisions that seem illogical or inconsistent. One of the pioneers of this research was Stanford sociologist R. T. LaPiere. He studied prejudice—a negative opinion about a social group or issue that people hold without examining the facts available to them. In one of his studies, most restaurant and hotel owners, answering to a mailed questionnaire, said that they would not host people of "Chinese race" in their establishments. Nevertheless, the same owners were very cordial and welcoming when LaPiere, accompanied by a Chinese couple, showed up at the door (LaPiere, 1934). In another survey, he showed that people develop negative perceptions about the alleged behavior of minority groups (such as the criminality of Armenian immigrants in California) even though these groups did not display such behavior (LaPiere, 1936).

Principles of Gestalt psychology made a distinct impact on the early research of social judgment. An Austria-born American psychologist, Fritz Heider (1896–1988), used the principle of balance to argue that people seek consistency among their judgments. Heider argued that perception of social situations follows many of the same rules as perception of physical objects. The organization found in object perception is also found in social perception (Heider, 1944, 1958). To maintain their perception in a "good form," people tend to seek explanations for their judgment, thus creating perceptual distortions (like perceptual illusions in Gestalt psychology). For example,

Heider made an empirical observation that when observing the behavior of other people, people tend to overestimate their internal causes and pay less attention to external causes or circumstances affecting their behavior. This phenomenon later became known as the *fundamental attribution error.*

Principles of social perception received further development in the studies by Leon Festinger (1919–1989), the author of the theory of cognitive dissonance, one of the most recognizable theories in social psychology today. Festinger found that people tend to experience psychological tension when they perceive mismatch (dissonance) between their judgments or between their judgment and behavior (Festinger, 1957). Whenever we must decide between two or more alternatives, the final choice will be inconsistent—to some extent—with some of our beliefs or previous decisions. This inconsistency generates dissonance, an unpleasant state of emotions. To reduce or eliminate this tension, people change their judgments or modify behavior (Festinger, Riecken, & Schachter, 1956). This theory generated significant research in social psychology and found tremendous applications in therapy and marketing.

Assessments

Psychoanalysis, behaviorism, and Gestalt psychology were three popular branches of psychology typically associated with the first half of the 20th century's psychology. However, the discipline developed in many other directions, both theoretical and practical. Psychology departments began to appear in practically every large university in the United States and other countries.

Psychological testing received significant attention from psychologists as well as support of sponsors from both private companies and government institutions. Not everything in this process went smoothly for psychology. First, psychologists argued about the interpretation and practical applicability of their empirical findings. Next, research methodologies continued to have serious flaws, including problems with sampling and measurement. Furthermore, some professionals, while welcoming psychological research, did not want psychologists to affect some established business practices and procedures.

Despite these and other setbacks, testing became a widely accepted method. Industrial experiments showed the importance of human relations and their impact on productivity and job satisfaction. A prevailing belief was that psychologists were capable of somewhat exact measurements of human capacities. They continued to apply science to practical matters, including education. While scores of psychologists worked on creating new testing instruments, others began to build specialized centers to provide diagnosis and treatment for retarded children and injured workers. Many psychologists moved to the field of applied studies and training such as road traffic problems, vocational guidance, management, or consumer behavior (Carpintero & Herrero, 2002). Psychologists as professionals were gaining confidence in many areas of life.

It was an increasingly accepted view that a person, either young or mature, develops in a complex and interconnected world. Psychologists continued to pay serious attention to the creative interaction between biological and social factors shaping an individual's mind. Research of intelligence began to develop in multiple directions and certainly enriched our perception of intelligence and its many forms, cultural biases in testing, and interpretations of intelligence tests. Developmental psychology had made a significant progress in that direction thanks to the works of Piaget, Vygotsky, and their followers and critics.

New branches of psychology, such as psychology of personality and social psychology, emerged early in the 20th century and developed further in theoretical and experimental studies.

Conclusion

The United States, as a result of a number of social and political developments, was turning into a leading industrial nation. University research flourished and attracted many new scholars both from other countries and "homegrown." Most psychologists were engaged in empirical and theoretical research within already "established" fields of behaviorism and psychoanalysis, to which we will turn in the next chapter.

Summary

- Before World War I, West European psychology played a leading role in the world as a theoretical, academic, and applied field. The postwar developments beginning in the early 1920s have changed this balance of scholarly power in favor of the United States.

- In post–World War I professional psychology, progressive ideas remained strong. They were based on an assumption that science could provide social recipes. Mental hygiene and eugenics remained popular.

- Although the participation of women and minority individuals in American psychology after the 1920s was increasing, most of them choosing a career in psychology faced significant institutional obstacles.

- Psychological testing was a field of research where psychologists could combine both theory and applied knowledge. Among practical goals of testing were evaluation, selection, and training people for various purposes ranging from education to sports and business to manufacturing. Testing stimulated the development of industrial and organizational psychology.

- The Army Testing Project and the Ellis Island studies revealed both accomplishments and weaknesses of psychology. Mental surveys became popular tools of measurement of educational skills and mental abilities in children and adolescents. The Iowa Child Welfare Station became an illustration of studies of behavior and skills of ordinary children under everyday conditions.

- The Hawthorne experiment was a landmark study initially designed to investigate the effects of several improved working conditions on factory productivity. The results of the experiment underlined the importance of psychological factors in productivity, work relations, and job satisfaction.

- Jean Piaget from Switzerland and Lev Vygotsky from Russia studied child development. Vygotsky's observations of parent-child interactions led him to a conclusion about an active and adaptive role of the child's adjustment to the changing conditions and demands of life. Piaget's theory emphasized children's inner developmental mechanisms and their adaptive role. Both theories gained significant international recognition.

- A growing number of psychologists in the 1920s began to pay attention to studies and problems focusing on individuality. Personality as a psychological phenomenon was described in both measurable and descriptive terms.

- Early studies in social psychology focused on social instincts, experimental studies of individuals in groups, and mechanisms of social judgment.

Key Terms

Army Alpha and Army Beta

Assimilation and accommodation

Genetic epistemology

Hawthorne effect

Hawthorne experiment

Iowa Child Welfare Station

Mental hygiene

Mental surveys

Psychotechnics

Trait theory of personality

Zone of proximal development

Behaviorism and Psychoanalysis in the Mid-20th Century

Theoretical and Applied Paths

I shall devote the body of this paper to a description of experiments with rats. But I shall also attempt in a few words at the close to indicate the significance of these findings on rats for the clinical behavior of men.

Edward Tolman (1948)

I was always looking outside myself for strength and confidence but it comes from within. It is there all the time.

Anna Freud (1936/1966)

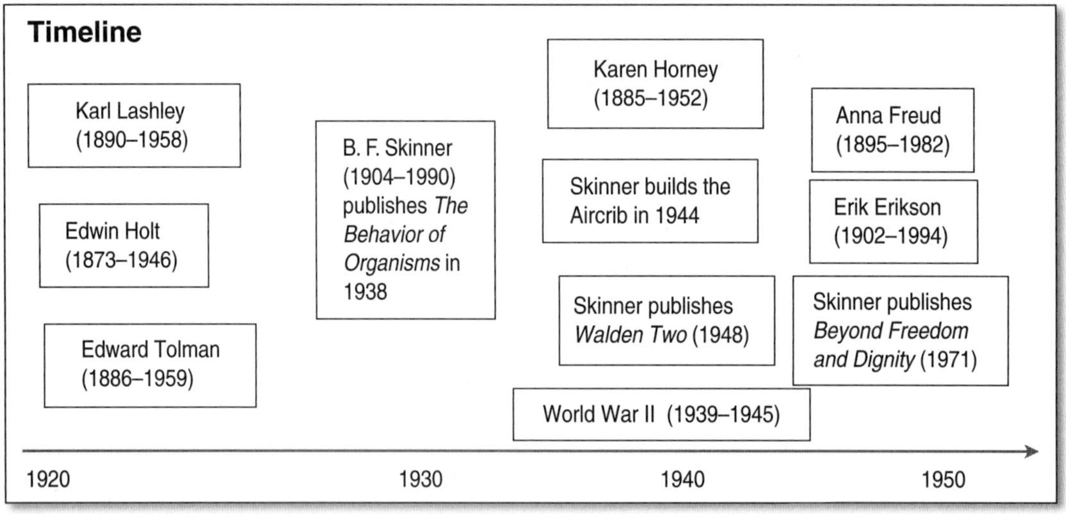

CHAPTER OUTLINE

B. F. Skinner uniquely combined the qualities of a researcher, engineer, writer, and public figure.

Travelling on a train to a 1940 conference in Chicago, a 36-year-old professor, Burrhus Frederic Skinner, from the University of Minnesota, was thinking about the unfolding war in Europe and the threat it posed to America. His attention switched to a flying flock of birds. A thought crossed his mind: Can one use a bird to navigate a missile into an enemy's aircraft? Skinner could already train pigeons in his lab to push buttons or even play a simple piano tune. But can one teach a pigeon to navigate a missile? Back in his lab in Minneapolis, he bought several pigeons to test his ideas. He thought he could train a pigeon connected to a steering device to peck a paper target a few inches away. The pigeons then were trained with aerial photographs to keep pecking the crosshairs on the target. Now Skinner assumed that in a real battle situation, the bird's sharp vision should help guide a flying rocket right into the real target. If the rocket moved away from a target, the bird's moving neck would produce steering movements and thus move the rocket back to the right trajectory. Skinner immediately applied for funding to experimentally test his ideas. Eventually, top experts from the federal government expressed interest in his potentially important defense-related research.

Approximately at the same time, psychologist Henry Murray, who had previously served as director of the Harvard Psychological Clinic, was asked by the Office of Strategic Services (a new U.S. intelligence agency) to compose a psychological profile of German dictator Adolf Hitler. The intelligence experts wanted to learn more about the personality of the German leader. Murray, as scores of other psychiatrists and psychologists of his generation, was already serving in the military. He and his colleagues gathered information from many sources and prepared a detailed psychoanalytic report describing Hitler's intolerance, envy, aggression, and contempt. Murray concluded in the report that Hitler had developed megalomania—the belief in own absolute superiority. Murray also predicted Hitler's increasing insecurity and ruthless behavior in the future. He also suggested Hitler's possible suicide (which happened in actuality in 1945). At the end of the analysis, Murray suggested how the

United States and its allies could increase anti-Hitler propaganda to discredit his image in the minds of the German people.

Both Skinner and Murray represented two different approaches to the study of behavior and motivation, yet they both tried to find practical applications for their studies.

Sources: Skinner (1960); Bjork (2003); Cornell University Law Library (http://library.lawschool.cornell.edu).

Further Development of Behaviorism

Like the research on the *Drosophila* fly in the past proved extremely helpful in understanding basic chromosomal mechanics, the animal studies appeared promising in understanding human behavior. From the first quarter of the 20th century and until the 1960s, a significant number of experimental psychologists accepted the view that the basic research on animals (and experiments on white rats in particular) could yield major insights into the fundamental processes underlying behavior of humans. Differences between species in psychological processes were assumed to be minimal, and rats were considered "model animals." As experimental material, they were inexpensive and easy to take care of. Psychologists studying rats could also investigate their behavior and learning processes with some precision (Logan, 1999). Accuracy of measurement in behavioral research was an inspiring factor attracting many new scholars (Munn, 1933). They believed that behavioral measurement and new discoveries in the brain physiology could help them describe general mechanisms of simple reflexes and complex responses.

Thorndike, Watson, Pavlov, and others provided a solid foundation for future behavioral research. Many new scholars agreed about the major principles of behaviorism but differed in the ways they interpreted it. They were often called neo-behaviorists, although very few of them wanted to accept this one-dimensional label. Besides the differences among them, at least two assumptions unified neo-behaviorists: their unrestrained belief in the possibility and necessity of objective measurement of behavior and their support for the reductionist beliefs that psychology should be a science of behavior and conditioning.

Several researchers made their studies recognizable because of valuable theoretical and practical innovations they added to the mainstream assumptions of behaviorism.

Attempting the Science of Behavior

Studies of conditioning continued, and many of them pursued practical results that could be used in education and treatment. Mary Cover Jones (1897–1987) became known for her research of conditioning related to treatment of fear in infants. Her name frequently appears in conjunction with the famous "little Albert" experiment by John Watson and Rosalie Rayner (see Chapter 7). This experiment illustrated how a fearful reaction could be produced experimentally under laboratory conditions. Jones's goal was different: she wanted to eliminate an existing fear in a 3-year-old child who was conditioned to fear a rabbit. Through the presence of the pleasant stimulus (food) whenever the "scary" rabbit was shown, the fear was gradually gone. She created a chain of conditioned reactions. First, they were fearful responses. Then toleration appeared. After that, fearful responses were eliminated (M. C. Jones, 1924). Later in life, working at the University of California at Berkeley, Jones focused on adolescent psychology and conducted a series of studies on the long-term behavioral effects of early and late physical maturation in adolescence (M. C. Jones, 1957). Her research laid an important foundation for behavioral therapy, one of the most accepted and effective therapeutic methods today, especially in dealing with emotional problems. Many clinical psychologists of the past three decades were working on the problem of fear extinction and its applications in therapy (K. M. Myers & Davis, 2002).

Many psychologists supported behaviorism in general but wanted to alter its focus. For example, Edwin Holt (1873–1946), who served as a professor at Harvard and later at Princeton, criticized Watson's and Pavlov's approaches as behavioral "elementarism" and reductionism for their focus mostly on individual responses. Holt argued that in reality, behavior is different and must be understood as a complex unity of many behavioral acts. Holt introduced the concept of **molar responses.** To respond to a situation, both humans and animals have to interpret it. The response reaction takes time because the response requires interpretation. The concept of "interpretation" signaled a departure from a traditional behaviorism that generally ignored the idea the behavior should have a goal or purpose. Holt's views found support among his many followers. One of Holt's students was Edward Tolman.

Purposeful Behavior. Edward Tolman (1886–1959) earned his reputation as a scientist and a citizen. Back in the early 1950s, he refused to sign a loyalty oath—a symbolic practice that many businesses and institutions accepted at that time as a compliant response to a massive anticommunist campaign across the United States. Not only did Tolman believe that he should not have to take an oath to the government because it violated his legal rights as a citizen, but he also thought that any loyalty oath was an infringement on academic freedom of a scholar. When the authorities attempted to pressure him, he took his case to the California's Supreme Court and won (*Tolman v. Underhill,* 1952). His name and work remain in the history of psychology for this and several other reasons. He was a prominent psychologist who enriched and expanded the initial ideas of behaviorism and gave them a new impulse.

Trained in engineering early in his life, Tolman later became interested in psychology. He studied psychology at Harvard University and traveled to Germany (as you remember, it was a popular destination for psychologists to study at that time). After earning his doctorate degree in 1915, Tolman became an early follower of Watson's behaviorism and one of his enthusiastic promoters. However, as it frequently happens with scientific theories, Tolman found many of the original principles of Watson's behaviorism unsatisfactory. He offered a new set of principles, which he and his new supporters believed represented an improvement and strengthening of the original theory. Working as professor of psychology at the University of California at Berkeley, Tolman began to depart from the traditional view of John Watson's classical behaviorism. Reviewers frequently labeled Tolman as purposive behaviorist, and his views were called **purposive or operational behaviorism.**

What was the essence of Tolman's revision? He believed that when rats or cats push buttons or run through a maze, their actions are not just mechanical responses to some stimuli. There is something in an animal's behavior that maintains its action, its movement toward a goal. This something is a drive, which is located somewhere within an animal's organism. Classical "mental" psychology always taught about the existence of a subjective image of purpose. However, Tolman was not interested in concepts such as "image" or "will." He wanted to use behavioral methods to gain a new understanding of the factors maintaining behavior. He wanted to find measurable variables in the spirit of behaviorism.

He found these variables using the example of frustration. Imagine a person trying to overcome an obstacle. Think in today's terms: You are trying to enter a password to get access to a site. Unfortunately, you are out of luck: Although you remember many passwords, you do not know which one is the right one. After a few minutes of trying, you get more frustrated. As a result, you begin to increase your efforts to find the right password. You check your cell phone's storage file. You try to find the password on a Post-it note somewhere on top of your desk. Meanwhile, frustration does not go away. But what is frustration? Can we see it? No. However, we can perfectly describe frustration in operational terms as a degree of tension caused by an inability to reach a goal. The more time you spend or the more attempts you make unsuccessfully to achieve your goal, the stronger your frustration is. Although frustration causes unpleasant emotions, it continues to direct your behavior for some time.

Tolman suggested an expansion of the traditional S → R (stimulus-reaction) model and added S → O → R, in which "O" stood for measurable processes or variables within an organism. These variables are heredity (some animals or individuals have certain inborn abilities), age (strength of responses may decline with age, for example), quality of previous training (some of us develop specific habits), features of stimuli (responses depend on various signals), and an organism's drive. Tolman believed that the business of psychology was to study the functional relations among these variables, as he described in his most famous book, *Purposive Behavior in Animals and Men* (Tolman, 1932). In his studies of rats' learning, Tolman sought to demonstrate that animals could learn in a flexible manner; they do not necessarily and always learn to develop automatic responses triggered by environmental stimuli. Tolman also used principles borrowed from Gestalt psychology to describe latent learning. He argued that animals could learn the connections between stimuli and did not need any biologically significant event to make their learning occur (see Figure 11.1).

Figure 11.1 Tolman's Modification of the Traditional Behaviorist "Formula"

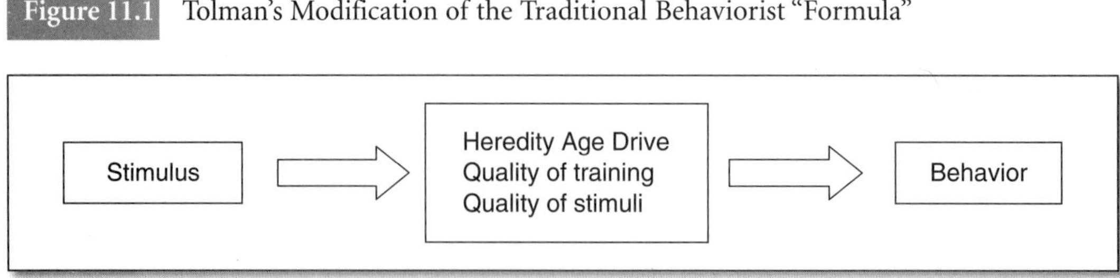

Tolman moved further away from traditional behaviorism by introducing the concept called a **cognitive map,** which later found support among many psychologists (Tolman, 1948). This term stands for internal processing by which individuals code, store, recall, and decode information about particular elements of their experience. It is not just a memory of vivid events. Cognitive maps represent a holistic pattern that guides a person's present behavior based on many previously learned patterns. Tolman and his followers believed that the concept of cognitive maps could explain a wide range of psychological phenomena, ranging from learning disabilities to prejudice. Tolman looked for practical use of the cognitive map concept. For example, by forming new cognitive maps (or learning strategies) in a student, teachers can overcome many learning problems because they had been based on old cognitive maps. Similarly, individuals can overcome prejudice if they approach their previously negative knowledge about a social group from a different perspective. This new perspective will be a new cognitive map that should result in a new behavior (Tolman, 1948).

Tolman's work sparked interest among many psychologists worldwide. Tolman's research of cognitive maps was used in other fields of psychology, particularly in the studies of attitudes, values, and prejudice. Tolman hoped that psychology should be applied to real social and individual problems. In addition to many of his scholarly publications, he wrote *Drives Toward War* (Tolman, 1942), in which he analyzed human propensity to violence. He remained a dedicated and humble scholar. For example, in 1937, while president of the American Psychological Association, he said in a public lecture that psychology, despite its remarkable progress, could not predict accurately the behavior of a rat in a maze; therefore, psychology was even less likely to be used to explain and predict behavior of human beings (Clifford, 1968). Tolman was not a disgruntled scholar. As a true researcher, he simply wanted to state how much psychology should achieve to earn its reputation.

Brain and Behavior. Many followers of behaviorism decided to seek new data not only in laboratory experiments of rats' behavior but also in the fields of biology and physiology. Karl Lashley (1890–1958) was a student and follower of John Watson. Inspired by behaviorism's main principles, he dedicated his life to the study of brain mechanisms of animal behavior. His work included research on brain regulations of sensory receptors and the cortical basis of motor activities. He studied many animals, including primates, but his major work was done on the measurement of behavior before and after specific, carefully quantified, induced brain damage in rats. He trained rats to perform specific tasks, then made cuts in specific areas of the rat cortex, either before or after the animals received the training. The cortical lesions had specific effects on acquisition and retention of knowledge. His main contribution to psychology was his theory about principles of behavioral responses (Lashley, 1929). He showed that the brain cortex functions not as an assemblage of different centers responsible for different action but rather as one mechanism. His experiments revealed that if certain parts of the brain are damaged, other parts may take on the role of the damaged regions. These views reflected a step forward from Watson's positions because Lashley emphasized the complexity of the brain and its special role in reflex formation, which Watson underemphasized.

Behaviorism and Physics. Another approach was based on the deepening of a scientific method of studying behavior based on rigorous methods of mathematics and physics. Clark Hull (1884–1952) could have been a "model" patient for psychoanalyst Alfred Adler (remember his views of psychological compensation): the young Hull was in very poor health. Yet his afflictions did not bring him down. He overcame all the obstacles and became a renowned scientist. He earned a PhD in psychology at the University of Wisconsin in 1918 at the age of 34. After spending 10 years there as a professor, he moved to Yale University. His interests were multiple. He studied, for example, the effects of tobacco on behavior and examined hypnosis and suggestibility (Hull, 1933/2002). Nevertheless, his main research interest was in objective methods of measurement and interpretation of behavior. He began to use rats for his experiments at Yale. He studied conditioning, inspired by Pavlov, and wanted to show that basic conditioning principles could explain the most complex forms of human action (Hull, 1943). He believed in a unification of all psychological studies under the principle of an objective measurement of behavior.

It was definitely a reductionist approach. Hull tried to reduce practically every aspect of human existence to mechanical, physical terms. He wasn't afraid of criticism when he was comparing human beings to extraordinary machines. He emphasized that the "machine" was a metaphor, yet the basic principles of physics according to which machines and human bodies function are the same (Hull, 1935). Behavior, from his view, is a process of constant adaptation to environmental conditions. If adaptation is threatened (absence of food, for example), the organism is in a state of need. This state produces a drive that activates and energizes food-searching behavior. When food is found, the need is satisfied. Organisms constantly generate drives that energize behavior and ultimately reduce needs. The strength of a drive can be measured. Among three factors affecting drives are the number of reinforcements, a degree of deprivation of a need (measured in the number of hours of deprivation), and the incentive value of the stimulus. How does learning work? If an organism responds to a stimulus by a drive reduction, then this response is likely to be retained and repeated. Reinforcement can be defined in terms of reduction of a primary need. The way to strengthen the stimulus-reaction response (or habit strength) is to increase the number of reinforcements.

Hull also believed that mathematics and logic are two disciplines that should help in designing experiments and interpreting them. Studying behavior experimentally, a scientist should establish first a research postulate, or a proposition that requires no additional proof. The next step is to use this postulate to propose a testable idea. Then a test is conducted to support or dismiss this idea. As a result, the initial postulate is reexamined. This approach is common in psychology today.

Many scholars around the world became ardent supporters of behaviorism. For example, Zing-Yang Kuo (1898–1970) worked both in the United States in China and was a passionate follower of behaviorism's methods. He criticized, for instance, the use of the term *instinct* in psychology and preferred to interpret instinct as behavioral changes that accompany maturation (G. Blowers, 2001). In one experiment, he could raise kittens and rats together so that the cats did not chase and kill the rats as they normally do in different conditions. He wanted to demonstrate that all forms of instinctual behavior are learned responses. However, the most remarkable and productive supporter of behaviorism in the mid-20th century was B. F. Skinner.

✓ CHECK YOUR KNOWLEDGE

What is a cognitive map?

What were the main differences between the views of behaviorists described earlier and the ideas of John Watson?

Behaviorism According to B. F. Skinner

Burrhus Frederick Skinner (1904–1990) was one of the most prominent psychologists of the 20th century. His theory and especially his proposed social applications have generated support, heated debates, and critical reactions. His name today is frequently quoted in popular literature and scholarly journals around the world. Skinner's views are frequently simplified and misinterpreted, which happens with controversial theories. Although he continued the line of experimental and theoretical research started by John Watson, Skinner moved further ahead of his prominent predecessor.

He was born in a small town in Pennsylvania and studied philosophy and literature in college. He hoped to become a writer. However, Skinner soon abandoned this plan. He hoped to become a scientist when he went to Harvard to continue his graduate studies. He chose experimental psychology and began to study animals' behavior in experimental conditions. During his long and productive career, he worked at several universities in the United States, including the University of Minnesota and Indiana University. In 1948, he returned to Harvard as a professor and remained there until his retirement. But even after his formal retirement, he remained actively engaged in research and writing.

ON THE WEB

Read B. F. Skinner's brief biographical sketch on the book website.

Several theories influenced his research. He accepted German philosopher Ernst Mach's view of science as a practical tool that had evolved because people needed to make necessary adjustments for their survival. To Skinner, science and technology were useful adaptation tools. Skinner also liked Jacques Loeb's theory of tropism emphasizing the importance of studying the entire organism, not just responses (Chapter 7). Early in his educational career, Skinner developed the view that the scientist has the right not only to observe phenomena but also use and control them. He was an optimist. According to Skinner, psychologists have the right to influence people's lives and make them better. Despite his belief in scientists' ability to improve social life, for the most of his career, he did not say much publicly about domestic politics and stayed away from it.

Two major interests influenced his future research orientation. One was behaviorism. He believed that psychology as a scientific discipline should be based on scientific facts obtained through quantitative research. The other influence was his exceptional craftsmanship skills.

Continuing Watson's Tradition. Skinner was already interested in behaviorism when he became a graduate student at Harvard in 1928. Influenced by the ideas of René Descartes and John Watson and Ivan Pavlov's work on reflexes translated into English in 1927, Skinner became increasingly convinced that accurate measurement of behavior was a challenge he wanted to tackle. Impressed with Pavlov's experimental procedures, Skinner moved in a different direction: He embraced the idea that psychologists in their experiments need not rely so much on physiology (remember, Pavlov collected saliva) but can focus on overt behavior instead. He was not really interested in what was going "inside" the brain. Skinner turned to descriptive behaviorism.

Since his childhood, Skinner loved to make things with his hands. As a young man, he developed remarkable skills of a craftsman. He always liked to design and build things from toys to small furniture and house appliances. These skills became helpful in building his experimental equipment. In the beginning, he studied the behavior of young squirrels and wanted to see how they formed their insights: he was trying to find further evidence to support Köhler's research of monkeys. After switching from squirrels to rats, Skinner realized that a typical rat maze used by other researchers was not good enough for him: he could not measure precisely an animal's behavior in it. Something else was needed, simple and inexpensive, that would allow him to conduct precise measurements. He knew he could accurately measure behavior if only he could build an appropriate measurement device.

He began to design boxes with tunnels, holes, or lever presses, studying responses of rats to different experimental conditions. One device was particularly successful. A mouse placed inside a specially made box was free to move around it. As soon as the animal pressed a lever (at first accidentally), a small food pellet was automatically released on a tray so the mouse could eat it. In behaviorist terms, the mouse's lever-pressing act was reinforced by the food delivered immediately after. Skinner next realized that he could measure many elements (or variables) of the process: the time elapsing before the mouse presses the lever, the number of repetitions before the animal learns a habit, and so forth. Years later, psychologists and laypeople began to call this type of device the *Skinner box.* He did not like this term and preferred to use *experimental space.*

All Behavior Is Conditioned. Using his experimental devices, Skinner became convinced that there is nothing accidental in the behavior of the rat. It is completely conditioned. It is all subject to natural laws as, for example, the rate of heart beat. He began to study different behavioral reinforcements. He borrowed this term from Pavlov. One substantial difference between him and Pavlov emerged. In the studies of the Russian physiologist, the dogs were conditioned to salivate at the presence of certain stimuli while being literally detained motionless standing on an experimental platform. In Skinner's experiments, the animals had enough freedom to move within the box, which was a condition more "natural" to them. The rats would develop their reflexes by achieving certain goals such as getting food after pushing a button. They would quickly learn about the consequences of their behavior. Rewards or punishments follow certain actions. This type of learning has received the name **operant conditioning.** The word *operant* has several meanings, but in the context of Skinner's ideas, it meant activities producing effects. The rat in the box presses the button (an activity), and then the food is delivered (an effect).

Both animals and humans face the consequences of their actions. People act and then see the results of their deeds. How do they learn from this experience? What are the connections between the outside conditions and behavior? Many scholars in the past had already asked this question and offered their own experimental procedures to test their hypotheses. Remember, Thorndike, for example, timed how fast animals escaped from the puzzle box. Pavlov measured the amount of saliva to judge the reflexes of his experimental dogs. Skinner's experiments also allowed him to change the experimental variables in precise terms—for example, the number of pellets given or the frequency of reinforcement. It was almost an experimenter's dream to be able to deal with the measurable variables of experimental conditions and the following responses.

Skinner came up with the idea of **schedules of reinforcement** or conditions involving different rates and times of reinforcement. By changing the conditions of different schedules of reinforcement, Skinner was able to measure behavioral responses. For example, at the beginning of an experiment, the rat would get food every time it pushed the button. Next, Skinner would give reinforcement precisely within 1-minute intervals regardless of how many times the rat pushed the button. Or, he would release food exactly after the rat pushed the button three consecutive times. Now he could measure the behavior of his experimental animals in precise terms.

Between 1928 and 1930, Skinner conducted numerous experiments involving rats. He did not study isolated reflexes or muscle movements. He wanted to study an animal's behavior influenced by multiple measurable factors. In several articles published in the 1930s, he showed that the seemingly spontaneous behavior of an animal—remember the studies of the insight in Gestalt psychology—was in fact determined almost exclusively by its reinforcing conditions (Skinner, 1938). The relationship between such reinforcing conditions in behavior appeared to Skinner as universal laws of behavior (Skinner, 1965). The inside content of the reflex—the brain mechanisms or other factors—no longer interested Skinner. He described reflex as a correlation between stimulus and response and other variables outside the organism (Bjork, 2003).

CASE IN POINT

Superstitions and Learning. One of Skinner's experiments examined the formation of superstition in one of his favorite experimental animals, the pigeon. Skinner placed a series of hungry pigeons in a cage attached to an automatic mechanism that delivered food to the pigeons at regular intervals regardless of the birds' behavior. He discovered that the pigeons associated the delivery of the food with whatever chance actions they had been performing as it was delivered (turning around, rocking, etc.) and that they subsequently continued to perform these same actions in anticipation to get food. Skinner believed that human beings develop their superstitions in similar ways.

From Animals to Humans. Skinner's early major work, *The Behavior of Organisms* (1938), received a largely unenthusiastic review from American psychologists. Only a few behavioral scientists extended their praise to Skinner. As a scholar, he felt that he was underappreciated. Yet he was deeply convinced that the results of his studies on rats could be used to study human beings. Skinner believed, for example, that speech is the process of interaction among humans through the means of their behavior. People are both speakers and listeners engaged in verbal behavior. They use language to influence other people's behavior and receive constant reinforcement by listening to the speech of other people. Speakers and audiences have reinforcing qualities. People use verbal and nonverbal signals to convey their intentions and receive reinforcement often through reading. Language can be learned through imitation almost in the same way people learn about other forms of behavior (Skinner, 1957).

Skinner was a scholar and professor. He experimented in his university laboratory and wrote in the basement of his home almost daily. He was also an avid inventor and designer, trying to make practical use of his many ideas. Remember the opening vignette of this chapter that described ideas about pigeon-controlled missiles? What happened to this unusual idea? At first, almost everyone was skeptical about Skinner's missile project. However, after the devastating attack against the United States in Pearl Harbor in 1941, the University of Minnesota and a local business decided to sponsor this unusual project to see if it could bring some encouraging results for defense research. Skinner received a $5,000 grant and hired several graduate students to assist him. He trained many pigeons to keep pecking on a target. In the spring of 1943, his experiments drew the attention of government officials. Skinner received a larger grant of $25,000 to continue his work. The main challenge was mechanical: he needed to find a way to transform the birds' movements into a usable signal to provide steering. Another problem was the accuracy of the missile and the time necessary to readjust course on a moving target. Skinner also realized that he had to train his pigeons to function aboard a flying rocket or bomb. It was a daunting task, but Skinner believed he was succeeding (Bjork, 2003).

Unfortunately, the pigeon project had to be abandoned by 1944. The official explanation was that the country had to spend funds on more important defense studies with more immediate applications on the battlefield. However, in reality, the members of the National Defense Research Committee remained skeptical about the ability of an animal to carry out a very sophisticated military operation such as navigating a missile. The country's top scientists at that time were working on the Manhattan Project, a super-sophisticated venture to develop nuclear weapons. The idea of a bird geared with steering devices and sitting in the front of the missile seemed a bit unrealistic. The skeptics also believed that it would be too risky to let psychologists be in charge of a defense project. Skinner was extremely upset about the unfortunate fate of this undertaking. Yet he was convinced that it would be just a matter of time when everyone could see the practical value of his behavioral research. He was convinced that psychology, as he saw it, was developing in the right direction (Skinner, 1960).

He worked on many other projects. In 1944, Skinner built a thermostatically controlled crib with a safety glass front and a stretched-canvas floor for his second daughter, Deborah. The box-like crib contained soundproof walls and a window. It had warming and moistening devices and also air filters to control the quality of the air inside. Skinner wanted to have a crib that would provide both safety and freedom of movement for a baby. As a behaviorist, he believed that this crib would create a more controlled environment for the child and better opportunities for parents to develop good habits in their children.

Skinner wanted to attract potential investors and manufacturers for his device. He published an article in the popular *Ladies' Home Journal* describing his baby crib. For commercial purposes, Skinner agreed to pick a catchy name for his device. First it was labeled *Heir Conditioner* (as if the crib was supposed to "condition" a family heir). Then another name was chosen, *Aircrib.* In the end, despite his relentless efforts, Skinner's commercial enterprise was unsuccessful. Both manufacturing companies and consumers remained somewhat skeptical about the usefulness and safety of his invention.

☞ CASE IN POINT

Aircrib. Aircrib was an easily cleaned, temperature- and humidity-controlled box that Skinner designed to assist parents in raising their babies. It was built to make early child care simpler. The temperature inside was regulated and the air circulated properly. The child would have freedom to move and develop confidence. Cleaning and drying devices would simplify the diaper-changing procedures. If a baby cried, the insulation would reduce the noise yet the parent could hear the baby very well. Unfortunately for Skinner, the public did not embrace this invention with great enthusiasm. Most parents felt uncomfortable putting their babies into boxes with electric devices. Lawyers warned about liability in case something went wrong with the crib. Many people also thought of the Aircrib as a small boxed "jail" for babies. The history of the Aircrib shows that many seemingly great inventions have to find public approval, and the researchers' great reputation is not a guarantee for the market success of their ideas.

Later in his life, Skinner designed and built various learning machines based on the concept of positive reinforcement. His early inventions were card-and-plastic devices for children to take simple arithmetic tasks, give answers, and see the immediate results. Seeing the result immediately, from Skinner's view, would provide additional reinforcement to the children and improve their learning. Early machines were crude but later grew in complexity and sophistication. Later versions, such as one called *Didak,* were commercially produced and received encouraging reviews. However, companies were reluctant to commit substantial funds to sell this product simply because it was unclear to them how many parents and schools would purchase it. There were other similar competing devices on the market, and the emerging personal computers had already presented a serious competition to plastic gadgets. You know how this competition ended.

From an Individual to Society. Skinner was also a social designer. Two of his most famous books, *Walden Two* (1948/2005) and *Beyond Freedom and Dignity* (1971), brought him worldwide fame. They also sparked heated discussions. In *Walden Two,* Skinner returns to the question posed by the 19th-century philosopher and writer Henry D. Thoreau. In *Walden,* published in 1854, Thoreau showed the psychological and moral benefits of a simple lifestyle. Skinner, in turn, described a fictional idyllic community of about 1,000 people. They live simple lives and own property collectively. Their economy is mostly agricultural. They educate children together. Everyone works for 4 hours daily. People recycle, consume only what is necessary, and do not overproduce. There is almost no government and very little religion. One of the key points of the story is that this community uses key principles of conditioning and positive enforcement to achieve societal harmony. Skinner emphasized that one of the problems of human civilization is that across centuries, the power of conditioning belonged to the wrong people: kings, presidents, and other authorities. They were, for the most part, incompetent people who continuously abused power to advance their own selfish interests. In Skinner's version of the world, as soon as educated behaviorists take over, they would create a better society for everybody.

Skinner's ideas received a storm of criticism. Critics believed that this utopian theory was no more than a disguised attempt to justify the necessity to transfer political power to scientists who would use behavioral methods to advance their own sinister interests. Some compared Skinner's ideas to communism. Yet to others, *Walden Two* was a naive vision of a culture shaped by behavioral engineers such as Skinner, who was simply a misguided scientist believing in conditioned slavery (Jessup, 1948). The book didn't sell well until the 1960s, the time of social and cultural experimentation in the West. Then *Walden Two* was "rediscovered" by a younger generation. Several volunteers even attempted to create a real-life community based on Skinner's book.

But the biggest Skinner's hit was the other book, *Beyond Freedom and Dignity.* It was featured in *Time* magazine on September 20, 1971. Skinner insisted that people are misguided in their overconfident belief in freedom. To solve mounting social problems, including the threat of a nuclear war, environmental problems, and overpopulation, human beings have to choose a different path of development based on the principles of behavioral conditioning. He argued that the problem was not freedom itself: human cultures in the past had survived without freedom. The problem is in government institutions that define freedom and make people follow those definitions. Freedom, in fact, should come from scientists. They would show that human evolution was a gigantic exercise in self-control, which should continue.

The book came out during the time when many American intellectuals demanded even greater freedom than they had. Criticism of his book came from scholars and philosophers, including a champion of liberal ideas, Noam Chomsky, and a top conservative intellectual, Ayn Rand. They both criticized Skinner for his alleged disbelief that human beings should pursue freedom. Skinner, of course, defended his work. He claimed that the alleged freedom that Americans thought they possessed was merely a set of conditioned reactions called consumerism. Consumerism is destructive. True freedom can occur only when people invite science to identify the morally "right" kinds of conditioning based on moderation, rational choice, and common good. Skinner wanted to free people from the abusive forces of contemporary life.

An Overview of Neo-Behaviorism. The main principles of behaviorism introduced by animal psychologists and developed by Thorndike, Watson, Pavlov, and others found a continuous support in the work of behaviorists in the mid-20th century. If you find many of these views somewhat similar to one another, you are right. In modern psychology textbooks, these researchers are frequently called neo-behaviorists as if they had represented the second generation of the "original" behaviorists. One of the key features of the neo-behaviorist orientation was its acceptance of the mediating variable in the classical S → R model. More behaviorists accepted the importance of the additional, cognitive component in their formulas and invited concepts such as purpose and goal in their interpretations of behavior (Staddon, 2001).

Several reasons explain the exceptional status that B. F. Skinner has earned in American and world psychology. The first was his uncompromising view of psychology as a scholarly discipline. He became interested in it relatively late in life and therefore, as he admitted himself, was not much impressed with the old, traditional "mental" psychology. Skinner developed a branch of investigation based exclusively on empirical facts and data-driven research. He downplayed the importance of a theoretical platform and turned to the deductive method: He wanted to obtain facts first and only then turn to their interpretation. Unlike many prominent behaviorists discussed earlier, including Tolman, Hull, and Clark, Skinner did not pay attention to so-called mediating factors in the classical behaviorist formulas. As Watson before him, Skinner excluded the subjective mental element from his investigation. He believed that two key processes, natural selection and operant conditioning, shape both the past and present of animals and human beings. As a scientist, he did not believe in free will and subjective intentions. All of them are just a person's reactions to stimuli. People have to adjust to changing conditions. The environment *selects* successful behavior.

Overall, behavioral principles have found important applications in today's behavioral methods of treatment of psychological disorders, including chemical addictions, anxiety, and mood problems. Behavioral theories generally suggest that circumstances,

ON THE WEB

Learn more about contemporary applications of behavioral models to clinical practice of Martin E. P. Seligman and his colleagues. We will return to Seligman's work in Chapter 13.

such as stress, may lead to constant anxiety or depressive symptoms because they reduce the number of positive stimuli in a person's environment. Certain conditions in our lives may either increase or decrease the probability of abnormal or dysfunctional emotional symptoms. Behavior therapies based on basic principles of operant conditioning often have been very effective in the treatment of phobias, anxiety, and mood problems (Lewinsohn, Rohde, Seeley, Klein, & Gotlib, 2003; Nolen-Hoeksema, 1991).

✓ CHECK YOUR KNOWLEDGE

In which way did Skinner continue Watson's tradition in psychology?

What is the difference between the Skinner's box and Thorndike's puzzle box?

What was the main idea of the book *Beyond Freedom and Dignity?*

A Winding Road of Psychoanalysis

Psychoanalysis as a theory and therapeutic method was evolving in the mid-20th century. Although many university professors treated psychoanalysis with serious apprehension, many others saw the works of Freud, Adler, and Jung as an innovative contribution to psychology. Some even considered psychoanalysis a step forward and away from traditional laboratory psychology of sensation, memory, or reflexes. In the clinical field, psychoanalysis initially remained a controversial but intriguing approach to the treatment of psychological problems. Later, it was becoming an increasingly accepted method of treatment of mental illness.

Psychoanalysis in the second quarter of the 20th century developed in several directions. The first path was related to therapy and clinical practice in general. The second path was associated with the development of the original psychoanalytic concepts of Freud, Jung, and Adler and the advancement of new theories. The third path was related to the expansion of psychoanalysis in the fields of social sciences.

Psychoanalysis and Society

Not everything was developing smoothly for the supporters of psychoanalytic theory and methods. Over the years, many psychologists continued to see psychoanalysis as just a fashionable trend. In articles published in American academic journals, specialists evaluated psychoanalysis as something similar to the Emmanuelle movement blending moral education and therapy: It was interesting and entertaining but eventually doomed to fade away (Scott, 1908). Others saw psychoanalysis not as a groundbreaking theory but rather as a sophisticated persuasion technique that could be used in clinical practice. Still others reserved their judgments and wanted to study psychoanalysis in some detail before expressing their opinion (Dunlap, 1920). However, despite criticisms and reservations, psychoanalysis generated huge public interest worldwide and motivated many young people to take psychology classes.

Popular Appeal. Few psychologists in the early 1900s could foresee a rapid growth of public fascination with psychoanalysis two decades later. Newspaper articles, magazine stories, and pop-psychology books contributed to this frenzy. A new fashion trend was emerging among the educated circles in the United States and Europe in the 1920s. Upper-middle-class professionals, students, professors, and artists wanted to be psychoanalyzed or "psyched" (as people called it then). People began to analyze one another at home parties and other informal gatherings. Words such as *complex* or *libido* from the Freudian dictionary penetrated the vocabulary of educated people. In a spirit of American entrepreneurship, some business-minded people in the United States began to register educational companies to offer crash courses in psychoanalysis. They promised their potential graduates advanced knowledge, full access to the therapeutic profession, and, of course, a great income in the future. Criminologists turned to psychoanalysis to interpret the behavior of violent criminals, habitual sex offenders, and swindlers. Educators were searching for lesser known hidden biographical facts to explain learning problems and deviant behavior. To attribute an individual's problems back to parents (as Freud taught), inferiority problems (as Adler suggested), or archetypes (based on Jung's theory) was intriguing. Discussions of human sexuality and revelations related to the most fascinating details of people's personal lives generated magazines sales. Great writers such as Fyodor Dostoevsky, Franz Kafka, and Stefan Zweig were fine "analysts" in their own way because they revealed to the reading public the intimate world of their literary characters. Yet their method was artistic imagination. Psychoanalysts, on the other hand, were doctors and scientists. They studied real, not imaginary, people having real problems (Karon & Widener, 2001). This was helping psychoanalysis to gain reputation and claim scientific legitimacy.

Money and Turf Battles. Scores of professionals turned to psychoanalysis not only because it was an interesting theory and seemingly useful method. Psychologists, psychiatrists, anthropologists, literary critics, journalists, and people of many other professions gradually discovered that their use of psychoanalysis generated money and could even bring a stable income. Where did the money come from? Primarily, they were paying clients with psychological problems who needed therapy. Others were average customers. They were buyers of books, journals, and magazines. They attended lectures for a fee. Students paid tuition to study psychoanalysis or develop therapeutic skills. Demand drives supply in a market economy. Psychoanalysis, in a way, became a "product" for sale and purchase. Psychoanalysts could advertise their ideas, generate the demand for them, and create jobs.

In other countries, psychoanalysis also attracted initial attention and support. The reasons for such support were different. In the Soviet Union in the 1920s, several psychologists and physicians were allowed to organize psychoanalytic centers and even received state funding. For example, Jung's former patient and confidante, Sabrina Spielrein (1885–1942), returned to the Soviet Union and hoped to use psychoanalysis in a newly developing child psychology field. Initially, government officials there supported psychoanalysis. They thought that this science created by Western scholars could help the Soviet officials to understand all the weaknesses of the capitalist society (Mursalieva, 2003). Later, however, the official support ended for ideological reasons: psychoanalysis could not fit into communist ideology and was prohibited (Etkind, 1993). In Germany, after the Nazi power came to power, psychoanalysis was prohibited as a "Jewish" science, and most therapists were forced to immigrate.

Meanwhile, in Europe and North and South America, many followers of psychoanalysis began to apply its theoretical assumptions to study and treat a variety of psychological problems. Practicing therapists opened private clinics. Such facilities were founded in most European capitals. Clinicians used these centers for two purposes: to treat their clients and train professionals. One such clinic was founded in London in 1920 to become an important center for training specialists dealing with mental illness (Fraher, 2004). Although many psychologists, such as J. Cattell in the United States, believed that psychoanalysis was no more than an educated obsession, psychoanalysis was winning a growing recognition in the 1920s and 1930s as a legitimate form of therapy. University students saw in psychoanalysis an interesting and rewarding career.

However, as soon as psychoanalysis appeared as a legitimate and profitable enterprise, the battle among various professional groups for the influence within its ranks was certainly assured. Opinions clashed. Actions followed. Some specialists referred to the original Freudian view that any willing person could become an educated analyst and a medical degree should not be a prerequisite. Others disagreed. In the 1920s, in Europe and the United States, legal cases were filed against practicing psychoanalysts who did not have a medical degree. Furthermore, professional medical organizations in several countries, including the United States, made a clever legal maneuver. They agreed to accept psychoanalysis as a legitimate form of therapy, which they had initially opposed. Yet an important condition was set. Now individuals who practiced psychoanalysis must have applied for a medical license. As a result, the medical establishment could limit the number of individuals who were permitted to practice psychoanalysis. This was a way to reduce competition in the field.

Analysts themselves wanted to limit the number of people allowed to practice psychoanalysis. The demands to regulate it grew in many countries. For example, in 1926, the New York Psychoanalytic Society restricted the use of psychoanalysis for medicinal purposes only to medical doctors properly trained and accredited. In the atmosphere of the medicalization of psychological knowledge related to mental illness (see Chapter 10), the debates about psychoanalysis deepened the rift between medical doctors who demanded restrictions, on one side, and psychologists who wanted more choices for themselves, on the other. Doctors continued to win legal cases to ensure that fewer psychologists and other nonmedical professionals remained in competition. This was a continuous turf battle, a struggle for money, jobs, grants, private funds, and government commissions. As a result, medical doctors pushed psychologists to play only secondary, supportive roles in psychoanalysis. For the young discipline of clinical psychology, it was a difficult struggle for legitimacy and survival.

Each country's conditions influenced the fate of psychoanalysis. In the United States, most psychoanalysts were medical doctors, educated in medical schools and properly licensed. Medical doctors were largely responsible for theoretical developments of psychoanalysis.

Theoretical Expansions: Ego Psychology

The revisions of the classic Freudian theory continued. New generations of his followers accepted the general idea that the infantile conflicts should affect the experiences of an adult. They also acknowledged that the recognition of such conflicts should be achieved in therapy. After this point, positions and interests differed. Several trends emerged (Fairbairn, 1963). Many psychoanalysts began to focus on the analysis of the ego. They acknowledged the existence of the unconscious drives shaped in early childhood. However, instead of speculating about these drives, analysts now approached a person as functioning in real-life circumstances. As you remember, in the Freudian classification, the ego represents mostly the conscious aspects of the individual's mental world. A new field of research called **ego psychology** was focusing on facts related to the ego's interaction with its social environment.

Anna Freud did not live in the shadow of her prominent father. She became one of the most respected psychologists of the 20th century as a theorist, innovator, and clinical practitioner.

Ego psychology was in some ways a reasonable compromise that allowed psychoanalysts to claim more legitimacy in the mainstream university psychology. In this new way, the classic Freudian theory could be applied not only to mental illness but also to a wide range of social and developmental issues. Subsequent psychologists interested in ego psychology emphasized the role of defenses, early childhood experiences, and the importance of sociocultural influences in a person's life. Ego psychology also reintroduced consciousness as a legitimate area of study (Hartmann, 1958). Because of its emphasis on rational factors, its basic principles were applied to psychological research in the fields of learning, education, and testing (Sandler, 1985).

What were the most important findings of ego psychology? It has never been a cohesive theory with established definitions. This term was frequently used to describe a wide range of studies focusing on the mechanisms of the ego functioning. To illustrate, we will examine the work of two remarkable psychologists, Anna Freud and Erik Erikson.

Work of Anna Freud. In the history of psychology, only a few children of famous psychologists continued the successful work of their parents. One was Anna Freud (1895–1982), the youngest of Sigmund Freud's six offspring. Born and raised in Vienna, she started reading her father's papers and books at age 15. She chose a professional career as a schoolteacher. Anna continued to study psychoanalysis, participated in analytical interviews with her father, and became a member of the Vienna Psychoanalytical Society in 1922, after which she was actively involved in theoretical and practical work for many years. Anna escaped persecution by the Nazis and emigrated with her parents from Austria to London in 1938. A founder of a child therapy clinic—now called the Anna Freud Centre—she continued to work in Great Britain for many years, earning many awards and honorary degrees.

ON THE WEB

Learn more about the Anna Freud Centre in London on the book website.

But it wasn't her father's reputation alone that brought Anna worldwide recognition. She was a talented scholar, instructor, and therapist. Anna Freud believed that children could not explain their psychological problems in the way many adults could. Therapists should develop special knowledge and skills to understand children's stories and explanations and interpret their symptoms. She developed different techniques of assessment and treatment of childhood disorders, thereby contributing to contemporary views of anxiety and depression in children. Anna Freud was one of pioneers of child clinical psychology.

Her most influential book was *The Ego and the Mechanisms of Defense* (A. Freud, 1936/1966). In this mostly theoretical work, she focused on the struggle of the ego with the overwhelming demands of the id and other powerful restrictions imposed by reality. The function of the ego is to regulate and defend itself from these contradictory demands. Such defense is set to protect a person's ego against anxiety, shame, or any form of unpleasantness. The defense is launched automatically and remains mostly unconscious. This means that a person's defenses occur without a person's awareness about them. Quite often, for an observer, there is little relation between a set of circumstances and the person's responses to them. This happens because the defenses are launched to protect this person's ego and not necessarily to produce a rational response to a situation. For example, we all know that a serious relationship involves responsibility. Why does a person in a relationship often act in a very immature, even childish manner? Behavioral immaturity is responsibility avoidance. This person does not want to accept responsibility and protects the ego by acting immature. Ego defenses can be described as **defense mechanisms** or specific unconscious structures that enable an individual to avoid awareness of anxiety-arousing issues. How can one detect and study defense mechanisms? A trained analyst is capable of doing so in the process of a clinical interview and by examining a person's everyday behavior and decisions. There are no experimental facilities or measuring devices. Analysts needed only paper and pencil to record their observations and interpretations (see Figure 11.2).

The overall idea about the existence of special "protective mechanisms" helping an individual to cope with reality was generally well received. It seemed to complement

Figure 11.2 How Defense Mechanisms Function

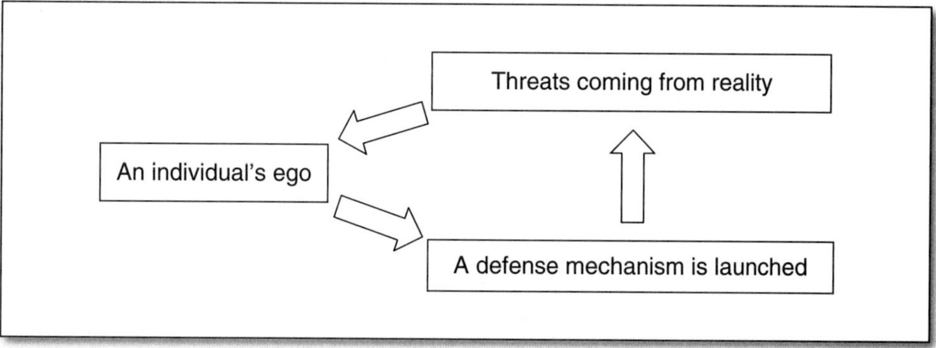

other theories. For example, a child psychologist or specialist in human evolution could see the defense mechanisms as special forms of coping, allowing individuals to adjust to changing environmental conditions.

One of Anna Freud's followers was Erik Erikson (1902–1994), whom she had met back in Vienna. Erikson was born in Germany and received initial training at the Vienna Psychoanalytic Institute before his immigration to the United States. He worked in America as a practitioner and professor teaching in different schools, including Yale, the University of California at Berkeley, and Harvard. Erik Erikson developed psychoanalysis by including his explorations of sociocultural influences on an individual's development.

Erik Erikson's Stages of Development. On the basis of his observations of hundreds of patients, Erikson theorized that all people pass through eight developmental stages that stretch from birth to death. In each stage, the ego faces a developmental conflict or crisis. If the crisis has a positive resolution, the person's ego is strengthened by gaining greater adaptation (Erikson, 1950). But if the crisis has a negative resolution, the ego loses strength, which results in poor adaptation. For instance, if a young girl's conflict between a desire to skip lunch and play and fear of retribution from parents has a positive resolution (parents allowed her to do what she wanted), she will emerge with the virtue of purpose. Contrary, a negative outcome would result in a sense of unworthiness. Erikson thus defined the healthy or mature personality as one whose ego possesses the eight virtues—namely, hope, will, purpose, competence, fidelity, love, care, and wisdom. These virtues emerge in progression, from a positive resolution at each stage of development. Psychotherapy, from his view, was to encourage the growth of whatever virtues the person was missing to achieve happiness (Erikson, 1968).

Erikson's views allow us to approach the issue of global applicability of psychological ideas established in one culture. Initially, Erikson's ideas generated interest and found support of many psychologists in the West. Studies showed that his theory of the developmental stages could be applicable to a wide variety of people in various cultures

(Gardiner et al., 1998). Erikson's views correspond in many ways with Indian philosophical traditions aiming at self-transformation through insight into the nature of self (Paranjpe, 1998). However, Erikson's developmental stages indicate a very general sequence that cannot always be paralleled in other countries. Unlike most adults in economically developed societies, people in many parts of the world face a very insecure reality. Hunger, violence, and oppression imposed by authorities, chronic ecological problems, and other cataclysms are the permanent focus of these people's daily concerns. Various erratic disturbances present a wide range of unpredictable problems, and the sequence of these problems is different from what appears in Erikson's classification. Therefore, more immediate strategies of survival "here and now" are likely to dominate these people's lives, not necessarily the long-term inner conflicts related to the past. Furthermore, the issue of an individual's identity is not over by adolescence, as Erikson suggested. Studies of immigrants to the United States show that identity continues to evolve in many people during adulthood, long after the period Erikson had proposed in his classification (Shiraev & Levy, 2009). With increasing global migration, the identity is likely to undergo changes in many people going through social transition in their lives.

On the other hand, Erikson based his ideas on the assumption that people should have choices in terms of their identity or beliefs. However, in many parts of the world, people's identities and lifestyles are prescribed at birth. They have to accept a particular religion, social status, profession, and place to live. People have fewer choices, and therefore their transition from one stage to another may be "smoother" than for people in the Western cultures who have more choices. It is also important to realize that in some cultures, social maturation is not associated with increased independence, as it happens in the West, but rather with increased interdependence. In India, for example, the Hindu concept of self is not focused on one's autonomy but rather on being an integral part of a larger whole or group (Kurtz, 1992). In general, when applying Erikson's theory to specific cultural conditions, we have to analyze how each culture views each life crisis—assuming, of course, that the crisis takes place—and what is generally expected of an individual to perform, believe in, or reject to solve the crisis.

To learn more about the increasing diversity of psychoanalysis, we should review the work of several prominent scientists who preserved the initial ideas of psychoanalysis but, like Anna Freud and Erik Erikson, moved farther away from it.

Theoretical Expansions: Away From the Libido Concept

This section will pay attention to the works of Karen Horney, Henry Murray, Harry Stack Sullivan, and Jacques Lacan, who all made significant contributions to theoretical and clinical psychology in the mid-20th century. The significance of their views for psychology's history was partly based on the extent of their departure from the original Freudian ideas. One of major areas of revision was the libido concept.

Studies of Coping and Development. A significant revision of the Freudian concept of libido came from Karen Horney (1885–1952). Born and raised in Germany, she received a medical degree from the University of Berlin in 1913. In 1920, Horney took up a position within the Institute for Psychoanalysis in Berlin, where she lectured on psychoanalysis for several years. She immigrated to the United States in 1930 where she continued her medical work and research. Having been trained within the main framework of psychoanalysis, she recognized the power of unconscious conflicts, their roots in infancy and childhood, and the role of the therapist in the treatment of mental illness. Yet, she moved beyond the traditional views of psychoanalysis.

She criticized Freud's approach to sexuality and the concept of libido. She rejected the view that the source of female unconscious conflicts is rooted in the woman's sense of inferiority. Men have all the reasons to feel inferior to and envious of women, she insisted. One of several reasons for envy is based on men's inability to bear children. She also criticized the concept of the Oedipus complex, suggesting that children's ambivalent relationships with their parents most likely are caused by specific circumstances of their life and not necessarily by sexual factors alone (Horney, 1950).

Karen Horney broadened the traditional understanding of neurosis (see Chapter 6) and considered it a more common phenomenon than most analysts believed. Neurosis in her view was a general maladjustment between an individual and traumatic events. People pursue their basic needs, including affection, power, companionship, perfection, achievement, and so forth. Individuals tend to satisfy these needs by developing coping strategies: in some cases, people move forward, but in other situations, people shift away from their needs or go against them. For example, a person feeling lonely may try to find a new friend. Under different circumstances, however, loneliness can lead to this person's further social isolation or aggressive behavior. Horney used the term **basic anxiety** to describe a person's feelings of loneliness, hopelessness, and counterhostility, which is a person's emotional response to intimidating situations. Such negative feelings originate during childhood and are based on the child's relationships with the parents. The nature of traumatic events does not have to be sexual. A person's fear of becoming helpless or lonely creates anxiety, which may produce abnormal responses, which constitute the foundation for a neurosis.

As a psychoanalyst, she focused on broad social and cultural factors affecting the child's development (Paris, 1994). As a scholar and practitioner, she paid special attention to women and examined problems they faced in society. She pointed out that many psychological problems relating to women's self-esteem, confidence, and psychological stability are rooted in old customs and societal expectations. In her view, society encourages women to depend on men and worship their strength and wealth. She also saw the solution of social inequalities between men and women in therapy, including self-therapy. She was one of the early creators and promoters of this method.

Another analyst who made an important contribution to the study of anxiety was Harry Stack Sullivan (1892–1949). Born in the United States, he enriched and expanded psychoanalysis based on his theoretical research and practical work with patients. He preserved several core concepts of the Freudian system by emphasizing the importance of unconscious mechanisms and dedicating significant attention to a person's early childhood experiences. Like Karen Horney, he studied loneliness and its early impact on psychological development of the child. Like Anna Freud, he believed that defenses reduce an individual's anxiety, yet they often lead to inaccurate interpretations of reality.

During early development, children develop certain self-perceptions and thus construct the world based on such perceptions. For example, early in life, the child develops the concept of the **bad-me:** an early awareness of self as disapproved by the adults. This awareness is a center for the development of later anxiety. However, children can see themselves from a different angle. The **good-me** is the child's awareness of an aspect of self that brings rewards such as approval or kindness from the parents or other adults. This awareness serves a foundation for understanding the whole self as good. The **not-me** refers to awareness of certain individual features that the child does not want to consider as part of his or her life and experience. The not-me is kept out of awareness by pushing it deep into the unconscious. An individual's personality is formed through the complex set of relationships and interactions. Sullivan maintained that people develop their psychological traits during adolescence and even later during adulthood.

French psychiatrist and social scientist Jacques Lacan (1901–1981) made a further contribution to psychoanalysis by studying the development of identity in children. He retained one of the main Freudian postulates that human beings are born into the world with essential needs that require constant gratification. However, other people begin to play a crucial role in the development of these needs. Early in life, we learn how to desire things not because we need them but rather because other people tell or show to us that *they* need them. As a result, what is important or not in our life is largely decided by others. If they, for example, show little interest in an object, it loses its attraction to us too. Lacan was a practicing therapist and author whose educational seminars in the 1950s attracted significant attention in France and beyond.

Psychoanalytic Ideas in Testing. Main ideas of psychoanalysis influenced testing methods used in clinical practice. A noticeable contribution here belongs to Henry Murray (1893–1988). Educated in history, biology, and medicine, he developed interests in psychoanalysis following a meeting with Jung. After competing his training, Murray began teaching psychology and psychoanalytic theory at Harvard. He remained there for the rest of his professional career. One of Murray's major contributions to psychology was the Thematic Apperception Test (TAT) developed together with Christina Morgan (H. A. Murray, 1938).

In its original form, the test contained 19 pictures. A person undergoing testing was asked to tell a story about each of these pictures. The pictures were sufficiently vague to leave enough to the imagination of the person taking the test. Murray's main idea was that the test taker in the process of picture interpretation would reveal specific psychological needs that are difficult to identify by other methods. Murray used the term **themas** to describe stories or interpretations projecting fantasy imagery onto an objective stimulus, such as a picture. When a person experiences a press (an external influence) on his or her needs, a thema is activated to bring this person satisfaction and the sense of power, affiliation, and achievement. By studying these themas, a trained psychologist could reveal the true nature of this person's hopes, wishes, or specific psychological problems (H. A. Murray, 1938). The Thematic Apperception Test received global recognition and was translated in many languages.

ON THE WEB

You can examine Murray's work, located in Cornell University archives. Link is provided on the book website.

Murray was also known for laying foundations for **political psychology**, the field examining psychological factors in politics and political behavior. Although systematic research in political psychology began much later, in the early 1970s, Murray was among early researchers who attempted a scholarly analysis of political leaders. As you remember from the opening of this chapter, he and his colleagues wrote a psychological profile of German dictator Adolf Hitler (H. Murray, 1943). Their report was a descriptive psychological examination of a number of known facts about Hitler mixed with psychoanalytic assumptions about the causes of his violent and erratic behavior. Specific recommendations for anti-Hitler propaganda followed. This highly speculative portrayal of a political leader was one of the earliest attempts at "long-distance" psychological profiling—a method that is used today by practitioners as a source of supplementary information about certain individuals such as political leaders.

Expanding Psychoanalysis Into Social Sciences

Many ideas of psychoanalysis found positive response among social scientists. Special attention was received in analytical studies attempting to explain how psychological factors affect human society and its functioning.

Several analysts attempting to apply psychoanalysis to social sciences stand out. One was Helene Deutsch (1884–1982), Freud's favorite student and a follower. After working in Vienna as a therapist, she moved to the United States in 1935. There she published a number of scholarly papers but became well known for her two-volume book, *The Psychology of Women* (Deutsch, 1944, 1945). The books received significant attention from many professionals. Like Karen Horney, she was both praised and criticized for her vision of the woman's role in contemporary society. She described women as motivated by the unconscious desire to overcome psychological deficiencies associated with the girl's realization of her destiny as a wife and mother. Deutsch believed that women have to overcome many complexes associated with their biological and social roles. Among such problems were their unconscious tendency to masochism (self-inflicted pain and suffering) and self-enslavement. Critics, expectedly, rejected these ideas and believed that Deutsch focused on the wrong causes of societal injustice. While most social scientists at that time were looking into social and political causes of gender inequality, Deutsch emphasized psychological ones.

A creative blend of psychoanalysis, sociology, and political science emerged in the works of one of the most remarkable social thinkers of the 20th century, Erich Fromm (1900–1980). His *Escape From Freedom* (published first in Britain as *Fear of Freedom*) is one of the early significant contributions to social and political psychology (Fromm, 1941/1994). To be free from something or somebody, Fromm wrote, is not to be free completely. To be actually free, human beings have to embrace another kind of freedom: their ability to have power and resources to realize their own potentials.

Unfortunately, many people cannot embrace their freedom because they cannot cope with many uncertain elements of freedom and choice. As a result, they try to avoid their freedom and escape from it. They follow three destructive paths: conformity, authoritarianism, and destruction. When people conform, they avoid anxiety by uncritically accepting someone else's ideas and actions. People also may accept authoritarianism as an uncritical, judgmental form of intolerance against other people and ideas. Ultimately, some people turn to destruction of social reality around them because the social order causes their anxiety and insecurity (Fromm, 1947).

Fromm criticized dictatorship, Nazism, fascism, and communism as abusive forms of government and destroyers of freedom. He also was critical about capitalism and people's inability to overcome consumerism and striving for material success. Fromm believed that capitalism could be improved if it embraced collectivist norms and policies of communist countries. On the other hand, he also believed that communism could be improved if it accepted openness and political freedoms of a capitalist society. You can imagine that these ideas were heavily criticized as unrealistic by his opponents.

Psychoanalysis and the Jews

Claims that psychoanalysis was a cultural creation of the Jews are as old as psychoanalysis itself. Sigmund Freud was aware of this critical view and constantly denied that psychoanalysis has something to do with Judaism (Freud, as you remember, did not practice his religion). Two points of view exist on this matter.

Some historians believe that psychoanalysis as a theory and movement was rooted in Jewish cultural and group identity. For the Jews, psychoanalysis of the early 20th century appeared as a cultural affair, a source of confidence and collective self-verification. It was a suitable way out of the collective mentality of an oppressed people (Cuddihy, 1974). Up until the 20th century, most European countries had legal restrictions limiting the participation of Jews in public education, politics, and social life. Russia simply restricted most Jews from moving into big cities. The rapid development of psychoanalysis coincided with both political and social liberation of the European Jews. Many young Jewish college graduates and doctors turned to psychoanalysis because it offered them inspiration, possible occupation, and a stable income.

A critical thinker, however, should express caution about an automatic connection of psychoanalysis to the Jewish culture. Fechner, Wundt, James, Watson, and Bekhterev were Christians, but there is little reason to define experimental psychology as a Christian scientific phenomenon. Furthermore, in countries such as England, Russia, and Switzerland before the 1920s, there were only few Jews among psychoanalysts (Leibin, 1994; Shorter, 1997). An influx of Jewish psychoanalysts to North America in the 1930s was part of

ON THE WEB

Many psychoanalysts were both theorists and dedicated practitioners. The William Alanson White Institute in New York is an example of this interaction between theory and practice. Learn more about the institute on the book's website.

a massive emigration of European Jews from Germany and Austria. However, the vast majority of these psychoanalysts as well as other scientists and professionals were secular. Some of them were distinct atheists.

✓ CHECK YOUR KNOWLEDGE

In which ways did psychoanalysts of the 1930s and 1940s develop the ideas of Sigmund Freud?

What is the defense mechanism?

What is the main idea of the book, *Escape From Freedom?*

Overview of Psychoanalysis

Most psychoanalysts, despite disagreements, shared several basic views. First, they focused on unconscious processes regulating an individual's experience and action. They also emphasized the crucial role of unconscious factors in psychological disorders. Second, they all stressed the crucial role of childhood and its impact on an individual's psychological development. Third, they offered a therapeutic method allowing their fellow analysts to address a patient's psychological problems and treat them. Psychoanalysts maintained that people were generally incapable of understanding their inner conflicts, yet they could achieve this understanding through therapy. This view had a significant impact on contemporary views about the causes and treatment of a wide range of anxiety, mood, and personality disorders (Mills, 2001). Finally, many psychoanalysts also maintained the view that not only an individual's life but also society and culture could be explained with the help of psychoanalytic ideas.

The main reformation of "classical" psychoanalysis in the mid-20th century was taking place in several areas. A range of psychoanalysts, including Anna Freud and Karen Horney, turned to a more rational or conscious aspect of an individual's experience and began to examine the functioning of the ego. This focus allowed them to turn to empirical data accessible through direct observation, which improved the reputation of psychoanalysis among psychologists. Next, most psychoanalysts expanded or moved away from the Freudian assumptions about the sexual nature of the unconscious conflicts. Furthermore, social scientists such as Helene Deutsch and Erich Fromm began to apply psychoanalytic ideas to other fields of social sciences and humanities. Psychoanalytic ideas entered the fields of history, sociology, and political science. Although psychoanalysis did not find an overwhelming support from the specialists in these fields, it was able to stimulate significant interest in psychological factors affecting society.

As a method of treating mental illness, psychoanalysis maintained its dominant position in economically advanced countries until the late 1950s. At least three factors contributed to its substantial weakening in the second half of the 20th century. The first one was the "drug revolution": the discovery and manufacturing of pills capable of changing the symptoms of some abnormal psychological symptoms. The second factor was the emerging new and effective forms of psychological treatment based on behavior modification and other techniques. Combined, the new pills and therapeutic methods were more effective than the lengthy and expensive analytical sessions. And finally, psychoanalysis did not address its old and chronic problem: the lack of scientific validity of its theoretical assumptions.

Assessment of Behaviorism and Psychoanalysis

In the early 1930s, the government officials in charge of science in the Soviet Union declared Pavlov's theory of reflexes the only "correct" theory capable of interpreting human behavior. At the same time, psychology as a university discipline and profession was officially dismantled. Psychology departments, laboratories, and psychoanalytic clinics were closed. Although some departments would reopen in the late 1950s, the damage to psychology in that country was significant. In effect, several government ideologues shut down the debates in psychology and picked the "winner." This historic example fortunately is a rare case of how scientists were forced to accept one theory over others. In most countries, the exchange of ideas continued, and the supporters of behaviorism and psychoanalysis—while freely debating their ideas in publications and lectures—revealed strengths and weaknesses of these approaches, thus shaping the developing psychology of the 20th century. In summary, what was the overall contribution of psychoanalysis and behaviorism?

Position Within "Mainstream" Science

Behaviorism and psychoanalysis stood for two distinctly different ways to understand psychology. One way was to study discrete and measurable responses. Supporters of this approach declared that such responses could stand for the complexity of human action. The other way was to focus on the depth of experience, suggesting the existence of inner mechanisms hidden from direct observation but available for analysis.

Early supporters of behaviorism suggested that their ideas were revolutionary because they changed the mainstream psychology of the past century. It is true that Bekhterev, Watson, Pavlov, and Skinner hoped to establish a new science or at least an academic discipline focusing exclusively on behavior. Pavlov, for instance, believed that his experimental method would open like a "key" the deepest secrets of human behavior. At the same time, behaviorism did not face significant resistance from most experts in psychology: The study of behavior and the use of objective methods of its measurement gained universal acceptance (Leahey, 2002). Behavioral studies became highly quantitative based on sophisticated experimental procedures. Gradually, behaviorism, refined and expanded, became part of the mainstream academic psychology and part of psychology's educational curriculum on the university campus. Psychoanalysis met a somewhat different fate.

While behaviorists questioned subjectivity, psychoanalysts declared it "scientific" and thus available for investigation called analysis. Willpower, resistance, guilt, and dream contents were brought to the researchers' attention. Psychoanalysts began to focus on neurotic symptoms and study them. Remember that Freud compared psychoanalysis to archeology (Chapter 8). Like an archaeologist, an analyst must be attentive, patient, and creative. An analyst first examines several clinical cases. Then the information is put together and compared with similar cases obtained from other analysts to establish common trends and discuss new evidence. However, one of the most obvious problems of psychoanalysis was its reluctance to advance research methodology, especially quantitative methods. Neither controlled experiments nor correlational studies interested most psychoanalysts throughout the 20th century. They persistently stayed away from any kind of statistical analysis, which in part determined their diminishing position on university campuses, especially in the United States (Sears, 1943). However, psychoanalysis gained substantial strength in medicine for some time and became the mainstream theory and method to study and treat psychological problems. Most psychiatrists in American medical schools by the mid-1950s were psychoanalysts (Chessick, 2007).

Determinism

Behaviorism and psychoanalysis were based on scientific determinism, a fundamental position according to which mental processes are determined by past events. Even early critics of psychoanalysis agreed that its goal was deterministic (Bjerre, 1916). For that reason, many behaviorists initially felt enthusiastic about psychoanalysis. They even attempted to interpret it in behaviorist terms. For example, John Watson explained the unconscious as a process that could not reach the level of verbalization (Watson, 1927). Watson popularized Freud and encouraged the rigorous scientific testing of his ideas in the laboratory (Rilling, 2000). In the 1920s, some enthusiasts began to translate psychoanalytic terms into the behaviorist vocabulary. For example, therapy became *reconditioning,* repression was *avoidance reaction,* and complexes became *conditioned reflexes* (Hornstein, 1992). Behaviorists as well as many other psychologists believed that there must be a special kind of psychological or spiritual energy that would be measured one day.

The overall belief that human behavior and experience could be explained in terms of their predetermining causes—the idea defended in behaviorism and psychoanalysis—is a mainstream view of today's academic psychology.

Adaptation and Progressivism

Psychoanalysis and behaviorism portrayed behavior as the process of constant adaptation of the individual to changing conditions. The idea of reflex, a conceptual foundation of behavior, is rooted in the fundamental assumption that behavior serves an important adaptive function. This was a view that continued the popular tradition of Charles Darwin and Herbert Spencer. This was also a position that strengthened the foundation of the functionalist view of psychology. From the behaviorist's view, animals and humans learn a habit not because they "understand" the purpose of learning.

They retain useful habits because they are likely to secure food, shelter, pleasure, or safety. People and animals alike adapt to changing conditions by constantly modifying their reflexes. If this is true, as behaviorists believed, then it would be possible to design educational and social programs to develop people's healthy habits and effective decision-making strategies.

Psychoanalysts also shared a view that an individual should adjust to the demands of the internal drives and societal restrictions. Mental illness reflects a person's inability to adjust. The major goal of psychoanalysis as a therapeutic method is to restore the lost balance or reduce the suffering caused by the inner conflict. While behaviorists insisted on replacing useless or unhealthy habits, psychoanalysts believed in guided therapies, deeper self-understanding, and gradual self-improvements. Furthermore, many analysts expanded the earlier suggestions of Freud about the necessity to improve humanity via societal changes. This was not about a social revolution. The main idea was that people could improve as human beings if they encounter fewer restrictions and social taboos related to gender roles, unlearn their ethnic and religious prejudices, and find socially accepted ways to display their aggressive tendencies.

Because of their belief in the possibility to improve humanity through social changes, both psychoanalysis and behaviorism shared similar progressive ideas. As you remember from Chapter 5, psychologist supporters of progressivism believed in the opportunity to apply scientific knowledge to improve many spheres of social life. Progressivism also emphasized the importance of applied psychological knowledge in three areas: health care, education, and social services. Both behavioral psychologists and psychoanalysts believed in their science as a new force capable of changing society and providing people with a new vision of a peaceful and healthy life. Psychology today is rooted in the same genuinely progressive view.

Cross-Cultural Applications

One of behaviorism's main goals was the establishment of universal scientific principles to explain behavior. Environment, educational conditions, cultural norms—all were the factors that condition people's responses to stimuli and direct their actions. Behaviorism appeared as a set of universal principles applicable in any cultural settings. Psychoanalysis, however, earned a reputation as a theory and method valid primarily within the Western culture. In the center of attention was a White person from the upper social class who was trapped in an internal conflict related to childhood and relationships. Although Freud understood the necessity of examining psychoanalysis in non-Western cultural conditions, he did not do much in this direction (Da Conceição & De Lyra Chebabi, 1987). In 1929, Girindrasekhar Bose, the founder and first president of the Indian Psychoanalytical Society, wrote to Freud on some differences in the psychoanalytic treatment of Indian and Western patients. One of the differences was that Indian people were less preoccupied with gender identity and had greater tolerance for feminine and masculine features within themselves (Kakar, 1989).

Over years, some psychoanalytic ideas were critically examined in different countries (Devereux, 1953; Kakar, 1995). Jung focused on non-Western cultural traditions.

There were psychoanalytic studies of African witchcraft, social customs of Australian aboriginal natives, the impact of mainstream culture on African Americans, or ego defenses in people from Buddhist communities (Tori & Bilmes, 2002). Some studies suggested that the Western psychoanalytic tradition has difficulty interpreting, for example, the complexity of gender relations in Muslim communities, the importance of male bondage common in South Asia, or the role of religious identity (Kurtz, 1992). Criticism was also directed at the cultural applicability of psychoanalysis as a therapeutic method. For many years, the principles of interactions between the therapist and the client in the West were generally based on the assumption that both patient and analyst are essentially equal, although the latter is more knowledgeable. It is not always the case in other cultural environments. Many immigrants from traditional cultures, for instance, expect a great deal of advice and direct guidance from the therapist like they expect guidance from the authority figure or family elders (Roland, 2006). Unlike behaviorism, in the 20th century, psychoanalysis remained, for most part, a psychological theory rooted in the Western cultural tradition.

✓ CHECK YOUR KNOWLEDGE

How did behaviorist supporters of psychoanalysis interpret some of its concepts?

Conclusion

During the 20th century, behaviorism and psychoanalysis grew into mainstream approaches to human behavior and experience. Over many years, most professionals working in the area of psychoanalysis moved into the clinical field and found employment in medical institutions. By the 1950s, most psychiatrists in the United States were working in the fields of psychoanalysis and its many branches. However, the inability of psychoanalysis to adopt contemporary methods of experimental research and poor statistical interpretation of therapeutic effectiveness weakened the position of psychoanalysis in most American universities. Psychoanalysis retained its power as an academic discipline and therapeutic method until the 1960s, after which the impact of psychoanalysis started to decline. However, its major assumptions about the importance of early childhood experiences, the significance of inner conflicts hidden from an individual conscious awareness, and the ability of human beings to overcome their own deficiencies became well-accepted ideas in contemporary psychology.

Behaviorism as a distinct school of thought and research based on experimentation and the statistical analysis of data eventually blended into mainstream academic psychology. Its principles became foundations of contemporary theories of learning, motivation, and therapy.

Summary

• Neo-behaviorists such as Jones believed in the possibility and necessity of objective measurement of behavior. They supported the reductionist beliefs that psychology should be a science of behavior and conditioning. Their research, however, contributed to educational methods and behavior therapy.

• One of the key features of the neo-behaviorist orientation was its acceptance of the mediating variable in the classical S → R model. More behaviorists, including Tolman, Hull, and Clark, accepted the importance of the additional cognitive component in their formulas and invited concepts such as purpose and goal in their interpretations of behavior.

• Unlike many prominent behaviorists, Skinner did not pay attention to so-called mediating factors in the classical behaviorist formulas. As Watson before him, Skinner excluded the subjective mental element from his investigation. He believed that two key processes, natural selection and operant conditioning, shape both the past and present of animals and human beings.

• In the age of the media, Skinner became one of the most popular psychologists of the 20th century. As many psychologists before and after him, he attempted broad and often controversial generalizations about education, the nature of human society, government, and social justice.

• Psychoanalysis in the second quarter of the 20th century developed in several directions. One was related to therapy and clinical practice. Another was associated with the development of the original psychoanalytic concepts of Freud, Jung, and Adler and the advancement of new theories. The third path was related to the expansion of psychoanalysis in the fields of social sciences. Karen Horney, Henry Murray, Harry Stack Sullivan, and Jacques Lacan made their contributions in all these fields.

• Despite the lack of experimental validity and selective attention to facts, psychoanalysis in the 20th century created valuable ideas about the importance of early childhood experiences, the significance of inner conflicts hidden from an individual conscious awareness, and the ability of human beings to overcome their own deficiencies and became well-accepted ideas in contemporary psychology.

Key Terms

Bad-me, good-me, and not-me

Basic anxiety

Cognitive map

Defense mechanisms

Ego psychology

Molar responses

Operant conditioning

Political psychology

Purposive or operational behaviorism

Schedules of reinforcement

Themas

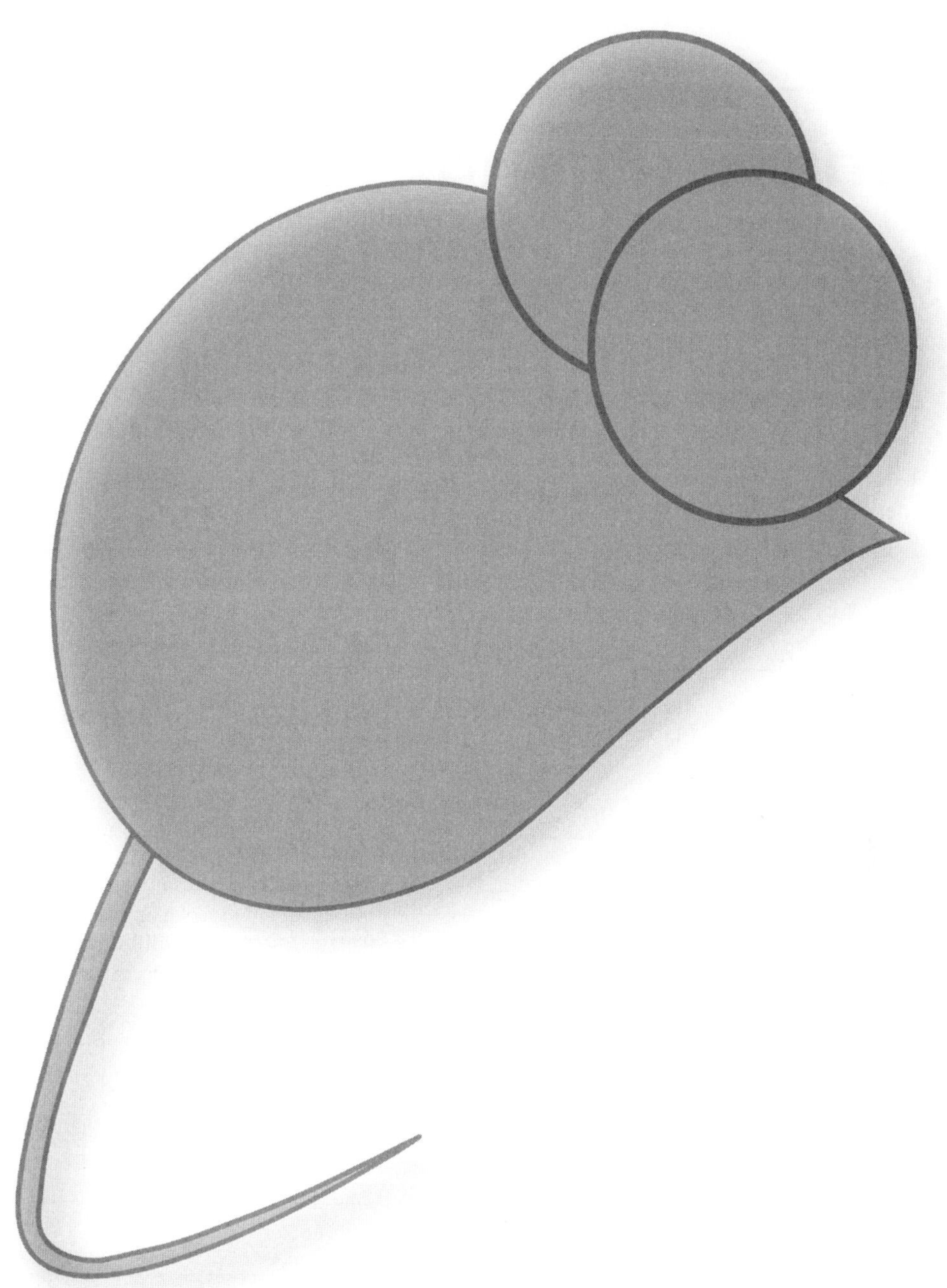

12

Humanistic and Cognitive Psychology

We don't know the details about how it works and it may well be a long time before we understand the details involved.

John Searle

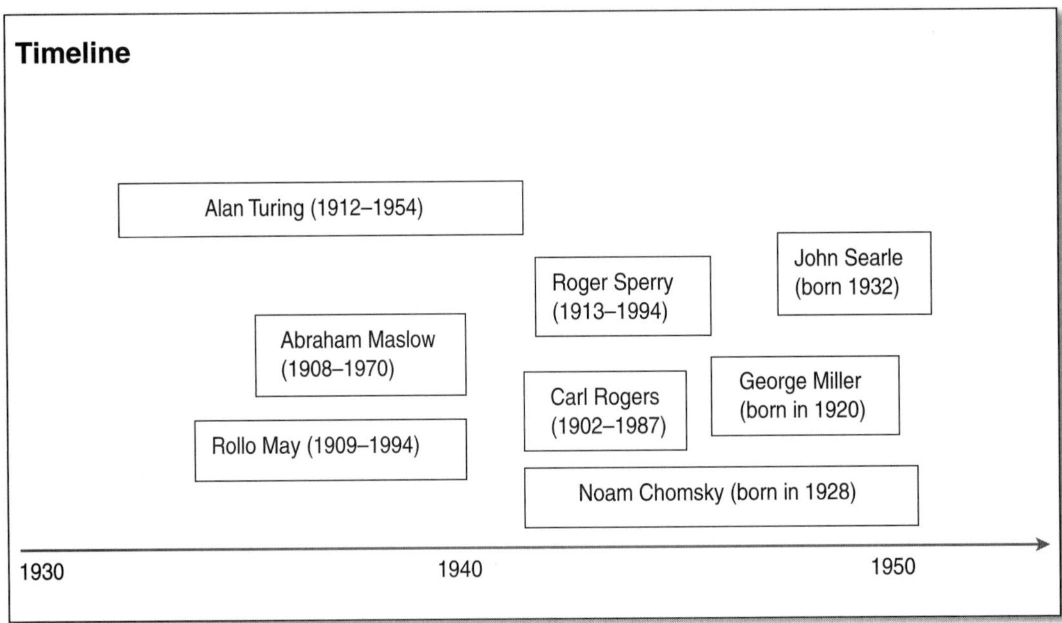

CHAPTER OUTLINE

Christopher Nolan had cerebral palsy since birth. He couldn't walk. Neither could he talk, write, or even touch his face. He needed help moving around. The muscles did not support his body. People pitied him because of his disability. What would you do in this unfortunate situation? Would you give up? He didn't. Immobile and helpless, he had an active, sharp, and creative mind. His curious brain was gradually absorbing the words, formulas, rhymes, and images of life unfolding through his eyes and ears. Unable to play tag or football, he studied math, science, and literature like every child. He began to write poetry and prose. He did it with a rubber-tipped stick attached to his forehead and stubbornly typed letters on a typewriter. It was hard and slow. Some words would take several minutes to produce. His novel, *The Banyan Tree,* took about 10 years to finish. A random quote from the poem hints about the elegance of his talent: "There in its innocence it would wait until, holding a spade-pen fashion, she'd inscribe her name upon it in a pattern of dots and dashes."

He began to publish his work at age 15. Recognition, raving reviews, and literary awards followed. He could master the words that he could never say. One reviewer wrote, "The language takes hold and doesn't let go." Christopher's physical disability shut down his body. Yet his stubborn mind kept on fighting and finding the strength to rhyme and toss the metaphors of his experience and imagination into the unspoken world of his resourceful talent.

Christopher died when he was 43. People say his life was a miracle.

It was a miracle of the living brain uninhibited by a physical disability. It was true magic performed by billions of his brain cells transforming physiological reactions into a literary marvel. His life was also a miracle of humanism that has given thousands of the afflicted, the unfortunate, and the unlucky a new inspiration to live. Christopher's physical problems make some of our own grievances simply minuscule in comparison. His zest for life makes our own hopes stronger.

This chapter is about two major themes in the late history of psychology that deal with two seemingly dissimilar topics reflected in this brief story of Christopher Nolan. One is about the precision of physiological reactions and algorithms of the brain. The other is about the meaning of life and inspiration. These two themes, in fact, are associated with two major endeavors that 20th-century psychology undertook at the closing of the millennium.

In the second half of the 20th century, psychology moved forward in a rapidly changing and increasingly anxious world. At least two major global conditions are important to mention. The first is the devastating impact of World War II and the following recovery period. The second was the emerging cold war and an increasing ideological struggle between two social and political systems, the struggle that directly and indirectly affected science and education, including psychology.

The Social Landscape

World War II (1939–1945) was probably the most devastating war of all times. It took more than 70 million lives globally. It had brought an unprecedented destruction followed by a period of a prolonged economic and social instability. Europe and East Asia, including China and Japan, were particularly overwhelmed. For several years, with unemployment levels high, crime rates rampant, and social problems mounting, much of Europe was in disarray.

Economic recovery began in the late 1940s. Historians mention clever economic policies of European countries coupled with the massive financial help from the United States (the Marshall Plan) as main sources of the revival. For the United States, it was a stage of economic boom and social stability. Higher education witnessed positive changes too. After years of low enrollment and underfunding, the 1944 Servicemen's Readjustment Act provided federal money for college or professional education of returning war veterans. Private funds and taxes were also redirected to support science and education. American universities experienced a postwar boom due to significant enrollment increases and federal, state, and private funds increasingly available to many people. The National Institute of Mental Health, established in 1946, and the National Science Foundation, founded in 1950, provided additional funding for psychological research (B. G. Holliday & Holmes, 2003).

The world was changing. Just 20 years after the end of the World War II, the world witnessed a series of dramatic events and developments. Although Europe remained war free, many small devastating conflicts continued across the globe. The colonial system had disintegrated by the 1960s. Yet this did not bring stability and peace to Africa and Asia. The gap between the prosperous West and the majority of the countries had increased. This was the period of the so-called cold war, a global rivalry between the Soviet Union and other communist countries on one side and the United States and its allies on the other. During almost 40 years of the cold war, enormous financial and intellectual resources were committed by both sides to build and develop weapons. Historians disagree today about whether the cold war was inevitable. It is clear, however, that if this global confrontation had not taken place, trillions of dollars could have been invested in science and education instead of armaments.

What did all these developments mean to psychology as a discipline?

Psychology and Global Developments

In the early 1950s, the United States became a powerful center of world education and science. Economically, most colleges and universities in the United States were in much better shape than other academic institutions and educational centers around the world. A significant influx of immigrants from Germany and other European countries in the 1930s and after the war had brought to America a fresh new wave of college-educated specialists. Continuously, since the mid-20th century, many psychologists from different countries were choosing the United States to study, work, and settle in. English was becoming the most accepted language of choice around the world, which certainly was beneficial to English-speaking psychologists: they did not have to translate their papers! Most prestigious publications in psychology were now in English (and not in German and French as in the late 1800s). The rapid development of communication technologies and increased travel and international contacts among scientists had also increased both educational and research opportunities. Psychology was becoming increasingly global. Publications of many European psychologists, including Piaget and Vygotsky, were gaining a good reputation in North America. Through various federal and private programs (such as the Fulbright program for scholars), especially after the early 1960s—the years of John Kennedy's administration—American professors began to travel around the world promoting psychological knowledge and, eventually, recruiting new students and specialists.

New intriguing debates about the role of psychology in contemporary society emerged. On one hand, it was clear to many psychologists that their discipline had to create, develop, and advance new sophisticated scientific methods of research, analysis, and prediction of various manifestations of human behavior and experience. Following the tradition of positivism, scores of professionals believed that psychology had to use primarily experimental methods of investigation. In their view, psychology should be based on science, including mathematics, biology, and neurophysiology. The global success of behaviorism reflects this belief. Moreover, the rapid development of mathematics and computer science had given psychologists a new challenge and opportunity at the same time: to use mathematical and computer science models and carefully examine the work of the human mind that involved the most elusive and least understood element, which was subjectivity. From the study of behavior, psychology turned again to the study of the human mind.

On the other hand, many psychologists argued that psychology, in addition to applying measurement to study human functioning, had to turn to the "other," relatively unexplored side of human existence. When behaviorists discussed useful habits and psychoanalysts emphasized childhood traumas, a new generation of psychologists turned to the fundamental question about the ultimate purpose of human existence. They argued that psychology must change its focus and embrace happiness, moral choice, self-improvement, and compassion as the major topics of research and practical applications. In the early 1960s, a significant number of psychologists began to emphasize the importance of humanitarian and moral issues in psychology. Group seminars on healthy relationships, sensitivity training about conflict resolution, and educational sessions on self-esteem improvement became increasingly popular. Psychologists argued that the mathematical precision of behavioral studies was running a risk of losing the essence of human existence: eternal search for love, kindness, compassion, and happiness. The focus of research was turning toward a comprehending, companionate, and ever-growing individual, a person who is not necessarily "responding" to stimuli but rather "growing" (Aanstoos, Serlin, & Greening, 2000).

Many psychologists also believed that their discipline should remain an increasingly progressive science pursuing an ambitious goal to make society better. Substantial cultural changes were taking place in the Western world in the 1960s. Dissatisfied with war, injustice, and unequal opportunity, scores of people, especially the young "baby-boomer" generation, began to question the rules of traditional establishment, as well as its practices and policies. The focus of their attention was shifting toward civil rights and social obstacles, including inequality, prejudice, racism, sexism, and bigotry. Many professors and students alike shared a popular opinion that psychology as a discipline should bring practical solutions to lingering societal problems, especially in the fields of education, mental health, and individual development.

Academic Traditions. Several trends developed within the mainstream, university-based psychology. Gradually, theoretical psychoanalysis was moving out of psychology departments in most academic institutions of higher education. Lacking experimental basis, psychoanalysis meanwhile continued to maintain its influence among practicing clinicians. Behavioral studies continued attracting new students and researchers. Behavioral psychologists used the traditional experimental research and offered new and increasingly sophisticated methods of investigation of animal and human behavior. Child psychology had finally established itself as the mainstream discipline in most departments. Clinical psychology continued to search for its own identity away from psychiatry taught primarily in medical schools for medical students.

Among several new developments, two will receive our attention in this chapter: cognitive psychology and humanistic psychology. Both cognitive and humanistic traditions, being quite dissimilar in terms of their research approaches and methodologies, have been similar in one important aspect. Researchers working within these traditions treated psychology from a similar perspective of subjectivity. Unlike behaviorists, both cognitive and humanistic psychologists turned to cognition. They were both interested in the "inner" side of human existence. We will begin with humanistic psychology.

✓ CHECK YOUR KNOWLEDGE

What was the "progressive" role for psychology that many scientists envisioned in the 1960s?

Humanistic Psychology

Humanistic psychology is a theoretical and practical field that concerns primarily the human dimension in psychology and calls for renewed efforts to study the phenomena that distinguish human beings—love, happiness, self-growth. Humanistic psychology focuses on long-term values instead of tangible and immediate rewards. It focuses on issues such as "being and becoming" somebody rather than "having and accumulating something." This field unified psychologists and their followers from other disciplines who challenged all the pragmatic, behavioral, and computational orientations of modern psychology. Humanistic psychologists were not against rationality. They simply wanted to focus on a different side of rationality, the one rooted in caring for others, self-growth, and uniqueness of individual experiences.

Humanistic principles are extraordinarily diverse and broad and have deep roots in the history of psychology. Almost every contributor to psychological thought in the past had addressed humanistic ideas one way or another. These principles have been expanding over the years. The very term *humanistic* is imprecise and has several interpretations, which multiply in foreign translations. Looking at many existing views and approaches, we will focus primarily on the general roots from which humanistic psychology grew at the early stages of its development. Then we will take a look at humanistic psychology's principles. The first one was critical and concerned the emerging situation in psychology in the 1950s. The second identified the main subject of attention and studies for humanistic psychologists. The third principle referred to the main area of psychological applications.

The Roots of Humanistic Psychology

The roots of humanistic psychology are found in critical examinations of many existing approaches, especially behaviorism and psychoanalysis. Also, several fundamental ideas of so-called existential psychologists had found their way into humanistic theories.

A Critical View of Psychology. Humanistic psychology is sometimes referred to as the **third force in psychology,** in contrast to two major forces and orientations, such as behaviorism and psychoanalysis. The latter two came gradually under growing criticism from several theorists and practitioners. These critics believed that contemporary psychology of the mid-20th century had been losing its main focus. The main concern of the commentators was that the ongoing research had essentially lost the main subject of psychology: the human being.

Behaviorism was the first target of criticism. A large group of psychologists in the 1950s grew increasingly dissatisfied with the mainstream psychology for its acceptance of behavioral studies and formal models of action and decision making. As far as their critical argument went, psychology was losing its subject behind sophisticated behavioral experiments, mathematical formulas, statistics, and formal logic. They argued that correlation numbers describing an individual could provide some information about this person. However, this information is sketchy because it does not describe the sophisticated inner world of that individual. Behaviorists, of course, disagreed. The claimed that behaviorism as the "first force" in psychology had already demonstrated in experimental research the tremendous power of learning and the formative role of circumstances in human life. In essence, we as humans are complex "products" whose behavior is predetermined by our genetic makeup and shaped by various environmental conditions. Nevertheless, this widely accepted approach was not satisfactory enough to those psychologists who believed in the power of individuals to shape their own lives. Moreover, behaviorism practically ignored consciousness and much information related to the "inner" world of the feeling and striving individual.

Psychoanalysis was the second target. Psychoanalysis as the "second force" in psychology was focusing primarily on psychological anomalies. An individual had to address them through a dialogue with a therapist, self-discovery, and a sustained mental effort. In fact, many supporters of the humanistic agenda in psychology came from psychoanalysis, and they could be called psychoanalysts of the "second generation." However, as psychoanalysts, they acknowledged that psychoanalysis had overemphasized the importance of unconscious processes and devalued the meaning of conscious, purposeful acts. The individual in many psychoanalytic theories appeared overwhelmed with the heavy weight of traumatic unconscious experiences. He or she would appear helpless to find his or her own strength and new resources for growth.

Challenging both behaviorism and psychoanalysis, humanistic psychologists began to emphasize the importance of individual responsibility, free choice, and intellectual freedom as fundamentally human forces guiding a person through life. It was a very optimistic orientation, assuring people of the strength of their own unrealized power. Describing these and other potentials, humanistic psychologists used many constructive ideas of so-called existential psychology.

Existential Psychology. You can imagine existential psychology as a branch on the tree of existential philosophy, a discipline focusing primarily on the thinking, willing, and independent individual. The philosophical bases for existential philosophy appeared thanks to Søren Kierkegaard (1813–1855) from Denmark and Martin Heidegger (1889–1976) from Germany. They both questioned an established belief that human beings are largely products of their environment and circumstances. Existential philosophers focused instead on independent minds of acting, hoping, and willing human beings. In a short way, existential philosophy celebrates and mourns the tragic uniqueness of each individual's experience.

The term *existential* refers, above all, to existence and being. What are they? They are difficult to interpret precisely. By itself, **existential psychology** is an eclectic and diverse field of studies embracing a great variety of views and beliefs. Despite this rich assortment of ideas, several important themes identifying existential psychology have emerged.

First, our individual existence and experience are unique, exceptional, and unrepeatable. Each one of us is a universe in itself. When you go, there will never be another "you." This is both inspiring and tragic: we can celebrate our uniqueness and bemoan the shortness of our existence. The second assumption emphasized the importance of individual free choice and independent will. We make our own choices and take responsibility for them. The third assumption is the necessity to consider each and every person a unique entity in the context of his or her circumstances, relationships, conditions, influences, and own internal forces (Binswanger, 1963). Although these principles might appear somewhat eclectic and broad, their practical application could lead to several important possibilities.

Unlike existential philosophers, most of whom considered the world disorganized, tragic, and confused, existential psychologists were more optimistic. True, the world seems chaotic. True, our lives are short. But there is always a path for every one of us to achieve confidence and happiness. Each individual can discover this path. This discovery can take place naturally, in the process of our individual growth. However, many people feel helpless because they are trapped in their daily routines and cannot break their habits. The path to happiness is in therapy. In fact, major theoretical assumptions of existential psychology lead toward **existential therapy.** This is the healing method based on the assumption that we, as human beings, make our own choices and should assume full responsibility for the outcomes of our behavior and our own feelings. Life often treats us in a very unkind way. Still, every individual possesses the freedom to create own goals and reach them. This freedom could generate in every one of us the sense of purpose and meaning. The job of the psychotherapist is to understand the four basic dimensions of human existence (the physical, the social, the psychological, and the spiritual) and help people set, reset, and eventually achieve their ultimate individual goal, which is happiness.

One of the leading representatives of existential psychology was American psychologist Rollo May (1909–1994). He accepted the basic philosophical assumption about the tragic nature of the world: our life is filled with uncertainty and anxiety. We constantly worry because our fundamental values or principles, many of which we hold essential to our existence, are constantly under threat from others (May, Angel, & Ellenberger, 1958). As the result, we tend to seek protection against anxiety and find a psychological shelter in our own selfishness or apathy: we either disregard other people's interests or stop pursuing our own dreams. May encouraged his generation to rediscover the importance of caring for one another as a way to reduce anxiety and diminish apathy. He believed, however, that joy and freedom come to people only when they confront the difficult circumstances of their lives (May, 1967).

Overall, being critically aware of the shortcoming of behaviorism and psychoanalysis, humanistic psychologists encouraged their colleagues to turn to the most important question that psychology should have studied, from their point of view: the meaning of human existence. Their main assumption was the following: if psychologists were able to turn to this subject, they would eventually be able to offer to other people a general path to a more productive, happy, peaceful, and humane existence. Finding and teaching about this path was the ultimate task of psychology.

✓ CHECK YOUR KNOWLEDGE

Humanistic psychology is sometimes called "the third force." Why?

Describe in a few sentences existential psychology.

Principles of Humanistic Psychology

In a nutshell, humanistic psychology is a school of thought that treats individuals as uniquely human. Humanistic psychologists themselves often define it as a value orientation that holds a hopeful and constructive view of people and of their substantial capacity to be self-determining (Association for Humanistic Psychology [AHP], 2001). Despite a great variety of influences, humanistic psychology is based on several theoretical principles. It uses a set of specific methods to gather, analyze, and interpret information. It also makes consistent suggestions about how to apply this knowledge. That is why it is common in the history of psychology to call it a "school" of thought. Most applications of humanistic psychology are found in clinical and educational practice. Let's consider these points in sequence.

Early Beginnings. The term *humanistic psychology* began to emerge in publications and presentations in the 1950s. Several psychologists, psychiatrists, and educators began to express their concerns about the growing and problematic trend in the mainstream academic psychology. As you remember, from these concerned critics' view, the problem was that the true human context of psychology was gradually disappearing. The intriguing, provocative, controversial, and inspirational essence of human existence appeared to them lost in theories of learned reactions and defense mechanisms. To reverse this negative trend, the critics believed they needed to take at least two steps.

Step 1: They hoped to consolidate their ranks and generate support from other psychologists. They needed an efficient professional association. In the late 1950s, a group of American psychologists, including Clark Moustakas, Abraham Maslow, Carl Rogers, and several others, began to gather a professional association specifically focused on humanistic principles of dignity, freedom, choice, love, and self-worth. This focus received a broad and growing acceptance among many psychologists.

Step 2: To promote their ideas, humanistic psychologists needed to appeal to both professionals and a larger audience. Before the Internet (remember, it was the middle of the past century), one of the best sources of publicity in the academic world was a journal. To publish a journal is not easy. You have to have financial backers, editorial staff, promoters, and distributors. These and many other organizational issues take significant time. The *Journal of Humanistic Psychology* was finally launched in 1961. Next, the inaugural meeting of the Association for Humanistic Psychology (AHP) was held in Philadelphia in 1963. More psychologists began to embrace humanistic ideas and use them in their clinical practice and teaching. An important development was formal recognition within the leading psychological organization. The American Psychological Association gives its members an opportunity to initiate new associations and groups so long as these groups receive enough endorsements. As a result, in 1971, humanistic psychology as a field was formally recognized by the American Psychological Association and granted its own division (Division 32).

Main Points. Despite a variety of approaches and methods within humanistic psychology, several basic principles can be identified. First, human beings should be viewed from a holistic perspective. Humans are more than the sum of their habits, reflexes, mental operations, or decision-making strategies. This statement seems trivial after it was emphasized in Gestalt psychology. It probably would be difficult to find any psychologist in the 1960s who would state that a human being is "just a sum of several parts." Nevertheless, the focus on holism was another way to express criticism of behaviorism. The message was this: in our humanistic study, we should focus on all aspects of an individual's existence and not necessarily isolated behavioral acts no matter how complex they are (Bugental, 1964, pp. 19–25).

Second, human beings are aware of their existence. They are also conscious: they are aware of being aware. This statement was a direct challenge to psychoanalysis and its fundamental assumption about the power of the unconscious side of human experience. Although many humanistic psychologists were trained within the psychoanalytic tradition and not all of them had abandoned the belief in the power of unconscious processes, the emphasis of humanistic psychology was shifting toward consciousness. This was their focal point of interest: the knowledgeable, thinking individual who is aware of his or her own psychological processes.

Third, human beings live in a uniquely human context that is not limited to their immediate surroundings such as an office at work, classroom, or dining room. To fully understand an individual's inner world, we have to expand the scientific view of individuals. We have to examine an individual's "cosmic ecology" involving its material, social, cultural, and spiritual dimensions.

Fourth, rational and knowledgeable individuals are capable of exercising their choices. They select their goals, pursue dreams, implement some projects, and abandon others. With those choices, however, comes individual responsibility. People make mistakes and learn from them. Humanistic psychologists, contrary to some assumptions of their critics, did not believe in total freedom of choice without responsibility.

And finally, if human behavior is generally intentional, deliberate, and goal directed, human beings are usually aware that their actions can cause certain outcomes. Overall, being aware of their goals, people tend to and seek meaning, value, and creativity in their lives.

As you can see, taken as a whole, the main message of humanistic psychology was constructive. People are not necessarily "products" of stimuli and circumstances. Neither do they follow the imperatives of the unconscious mind. People are generally rational and logical in setting their goals and choosing the methods to achieve them. Humanistic psychology is inherently optimistic. Circumstances can affect all of us, but we, as humans, have the power to overcome the challenges. However, there are individuals who fail to achieve their goals despite their efforts and good intentions. Many people in pursuing their goals simply choose the wrong methods. Such failures cause suffering. Persistent failures cause persistent suffering, which is labeled a psychological disorder. Fortunately, help is available.

Therapy. Humanistic psychology was not only a theoretical discipline. It also established the main principles of therapy, aiming to reduce or eliminate suffering. In their efforts to apply humanistic ideas to psychotherapy, psychologists offered a different approach to the therapist-client interaction compared to mainstream clinical psychology at the time. One major feature of the new method was that the therapist generally downplays the pathological aspects of a client's symptoms and focuses on healthy aspects of existence and the ways to achieve recovery (Clay, 2002). A key ingredient in this approach is the process of interaction between therapist and client and the achievement of a productive dialogue. Major therapeutic principles of the humanistic approach are very inclusive. A therapist here may embrace any form of treatment directed at an individual's personal improvement, enlightenment, and moral growth. For example, a combination of physical and talk therapy is welcome if they help the client to overcome persistent anxiety or chronic pain. Physical therapy may reduce a client's persistent anxiety, thus easing a therapeutic dialogue. To achieve deep relaxation or concentration, people can use various forms of meditation. In fact, back in the 1960s and 1970s, methods rooted in Eastern philosophies and religious traditions, including Hinduism and Buddhism, gained significant popularity (Aanstoos et al., 2000). These methods were very popular because they placed self-awareness, forgiveness, and growth-seeking experiences at the center of therapeutic treatment. Humanistic psychology has inadvertently invited psychologists to discover the incredible world of Indian and Asian philosophy and mythology.

Methods. According to its founders, the main approach of humanistic psychology involves an emphasis on the actual experience of individuals (Greening, 1971). In terms of methodology, humanistic psychology preferred qualitative research methods in contrast to quantitative procedures. It also acknowledged several limitations of the experimental method and, above all, its formalized, statistics-based view of the individual. Instead, psychologists stressed the importance of in-depth, detailed examinations of human experience, concerns, feelings, and actions taken in unity. Such an emphasis does not mean that early humanistic psychologists rejected experimental methods. They simply considered that quantitative experimental procures did not allow examining the diversity and complexity of an individual's inner world. For example, the fact that 50 percent of patients show improvements in their symptoms after undergoing a certain kind of psychotherapy does not say much about what these individuals feel, how they understood their own symptoms, and whether the changes in their behavioral symptoms affected their overall existence.

One of the brightest representatives of this school of thought, whose name is inseparable from humanistic psychology, was American psychologist and humanist Abraham Maslow.

Humanistic Psychology of Abraham Maslow

As an experimental psychologist early in his career, Brooklyn-born Abraham Maslow (1908–1970) developed a research program at Brandeis University in Massachusetts. His studies helped him to develop his own theory of motivation. Maslow was also influenced by German psychologist Kurt Goldstein (see Chapter 9) and a fundamental assumption of Gestalt psychologists that an organism must be analyzed in terms of the totality of its whole behavior and complex interaction with its environment. Motivation is a force within an organism that initiates and maintains behavior.

Abraham Maslow as a founder of Humanistic Psychology. He called for psychologists' attention to compassion, hope, and goodwill as key features of human existence.

How does this motivation work? Maslow argued that people are motivated by certain needs, indicating some deficiency. Hunger, for example, is an indicator of food deficiency. An individual will eat to eliminate this deficiency, which will end the subjective experience of hunger. However, other needs are distinctly human. They are not necessarily about obtaining something tangible or material. These are needs related to being or becoming: a better student, a caring husband, a loving daughter, a decent human being, and so forth.

Maslow further proposed that humans have a number of needs that can be arranged in a hierarchy in terms of their potency (Maslow, 1970). Maslow grouped these needs into five categorical levels: physiological, safety, love, esteem, and self-actualization. Once an individual has satisfied the cluster of needs at a particular level, he or she is able to progress to the next hierarchical level. Thus, for example, people typically are not prompted to seek acceptance and esteem until they have met their needs for food, water, shelter, and safety. Maslow noted that as one ascends the hierarchy of needs, this person becomes less animal-like and more human. If a woman, for example, has been able to satisfy adequately the needs on the first four levels, she is in a position to fulfill the highest order needs—namely, to actualize her unique potential. According to Maslow, once she enters the realm of **self-actualization,** she becomes qualitatively different from those who are still attempting to meet their more basic needs.

IN THEIR OWN WORDS

Abraham Maslow: If I were dropped out of a plane into the ocean and told the nearest land was a thousand miles away, I'd still swim. And I'd despise the one who gave up.

The self-actualizing person's life is governed by the search for "being-values" (B-values), such as truth, goodness, beauty, wholeness, justice, and meaningfulness. His interest in self-actualizing people began with his great admiration for Max Wertheimer, one of the pioneers of Gestalt psychology, and Ruth Benedict (1888–1948), the renowned American cultural anthropologist and one of the most ardent critics of the early 20th-century racist theories in social sciences. After discovering that these two individuals had many characteristics in common, such as optimism, efficiency, kindness, and generosity, Maslow began to search for others with similar qualities. The group that he finally isolated for more detailed study included American presidents Abraham Lincoln and Thomas Jefferson, physicist Albert Einstein, Eleanor Roosevelt (wife of President Franklin D. Roosevelt), philosophers Benedict Spinoza and Albert Schweitzer, politician Adlai Stevenson, and educator Martin Buber—all Europeans or European Americans. On the basis of his research, Maslow developed a composite, impressionistic profile of an optimally functioning, mature, and healthy human being. Maslow concluded that self-actualizing persons exhibit a number of similar characteristics, including (a) an accurate perception of reality, (b) a continued freshness of appreciation and openness to experience, (c) spontaneity and simplicity, (d) a strong ethical awareness, (e) a philosophical (rather than hostile) sense of humor, (f) a need for privacy, (g) periodic mystical ("peak") experiences, (h) democratic leadership traits (see Chapter 9), (i) deep interpersonal relations, (j) autonomy and independence, (k) creativeness, (l) a problem-centered (rather than self-centered) orientation, (m) a resistance to enculturation, and (n) an acceptance of self, others, and nature.

Maslow's views were innovative. In contrast to many psychoanalytic theorists preceding him, focusing on clinical cases, Maslow created his theory by studying healthy and successful people. His influence within humanistic psychology was significant. Again, instead of focusing on symptoms of mental illness and the ways to reduce and eliminate them, he wanted to understand the nature of mental health. He approached clinical psychology from a different angle by asking, "What does it mean to be mentally healthy?" His approach stimulated the development of numerous studies and creation of several therapeutic methods. One of them was developed by Carl Rogers.

Person-Centered Approach

American psychologist Carl Rogers (1902–1987) offered a so-called person-centered approach to an individual, the approach that had found remarkable and well-received applications in therapeutic practice worldwide. One of the principles of Rogers's approach to psychology was his emphasis on the self-actualizing, fully functioning individual (Rogers, 1951). Like Maslow, he saw self-actualization as the highest level of psychological health. Self-actualization, however, does not occur simply because an individual wants it. To achieve self-actualization, people have to make a continuous and conscious effort (Rogers, 1961). Specifically, they have to try to be open to experience, live each day fully, have trust in their own decisions, enjoy freedom to choose, remain creative without the feeling of conformity, balance their own needs, and participate in the opportunities that life constantly offers to them.

Person-Centered Therapy. Person-centered therapy is an application of the person-centered approach to therapy. Rogers taught therapists to show their clients genuineness, empathy, and unconditional positive regard. On the basis of these basic elements, the therapist creates a supportive, nonjudgmental environment in which clients are encouraged to think about their own problems, discuss them, prepare a

ON THE WEB

Read more about approaches and methods embraced by humanistic therapists.

course of action, and then reach their full potential (Rogers, 1959). A healthy, friendly relationship between client and therapist must be achieved. It should be based on openness, trust, and mutual respect. The therapist accepts the client without disapproval or approval. This attitude should facilitate increased self-respect in the clients, which they often lack when they enter therapy. Person-centered therapy became a very popular method in psychology worldwide.

✓ CHECK YOUR KNOWLEDGE

What are the main theoretical principles of humanistic psychology?

Is it possible for every person to achieve self-actualization?

What is humanistic therapy?

Assessment of Humanistic Psychology

Humanistic psychology expanded its influence rapidly in the 1970s and the 1980s. It had gained a large number of active followers and supporters internationally. The overall success was due to many innovative ideas and practical applications that this discipline was offering to many other branches of psychology. What particular ideas and applications have gained most recognition?

Accomplishments. Humanistic psychologists directed attention of many psychologists to a few fundamental questions about their discipline. For example, what is the major goal of psychology as science? What do we, as psychologists, try to understand in our research? A major critical complaint of the pioneers of humanistic psychology was that the mainstream discipline was losing its focus. They hoped to redirect attention to the human factor and the issues that are ultimately human, unique to people's experience. This was a quite reasonable and timely argument. Although most professional psychologists in the 1960s did not switch their research interests dramatically in favor of humanistic principles, many of them began to pay serious attention to the problems that humanistic psychology was putting forward.

One of the signs of success of humanistic psychology as a discipline was the development of psychological humanistic-oriented research in several theoretical and applied fields. Consider just a few examples of research studies and academic programs developed under the influence of humanistic psychology.

One rapidly growing field was **positive psychology**—a branch that studies the strengths and virtues that enable individuals and communities to thrive (Compton, 2004). Back in the 1960s, Maslow not only urged psychologists to focus on psychological problems and mental illness but also asked them to promote success and accomplishment, nurture talent, support great initiatives, and set examples of happiness. Many psychologists turned to studies of happiness, meaningful life, and achievement. Psychology professionals began to use methods of positive psychology in the classroom and workplace. The main focus of their work was not on problems or weaknesses but mostly on sources of growth and improvement. Practical applications of positive psychology included helping individuals find their strength and organizations identify their potentials.

An important contribution of humanistic psychology was the concept of positive mental health. Instead of studying, almost exclusively, psychopathological symptoms and traumatic conditions causing such symptoms, humanistic psychologists turned to the healthy side of an individual, the optimal state of functioning and experience. The concept of self-actualization has become a widely accepted idea in contemporary psychology.

Humanistic principles of the necessity of care and dignity in an individual existence were also crucial in the development of **hospice care,** a complex medical and psychological system of help focusing on palliative and other humane principles of medical care. The major goal of palliative care is to prevent and relieve the suffering of individuals affected by a serious illness and to improve their well-being when it is possible (Callanan & Kelly, 1997). Today, hospice care in the United States and many other countries has become a very important part of the health care system.

ON THE WEB

Learn more about hospice care on the textbook's website.

Humanistic principles had contributed to the **holistic health movement,** a multidisciplinary field or approach focusing on the fundamental assumption that physical, mental, and spiritual factors contributing to illness are interconnected and equally important in treatment. In fact, the holistic approach in medicine elevates the importance of psychological factors in medical treatment and prevention of illness (Remen, 1996). Since 1960, scores of new centers of holistic treatment began to appear in North America and western Europe and across the world. Many trained professionals with medical and psychology degrees began to study spirituality, classic literature, folk stories, and traditional methods of healing to identify and use the effective methods of treatment involving both the body and mind. Supporters of holistic treatment used humanistic principles and no longer saw their clients and patients as "sets of symptoms" but rather emphasized the uniqueness of every individual's history of illness and every therapeutic method used in every individual case.

For example, basic humanistic principles found a grateful recipient in **narrative medicine,** a clinical field that helps medical professionals to recognize, absorb, interpret, and be moved by the stories of illness (Charon, 1992). Several medical schools and residency programs began to train physicians to treat medical problems not merely as problems to be solved. Doctors and nurses learn how to take into account the specific psychological and personal history of the patient. Narrative medicine helps doctors, nurses, social workers, and therapists to improve the effectiveness of care by developing the capacity for attention, reflection, representation, and affiliation with patients and colleagues (Charon, 1993).

Principles of humanistic psychology influenced **peace psychology,** a theoretical and applied field that tries to understand ideological and psychological causes of war and develops educational programs to reduce the threat of violence in international relations and domestic policies of some countries. Psychologists working in this field also conducted research on a wide range of social issues and topics, including forgiveness, social awareness, altruism, and conflict resolution. Specifically, positive psychology teaches that most causes of war and violence are preventable. It takes both political leaders and ordinary people to give up their old images of the enemy and try to find possibilities for dialogue with their adversaries. Several pioneers of peace psychology, including Thomas Greening, have made an important contribution to the U.S.-Soviet relations during the cold war and especially during the period of relaxation of international tensions in the 1980s (Greening, 1986). They organized face-to-face meetings between officials, students, teachers, and other professionals in the United States and the Soviet Union to "deconstruct" the old enemy image and promote the new atmosphere of trust. This psychological approach to conflict resolution may appear to some a bit too naive and impractical.

You may ask, "How is it possible to affect international relations by conducting interpersonal group seminars?" Peace psychologists insist that psychological changes could influence policy and global outcomes. In fact, studies in public diplomacy, one of the growing areas of 21st-century international relations, showed that a gradual reduction of international tensions is possible to achieve by turning to, among other issues, individual contacts between opinion leaders, including scientists, journalists, and business leaders.

Skeptics disagree. They have long maintained that social and political changes cause psychological transformations, not the other way around. To achieve peace, for example, one side has to impose it first, and then people change their attitudes and behavior to adjust to the reality of peace. Which side would you support in this argument? Do psychologists have enough intellectual power to affect social conflicts and promote peace?

Some fields of research turned to empirical studies of specific mechanisms of socialization and development. For example, *narrative psychology* began to focus on how published stories and essays shape lives (K. Murray, 1985). Psychologist James Liu, who was born in Taiwan and now works in New Zealand, showed in his cross-national studies that despite popular assumptions about the existence of profound differences in the way people of different cultures perceive history and major world events, the similarities are overwhelming. We focus on the recent past, which is generally centered on politics and war (Liu et al., 2005).

During the 1970s and 1980s, the ideas and values of humanistic psychology became very popular and well accepted in Western countries and around the world. Humanistic psychologists offered a new, optimistic vision of human nature and experiences. The emphasis on a free, rational, and ever-growing individual was innovative and promising compared to the widely accepted psychoanalytic assumption about the predetermined trouble hidden in the dungeon of an individual's unconscious mind. Humanistic psychology was also inspirational. It offered a new set of values for approaching an understanding of an individual's nature and development.

Shortcomings and Criticisms. One of the obvious shortcomings of humanistic psychology, from the critics' viewpoint, was its relatively poor record of experimental research. You remember that the founders of this school back in the 1950s were disappointed with the status of what appeared to be mainstream psychology. Psychology as a discipline, they believed, was losing the "tree" human element in the "forest" of experimental procedures. Critics, however, fired back and maintained that humanistic psychology had distanced itself carelessly from empirical studies and statistical interpretations of experimental data. As a result, most empirical facts obtained in this field are based on individual observations, stories, and interviews—all imprecise and probably biased. Like introspection in the 19th century, most research methods of humanistic psychology were very subjective. The weakness of its experimental base was among several factors affecting the declining interest in humanistic psychology beginning in the 1990s.

Serious criticisms came from specialists in theoretical science. The criticism was rather serious: humanistic psychology and related research orientations in social sciences are not necessarily scientific. The central argument was that a theory should be considered scientific if and only if it is falsifiable (Popper, 1950/1992). What does it mean to be falsifiable? Consider, for example, the following statement: "Every person has the right to be happy." It is an unfalsifiable statement because it would be almost impossible to demonstrate its falsehood and prove, for example, that "this person or that individual does not have the right to be happy." A falsifiable statement would be "this therapeutic method provides successful outcomes 70 percent of the time" because it is possible to verify empirically. If major statements and findings of humanistic psychology are not falsifiable, the discipline is likely to be just a set of inspirational ideas that exist at the mercy of their creators and supporters. Furthermore, the validity of their assumptions is only the matter of individual taste or social perspective. Critics maintained that humanistic principles became widely acceptable because they were fitting well in the social climate of the 1960s and the rapidly growing awareness among intellectual elites about social justice, international peace, nonviolence, spirituality, and continuous self-improvement. As soon as social fads go away, so does a fashionable trend in psychology.

Another critical argument is based on an assumption that instead of presenting objective data, most humanistic psychologists tried to promote their own subjective value systems. Take Maslow, for example. Do you think that Maslow's theory is a valid depiction of a fully functioning person or, instead, a reflection of Maslow's own subjective value system? Did Maslow mix ethical and moral considerations with his logic? Consider, for instance, his portrayal of self-actualizing people as open, realistic, spontaneous, possessing democratic leadership traits, resistant to enculturation, and accepting of self, others, and nature. Is this an objective description of human fulfillment?

Or is it a prescription—masked as a description—of Maslow's own subjective ideals? As noted by M. B. Smith (1978), perhaps Maslow simply selected his personal heroes and offered his impressions of them. He simply selected people who shared his moral code and his conception of fulfillment and thus assigned them the honorific status of being self-actualized (Kendler, 1999).

Another weakness of humanistic views is their relatively weak cross-cultural validity. For example, although the structure of needs presented by Maslow may be appropriate for individuals of all cultures, the relative strengths of the needs are culture specific. Self-preoccupation could be seen as a Western characteristic not so dominant in some other cultures. The Chinese hierarchy of values, for instance, includes the promotion of interconnectedness, in contrast to the emphasis on self-development in Maslow's version. In one study, Nevis (1983) revised Maslow's hierarchy of needs and argued that one of the most basic needs of people in communist China is the need to belong, rather than physiological needs. Moreover, self-actualization could manifest as a devoted service to community. If a person self-actualizes by contributing to the group, this individual is realizing the value of collectivist self-actualization.

A similar theory of motivation was formulated and empirically tested within a different cultural environment by the Soviet psychologist Arthur Petrovsky (1978), who studied in the 1970s a collectivist orientation in Soviet people. He found that in the Soviet Union, the individual was able to fulfill maximum potential when he or she accepted the goals and values of the communist society. In both Chinese and Russian examples, environmental demands, socialist ideology, and traditions (like the Confucian work ethic in China or a communist moral code of behavior in the Soviet Union) advocated harmony and cooperation, but not a kind of self-determination emphasized at that time by many humanistic psychologists in the West (Shiraev & Levy, 2009).

Maslow himself acknowledged that his creative theorizing and research lacked the rigor of strict empirical science. He and his colleagues who pioneered humanistic psychology fervently believed, however, that it was imperative to begin the process of rounding out the field of psychology by attending to "the highest capacities of the healthy and strong man as well as with the defensive maneuvers of crippled spirits" (Maslow, 1954, p. 33). Furthermore, Maslow maintained that it would be misleading to believe that science is value free since its methods and procedures are developed and used for human purposes.

✓ CHECK YOUR KNOWLEDGE

Explain positive psychology.

What is the holistic health movement?

Name a basic weakness of humanistic psychology related to experimental research.

As it was stated in the beginning of this chapter, humanistic psychology attempted to redirect psychology as a discipline to the issue of subjectivity. Cognitive psychology, to which we are turning now, pursued a relatively similar goal. Despite this common interest, cognitive and humanistic psychologists were very different in how they approached subjectivity. In short, they asked different questions. And this was the crucial difference between the two groups. Psychologist-supporters of the humanistic tradition were mostly interested in *why* people do what they do. The cognitive tradition in psychology was studying *how* the individual processes information. Not surprisingly, the first group (humanistic psychologists) had turned to moral values and ethical prescriptions. The other group (cognitive psychologists) was turning to formal operations, physiological and mathematical models describing cognitive processes.

Cognitive Psychology

Throughout the first half of the 20th century, the behavioral tradition within American and world psychology was becoming increasingly influential. In a simple way, behaviorism as a research approach made sense. It was easy to understand. Behaviorism's simple assumptions, clear-cut methods of measurement, and general scientific optimism (psychology can provide knowledge to influence behavior) appealed to many individuals choosing psychology as a career. Globally, behaviorism by the 1940s had achieved the status of the mainstream approach. Scientists such as Watson, Pavlov, Tolman, Skinner, and many others had advanced this tradition through basic research and practical applications. Psychology appeared to both insiders and outsiders as a complex study of human behavior. Although behaviorism was continuously under criticism for being reductionist, simplistic, and one-sided, America's leading position in world psychology had influenced a substantial shift of interest toward behaviorism globally.

Nevertheless, in the United States, a significant change of course—a strategic correction—was taking place between the late 1950s and the 1970s. The change was associated with the so-called **cognitive revolution,** the term referring to the shift within psychology from being primarily behavioral to being increasingly cognitive. Of course, the term *revolution* sounds vividly dramatic. From a critical observer's view, it is largely inaccurate to apply revolutionary analogies to the actual course of events lasting for almost two decades. In fact, there had not been any violent and rapid takeover of psychology departments by a new generation of psychologists demanding change. Nevertheless, the term *cognitive revolution* has survived because it refers to a dynamic shift or reorientation in both the main focus and basic research methods of psychological studies.

As you well remember, in the 19th century, the great minds of psychology, including Fechner, Ebbinghaus, Wundt, Titchener, and others, tried to find a way to measure the elusive "internal" mechanisms of mental functioning. It was a frustrating task. Such mechanisms appeared difficult to examine with the methods borrowed from physics or chemistry. The "founding fathers" of experimental psychology focused on introspection instead. It seemed to them that introspection had given them a sense of experimental validity of their experimental studies. It was a method to measure human experience. Numbers and mathematical formulas appeared suitable to describe the mind's action. Yet overall, the method of introspection had failed to provide sufficient and reliable information about the mind's work (see Chapter 4).

Behaviorism, on the other hand, appeared as an attractive and modern approach to study the manifestations of the work of human mind, the overt reactions of the body. Some behaviorists, such as Watson and Skinner, were simply disinterested in examining the contents of the *black box* of mental activities. What was inside of that box, what was within an individual's mental operations, did not interest most behaviorists. They found satisfaction in examining only the input (the signals) and the output (the responses) coming out of the black box. Sure, some behaviorists assumed the existence of a mediating variable between stimulus and reaction. Yet they continued to study memory, intelligence, learning, and motivation by behavioral methods.

It is erroneous to think that the entire world of psychology turned to behaviorism by the last century's second half. True, it was a mainstream orientation of most psychology departments in North America. Yet the studies of the "subjective" element of human existence continued. Remember the Gestalt tradition in psychology. Wertheimer, Köhler, and Koffka continued the experimental study of experience (G. Mandler, 2007). In Europe, Piaget and Vygotsky (and many others) examined the works of the developing mind. Psychoanalysts, along with examining a range of clinical symptoms, also paid attention to the various manifestations of the mind's work. So what was specifically innovative in the new wave of empirical studies of the human mind in the mid-20th century? What was the origin and essence of a new branch that we call today cognitive psychology?

In the beginning, we will examine the most fundamental principles of this approach formulated in its founders' early studies. Then we will consider cognitive psychology in the context of a larger field of cognitive science. After that, we will briefly describe several major areas and directions of research in cognitive psychology.

Rebirth of the Tradition

Cognitive psychology is the scientific study of human mental processes and their role in thinking, emotions, and behavior (Kellogg, 2003). Cognitive psychology's main concern is how we, as individuals, process information. What behaviorists ignored and put aside time after time had become the subject of interest of cognitive psychologists in the 1950s. But does epistemology do the same? Does epistemology study how individuals process information? Let's return to Chapter 2 and recall that epistemology as a branch of philosophy examines the nature of knowledge, its foundations, extent, and validity. Cognitive psychologists from the start pursued a different goal. They wanted to examine the internal mechanisms, the functioning, and the operational performance of the mind. They turned to cognitive processes such as thinking, memory, perception, and others. Most important, in these examinations, psychologists began to use specific methods, including popular behavioral methods, such as time reaction measurement. They also used new methods developed in the 20th century, including brain imaging, mathematical models, and sophisticated computer simulations. One of the most distinct features of cognitive psychology was its emphasis on meaning, which behaviorists generally overlooked or simply ignored for the same reason they did not accept subjectivity: To them, it seemed impossible to measure phenomena such as "meaning" experimentally.

To summarize, cognitive psychology represented in many ways a switch of attention from behavior to consciousness, from habits and reflexes, to meaning and subjectivity. In the process, cognitive psychology was becoming a dominant approach in psychology in the late 20th century (Kellogg, 2003).

Early Founders. Several great scholarly minds working in various fields of science have contributed to the development of cognitive psychology. American professor George Miller (born in 1920) was one of them. Although it is impossible to establish the exact birthday of cognitive psychology, many historians of psychology refer to a symbolic "square one" in 1960, when Miller and his colleagues founded the Center for Cognitive Studies at Harvard University. It also was the year when Miller, together with Eugene Galanter and Karl Pribram, published their groundbreaking work, *Plans and the Structure of Behavior* (G. Miller, Galanter, & Pribram, 1960). In this book, the authors underlined and explained several important principles of their approach to psychology. In essence, several principal assumptions from this book stand out clearly.

First, the authors believed that what people commonly called "mental life" could be studied from the standpoint of information. Other psychologists continued to underline the importance of studies of reflexes, learning mechanisms, or individual actions; physiologists used complex physiological mechanisms to explain psychological processes; and many psychoanalysts continued to use the concept of psychological energy, but what Miller and colleagues considered "mental" was pure information processing. If the nature of everything we call subjective (or psychological) is rooted in information processing, then it would be possible to approach psychology from an entirely different perspective. Consider the concept of an "image," for example. From the standpoint of the new cognitive approach, this image now could be understood as a quantitative measure of information, which an individual receives, stores, and processes.

Second, the pioneers of cognitive psychology introduced an assumption that human beings are extremely complex computing devices. It was quite a logical suggestion: if the nature of all mental is in information processing, then human beings should become natural processors of such information. In the 1950s, science was rapidly developing new theories about information-processing operations of machines. If we know how machines process information, then by analogy we could use this knowledge to understand the work of the human mind. This discourse leads to the third assumption.

Mathematicians, engineers, and computer scientists have already advanced their knowledge about information-processing devices and computers. Such devices conduct operations based on a set of instructions or programs. If there is no instruction or program, there is no corresponding operation. When a program is given to a computing device, it does not deviate from this program. The program compels the device's every step, every operation in solving a particular problem or performing a task. When programming instructions change, the operations change accordingly. In general terms, every operation of the device refers to an underlying program. What is a program? It is a set of commands. Therefore, using these definitions and applying them to psychology, we can propose that any element of mental life, such as an image, any psychological process such as memory or daydreaming, can be explained, in theory, as information processing based on a set of specific instructions or programs.

Fourth, such instructions underlying the work of the mind are very sophisticated. They represent a certain multilevel plan, a long chain of operations. Each operation can be described as either action or inaction. Every psychological phenomenon, like thinking, for example, is a complex process giving individuals special tools to control the schedule according to which each chain of operations takes place. How does this chain function?

Remember, behaviorists used a generic principle expressed in the popular S → R model, where S stood for the stimulus and R represented reactions. The "inside" processes were of little interests to behaviorists: They claimed they could measure external reactions without the need to look inside. The cognitive psychologists offered a different approach. The organization of behavior as well as any mental process should be understood as a strategy organized under the "test-operate-test-exit" principle or **T.O.T.E.**

> **ON THE WEB**
>
> Check George Miller's work on WordNet.

Keep in mind, an individual acts according to a given program or plan. To verify whether this individual follows the plan correctly (or whether the individual achieves certain results), we need a test: How far is the individual from the destination point? How far is this person from solving the problem? Several outcomes are possible. If there is a deviation from the proposed course, if the plan is followed incorrectly, a change or operation is needed. After this operation is performed, another test follows. If everything goes according to the plan, no further changes are needed. It is time to "exit." However, if the desired result has not been achieved, it is time to loop back to the "operate" stage and try again. This principle is applicable to both simple as well as super-complex tasks that we, as humans, perform (see Figure 12.1).

Figure 12.1 The T.O.T.E. Principle of Behavior Organization

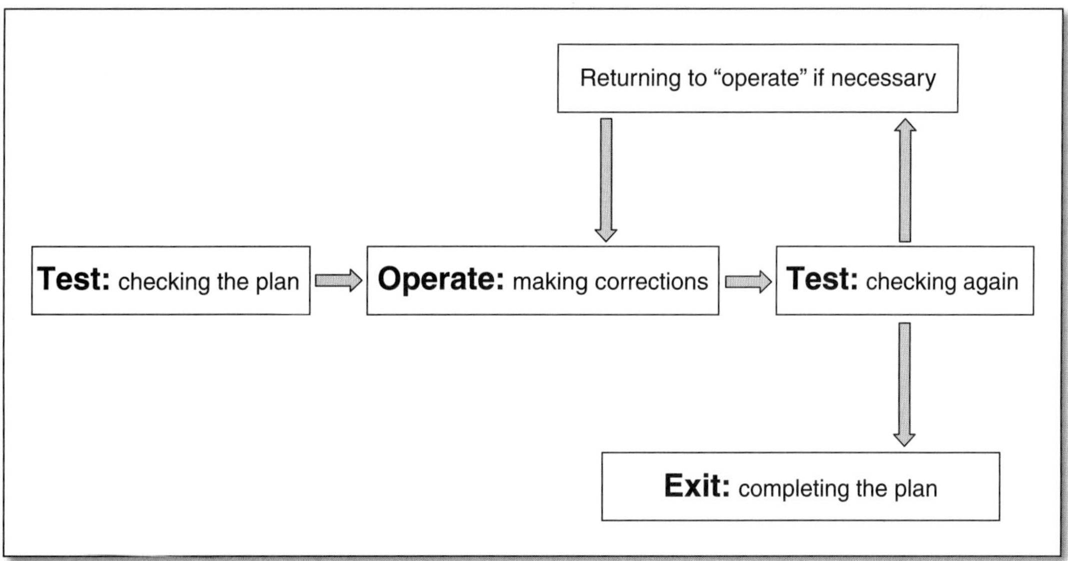

CASE IN POINT

The Number Seven. In 1956, psychologist George Miller found support for earlier assumptions made by psychologists that seven was the "magic" number that characterized people's optimal memory performance on random lists of letters, words, numbers, or almost any kind of meaningful familiar item. He also noticed that the memory span of young adults was around seven elements, called "chunks," regardless of whether the elements were digits, letters, words, geometrical units, or symbols. From the view of popular psychology, "seven" is a very popular number. There are seven days in a week. There are also seven days of creation in Christianity. The menorah, one of the oldest symbols of the Jewish people, has seven branches. We often say "seventh heaven." In Islam, there are seven heavens and seven earths. We travel the "seven seas." There are seven notes in the traditional Western music scale. There are seven deadly sins. In Hinduism, there are seven Chakras. Seven is also the number of stellar objects in the solar system visible to the naked eye. There are the seven colors of the rainbow. Is this a coincidence between our memory span and the number seven?

Probably not. Later research revealed that our memory capacity does depend on the category of chunks used. For example, it is seven if we use digits, six if we use letters, and five if we use words. The position of such chunks has an impact as well (Gestalt psychologists were right). Besides, the attention to the number seven is probably exaggerated. Every number may have a special cultural meaning. Think, for example, about the number three. Could you find similar cultural, everyday examples involving this number? How about the three traffic lights or three strikes for starters?

Source: G. Miller (1956)

Psychology and Cognitive Science

Cognitive psychology belongs to the line of research that is commonly regarded today as part of an interdisciplinary field of **cognitive science.** This field includes studies in several fields, particularly cognitive neuroscience, computer science, philosophy, and linguistics, among other fields. To better understand cognitive psychology, let's examine briefly some key studies involved in the early development of cognitive science.

Cognitive Neuroscience. The 1950s was a period in the history of psychology and physiology marked by the inauguration of **cognitive neuroscience,** an academic field that examines the brain mechanisms supporting mental functions. During that period, a growing flow of new research data related to the brain's physiology continued. At least three sources of new information existed.

First, it was traditional experimental research in neurophysiology conducted in university and hospital-based laboratories. Physiologists used increasingly sophisticated methods and experimental devices to learn more about the mechanisms of neurophysiological processes and the brain's chemistry. For example, new studies in electrophysiology produced better and more effective ways to measure the electric and magnetic fields generated by neurons and neuronal networks in the brain.

Second, clinical data based on the studies of brain pathology also provided valuable knowledge about the brain's normal functioning as well as its dysfunctions. One of many efficient methods involved studies of lesions (using clinical observations of people as subjects who have suffered damage to their brains).

Third, the rapidly developing methods of brain imaging provided cognitive neuroscientists with new remarkable facts. For example, by examining the location of neural activation generated by a cognitive task, researchers could learn more about the brain's functioning and the role of psychological processes in thinking, emotions, and decision making.

Cognitive neuroscientists began to offer psychologists new and increasingly rich information related to the brain's performance. Psychologists, in turn, had to face no less challenging tasks of interpreting such newly acquired research data. The challenge was clear: an experimental fact that one portion of the brain is more active than several adjacent areas during a certain mental operation could be interpreted in a variety of ways.

☞ A CASE IN POINT

Amygdala and Information Processing Related to Emotion. It has been accepted from the 1950s that brain damage restricted to the amygdala may produce significant emotional disturbance (Weiskrantz, 1956). More recent research on emotional processing in animals and humans with brain lesions provides additional and compelling evidence that the amygdala is critical to fear responses (Adolphs, Tranel, & Damasio, 1998). It has been shown that electrical stimulation of the amygdala elicits a pattern of behaviors that mimic natural or conditioned fear, even in the absence of any obvious eliciting stimuli (Davis, 1997). Direct projections (connecting pathways) from this part of the brain to the hypothalamus appear to be involved in the activation of the sympathetic autonomic nervous system seen during fear and anxiety. Projections from amygdala also innervate multiple brain systems involved in the behavioral responses to fear. As a result, the body responds to threats by activating numerous protective "shields." For some individuals, certain hormones can suppress subjective feelings of pain in an emergency; in others, various defensive responses are activated, such as "freezing," crying, hiding, and so forth. It is known today that lesions of the amygdala may block fear, as well as various measures of attention. Local infusions of specific drugs into the amygdala may reduce anxiety, which is called an *anxiolytic effect* (Breiter et al., 1996).

Two important principles used in cognitive neuroscience became essential for psychologists. As a general rule, cognitive neuroscience began to treat psychological processes as the product of the brain's physiological processes. This materialist point of view attracted many researchers over the years. However, most of them attempted to avoid reductionism: they firmly believed that physiological processes are not identical to mental ones. For example, one of the pioneers of cognitive neuroscience, American neuroscientist and the Nobel Prize-winner Roger Sperry (1913–1994), maintained that the higher order mental processes function according to their own specific laws and principles, which cannot be simply reduced to physiological processes, even the most complicated ones (Sperry, 1961). A mental function is more than a combination of billions of neurons firing. To understand psychology, one has to understand the complexity of multilevel interactions of physiological processes and mechanisms by which they interact. Like Sperry, most cognitive neuroscientists wanted to adopt a holistic viewpoint on psychology and physiology: the total is greater than the sum of its parts.

Next, cognitive neuroscientists proposed various models of brain processing, largely comparing it to the way computers process data. In a nutshell, the brain receives information from the senses, encodes it, stores it, and then exercises decision making and response selection. But how and where does all this information travel within the brain? Cognitive neuroscience comes to help and uses the model of neural networks to explain these dynamics. What are these neural network models? The brain neurons can be presented as "nodes." A node stands for a device of some sorts, which is connected to other nodes and attached to a larger network. Such a node is able to send, receive, block, and forward information through various communication channels. In terms of the brain's operations, cognitive neuroscientists examine mental functions from the standpoint of these nodes functioning in networks (Glynn, 1999).

Of course, the brain is composed of billions of cells engaged in complex physiological processes, and computers are just electronic machines. Nevertheless, as cognitive neuroscience maintained, both the machines and the brain have to share virtually similar principles of functioning. By studying these principles, scientist can learn more about the devices and, most important, about the brain's functions. Here, neurophysiology was adopting many fundamental assumptions used in the new and fast-growing field of computer science.

Computer Science. For psychologists, the most important assumption of the rapidly developing new discipline called computer science was that computers and human beings process information similarly. In a way, computer science represents a computational approach to psychology. One of the most prominent pioneers of the computational approach was British scientist Alan Turing (1912–1954), an intellectual genius whose life tragically ended at 42. Historians of science agree that his work serves the theoretical and practical basis of modern computer science and the artificial intelligence program (Hodges, 1983).

Turing was a unique scientist combining the talents of an engineer, mathematician, philosopher, logician, and a criminal investigator. Educated in Great Britain

Alan Turing brought computational principles to the study of cognitive processes. Pictured: The Alan Turing Memorial in Manchester, England.

and the United States, he worked during World War II for the British government. One of his responsibilities was the creation of programs and machines to break German secret codes used in the Nazi's military and government communications. His theoretical quests and remarkable practical accomplishments had convinced him that human judgment, the sophisticated work of the mind, can be explained with absolute certainty from the standpoint of mathematics and logic.

His paper "Computing Machinery and Intelligence," which appeared in the journal *Mind* in 1950, brought him notoriety. His research received global attention. Although he had never considered himself a psychologist, several of Turing's ideas were essential to the young field of cognitive psychology (Turing, 1950; Weizenbaum, 1976). What were these fundamental ideas?

First, to operate, the brain has to use information from a variety of sources inside and outside the body. In the process, the brain has to store this information. A crucial point here is that this information is not infinite or incalculable as it may appear. It is, in fact, limited and measurable.

Second, the brain uses this information to solve problems. Therefore, mental functions can be viewed as problem-solving operations, programs, or procedures. If the information is finite and measurable, then each and every problem that the brain solves using this information is essentially a mathematical one.

Third, each problem-solving method should be based on a particular rule or algorithm. Each algorithm can be viewed as a computable operation. Essentially, all mental operations are computable. Overall, such computable operations should be sufficient enough to explain all mental functions that the brain performs.

Turing believed that if these assumptions were correct, then computer science could provide new insights into the mechanisms of the central nervous system. Sometime in the future, he thought, it would be possible to describe mathematically and simulate virtually all operations taking place in a person's brain. Yet another intriguing possibility had occurred to him. If any problem solving was a computable operation, such operations should be available for a machine if only it was given a sufficient algorithm. It was a truly intriguing proposition resembling a fantasy: a machine capable of thinking.

Turing's work had given a significant boost to the fields of studies of so-called **artificial intelligence.** This term had several meanings. In general terms, it stood for the study and design of intelligent machines. In the context of cognitive neuroscience, artificial intelligence is the study and creation of systems that perceive their environment and make decisions to maximize success. In 20th-century popular culture, scores of authors have long entertained the literary idea that "thinking" machines would eventually compete with humans in all intellectual and practical fields. In the 1950s, after Turing proposed his ideas, artificial intelligence was becoming a reasonable possibility. Even skeptics had to lower their critical voices.

Chess was one of several areas where computers began to gain both strength and public attention. Digital computers provided both mathematical and sophisticated technical solutions for this game. Soon enough, chess computers began to compete with humans. Today, some computers can compete on the highest level of the game, winning against world chess champions. Creative writing was another field. Some assumed that poetry would become a routine procedure for machines as soon as mathematicians wrote clever programs for metaphors and rhyming. It didn't happen, however. Computer-produced poetry was sophisticated grammatically but awful as an art. Yet doomsday scenarios involving smart but evil computers became a source of inspiration for fiction writers. Despite differences in their plots, all these scenarios were based on an assumption that some day in the future, the "clever" computers and machines would go out of control and rebel against humans. One of the most famous works of the not-so-distant past has been the movie *The Terminator*, featuring Arnold Schwarzenegger and other famous performers.

ON THE WEB

Researchers claim that telepathy exists. Sort of. Read more on the website.

By the 1960s, computing became a well-recognized and acceptable model to explain many aspects of the mind's work. Cognitive processes were routinely compared or even sometimes equated with the programs that could be run on a computational device.

Philosophy and Consciousness. In addition to computer science, cognitive psychology secured another source of knowledge and inspiration. It was philosophy. As you remember, since the end of the 19th century, experiment-oriented scientists representing a "new" psychology pursued a peaceful separation with philosophy. For a number of years, experimental and then, to a large degree, mainstream psychology ignored and avoided philosophical discussions about the activities of the rational mind and the awesome power of human will. The situation started to change in the 1950s, when psychology as an experimental discipline became more confident and secure. One of the most difficult questions coming from the philosophers was, *How exactly do neurobiological processes in the brain result in consciousness?* Now, supported by neuroscience and computer science, philosophers turned again to a holistic perspective on the functioning of the mind. A leading philosopher of the 20th century, John Searle (born 1932) believed that psychological functions such as consciousness can be studied perfectly by physics or biology. Above all, consciousness is a biological phenomenon. However, it has some important and unique features that cannot be understood by biology alone. The most important of these features is "subjectivity." Searle used a specific example to demonstrate subjectivity. If somebody asked him what it feels like to give a lecture in front of a large audience, he could answer that question. But if somebody asked what it feels like to be a stone, there is no answer to that question because stones are not conscious (Searle, 1998).

Thus, Searle avoided reductionism and reiterated the idea that physiological processes in the brain are not consciousness. He approached the issue of consciousness from a different direction: physiology causes consciousness. In other words, processes at the level of individual neurons and changes on the macro-level of the whole brain produce consciousness. This was Searle's approach to the solution of the mind-body problem. To clarify, he used the following analogy. We cannot consider a molecule of water to be cold and wet. Similarly, a firing neuron does not allow us to say that this neuron produces an image of a veggie sandwich. Consciousness is a higher level feature of the whole system of chemical and physiological processes of the brain. In the world of physics, features such as liquidity or coldness occur at a much higher level than that of single molecules. Similarly, our thoughts about sandwiches (or anything else) occur at a much higher level than that of the single neuron or synapse. Searle's views can be summarized briefly as follows: At least two crucial relationships between consciousness and the brain can be established. First, lower level neuronal processes in the brain cause consciousness. Second, consciousness is simply a higher level feature of the system that is made up of the lower level neuronal elements (Searle, 1992).

Another support for cognitive psychology came from linguistics, the scientific approach to the study of language. A particularly significant role here was played by the studies of language acquisition (i.e., how children and adults learn a language).

Linguistics. In the middle of the past century, despite variations and details, the main message of the behavioral approach to language acquisition was that learning a language was in essence habit formation. We remember words and then remember habits of putting those words in grammatically correct phrases. Misspellings and verbal errors go away gradually while we develop linguistic skills. One of the researchers who questioned this approach was Noam Chomsky (born in 1928), widely recognized today as one of the world's most prominent linguists. In 1959, Chomsky published an influential review of B. F. Skinner's book *Verbal Behavior,* in which Skinner explained language in strict behavioral terms. Chomsky used this review not only to criticize behaviorism and its approach to language but also to introduce his own ideas. Little he knew that these ideas would become most influential in cognitive psychology for many years.

What was the essence of his approach? Two of his arguments are essential for psychology. Notice here several themes already familiar to you. First, Chomsky emphasized that any language consists of a finite set of words and terms and a fixed number of rules according to which people put these words together. Nevertheless, using this limited set of grammar rules and terms, humans can produce an endless number of sentences and phrases, including sentences no one has said previously. (Try to put such a sentence together right now and you see how easy it is.) Chomsky suggested the existence of a universal grammar: the general grammatical principles underlying all languages. Sure there are differences among languages, but they are in details and specific rules. For example, the order of nouns and verbs in a sentence, the changing endings of words, or the existence or absence of indefinite and definite articles could be different in different languages. Wilhelm Wundt early in the 20th century (see Chapter 4) had considered these linguistic details essential in our understanding of national character and culture. For Chomsky, these were details underlying the importance of the universal grammar (Chomsky, 1995).

Second, Chomsky argued that most of the important properties of language are innate. This does not mean that humans are born with some preexisting knowledge of a language. The acquisition and development of a language is a result of the unfolding of internal potential to speak and understand a language—all triggered by the external environment. In other words, the developing child's brain is normally ready to acquire a language. But the brain needs external influences to start the acquisition process. This view explains why young children learn languages so quickly and without significant effort. This capacity for languages diminishes with age.

Several early studies supported Chomsky's assumption about the innate capacity for language acquisition. For example, his wife, professor Carol Chomsky (1930–2008), studied the acquisition of grammar in children (C. Chomsky, 1963) and how they interpret sentences of increasing complexity as they get older. Despite earlier assumptions that children complete their acquisition of syntax by age 5, Chomsky's research showed that children continue to develop the skills needed to understand complex constructions beyond that age.

✓ CHECK YOUR KNOWLEDGE

What knowledge did computer science as a theoretical field give to cognitive psychology?

What was the main impact of Alan Turing to cognitive science?

What is Searle's view of consciousness?

Assessment of Cognitive Psychology

Cognitive psychology found many enthusiastic supporters in most universities, research centers, and teaching facilities across the world. Successes in cognitive sciences have inspired research in many areas of cognition.

Basic Studies. When some psychologists turned to perception and its patterns, what was the difference between their work and the research of the 19th century? The main difference was that modern psychologists were equipped with substantially more accurate knowledge about neural pathways in the brain and the association areas of the cortex involved in information processing. Clinical studies of various abnormalities of perception provided new facts. *Agnosia,* the term for substantial disturbances of perception, received significant attention. Psychologists provided new information about its symptoms and helped thousands of patients suffering from this difficult medical condition. Interest in the early studies of Gestalt psychology was back. Different experimental procedures showed that so-called holistic information processing plays a crucial role in the way we recognize information and learn from experience (Kellogg, 2003).

Many psychologists turned to the study of memory and its mechanisms, including encoding, storage, retrieval, and forgetting. Compared to the classical studies of Ebbinghaus (see Chapter 4), memory appeared as a complex hierarchical system, organized on at least three levels: sensory, short term, and long term. Different neurophysiological mechanisms are likely to support the functioning of memory on those levels. Psychologists also examined various serial position effects of memory or the specific conditions affecting both efficient memorization and forgetting. Significant resources went to the study of amnesia or severe memory loss, which can be caused by aging factors, a neurological illness, or trauma (either emotional or physical). Studies of memory were helping tens of thousands of patients in their recovery, adjustment, or rehabilitation process.

Further research in the fields of memory, decision making, and thinking created various theories and practical applications that were widely used in schools, universities, and in the fields of business training, design, counseling, and rehabilitation therapy. New facts were obtained in diverse areas such as the impact of aging on cognitive functions (Budson & Price, 2005), cognitive and motor rehabilitation after illness or injury (Riley & Turvey, 2002), eyewitness memory in testimony (Benton, Ross, Bradshaw, Thomas, & Bradshaw, 2006), or decision making in engineering (Levin, 2006) and driving (C. L. Baldwin, 2007; Gray, Regan, Castaneda, & Sieffert, 2006). Applied cognitive psychology is one of the fastest growing fields in global psychology today.

Critical Assessments. One of the most essential points of criticism was cognitive psychology's alleged preoccupation with digital and other formal models of cognition. To some, cognitive psychology was turning to computer science but losing psychology. One of the critical commentators was Jerome Bruner (born in 1915), who received his doctoral degree in 1941 under supervision of Gordon Allport at Harvard University. Bruner argued that the cognitive revolution, with its fixation on mind as an "information processor," was pulling psychology away from the deeper objective of understanding the mind as a creator of subjective meanings. Bruner hoped to establish meaning as the central concept of cognitive psychology, which would focus on the symbolic activities that human beings employed in constructing and making sense of the world and themselves (Bruner, 1990).

Other critics believed that cognitive psychology did not pay enough attention to practical, applied issues of everyday's life. Renowned cognitive psychologist Ulrich Neisser (born in 1928) expressed dissatisfaction with his discipline's excessive reliance on laboratory work rather than real-life situations. In his writings in the 1970s and later, he was critical of cognitive psychology for its relative detachment from human environment (Neisser, 1976). Studying cognitive issues is only part of psychology's task, in his view. He praised the computational approach to psychology but believed it was not enough to understand the complexity of mental processes without taking them in the context of specific human activities in real-life contexts. A similar view was expressed by Searle (1992) suggesting the limitations of the computational approach to consciousness.

Many critics also maintained that cognitive psychology overemphasizes cognition and pays significantly less attention to emotion and motivation and especially to the issues involving ultimately "human" attributes of people's existence and experience: ideals, moral choices, and values.

Conclusion

Both cognitive and humanistic psychology appeared approximately at the same time and pursued seemingly unrelated strategies. Cognitive psychology examined how the mind works. It became a distinct part of an interdisciplinary field of cognitive science. This field includes studies in several fields, particularly cognitive neuroscience, computer science, philosophy, and linguistics. One of the main assumptions of cognitive psychology is that the operations of our mind are generally computable. Humanistic psychology, on the other hand, is both a school of thought and a value orientation that holds a hopeful, constructive view of human beings and of their substantial capacity to be self-determining. It is guided by a conviction that ethical values are strong determinants of human behavior. This belief leads to an effort to emphasize human qualities as choice, imagination, the interaction of the body and mind, and the capacity to become free and happy. Humanistic psychologists have transformed the field of psychotherapy, introducing principles of positive psychology that are gaining respect and popularity in the 21st century. The reputation of positive psychology may match the popularity of contemporary cognitive psychology closely associated with cognitive neuroscience and computer science.

Summary

- In the early 1950s, the United States became a powerful center of world education and science. Economically, most colleges and universities in the United States were in much better shape than other academic institutions and educational centers around the world. A significant influx of immigrants had brought to America a fresh new wave of college-educated specialists.

- New intriguing debates about the role of psychology in contemporary society emerged. They often challenged the traditional behavioral and psychoanalytic approaches.

- Both cognitive and humanistic traditions, being quite dissimilar in terms of their research approaches and methodologies, have been similar in one important aspect. Researchers working within these traditions treated psychology from a similar perspective of subjectivity.

- Humanistic psychology is sometimes referred to as the third force in psychology, in contrast to behaviorism and psychoanalysis. Humanistic psychologists encouraged their colleagues to turn to the most important question that psychology should have studied, from their point of view: the meaning of human existence.

- Among several basic principles of humanistic psychology are the following: human beings should be viewed from a holistic perspective, are aware of their existence, and live in a uniquely human context that is not limited to their immediate surroundings.

- Humanistic psychology established the main principles of therapy, aiming to reduce or eliminate suffering. One of major features of the new method was that the therapist generally downplays the pathological aspects of a client's symptoms and focuses on healthy aspects of existence and the ways to achieve recovery.

- Among many representatives of humanistic psychology, Abraham Maslow and Carl Rogers stood out.

- The term *cognitive revolution* refers to a dynamic shift or reorientation in both the main focus and basic research methods of psychological studies. Cognitive psychology is the scientific study of human mental processes and their role in thinking, emotions, and behavior. Cognitive psychology's main concern is how we, as individuals, process information. It also represented in many ways a switch of attention from behavior to consciousness, from habits and reflexes, to meaning and subjectivity.

- Cognitive psychology belongs to the line of research that is commonly regarded today as part of an interdisciplinary field of cognitive science. This field includes studies in several fields, particularly cognitive neuroscience, computer science, philosophy, and linguistics, among other fields.

- Several great scholarly minds working in various fields of science have contributed to the development of cognitive psychology. George Miller founded the Center for Cognitive Studies at Harvard University. One of the most prominent pioneers of the computational approach to cognition was Alan Turing. His work gave a significant boost to the fields of studies of artificial intelligence. John Searle considered consciousness a biological phenomenon. Noam Chomsky suggested the existence of the general grammatical principles underlying all languages. He argued that most of the important properties of language are innate.

Key Terms

Artificial intelligence	Existential psychology	Peace psychology
Cognitive neuroscience	Existential therapy	Positive psychology
Cognitive psychology	Holistic health movement	Self-actualization
Cognitive revolution	Hospice care	T.O.T.E.
Cognitive science	Narrative medicine	Third force in psychology

13

Focusing on Contemporary Issues

Glendower: I can call spirits from the vasty deep.
Hotspur: Why so can I, or so can any man; But will they come when you do call them?

William Shakespeare, Henry IV, *Part 1*

CHAPTER OUTLINE

Fifty years from now, several names of contemporary psychologists will appear in history books. Whose names will emerge on the pedestal of psychological science? Will it be Phil Zimbardo? Let's assume so. If mentioned, he would probably receive recognition for his *prison study* in which he demonstrated that people tend to act unethically when they are allowed to. Zimbardo called it the *Lucifer effect.* It is also probable that college students born in the 2030s will read about Zimbardo's fundamental studies of shyness.

Will the books and sites mention Daniel Kahneman simply because he would remain the only psychologist-winner of the Nobel Prize in . . . economics? It would also be interesting to see if Kahneman's work on *hedonic psychology*—the study of what makes people happy or unhappy—is retained by history too.

Will history books preserve the name of Cheryl Koopman for her exceptional research on trauma survivors? Or maybe her name will be forever associated with her studies of support groups for patients with serious illnesses.

Will future students learn about Karen Mathews for her fundamental research of mind-body interaction? Yet it is quite possible that her applied work on psychological risk factors of illness also will become a classic.

How will history judge James Sidanius? Probably your children will read about Sidanius's main creation: his *social dominance* theory that explains fundamental psychological mechanisms of social discrimination. But he is also known for his role in the development of the new academic discipline—*political psychology*.

Who and what will psychology retain in its selective memory?

Of course, we cannot predict anything with certainty. Future psychologists will evaluate our contemporaries using their own criteria and methods of assessment. What appears important today may easily be overlooked tomorrow. Likewise, some seemingly obscure studies will be "rediscovered" in the future. Such delayed recognitions are quite common in psychology (L. Lange, 2005). Wundt believed one hundred years ago that history would treat very well his fundamental multivolume tractate. However, few psychologists read that work today. Milgram in the 1960s conducted several experiments on obedience. He remains among the most quoted psychologists of all time. People tomorrow will judge today's work from the positions of their time.

In the present day, however, we can make some preliminary evaluations relevant to contemporary issues. This chapter will attempt to describe several current developments in psychology from a historic context. Most of the names mentioned here are psychologists formally recognized by their professional groups for their noticeable contribution to psychology. Some of the people are at the peaks of their academic careers, while others are only at early stages of their professional life. Let's wish their work is here to stay.

Probably all of us studying psychology's past can draw our own lessons and come up with different opinions about the impact of previous psychological knowledge on contemporary psychology. To some of us, the knowledge accumulated over centuries is a clear demonstration of how little people knew about their bodies and minds and how insignificant our knowledge remains today. To others, the history of psychology is a remarkable example of a triumph of science over fiction, experiments over abstract discourses, and compassion over indifference. Yet to others, psychology's history is a continuous work in progress, a never-ending story of promise, frustration, and hope. How significant were all those views and theories for our knowledge today? What are the main lessons of psychology's history that we are learning today?

Let's go over again through the centuries and relatively recent times and try to find some general lessons that contemporary psychologists continued to draw from history. As a sample of contemporary research, as it is already mentioned, we will refer to the work of today's psychologists awarded not long ago by the American Psychological Association's Annual Awards for Distinguished Scientific Applications of Psychology and Awards for Distinguished Scientific Early Career Contributions to Psychology. In addition to this list of scholars, we also chose several psychological studies that already have attracted global attention and discussions in the 21st century.

Lesson 1. Psychology Continues to Address Its "Traditional Themes"

Return for a moment to the first chapter and recall three general historical and incessant problems of psychology: the body-mind relationship, the nature-nurture question, and the theory-practice concerns. Today it will probably be inaccurate to assume that contemporary psychology has already solved these classical problems and moved on to examine other issues. Quite to the contrary, psychologists today continue both theoretical and experimental research associated with these classical themes. Consider several brief illustrations.

The Mind-Body Problem

As you remember, philosophers and psychologists described the body-mind relationship along the lines of at least four principal directions: monism, materialism, dualism, and idealism. The debates about the mind-body problem dominated discussions connecting the work of the human brain (the matter or body) with the richness of human experiences (the ideas or mind). By the end of the 19th century, primarily due to the advancements of biology and medicine, a large group of psychologists turned to physiology. These psychologists believed that the mind was working in a quite understandable way: nerve endings pick up most physical qualities of the objects outside human body, including the body itself. Then an electrical or chemical reaction transforms the signals and moves them into the brain, which decodes these signals and produces what we call subjective experience. How is that view different from your vision today?

Despite serious objections of philosopher-idealists who claimed the leading role of subjectivity and experience, the materialist point of view became dominant in mainstream academic psychology, developing primarily within universities and clinics. With the advancement of behaviorism, the idea of "subjectivity" began to disappear from psychology's vocabulary. However, psychoanalysts, Gestalt psychologists, and psychologists who studied the "self" continued to examine the work of the human mind and its subjective mechanisms. Scores of psychologists maintained the view that physiological processes in the brain are not necessarily equal to subjective experience.

In the mid-20th century, cognitive psychology gave a boost to studies of "subjectivity," giving them quite clear scientific strength of a computational science. Searle's position that the brain processes cause (or produce) psychological phenomena gave an intellectual boost to many psychologists attempting to connect the brain's physiology and psychology. Most of the research, however, does not separate the body and mind. The focus of interests is in the investigation of how the mind and body interact (see Figure 13.1).

Contemporary research shows that not only immediate experiences "here and now" but also the brain's complex memories participate in experiences forming. Present-day studies of pain and itching, for instance, demonstrate that these unpleasant sensations can be caused by both skin abnormalities and also by the brain's own mechanisms producing memories of the itching pain (Oaklander, 2008). The body and mind interact in remarkable ways. Other studies show that an individual's higher sense of personal control has a significant impact on health. What does this mean? Individuals who believe that they are in charge of their lives tend to stay healthier than

Figure 13.1 The Mind-Body Problem

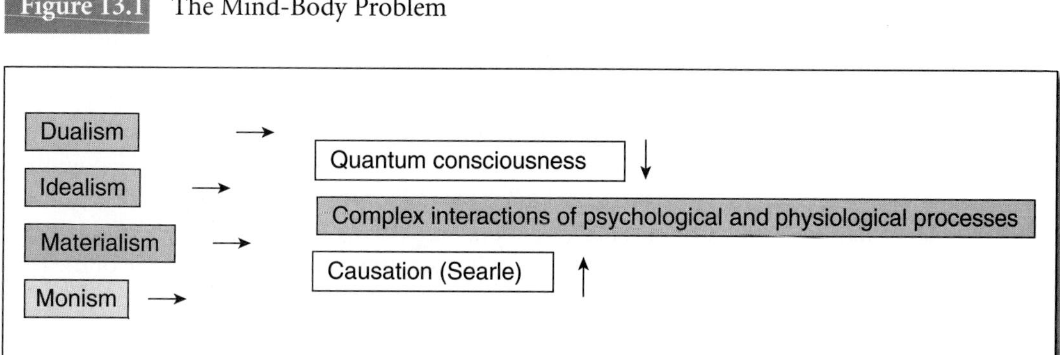

those who are not so sure about their lives (W. Johnson & Krueger, 2005). The mind can affect the body's fundamental physiological processes. Psychologist Angela Bryan showed experimentally that optimism and high self-esteem are important factors contributing to healthy habits (Bryan et al., 2004). People who really believe that they will get healthier tend to achieve more positive results compared to bitter pessimists. Psychologist and author David Myers find supportive evidence about the positive impact of our spiritual beliefs on health and behavior (D. Myers, 2008).

The mind-body interaction is also described in a remarkable line of research by Martin Seligman. His studies convey a very powerful and intriguing message: you can be a happy person if you want to be one. Happiness from his point of view consists of positive emotion (the pleasant life), engagement (the engaged life), and meaning (the meaningful life). On the basis of these assumptions, Seligman constructed a therapeutic procedure called **positive psychotherapy** based on the premise that the human mind is capable of changing itself: The right state of mind affects behavior; the behavior then produces the changes within the mind (Seligman, Rashid, & Parks, 2006). Dutch professor Ruut Veenhoven (2008) showed through his research that, despite common assumptions, happiness is not entirely based on economic factors alone such as jobs or prices. In Great Britain, for instance, different indicators of happiness have not changed much for 40 years despite economic ups and downs. Brits steadily score as one of the happiest nations.

It may appear that psychology is more interested in interactions between the mind and the body but stays away from explaining the nature of psychological experience. This is incorrect. Contemporary cognitive psychology actively cooperates with philosophy, neurophysiology, and physics to deepen our knowledge of the mind. Remember, one of the postulates of cognitive psychology was that all mental operations are essentially computable. Likewise, cognitive neuroscience assumed that the human mind as a sophisticated computer is driven solely by algorithms, the number of which is as finite as the number of mental operations.

These fundamental assumptions face tremendous support and relentless challenges. For example, Roger Penrose and many followers of the **quantum mind tradition** challenge some assumptions of cognitive neuroscience. They argue that the brain has the ability to conduct more sophisticated operations than the algorithms suggest

(Penrose, 1989). This means that the mind has some additional function not based on algorithms (or systems or rules of calculation). In short, the brain could perform functions that no computer could perform. The challengers claim that the work of the brain may not be driven by a finite number of algorithms and operations. The secret of the brain's work does not necessarily lie within the laws of chemistry or physiology. The puzzle of human consciousness is in its "quantum" nature. Like quantum mechanics challenges the main principles of mechanics, the quantum mind tradition challenges traditional molecular physiology and turns to the principles of quantum mechanics (Wendt, 2006). Supporters of the quantum theories say that one of the reasons psychologists historically have a problem measuring "subjective" elements of experience is that the brain functions on both physiological and quantum levels. It is the latter that we don't understated well yet.

Biological and Social Factors

The debates about complex interactions of natural (biological) factors and social (cultural) influences have always been in the focus of psychology's attention. Reductionist views emphasized the importance of biological factors affecting human development, behavior, and experience. Determinist ideas underlined the crucial role of social factors. Later, these views somewhat merged. As you remember from Chapter 1, by the 20th century, most psychologists viewed human beings as an indivisible part of the natural world and social environment (Münsterberg, 1915). The dual impact of natural and social factors is commonly accepted today (see Figure 13.2). The question

Figure 13.2 The Nature-Nurture Debate in Psychology

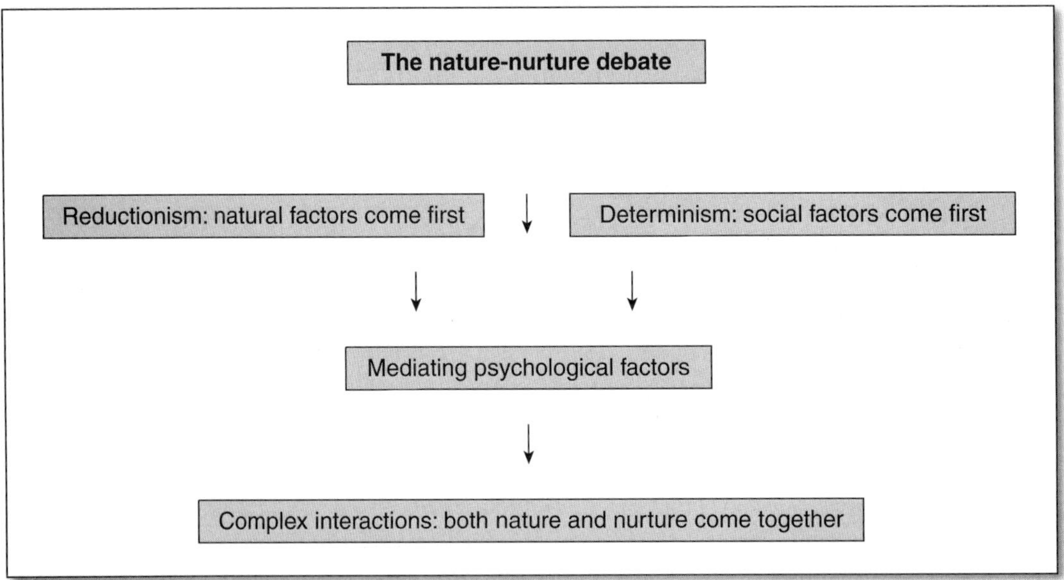

remains open about the specific mechanisms of interaction of biological and social factors in our behavior and experience. Consider several examples of contemporary research of award-winning psychologists.

Did you ever notice how quickly U.S. presidents age right before your eyes? In the middle of the 4-year term, they already look tired, their faces are wrinkled, and their eyes signal fatigue. Their entire body language conveys a silent but desperate call for a vacation. Science has established that aging is a biologically programmed mechanism. However, today's science also shows that nonbiological factors may play a significant role in our bodies' wear and tear. Psychologist Elissa Epel, in a series of studies, showed how chronic stress or inactive lifestyle can affect aging (Epel, 2009). But there is good news. For example, those of us who spend an average of 30 minutes a day exercising have cells that appear up to 10 years younger than those who do not exercise. There is no mystery in her findings. Epel's research shows that regular exercise protects our body from the risk of cell inflammation, the process that shortens our life (Epel, Burke, & Wolkowitz, 2007). In other words, aging may be programmed genetically, yet we can increase or decrease the speed of it by a lifestyle we maintain. A lifestyle we choose is based on many psychological factors. In effect, your decision to exercise regularly may increase your life expectancy.

ON THE WEB

Learn more about Elissa Epel and her research on the book website.

Elissa Epel received special recognition from the American Psychological Association for her studies showing how chronic stress or inactive lifestyle affect aging.

Contemporary studies show the complex interaction of biological, psychological, and social factors in our life. For instance, there is evidence about the existence of so-called **latent vulnerability traits,** specific psychological features that we may develop early in life (e.g., certain avoidant tendencies or hostile behavior) and that may later develop into serious psychopathological symptoms (Beauchaine & Marsh, 2006). Psychologist Karen Matthews demonstrates in her research how factors including smoking, continuous stress, or immobility contribute to physical changes in the cardiovascular system and lead to thrombosis and heart attack (Matthews, 2005). John Curtin and colleagues advance the view of addictive behavior as rooted in both biological and social factors. To illustrate, a person who intoxicates his or her body (a conscious decision) puts the nervous system under a "stress test." An anxiety response to this stress results in a craving for more substance. This eventually leads to substance-seeking behavior (Curtin, McCarthy, Piper, & Baker, 2005). These studies suggest that people who abuse drugs launch the body's automatic addictive response. As another example, Linda Gallo's research reveals that both psychological and social factors affect patients with chronic health problems (Gallo & Matthews, 2003). Conducting studies on Latina women, she explains how socioeconomic, cultural, and psychological risks directly affect these women's health (Gallo, Espinosa de los Monteros, Ferent, Urbina, & Talavera, 2007).

In summary, the idea that both a person's lifestyle and certain biological predispositions affect this person's health has been discussed for centuries. Today's psychologists continue this discussion but also provide sophisticated experimental evidence to support or dismiss some of those assumptions.

Combining Theory and Practice

Should psychologists constantly look for practical applications of their research? Should psychology remain neutral, "objective" science untouched by social developments, or should it become actively involved in social life? As you remember, many psychologists in the 20th century thought that their findings should help to develop a just, democratic, and efficient society (F. Allport, 1924). Others disagreed and emphasized the importance of psychology's main role in providing scientific data and not making policy (Atkinson, 1977; G. Miller, 1969). Psychologists today provide a balanced answer regarding theoretical and practical goals of psychological research. In most cases, they pursue both.

Life constantly asks new questions that psychologists attempt to answer. Their applied research, in turn, adds new lines in the book of psychological theory. For example, psychologist Jodi Quas studies bias in human judgments. Yet besides studying this important issue, she pursues a very practical goal: by using studies of bias to increase fairness of courtroom decisions. In particular, she studies children's testimonies in criminal cases and their accuracy of the reported facts. Quas also examines the jurors' reactions to these testimonies and the role of some of their uncritical beliefs on legal judgments (Quas et al., 2007; see Figure 13.3).

Figure 13.3 The Balance Between Theoretical Knowledge and Its Practical Applications

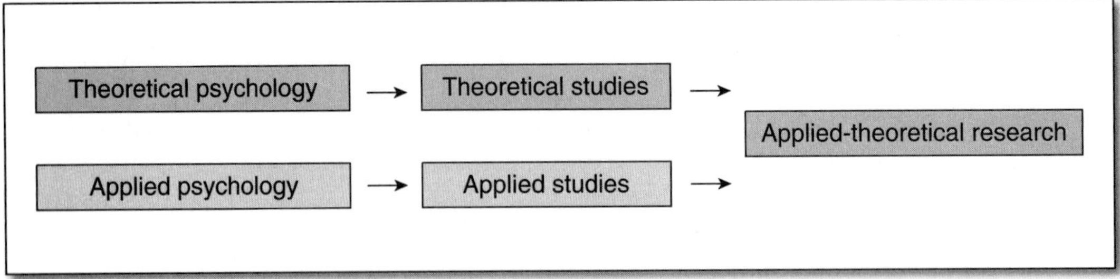

Theoretical and practical goals of research are frequently inseparable. Professor Hendree Jones combines her top-rated research of drug addiction in pregnant women with sophisticated therapeutic methods of clinical intervention, the methods that help her patients discontinue dangerous habits of drug abuse. Such intervention methods would be impossible to create without a serious theoretical investigation of the problem (H. E. Jones, 2008). Psychologist Samuel Gosling helps to increase the effectiveness of shelter dog adoptions and helps in training of dogs in detecting explosives. Such practical steps would be impossible without his theoretical interest in the animals' personality—a predominant set of behavioral traits and responses (Gosling, 2008). Martin Seligman's theoretical work on human happiness is always connected with his highly effective therapeutic program (Seligman et al., 2006). Studying cognitive changes associated with aging allows psychologists to make practical recommendations to car manufacturers about safety displays and devices that should allow the elderly to remain safe drivers (C. L. Baldwin, 2002). Therapists use theoretical and applied studies of cognition to develop rehabilitation techniques for patients recovering from illness or injury (Riley, Baker, Schmit, & Weaver, 2005). New laboratory studies of motion perception are very important in understanding and preventing certain driving accidents: these psychologists show, for example, that an extended period of driving on a straight, open highway can lead to an accident if a driver attempts to pass another vehicle or take a left turn at an intersection (Gray et al., 2006).

Cognitive psychologists always seek practical applications of the knowledge accumulated within theoretical studies. One of the leading cognitive neuroscientists, Michael Gazzaniga, put together a team of more than 30 scholars to examine how people make legal decisions in court: how they select evidence, decide someone's guilt, explain criminal behavior, and assign responsibility for the crime (Hotz, 2009). One of theoretical goals of this project is to understand physiological mechanisms in the brain responsible for important moral decisions (Gazzaniga, 2005). From a practical standpoint, the project aims to limit the number of biased decisions in court verdicts.

Lesson 2. Psychology Welcomes Interdisciplinary Science

Japanese researcher-physicists studying human locomotion found that people with symptoms of clinical depression move differently than people without depressive symptoms. That discovery may provide another way of diagnosing major depressive disorders. In addition to clinical interviews, therapists can probably look at mathematical formulas describing an individual's movements (Nakamura et al., 2007). Physics and mechanics contribute to psychology. Psychology itself saw the birth, development, transformation, and decline of several popular schools and research orientations. Some trends in psychological research would become fashionable, while the attractiveness of others diminished (Rozin, 2007). Studying the history of psychology, you can see how psychologists changed their theoretical preferences and switched to new methods. Since the beginning of the 20th century, some psychologists have chosen experimental research in university laboratories. Others have preferred clinical interviews involving patients. Some psychologists have preferred studying animal behavior. Yet others have begun explorations in the field of psychoanalysis, thus moving away from experimentation. The Gestalt tradition was born out of advanced experimental research of sensation and perception. Many areas of developmental psychology took their roots in early studies of mental abilities of children.

Year after year, decade after decade, psychologists, like prospectors or gold seekers, tried different theories, concepts, methods, and approaches to advance their knowledge. Offering their findings for critical peer review or other forms of evaluation, psychologists began to "filter" and accumulate the best, most successful, and effective methods of investigation and psychological intervention. Travel and publications made this knowledge available to more psychologists and in more countries. More psychologists began to combine various methods received from different schools to examine specific psychological issues. Beside psychology, other disciplines could provide reliable and relevant methods for the purposes of psychological research. Thus, comprehensive and multidisciplinary methods were becoming increasingly popular in the 20th century. The main question that psychologists began to ask was not whether a particular psychological school was right or wrong in understanding human behavior and experience. Rather, the question was, "Which findings and methods of that school can be used in my research to advance my study?" (see Figure 13.4).

Many contemporary psychologists increasingly often take an interdisciplinary approach to design comprehensive research methods. Psychologist Seth Pollak, as an example, studies the mechanisms of emotional development in children through an innovative combination of methods from psychophysics, neuroscience, and behavioral endocrinology (Pollak, 2003, 2005). Marcia Johnson studies false memories by

Figure 13.4 The "Blending" of Traditional Approaches Into the Mainstream Field

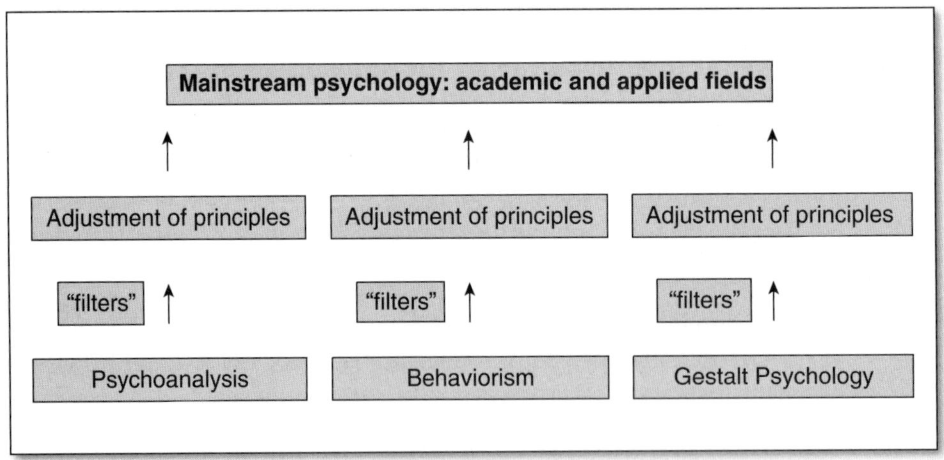

applying methods of behavioral sciences, cognitive psychology, and cognitive neuropsychology (M. K. Johnson, 2006; M. K. Johnson & Raye, 2000).

Psychologists began to examine their specific psychological problems by simply turning to the best methods available in the field, thus using comprehensive and multidisciplinary methods in their investigations. To illustrate, let's exemplify how contemporary psychologists approach the issue of decision making.

Studying How People Make Decisions

Did you remember that only one psychologist has won the Nobel Prize? It was Daniel Kahneman. Together with Amos Tversky (1937–1996), he designed a theory that described how people make decisions involving risk (Kahneman & Tversky, 1979). They designed a number of cognitive and behavioral experiments and applied advanced mathematical analysis to understand the collected data. The overall conclusion of their **prospect theory** was that people, despite seemingly acting in a rational and logical way, make constant mistakes in evaluating their chances to win or lose. People tend to show a consistent tendency—based on specific circumstances—to overestimate or underestimate their chances of success and failure.

Dutch scholar Albert Dijksterhuis shows in his studies that people tend to like their decisions made spontaneously, without a lengthy deliberation, more than the decisions they make very carefully. In the studies combining behavioral and cognitive methods, he showed that "deliberation without attention" works very well when people make decisions about complex and sophisticated products, such as buying kitchen furniture or a car (Dijksterhuis, 2004). However, when we buy simple products, careful, deliberate decision making is better than spontaneous decisions (Dijksterhuis, Bos, Nordgren, & van Baaren, 2006). The researcher claims that this type of decisions "without attention" is also typical for many other areas of human behavior, including management and even voting. Other research shows that people tend to display emotional tensions and regrets for making inappropriate or controversial decisions even though they do not remember these decisions (Lieberman, 2007). Studies by Josh Tenenbaum and his colleagues show that people are capable of making accurate predictions about the duration or extent of everyday phenomena despite having only limited knowledge about such events. Such predictions reflect people's accurate perceptions of statistical probabilities (Griffiths & Tenenbaum, 2006; Tenenbaum, Griffiths, & Kemp, 2006). Experiments by Joris Lammers from the Netherlands and Adam Galinsky from the United States show that people with power break rules not only because they can but also because they feel at some intuitive level that they are entitled to do so. Knowing that you have power may transform our views of moral values (Lammers & Galinsky, 2010).

These and other studies of decision making demonstrate that today's psychologists tend to approach their research problems from a clearly pragmatic position: they choose the best, from their point of view, methods available and then combine different kinds of research to achieve their goal (see Figure 13.5).

Figure 13.5 Theories of Decision Making: Choosing the Best Model

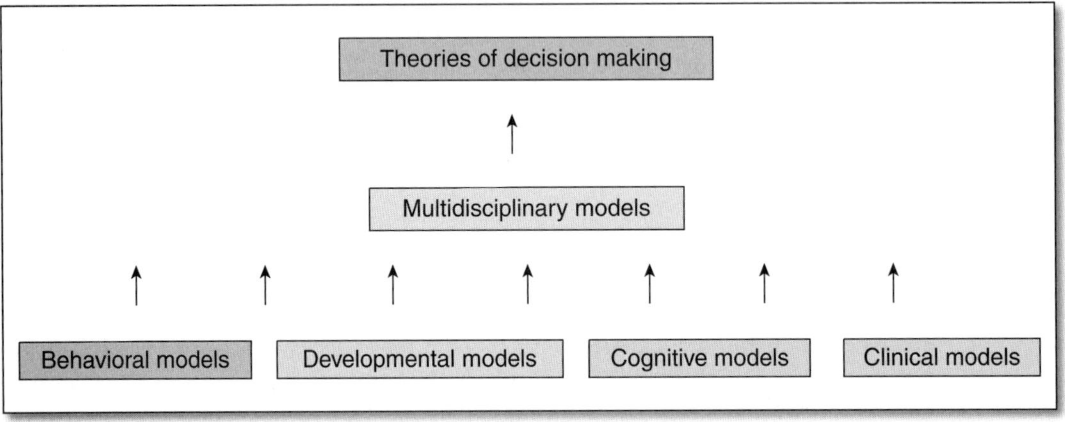

Lesson 3. Psychology Did Not Abandon Its Established Traditions

Psychologists have not abandoned the traditional approaches of the 20th century. Many of them continue to develop those traditions further. A noticeable difference between today's research and the studies conducted earlier in history is in the substantially increased sophistication of contemporary methods, especially in the fields of measurement.

Increased Sophistication of Studies

In the classical tradition of behaviorism, today's psychologists continue to examine specific mechanisms of learning in specific contexts. One such context is clinical and involves people who suffer from anxiety-related problems. Contemporary studies show that extinction—which can involve forgetting a habit or a decrease in a fearful reaction—is not just a disappearance of something previously learned. Behavioral experimental studies indicate that extinction is a form of learning in its own right, rather than an "unlearning" or forgetting (K. M. Myers & Davis, 2002).

Contemporary technologies allow researchers to conduct sophisticated studies that were almost impossible 10 years ago. Jorn Diedrichsen shows in his carefully crafted research the mechanisms of several automatic functions of bodily coordination: when people operate objects, one hand often plays a supportive role, while the other hand manipulates the object. He showed that the supporting hand anticipates the consequences of the other hand's actions by changing the forces with which it supports the object. Diedrichsen's work also highlights the importance of the cerebellum in our ability to predict our own actions (Diedrichsen, Verstynen, Lehman, & Ivry, 2005).

As you remember from Chapter 12, one of the blossoming areas of contemporary psychology is cognitive. Many psychologists work today in the field of cognitive neuroscience, an academic field that examines the brain mechanisms supporting mental functions. They try to identify specific portions of the brain and even clusters of cells that have something to do with psychological manifestations. For example, a series of studies by C. G. Gross and his colleagues over the years revealed complex cortex mechanisms involved in facial recognitions (Gross, 1998, 2005). Some cognitive neuroscientists have attempted to expand the area of interest of their field and applied the fundamental knowledge to other areas of psychology. As an example, Matthew Lieberman (2006) has developed a brand-new field called social cognitive neuroscience. He uses neuropsychology and neuroimaging techniques to research social cognition, including attitudes and their change, guilt, and regrets for making wrong decisions (Lieberman, 2007).

Brian J. Scholl continues the experimental tradition of Gestalt psychology in his research. He demonstrates that people may process visual information without awareness. Because of the massive amount of incoming visual information at any moment, we cannot be consciously aware of everything simultaneously. As a result, our perception of the world is a complex give-and-take between physical reality and the inferences made by our brains. This creates room for error, and past research has demonstrated that we can sometimes fail to become consciously aware of objects right in front of us (Mitroff & Scholl, 2005). In his carefully crafted experiments made in the spirit of the well-designed traditions of Gestalt psychology, Scholl demonstrates, for example, that people can report a paradox: the disappearance of an object that they did not see. His experiments demonstrate how our experience combines various sensations into meaningful patterns—something that Gestalt psychology began to examine almost 100 years ago (Scholl, 2005).

Revisiting Theories and Clarifying Knowledge

Consider how the definitions of psychology changed. One hundred and twenty years ago, there were at least three types of definitions from natural science, mental science, and social science perspectives (Robinson, 1986). Most definitions of psychology of the early 20th century referred to a scientific description of mind, mental activity, or, as they were called then, mental products. None of those definitions referred to behavior (Griffith, 1921). Just one decade later, many psychologists switched attention to behavior. They were virtually ignoring everything containing the adjective *mental* in reference to psychology (Watson, 1913). Which definitions were correct? Every one of them, to some degree.

Psychology constantly clarifies and explains topics and issues from the past. Some unanswered questions are addressed. Easy answers become more sophisticated. Simple explanations get clarifications. New questions occur. In developmental psychology, for example, new discoveries help with better interpretations of the mechanisms of learning and cognitive development. The *overlapping waves* theory of cognitive development posits that at any given time, children tend to use not just one but a variety of approaches to solve one class of problems. The more effective approaches become increasingly common with age. Children learn which approaches work better and use them more often. With age and experience, some strategies become less frequent (Siegler, 1996). In other words, this theory suggests that the child does not simply move from one developmental stage to another. There is a complicated process of selection of the best approach available in present conditions.

Wundt (1916) suggested that languages might contain important information about how people in different cultures perceive reality. He believed, for example, in Germans' behavioral orderliness, reflected in the German language. Was he completely wrong? Maybe not. Aanne Maass, Minoru Karasawa, and their colleagues from Italy and Japan showed in their studies that when we describe other people, different national groups rely on and use different linguistic tools. Italians, for example, when they guess about other people, rely more on adjectives compared to people from Japan (Maass, Karasawa, Politi, & Suga, 2006).

The Gestalt tradition continues. Research by Jean Mandler, for instance, shows that the perceptual principles introduced a century ago can explain an infant's perceptual development. Early in development, infants often do not pay attention to the details of the appearance of many objects. They begin with big concepts and then begin paying attention to fine perceptual details. Attention to details increases when the child begins to learn a language (J. M. Mandler, 2004).

ON THE WEB

Read "The Myth of Mental Illness" by Thomas S. Szasz, first published in 1960 in *American Psychologist, 15,* 113–118.

Do you agree with his view that mental illness is "a name for problems in living"?

The clinical tradition in psychology has long roots. You remember that historically, researchers and practitioners had changing perceptions of psychopathology and its causes. In the 20th century, psychopathology was understood in terms of putatively distinct categories, where "membership" in a category was a matter of having a sufficient number of symptoms. Psychologist Robert Krueger is developing a new approach to psychopathology based on the concept of comorbidity. He sees specific mental disorders resulting from more general *overarching liabilities* and their manifestations. For example, so-called internalizing liabilities are linked to emotional problems; externalizing liabilities refer to behavioral conduct such as lack of inhibition or aggressiveness (Krueger & Markon, 2006).

Responding to Pseudo-Science

Beliefs in supernatural forces, spiritual healing, or occult phenomena continue to attract attention around the world. In particular, people in many traditional communities believe that various physical and psychological problems occur as a form of god's punishment for evil acts. A remedy for the punishment is typically sought in symbolic actions, including ritualistic prayer or meditation involving "healers."

In history, scientific psychology dealt with and dismissed most of the emerging "popular" trends such as mesmerism, phrenology, clairvoyance, and telepathy. The criticism was based on careful verifications of facts. Like 100 or 50 years ago, psychologists today pay careful attention to such verifications. For example, in the United States, there is a federally funded agency called the National Center for

Visit the National Center for Complementary and Alternative Medicine on the book website.

Complementary and Alternative Medicine. This center examines claims related to nontraditional methods of healing.

As you might expect, so far all the emerging and reemerging approaches claiming the existence of healing energy fields, distance healing, and chakras (force centers) on the human body have been assessed as nonscientific. There is no research-supported evidence, for example, that a healer's willpower could cure an acute illness, a mantra would cause a person to lose weight, or focusing on a specific thought would eliminate a cardiovascular problem or cure a person from his or her cocaine addiction. Referring to Chapter 1, we can place these and similar approaches within the tradition of folk knowledge.

However, psychologists today, like they did in the past, pay serious attention to studies from so-called nontraditional fields. Consider **spirituality,** for example, a field referring to a broad range of phenomena concerning "nonmaterial" matters related to faith, trust, and hope, in contrast to "material" matters related to ownership, accumulation of possessions, and competition (Shiraev & Levy, 2009). For contemporary psychologists studying this field, spirituality emphasizes mind over matter, being over having, and mental effort over physical action. Individuals emphasizing spirituality in their lives develop a strong belief in the existence of a spiritual or similar essence that fills and guards everything in the universe, including human beings. Over the span of several generations, contemporary university-based psychological science in most Western countries treated spirituality with caution. The situation began to change in the 1990s. Using a multidisciplinary scientific approach and inviting anthropologists, medical doctors, and historians into the discussion, psychologists try to understand spirituality and its effects on behavior, health, and community life (T. Hall, 1997). Psychologists currently try to apply scientifically sound methods of comparative analysis. On the basis of such comparative studies, researchers have found evidence that meditation and prayer are associated with and cause lower blood pressure and pulse, lower endocrine activity, and overall lower body metabolism.

Some researchers turned toward the spiritual side of human existence. *Transpersonal psychology* as a theoretical and applied field, focusing on spiritual and transcendent states of consciousness (Vich, 1988), continues to attract attention in this century. Overall, the contemporary view of spirituality is that spiritual factors such as strong religious beliefs, prayer, meditation, and combinations of these affect at least four interacting physiological systems: the brain, the endocrine system, the peripheral nervous system, and the immune system. These data are published in top peer-reviewed psychology journals (Powell, Shahabi, & Thoresen, 2003; Ray, 2004).

Lesson 4. Psychology Can Correct Its Past Mistakes

Carriers of educated psychological knowledge did not always promote humanism, reason, equal justice, and compassion. To illustrate, ancient Greeks made spectacular observations about emotions, motivation, sensations, sleep, and psychological disturbances. At the same time, the Greeks gave rational justifications to inequality among human races, male superiority over women, and the innate inferiority of slaves. The Renaissance period, typically associated with a revolution in arts and sciences, was also the time of witch hunts, occultism, and deep-seated beliefs in the power of supernatural forces. Psychological investigations of the human mind in the 19th century had brought an enormous breakthrough in understanding learning, intelligence, and skill formation. In contrast, many specialists at that time also believed that human mental capacities are rooted in ethnicity, gender, and race. Psychoanalysis deserves credit for its attention to the child's development, anxiety, and the unconscious roots of human experience and behavior. Yet psychoanalysis, lacking control experiments and self-criticism, produced a number of bizarre assumptions uncritically accepted by their followers.

Nevertheless, despite occasionally taking wrong paths, the psychology discipline has learned from its mistakes and revisited its own missteps. One of psychology's strengths is the ability to learn from its past. Consider a couple of examples related to some later developments of evolutionary ideas and psychoanalysis.

Evolutionary Ideas in Psychology

More than a hundred years ago, the evolutionary theory introduced the idea of natural selection. Some supporters of evolutionary views in psychology began to use the natural selection principle to justify racial and national superiority. Others embraced eugenics and the methods of scientific selection and exclusion of "inferior" groups and individuals. Fortunately, most psychologists understood the lack of scientific validity of eugenics and the harmful impact of its applications. Although behaviorism and several learning theories accepted various evolutionary ideas, the overall interest to evolutionary theories in psychology was insignificant.

Today psychologists reject eugenics but acknowledge the validity of some evolutionary ideas studied in **evolutionary psychology.** The task of this developing discipline is to explore the ways in which complex evolutionary factors affect behavior and experience. For example, it is possible that some behavioral patterns that promoted human survival could have been transmitted genetically. Classic evolutionary theories emphasized primarily aggression and greed as natural phenomena. Today's psychologists offer evolutionary explanations for a much diverse array of human behaviors, including cooperative and moral behavior, altruism, and curiosity (see Figure 13.6).

The main idea of evolutionary psychology is that certain elements of human behavior should be biologically useful. Cooperation and altruism, for example, did not appear in people living only in modern civilization. An altruistic gesture, a self-sacrifice on behalf of the family or community, was in many cases evolutionarily useful. In other words, human kindness could be a "product" of natural selection. Take, for instance, the case of interpersonal attraction. According to evolutionary theorist Geoffrey Miller, the brain, like the peacock's tail, is designed through evolution to attract the opposite sex.

Figure 13.6 Evolutionary Ideas in Psychology

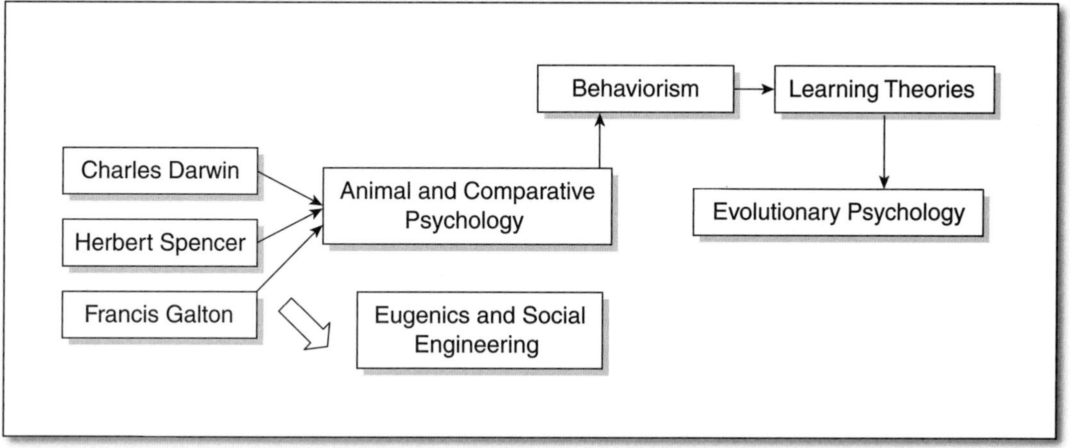

Both sexes have a reason to "show off" in an attempt to attract a mate, but men and women have different criteria for making their choices. The difference between men and women, according to Miller, is that women naturally tend to act altruistically to show that they can share resources. Men tend to act greedy to demonstrate that they can protect these resources (G. Miller, 2000).

Marilynn Brewer's contribution to psychology is based on her application of evolutionary views in the study of group behavior including intolerance and conflict.

Darwin and his followers suggested a universal evolutionary root of human emotions. Studies by Paul Rozin and his colleagues go further and demonstrate how evolutionary and cultural factors act together in shaping emotions (Rozin, Haidt, & McCauley, 1993). Take disgust, for example. This emotion, associated initially with food rejection, has been transforming during human history. Cultures began to use disgust as a mechanism to limit certain behaviors deemed inappropriate or immoral. This emotion later emerged as an evolutionary mechanism of moral censorship. Think for a second about anything you consider "disgusting behavior." It could be an inappropriate joke, sloppy manners, dishonesty, or something else. In many cases, however, this behavior will have nothing to do with food. In other terms, disgust during social evolution and individual development became associated with many culturally rejected ideas, objects, and behaviors (Rozin & Fallon, 1987).

Another psychologist, Marilynn Brewer, incorporates evolutionary views in her study of group behavior. Her social-psychological theory portrays humans as driven by two natural and opposing needs. The first is a need for assimilation and inclusion, a desire for belonging that motivates immersion in social groups. The second is a need for differentiation from others that operates in opposition to the need for immersion (Brewer, 1991). The needs for inclusion and independence, according to her theory, may become major causes of prejudice, group conflict, and intolerance (Brewer & Pierce, 2005). Brewer's ideas find many applications in studies of conflict resolution.

Psychoanalysis is another theory and practice to which psychologists return today but make major revisions. What kind of revisions?

A New Psychoanalysis?

More than 50 years ago, E. G. Boring, a student of Wundt and die-hard supporter of experimental psychology, admitted that he had suffered from depression. He went through a series of psychoanalytic sessions, paying out of his pocket to a prominent émigré analyst Hanns Sachs. Boring called Freud a man "with attributes of greatness," a "pioneer in the fields of thought," and an "originator" (Boring, 1950, p. 706). He compared Freud to Darwin. Boring conveyed a common view at that time that psychoanalysis was an effective method of treatment.

However, as you remember, in the second half of the 20th century, many psychologists began to distance themselves from psychoanalysis. Psychoanalytic techniques began to lose popularity among therapists. Two main reasons: poor scientific validity and the lack of controlled studies of psychoanalysis' therapeutic effectiveness have contributed to its diminishing status in the academic community. Contemporary psychoanalysts, however, believe that they have found the way for the return of psychoanalysis to university-based psychology. They base their research and practical work on three principles or imperatives. These are (a) use clinical data to generate testable hypotheses, (b) test these hypotheses by scientific methods, and (c) look outside the discipline to exchange data with other fields in psychology (Bornstein, 2001; Mills, 2001). Many analysts began to implement these principles in their studies. Jonathan Metzl (2005), for example, in the book *Prozac on the Couch*, provides evidence of the effective use of psychoanalysis in combination with prescribed medication. Other researchers began to analyze the effectiveness of psychoanalysis as a therapeutic method using controlled methods and statistical analysis (Karon & Widener, 2001). A renewed discussion about the place of psychoanalysis in history and possible developments will be based, in part, on the result of these and other studies.

Lesson 5. Psychology Remains a Progressive Science

It will probably be accurate to assume that most psychologists in the past hoped to make the world around them better. Take a random psychology book from the library shelf and you will see various suggestions on how to make one's life healthier, happier, or more productive. Some ideas are limited to one area, such as elementary education, skill development, or treatment of anxiety. Other ideas are far-reaching and relate to the global society. In fact, many psychologists in the past allowed their imagination to blend with their scientific knowledge and create theories about a different, distant, but very possible world of **social utopia,** which is a model of an ideally perfect human society. Of course, from the scientists' view, such a utopian society will entrust its laws and customs to psychologists. The best of them, as smart and benevolent managers, will be in charge of the utopian government. Science will take over politics.

Some prominent utopian ideas developed in the atmosphere of the progressive era in the beginning of the 20th century (described in Chapter 5). Supporters of progressive views believed that societal advancement should be placed under control of the educated. They also believed that smart social policies based on science could cure many social ills, including poverty, illiteracy, and violence. An ideal society would become achievable (Gergen, 2001). Psychologists in the 20th century created many remarkable theories about such as a perfect, utopian society of the future. In these theories, psychologists had hoped for a bigger, more efficient role for psychologists in society. Remember Skinner's utopian views described in Chapter 11? Consider some other examples.

- Hugo Münsterberg (1916) believed that an ideal society could be built on social policies promoting the most fundamental values of peace and harmony. He also believed that psychologists will have to assume unique obligations in serving society. They, as trained professionals, would help other people strive for truth, beauty, progress, and morality.

- G. Stanley Hall (1920) maintained that human beings are responsible for guarding the process of evolution. Those who have power, including psychologists, should have even greater responsibility for the progress of humankind. In his version of an ideal society, trained psychologists should occupy a special position in society, being relieved from many social duties. Public policy would be conducted according to scientific research.

- John Watson (1929) designed a utopian society in which people's happiness is based on behaviorist principles: people are conditioned to feel happy. There is no government because people are also conditioned to act appropriately: they all work hard and contribute to community. Training should correct deviant and criminal behavior. Trained *behaviorist physicians* would guard the community in the same way that physicians would conduct preventive care.

- From W. McDougall's (1934) point of view, psychologists, because they know life from a scientific side, should come to rescue the collapsing human civilization. In his view, an ideal society could be created on a special island. A group of

ON THE WEB

To learn more about psychologists' progressive views, some of their specific ideas of creating an idealistic society, and the role of educated researchers, visit the book website.

selected people would arrive on the island to join a welcoming atmosphere for education, science, monogamy, traditional family values, and productive work. The primary government institutions on the island would be research centers focusing on psychology.

As you can see, these utopian ideas of some 20th-century psychologists were largely naive and impractical. People generally disagree about what happiness is. Some look for a busy, ambitious, and mistake-prone life while others seek calm, tranquility, and harmony. Second, if we imagine for a second that psychologists have shown convincingly what happiness *is,* can we compel everyone to live according to these standards? The idea of special "happiness camps" where people learn about happiness and are guarded by psychologists is as impractical as it is scary.

Contemporary psychologists offer their utopian ideas from time to time. Most efforts, however, continue to focus on real, incremental steps to improve individuals, communities, and society. Psychologists' main resource is education and information. Just as 100 years ago, psychology remains largely a progressive discipline engaged in an important mission of promotion of science, reason, and educated social action. If we look at social policies in many countries, we will find that psychology continues to play an increasingly bigger role in changing local and global worlds through educated action (Jansz & van Drunen, 2003; Singh, 2005). On one hand, historically, psychologists praised a free individual independent and self-sufficient. On the other, psychology views individuals as inseparable part of a larger community.

Psychology today tries to perform at least three major progressive functions: promotion of awareness, incremental improvements, and social initiative. How successful is its performance? It's up to you to make a judgment.

The journey continues.

Summary

- Future psychologists will evaluate our contemporaries using their own criteria and methods of assessment. What appears important today may easily be overlooked tomorrow. Likewise, some seemingly obscure studies will be "rediscovered" in the future.

- Among the main lessons of psychology's history is that it continues both theoretical and experimental research associated with the classical themes of the body-mind relationship, the nature-nature question, and the theory-practice concerns.

- Many contemporary psychologists increasingly often take an interdisciplinary approach to design comprehensive research methods.

- Psychologists have not abandoned the traditional approaches of the 20th century. Many of them continue to develop those traditions further. The sophistication of contemporary methods has increased, especially in the fields of measurement.

- Despite occasionally taking wrong paths, the psychology discipline has learned from its mistakes and revisited its own missteps. One of psychology's strengths is the ability to learn from its past.

- Psychology remains largely a progressive discipline engaged in an important mission of promoting science, reason, and educated social action.

Key Terms

Evolutionary psychology

Latent vulnerability traits

Positive psychotherapy

Prospect theory

Quantum mind tradition

Social utopia

Spirituality

References

Aanstoos, C., Serlin, I., & Greening, T. (2000). History of Division 32 (Humanistic Psychology) of the American Psychological Association. In D. Dewsbury (Ed.), *Unification through division: Histories of the divisions of the American Psychological Association* (Vol. V). Washington, DC: American Psychological Association. http://www.apa.org/divisions/Div32/pdfs/ history.pdf

Abbott, A. H. (1900). Experimental psychology and the laboratory in Toronto. *University of Toronto Monthly, 1,* 85–98, 106–112.

Abbott, A. D. (1988). *The system of professions: An essay on the division of expert labor.* Chicago: University of Chicago Press.

Adair, J. G. (1984). The Hawthorne effect: A reconsideration of the methodological artifact. *Journal of Applied Psychology, 69,* 334–345.

Adler, A. (1930). Individual psychology: Some other problems fundamental to all psychology. In C. Murchison (Ed.), *Psychologies of 1930* (pp. 395–405). Worcester, MA: Clark University Press.

Adolphs, R., Tranel, D., & Damasio, A. (1998). The human amygdala in social judgment. *Nature, 393,* 470–474.

Adorno, T. W., Frenkel-Brunswik, E., Levinson, D. J., & Sanford, R. N. (1950). *The authoritarian personality.* New York: Harper & Row.

Allport, F. (1920). The influence of the group upon association and thought. *Journal of Experimental Psychology, 3,* 159–182.

Allport, F. (1924). *Social psychology.* New York: Houghton Mifflin.

Allport, G. (1924). The study of undivided personality. *Journal of Abnormal and Social Psychology, 19,* 132–141.

Allport, G. (1937). *Personality: A psychological interpretation.* New York: Henry Holt.

American Psychological Association (APA). (2009). *APA membership: Past, present, and possible futures.* http://www.apa.org/workforce/presentations/2009-membership-data.pdf

Angell, J. R. (1907). The province of functional psychology. *Psychological Review, 14,* 61–91.

Annas, J. (1994). *Hellenistic philosophy of mind.* Berkeley: University of California Press.

Ardila, R. (1968). Psychology in Latin America. *American Psychologist, 23,* 567–574.

Arnheim, R. (1998, February). Wolfgang Köhler and Gestalt theory: An English translation of Köhler's Introduction to *Die physischen Gestalten* for philosophers and biologists. *History of Psychology, 1*(1), 21–26.

Asch, S. (1961). *Social psychology.* New York: Prentice Hall. (Original work published 1952)

Ash, M. (1992). Cultural contexts and scientific change in psychology: Kurt Lewin in Iowa. *American Psychologist, 47*(2), 198–207.

Association for Humanistic Psychology. (2001). *Humanistic psychology overview.* http://www.ahpweb.org/aboutahp/whatis.html

Atkinson, R. C. (1977). Reflections on psychology's past and concerns about its future. *American Psychologist, 32,* 205–210.

Bagdonas, A., Pociūt, B., Rimkut , E., & Valickas, G. (2008). The history of Lithuanian psychology. *European Psychologist, 13,* 227–237.

Baldwin, C. L. (2002). Designing in-vehicle technologies for older drivers: Application of sensory-cognitive interaction theory. *Theoretical Issues in Ergonomic Science, 3,* 307–329.

Baldwin, C. L. (2007). Cognitive implications of facilitating echoic persistence. *Memory & Cognition, 35,* 774–780.

Baldwin, J. M. (1892). The psychological laboratory in the University of Toronto. *Science, 19*(475), 143–144.

Baldwin, J. M. (1895a). *Mental development in the child and the race.* New York: Macmillan.

Baldwin, J. M. (1895b). Types of reaction. *Psychological Review, 2,* 259–273.

Baldwin, J. M. (1902). *Development and evolution.* New York: Macmillan.

Baldwin, J. M. (1926). *Between two wars (1861–1921) being memories, opinions and letters received.* Boston: Stratford.

Bascom, J. (1869). *Principles of psychology.* New York: Putnam.

Battie, W. (1962). *A treatise on madness.* London: Dawsons of Pall Mall. (Original work published 1758)

Bayton, J. A. (1975). Francis Sumner, Max Meenes, and the training of Black psychologists. *American Psychologist, 30,* 185–186.

Beard, G. (1881). *American nervousness.* New York: Putnam.

Beauchaine, T. P., & Marsh, P. (2006). Taxometric methods: Enhancing early detection and prevention of psychopathology by identifying latent vulnerability traits. In D. Cicchetti & D. Cohen (Eds.), *Developmental psychopathology* (2nd ed., pp. 931–967). Hoboken, NJ: John Wiley.

Beck, H. P., Levinson, S., & Irons, G. (2009). Finding little Albert: A journey to John B. Watson's infant laboratory. *American Psychologist, 64,* 605–614.

Beers, C. (1907). *A mind that found itself: An autobiography.* New York: Longmans.

Bekhterev, V. M. (1888). *Soznanie I ego granitsy* [Consciousness and its limits]. Kazan, Russia: Kazan University Press.

Bekhterev, V. M. (1904). *Psikhicheskaia deiatelnost i Zhizn* [Psychological activity and life]. St. Petersburg, Russia: Military Medical Academy.

Bekhterev, V. M. (1933). *General principles of human reflexology: An introduction to the objective study of personality.* A translation of the 4th Russian edition. London: Jarrolds. (Original work published 1918)

Bekhterev, V. M. (1998). *Suggestion and its role in social life* (L. Strickland, Ed. & Trans.). New Brunswick, NJ: Transaction. (Original work published 1903)

Bekhterev, V. M. (2001a). *Collective reflexology: The complete edition* (E. Lockwood & A. Lockwood, Trans.). New Brunswick, NJ: Transaction. (Original work published 1921)

Bekhterev, V. M. (2001b). Immortality from a scientific point of view. *Journal of Russian and East European Psychology, 39*(5), 34–70. (Original work published 1916)

Bekhterev, V. M. (2003). From darkness to light. *Journal of Russian and East European Psychology, 41*(2), 76–79. (Original work published 1916)

Bekhtereva, N. (1995, September). An interview. *Argumenty I Facty,* n. 39 (780), 3.

Bemak, F., Chung, R. C-Y., & Pedersen, P. B. (2003). *Counseling refugees: A psychosocial approach to innovative multicultural interventions.* Westport, CT: Greenwood.

Benjamin, L. (2002). Organized industrial psychology before Division 14: The ACP and AAAP (1930–1945). In W. Pickren & D. Dewsbury (Eds.), *Evolving perspectives on the history of psychology* (pp. 369–384). Washington, DC: American Psychological Association.

Benjamin, L. T., Durkin, M., Link, M., &Vestal, M. (1992). Wundt's American doctoral students. *American Psychologist, 47*(2), 123–131.

Benjamin, L. T., Rogers, A. M., & Rosenbaum, A. (1991). Coca-Cola, caffeine, and mental deficiency: Harry Hollingworth and the Chattanooga Trial of 1911. *Journal of the History of the Behavioral Sciences, 27,* 42–55.

Benton, T., Ross, D., Bradshaw, E., Thomas, W., & Bradshaw, G. (2006). Eyewitness memory is still not common sense: Comparing jurors, judges and law enforcement to eyewitness experts. *Applied Cognitive Psychology, 20,* 115–129.

Berkeley, G. (1975). *Philosophical works, including the works on vision* (M. R. Ayers, Ed.). London: J. M. Dent. (Original work published 1710)

Berridge, V., & Edwards, G. (1981). *Opium and the people.* London: Allen Lane.

Betts, R. (2005). *Conflicts after the cold war.* New York: Longman.

Binet, A., & Simon, T. (1913). *A method of measuring the development of the intelligence of young children* (C. H. Town, Trans.). Chicago: Chicago Medical Book. (Original work published 1911)

Binswanger, L. (1963). *Being-in-the-world: Selected papers of Ludwig Binswanger* (J. Needleman, Trans.). New York: Basic Books.

Bjerre, P. (1916). *The history and practice of psychoanalysis.* Boston: Richard Badger.

Bjork, D. (2003). *B. F. Skinner: A life.* Washington, DC: American Psychological Association.

Blass, T. (1992). The social psychology of Stanley Milgram. In M. P. Zanna (Ed.), *Advances in experimental social psychology* (Vol. 25, pp. 277–328). San Diego: Academic Press.

Bloch, S., & Reddaway, P. (1977). *Psychiatric terror.* New York: Basic Books.

Blowers, G. (2001). "To be a big shot or to be shot": Zing-Yang Kuo's other career. *History of Psychology, 4,* 367–387.

Blowers, J. (2000). Learning from others: Japan's role in bringing psychology to China. *American Psychologist, 55,* 1433–1436.

Boakes, R. (2008). *From Darwin to behaviourism: Psychology and the minds of animals.* New York: Cambridge University Press.

Boas, F. (2010). *The mind of primitive man.* Berlin: Nabu Press. (Original work published 1911)

Bode, B. H. (1914). Psychology as a science of behavior. *Psychological Review, 21,* 46–61.

Bokenkamp, S. (1997). *Early Daoists scriptures.* Berkeley: University of California Press.

Boring, E. G. (1929). The psychology of controversy [Boring's 1928 APA presidential address]. *Psychological Review, 36,* 97–121.

Boring, E. G. (1950). *A history of experimental psychology* (2nd ed.). New York: Century. (Original work published in 1929)

Bornstein, R. F. (2001). The impending death of psychoanalysis. *Psychoanalytic Psychology, 18,* 3–20.

Bos, J. (2003). A silent antipode: The making and breaking of psychoanalyst Wilhelm Stekel. *History of Psychology, 6,* 331–361.

Bower, G. H. (1993). The fragmentation of psychology? *American Psychologist, 48,* 905–907.

Bowman, M. L. (1989). Testing individual differences in ancient China. *American Psychologist, 44,* 576–578.

Braid, J. (2008). *Neurypnology, or, the rationale of nervous sleep: Considered in relation with animal magnetism.* Whitefish, MT: Kessinger (Original work published 1843)

Breiter, H. C, Etcoff, N. L, Whalen, P. J, Kennedy, W. A., Rauch, S. L., Buckner, R. L., et al. (1996). Response and habituation of the human amygdala during visual processing of facial expression. *Neuron, 17,* 875–887.

Brentano, F. (1995). *Psychology from the empirical standpoint.* London: Routledge & Kegan Paul. (Original work published in 1874)

Brewer, M. B. (1991). The social self: On being the same and different at the same time. *Personality and Social Psychology Bulletin, 17,* 475–482.

Brewer, M. B., & Pierce, K. P. (2005). Social identity complexity and outgroup tolerance. *Personality and Social Psychology Bulletin, 31,* 428–437.

Broca, P. (1861). Remarques sur le siége de la faculté du langage articulé, suivies d'une observation d'aphemie (perte de la parole). *Bulletins de la société anatomique de Paris, 36,* 330–357.

Bronfenbrenner, Y. (1979). *The ecology of human development: Experiments by nature and design.* Cambridge, MA: Harvard University Press.

Brooks, J. I. (1993). Philosophy and psychology at the Sorbonne, 1885–1913. *Journal of the History of the Behavioral Sciences, 29,* 123–145.

Browne, E. (1962). *Arabian medicine.* Cambridge, UK: Cambridge University Press.

Bruner, J. (1960). *The process of education.* Cambridge, MA: Harvard University Press.

Bruner, J. (1990). *Acts of meaning.* Cambridge, MA: Harvard University Press.

Bryan, A., Aiken, L. S., & West, S. G. (2004). HIV/STD risk among incarcerated adolescents: Optimism about the future and self-esteem as predictors of condom use self efficacy. *Journal of Applied Social Psychology, 34,* 912–936.

Brumbaugh, R. (1981). *The philosophers of Greece.* Albany: State University of New York Press.

Buckley, K. W. (1994). Misbehaviorism: The case of John B. Watson's dismissal from Johns Hopkins University. In J. T. Todd & E. K. Morris (Eds.), *Modern perspectives on John B. Watson and classical behaviorism* (pp. 37–63). Westport, CT: Greenwood.

Budson, A. E., & Price, B. H. (2005). Memory dysfunction. *New England Journal of Medicine, 352,* 692–699.

Bugental, J. (1964). The third force in psychology. *Journal of Humanistic Psychology, 4*(1), 19–25.

Burckhardt, J. (2002). *The civilization of the Renaissance in Italy.* New York: Modern Library. (Original work published 1860)

Butler, P. (2008). *Talking to yourself: How cognitive behavior therapy can change your life.* Charleston, SC: BookSurge.

Byrnes, J. P. (1988). Formal operations: A systematic reformulation. *Developmental Review, 8,* 66–87.

Calkins, M. W. (1892). Experimental psychology at Wellesley College. *American Journal of Psychology, 5,* 464–271.

Calkins, M. W. (1906). A reconciliation between structural and functional psychology [Calkins' APA presidential address]. *Psychological Review, 8,* 61–81.

Calkins, M. W. (1913). Psychology and the behaviorist. *Psychological Bulletin, 10,* 288–291.

Calkins, M. W. (1930). Autobiography of Mary Whiton Calkins. In C. Murchison, *History of psychology in autobiography, Vol. 1* (pp. 31–61). Worcester, MA: Clark University Press.

Callanan, M., & Kelly, P. (1997). *Final gifts: Understanding the special awareness, needs, and communications of the dying.* New York: Bantam.

Campbell, D. (2006). *Inner strength defies the skeptic: A psychological and spiritual guide from fear to freedom inner strength defies the skeptic.* Los Angeles: Immediex.

Cannon, W. B. (1927). The James-Lange theory of emotions: A critical examination and an alternative theory. *American Journal of Psychiatry, 39,* 106–124.

Caplan, B. (2008). *The myth of the rational voter.* Princeton, NJ: Princeton University Press.

Caplan, E. (1998a). *Mind games: American culture and the birth of psychotherapy.* Berkeley: University of California Press.

Caplan, E. (1998b). Popularizing American psychotherapy: The Emmanuel movement, 1906–1910. *History of Psychology, 1,* 289–314.

Cardano, G. (2002). *The book of my life [De vita propria liber].* (J. Stoner, Trans.). New York Review of Books. (Original work published 1576)

Carpintero, H., & Herrero, F. (2002). Early applied psychology: The early days of the IAAP. *European Psychologist, 7*(1), 39–52.

Casmann, O. (1594). *Psychologia anthropologica.* http://books.google.com/books?id=ytU5AAAAcAAJ&printsec=frontcover&dq=Psychologia+Anthropologica&source=bl&ots=fmGepDjrz-&sig=cQQh-n5XozyVUSnlEh3Id5_sGc&hl=en&ei=H48hTI6rEMKAlAeHs6iTAQ&sa=X&oi=book_result&ct=result&resnum=1&ved=0CBEQ6AEwAA#v=onepage&q&f=false

Cattell, J. M. (1885). The influence of the intensity of the stimulus on the length of the reaction time. *Brain, 8,* 512–515.

Cattell, J. M. (1928). Early psychological laboratories. *Science, 67,* 543–548.

Charcot, J. M. (1888). *Clinical lectures on certain diseases of the nervous system.* Detroit, MI: G. S. Davis.

Charle, C. (2004). *Patterns: A history of the university in Europe: Vol. III. Universities in the nineteenth and early twentieth centuries.* New York: Cambridge University Press.

Charon, R. (1992). To build a case: Medical histories as traditions in conflict. *Literature and Medicine, 11*(1), 93–105.

Charon, R. (1993). The narrative road to empathy. In H. Spiro (Ed.), *Empathy and the medical profession: Beyond pills and the scalpel* (pp. 147–159). New Haven, CT: Yale University Press.

Chessick, R. (2007). *The future of psychoanalysis.* Albany: State University of New York Press.

Cheyne, G. (1740). *An essay on regimen.* London: C. Rivington.

Chiarugi, V. (1987). *On insanity and its classification.* Nantucket, MA: Watson. (Original work published 1793)

Chomsky, C. (1963). *The acquisition of syntax in children from 5 to 10.* Cambridge, MA: MIT Press.

Chomsky, N. (1959). Verbal behavior by B. F. Skinner. *Language, 35,* 26–58.

Chomsky, N. (1995). *Language and thought.* Kingston, RI: Moyer Bell.

Clay, R. A. (2002). A renaissance for humanistic psychology: The field explores new niches while building on its past. *American Psychological Association Monitor, 33*(8), 42.

Clifford, G. (1968). E. L. Thorndike: The psychologist as professional man of science. *American Psychologist, 23,* 434–446.

Clower, W. T. (1998). The transition from animal spirits to animal electricity: A neuroscience paradigm shift. *Journal of the History of the Neurosciences, 7,* 201–218.

Compton, W. C. (2004). *An introduction to positive psychology.* Belmont, CA: Wadsworth.

Condillac, E. B. (2002). *Treatise on the sensations.* Manchester, UK: Clinamen Press. (Original work published 1754)

Coon, D. J. (1992). Testing the limits of sense and science: American experimental psychologists combat spiritualism, 1880–1920. *American Psychologist, 47*(2), 143–151.

Cooper, D. (2003). *World philosophies.* Malden, MA: Blackwell.

Cottingham, J., Stoothoff, R., & Murdoch, D. (1984). *The philosophical writings of Descartes.* Cambridge, UK: Cambridge University Press.

Cox, C. (1926). *Early mental traits of three hundred geniuses* (Genetic Studies of Genius Series). Stanford, CA: Stanford University Press.

Cravens, H. (2002). *Before Head Start: The Iowa station and America's children.* Chapel Hill: University of North Carolina Press.

Cuddihy, J. M. (1974). *The ordeal of civility: Freud, Marx, Levi-Strauss, and the Jewish struggle with modernity.* New York: Basic Books.

Curtin, J. J., McCarthy, D. E., Piper, M. E., & Baker, T. B. (2005). Implicit and explicit drug motivational processes: A model of boundary conditions. In R. Reinout & A. Stacy (Eds.), *Handbook on implicit cognition and addiction* (pp. 233–250). Thousand Oaks, CA: Sage.

Da Conceição, C. G., & De Lyra Chebabi, W. (1987). Psychoanalysis and the role of Black life and culture in Brazil. *International Review of Psycho-Analysis, 14,* 185–202.

Dahlsgaard, K., Peterson, C., & Seligman, M. (2005). Shared virtue: The convergence of valued human strengths across culture and history. *Review of General Psychology, 9,* 203–213.

Danziger, K. (1990). *Constructing the subject: Historical origins of psychological research.* Cambridge, UK: Cambridge University Press.

Danziger, K. (1997). *Naming the mind: How psychology found its language.* London: Sage.

Darwin, C. (1859). *The origin of species.* London: John Murray.

Darwin, C. (1871). *The descent of man and selection in relation to sex.* London: Murray.

Darwin, C. (1872). *The expression of the emotions in man and animals.* London: John Murray. http://pages.britishlibrary.net/charles.darwin3/expression/expression_intro.htm

Darwin, C.. (1877). A biographical sketch of an infant. *Mind, 2,* 285–294.

Dasen, P. R. (1994). Culture and cognitive development from a Piagetian perspective. In W. J. Lonner & R. Malpass (Eds.), *Psychology and culture* (pp. 145–149). Boston: Allyn & Bacon.

David, D., Moore, M., & Domuta, A. (2002). Romanian psychology on the international psychological scene: A preliminary critical and empirical appraisal. *European Psychologist, 7*(2), 153–160.

Davidson, D. (1999). Spinoza's causal theory of the affects. In Y. Yovel (Ed.), *Desire and affect: Spinoza as psychologist* (pp. 95–112). New York: Little Room Press.

Davis, M. (1997). Neurobiology of fear responses: The role of the amygdala. *Neuropsychiatry and Clinical Neuroscience, 9,* 382–402.

Descartes, R. (1989). *Passions of the soul.* Indianapolis: Hackett. (Original work published 1646)

Descartes, R. (2000). *Treatise of man: Philosophical essays and correspondence.* Indianapolis: Hackett. (Original work published 1662)

Deutsch, H. (1944). *The psychology of women: A psychoanalytic interpretation: Vol. 1. Girlhood.* New York: Grune & Stratton.

Deutsch, H. (1945). *The psychology of women: A psychoanalytic interpretation: Vol. 2. Motherhood.* New York: Grune & Stratton.

Devereux, G. (1953). Cultural factors in psychoanalytic therapy. *Journal of the American Psychoanalytic Association, 1,* 629–655.

Dewey, J. (1884). The new psychology. *Andover Review, 2,* 278–289.

Dewey, J. (1896). The reflex arc concept in psychology. *Psychological Review, 3,* 357–370.

Dewsbury, D. (2002). The Chicago five: A family group of integrative psychobiologists. *History of Psychology, 5*(1), 16–37.

Dewsbury, D. (2003). The 1973 Nobel Prize for physiology or medicine: Recognition for behavioral science? *American Psychologist, 58,* 747–752.

Diedrichsen, J., Verstynen, T., Lehman, S. L., & Ivry, R. B. (2005). Cerebellar involvement in anticipating the consequences of self-produced actions during bimanual movements. *Journal of Neurophysiology, 93,* 801–812.

Dijksterhuis, A. (2004). Think different: The merits of unconscious thought in preference development and decision making. *Journal of Personality and Social Psychology, 87,* 586–598.

Dijksterhuis, A., Bos, M. W., Nordgren, L. F., & van Baaren, R. B. (2006). On making the right choice: The deliberation-without-attention effect. *Science, 311,* 1005–1007.

Dobreva-Martinova, T., & Strickland, L. H. (Eds.). (2001, September–October). The many sides of Bekhterev [Special issue]. *Journal of Russian and East European Psychology, 39,* 5.

Driver-Linn, E. (2003). Where is the psychology going? Structural fault lines revealed by psychologists' use of Kuhn. *American Psychologist, 58,* 269–278.

Drob, S. L. (1999). Jung and the kabbalah. *History of Psychology, 2*(2), 102–118.

Dufresne, T. (2003). *Killing Freud.* London: Continuum International.

Dunlap, K. (1920). *Mysticism, Freudianism, and scientific psychology.* St. Louis, MO: Mosby.

Durkheim, É. (1997). *Suicide.* New York: Free Press. (Original work published 1897)

Eaton, V. (1888). How the opium habit is acquired. *Popular Science Monthly, 33,* 663–667.

Ebbinghaus, H. (1964). *On memory.* New York: Dover. (Original work published 1885)

Einstein, A. (1905). On the electrodynamics of moving bodies. *Annalen der Physik, 17,* 891–921.

Eisold, K. (2002). Jung, Jungians, and psychoanalysis. *Psychoanalytic Psychology, 19,* 501–524.

Ellenberger, H. (1970). *The discovery of the unconscious.* New York: Basic Books.

Elliotson, J. (1843). *Numerous cases of surgical operations in the mesmeric state without pain.* Philadelphia: Lea and Blanchard.

Ellis, H. H. (1929). *Man and woman: A study of secondary and tertiary sexual characteristics.* New York: Houghton & Mifflin. (Original work published 1894)

Ellis, H. H., & Symonds, J. A. (2006). *SexualiInversion.* Biblio Bazaar. (Original work published 1897)

Enegolm, I. I. (1815). *Kratkoe obozrenie ipohondrii I ee lechenir* [A brief observation of ipochondria and its treatment]. St. Petersburg, Russia: Imperial Print.

English, H., & English, A. C. (1958). *A comprehensive dictionary of psychological and psychoanalytical terms.* New York: Longmans, Green.

Epel, E., Burke, H., & Wolkowitz, O. (2007). The psychoneuroendocrinology of aging: Anabolic and catabolic hormones. In C. M. Aldwin, C. L. Park, & A. Spiro III (Eds.), *Handbook of health psychology and aging* (pp. 119–141). New York: Guilford.

Epel, E. S. (2009). Psychological and metabolic stress: A recipe for accelerated cellular aging? *Hormones (Athens), 8,* 7–22.

Erikson, E. (1950). *Childhood and society.* New York: Norton.

Erikson, E. (1968). *Identity: Youth and crisis.* New York: Norton.

Esterson, A. (2002). The myth of Freud's ostracism by the medical community in 1896–1905: Jeffrey Masson's assault on truth. *History of Psychology, 5*(2), 115–134.

Etkind, L. (1993). *Eros nevozmozhnogo. Oastoriya psychonalyza v Rossii* [Eros of impossible: A history of psychoanalysis in Russia]. Moscow: Meduza.

Ewin, R. E. (1991). *Virtues and rights: The moral philosophy of Thomas Hobbes.* Boulder, CO: Westview.

Fairbairn, W. R. D. (1963). Synopsis of an object-relations theory of the personality. *International Journal of Psycho-Analysis, 44,* 224–225.

Fairbank, J., & Reischauer, E. (1989). *China: Tradition and transformation* (Rev. ed.). Boston: Houghton Mifflin.

Fakhry, M. (1983). *A history of Islamic philosophy.* London: Longman.

Fancher, R. E. (1985). *The intelligence men: Makers of the IQ controversy.* New York: Norton.

Fara, P. (2009). *Science: A four thousand year history.* New York: Oxford University Press.

Farber, P. (2000). *Finding order in nature: The naturalist tradition from Linnaeus to E. O. Wilson.* Baltimore: The Johns Hopkins University Press.

Farmer, R., & Chapman, A. (2007). *Behavioral interventions in cognitive behavior therapy: Practical guidance for putting theory into action.* Washington, DC: American Psychological Association.

Farr, R. (1988). The shaping of modern psychology and the framing of historical accounts. *History of the Human Sciences, 1,* 113–121.

Fechner, G. (1966). *Elements of psychophysics.* Austin, TX: Holt, Rinehart & Winston. (Original work published 1860)

Ferguson, G. A. (1982). Psychology at McGill. In M. J. Wright & C. R. Myers (Eds.), *History of academic psychology in Canada* (pp. 33–67). Toronto, ON: Hogrefe.

Ferrier, D. (1873). Experimental researches in cerebral physiology and pathology. *West Riding Lunatic Asylum Medical Reports, 3,* 30–96

Festinger, L. (1957). *A theory of cognitive dissonance.* Stanford, CA: Stanford University Press.

Festinger, L., Riecken, H. W., & Schachter, S. (1956). *When prophecy fails: A social and psychological study of a modern group that predicted the destruction of the world.* Minneapolis: University of Minnesota Press.

Fisher, R. (1971). *The design of experiments.* New York: Macmillan. (Original work published 1935)

Flanagan, M. (2006). *America reformed: Progressives and progressivisms, 1890s–1920s.* New York: Oxford University Press.

Flourens, P. (1824). *Researches experimentale sur les propriete les fonctions du systeme nerveux dans les animaux vertebris.* Paris: Bulliere.

Flournoy, T. (1994). *From India to the planet Mars.* Princeton, NJ: Princeton University Press. (Original work published 1900)

Foote, E. B. (1896). *Plain home talk: About the human system--the habits of men and women—the causes and prevention of disease—our sexual relations and social natures: Embracing medical common sense.* New York: Murray Hill.

Foucault, M. (1965). *Madness and civilization.* New York: Vintage.

Fox, R. J., Kasner, S. E., Chatterjee, A., & Chalela, J. A. (2001). Aphemia: An isolated disorder of articulation. *Clinical Neurology and Neurosurgery, 103,* 123–126.

Fraher, A. (2004). Systems psychodynamics: The formative years of an interdisciplinary field at the Tavistock. *History of Psychology, 7*(1), 65–84.

Franz, S. I. (1912). New phrenology. *Science, 35,* 321–328.

Freedman, L. (Ed.). (1983). *By reason of insanity: Essays on the psychiatry and the law.* Wilmington, DE: Scholarly Resources.

Freud, A. (1966). *The ego and the mechanisms of defense.* Madison, CT: International Universities Press. (Original work published 1936)

Freud, S. (1955). *Moses and monotheism.* New York: Vintage. (Original work published 1939)

Freud, S. (1957). On the history of the psychoanalytic movement. In J. Strachey (Ed. & Trans.), *The standard edition of the complete psychological works of Sigmund Freud* (Vol. 14, pp. 3–66). London: Hogarth. (Original work published 1914)

Freud, S. (1990a). *Civilization and its discontents.* New York: Norton. (Original work published 1930)

Freud, S. (1990b). *The ego and the id.* New York: Norton. (Original work published 1923)

Freud, S. (1990c). *The future of an illusion.* New York: Norton. (Original work published 1927)

Freud, S. (2000). *Three essays on the theory of sexuality.* New York: Basic Books. (Original work published 1905)

Freud, S. (2008). *The interpretation of dreams.* New York: Oxford University Press. (Original work published 1899)

Freud, S. (2009a). *Beyond the pleasure principle.* Eastford, CT: Martino Fine Books. (Original work published 1920)

Freud, S. (2009b). *The psychopathology of everyday life.* General Books LLC. (Original work published 1901)

Freud, S. (2010). *Totem and taboo.* Nabu Press. (Original work published 1913)

Fritsch, G., & Hitzig, E. (1870). Über die elektrische Erregbarkeit des Grosshirns. *Archiv für Anatomie, Physiologie, und wissenschaftliche Medicin,* 300–322.

Fromm, E. (1947). *Man for himself: An inquiry into the psychology of ethics.* New York: Rinehart & Co.

Fromm, E. (1994). *Escape from freedom.* New York: Holt. (Original work published 1941)

Frost, E. P. (1912). Can biology and physiology dispense with consciousness? *Psychological Review, 19,* 246–252.

Fuchs, A. H. (2000). Contributions of American mental philosophers to psychology in the United States. *History of Psychology, 3*(1), 3–19.

Fullerton, H. S. (1921). Why Babe Ruth is greatest home-run hitter. *Popular Science Monthly, 99*(4), 19–21, 110.

Gallo, L. C., Espinosa de los Monteros, K., Ferent, V., Urbina, J., & Talavera, G. (2007). Education, psychosocial resources, and metabolic syndrome variables in Latinas. *Annals of Behavioral Medicine, 34,* 14–25.

Gallo, L. C., & Matthews, K. A. (2003). Understanding the association between socioeconomic status and physical health: Do negative emotions play a role? *Psychological Bulletin, 129,* 10–51.

Galton, F. (1869). *Hereditary genius. London:* Macmillan.

Galton, F. (1875). The history of twins, as a criterion of the relative powers of nature and nurture. *Fraser's Magazine, 12,* 566–576.

Galton, F. (1880). Statistics of mental imagery. *Mind, 5,* 301–318.

Galton, F. (1883). *Inquiries into human faculty and its development.* New York: Macmillan.

Gardiner, H., Mutter, J., & Kosmitzki, C. (1998). *Lives across cultures: Cross-cultural human development.* Boston: Allyn & Bacon.

Gaukroger, S., Schuster, J., & Sutton, J. (Eds.). (2000). *Descartes' natural philosophy.* New York: Routledge.

Gay, P. (1998). *Freud: A life for our time.* New York: Norton.

Gazzaniga, M. S. (2005). *The ethical brain: The science of our moral dilemmas.* New York: Dana Press.

Gelb, A., & Goldstein, K. (1918). Analysis of a case of figural blindness. In W. D. Ellis (Ed.), *A source book of gestalt psychology* (pp. 315–325). New York: Harcourt, Brace.

Gergen, K. (2001). Psychological science in a post-modern context. *American Psychologist, 56,* 803–813.

Geuter, U. (1987). German psychology during the Nazi period. In M. C. Ash & W. R. Woodward (Eds.), *Psychology in twentieth-century thought and society* (pp. 164–187). Cambridge, UK: Cambridge University Press.

Gibson, M. (2002). *Born to crime: Cesare Lombroo and the origins of biological criminology.* Westport, CT: Praeger.

Gillespie, R. (1991). *Manufacturing knowledge: A history of the Hawthorne experiments.* Cambridge, UK: Cambridge University Press.

Gilman, S. L. (1988). *Disease and representation: Images of illness from madness to AIDS.* Ithaca, NY: Cornell University Press.

Gilman, S. L., King, H., Porte, R., Rousseau, G. S., & Showalter, E. (1993). *Hysteria beyond Freud.* Berkeley: University of California Press.

Gleaves, D. H., & Hernandez, E. (1999). Recent reformulations of Freud's development and abandonment of his seduction theory: Historical/scientific clarification or a continued assault on truth? *History of Psychology, 2,* 324–354.

Glynn, I. (1999). *An anatomy of thought.* Oxford, UK: Oxford University Press.

Goddard, H. H. (1916). *Feeble-mindedness: Its causes and consequences.* New York: Macmillan.

Goddard, H. H. (1950). *The Kallikak family.* New York: Macmillan. (Original work published 1912)

Goclenius, R. (1598). *Isagoge in peripateticorum et scholasticorum primam philosophiam* (Latin ed.). Frankfurt: Olms. (Original work published 1976)

Goldberg, A. (2004). *Misunderstanding Freud.* New York: Other Press.

Goldney, R. D., & Schioldann, J. A. (2002). *Pre-Durkheim suicidology: The 1892 reviews of Tuke and Savage.* Burnside, Australia: Adelaide Academic Press.

Goldstein, K. (1963). *The organism: A holistic approach to biology.* New York: American Book Co. (Original work published 1939)

Golubovsky, M. D. (1998). Ivan Pavlov. *Znaznie-Sila,* pp. 8–11, 29.

Goodchild, L. (1996). G. Stanley Hall and the study of higher education. *The Review of Higher Education, 20,* 69–99.

Gosling, S. D. (2008). Personality in non-human animals. *Social and Personality Psychology Compass, 2,* 985–1002.

Gray, R., Regan, D., Castaneda, B., & Sieffert, R. (2006). Role of feedback in the accuracy of perceived direction of motion-in-depth and control of interceptive action. *Vision Research, 46,* 1676–1694.

Green, C. D. (2002). Toronto's "other" original APA member James Gibson Hume. *Canadian Psychology, 43*(1), 35–45.

Green, C. D. (2003). Psychology strikes out: Coleman R. Griffith and the Chicago Cubs. *History of Psychology, 6,* 267–283.

Green, C. D. (2004). The hiring of James Mark Baldwin and James Gibson Hume at the University of Toronto in 1889. *History of Psychology, 7,* 130 –153.

Green, C. D., Shore, M., & Teo, T. (Eds.). (2001). *The transformation of psychology: Influences of 19th-century philosophy, technology, and natural science.* Washington, DC: American Psychological Association Press.

Greening, T. (1971). *Existential humanistic psychology.* Belmont, CA: Brooks/Cole.

Greening, T. (1986). Passion bearers and peace psychology. *Journal of Humanistic Psychology, 26*(4), 98–105.

Greenwood, J. (2003). Wundt, Völkerpsychologie, and experimental social psychology. *History of Psychology, 6*(1), 70–88.

Gregory, R. L. (1997) *Mirrors in mind.* New York: W. H. Freeman.

Griffith, C. R. (1921). Some neglected aspects of a history of psychology. *Psychological Monographs, 30,* 17–29.

Griffith, C. R. (1922). Contributions to the history of psychology—1916–1921. *Psychological Bulletin, 19,* 411–428.

Griffiths, T. L., & Tenenbaum, J. B. (2006). Optimal predictions in everyday cognition. *Psychological Science, 17,* 767–773.

Grob, G. (1994). *The mad among us.* New York: Free Press.

Gross, C. G. (1998). *Brain, vision, memory: Tales in the history of neuroscience.* Cambridge, MA: MIT Press.

Gross, C. G. (2005). Processing the facial image: A brief history. *American Psychologist, 60,* 755–763.

Habermas, T. (1989). The psychiatric history of anorexia nervosa and bulimia nervosa: Weight concerns and bulimic symptoms in early case reports. *International Journal of Eating Disorders, 8,* 259–273.

Hall, G. S. (1904). *Adolescence: Its psychology and its relations to physiology, anthropology, sociology, sex, crime, religion, and education* (2 vols.). New York: Appleton.

Hall, G. S. (1920). *Recreations of a psychologist.* New York: Appleton.

Hall, S., Held, D., Hubert, D. & Thompson, K. (Eds.). (1996). *Modernity: An introduction to modern societies.* New York: Wiley-Blackwell.

Hall, T. (1997). Gender differences: Implications for spiritual formation and community life. *Journal of Psychology and Christianity, 16,* 222–232.

Hardcastle, G. (2000). The cult of experiment: The psychological round table, 1936–1941. *History of Psychology, 3,* 344–370.

Harrington, A. (1996). *Reenchanted science: Holism in German culture from Wilhelm II to Hitler.* Princeton, NJ: Princeton University Press.

Hartley, D. (1999). *Observations on man, his frame, his duty, and his expectations* (2 vols.). Bath, UK: Samuel Richardson. (Original work published 1749)

Hartmann, H. (1958). *Ego psychology and the problem of adaptation.* New York: International Universities Press.

Harvey, W. (1965). *The works of William Harvey.* New York: Johnson Reprint. (Original work published 1628)

Haslam, J. (1976). *Observations on madness and melancholy.* New York: Arno. (Original work published 1810)

Haven, J. (1882). *Mental philosophy.* New York: Sheldon and Company.

Hayman, R. (1999). *A life of Jung.* New York: Norton.

Heckel, R. V., & Paramesh, C. R. (1974). Applied psychology in India. *Professional Psychology,* 5(1), 37–41.

Heider, F. (1944). Social perception and phenomenal causality. *Psychological Review, 51,* 358–374.

Heider, F. (1958). *The psychology of interpersonal relations.* New York: John Wiley.

Helson, H. (1973). Why did their precursors fail and the Gestalt psychologists succeed? In M. Henle, J. Jaynes, & J. Sullivan (Eds.), *Historical concepts of psychology* (pp. 74–82). New York: Springer.

Helson, H. (1987). The psychology of Gestalt. *American Journal of Psychology, 100,* 537–566.

Hendstrom, J. (1994). Morita and Naikan therapies: American applications. *Psychotherapy: Theory, Research, Practice, Training, 31*(1), 154–160.

Henle, M. (1978). One man against the Nazis: Wolfgang Köhler. *American Psychologist, 33,* 939–944.

Henle, M. (2006). Robert M. Ogden and Gestalt psychology in America. *Journal of the History of the Behavioral Sciences, 20*(1), 9–19.

Herman, E. (2001). How children turn out and how psychology turns them out. *History of Psychology, 4,* 297–316.

Herrnstein, R. (1967). *Introduction to John B. Watson's comparative psychology.* New York: Holt, Rinehart, & Winston.

Higgins, L. T., & Zheng, M. (2002). An introduction to Chinese psychology: Its historical roots until the present day. *Journal of Psychology, 136,* 225–239.

Hodges, A. (1983). *Alan Turing: The enigma.* London: Burnett.

Hoffman, C. (2004, December). Dumuzi's dream: Dream analysis in ancient Mesopotamia. *Dreaming,* pp. 240–251.

Holbach, P.-H. (1970). *System of nature* (H. D. Robinson, Trans.). New York: Burt Franklin. (Original work published 1770)

Holliday, B. (2009). The history and visions of African American psychology: Multiple pathways to place, space, and authority. *Cultural Diversity and Ethnic Minority Psychology, 15,* 317–337.

Holliday, B. G., & Holmes, A. L. (2003). A tale of challenge and change: A history and chronology of ethnic minorities in psychology in the United States. In G. Bernal, J. Trimble, A. Burlew, & F. Leong (Eds.), *Handbook of racial and ethnic minority psychology* (pp. 15–64). Thousand Oaks, CA: Sage.

Hollingworth, H. L. (1913). *Advertising and selling: Principles of appeal and response.* New York: Appleton.

Hooker, R. (1982). *The complete works of Richard Hooker.* Cambridge, MA: Harvard University Press.

Horney, K. (1950). *The collected works of Karen Horney* (2 vols.). New York: Norton.

Hornstein, G. (1992). The return of the repressed: Psychology's problematic relations with psychoanalysis, 1909–1960. *American Psychologist, 47,* 254–263.

Hotta, M., & Strickland, L. (1991). Social psychology in Japan. *Canadian Psychology, 32,* 596–611.

Hotz, R. (2009, January 15). The brain, your honor, will take the witness stand. *Wall Street Journal,* p. A7.

Hsueh, Y. (2002). The Hawthorne experiments and the introduction of Jean Piaget in American industrial psychology, 1929–1932. *History of Psychology, 5*(2), 163–189.

Hubbard, L. R. (1955). *Dianetics: The evolution of a science.* Los Angeles: Bridge Publications.

Hull, C. (1935). The conflicting psychologies of learning—a way out. *Psychological Review, 42,* 491–451.

Hull, C. (1943). *Principles of behavior.* New York: Appleton.

Hull, C. (2002). *Hypnosis and suggestibility: An experimental approach.* Carmarthen, UK: Crown House Publishing. (Original work published 1933)

Hume, D. (1987). *Essays: Moral, political, and literary.* Indianapolis, IN: Liberty Classics. (Original work published 1777)

Ingram, A. (Ed.). (1998). *Patterns of madness in the eighteenth century: A reader.* Liverpool, UK: Liverpool University Press.

Isaeva, N. (1999). *From early Vedanta to Kashmir Shaivism.* Albany: State University of New York Press.

Jackson, J. H. (1931). Evolution and dissolution of the nervous system. In J. Taylor (Ed.), *Selected writings of John Hughlings Jackson* (Vol. 2, pp. 92–118). London: Hodder & Stoughton. (Original work published 1884)

Jackson, L. A. (2000). *Child sexual abuse in Victorian England.* London: Routledge.

James, W. (1906). *The moral equivalent of war.* Speech delivered at Stanford University. Retrieved August 7, 2010, from http://www.constitution.org/wj/meow.htm

James, W. (1920). *Collected essays and reviews.* New York: Longmans. (Original work published 1892)

James, W. (1950). *The principles of psychology.* Mineola, NY: Dover. (Original work published 1890)

James, W. (1995). *Pragmatism.* Mineola, NY: Dover. (Original work published 1909)

Janet, P. (1924). *Principles of psychotherapy.* New York: Macmillan.

Jansz, J., & van Drunen, P. (Eds.). (2003). *A social history of psychology.* New York: Wiley-Blackwell.

Jastrow, J. (1935). Has psychology failed? *American Scholar, 4,* 261–269.

Jessup, J. (1948, June 28). The newest utopia. *Life,* p. 38.

Jilek, W. (1994). Traditional healing in the prevention and treatment of alcohol and drug abuse. *Transcultural Psychiatric Research Review, 31,* 219–258.

Johnson, M. K. (2006). Memory and reality. *American Psychologist, 61,* 760–771.

Johnson, M. K., & Raye, C. L. (2000). Cognitive and brain mechanisms of false memories and beliefs. In D. Schacter & E. Scarry (Eds.), *Memory, brain, and belief* (pp. 35–86). Cambridge, MA: Harvard University Press.

Johnson, W., & Krueger, R. F. (2005). Higher perceived life control decreases genetic variance in physical health: Evidence from a national twin study. *Journal of Personality & Social Psychology, 88,* 165–173.

Johnston, T. D. (2002). An early manuscript in the history of American comparative psychology Lewis Henry Morgan's "Animal Psychology" (1857). *History of Psychology, 5,* 323–355.

Jones, E. (1953). *The life and work of Sigmund Freud.* London: Hogarth.

Jones, H. E. (2008). Scientific evidence and practical experience with methadone-assisted withdrawal of heroin-dependent pregnant patients. *Heroin Addiction and Related Clinical Problems, 10,* 33–38.

Jones, M. C. (1924). A laboratory study of fear: The case of Peter. *Pedagogical Seminary, 31,* 308–315.

Jones, M. C. (1957). The later careers of boys who were early- or late-maturing. *Child Development, 28,* 113–128.

Jung, C. G. (1961). *Memories, dreams, reflections* (recorded and edited by Aniela Jaffe). New York: Random House.

Jung, C. G. (1964). *Man and his symbols.* New York: Dell.

Jung, C. G. (1967). *C. G. Jung collected works: Alchemical studies.* Princeton, NJ: Princeton University Press. (Original work published 1929)

Jung, C. G. (1924). *Psychological types or the psychology of individuation.* New York: Random House.

Jung, C. G., & Hinkle, B. M. (1912). *Psychology of the unconscious: A study of the transformations and symbolisms of the libido, a contribution to the history of the evolution of thought.* London: Kegan, Paul, Trench, Trubner.

Kahneman, D. (2003). A perspective on judgment and choice: Mapping bounded rationality. *American Psychologist, 58,* 697–720.

Kahneman, D., & Tversky, A. (1979). Prospect theory: An analysis of decisions under risk. *Econometrica, 47,* 313–327.

Kakar, S. (1989). The maternal-feminine in Indian psychoanalysis. *International Review of Psycho-Analysis, 16,* 355–362.

Kakar, S. (1995). Clinical work and cultural imagination. *Psychoanalytic Quarterly, 64,* 265–281.

Karon, B. P., & Widener, A. J. (2001). Repressed memories: Avoiding the obvious. *Psychoanalytic Psychology, 18,* 161–164.

Katz, D. (1968). David Katz. In E. G. Boring, H. S. Langfeld, H. Werner, & R. M. Yerkes (Eds.), *History of psychology in autobiography* (Vol. 4, pp. 189–211). Worcester, MA: Clark University Press. (Original work published 1952)

Katz, D. (1979). Floyd H. Allport (1890–1978). *American Psychologist, 34,* 351–353.

Kavanaugh, P. B. (1999, November). *Thinking about psychoanalytic thinking: An historical approach to hysterical symptoms.* President's address at the 10th annual congress of the International Federation for Psychoanalytic Education, San Francisco.

Keegan, E. (2003). Flechsig and Freud: Late 19th-century neurology and the emergence of psychoanalysis. *History of Psychology, 6*(1), 52–69.

Keel, P., & Klump, K. (2003). Are eating disorders culture-bound syndromes? Implications for conceptualizing their etiology. *Psychological Bulletin, 129,* 747–769.

Keller, E. F. (1985). *Reflections on gender and science.* New Haven, CT: Yale University Press.

Kellogg, R. (2003). *Cognitive psychology.* Thousand Oaks, CA: Sage.

Kendler, H. (1999). The role of value in the world of psychology. *American Psychologist, 54,* 828–835.

Kendler, H. (2000). Thorndike's science of values. *American Psychologist, 55,* 343–344.

Kendler, H. H. (2002). A personal encounter with psychology (1937–2002). *History of Psychology, 5,* 52–84.

Kenny, A. (1968). *Descartes: A study of his philosophy.* New York: Random House.

Kevles, D. J. (1985). *In the name of eugenics: Genetics and the uses of human heredity.* New York: Knopf.

King, P. L. (1991). *The life of John Locke: With extracts from his correspondence, journals, and common-place books.* Bristol, UK: Thoemmes.

Kinsey, A. (1998). *Sexual behavior in the human male.* Bloomington: Indiana University Press. (Original work published 1948)

Kirk, G. S., Raven J. E., & Schofield, M. (1995). *The presocratic philosophers: A critical history with a selection of texts.* New York: Cambridge University Press.

Kirkebøen, G. (2000). Descartes's regulae, mathematics, and modern psychology: "The noblest example of all" in light of Turing's (1936) On computable numbers. *History of Psychology, 3,* 299–325.

Klein, A. (2002). *A forgotten voice: A biography of Leta Stetter Hollingworth.* Scottsdale, AZ: Great Potential Press.

Kleinman, A., & Kleinman, J. (1991). Suffering and its professional transformation: Toward an ethnography of interpersonal experience. *Culture, Medicine, and Psychiatry, 15,* 275–301.

Klingenstein, S. (1991). *Jews in the American academy, 1900–1940: The dynamics of intellectual assimilation.* New Haven, CT: Yale University Press.

Knox, H. A. (1913). A test for adult imbeciles and six year old normals. *New York Medical Journal, 98,* 1017–1018.

Knox, H. A. (1915). Measuring human intelligence: A progressive series of standardized tests used by the Public Health Service to protect our racial stock. *Scientific American, 112,* 52–53, 57–58.

Kodama, S. (1991). Life and work: Y. J. Yan, the first person to introduce Western psychology to China. *Psychologia: An International Journal of Psychology in the Orient, 34,* 213–226.

Koenigsberg, R. (2007). *The nation: A study in ideology and fantasy.* New York: Information Age.

Koffka, K. (1922). Perception: An introduction to the *Gestalt-theorie. Psychological Bulletin, 19,* 531–585.

Koffka, K. (1924). *The growth of the mind* (R. M. Ogden, Trans.). London: Routledge & Kegan Paul. (Original work published 1921)

Köhler, W. (1925). *Mentality of apes* (E. Winter, Trans.). London: Routledge & Kegan Paul. (Original work published 1917)

Köhler, W. (1938). *The place of value in a world of facts.* New York: Livewright.

Köhler, W. (1959). Gestalt psychology today. *American Psychologist, 14,* 727–734.

Köpping, K.-P. (2005). *Adolf Bastian and the psychic unity of man: The foundations of anthropology in nineteenth-century Germany.* Berlin: Lit Verlag.

Korn, J., Davis, R., & Davis, S. (1991). Historians' and chairpersons' judgments of eminence among psychologists. *American Psychologist, 46,* 789–792.

Kosits, R. D. (2004). Of faculties, fallacies, and freedom: Dilemma and irony in the secularization of American psychology. *History of Psychology, 7,* 340–366.

Kotik-Friedgut, B., & Friedgut, T. H. (2008). A man of his country and his time: Jewish influences on Lev Semionovich Vygotsky's world view. *History of Psychology, 11,* 15–39.

Kraepelin, E. (1883). Compendium der psychiatrie. *American Journal of Insanity, 40,* 509–511.

Krafft-Ebbing, R. (1886). *Psychopathia sexualis.* Stuttgart: Verlag von Ferdinand Enke.

Krantz, D. L., & Wiggins, L. (1973). Personal and impersonal channels of recruitment in the growth of theory. *Human Development, 16*(3), 133–156.

Kressley-Mba, R. (2006). On the failed institutionalization of German comparative psychology prior to 1940. *History of Psychology, 9,* 55–74.

Krstic, K. (1964). Marko Marulic: The author of the term "psychology." *Acta Instituti Psychologici Universitatis Zagrabiensis, 36,* 7–13.

Krueger, R. F., & Markon, K. E. (2006). Reinterpreting comorbidity: A model based approach to understanding and classifying psychopathology. *Annual Review of Clinical Psychology, 2,* 111–133.

Kugelmann, R. (2001). Introspective psychology, pure and applied: Henry Rutgers Marshall on pain and pleasure. *History of Psychology, 4,* 34–58.

Kugelmann, R. (2005). Neoscholastic psychology revisited. *History of Psychology, 8,* 131–175.

Kuhn, T. (1962). *The structure of scientific revolutions.* Chicago: University of Chicago Press.

Külpe, O. (2008). *Outline of psychology: Based upon the results of experimental investigation.* Whitefish, MT: Kessinger. (Original work published 1885)

Kurtz, S. N. (1992). *All the mothers are one: Hindu India and the cultural reshaping of psychoanalysis.* New York: Columbia University Press.

Kurzban, R., & Houser, D. (2005). An experimental investigation of cooperative types in human groups: A complement to evolutionary theory and simulations. *Proceedings of the National Academy of Sciences, 102,* 1803–1807.

Lakatos, I. (1970). Falsification and the methodology of scientific research programmes. In I. Lakatos & A. Musgrave (Eds.), *Criticism and the growth of knowledge* (pp. 91–196). Cambridge, UK: Cambridge University Press.

La Mettrie, J. O. (1994). *Man a machine; man a plant* (R. A. Watson & M. Rybalka, Trans.). Indianapolis, IN: Hackett. (Original work published 1748)

Lamiell, J. T. (2009). Some philosophical and historical considerations relevant to William Stern's contributions to developmental psychology. *Zeitschrift für Psychologie/Journal of Psychology, 217*(2), 66–72.

Lammers, J., & Galinsky, A. (2010). Power increases hypocrisy: Moralizing in reasoning, immunity and behavior. *Psychological Science, 21,* 737–744.

Lange, C. G. (1912). The mechanism of the emotions. In B. Rand (Ed. & Trans.). (1912). *The classical psychologists* (pp. 672–684). Ann Arbor: University of Michigan Library. (Original work published 1885a)

Lange, C. G. (1922). The emotions: A psycho-physiological study. In C. G. Lange & W. James (Eds.), *Psychology classics* (Vol.1.). Baltimore: Williams & Wilkins. (Original work published 1885b)

Lange, L. (2005). Sleeping beauties in psychology: Comparisons of "hits" and "missed signals" in psychological journals. *History of Psychology, 8,* 194–217.

LaPiere, R. T. (1934). Attitude and action. *Social Forces, 13,* 230–237.

LaPiere, R. T. (1936). Type-rationalizations of group antipathy. *Social Forces, 15,* 232–237.

Laqueur, T. (2004). *Solitary sex: A cultural history of masturbation.* Cambridge, MA: Zone Books.

Lashley, K. (1929). *Brain mechanisms and intelligence.* Chicago: University of Chicago Press.

Laycock, T. (1976). *Mind and brain.* New York: Arno. (Original work published 1860)

Lea, M., & Spears, R. (1991). Computer-mediated communication, de-individuation and group decision-making. *International Journal of Man-Machine Studies, 34,* 283–301.

Leahey, T. (2002). History without the past. In W. Pickren & D. Dewsbury (Eds.), *Evolving perspectives on the history of psychology* (pp. 15–20). Washington, DC: American Psychological Association.

Le Bon, G. (1896). *The crowd: A study of the popular mind.* London: Ernest Benn.

Lee, W. O. (1996). The cultural context for Chinese learners: Conceptions of learning in the Confucian tradition. In D. A. Watkins & J. B. Biggs (Eds.), *The Chinese learner* (pp. 45–67). Hong Kong: Comparative Education Research Centre.

Leibin, V. M. (1994). *Zigmund Freid, psychoanalys, I russkaya mysl* [Sigmund Freud, psychoanalysis, and the Russian thought]. Moscow: Respublika.

Leibniz, G. (1951). *Philosophical writings.* London: J. M. Dent & Sons. (Original work published 1670)

Le Poidevin, R., & MacBeath, M. (Eds.). (1997). *The philosophy of time* (Oxford Readings in Philosophy). Oxford, UK: Oxford University Press.

Lerner, P. (2003). *Hysterical men, war, psychiatry, and the politics of trauma in Germany, 1890–1930.* Ithaca, NY: Cornell University Press.

Levy, D. (2010). *Tools of critical thinking: Metathoughts for psychology* (2nd ed.). Long Grove, IL: Waveland.

Levin, M. (2006). *Composite systems decisions.* New York: Springer.

Lewin, K. (1931). The conflict between Aristotelian and Galilean models of thought in contemporary psychology. *Journal of General Psychology, 5,* 141–177.

Lewin, K. (1936). *Principles of topological psychology.* New York: McGraw-Hill.

Lewin, K. (1939). Field theory and experiment in social psychology. *American Journal of Sociology, 44,* 868–896.

Lewin, K. (1942). *Field theory in social science.* Chicago: University of Chicago Press.

Lewin, K. (1943). Defining the "Field at a Given Time." *Psychological Review, 50,* 292–310. (Republished in *Resolving Social Conflicts & Field Theory in Social Science.* Washington, DC: American Psychological Association, 1997.)

Lewin, K. (1944). Constructs in psychology and psychological ecology. *University of Iowa Studies in Child Welfare, 20,* 1–29. (Republished in *Resolving Social Conflicts & Field Theory in Social Science.* Washington, DC: American Psychological Association, 1997.)

Lewin, K. (1948). *Resolving social conflicts: Selected papers on group dynamics.* New York: Harper & Row.

Lewin, K. (1997). *Field theory in social science.* New York: Harper & Row. (Original work published 1951)

Lewin, K., Lippitt, R., & White, R. (1939). Patterns of aggressive behavior in experimentally created social climates. *Journal of Social Psychology, 10,* 271–299.

Lewinsohn, P. M., Rohde, P., Seeley, J. R., Klein, D. N., & Gotlib, I. H. (2003). Psychosocial functioning of young adults who have experienced and recovered from major depressive disorder during adolescence. *Journal of Abnormal Psychology, 112,* 353–363.

Lewis, M. (2001). *Multicultural health psychology: Special topics acknowledging diversity.* Boston: Allyn & Bacon.

Lieberman, M. D. (2006). Social cognitive and affective neuroscience: When opposites attract. *Social Cognitive and Affective Neuroscience, 1,* 1–2.

Lieberman, M. D. (2007). Social cognitive neuroscience: A review of core processes. *Annual Review of Psychology, 58,* 259–289.

Lippmann, W. (1923). The great confusion. *New Republic, 34,* 145–146.

Liu, J. H., Goldstein-Hawes, R., Hilton, D. J., Huang, L. L., Gastardo-Conaco, C., Dresler-Hawke, E., et al. (2005). Social representations of events and people in world history across twelve cultures. *Journal of Cross-Cultural Psychology, 36,* 171–191.

Lock, A. (1981). Ingenious psychology and human nature: A psychological perspective. In P. Heelas & A. Lock. (Eds), *Indigenous psychologies* (pp. 183–204). London: Academic Press.

Locke, J. (1944). *An essay concerning human understanding.* Amherst, NY: Prometheus Books. (Original work published 1690)

Logan, C. (1999). The altered rationale for the choice of a standard animal in experimental psychology: Henry H. Donaldson, Adolf Meyer, and "the" Albino Rat. *History of Psychology, 2,* 3–24.

Lombardo, G., & Foschi, R. (2003). The concept of personality in the 19th-century French and 20th-century American psychology. *History of Psychology, 6,* 123–142.

Lombroso, C. (1911). *Criminal man: According to classification of Cesare Lombroso.* New York: Putnam.

Lombroso, C., & Ferrero, G. (1959). *The female offender.* New York: Appleton. (Original work published 1895)

Long, A., & Sedley, D. (1987). *The Hellenistic philosophers* (Vols. 1–2). Cambridge, UK: Cambridge University Press.

Louw, J., & Swartz, S. (2001). An English asylum in Africa: Space and order in Valkenberg Asylum. *History of Psychology, 4,* 3–23.

Ludmerer, K. M. (1978). Eugenics: History. In W. T. Reich (Ed.), *Encyclopedia of bioethics* (pp. 457–462). New York: Free Press.

Ludy, B. (1986). Why don't they understand us? A history of psychology's public image. *American Psychologist, 41,* 941–946.

Lukova, O. (1992, January–February). *V. M. Bekhterev on the effect of extreme situations on the psychological health of the individual.* Proceedings of the 5th Conference of the Russian Psychological Society, Psychology and Its Applications, Moscow.

Maass, A., Karasawa, M., Politi, F., & Suga, S. (2006). Do verbs and adjectives play different roles in different cultures? A cross-linguistic analysis of person representation. *Journal of Personality and Social Psychology, 90,* 734–750.

Macmillan, M. B. (2000a). Nineteenth-century inhibitory theories of thinking: Bain, Ferrier, Freud (and Phineas Gage). *History of Psychology, 3,* 187–217.

Macmillan, M. B. (2000b). Restoring Phineas Gage: A 150th retrospective. *Journal of the History of the Neurosciences, 9,* 42–62.

Maier, B. N. (2004). The role of James McCosh in God's exile from psychology. *History of Psychology, 7,* 323–339.

Mandler, G. (2007). *A history of modern experimental psychology: From James and Wundt to cognitive science.* Cambridge, MA: MIT Press.

Mandler, J. M. (2004). *The foundations of mind: Origins of conceptual thought.* New York: Oxford University Press.

Maslow, A. (1954). *Motivation and personality.* New York: Harper & Brothers.

Maslow, A. (1970). *Religions, values, and peak-experiences.* London: Penguin.

Matthews, K. (2005). Psychological perspectives on the development of coronary heart disease. *American Psychologist, 60,* 783–796.

Maudsley, H. (1870). *Body and mind: An inquiry into their connection and mutual influence, especially in reference to mental disorders.* London: Macmillan.

May, R. (1967). *Psychology and the human dilemma.* Princeton, NJ: Van Nostrand.

May, R., Angel, E., & Ellenberger, H. F. (Eds.). (1958). *Existence.* New York: Basic Books.

Mayer, S. (2005). The early evolution of Jean Piaget's clinical method. *History of Psychology, 8,* 362–382.

Mayo, E. (2003). *The human problems of an industrialized civilization.* New York: Routledge. (Original work published 1933)

McCormick, D. J. (2004). Galton on spirituality, religion, and health. *American Psychologist, 59,* 52.

McCosh, J. (1871). *Christianity and positivism: A series of lectures to the times on natural theology and apologetics.* New York: Robert Carter.

McCosh, J. (1880). How to deal with young men trained in science in this age of unsettled opinion. In J. B. Dale & R. M. Patterson (Eds.), *Report of the Proceedings of the Second General Council of the Presbyterian Alliance* (pp. 204–213). Philadelphia: Presbyterian Journal Co. and J. C. McCurdy.

McDougall, W. (1908). *An introduction to social psychology.* London: Methuen.

McDougall, W. (1912). *Psychology: The study of behavior.* New York: Holt.

McDougall, W. (1934). *Religion and the sciences of life with other essays on allied topics.* Durham, NC: Duke University Press.

McMillan, S., Stevens, S., & Kelloway, E. K. (2009). History and development of industrial/organisational psychology in the Canadian Forces: Personnel Selection Branch: 1938–2009. *Canadian Psychology, 50,* 283–291.

McReynolds, P. (1987). Lightner Witmer: Little-known founder of clinical psychology. *American Psychologist, 42,* 849–858.

McReynolds, P. (1996). Lightner Witmer: Father of clinical psychology. In G. Kimble, C. A. Boneau, & M. Wertheimer (Eds.), *Portraits of pioneers in psychology* (Vol. II). Washington, DC: APA and Lawrence Erlbaum.

Meaghers, J. F. W. (1929). Homosexuality; its psychobiological and psychopathological significance. *Urologic and Cutaneous Review, 33,* 505–518.

Meissner, S. J. W. W. (2006). Prospects for psychoanalysis in the 21st century. *Psychoanalytic Psychology, 23,* 239–256.

Mesmer, F. A. (1980). *Mesmerism, a translation of the original medical and scientific writings of F. A. Mesmer, M.D.* Los Altos, CA: William Kaufmann. (Original work published 1766)

Metzl, J. (2005). *Prozac on the couch.* Durham, NC: Duke University Press.

Milgram, S. (1963). Behavioral study of obedience. *Journal of Abnormal and Social Psychology, 67,* 371–378.

Mill, J. S. (1998). *Utilitarianism.* New York: Oxford University Press. (Original work published 1863)

Mill, J. S. (2010). *On the subjection of women.* Berlin: Nabu Press. (Original work published 1869)

Miller, A. G. (Ed.). (2004). *The social psychology of good and evil.* New York: Guilford.

Miller, G. (1956). The magical number seven, plus or minus two: Some limits on our capacity for processing information. *Psychological Review, 63,* 81–97.

Miller, G. (1969). Psychology as a means of promoting human welfare. *American Psychologist, 24,* 1063–1075.

Miller, G. (2000). *The mating mind: How sexual choice shaped the evolution of human nature.* London: Heineman.

Miller, G., Galanter, E., & Pribram, K. (1960). *Plans and the structure of behavior.* New York: Holt.

Mills, J. (2001). Reexamining the psychoanalytic corpse from scientific psychology to philosophy. *Psychoanalytic Psychology, 19,* 552–558.

Mitroff, S. R., & Scholl, B. J. (2005). Forming and updating object representations without awareness: Evidence from motion-induced blindness. *Vision Research, 45,* 961–967.

Mollon J. D., & Perkins, A. J. (1996, March 14). Errors of judgment in Greenwich in 1796. *Nature, 380,* 101–102.

Morawski, J. (2002). Assessing psychology's moral heritage through our neglected utopias. In W. Pickren & D. Dewsbury (Eds.), *Evolving perspectives on the history of psychology* (pp. 499–525). Washington, DC: American Psychological Association.

Morel, B. A. (1976). *Traite des degenerescence physique, et intellectuelles et morales de l'espece humaine* [Degenerative physical, intellectual and moral traits in human beings]. New York: Arno. (Original work published 1857)

Moreno, J. (1977). *Who shall survive? Foundations of sociometry, group psychotherapy, and sociodrama.* New York: Beacon House. (Original work published 1934)

Moreva, N. (1998). Voprosy muzykalnogo vospitania v psikhologo-pedagogicheskoi teorii [Musical education in the theory of psychology and pedagogy]. *Preschool Education, 2,* 114–116.

Morgan, P. (1896). A case of congenital word-blindness. *British Medical Journal, 2,* 1378.

Moser, G., & Rouquette, M.-L. (2002). Psychology in France: A popular discipline with a strong tradition and a somewhat uncertain future. *European Psychologist, 7,* 238–241.

Mote, F. (1971). *Intellectual foundations of China.* New York: Knopf.

Müller-Hill, B. (1988). *Murderous science: Elimination by scientific selection of Jews, Gypsies, and others, Germany, 1933–1945.* Oxford, UK: Oxford University Press.

Mungello, D. (2008). *Drowning girls in China: Female infanticide since 1650.* New York: Rowman & Littlefield.

Munk, H. (1878). Weitere Mittheilungen zur Physiologie der Grosshirnrinde [Further notes about the physiology of the cerebral cortex]. *Verhandlungen der Physiologischen Gesellschaft zu Berlin,* pp. 162–167.

Munn, N. (1933). *An introduction to animal psychology: The behavior of the rat.* Boston: Houghton-Mifflin.

Münsterberg, H. (1893). The new psychology and Harvard's equipment for teaching it. *Harvard Graduate Magazine, 1*(2), 201–209.

Münsterberg, H. (1913). *Psychology of industrial efficiency.* Boston: Houghton Mifflin.

Münsterberg, H. (1915). *Psychology: General and applied.* New York: Appleton.

Münsterberg, H. (1916). *Tomorrow: Letters to a friend in Germany.* New York: Appleton.

Münsterberg, H. (2009). *On the witness stand: Essays on psychology and crime.* Ann Arbor. Digital Collection, University of Michigan Library. (Original work published 1912)

Murchison, C. (Ed.). (1930). Autobiography of C. Lloyd Morgan. In *History of psychology in autobiography* (Vol. 2, pp. 237–264). Worcester, MA: Clark University Press.

Murray, H. (1943, October). *Analysis of the personality of Adolf Hitler.* http://library.lawschool.cornell.edu/WhatWeHave/SpecialCollections/Donovan/Hitler/Hitler-TOC.cfm

Murray, H. A. (1938). *Explorations in personality.* New York: Oxford University Press.

Murray, K. (1985). Life as fiction. *Journal for the Theory of Social Behaviour, 15*(2), 173–188.

Mursalieva, S. (2003, July 18). Sudba psychoanalyze v Rossii [Psychoanalysis' fate in Russia]. *Novaya Gazeta.* http://www.novayagazeta.ru/data/2002/51/21.html

Myers, D. (2008). *A friendly letter to skeptics and atheists: Musings on why god is good and faith isn't evil.* New York: Jossey-Bass/Wiley.

Myers, K. M., & Davis, M. (2002). Behavioral and neural analysis of extinction: A review. *Neuron, 36,* 567–584.

Nakamura, T., Kiyono, K., Yoshiuchi, K., Nakahara, R., Struzik, Z. R., & Yamamoto, Y. (2007). Universal scaling law in human behavioral organization. *Physical Review Letters, 99*(13), 138103.

Neisser, U. (1976). *Cognition and reality.* New York: Freeman.

Nerlich, B., & Clarke, D. D. (1998). The linguistic repudiation of Wundt. *History of Psychology, 1,* 179–204.

Nevis, E. C. (1983). Cultural assumptions and productivity: The United States and China. *Sloan Management Review, 24,* 17–29.

Nicholson, I. A. M. (1998). Gordon Allport, character, and "culture of personality," 1897–1937. *History of Psychology, 1,* 52–68.

Nicholson, I. A. M. (2000). "A coherent datum of perception": Gordon Allport, Floyd Allport, and the politics of "personality." *Journal of the History of Behavioral Sciences, 36,* 463–470.

Nicolas, S. (2002). *Histoire de la psychologie française* [History of French psychology]. Paris: In Press.

Nicolas, S., & Charvillat, A. (2001). Introducing psychology as an academic discipline in France: Théodule Ribot and the Collège de France (1888–1901). *Journal of the History of Behavioral Sciences, 37,* 143–164.

Nicolas, S., & Ferrand, L. (2002). Henry Beaunis (1830-1921): A psychologist among psychologists. *Journal of Medical Biography, 10,* 1–3.

Nietzsche, F. (1968). *The will to power.* New York: Vintage. (Original work published 1901)

Nolen-Hoeksema, S. (1991). Responses to depression and their effects on the duration of the depressive episode. *Journal of Abnormal Psychology, 100,* 569–582.

Noon, D. H. (2004). Situating gender and professional identity in American child study, 1880–1910. *History of Psychology, 7,* 107–129.

Novak, M. A., & Harlow, H. F. (1975). Social recovery of monkeys isolated for the first years of life. *Developmental Psychology, 11,* 453–465.

Nozdrachev, A. D., & Pastukhov, V. A. (1999). *Genialnyj vzmah fiziologicheskoj mysli* [A genius' sway of physiological thought]. *Priroda,* no. 11. http://vivovoco.rsl.ru/VV/ JOURNAL/NATURE/11_99/SECHENOV.HTM

Oaklander, A. (2008). Mechanisms of pain and itch caused by herpes zoster (shingles). *Journal of Pain,* 9(Suppl. 1), 10–18.

Oppenheimer, S. (2003). *The real Eve: Modern man's journey out of Africa.* New York: Carroll & Graf.

Orbeli, L. (1961). *Izbrannye Trudy* [Selected works]. Vol. I. Moscow: Academy of Sciences.

Osborne, L. (2001, May 6). Case study: Latah. *New York Times,* Section 6, p. 98.

Osipov, V. (1947). *Bekhterev: Vydaushiesia deiatelu Russkoi meditsiny* [Bekhterev: Prominent figures in Russian medicine]. Moscow: GIML.

Pagels, E. (1989). *Adam, Eve, and the serpent.* New York: Vintage.

Pandey, R. E. (1969). Psychology in India. *American Psychologist, 24,* 936–939.

Paranjpe, A. (1998). *Self and identity in modern psychology and Indian thought.* New York: Plenum.

Paris, B. (1994). *Karen Horney: A psychoanalyst's search for self-understanding.* New Haven, CT: Yale University Press.

Parot, F. (2000). Psychology in the human sciences in France, 1920–1940: Ignace Meyerson's historical psychology. *History of Psychology, 3,* 104–121.

Patnoe, S. (1988). *A narrative history of experimental social psychology: The Lewin tradition.* Berlin: Springer-Verlag.

Paulson, G. (2006). Death of a president and his assassin: Errors in their diagnosis and autopsies. *Journal of the History of the Neurosciences, 15*(2), 77–91.

Peng, K., & Nisbett, R. E. (1999). Culture, dialectics, and reasoning about contradiction. *American Psychologist, 54,* 741–754.

Penrose, R. (1989). *Emperor's new mind.* New York: Oxford University Press.

Perls, F. (1968). *Gestalt therapy verbatim.* Moab, UT: Real People Press.

Perls, F., Hefferline, R., & Goodman, P. (1951). *Gestalt therapy: Excitement and growth in the human personality.* New York: Julian.

Perrez, M., & Perring, W. (1997). Psychology in Switzerland. *World Psychology, 3,* 311–324.

Perry, C. (1723). *On the causes and nature of madness.* Cambridge, UK: Cambridge University Library.

Petrina, S. (2001). The "never-to-be-forgotten investigation": Luella W. Cole, Sidney L. Pressey, and mental surveying in Indiana, 1917–1921. *History of Psychology, 4,* 245–271.

Petrovsky, A. (1978). *Psichologicheskaya teorija kollektiva* [The psychological theory of the collective]. Moscow: Academy of Sciences.

Piaget, J. (1960). *The child's conception of the world.* Totowa, NJ: Littlefield, Adams. (Original work published 1926)

Pick, D. (1989). *Faces of degeneration: A European disorder, c.1848–c.1918.* New York: Cambridge University Press.

Pickren, W., & Dewsbury, D. (2002). Introduction: Methods of historical inquiry. In W. Pickren & D. Dewsbury (Eds.), *Evolving perspectives on the history of psychology* (pp. 21–44). Washington DC: American Psychological Association.

Pickren, W. E. (2003). An elusive honor: Psychology, behavior, and the Nobel Prize. *American Psychologist, 58,* 721–722.

Pinel, P. (2007). *A treatise on insanity.* Whitefish, MT: Kessinger Publishers. (Original work published 1801)

Pollak, S. D. (2003). Experience-dependent affective learning and risk for psychopathology in children. *Annals of the New York Academy of Sciences, 1008,* 102–111.

Pollak, S. D. (2005). Early adversity and the mechanisms of plasticity: Integrating affective neuroscience with developmental approaches to psychopathology. *Development and Psychopathology, 17,* 735–752.

Pols, H. (2002). Between the laboratory and life: Child development research in Toronto, 1919–1956. *History of Psychology, 5,* 135–162.

Popper, K. (1992). *The logic of scientific discovery.* New York: Routledge. (Original work published 1950)

Powell, L. H., Shahabi, L., & Thoresen, C. E. (2003). Religion and spirituality: Linkages to physical health. *American Psychologist, 58,* 36–52.

Prince, M. (2007). *The dissociation of a personality.* Whitefish, MT: Kessinger Publishers. (Original work published 1905)

Prinz, J. (2008). *The emotional construction of morals.* New York: Oxford University Press.

Quas, J. A., Malloy, L., Goodman, G. S., Melinder, A., Schaaf, J., & D'Mello, M. (2007). Developmental differences in the effects of repeated interviews and interviewer bias on young children's false reports. *Developmental Psychology, 43,* 823–837.

Quen, J. (1983). Psychiatry and the law: Historical relevance to today. In L. Freedman (Ed.), *By reason of insanity. Essays on the psychiatry and the law.* Wilmington, DE: Scholarly Resources.

Quinn, S. (2007). How southern New England became magnetic north: The acceptance of animal magnetism. *History of Psychology, 10,* 231–248.

Rafter, N. (2003, November). *Cesare Lombroso and the origins of criminology.* Paper prepared for annual meeting of the American Society of Criminology, Denver, CO.

Rao, V. (2000). Depression in Indian History. *Journal of the Indian Medical Association, 98*(5), 219–23.

Ray, O. (2004). How the mind hurts and heals the body. *American Psychologist, 59,* 29–40.

Reisenzein, R., & Schönpflug, W. (1992). Stumpf's cognitive-evaluative theory of emotion. *American Psychologist, 47,* 34–45.

Remen, R. N. (1996). *Kitchen table wisdom: Stories that heal.* New York: Riverhead Books.

Resick, P. (2001). *Stress and trauma: Clinical psychology, a modular course.* London: Psychology Press.

Reynolds, D. K. (1983). *Naikan psychotherapy.* Chicago: University of Chicago Press.

Richardson, J. (2003). Howard Andrew Knox and the origins of performance testing on Ellis Island, 1912–1916. *History of Psychology, 6,* 143–170.

Ridley, M. (1998). *The origins of virtue: Human instincts and the evolution of cooperation.* New York: Penguin.

Riger, S. (2002). Epistemological debates, feminist voices: Science, social values, and the study of women. In W. Pickren & D. Dewsbury (Eds.), *Evolving perspectives on the history of psychology* (pp. 21–44). Washington, DC: American Psychological Association.

Riley, M. A., Baker, A. A., Schmit, J. M., & Weaver, E. (2005). Effects of visual and auditory short-term memory tasks on the spatiotemporal dynamics and variability of postural sway. *Journal of Motor Behavior, 37,* 311–324.

Riley, M. A., & Turvey, M. T. (2002). Variability and determinism in motor behavior. *Journal of Motor Behavior, 34,* 99–125.

Rilling, M. (2000). John Watson's paradoxical struggle to explain Freud. *American Psychologist, 55,* 301–312.

Ringer, F. (1969). *The decline of the German mandarins: The German academic community, 1890–1933.* Cambridge, MA: Harvard University Press.

Ritvo, L. R. (1990). *Darwin's influence on Freud: A tale of two sciences.* New Haven, CT: Yale University Press.

Robinson, D. N. (1986). *An intellectual history of psychology.* Madison: University of Wisconsin Press.

Rogers, C. (1951). *Client-centered therapy.* Boston: Houghton-Mifflin.

Rogers, C. (1959). The essence of psychotherapy: A client-centered view. *Annals of Psychotherapy, 1,* 51–57.

Rogers, C. (1961). *On becoming a person: A therapist's view of psychotherapy.* Boston: Houghton-Mifflin.

Rogler, L. H. (2002). Historical generations and psychology: The case of the Great Depression and World War II. *American Psychologist, 57,* 1013–1023.

Roland, A. (2006). Across civilizations: Psychoanalytic therapy with Asians and Asian Americans. *Psychotherapy: Theory, Research, Practice, Training, 43,* 454–463.

Rolett, B. (1999). Psychology in Austria. *European Psychologist, 4,* 115–118.

Romanes, G. J. (1882). *Animal intelligence.* Whitefish, MT: Kessinger.

Rosenberg, C. (1989). *The trial of the assassin Guiteau: Psychiatry and the law in the gilded age.* Chicago: University of Chicago Press.

Ross, D. (1972). *G. Stanley Hall: The psychologist as prophet.* Chicago: University of Chicago Press.

Rousseau, J.-J. (1997). *The social contract and other later political writings.* Cambridge, UK: Cambridge University Press. (Original work published 1762)

Routh, D. (1996). Lightner Witmer and the first 100 years of clinical psychology. *American Psychologist, 51,* 244–247.

Rozin, P. (2007). Exploring the landscape of modern academic psychology: Finding and filling the holes. *American Psychologist, 62,* 754–766.

Rozin, P., Haidt, J., & McCauley, C. R. (1993). Disgust. In M. Lewis & J. Haviland (Eds.), *Handbook of emotions* (pp. 575–594). New York: Guilford.

Rozin, P., & Fallon, A. (1987). A perspective on disgust. *Psychological Review, 94*(1), 23–41.

Rudolph, F. (1990). *The American college and university.* Athens: University of Georgia Press.

Rush, B. (1979). *Diseases of the mind.* Bethesda, MD: The Classics of Medicine Library. (Original work published 1812)

Sahakian, W. (1968). *History of psychology: A source book in systematic psychology.* Itasca, IL: Peacock.

Sampson, E. (2000). Reinterpreting individualism and collectivism: Their religious roots and monologic versus dialogic person-other relationship. *American Psychologist, 55,* 1425–1432.

Sandler, J. (1985). *The analysis of defense: The ego and the mechanisms of defense revisited.* New York: International Universities Press.

Sato, K., & Graham, C. H. (1954). Psychology in Japan. *Psychological Bulletin, 51,* 443–464.

Sawyer, T. (2000). Francis Cecil Sumner: His views and influence on African American higher education. *History of Psychology, 3,* 122–141.

Scarborough, J. (1988). Galen Redivivus: An essay review. *Journal of the History of Medicine and Allied Sciences, 43,* 313–321.

Scarborough, E., & Furumoto, L. (1987). *Untold lives: The first generation of American women psychologists.* New York: Columbia University Press.

Schioldann, J. A. (2001). *In commemoration of the centenary of the death of Carl Lange. The Lange theory of "periodical depressions": A landmark in the history of lithium therapy.* Burnside, Australia: Adelaide Academic Press.

Schmit, D. (2005). Re-visioning antebellum American psychology: The dissemination of mesmerism, 1836–1854. *History of Psychology, 8,* 403–434.

Schniermann, A. (1930). Bekhterev's reflexological school. In C. Murchinson (Ed.), *Psychologies of the 1930s* (pp. 221–242). Worchester, MA: Clark University Press.

Scholl, B. J. (2005). Innateness and (Bayesian) visual perception: Reconciling nativism and development. In P. Carruthers, S. Laurence, & S. Stich (Eds.), *The innate mind: Structure and contents* (pp. 34–52). Oxford, UK: Oxford University Press.

Schwartz, S. H. (1994). Are there universal values in the structure and contents of human values? *Journal of Social Issues, 50,* 19–45.

Schwartz, J. (1997). *Brain lock: Free yourself from obsessive-compulsive behavior.* New York: Harper.

Scott, W. D. (1908). And interpretation of the psychoanalytic method in psychotherapy with a report on a case so treated. *Journal of Abnormal Psychology, 3,* 371–379.

Scott, W. D. (2009). *The psychology of advertising.* General Books LLC. (Original work published 1908)

Scott, W. D. (2010). *The theory of advertising.* Berlin: Nabu Press. (Original work published 1903)

Seal, K. H., Bertenthal, D., Miner, C. R., Sen, S., & Marmar, C. (2007). Bringing the war back home: Mental health disorders among 103,788 US veterans returning from Iraq and Afghanistan seen at Department of Veterans Affairs facilities. *Archives of Internal Medicine, 167,* 476–482.

Searle, J. (1983). *Intentionality.* Cambridge, UK: Cambridge University Press.

Searle, J. (1992). *The rediscovery of the mind.* Cambridge, MA: MIT Press.

Searle, J. (1998). *The mystery of consciousness.* London: Granta Publications.

Sears, R. R. (1943). *Survey of objective studies of psychoanalytic concept.* New York: Social Science Research Council.

Sechenov, I. M. (1965). *Reflexes of the brain.* Cambridge, MA: MIT Press. (Original work published 1876)

Sechenov, I. M. (2004). *Sechenov I.M. Biographia. Glavnye Trudy.* Moscow: Dean [Sechenov, I.M. Biography. Major Works], 479-584. (Original work published 1873)

Seitelberger, F. (1997). Theodor Meynert (1833–1892), pioneer and visionary of brain research. *Journal of the History of the Neurosciences, 6,* 264–274.

Seligman, M. E. P., Rashid, T., & Parks, A. C. (2006). Positive psychotherapy. *American Psychologist, 61,* 774–788.

Shapiro, E. S. (1992). *A time for healing: American Jewry since World War II.* Baltimore: Johns Hopkins University Press.

Shedrovitsky, P. (2009). Lev ygotsky I sovremennaja pedagogicheskaya antropologiya [Lev Vygotsky and modern pedagogical anthropology]. *Russian Archipelago.* http://www.archipelag.ru/authors/shedrovicky_ petr/? library=1308

Sherif, M. (1936). *The psychology of social norms.* New York: Harper & Brothers.

Shiraev, E., & Levy, D. (2009). *Cross-cultural psychology: Critical thinking and contemporary applications.* Boston: Pearson.

Shlapentokh, V. (2004). *An autobiographical narration of the role of fear and friendship in the Soviet Union.* Lewiston, NY: Edwin Mellen.

Shnol, S. E. (1997). *Genii I Zlodei Rossijskij nauki* [Geniuses and villains of Russian science]. http://www.cellbiol.ru

Shorter, E. (1997). *A history of psychiatry.* New York: John Wiley.

Sidis, B. (1907). *The psychology of suggestion.* New York: Appleton.

Siegel, P. F. (2003). Dissociation and the question of history: "What, precisely, are the facts?" *Psychoanalytic Psychology, 20,* 67–83.

Siegler, R. S. (1992). The other Alfred Binet. *Developmental Psychology, 28,* 179–190.

Siegler, R. S. (1996). *Emerging minds: The process of change in children's thinking.* New York: Oxford University Press.

Simon, B. (1978). *Mind and madness in ancient Greece: The classical roots of modern psychiatry.* Ithaca, NY: Cornell University Press.

Simonton, D. K. (1994). *Greatness: Who makes history and why.* New York: Guilford.

Singh, M. (2005). *Meeting basic learning needs in the informal sector: Integrating education and training for decent work, empowerment and citizenship.* Heidelberg, Germany: UIE/UNEVOC/ Springer.

Skinner, B. F. (1938). *The behavior of organisms.* New York: Appleton-Century-Crofts.

Skinner, B. F. (1957). *Verbal behavior.* New York: Copley.

Skinner, B. F. (1960). Pigeons in a pelican. *American Psychologist, 15,* 28–57.

Skinner, B. F. (1965). *Science of human behavior.* New York: Free Press.

Skinner, B. F. (1971). *Beyond freedom and dignity.* New York: Bantam Vintage.

Skinner, B. F. (2005). *Walden two.* Indianapolis: Hackett. (Original work published 1948)

Slife, B. (1993). *Time and psychological explanation.* New York: State University of New York Press.

Smart, N. (2001). *World philosophies.* New York: Routledge.

Smith, M. B. (1978). Psychology and values. *Journal of Social Issues, 34,* 181–199.

Smith, M. B. (1991). *Values, self, and society: Toward a humanist social psychology.* New Brunswick, NJ: Transaction.

Smith, R. (1997). *The Norton history of the human sciences.* New York: Norton.

Sokal, M. M. (1984). The Gestalt psychologists in behaviorist America. *American Historical Review, 89,* 1240–1263.

Sokal, M. M. (1990). G. Stanley Hall and they institutional character of psychology at Clark, 1889–1920. *Journal of the History of Behavioral Sciences, 26,* 114–124.

Sokal, M. M. (1992). Origins and early years of the American Psychological Association, 1890–1906. *American Psychologist, 47,* 111–122.

Spearman, C. (1904). General intelligence, objectively determined and measured. *American Journal of Psychology, 15,* 268–285.

Spearman, C. E. (1927). *The abilities of man* (6th ed.). London: Macmillan.

Spencer, H. (1891). *Essays scientific, political & speculative.* London: Williams and Norgate. (Original work published 1852)

Sperry, R. (1961). Cerebral organization and behavior. *Science, 133,* 1749–1757.

Spielvogel, J. J. (2006). *Western civilization.* New York: Wadsworth.

Spinoza, B. (1985). *The collected works of Spinoza* (Vol. I; E. Curley, Ed. & Trans.). Princeton, NJ: Princeton University Press. (Original work published 1677)

Spurlock, J. C. (2002). From reassurance to irrelevance: Adolescent psychology and homosexuality in America. *History of Psychology, 5,* 38–51.

Staddon, J. (2001). *The new behaviorism: mind, mechanism, and society.* London: Taylor & Francis.

Stern, W. (1903). Angewandte Psychologie [Applied psychology]. *Beiträge zur Psychologie der Aussage, 1,* 4–45.

Starcevic, V. (1999). Neurosthenia: Cross-cultural and conceptual issues pertaining to chronic fatigue syndrome. *General Hospital Psychiatry, 21*(4), 249–255.

Sternberg, R. (2004). Why smart people can be so foolish. *European Psychologist, 9,* 145–150.

Sternberg, R. (2007). *Wisdom, intelligence, and creativity synthesized.* New York: Cambridge University Press.

Sternberg, R. J., & Grigorenko, E. L. (2001). Unified psychology. *American Psychologist, 56,* 1069–1079.

Strickland, L. H. (1997). "Who? V. M. Bekhterev? A field theorist?" *SAFT Newsletter, 13,* 1, 2–3.

Strickland, L. H. (2001). Introduction. In L. Strickland, *L. Bekhterev's collective reflexology: The complete edition* (E. Lockwood & A. Lockwood, Trans., pp. 15–19). New Brunswick, NJ: Transaction.

Stumpf, C. (1907). Über Gefühlsempfindungen [On affective sensations]. *Zeitschrift für Psychologie und Physiologie der Sinnesorgane, 44,* 1–49.

Sumner, F. C. (1920). Psychoanalysis of Freud and Adler. *Pedagogical Seminary, 29,* 139–168.

Sutton, J. (1998). *Philosophy and memory traces: Descartes to connectionism.* New York: Cambridge University Press.

Synnott, M. G. (1986). Anti-Semitism and American universities: Did quotas follow the Jews? In D. A. Gerber (Ed.), *Anti-Semitism in American history* (pp. 233–171). Urbana: University of Illinois Press.

Taft, R., & Day, R. H. (1988). Psychology in Australia. *Annual Review of Psychology, 39,* 375–400.

Taine, H. (1870). *De l'intelligence* [On intelligence] (Vols. 1–2). Paris: Hachette.

Tangney, J. P., & Dearing, R. L. (2003). *Shame and guilt: Emotions and social behavior.* New York: Guilford.

Tarde, G. (1903). *The laws of imitation.* New York: Holt.

Taves, A. (1999). *Fits, trances, and visions: Experiencing religion and explaining experience from Wesley to James.* Princeton, NJ: Princeton University Press.

Taylor, F. W. (1911). *The principles of scientific management.* New York: Harper Bros.

Tellenbach, H. (1980). *Melancholy.* Pittsburgh: Duquesne University Press.

Tenenbaum, J. B., Griffiths, T. L., & Kemp, C. (2006). Theory-based Bayesian models of inductive learning and reasoning. *Trends in Cognitive Sciences, 10,* 309–318.

Thompson, H. T. (1903). *The mental traits of sex: An experimental investigation of the normal mind in men and women.* Chicago: University of Chicago Press.

Thorndike, E. L. (1911). *Animal intelligence: Experimental studies.* New York: Macmillan.

Thorndike, E. L. (1935). The paradox of science. *Proceedings of the American Philosophical Society, 75,* 287–294.

Thurstone, E. L. (1938). *Primary mental abilities.* Chicago: University of Chicago Press.

Titchener, E. B. (1898). The postulates of a structural psychology. *Philosophical Review, 7,* 449–465.

Titchener, E. B. (1914). On "psychology as the behaviorist views it." *Proceedings of the American Philosophical Society, 53,* 1–17.

Tolman, E. (1932). *Purposive behavior in animals and men.* New York: The Century Company.

Tolman, E. C. (1942). *Drives beyond war.* New York: Appleton.

Tolman, E. C. (1948). Cognitive maps in rats and men. *Psychological Review, 55,* 189–208.

Tolman v. Underhill, 39 C 2d, 709–13 (1952).

Tori, C. D., & Bilmes, M. (2002). Multiculturalism and psychoanalytic psychology: The validation of a defense mechanisms measure in an Asian population. *Psychoanalytic Psychology, 19,* 701–721.

Trahair, R. (1984). *The humanist temper: The life and work of Elton Mayo.* New Brunswick, NJ: Transaction.

Triplett, N. (1898). Dynamogenic factors in peacemaking and competition. *American Journal of Psychology, 9,* 507–533.

Truog, R. D., & Miller, F. G. (2008). The dead donor rule and organ transplantation. *New England Journal of Medicine, 359,* 674–675.

Tryon, W. W. (2002). Contributions of connectionism to postmodern psychology. *American Psychologist, 57,* 455–456.

Tu, W. M. (1979). *Humanity and self-cultivation: Essays in Confucian thought.* Berkeley, CA: Asian Humanities Press.

Turing, A. (1950). Computing machinery and intelligence. *Mind, 50,* 433–460.

Turner, T. (1997, October). Ethnicity and psychiatry. *The Practitioner,* pp. 612–615.

Uyeno, Y. (1924). Present status of industrial psychology in Japan. *Psychological Bulletin, 21,* 225–226.

Vaihinger, H. (1952). *The philosophy of "as if."* London: Routledge. (Original work published 1924)

Vaill, P. (2007). F. J. Roethlisberger and the elusive phenomena of organizational behavior. *Journal of Management Education, 31,* 321–338.

van Campen, C. (1997). Early abstract art and experimental Gestalt psychology. *Leonardo, 30,* 133–136.

Vande Kemp, H. (1980). Origin and evolution of the term psychology: Addenda. *American Psychologist, 35,* 774.

van Strien, P. (1998). Early applied psychology between essentialism and pragmatism: The dynamics of theory, tools, and clients. *History of Psychology, 1,* 205–234.

Vartanian, A. (1960). *L'Homme machine: A study in the origins of an idea.* Princeton, NJ: Princeton University Press.

Veenhoven, R. (2008). Sociological theories of subjective well-being. In M. Eid & R. Larsen (Eds.), *The science of subjective well-being: A tribute to Ed Diener* (pp. 44–61). New York: Guilford.

Vernon, P. (1969). *Intelligence and cultural environment.* London: Methuen.

Vich, M. A. (1988). Some historical sources of the term "transpersonal." *Journal of Transpersonal Psychology, 20,* 107–110.

von Brücke, E. W. (1866). *Die Physiologie der Farben für die Zwecke der Kunstgewerbe* [The physiology of colors for the purposes of arts]. Leipzig: S. Hirzel.

von Mayrhauser, R. (2002). The mental testing community and validity: A prehistory. *American Psychologist, 47,* 244–253.

Vygotsky, L. (1933, April 20). *Kriticheskie vozrasta* [Critical periods]. Leningrad: Leningrad Pedagogical Institute's Archive.

Vygotsky, L. (2005a). Development of higher psychological functions. In *Psychology of the individual's development.* Moscow: Smysl. (Original work published 1931)

Vygotsky, L. (2005b). Myshlenie i rech [Thought and language]. In *Psychology of the individual's development.* Moscow: Smysl. (Original work published 1934)

Vygotsky, L., & Luria, I. (2005). Orudie I znak v razvitii regenka [Tool and sign in child's development]. In *Psychology of the individual's development.* Moscow: Smysl. (Original work published 1930)

Wallerstein, R. (1988). One psychoanalysis or many? *International Journal of Psychoanalysis, 69,* 5–21.

Wallin, J. E. W. (1955). *The education of mentally handicapped children.* Boston: Houghton Mifflin. (Original work published 1924)

Wampold, B. E., & Bhati, K. S. (2004). Attending to the omissions: A historical examination of evidence-based practice movements. *Professional Psychology: Research and Practice, 35,* 563–570.

Watson, J. (1913). Psychology as the behaviorist views it. *Psychological Review, 20,* 158–177.

Watson, J. (1929). Should a child have more than one mother? *Liberty Magazine,* pp. 31–35.

Watson, J., & Rayner, R. (1920). Conditioned emotional responses. *Journal of Experimental Psychology, 3,* 1–14.

Watson, J. B. (1916). Behavior and the concept of mental disease. *Journal of Philosophy, Psychology, and Scientific Methods, 13,* 589–597.

Watson, J. B. (1919). *Psychology from a standpoint of a behaviorist.* Philadelphia: Lippincott.

Watson, J. B. (1922). What cigarette are you smoking and why? *J. Walter Thompson News Bulletin, 88,* 1–17.

Watson, J. B. (1927). The myth of the unconscious. *Harpers, 155,* 214–218.

Weber, M. (2003). *The Protestant ethic and the spirit of capitalism.* Mineola, NY: Dover. (Original work published 1904)

Weininger, O. (2009). *Sex and character.* Charleston, SC: BiblioLife. (Original work published 1903)

Weiskrantz, L. (1956). Behavioral changes associated with ablation of the amygdaloid complex in monkeys. *Journal of Comparative and Physiological Psychology, 49,* 381–391.

Weiss, S. F. (1987). *Race hygiene and national efficiency: The eugenics of Wilhelm Schallmayer.* Berkeley: University of California Press.

Weissberg, R., Kumpfer, K., & Seligman, M. (2003). Prevention that works for children. *American Psychologist, 48,* 425–432

Weizenbaum, J. (1976). *Computer power and human reason.* London: Freeman.

Welch, H. (1957). *Taoism: The parting of the way.* Boston: Beacon.

Wellmann, K. A. (1992). *La Mettrie: Medicine, philosophy, and enlightenment.* Durham, NC: Duke University Press.

Wendt, A. (2006). Social theory as Cartesian science: An auto-critique from a quantum perspective. In S. Guzzini & A. Leander (Eds.), *Constructivism and international relations* (pp. 181–219). London: Routledge.

Wertheimer, M. (1938). Gestalt theory. In W. Ellis (Ed.), *A source book of Gestalt psychology.* London: K. Paul, Trench, Trubner. (Original work published 1925)

Wertheimer, M. (1961). Experimental studies on the seeing of motion. In T. Shipley (Ed.), *Classics in psychology* (pp. 1032–1065). New York: Philosophical Library. (Original work published 1912)

What America thought in 1937: Men and machines compile public opinion. *Life,* Vol. 4, No 1, January 3, 1938.

Whitaker, H. A., & Etlinger, S. C. (1993). Theodor Meynert's contribution to classical 19th century aphasia studies. *Brain and Language, 45,* 560–571.

White, S. (2000). Conceptual foundations of IQ testing. *Psychology, Public Policy, and Law, 6*(1), 33–43.

Whittaker, J. (1970). Psychology in China: A brief survey. *American Psychologist, 25,* 757–759.

Whyte, W. F. (1968). Elton Mayo. *International Encyclopedia of the Social Sciences, 10,* 82–83.

Williams, E. H. (1914, Sunday February 8). Murder and insanity increasing among lower class because they have taken to "sniffing" since being deprived of whisky by Prohibition. *The New York Times.*

Wilson, D. (1975). *Stranger and traveler.* Boston: Little, Brown.

Wilson, D. (2003). British female academics and comparative psychology: Attempts to establish a research niche in the early 20th century. *History of Psychology, 6,* 89–109.

Winks, R. W., & Neuberger, J. (2005). *Europe and the making of modernity: 1815–1914.* New York: Oxford University Press.

Winslow, L. S. F. (1880). Fasting and feeding: A detailed account of recorded instances of unusual abstinence from food, and of cases illustrating inordinate appetite. *Journal of Psychological Medicine and Mental Pathology, 6,* 253–299.

Winston, A. (1998). The defects of his race: E. G. Boring and anti-Semitism in American psychology, 1923–1953. *History of Psychology, 1,* 27–51.

Witmer, L. (1896). Practical work in psychology. *Pediatrics, 2,* 462–471.

Witmer, L. (1907a). Clinical psychology. *Psychological Clinic, 1,* 1–9.

Witmer, L. (1907b). A case of chronic bad spelling–Amnesia visualis verbalis, due to arrest of post-natal development. *Psychological Clinic, 1,* 53–64.

Witmer, L. (1915). *The Nearing case.* New York: Huebsch.

Worcester, E., McComb, S., & Coriat, I. (2003). *Religion and medicine: The moral control of nervous disorders.* Whitefish, MT: Kessinger Publishing. (Original work published 1908)

Wozniak, R. H. (1992). *Mind and body: René Descartes to William James.* Bethesda, MD, and Washington, DC: National Library of Medicine and American Psychological Association.

Wozniak, R. H. (1993a). Jacques Loeb, comparative physiology of the brain, and comparative psychology. In J. Loeb, *Comparative physiology of the brain and comparative psychology.* London: Routledge Thoemmes.

Wozniak, R. H. (1993b). Theoretical roots of early behaviorism: Functionalism, the critique of introspection, and the nature and evolution of consciousness. In R. H. Wozniak (Ed.), *The theoretical roots of early behaviorism: Functionalism, the critique of introspection, and the nature and evolution of consciousness* (pp. ix–xiii). London: Routledge/Thoemmes Press.

Wozniak, R. H. (1997). *Floyd Henry Allport and the social psychology.* http://www.brynmawr.edu/Acads/Psych/rwozniak/allport.html

Wright, M. J. (2002). Flashbacks in the history of psychology in Canada: Some early "headline" makers. *Canadian Psychology, 43,* 21–34.

Wundt, W. (1904). *Principles of physiological psychology* (E. B. Titchener, Trans.). New York: Macmillan.

Wundt, W. (1916). *Elements of folk psychology: Outlines of a psychological history of the development of mankind* (E. L. Schaub, Trans.). New York: Macmillan.

Yakunin, V. (2001). *Istoriya Psikhilogii* [A history of psychology]. St. Petersburg, Russia: Mikhailov.

Yanchar, S., & Slife, B. (1997). Pursuing unity in a fragmented psychology: Problems and prospects. *Review of General Psychology, 1,* 235–255.

Yaroshevsky, G. (1996). *Istoria Psikhologii* [A history of psychology]. Moscow: Nauka.

Yates, F. A. (1966). *The art of memory.* Middlesex, UK: Penguin.

Yerkes, R. M. (1910). Psychology in its relations to biology. *Journal of Philosophy, Psychology and Scientific Methods, 7,* 113–124.

Yerkes, R. M. (1921). *Psychological examining in the United States Army: Memoirs of the National Academy of Sciences* (Vol. XV). Washington, DC: Government Printing Office.

Yew, E. (1980). Medical inspection of immigrants at Ellis Island, 1891–1924. *Bulletin of the New York Academy of Medicine, 56,* 488–510.

Young, R. K. (1985). Ebbinghaus: Some consequences. *Journal of Experimental Psychology: Learning, Memory, and Cognition, 11,* 491–495.

Zaidi, S. M. H. (1959). Pakistan psychology. *American Psychologist, 14,* 532–536.

Zajonc, R. B. (1965). Social facilitation. *Science, 149,* 269–274.

Zeigarnik, B. (1988). An interview given to Yaroshevsky, M. From conversations with B. Zeigarnik [in Russian]. http://www.voppsy.ru/issues/1988/883/883172.htm

Zenderland, L. (1998). *Measuring minds: Henry Herbert Goddard and the origins of American intelligence testing.* New York: Cambridge University Press.

Zilboorg, G. (1941). *A history of medical psychology.* New York: Norton.

Zimbardo, P. (2008). *The Lucifer effect: Understanding how good people turn evil.* New York: Random House.

Glossary

Agility of the nervous system In Pavlov's theory, refers to the quickness of the activation of excitement or the quickness of change between the two states of inhibition and excitement.

Analysant A person undergoing psychoanalysis; also, a therapeutic patient or client.

Analytical psychology The term used by Jung to distinguish his views from Freud's.

Anorexia First described in 1874 (William Gull), symptoms of deliberate weight loss through self-starvation.

Anthropomorphism A type of description or scientific approach to portray animal behavior in human terms.

Apperception The process of organizing mental elements together; the active (selective and constructive) process of attention.

Archetypes The content of the collective unconscious, which consists of images of the primordial (elemental, ancient) character. People, according to Jung, share similar ancestral experiences. These archetypes manifested in three universal ways: dreams, fantasies, and delusions.

Army Alpha and Army Beta Tests the U.S. Army used for recruits during World War I; the Alpha test was designed for literate groups; the Beta test was used with illiterate, poor English speakers, non-English speakers, or those who failed the Alpha test.

Artificial intelligence In general terms, this is the study and design of intelligent machines. In the context of cognitive neuroscience, artificial intelligence is the study and creation of systems that perceive their environment and make decisions to maximize success.

Assimilation and accommodation In Piaget's system, the two sides of the process of adaptation or learning. Assimilation is adopting operations with new objects into old mind patterns. Accommodation is modifying one's mental structures to fit the new demands of the environment.

Atomism The notion that matter is made up of small, indivisible particles.

Bad-me, good-me, and not-me In Sullivan's system, various types of awareness related to self seen from different angles.

Balance of the nervous system Refers to equilibrium between excitement and inhibition within the nervous system.

Basic anxiety In Karen Horney's system, feelings of loneliness, hopelessness, and counterhostility (emotional responses to hostile situations).

Caritas and **cupiditas** The key concepts in the teaching of Augustine referring to "good" and "evil" types of will possessed by individuals.

Castration anxiety The irrational fear in men of loss of the genitals.

Clairvoyance A term originated in the French language meaning "clear seeing"; this was the supposed extrasensory power of an individual, that is, the power to see or feel objects or events that could be perceived by the senses or measured objectively.

Clinical-pathological method A procedure based on comparing clinical observations of a patient's abnormal symptoms with the reliable data about brain pathology, most likely obtained during the autopsy on this patient's brain.

Cognitive map In Tolman's system, internal processing by which an individual can code, store, recall, and decode information about particular elements of this person's experience.

Cognitive neuroscience An academic field that examines the brain mechanisms supporting mental functions.

Cognitive psychology The scientific study of human mental processes and their role in thinking, emotions, and behavior.

Cognitive revolution The term referring to the shift within psychology from being primarily behavioral to being increasingly cognitive.

Cognitive science An interdisciplinary field that involves studies in cognitive neuroscience, computer science, philosophy, and linguistics, among other fields.

Collective reflexology In Bekhterev's theory, the study of the emergence, development, and behavior of groups that display their collective activity in unity.

Collective unconscious In Jung's theory, an impersonal layer in the human psyche, different from the individual unconscious, inherited and shared with other members of the species.

Compensation In Adler's vocabulary, attempts to overcome the discomfort and negative experiences caused by their inferiority.

Conditioned reflexes In Pavlov's theory, the reflexes that appear only under certain conditions.

Creationist approach (also called **creationism**) The view that explains the creation of the universe and of all living organisms as an act of God.

Death wish (often labeled as death instinct or death drive) The repressed instinctual tendencies that lead toward destruction.

Defense mechanisms In Anna Freud's system, specific unconscious structures that enable an individual to avoid awareness of anxiety-arousing issues.

Deism The belief that God has created the universe but abandoned earthly affairs afterward.

Degeneration A term referring to a generational regress in physical and psychological traits.

Dualism The philosophical tradition that claimed the existence of "parallel" spiritual and material realities.

Ego The component of the psyche that makes compromises between the id and the environment and is guided by the reality principle. During an individual's development, the ego starts within the id but gradually changes to accept reason.

Ego psychology A branch of psychoanalysis focusing on a wide variety of facts related to a person's interaction with the social environment.

Emanation theory The view according to which objects release substance that makes an impression on human senses thus evoking sensation then thought.

Emmanuel Church Healing Movement A social movement and therapeutic practice based on psychological assessment and spiritual advice.

Empiricism The scientific belief that experience, especially sensory processes, is the main source of knowledge.

Epistemology The branch of philosophy that studies the nature of knowledge, its foundations, extent, and validity—were result of observation and speculation.

Eros Or life instinct, all the tendencies that strive toward the integration of living substance. The psychic energy of this instinct was often called libido in psychoanalysis.

Ethnocentrism The tendency—sometimes deliberate but often unintentional—to view psychological knowledge from one's own national or ethnic position.

Eugenics A theory proposing the ways of societal improvement by improving people's hereditary features.

Evolutionary psychology A discipline attempting to explore the ways in which complex evolutionary factors affect behavior and experience.

Existential psychology Is an eclectic and diverse field of studies embracing the idea of the exceptionality of human existence, the importance of individual free choice and independent will, and the necessity to consider each and every person as a unique entity.

Existential therapy The therapeutic method based on the assumption that we, as human beings, make our own choices and should assume full responsibility for the outcomes of our behavior and our own feelings.

Experimental introspection The method according to which the researcher had to carefully observe his own experience as a response to a physical stimulus delivered in laboratory surroundings.

Feebleminded children The term used in early 20th century to describe serious developmental problems identified today as mental retardation.

Force field analysis A method introduced by Kurt Lewin to look at the factors or forces influencing an individual's behavior in a particular situation. Every act can be viewed as an interplay of forces either moving an individual toward a goal (helping forces) or blocking his or her movement toward a goal (hindering forces).

Forensic psychology A discipline that applies psychological principles to the criminal justice system.

Founding principles of behaviorism In Watson's theory, stimulus and response (behavior is a set of responses to specific signals), habit formation (behavioral responses become useful and retained), and habit integration (simple reactions develop in complex acts).

Free associations The method of free association is labeled based on an apparently inaccurate translation from German, in which the term has the meaning of "free occurrences," as if the patient reproduces thoughts and images that "occur" in her freely. The patient is asked to make a chain of associations, starting from a word suggested by the therapist and then naming anything that comes to mind.

Functionalism A theoretical and methodological view focusing on the dynamic purposes of psychological experience rather than on its structure; functionalism claimed that an individual's mental states are interrelated and influenced by ever-changing behavior within a complex environment.

Genetic epistemology A field that attempts to explain knowledge (scientific knowledge in particular) from the standpoint of knowledge's history.

Gestalt laws Several general principles of Gestalt theory, referring to perceptual functioning.

Gestalt therapy A therapeutic method, the initial assumptions of which were based on the holistic principles of Gestalt psychology.

Hawthorne effect Any positive effect of properly organized work relationships on workers' productivity and satisfaction.

Hawthorne experiment A series of experiments initially designed to investigate the effects of several improved working conditions on factory productivity. Later these experiments focused on human interaction within the work group. The experiments began in 1924. In collaboration with the National Research Council, the Western Electric Company conducted research at its Hawthorne manufacturing plant in Chicago.

Highest nervous activity The term in Pavlov's theory to describe physiological activities of the brain's cortex; Pavlov commonly called it *behavior.*

Historiography The study of the ways by which people obtain and disseminate historical knowledge.

Hodological space A finitely structured space; its parts are composed of certain regions; direction and distance within this space are defined as paths.

Holism The concept holding that everything is interconnected in the world and body.

Holistic health movement A multidisciplinary field or approach focusing on the fundamental assumption that physical, mental, and spiritual factors contributing to illness are interconnected and equally important in treatment.

Homology The theory that all animals have similar organs and differ only in complexity.

Hospice care A complex medical and psychological system of help focusing on palliative and other humane principles of care.

Humanism The view emphasizing the uniqueness of the subjective side of the individual: the sense of freedom, beauty, and moral responsibility.

Hylomorphism From the Greek words matter (*hulê*) and form (*morphê*), the view that recognized the existence of two fundamental principles: one potential, that is, primary matter, and one actual, that is, substantial form.

Hypnology The study of causes and effects of nervous sleep.

Hysteria A term to describe a wide range of psychological and physical complaints without an identifiable anatomical defect of physiological malady.

Id The component of the psyche that contains inborn biological drives (the death wish and life instinct); the id seeks immediate gratification of its impulses.

Idealism The fundamental view suggesting that the facts of mental life can be sufficiently explained in mental terms.

Ideological (value-based) knowledge A cohesive and stable set of beliefs about the world, the nature of good and evil, right and wrong, and the purpose of human life—all based on a certain organizing principal or central idea.

Individuation The process of a person's psychological growth and awareness of his or her own individuality.

Induction The process, according to Pavlov, of coinfluence between excitement and inhibition.

Insight The ability of seeing into a situation, understanding its "inner" nature; a sudden, intuitive perception or grasping of useful relations in a given situation.

Instrumentalism A philosophical view suggesting that any human action is rational so long as it is justified by the goal an individual pursues.

Iowa Child Welfare Station Founded in 1917, it was one of the first research institutions designed to study the behavior and skills of ordinary children under everyday conditions.

Isomorphism In Gestalt theory, the correlated phenomena that people experience and the underlying processes in the brain.

Knowledge Information that has a purpose or use.

Latent vulnerability traits Specific psychological features that we may develop early in life (e.g., certain avoidant tendencies or hostile behavior) and that may later develop into serious psychopathological symptoms.

Leadership style The predominant type of communications established by the group leader.

Learning curve A concept in Thorndike's theory to describe the dynamic of learning a habit; it also indicates the connection between learning and the time it takes to learn.

Legal knowledge Knowledge encapsulated in the law and detailed in official rules and principles related to psychological functioning of individuals.

Level of aspiration The degree of difficulty of the goal toward which a person is striving.

Libido A universal kind of energy, an instinctual and irrational determiner of both conscious and unconscious processes.

Madness (also called *insanity* or *lunacy*) Term referring to symptoms of gross excessiveness or overwhelming deficiency of certain features in an individual's behavior and experiences.

Mastery values The belief that an individual using the power of science and technology must exercise control over the environment, society, and own body.

Material monism The view according to which all things and developments, including psychological processes, no matter how simple or complicated they are, have one similar material origin.

Materialism The view about the human soul that holds that it originated from the same matter as any other material object. From the materialists' view, the soul was part of the natural world and could be studied by the methods used for the study of nature.

Mechanism A school of thought suggesting that almost everything about human beings can be effectively explained in mechanical terms.

Medicalization The process of identification and categorization of a condition or behavior as a medical disorder requiring medical treatment or intervention.

Melancholy (often **melancholia**) The most common label in ancient Greece for symptoms today called depressive.

Mental hygiene A theoretical discipline and a social movement involving health care professionals, social activists, and charitable organizations. Their goal was to promote innovations and create conditions under which individuals could pursue their professional and educational goals without excessive stress, unhealthy conditions, and inefficient educational techniques.

Mental surveys Special measurements of mental capacities of a large population (most typically children).

Metaphysics The branch of philosophy that examines the nature of reality, including the relationship between mind and matter.

Molar responses In Holt's system, the response reaction has something to do with the meaning of the situation, that is, the way an animal or human interprets the situation.

Monads Windowless entities each reflecting the state of every other according to the established principle of harmony.

Mood disorders Term referring to states of human mood considered abnormal; symptoms should be profoundly different from normal mood fluctuations, and such fluctuations should be frequent or long lasting.

Moral therapy A therapeutic principle based on an assumption that to return to a normal mental state, the patient should be given a chance to do it in the atmosphere of compassion and trust. Only then, through learning and trust, he or she could restore the lost qualities of good behavior.

Mysticism A belief in the existence of realities beyond perceptual reflection or scientific explanations, but accessible by subjective experience.

Narrative medicine A clinical field that helps medical professionals to recognize, absorb, interpret, and be moved by the stories of illness.

Natural selection The process, first suggested by Charles Darwin, by which only the organisms best adapted to their environment tend to survive and transmit their adaptive characteristics to succeeding generations, while those less adapted tend to be eliminated.

Naturalism The view that observable events should be explained only by natural causes without assuming the existence of divine, paranormal, or supernatural causes such as "magic" or "evil eye."

Neurasthenia The term meaning the weakness of nervous system, used by clinicians to explain the etiology of several dysfunctions, mostly including forms of anxiety and depression.

Neurosis Term referring to an individual's persistent, overwhelming anxiety and avoidant behavior. Most neurotic patients were aware of their problems and acknowledged the oddness of their symptoms.

"Noble savage" The term coined by Rousseau suggesting that people were essentially good when they lived under the rules of nature, before modern civilizations were created.

Nonsense syllables The words containing two consonants and one vowel that would have no apparent meaning in the German language.

Oedipus complex The repressed desire of a person for sex relations with the parent of the opposite sex.

Operant conditioning In Skinner's system, this is conditioning based on activities producing effects.

Organ inferiority The term stands for a wide range of difficulties that become impediments. They can be physical or psychological. They appear at birth but may develop later in life.

Parsimony The scientific principle standing for the necessity to seek the simplest explanations available to explain complex phenomena.

Peace psychology A theoretical and applied field that tries to understand ideological and psychological causes of war and develops educational programs to reduce the threat of violence in international relations and domestic policies of some countries.

Personal equation The existence of remarkably consistent differences in measurement between two observers, established in several experiments.

Phi-phenomenon The observable fact of pure motion when two images are projected in succession; a perceptual illusion in which two stationary but alternately flashing lights appear to be a single light moving from one location to another.

Phrenology (or *cranioscopy*) A theory connecting the size and shape of the brain with human behavior and the individual's personality.

Placebo effect The effect of a change caused by an anticipation of a change.

Pleasure principle The demand that an instinctual need be immediately gratified.

Political psychology The field examining psychological factors in politics and political behavior.

Pop psychology Psychological knowledge that is simplified and sensationalized.

Popular (or folk) beliefs Everyday assumptions ranging from widespread beliefs to individual opinions about psychological phenomena.

Positive psychology A branch that studies the strengths and virtues that enable individuals and communities to thrive.

Positive psychotherapy A theory and therapy based on the premise that the human mind is capable of changing itself: the right state of mind affects behavior; the behavior then produces the changes within the mind.

Pragmatism The doctrine that holds that the meaning of an idea or a proposition lies in its observable practical consequences. In a broader sense, this is a way of approaching situations or solving problems that emphasize practical applications and consequences.

Progressivism A general way of thinking and a social movement based on the deep belief that human beings and their society can be improved through social reform, education, and opportunity available to all people.

Prospect theory A theory suggesting that people, despite seemingly acting in a rational and logical way, make constant mistakes in evaluating their chances to win or lose.

Psychoanalysis In its original form, the method of an imaginative construction and reconstruction of the person's past and present reality. The therapist (a) collects the reported reflections, (b) analyzes them, and then (c) interprets them to the patient.

Psychological compounding The process that connects psychological elements by association.

Psychological parallelism The view suggested that physical and mental processes develop in parallel courses.

Psychopathology A term used to reflect the competition between psychology and medicine. From a psychological standpoint, psychopathology is the branch of psychology concerned with abnormal behavior; this is a study of the origin, development, and manifestations of psychological dysfunctions. From the medical standpoint, psychopathology is the branch of medicine dealing with the diagnosis and treatment of mental disorders.

Psychophysics According to Fechner, an exact science of the functional relations of dependency between body and mind.

Psychotechnics Term coined by German psychologist William Stern and stood for the branch of applied psychology directed toward treatment of human problems.

Purposive or operational behaviorism In Tolman's system, a type of behaviorism involving the idea of purpose or goal.

Quantum mind tradition A theory of the mind-body interaction suggesting the quantum nature of neurophysiological and psychological processes.

Rationalism A position in epistemology suggesting that reason is the prime source of knowledge and the thinking mind, not sensations alone, should provide justification of truth.

Reaction time The interval between the presentation of a stimulus and the response to it.

Reality principle The realization of the demands of the environment and the adjustment of behavior to these demands.

Recapitulation theory S. Hall's theory holding that children, as they develop, repeat the development of humankind.

Reductionism An approach to explaining the nature of complex processes by reducing them to the interactions of their elements or underlying processes, such as psychological functions are described as simple physiological reactions or reflexes.

Reflexology The name of Bekhterev's theory, the central concepts of which were reflex and adaptation.

Reversible figure A figure such as the Rubin vase that can you can see either as a white vase on a black background, or black profiles of two human faces on a white background.

Romanticism A comprehensive viewpoint of society and human behavior based on the idealistic enchantment with the individuality, spontaneity, and passion.

Schedules of reinforcement Conditions involving different rates and times of reinforcement.

Scholasticism The principal Western Christian theological and philosophical school of thought based on the authority of the church and teachings of Aristotle and his commentators.

School psychology movement A collective attempt by a wide range of professionals in the United States to bring psychology into the classroom and to use psychology to develop solutions for practical problems.

Scientific knowledge Knowledge accumulated through research, systematic empirical observation, and evaluation of a wide range of psychological phenomena.

Scientific rationalism The view that focuses on the mechanical character of the universe and human beings as the consequence.

Second signaling system In Pavlov's theory, this is language as a form of communication in contrast to the first signaling system, such as the sight of food, for example.

Self-actualization The highest stage of individual development governed by the search for truth, goodness, beauty, wholeness, justice, and meaningfulness.

Social engineering A broad term standing usually for the use of science by the government to improve society.

Social hygiene movement An eclectic conglomerate of intellectuals and health care professionals whose beliefs were driven by a mix of Darwinism, progressivism, and social engineering.

Social interest The desire, according to Adler, to be connected with other people.

Social utopia A model of an ideal and perfect human society.

Solipsism The theory claiming the self as the only entity that can be known and verified.

Spiritualism A set of folk beliefs that held that the living could communicate with the deceased through special channels of communication.

Spirituality A field referring to a broad range of phenomena concerning "nonmaterial" matters related to faith, trust, and hope, in contrast to "material" matters related to ownership, accumulation of possessions, and competition.

Strength of the nervous system A reflection of the functional ability of the neurons to maintain the state of activation or excitement without developing self-protecting inhibition. Described by Pavlov.

Striving toward superiority In Adler's view, an individual's vigorous exertion or effort to achieve security, improvement, control, and conquest.

Structural psychology or **structuralism** The term invented by its critics and observers who thought of structuralism as a special school in psychology. In general, a "structural" psychologist studies an individual by paying attention to elements of this individual's experience that are further irreducible.

Style of life In Adler's view, a technique for dealing with one's inadequacies and inferiorities and for gaining social status.

Subjective culture The term to describe connections between individuals and environment and manifested in various forms including early religion, arts, education, and science.

Superego The component of the psyche acting as the moral guide with unconscious features. This guide tells us what we should and should not do.

Tabula rasa or "clean board" The Latin term used by Locke who believed that the child's mind can record experiences in a fashion similar to the way in which teachers use a piece of chalk to write on the board.

Thanatos Or death instinct, a collective name for all the instinctual tendencies that lead away from full expression of pleasure toward constriction, destruction, and death.

Themas In Murray's system, stories or interpretations projecting fantasy imagery onto an objective stimulus.

Theology The study of the nature of God and religious truth.

Third force in psychology Term referring to humanistic psychology in contrast to behaviorism and psychoanalysis.

Time perspective According to Lewin, the totality of an individual's views of his psychological future and past.

Topology The complex study of the properties of geometric figures and spaces in terms of their connectedness, continuity, and orientation.

T.O.T.E. The "test-operate-test-exit" principle or strategy that organizes behavior and mental processes.

Trait theory of personality An approach initiated by Allport who argued that personality consists of a potent collection of qualities or traits.

Transferences The process by which patients shift emotions applicable to another person onto the psychoanalyst.

Transposition The ability to transfer one's initial experience to new circumstances.

Tropism A physical and chemical reaction of orientation of the organism in a field of force.

Unconditioned reflexes In Pavlov's theory, the reflexes associated with the direct influence of a substance on the receptors within the mouth.

Unconscious (adjective) Mostly repressed desires and memories of a person.

Unconscious (noun) The activities not open to direct conscious scrutiny but influencing conscious process and behavior. This was a complicated dynamic of wishes and drives fighting against restrictions, logic, and delays of gratification of these wishes.

Unfinished actions Describes unfinished behavior that is remembered better than accomplished actions; also known as the Zeigarnik effect.

Utilitarianism The approach suggesting that the value of an object or action is determined by its utility or usefulness.

Values Knowledge that stems from established, stable perceptions about the world, the nature of good and evil, right and wrong behavior, purpose of human life, and so forth.

Vitalism The view that life processes arise from or contain a nonmaterial vital principle and cannot be explained entirely as physical and chemical phenomena.

Wish fulfillment A symbolic attempt to realize an unfulfilled desire; the discharge of a tension by imagining a satisfying situation.

Witchcraft Usually, the alleged practices or arts of witches.

Zeitgeist A special term in sociology meaning the general social climate, the spirit of a particular time or generation.

Figure and Photo Credits

Chapter 1

Photo page 10. Hulton Archive/Getty Images.

Photo page 10. Fotosearch/Archive Photos/Getty Images.

Chapter 2

Photo page 39. © Getty Images.

Photo page 52. © Getty Images.

Chapter 3

Photo page 74. ThinkStock.

Photo page 78. Science & Society Picture Library/SSPL/Getty Images.

Figure 3.1, page 79. Wikipedia: http://en.wikipedia.org/wiki/File:The_Anatomy_of_Melancholy_by_Robert_Burton_frontispiece_1638_edition.jpg

Figure 3.2, page 87. SAGE.

Photo page 101. Wikipedia: http://en.wikipedia.org/wiki/File:Paul_Heinrich_Dietrich_Baron_d%27Holbach_Roslin.jpg

Chapter 4

Photo page 124. Hulton Archive/Getty Images.

Photo page 128. Hulton Archive/Getty Images.

Photo page 129. Archives of the History of American Psychology–The University of Akron.

Chapter 5

Photo page 163. FPG/Archive Photos/Getty Images.

Photo page 168. Archives of the History of American Psychology–The University of Akron.

Photo page 173. Hulton Archive/Getty Images.

Photo page 177. Archives of the History of American Psychology–The University of Akron.

Photo page 184. Archives of the History of American Psychology–The University of Akron.

Chapter 6

Photo page 209. Hulton Archive/Getty Images.

Photo page 225. Apic/Hulton Archive/Getty Images.

Photo page 228. Archives of the History of American Psychology–The University of Akron.

Chapter 7

Photo page 237. Sergei Pavlov.

Photo page 254. Sergei Pavlov.

Photo page 263. Archives of the History of American Psychology–The University of Akron.

Chapter 8

Photo page 275. Eric Shiraev.

Photo page 280. Wikipedia: http://en.wikipedia.org/wiki/File:Sigmund_Freud_LIFE.jpg

Photo page 296. Popperfoto/Getty Images.

Photo page 301. Hulton Archive/Archive Photos/Getty Images.

Chapter 9

Photo page 329. ThinkStock.

Photo page 329. ThinkStock.

Photo page 333. Archives of the History of American Psychology–The University of Akron.

Photo page 336. Wikipedia: http://en.wikipedia.org/wiki/File:Kurt_Lewin.jpg

Chapter 10

Photo page 357. Archives of the History of American Psychology–The University of Akron.

Photo page 372. Archives of the History of American Psychology–The University of Akron.

Chapter 11

Photo page 389. Wikipedia: http://en.wikipedia.org/wiki/File:B.F._Skinner_at_Harvard_circa_1950.jpg

Photo page 405. Wikipedia: http://en.wikipedia.org/wiki/File:Sigmund_en_Anna.jpg

Chapter 12

Photo page 431. Wikipedia: http://en.wikipedia.org/wiki/File:Abraham_maslow.jpg

Photo page 445. Wikipedia: http://en.wikipedia.org/wiki/File:Alan_Turing_Memorial_Closer.jpg

Chapter 13

Photo page 457. Elissa Epel.

Photo page 467. Marilyn Brewer.

Author Index

Subject Index